Organizational Behavior and Management
A Contingency Approach

Organizational Behavior and Management
A Contingency Approach

Henry L. Tosi
W. Clay Hamner
Michigan State University

St. Clair Press
3 East Huron Street
Chicago 60611

Fourth Printing May 1976

Organizational Behavior and Management
A Contingency Approach

Library of Congress Catalog Card Number 73-91196
ISBN   00-914292-00-5

Cover design by H.B. Smith

To Rosemary and Patti

Preface

This book is designed to bring present and potential managers into first hand contact with the knowledge currently available in the area of organizational behavior. In the past decade there has been an increase in information concerning organizational and environmental influences on performance and satisfaction in industry.

The primary objective of the text is to provide students with a basis for analyzing how the determinants of individual and group behavior enable individuals to accommodate to varying types of organizational environments and for analyzing the managerial implications of those modes of accommodation. Thus, the book seeks to develop and relate contingency models at all levels of the organization.

We have selected and edited the readings from classical and contemporary sources to present a wide range of concepts and to treat important areas in the field of organizational behavior. With only one or two exceptions, we have eliminated all empirical data so that we may reach students who have not yet completed courses in statistical analysis and so that the emphasis in the book will be, hopefully, upon the power of theory and concepts. We have attempted to arrange the material in such a way that the student can relate each reading to the topic under consideration. Our hope is that we have provided a conceptual view that will be useful to students as a foundation for more advanced study or as a basis for creative management practice.

The book is intended for courses in management, organizational behavior, organization theory, personnel and industrial relations, and industrial psychology, and it presumes that students have taken an introductory course in psychology, sociology, or a related area. The book can be used as a primary text or as a supplement to most texts in management, human relations, personnel, or organizational behavior.

We wish to express our gratitude to Andre L. Delbecq, Steven Kerr, Jonathan S. Monat, George Strauss, and Charles E. Summer, all of whom reviewed the plans for the book and offered valuable suggestions. We also thank Marie Dumeney for her time and patience in the typing, proofreading, and correspondence which are part of the hard work in the preparation of a book.

Henry L. Tosi
W. Clay Hamner

Contents

INTRODUCTION

A Contingency Model
of Organizational Behavior

To understand behavior in an organization, administrators should have a systematic set of concepts. The contingency approach to organizational behavior assumes that an organization is a system, or unit, of behavior composed of subsystems or subunits that have identifiable boundaries within the system. Each subsystem can be analyzed as a unit of behavior in its own right, or as a subunit of behavior interacting with other subunits.

When a subsystem in an organization "behaves" in response to another system or subsystem, we say that the response was "contingent" on the environment (in this case, the other system). Hence, a "contingency" approach is an approach where the behavior of one subunit is dependent on its environmental relationship to other units or subunits that have some control over the consequences (e.g., profit for the organization or recognition and praise for the individual) desired by that subunit.

In this text, we discuss three units of behavior: the individual as he behaves within the group, the group as it behaves within the organization, and the organization as it behaves within society. An underlying concept is that the components of the contingency approach are similar at the various levels of behavior. These components at each level are the *environment*, the *behavior* which occurs within that environment, and the *consequences* of that behavior *from* the environment. Consequences are always contingent upon the behavior within the environment, a theme that is developed in the body of this text.

We seek, therefore, to explain the interrelationships within, *and among*, the various subunits in the organization as well as between the organization and its environment, by examining the contingency relationship.

Although the emphasis is on dealing with determinants of *human* behavior within organizations, the *structure* of the organization is an important influence on behavior. As a consequence, behavioral responses can be best understood in terms of such topics as organizational structure, compensation systems, and other environmental factors.

In building the contingency model, we include four major topics related to understanding behavior in organizational settings. These are:

1. psychological determinants of individual and group behavior;
2. organizational determinants of individual and group behavior;

1

3. internal characteristics of the organizational system; and
4. environmental determinants of the organizational system.

Most uses of a contingency approach center on psychological determinants of individual behavior[1] or on environmental determinants of the organizational system.[2] The approach here is a contingency view of behavior in each unit within the organization (see fig. 1).

Psychological Determinants of Individual and Group Behavior

Whether he is aware of it or not, every manager makes assumptions about those he supervises and those with whom he works. These assumptions, to a large extent, influence how he behaves toward his employees. If a manager understands the psychological determinants of individual and group behavior, he is very much more likely to influence behavior in desired directions than if he does not. Three parts of this book are devoted to this topic.

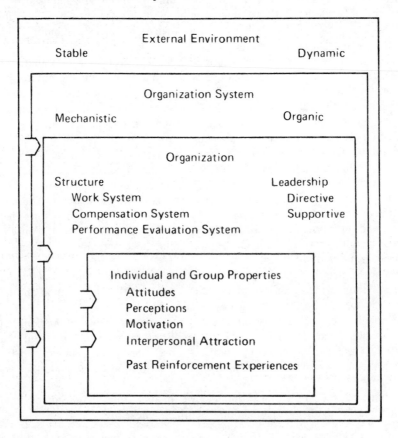

Figure 1. Contingency model of organizational behavior.

The smallest box in figure 1 illustrates the framework presented in parts 2 and 3 on the psychological determinants of individual behavior. This is the core of the contingency model for two reasons: First, organizational behavior can be better understood when the determinants of individual behavior are clear. Second, the first level of analysis in the system is the individual; all other subsystems influence groups of individuals in order to accomplish the goals of the organization.

Part 2, entitled "Individual Learning and Socialization," explains how individuals learn to adapt to their environment. The framework is learning theory, used to explain how the history of the individual is instrumental in determining the behavior patterns brought to the organization and how rearrangement of the contingencies of reinforcement can modify these behavioral patterns.

In Part 3, "Individual Behavior in the Organization," the individual's attitudes, needs perceptions, and total motivational state are considered. The importance of these complex psychological factors as determinants of the individual's behavior in the organization is also discussed.

In Part 4, "Group Behavior and Intergroup Conflict in the Organization," the topics shown in figure 1 are again considered, but from a group point of view. Again, as with the individual, the environment of the group must be understood in order to determine why groups behave as they do. In this part, therefore, we examine those factors instrumental in shaping the work group's behavior, and how the group is instrumental in affecting individual behavior.

Organizational Determinants of Individual and Group Behavior

Individuals function in an organization setting, where pressures are imposed by the work environment (see the next largest box in fig. 1). Individual attitudes, values, beliefs, and skills developed in early experiences are affected by two sets of organization determinants—structure and leadership.

Structure

Structure consists of the work procedures and rules that affect all individuals in an organization. These effects are discussed in part 5. The tasks that are performed may range in repetitiveness from routine to highly varied. Broad discretion in decision-making may be associated with some positions, and narrow discretion in others. What someone does, and how he does it, may have a considerable impact on his attitudes. Repetitive jobs may be boring. Broad discretion may be perceived as associated with high status, resulting in positive feelings. The upper limit of machine capacity restricts output to a given level, regardless of how highly motivated a person may be.

The way compensation is made, and the reasons that salaries are increased may condition behavior. For example, when salary increases can only be given annually, it may be difficult for a person to regard an increase as a reward for behavior of merit at other times in the year. This means that an increase may not reinforce desired behavior. Yet such a compensation system may be in effect because it is difficult to design it any other way. This type of system can be contrasted to a commission plan for salesmen, where pay is related to sales volume, or piecework pay where each unit produced results in added income. These different payment methods will condition different individual reactions. The manager must know how the method he must live with affects attitudes and performance.

Performance evaluation may also have significant effects on behavior. For instance, where there are relatively widely accepted measures used to assess effectiveness, such as unit costs or cost savings, individuals are likely to work toward achieving them, rather than worrying about *how* they are achieved. In other cases, goals may be ambiguous, leaving the individual uncertain about what is expected. This uncertainty has different effects on different people.

Leadership

The interpersonal relationship on which we focus is leader/subordinate interaction, discussed in part 6. This is not to imply that other relationships are less important, but simply that this aspect is of greatest interest. The power of a manager to make decisions, the way he reinforces subordinate behavior, and the style he uses in providing feedback, are factors in the organization setting which affect an individual's performance.

Organization System Characteristics

The form and shape of structural factors and the nature of interpersonal relationships can be generally categorized as either *organic* or *mechanistic*. These concepts are treated in detail in part 1. They describe the different types of relationships between systemic properties (see the next to largest box in fig. 1).

Mechanistic Systems

Organizations characterized by relatively routine, repetitive activities at the lowest operating levels are called mechanistic. There is a high level of task specialization, with most of the operating activities broken down into relatively small sets requiring moderate to low levels of skill and ability. The authority/responsibility relationships are fairly well defined and fairly fixed over time. Authority, or the right to command, is based on position. There are likely to be sharp status distinctions between hierarchical levels.

Jobs are apt to be fairly clearly specified, with limits on discretion, resulting in clear understanding of work relationships and responsibilities. Clear definition of the job, especially if it remains relatively stable over long periods of time, will aid the development of a compensation system in which base levels are defined by job evaluation. Jobs are priced according to their relative worth in an organization.

In mechanistic systems, policies and procedures are in evidence, and there are strong pressures for compliance. Individuals can use procedures and rules as a basis for knowing how to schedule and plan their work. For instance, when a procedure specifies that a report is to be submitted on the first of the month, the individual can plan his work around it. In mechanistic organizations there is likely to be a complex policy and procedural network on which members rely. Therefore, in order to maintain some degree of effectiveness, and for the system to work smoothly, there must be compliance.

Organic Systems

Organic systems are characterized by constantly changing work assignments. The hierarchical authority structure is less rigidly fixed, and authority is usually based on individual competence and skill. The individual, rather than the organizational system, is likely to have major control over what he does and how he does it.

In an organic organization, compensation is based upon the skill level and capability that an individual brings to the organization. In contrast to the mechanistic system, where the base rate is relative to other jobs, salary is usually individually negotiable.

In an organic organization, performance evaluation is less likely to be based on specific output indicators, as would be true in a mechanistic system, and is more probably a function of *what*, not how much, the individual does. For example, it is difficult to evaluate a research or development scientist on the basis of the results he obtains, especially in the short run. He is typically evaluated on whether or not he conducts his work in generally accepted scientific fashion.

There is more flexibility in an organic organization than in a mechanistic one. Individuals are less constrained by policy and procedures. They are more free to plan their own time and work.

Environmental Determinants of the Organization System

The form of the organization system is not simply a matter of managerial choice. The most appropriate form is a function of external circumstances. A mechanistic or organic form will not be effective, nor can it last for an extended period of time simply because someone chooses it as a structure. Organizational form is largely a function of, or contingent upon, the external environment (see the outside box in fig. 1).

The external environment is made up of those influences which are beyond the boundary of the organization, but which interact with it. The relevant environment includes knowledge, science, and cultural values on which the internal activities and processes of an organization are based. For instance, technological change which results in an alteration of the production system may come from the outside, but must be dealt with internally.

The specific type of environment is different for various kinds of organizations. Steel suppliers, anti-trust agencies, environmental protection legislation, and the car buying public are certainly relevant environmental components for the auto industry. Clients, federal and state funding agencies, and local communities may constitute the relevant environment for a welfare agency. It is the administrator's problem to define *what* his relevant environment is, and how to respond to it.

In this book we do not attempt to index the environment for different organizations, but rather to describe the primary environmental characteristic most likely to affect the organization; that is, *the environmental rate of change*. The external world of the organization may be relatively stable, with changes occurring at a moderately slow and predictable rate. For instance, changes in sales may be related only to changes in population; there may be no new markets to tap. Or the technology may be fairly well established, as in the steel industry, which has not been exposed to rapid technological changes. There have been no breakthroughs to change the character of the industry or any of the firms. Under environmental conditions of stability, the mechanistic organization is evidently appropriate. In fact, under conditions of high stability one could argue that the more mechanistic the structure, the more effective the organization.

On the other hand, the external world may be relatively dynamic. Changes may be extensive and unpredictable. Breakthroughs in technology may occur at any time. Markets may be in a state of flux, because of changing products, changing demand, or both. Under these conditions, the organic form of structure seems to work best. The rigidity of the mechanistic form restricts adjustment to change. Project management is used extensively in organic organizations so that specialists may be easily shifted from one assignment to another to meet changing needs.

Organizational Change

The themes developed to this point suggest that individual and group behavior may be changed as a result of inducing changes in the system at several different points. These ideas are represented in figure 2.

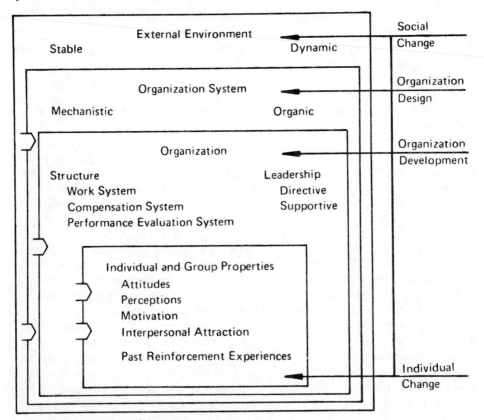

Figure 2. Application of organization change.

Individual Change

A number of different methods may be used to change individual or group attitudes, knowledge, and ability without regard to the organization setting. Lectures, group exercises, and skill training can alter individual beliefs, attitudes, and capabilities. They are likely to be successful as long as the change effort is consistent with the organizational environment. If, for instance, an effort is undertaken to improve an individual's budgeting skill, it is necessary that he use budgets in his job. Otherwise, the skills learned will quickly atrophy. If training is directed to teach how to allocate resources to increase output, but the performance evaluation system focuses on cost reduction, then the learning situation may be inconsistent with the work environment, and when the trainee returns to the job he is likely to adopt a mode of adaptation consistent with the work environment rather than with the content of training.

Organization Development

Organization development includes activities which focus on both organizational features and individual behavior. Diagnosis of how structural and interpersonal relationships affect individuals is undertaken to decide what kind of change effort is likely to be effective. Lectures, group exercises, and role playing may be used to change the individual, but attention is also given to the need for and implementation of changes in policy, procedure, work design, compensation, and evaluation.

Organization Design

This type of change is concerned primarily with structural considerations as they relate to the environment. Authority/responsibility relationships need to be different under different environmental circumstances. When an analyst examines the formal structure of an organization for its congruity with the environment, and recommends changes in reporting relationships and discretionary limits of jobs, he is engaging in organization redesign. This is the quite common consulting activity of reorganization. Perhaps the primary reason why most reorganization fails is that efforts are made to impose a design which does not square with the external situation.

Social Change

Social change is change in the environment, induced by factors beyond the control of an organization. Changes in social values and consumer preferences fall in this category. When consumers demand a different type of product, the organization must change, or fail to survive.

Summary

Individual and group behavior in an organization are determined by factors at different levels. Basic ideas from learning theory provide insights into comprehending how society socializes its members, especially their views about organizations, and how organizations can shape member behavior. Attitudes, perception, and motivation are important individual processes. They are regarded as relatively stable characteristics. Group structure and intergroup processes and conflict are a basic unit of analysis in organizational behavior.

All of the above are affected by the setting within which people operate. Organization structure and leadership shape the immediate environment within which the organization member must function. They serve to maintain or change the attitudes, perceptions, and motivation of individuals, singly and in groups. Further, knowing the nature of the external environment can be a basis for understanding the form of the organization system. Finally, to change the performance of the system, alterations can be made at any or all of the four levels above, by way of individual retraining, organization development, organization design, and social change.

In the first reading, Perrow presents an overview of the historical development of the theoretical perspectives which have shaped the structure of the approach presented in this book. His article discusses how thinking about organizations has evolved from viewing an organization strictly as a set of relationships among individuals constrained by line and staff authority to an open systems view which attempts to account for internal as well as external forces that shape the organization.

Notes

1. For example, see B.F. Skinner, *Contingencies of Reinforcement,* Appleton-Century-Crofts, 1969.
2. For example, see F. E. Kast and J. E. Rosenzweig, *Contingency Views of Organization and Management,* Science Research Associates, 1973.

THE SHORT AND GLORIOUS
HISTORY OF ORGANIZATIONAL THEORY

CHARLES PERROW

From the beginning, the forces of light and the forces of darkness have polarized the field of organizational analysis, and the struggle has been protracted and inconclusive. The forces of darkness have been represented by the mechanical school of organizational theory—those who treat the organization as a machine. This school characterizes organizations in terms of such things as:

- centralized authority
- clear lines of authority
- specialization and expertise

●marked division of labor

●rules and regulations

●clear separation of staff and line

The forces of light, which by mid-twentieth century came to be characterized as the human relations school, emphasizes people rather than machines, accommodations rather than machine-like precision, and draws its inspiration from biological systems rather than engineering systems. It has emphasized such things as:

●delegation of authority

●employee autonomy

●trust and openness

●concerns with the "whole person"

●interpersonal dynamics

The Rise and Fall of Scientific Management

The forces of darkness formulated their position first, starting in the early part of this century. They have been characterized as the scientific management or classical management school. This school started by parading simple-minded injunctions to plan ahead, keep records, write down policies, specialize, be decisive, and keep your span of control to about six people. These injunctions were needed as firms grew in size and complexity, since there were few models around beyond the railroads, the military, and the Catholic Church to guide organizations. And their injunctions worked. Executives began to delegate, reduce their span of control, keep records, and specialize. Planning ahead still is difficult, it seems, and the modern equivalent is Management by Objectives.

But many things intruded to make these simple-minded injunctions less relevant:

1. Labor became a more critical factor in the firm. As the technology increased in sophistication it took longer to train people, and more varied and specialized skills were needed. Thus, labor turnover cost more and recruitment became more selective. As a consequence, labor's power increased. Unions and strikes appeared. Management adjusted by beginning to speak of a cooperative system of capital, management, and labor. The machine model began to lose its relevancy.

2. The increasing complexity of markets, variability of products, increasing number of branch plants, and changes in technology all required more adaptive organization. The scientific management school was ill-equipped to deal with rapid change. It had presumed that once the proper structure was achieved the firm could run forever without much tampering. By the late 1930s, people began writing about adaptation and change in industry from an organizational point of view and had to abandon some of the principles of scientific management.

3. Political, social, and cultural changes meant new expectations regarding the proper way to treat people. The dark, satanic mills needed at the least a whitewashing. Child labor and the brutality of supervision in many enterprises became no longer permissible. Even managers could not be expected to accept the authoritarian patterns of leadership that prevailed in the small firm run by the founding father.

4. As mergers and growth proceeded apace and the firm could no longer be

viewed as the shadow of one man (the founding entrepreneur), a search for methods of selecting good leadership became a preoccupation. A good, clear, mechanical structure would no longer suffice. Instead, firms had to search for the qualities of leadership that could fill the large footsteps of the entrepreneur. They tacitly had to admit that something other than either "sound principles" or "dynamic leadership" was needed. The search for leadership traits implied that leaders were made, not just born, that the matter was complex, and that several skills were involved.

Enter Human Relations

From the beginning, individual voices were raised against the implications of the scientific management school. "Bureaucracy" had always been a dirty word, and the job design efforts of Frederick Taylor were even the subject of a congressional investigation. But no effective counterforce developed until 1938, when a business executive with academic talents named Chester Barnard proposed the first new theory of organizations: Organizations are cooperative systems, not the products of mechanical engineering. He stressed natural groups within the organization, upward communication, authority from below rather than from above, and leaders who functioned as a cohesive force. With the spectre of labor unrest and the Great Depression upon him, Barnard's emphasis on the cooperative nature of organizations was well-timed. The year following the publication of his *Functions of the Executive* (1938) saw the publication of F. J. Roethlisberger and William Dickson's *Management and the Worker*, reporting on the first large-scale empirical investigation of productivity and social relations. The research, most of it conducted in the Hawthorne plant of the Western Electric Company during a period in which the workforce was reduced, highlighted the role of informal groups, work restriction norms, the value of decent, humane leadership, and the role of psychological manipulation of employees through the counseling system. World War II intervened, but after the war the human relations movement, building on the insights of Barnard and the Hawthorne studies, came into its own.

The first step was a search for the traits of good leadership. It went on furiously at university centers but at first failed to produce more than a list of Boy Scout maxims: A good leader was kind, courteous, loyal, courageous, etc. We suspected as much. However, the studies did turn up a distinction between "consideration," or employee-centered aspects of leadership, and job-centered, technical aspects labeled "initiating structure." Both were important, but the former received most of the attention and the latter went undeveloped. The former led directly to an examination of group processes, an investigation that has culminated in T-group programs and is moving forward still with encounter groups. Meanwhile, in England, the Tavistock Institute sensed the importance of the influence of the kind of task a group had to perform on the social relations within the group. The first important study, conducted among coal miners, showed that job simplification and specialization did not work under conditions of uncertainty and nonroutine tasks.

As this work flourished and spread, more adventurous theorists began to extend it beyond work groups to organizations as a whole. We now knew that there were a number of things that were bad for the morale and loyalty of groups—routine tasks, submission to authority, specialization of task, segregation of task sequence, ignorance of the goals of the firm, centralized decision making, and so on. If these were bad for groups, they were likely to be bad for groups of groups—i.e., for organizations. So people like Warren Bennis began talking about innovative, rapidly changing organizations that were made up of temporary groups, temporary authority systems, temporary leadership and role assignments, and democratic access to the goals of the firm. If rapidly changing technologies and unstable, turbulent environments were to characterize industry, then the structure of firms should be temporary and decentralized. The forces of light, of freedom, autonomy, change, humanity, creativity, and democracy were winning. Scientific management survived only in outdated text books. If the evangelizing of some of the human relations school theorists was excessive, and if Likert's System 4 or MacGregor's Theory Y or Blake's 9 x 9 evaded us, at least there was a rationale for confusion, disorganization, scrambling, and stress: Systems should be temporary.

Bureaucracy's Comeback

Meanwhile, in another part of the management forest, the mechanistic school was gathering its forces and preparing to outflank the forces of light. First came the numbers men—the linear programmers, the budget experts, and the financial analysts—with their PERT systems and cost-benefit analyses. From another world, unburdened by most of the scientific management ideology and untouched by the human relations school, they began to parcel things out and give some meaning to those truisms, "plan ahead" and "keep records." Armed with emerging systems concepts, they carried the "mechanistic" analogy to its fullest—and it was very productive. Their work still goes on, largely untroubled by organizational theory; the theory, it seems clear, will have to adjust to them, rather than the other way around.

Then the works of Max Weber, first translated from the German in the 1940s—he wrote around 1910, incredibly—began to find their way into social science thought. At first, with his celebration of the efficiency of bureaucracy, he was received with only reluctant respect, and even with hostility. All writers were against bureaucracy. But it turned out, surprisingly, that managers were not. When asked, they acknowledged that they preferred clear lines of communication, clear specifications of authority and responsibility, and clear knowledge of whom they were responsible to. They were as wont to say "there ought to be a rule about this," as to say "there are too many rules around here," as wont to say "next week we've got to get organized," as to say "there is too much red tape." Gradually, studies began to show that bureaucratic organizations could change faster than nonbureaucratic ones, and that morale could be higher where there was clear evidence of bureaucracy.

What was this thing, then? Weber had showed us, for example, that bureaucracy was the most effective way of ridding organizations of favoritism, arbitrary authority, discrimination, payola and kick-backs, and yes, even incompetence. His model stressed expertise, and the favorite or the boss's nephew or the guy who burned up resources to make his performance look good was *not* the one with expertise.

Rules could be changed; they could be dropped in exceptional circumstances; job security promoted more innovation. The sins of bureaucracy began to look like the sins of failing to follow its principles.

Enter Power, Conflict, and Decisions

But another discipline began to intrude upon the confident work and increasingly elaborate models of the human relations theorists (largely social psychologists) and the uneasy toying with bureaucracy of the "structionalists" (largely sociologists). Both tended to study economic organizations. A few, like Philip Selznick, were noting conflict and differences in goals (perhaps because he was studying a public agency, the Tennessee Valley Authority), but most ignored conflict or treated it as a pathological manifestation of breakdowns in communication or the ego trips of unreconstructed managers.

But in the world of political parties, pressure groups, and legislative bodies, conflict was not only rampant, but to be expected—it was even functional. This was the domain of the political scientists. They kept talking about power, making it a legitimate concern for analysis. There was an open acknowledgement of "manipulation." These were political scientists who were "behaviorally" inclined—studying and recording behavior rather than constitutions and formal systems of government—and they came to a much more complex view of organized activity. It spilled over into the area of economic organizations, with the help of some economists like R. A. Gordon and some sociologists who were studying conflicting goals of treatment and custody in prisons and mental hospitals.

The presence of legitimately conflicting goals and techniques of preserving and using power did not, of course, sit well with a cooperative systems view of organizations. But it also puzzled the bureaucratic school (and what was left of the old scientific management school), for the impressive Weberian principles were designed to settle questions of power through organizational design and to keep conflict out through reliance on rational-legal authority and systems of careers, expertise, and hierarchy. But power was being overtly contested and exercised in covert ways, and conflict was bursting out all over, and even being creative.

Gradually, in the second half of the 1950s and in the next decade, the political science view infiltrated both schools. Conflict could be healthy, even in a cooperative system, said the human relationists; it was the mode of resolution that counted, rather than prevention. Power became reconceptualized as "influence," and the distribution was less important, said Arnold Tannenbaum, than the total amount. For the bureaucratic school—never a clearly defined group of people, and largely without any clear ideology—it was easier to just absorb the new data and theories as something else to be thrown into the pot. That is to say, they floundered, writing books that went from topic to topic, without a clear view of organizations, or better yet, producing "readers" and leaving students to sort it all out.

Buried in the political science viewpoint was a sleeper that only gradually began to undermine the dominant views. This was the idea, largely found in the work of Herbert Simon and James March, that because man was so limited—in intelligence, reasoning powers, information at his disposal, time available, and means of ordering his preferences clearly—he generally seized on the first acceptable alternative when deciding, rather than looking for the best; that he rarely changed things unless they really got bad, and even then he continued to try what had worked before; that he limited his search for solutions to well-worn paths and traditional sources of information and established ideas; that he was wont to remain preoccupied with routine, thus preventing innovation. They called these characteristics "cognitive limits on rationality" and spoke of "satisficing" rather than maximizing or optimizing. It is now called the "decision making" school, and is concerned with the basic question of how people make decisions.

This view had some rather unusual implications. It suggested that if managers were so limited, then they could be easily controlled. What was necessary was not to give direct orders (on the assumption that subordinates were idiots without expertise) or to leave them to their own devices (on the assumption that they were supermen who would somehow know what was best for the organization, how to coordinate with all the other supermen, how to anticipate market changes, etc.). It was necessary to control only the *premises* of their decisions. Left to themselves, with those premises set, they could be predicted to rely on precedent, keep things stable and smooth, and respond to signals that reinforce the behavior desired of them.

To control the premises of decision making, March and Simon outline a variety of devices, all of which are familiar to you, but some of which you may not have seen before in quite this light. For example, organizations develop vocabularies, and this means that certain kinds of information are highlighted, and others are screened out—just as Eskimos (and skiers) distinguish many varieties of snow, while Londoners see only one. This is a form of attention directing. Another is the reward system. Change the bonus for salesmen and you can shift them from volume selling to steady-account selling, or to selling quality products or new products. If you want to channel good people into a different function (because, for example, sales should no longer be the critical function as the market changes, but engineering applications should), you may have to promote mediocre people in the unrewarded function in order to signal to the good people in the rewarded one that the game has changed. You cannot expect most people to make such decision on their own because of the cognitive limits on their rationality, nor will you succeed by giving direct orders, because you yourself probably do not know whom to order where. You presume that once the signals are clear and the new sets of alternatives are manifest, they have enough ability to make the decision but you have had to change the premises for their decisions about their career lines.

It would take too long to go through the dozen or so devices, covering a range of decision areas (March and Simon are not that clear or systematic about them, themselves, so I have summarized them in my own book), but I think the message is clear.

It was becoming clear to the human relations school, and to the bureaucratic school. The human relationists had begun to speak of changing stimuli rather than changing personality. They had begun to see that the rewards that can change behavior can well be prestige, money, comfort, etc., rather than trust, openness, self-insight, and so on. The alternative to supportive relations need not be punishment, since behavior can best be changed by rewarding approved behavior rather than by punishing disapproved behavior. They were finding that although leadership may be centralized, it can function best through indirect and unobtrusive means such as changing the premises on which decisions are made, thus giving the impression that the subordinate is actually making a decision when he has only been switched to a different set of alternatives. The implications of this work were also beginning to filter into the human relations school through an emphasis on behavioral psychology (the modern version of the much maligned stimulus-response school) that was supplanting personality theory (Freudian in its roots, and drawing heavily, in the human relations school, on Maslow).

For the bureaucratic school, this new line of thought reduced the heavy weight placed upon the bony structure of bureaucracy by highlighting the muscle and flesh that make these bones move. A single chain of command, precise division of labor, and clear lines of communication are simply not enough in themselves. Control can be achieved by using alternative communication channels, depending on the situation; by increasing or decreasing the static or "noise" in the system; by creating organizational myths and organizational vocabularies that allow only selective bits of information to enter the system; and through monitoring performance through indirect means rather than direct surveillance. Weber was all right for a starter, but organizations had changed vastly, and the leaders needed many more means of control and more subtle means of manipulation than they did at the turn of the century.

The Technological Qualification

By now the forces of darkness and forces of light had moved respectively from midnight and noon to about 4 A.M. and 8 A.M. But any convergence or resolution would have to be on yet new terms, for soon after the political science tradition had begun to infiltrate the established schools, another blow struck both of the major positions. Working quite independently of the Tavistock Group, with its emphasis on sociotechnical systems, and before the work of Burns and Stalker on mechanistic and organic firms, Joan Woodward was trying to see whether the classical scientific principles of organization made any sense in her survey of 100 firms in South Essex. She tripped and stumbled over a piece of gold in the process. She picked up the gold, labeled it "technology," and made sense out of her otherwise hopeless data. Job-shop firms, mass-production firms, and continuous-process firms all had quite different structures because the type of tasks, or the "technology," was different. Somewhat later, researchers in America were coming to very similar conclusions based on studies of hospitals, juvenile correctional institutions, and industrial firms. Bureaucracy appeared to be the best form of organization for routine operations; temporary work groups, decentralization, and emphasis on interpersonal processes appeared to work best for nonroutine operations. A raft of studies appeared and are still appearing, all trying to show how the nature of the task affects the structure of the organization.

This severely complicated things for the human relations school, since it suggested that openness and trust, while good things in themselves, did not have much impact, or perhaps were not even possible in some kinds of work situations. The prescriptions that were being handed out would have to be drastically qualified. What might work for nonroutine, high-status, interesting, and challenging jobs performed by highly educated people might not be relevant or even beneficial for the vast majority of jobs and people.

It also forced the upholders of the revised bureaucratic theory to qualify their recommendations, since research and development units should obviously be run differently from mass-production units, and the difference between both of these and highly programmed and highly sophisticated continuous-process firms was obscure in terms of bureaucratic theory. But the bureaucratic school perhaps came out on top, because the forces of evil—authority, structure, division of labor, etc.—no longer looked evil, even if they were not applicable to a minority of industrial units.

The emphasis on technology raised other questions, however. A can company might be quite routine, and a plastics division nonroutine, but there were both routine and nonroutine units within each. How should they be integrated if the prescription were followed that, say, production should be bureaucratized and R&D not? James Thompson began spelling out different forms of interdependence among units in organizations, and Paul Lawrence and Jay Lorsch looked closely at the nature of integrating mechanisms. Lawrence and Lorsch found that firms performed best when the differences between units were *maximized* (in contrast to both the human relations and the bureaucratic school), as long as the integrating mechanisms stood half-way between the two—being neither strongly bureaucratic nor nonroutine. They also noted that attempts at participative management in routine situations were counterproductive, that the environments of some kinds of organizations were far from turbulent and customers did not want innovations and changes, that cost reduction, price, and efficiency were trivial considerations in some firms, and so on. The technological insight was demolishing our comfortable truths right and left. They were also being questioned from another quarter.

Enter Goals, Environments, and Systems

The final seam was being mined by the sociologists while all this went on. This was the concern with organizational goals and the environment. Borrowing from the political scientists to some extent, but pushing ahead on their own, this "institutional school" came to see that goals were not fixed; conflicting goals could be pursued simultaneously, if there were enough slack resources, or sequentially (growth for the next four years, then cost-cutting and profit-taking for the next four); that goals were up for grabs in organizations, and units fought over them. Goals were, of course, not what they seemed to be, the important ones were quite unofficial; history played a big role; and assuming profit as the pre-eminent goal explained almost nothing about a firm's behavior.

They also did case studies that linked the organization to the web of influence of the environment; that showed how unique organizations were in many respects (so that, once again, there was no one best way to do things for all organizations); how organizations were embedded in their own history, making change difficult. Most striking of all, perhaps, the case studies revealed that the stated goals usually were not the real ones; the official leaders usually were not the powerful ones; claims of effectiveness and efficiency were deceptive or even untrue; the public interest was not being served; political influences were pervasive; favoritism, discrimination, and sheer corruption were commonplace. The accumulation of these studies presented quite a pill for either the forces of light or darkness to swallow, since it was hard to see how training sessions or interpersonal skills were relevant to these problems, and it was also clear that the vaunted efficiency of bureaucracy was hardly in evidence. What could they make of this wad of case studies?

We are still sorting it out. In one sense, the Weberian model is upheld because organizations are not, *by nature*, cooperative systems; top managers must exercise a great deal of effort to control them. But if organizations are tools in the hands of leaders, they may be very recalcitrant ones. Like the broom in the story of the sorcerer's apprentice, they occasionally get out of hand. If conflicting goals, bargaining, and unofficial leadership exists, where is the structure of Weberian bones and Simonian muscle? To what extent are organizations tools, and to what extent are they products of the varied interests and group strivings of their members? Does it vary by organization, in terms of some typological alchemy we have not discovered? We don't know. But at any rate, the bureaucratic model suffers again; it simply has not reckoned on the role of the environment. There are enormous sources of variations that the neat, though by now quite complex, neo-Weberian model could not account for.

The human relations model has also been badly shaken by the findings of the institutional school, for it was wont to assume that goals were given and unproblematical, and that anything that promoted harmony and efficiency for an organization also was good for society. Human relationists assumed that the problems created by organizations were largely limited to the psychological consequences of poor interpersonal relations within them, rather than their impact on the environment. Could the organization really promote the psychological health of its members when by necessity it had to define psychological health in terms of the goals of the organization itself? The neo-Weberian model at least called manipulation "manipulation" and was skeptical of claims about autonomy and self-realization.

But on one thing all the varied schools of organizational analysis now seemed to be agreed: organizations are systems—indeed, they are open systems. As the growth of the field has forced ever more variables into our consciousness, flat claims of predictive power are beginning to decrease and research has become bewilderingly complex. Even consulting groups need more than one or two tools in their kit-bag as the software multiplies.

The systems view is intuitively simple. Everything is related to everything else, though in uneven degrees of tension and reciprocity. Every unit, organization, department, or work group takes in resources, transforms them, and sends them out, and thus interacts with the larger system. The psychological, sociological, and cultural aspects of units interact. The systems view was explicit in the institutional work, since they tried to study whole organizations; it became explicit in the human relations school, because they were so concerned with the interactions of people. The political science and technology viewpoints also had to come to this realization, since they dealt with parts affecting each other (sales affecting production; technology affecting structure).

But as intuitively simple as it is, the systems view has been difficult to put into practical use. We still find ourselves ignoring the tenets of the open systems view, possibly because of the cognitive limits on our rationality. General systems theory itself has not lived up to its heady predictions; it remains rather nebulous. But at least there is a model for calling us to account and for stretching our minds, our research tools, and our troubled nostrums.

Some Conclusions

Where does all this leave us? We might summarize the prescriptions and proscriptions for management very roughly as follows:

1. A great deal of the "variance" in a firm's behavior depends on the environment. We have become more realistic about the limited range of change that can be induced through internal efforts. The goals of organizations, including those of profit and efficiency, vary greatly among industries and vary systematically by industries. This suggests that the impact of better management by itself will be limited, since so much will depend on market forces, competition, legislation, nature of the work force, available technologies and innovations, and so on. Another source of variation is, obviously, the history of the firm and its industry and its traditions.

2. A fair amount of variation in both firms and industries is due to the type of work done in the organization—the technology. We are now fairly confident in recommending that if work is predictable and routine, the necessary arrangement for getting the work done can be highly structured, and one can use a good deal of bureaucratic theory in accomplishing this. If it is not predictable, if it is nonroutine and there is a good deal of uncertainty as to how to do a job, then one had better utilize the theories that emphasize autonomy, temporary groups, multiple lines of authority and communications, and so on. We also know that this distinction is important when organizing different parts of an organization.

We are also getting a grasp on the question of what is the most critical function in different types of organizations. For some organizations it is production; for others, marketing; for still others, development. Furthermore, firms go through phases whereby the initial development of a market or a product or manufacturing process or accounting scheme may require a non-bureaucratic structure, but once it comes on stream, the structure should change to reflect the changed character of the work.

3. In keeping with this, management should be advised that the attempt to produce change in an organization through managerial grids, sensitivity training, and even job enrichment and job enlargement is likely to be fairly ineffective for all but a few organizations. The critical reviews of research in all these fields show that there is no scientific evidence to support the claims of the proponents of these various methods; that research has told us a great deal about social psychology, but little about how to apply the highly complex findings to actual situations. The key word is *selectivity*: We have no broad-spectrum antibiotics for interpersonal relations. Of course, managers should be sensitive, decent, kind, courteous, and courageous, but we have known that for some time now, and beyond a minimal threshold level, the payoff is hard to measure. The various attempts to make work and interpersonal relations more humane and stimulating should be applauded, but we should not confuse this with solving problems of structure, or as the equivalent of decentralization or participatory democracy.

4. The burning cry in all organizations is for "good leadership," but we have learned that beyond a threshold level of adequacy it is extremely difficult to know what good leadership is. The hundreds of scientific studies of this phenomenon come to one general conclusion: Leadership is highly variable or "contingent" upon a large variety of important variables such as nature of task, size of the group, length of time the group has existed, type of personnel within the group and their relationships with each other, and amount of pressure the group is under. It does not seem likely that we'll be able to devise a way to select the best leader for a particular situation. Even if we could, that situation would probably change in a short time and thus would require a somewhat different type of leader.

Furthermore, we are beginning to realize that leadership involves more than smoothing the paths of human interaction. What has rarely been studied in this area is the wisdom or even the technical adequacy of a leader's decision. A leader does more than lead people; he also makes decisions about the allocation of resources, type of technology to be used, the nature of the market, and so on. This aspect of leadership remains very obscure, but it is obviously crucial.

5. If we cannot solve our problems through good human relations or through good leadership, what are we then left with? The literature suggests that changing the structures of organizations might be the most effective and certainly the quickest and cheapest method. However, we are now sophisticated enough to know that changing the formal structure by itself is not likely to produce the desired changes. In addition, one must be aware of a large range of subtle, unobtrusive, and even covert processes and change devices that exist. If inspection procedures are not working, we are now unlikely to rush in with sensitivity training, nor would we send down authoritative communications telling people to do a better job. We are more likely to find out where the authority really lies, whether the degree of specialization is adequate, what the rules and regulations are, and so on, but even this very likely will not be enough.

According to the neo-Weberian bureaucratic model, as it has been influenced by work on decision making and behavioral psychology, we should find out how to manipulate the reward structure, change the premises of the decision-makers through finer controls on the information received and the expectations generated, search for interdepartmental conflicts that prevent better inspection procedures from being followed, and after manipulating these variables, sit back and wait for two or three months for them to take hold. This is complicated and hardly as dramatic as many of the solutions currently being peddled, but I think the weight of organizational theory is in its favor.

We have probably learned more, over several decades of research and theory, about the things that do *not* work (even though some of them obviously *should* have worked), than we have about things that do work. On balance, this is an important gain and should not discourage us. As you know, organizations are extremely complicated. To have as much knowledge as we do have in a fledgling discipline that has had to borrow from the diverse tools and concepts of psychology, sociology, economics, engineering, biology, history, and even anthropology is not really so bad.

Selected Bibliography

This paper is an adaptation of the discussion to be found in Charles Perrow, *Complex Organizations: A Critical Essay*, Scott, Foresman & Co., Glenview, Illinois, 1972. All the points made in this paper are discussed thoroughly in that volume.

The best overview and discussion of classical management theory, and its changes over time is by Joseph Massie—"Management Theory" in the *Handbook of Organizations* edited by James March, Rand McNally & Co., Chicago, 1965, pp. 387-422.

The best discussion of the changing justifications for managerial rule and worker obedience as they are related to changes in technology, etc., can be found in Reinhard Bendix's *Work and Authority in Industry*, John Wiley & Sons, Inc., New York, 1956. See especially the chapter on the American experience.

Some of the leading lights of the classical view—F. W. Taylor, Col. Urwick, and Henry Fayol—are briefly discussed in *Writers on Organizations* by D. S. Pugh, D. J. Hickson and C. R. Hinings, Penguin, 1971. This brief, readable, and useful book also contains selections from many other schools that I discuss, including Weber, Woodward, Cyert and March, Simon, and Hawthorne Investigations, and the Human Relations Movement as represented by Argyris, Herzberg, Likert, McGregor, and Blake and Mouton.

As good a place as any to start examining the human relations tradition is Rensis Likert, *The Human Organization*, McGraw-Hill, New York, 1967. See also his *New Patterns of Management*, McGraw-Hill Book Company, New York, 1961.

The Buck Rogers school of organizational theory is best represented by Warren Bennis. See his *Changing Organizations*, McGraw-Hill Book Company, New York, 1966, and his book with Philip Slater, *The Temporary Society*, Harper & Row, Inc., New York, 1968. Much of this work is linked into more general studies, e.g., Alvin Toffler's very popular paperback *Future Shock*, Random House, 1970, and Bantam Paperbacks, or Zibigniew Brzezinsky's *Between Two Ages: America's Role in the Technitronic Era*, the Viking Press, New York, 1970. One of the first intimations of the new type of environment and firm and still perhaps the most perceptive is to be found in the volume by Tom Burns and G. Stalker, *The Management of Innovation*, Tavistock, London, 1961, where they distinguished between "organic" and "mechanistic" systems. The introduction, which is not very long, is an excellent and very tight summary of the book.

The political science tradition came in through three important works. First, Herbert Simon's *Administrative Behavior*, The Macmillan Co., New York, 1948, followed by the second half of James March and Herbert Simon's *Organizations*, John Wiley & Sons, Inc., New York, 1958, then Richard M. Cyert and James March's *A Behavioral Theory of the Firm*, Prentice-Hall, Inc., Englewood Cliffs, N.J., 1963. All three of these books are fairly rough going, though chapters 1, 2, 3, and 6 of the last volume are fairly short and accessible. A quite interesting book in this tradition, though somewhat heavy-going, is Michael Crozier's *The Bureaucratic Phenomenon*, University of Chicago, and Tavistock Publications, 1964. This is a striking description of power in organizations, though there is a somewhat dubious attempt to link organization processes in France to the cultural traits of the French people.

The book by Joan Woodward *Industrial Organisation: Theory and Practice*, Oxford University Press, London, 1965, is still very much worth reading. A fairly popular attempt to discuss the implications for this for management can be found in my own book, *Organizational Analysis: A Sociological View*, Tavistock, 1970, Chapters 2 and 3. The impact of technology on structure is still fairly controversial. A number of technical studies have found both support and nonsupport, largely because the concept is defined so differently, but there is general agreement that different structures and leadership techniques are needed for different situations. For studies that support and document this viewpoint see James Thompson, *Organizations in Action*, McGraw-Hill Book Company, New York, 1967, and Paul Lawrence and Jay Lorsch, *Organizations and Environment*, Harvard University Press, Cambridge, Mass., 1967.

The best single work on the relation between the organization and the environment and one of the most readable books in the field is Philip Selznick's short volume *Leadership in Administration*, Row, Peterson, Evanston, Illinois, 1957. But the large number of these studies are scattered about. I have summarized several in my *Complex Organizations: A Critical Essay*.

Lastly, the most elaborate and persuasive argument for a systems view of organizations is found in the first 100 pages of the book by Daniel Katz and Robert Kahn, *The Social Psychology of Organizations*, John Wiley and Co., 1966. It is not easy reading, however.

PART ONE

The Organization
and the Environment

Organizations exist in environments, and each environment takes part in shaping the internal structure of each organization within it. This is basically a systems point of view. An organization can be viewed as a set of subsystems related to one another. A change in one, whether internal or external, is likely to induce changes in the others. These subsystems, operating together as "transformation elements," act upon inputs, transforming them into outputs. In the process, outputs of the organization are exchanged with its external environment for inputs.

Terreberry focuses on the environment and its characteristics. She argues that there are conditions which occur externally to an organization over which it has little or no control. The organization must adapt to these conditions. She notes that the "capacity of any system for adapting to changing contingencies in the environment is inversely related to its dependence upon instinct, habit, or tradition. Adaptability exists, by definition, to the extent that a system can survive externally induced change in its transactional interdependencies." She concludes that organization change is, for the most part, externally induced, and that survival is a function of "the ability to learn and perform according to changing environmental contingencies." She describes the role that various organization activities, such as communication or information storage, play in the adaptation process. She is not, however, precise in describing the manner in which adaptive processes occur, or the form that the organization takes in various environmental situations.

Katz and Kahn describe five basic internal subsystems that absorb inputs and create and disperse outputs: production or technical, supportive, maintenance, adaptive, and managerial. These "generic" subsystems are useful descriptive categories for various internal organization activities.

These basic subsystems may take different forms depending upon the characteristics of the external environment. Thompson describes how the technical (production) subsystem may vary under different circumstances. He also provides a useful conceptual basis for determining the manner in which other systemic components may vary. For instance, the long-linked technology, characterized by repetitiveness and standardization, may well be an appropriate structural form under conditions in which the external environment is relatively stable, rather than turbulent. The "intensive" technology may be a more appropriate form in a turbulent, dynamic, or otherwise changing environment. For instance, Thompson suggests that "the

21

development of military combat teams, with the multiplicity of highly skilled capacities to be applied to the requirement of changing circumstances, represents a shift toward the intensive technology in military operations.''

Thompson also suggests ways in which the organization can minimize the internal impact of external environmental changes. For example, he notes that, ''under norms of rationality, organizations seek to seal off their core technologies from environmental influences.'' This is done by *buffering, leveling*, or *adaptation*. These concepts as defined in the Thompson article are useful in drawing inferences about how the adaptive and supportive subsystems defined by Katz and Kahn might function in different environmental settings. In a turbulent environment, for example, input and output transactions can be smoothed by supportive subsystems, an important process from a cost standpoint. For instance, where there are substantial cycles in the raw material markets, firms must inventory goods to maintain steady operation.

Lynton, in examining the problem of how innovation may be introduced into an organization, looks at the linkage mechanism which ties the organization to the external sector. The form of the linkage mechanism depends upon whether the need to adapt and change internally is important. Linking an organization to a dynamic or turbulent environment is a difficult, costly, and important function. Thus, the linking mechanism may need a great deal of power and control. When there is only a minimal need for change, as would be the case in a relatively quiet environment, the authority of the linking subsystem may be less important.

Burns and Stalker describe in some detail the characteristics of different organizations in different environmental circumstances. The characteristics of the ''organic'' organization would likely be found in an environment which is extremely dynamic and changing. The ''mechanistic'' organization is a more appropriate form in a tranquil and stable environment. The most important point made by Burns and Stalker is that ''the beginning of administrative wisdom is awareness that there is no one optimum type of management system.'' The utility of the ''notion of mechanistic and organic management systems resides largely in their being related as dependent variables to the rate of organization change.''

There is no one appropriate form of organization which cuts across all environmental circumstances. At the two extremes, a relatively rigid authority structure may be effective in adapting to a stable environment, while a flexible structure is likely to be effective in an unstable environment. The appropriate type is a function of the characteristics of the environment.

The readings in this part, then, show how the internal subsystems of the organization, as defined by Katz and Kahn, take on either mechanistic or organic characteristics. Organizations do so in response to the external environment. Terreberry describes turbulence as the important characteristic of the external environment. Yet, as Thompson points out, the organization provides a mechanism (buffering, leveling, and adapting) to ease the uncertainties.

Under any circumstances, the organization structure, mechanistic or organic, is the environment within which the individual must operate. In part 2 we present a set of concepts which can be used to understand how this individual adaption occurs.

THE EVOLUTION
OF ORGANIZATIONAL ENVIRONMENTS

SHIRLEY TERREBERRY

Darwin published *The Origin of Species by Means of Natural Selection* in 1859. Modern genetics has vastly altered our understanding of the variance upon which natural selection operates. But there has been no conceptual breakthrough in understanding *environmental* evolution which, alone, shapes the direction of change. Even today most theorists of change still focus on *internal* interdependencies of systems —biological, psychological, or social—although the external environments of these systems are changing more rapidly than ever before.

Introduction

Von Bertalanffy was the first to reveal fully the importance of a system being open or closed to the environment in distinguishing living from inanimate systems.[1] Although von Bertalanffy's formulation makes it possible to deal with a system's exchange processes in a new perspective, it does not deal at all with those processes in the environment *itself* that are among the determining conditions of exchange.

Emery and Trist have argued the need for one additional concept, "the causal texture of the environment."[2] Writing in the context of formal organizations, they offer the following general proposition:

That a comprehensive understanding of organizational behaviour requires some knowledge of each member of the following set, where L indicates some potentially lawful connection, and the suffix 1 refers to the organization and the suffix 2 to the environment:

$$L_{11} \quad L_{12}$$
$$L_{21} \quad L_{22}$$

L_{11} here refers to processes within the organization—the area of internal interdependencies; L_{12} and L_{21} to exchanges between the organization and its environment—the area of transactional interdependencies, from either direction; and L_{22} to processes through which parts of the environment become related to each other—i.e., its causal texture—the area of interdependencies that belong within the environment itself.[3]

We have reproduced the above paragraph in its entirety because in the balance of this paper, we will use Emery and Trist's symbols (i.e., L_{11}, L_{21}, L_{12}, and L_{22}) to denote intra-, input, output, and extra-system interdependencies, respectively. Our purpose in doing so is to avoid the misleading connotations of conventional terminology.

Reprinted by permission of the author and the publisher from *Administrative Science Quarterly*, vol. 12, no. 4 (March 1968), pp. 590-613.

Purpose

The theses here are: (*1*) that contemporary changes in organizational environ-ments are such as to increase the ratio of externally induced change to internally induced change; and (2) that *other* formal organizations are, increasingly, the impor-tant components in the environment of any focal organization. Furthermore, the evolution of environments is accompanied—among viable systems—by an increase in the system's ability to learn and to perform according to changing contingencies in its environment. An integrative framework is outlined for the concurrent analysis of an organization, its transactions with environmental units, and interdependencies among those units. Lastly, two hypotheses are presented, one about organizational *change* and the other about organizational *adaptability*; and some problems in any empirical test of these hypotheses are discussed.[4]

Concepts of Organizational Environments

In Emery and Trist's terms, L_{22} relations (i.e., interdependencies within the environment itself) comprise the "causal texture" of the field. This causal texture of the environment is treated as a quasi-independent domain, since the environment cannot be conceptualized except with respect to some focal organization. The compo-nents of the environment are identified in terms of that system's actual and *potential* transactional interdependencies, both input (L_{21}) and output (L_{12}).

Emery and Trist postulate four "ideal types" of environment, which can be ordered according to the degree of *system connectedness* that exists among the com-ponents of the environment (L_{22}). The first of these is a "placid, randomized" envi-ronment: goods and bads are relatively unchanging in themselves and are randomly distributed (e.g., the environments of an amoeba, a human foetus, a nomadic tribe). The second is a "placid, clustered" environment: goods and bads are relatively unchanging in themselves but clustered (e.g., the environments of plants that are subjected to the cycle of seasons, of human infants, of extractive industries). The third ideal type is "disturbed-reactive" environment and constitutes a significant qualitative change over simpler types of environments: an environment characterized by similar systems in the field. The extinction of dinosaurs can be traced to the emergence of more complex environments on the biological level. Human beings, beyond infancy, live in disturbed-reactive environments in relation to one another. The theory of oligopoly in economics is a theory of this type of environment.[5]

These three types of environment have been identified and described in the lit-erature of biology, economics, and mathematics.[6] "The fourth type, however, is new, at least to us, and is the one that for some time we have been endeavouring to identify."[7] This fourth ideal type of environment is called a "turbulent field." Dynamic processes "arise from the *field itself*" and not merely from the interactions of components; the actions of component organizations and linked sets of them "are both persistent and strong enough to induce autochthonous processes in the environ-ment."[8]

An alternate description of a turbulent field is that the accelerating rate and complexity of interactive effects exceeds the component systems' capacities for pre-diction and, hence, control of the compounding consequences of their actions.

Turbulence is characterized by complexity as well as rapidity of change in causal interconnections in the environment. Emery and Trist illustrate the transition from a disturbed-reactive to a turbulent-field environment for a company that had maintained a steady 65 percent of the market for its main product—a canned vegetable—over many years. At the end of World War II, the firm made an enormous investment in a new automated factory that was set up exclusively for the traditional product and technology. At the same time postwar controls on steel strip and tin were removed, so that cheaper cans were available; surplus crops were more cheaply obtained by importers; diversity increased in available products, including substitutes for the staple; the quick-freeze technology was developed; home buyers became more affluent; supermarkets emerged and placed bulk orders with small firms for retail under supermarket names. These changes in technology, international trade, and affluence of buyers gradually interacted (L_{22}) and ultimately had a pronounced effect on the company: its market dwindled rapidly. "The changed texture of the environment was not recognized by an able but traditional management until it was too late."[9]

Sociological, social psychological, and business management theorists often still treat formal organizations as closed systems. In recent years, however, this perspective seems to be changing. Etzioni asserts that interorganizational relations need intensive empirical study.[10] Blau and Scott present a rich but unconceptualized discussion of the "social context of organizational life."[11] Parsons distinguishes three distinct levels of organizational responsibility and control: technical, managerial, and institutional.[12] His categories can be construed to parallel the intraorganizational (i.e., technical or L_{11}), the interorganizational (i.e., managerial or L_{21} and L_{12}), and the extra-organizational levels of analysis (i.e., the institutional or L_{22} areas). Perhaps in the normal developmental course of a science, intrasystem analysis necessarily precedes the intersystem focus. On the other hand, increasing attention to interorganizational relations may reflect a real change in the phenomenon being studied. The first question to consider is whether there is evidence that the environments of formal organizations are evolving toward turbulent-field conditions.

Evidence for Turbulence

Ohlin argues that the sheer rapidity of social change today requires greater organizational adaptability.[13] Hood points to the increasing complexity, as well as the accelerating rate of change, in organizational environments.[14] In business circles there is growing conviction that the future is unpredictable. Drucker[15] and Gardener[16] both assert that the kind and extent of present-day change precludes prediction of the future. Increasingly, the rational strategies of planned-innovation and long-range planning are being undermined by unpredictable changes. McNulty found no association between organization adaptation and the introduction of purposeful change in a study of 30 companies in fast-growing markets.[17] He suggests that built-in flexibility may be more efficient than the explicit reorganization implicit in the quasi-rational model. *Dun's Review* questions the effectiveness of long-range planning in the light of frequent failures, and suggests that error may be attributable to forecasting the future by extrapolation of a noncomparable past. The conclusion is that the rapidity and complexity of change may increasingly preclude effective long-range planning.[18] These examples clearly suggest the emergence of a change in the environment that is suggestive of turbulence.

Some writers with this open-system perspective derive implications for interorganizational relations from this changing environment. Blau and Scott argue that the success of a firm increasingly depends upon its ability to establish symbiotic relations with other organizations, in which extensive advantageous exchange takes place.[19] Lee Adler proposes "symbiotic marketing."[20] Dill found that the task environments of two Norwegian firms comprised four major sectors: *customers*, including both distributors and users; *suppliers* of materials, labor, capital, equipment, and work space; *competitors* for both markets and resources; and *regulatory groups*, including governmental agencies, unions, and interfirm associations.[21] Not only does Dill's list include many more components than are accommodated by present theories, but all components are themselves evolving into formal organizations. In his recent book, Thompson discusses "task environments," which comprise the units with which an organization has input and output transactions (L_{21} and L_{12}), and postulates two dimensions of such environments: homogeneous-heterogeneous, and stable-dynamic. When the task environment is *both* heterogeneous and dynamic (i.e., probably turbulent), he expects an organization's boundary-spanning units to be functionally differentiated to correspond to segments of the task environment and each to operate on a decentralized basis to monitor and plan responses to fluctuations in its sector of the task environment.[22] He does not focus on other organizations as components of the environment, but he provides a novel perspective on structural implications (L_{11}) for organizations in turbulent fields.

Selznick's work on TVA appears to be the first organizational case study to emphasize transactional interdependencies.[23] The next study was Ridgway's 1957 study of manufacturer-dealer relationships.[24] Within the following few years the study by Dill[25] and others by Levine and White,[26] Litwak and Hylton,[27] and Elling and Halebsky[28] appeared, and in recent years, the publication of such studies has accelerated.

The following are examples from two volumes of the *Administrative Science Quarterly* alone. Rubington argues that structural changes in organizations that seek to change the behavior of "prisoners, drug addicts, juvenile delinquents, parolees, alcoholics [are] . . . the result of a social movement whose own organizational history has yet to be written."[29] Rosengren reports a similar phenomenon in the mental health field, whose origin he finds hard to explain: "In any event, a more symbiotic relationship has come to characterize the relations between the [mental] hospitals and other agencies, professions, and establishments in the community."[30] He ascribes changes in organizational goals and technology to this interorganizational evolution. In the field of education, Clark outlines the increasing influence of private foundations, national associations, and divisions of the federal government. He, too, is not clear as to how these changes have come about, but he traces numerous changes in the behavior of educational organizations to interorganizational influences.[31] Maniha and Perrow analyze the origins and development of a city youth commission: The agency had little reason to be formed, no goals to guide it, and was staffed by people who sought a minimal, no-action role in the community. By virtue of its existence and broad province, however, it was seized upon as a valuable weapon by other organizations for the pursuit of their own goals. "But in this very process it became an organization with a mission of its own, in spite of itself."[32]

Since uncertainty is the dominant characteristic of turbulent fields, it is not surprising that emphasis in recent literature is away from algorithmic and toward heuristic problem-solving models;[33] that optimizing models are giving way to satisficing models;[34] and that rational decision making is replaced by "disjointed incrementalism."[35] These trends reflect *not* the ignorance of the authors of earlier models, but a change in the causal texture of organizational environments and, therefore, of appropriate strategies for coping with the environment. Cyert and March state that "so long as the environment of the firm is unstable—and predictably unstable—the heart of the theory [of the firm] must be the process of short-run adaptive reactions."[36]

In summary, both the theoretical and case study literature on organizations suggests that these systems are increasingly finding themselves in environments where the complexity and rapidity of change in external interconnectedness (L_{22}) gives rise to increasingly unpredictable change in their transactional interdependencies (L_{21} and L_{12}). This seems to be good evidence for the emergence of turbulence in the environments of many formal organizations.

Interorganizational Environment

Evidence for Increasing Dependence on Environment
Elsewhere the author has argued that Emery and Trist's concepts can be extended to *all* living systems; furthermore, that this evolutionary process gives rise to conditions—biological, psychological, and social—in which the rate of evolution of environments exceeds the rate of evolution of component systems.[37]

In the short run, the openness of a living system to its environment enables it to take in ingredients from the environment for conversion into energy or information that allows it to maintain a steady state and, hence, to violate the dismal second law of thermodynamics (i.e., of entropy). In the long run, "the characteristic of living systems which most clearly distinguishes them from the nonliving is their property of progressing by the process which is called evolution from less to more complex states of organization."[38] It then follows that to the extent that the environment of some living system X is comprised *of other living systems*, the environment of X is *itself* evolving from less to more complex states of organization. A major corollary is that the evolution of environments is characterized by an increase in the ratio of externally induced change over internally induced change in a system's transactional interdependencies (L_{21} and L_{12}).

For illustration, let us assume that at some given time, each system in some set of interdependent systems is equally likely to experience an internal (L_{11}) change that is functional for survival (i.e., improves its L_{21} or L_{12} transactions). The greater the number of other systems in that set, the greater the probability that some system other than X will experience that change. Since we posit interdependence among members of the set, X's viability over time depends upon X's capacity (L_{11}) for adaptation to environmentally induced (L_{22}) changes in its transactive position, or else upon control over these external relations.

In the case of formal organizations, disturbed-reactive or oligopolistic environments require some form of accommodation between like but competitive organizations whose fates are negatively correlated to some degree. A change in the transactional position of one system in an oligopolistic set, whether for better or worse, automatically affects the transactional position of all other members of the set, and in the opposite direction (i.e., for worse or better, as the case may be).[39] On the other hand, turbulent environments require relationships between dissimilar organizations whose fates are independent or, perhaps, positively correlated.[40] A testable hypothesis that derives from the formal argument is that the evolution of environments is accompanied, in viable systems, by an increase in ability to learn and to perform according to changing contingencies in the environment.

The evolution of organizational environments is characterized by a change in the important constituents of the environment. The earliest formal organizations to appear in the United States (e.g., in agriculture, retail trade, construction, mining)[41] operated largely under placid-clustered conditions. Important inputs, such as natural resources and labor, as well as consumers, comprised an environment in which strategies of optimal location and distinctive competence were critical organizational responses.[42] Two important attributes of placid-clustered environments are: (1) the environment is itself *not* formally organized; and (2) transactions are largely initiated and controlled by the organization (i.e., L_{12}).

Later developments, such as transport technology and derivative overlap in loss of strength gradients, and communication and automation technologies that increased economies of scale, gave rise to disturbed reactive (oligopolistic) conditions in which similar formal organizations become the important actors in an organization's field. They are responsive to its acts (L_{12}) *and* it must be responsive to theirs (L_{21}). The critical organizational response now involves complex operations, requiring sequential choices based on the calculated actions of others, and counteractions.[43]

When the environment becomes turbulent, however, its constituents are a multitude of other formal organizations. Increasingly, an organization's markets consist of other organizations; suppliers of material, labor, and capital are increasingly organized, and regulatory groups are more numerous and powerful. The critical response of organizations under these conditions will be discussed later. It should be noted that *real* environments are often mixtures of these ideal types.

The evolution from placid-clustered environments to turbulent environments[44] can be summarized as a process in which formal organizations evolve: (*1*) *from* the status of systems within environments not formally organized; (2) *through* intermediate phases (e.g., Weberian bureaucracy); and (3) *to* to the status of subsystems of a larger social system.

Clark Kerr traces this evolution for the university in the United States.[45] In modern industrial societies, this evolutionary process has resulted in the replacement of individuals and informal groups by organizations as *actors* in the social system. Functions that were once the sole responsibility of families and communities are increasingly allocated to formal organizations; child-rearing, work, recreation, education, health, and so on. Events which were long a matter of chance are increasingly subject to organizational control, such as population growth, business cycles, and even the weather. One wonders whether Durkheim, if he could observe the current scene, might speculate that the evolution from "mechanical solidarity" to "organic solidarity" is now occurring on the *organizational level*, where the common values of organizations in oligopolies are replaced by functional interdependencies among specialized organizations.[46]

Interorganizational Analysis

It was noted that survival in disturbed-reactive environments depends upon the ability of the organization to anticipate and counteract the behavior of similar systems. The analysis of interorganizational behavior, therefore, becomes meaningful only in these and more complex environments. The interdependence of organizations, or any kind of living systems, at less complex environmental levels is more appropriately studied by means of ecological, competitive market, or other similar models.

The only systematic conceptual approach to interorganizational analysis has been the theory of oligopoly in economics. This theory clearly addresses only disturbed-reactive environments. Many economists admit that the theory, which assumes maximization of profit and perfect knowledge, is increasingly at odds with empirical evidence that organizational behavior is characterized by satisficing and bounded rationality. Boulding comments that "it is surprisingly hard to make a really intelligent conflict move in the economic area simply because of the complexity of the system and the enormous importance of side effects and dynamic effects."[47] A fairly comprehensive search of the literature has revealed only four conceptual frameworks for the analysis of interorganizational relations outside the field of economics. These are briefly reviewed, particular attention being given to assumptions about organization environments, and to the utility of these assumptions in the analysis of interorganizational relations in turbulent fields.

William Evan has introduced the concept of "organization-set," after Merton's "role-set."[48] Relations between a focal organization and members of its organization-set are mediated by the role-sets of boundary personnel. "Relations" are conceived as the flow of information, products or services, and personnel.[49] Presumably, monetary, and legal, and other transactions can be accommodated in the conceptual system. In general, Evan offers a conceptual tool for identifying transactions at a given time. He makes no explicit assumptions about the nature of environmental dynamics, nor does he imply that they are changing. The relative neglect of interorganizational relations, which he finds surprising, is ascribed instead to the traditional intraorganizational focus, which derives from Weber, Taylor, and Barnard.[50] His concepts, however, go considerably beyond those of conventional organization and economic theory (e.g., comparative versus reference organizations and overlap in goals and values). If a temporal dimension were added to Evan's conceptual scheme, then, it would be a very useful tool for describing the "structural" aspects of transactional interdependencies (L_{21} and L_{12} relations) in turbulent fields.

Another approach is taken by Levine and White who focus specifically on relations among community health and welfare agencies. This local set of organizations "may be seen as a system with individual organizations or system parts varying in the kinds and frequencies of their relationships with one another."[51] The authors admit that interdependence exists among these local parts only to the extent that relevant resources are not available from *outside* the local region, which lies beyond their conceptual domain. Nor do we find here any suggestion of turbulence in these local environments. If such local sets of agencies are increasingly interdependent with other components of the local community and with organizations outside the locality, as the evidence suggests, then the utility of Levine and White's approach is both limited and shrinking.

Litwak and Hylton provide a third perspective. They too are concerned with health and welfare organizations, but their major emphasis is on coordination.[52] The degree of interdependence among organizations is a major variable; low interdependence leads to *no* coordination and high interdependence leads to merger, therefore they deal only with conditions of moderate interdependence. The type of coordinating mechanism that emerges under conditions of moderate interdependence is hypothesized to result from the interaction of three trichotomized variables: the *number* of interdependent organizations; the degree of their *awareness* of their interdependence; and the extent of *standardization* in their transactions. The attractive feature of the Litwak and Hylton scheme is the possibility it offers of making different predictions for a great variety of environments. Their model also seems to have predictive power beyond the class of organizations to which they specifically address themselves. If environments are becoming turbulent, however, then increasingly fewer of the model's cells (a $3 \times 3 \times 3$ space) are relevant. In the one-cell turbulent corner of their model, where a large number of organizations have low awareness of their complex and unstandardized interdependence, "there is little chance of coordination,"[53] according to Litwak and Hylton. If the level of awareness of interdependence increases, the model predicts that some process of arbitration will emerge. Thus the model anticipates the interorganizational implications of turbulent fields, but tells us little about the emerging processes that will enable organizations to adapt to turbulence.

The fourth conceptual framework available in the literature is by Thompson and McEwen.[54] They emphasize the interdependence of organizations with the larger society and discuss the consequences that this has for goal setting. "Because the setting of goals is essentially a problem of defining desired relationships between an organization and its environment, change in either requires review and perhaps alteration of goals."[55] They do not argue that such changes are more frequent today, but they do assert that reappraisal of goals is "a more constant problem in an unstable environment than in a stable one," and also "more difficult as the 'product' of the enterprise becomes less tangible."[56]

Thompson and McEwen outline four organizational strategies for dealing with the environment. One is competition; the other three are subtypes of a cooperative strategy: bargaining, co-optation, and coalition. These cooperative strategies all require direct interaction among organizations and this, they argue, increases the environment's potential control over the focal organization.[57] In bargaining, to the extent that the second party's support is necessary, that party is in a position to exercise a veto over the final choice of alternative goals, and thus takes part in the decision. The co-optation strategy makes still further inroads into the goal-setting process. From the standpoint of society, however, co-optation, by providing overlapping memberships, is an important social device for increasing the likelihood that organizations related to each other in complicated ways will in fact find compatible goals. Co-optation thus aids in the integration of heterogeneous parts of a complex social system. Coalition refers to a combination of two or more organizations for a common purpose and is viewed by these authors as the ultimate form of environmental conditioning of organization goals.[58]

The conceptual approaches of Levine and White and of Litwak and Hylton therefore appear to be designed for nonturbulent conditions. Indeed, it may well be that coordination *per se*, in the static sense usually implied by that term is dysfunctional for adaptation to turbulent fields. (This criticism has often been leveled at local "councils of social agencies."[59]) On the other hand, Evan's concept of organization-set seems useful for describing static aspects of interorganizational relations in either disturbed-reactive *or* turbulent-field environments. Its application in longitudinal rather than static studies might yield data on the relationship between structural aspects of transactional relations and organizational adaptability. Lastly, Thompson and McEwen make a unique contribution by distinguishing different *kinds* of interorganizational relations.

As an aside, note that Evan's extension of the role-set concept to organizations suggests still further analogies, which may be heuristically useful. A role is a set of acts prescribed for the occupant of some position. The role accrues to the position; its occupants are interchangeable. If formal organizations are treated as social actors, then one can conceive of organizations as occupants of positions in the larger social system. Each organization has one or more roles in its behavioral repertoire (these are more commonly called functions or goals). The organization occupants of these social positions, however, are also interchangeable.

Integrative Framework

Model

It is assumed that the foregoing arguments are valid: (*1*) that organizational environments are increasingly turbulent; (*2*) that organizations are increasingly less autonomous; and (*3*) that other formal organizations are increasingly important components of organizational environments. Some conceptual perspective is now needed, which will make it possible to view any formal organization, its transactional interdependencies, and the environment itself within a common conceptual framework. The intent of this section is to outline the beginnings of such a framework.

A formal organization is a system primarily oriented to the attainment of a specific goal, which constitutes an output of the system and which is an input for some other system.[60] Needless to say, the output of any living system is dependent upon input into it. Figure 1 schematically illustrates the skeletal structure of a living system. The input and output regions are partially permeable with respect to the environment, which is the region outside the system boundary. Arrows coming into a system represent input and arrows going out of a system represent output. In Figure 2, rectangles represent formal organizations and circles represent individuals and *non*formal social organizations. Figure 2 represents the *statics* of a system X and its turbulent environment. Three-dimensional illustration would be necessary to show the *dynamics* of a turbulent environment schematically. Assume that a third, temporal dimension is imposed on Figure 2 and that this reveals an increasing number of elements and an increasing rate and complexity of change in their interdependencies over time. To do full justice to the concept of turbulence we should add other sets of elements even in Figure 2 above, although these are not yet linked to $X's$ set. A notion that is integral to Emery and Trist's conception of turbulence is that changes outside of $X's$ set, and hence difficult for X to predict and impossible for X to control, will have impact on $X's$ transactional interdependencies in the future. The addition of just one link at some future time may not affect the supersystem but may constitute a system break for X.

Figure 1. Structure of living systems such as a formal organization.

Figure 2. Illustration of system X in turbulent environment.

This schematization shows only one-way directionality and is meant to depict energic inputs (e.g., personnel and material) and output (e.g., product). The organization provides something in exchange for the inputs it receives, of course, and this is usually informational in nature—money, most commonly. Similarly the organization receives money for its product from those systems for whom its product is an input. Nor does our framework distinguish different kinds of inputs, although the analysis of interorganizational exchange requires this kind of taxonomic device. It seems important to distinguish energic inputs and outputs from informational ones. Energic inputs include machinery, personnel, clientele in the case of service organizations, electric power, and so on. Informational inputs are not well conceptualized although there is no doubt of their increasing importance in environments which are more complex and changeable. Special divisions of organizations and whole firms devoted to information collecting, processing, and distributing are also rapidly proliferating (e.g., research organizations, accounting firms, the Central Intelligence Agency).

An input called "legitimacy" is popular in sociological circles but highly resistant to empirical specification. The view taken here is that legitimacy is mediated by the exchange of other resources. Thus the willingness of firm A to contribute capital to X, and of agency B to refer personnel to X and firm C to buy $X's$ product testifies to the legitimacy of X. This "willingness" on the part of organizations A, B, and C, however, can best be understood in terms of informational exchange. For example, A provides X with capital on the basis of A's information about the market for X's product. Or B refuses to refer skilled workmen to X since B has information on X's discriminatory employment practices and also knows of consequences to itself from elsewhere if it is party to X's practice. Technology is also sometimes treated as an input to organizations. We use the term, however, to refer to the complex set of interactions among inputs which takes place in the internal region shown in Figure 1. It is technology which transforms the inputs of the system into the output of the system. Transportation and communication technologies, however, are of a uniquely different order; the former constitutes an energic and the latter an informational transcendence of space-time that enabled the evolution of the more complex environments (L_{22}) which concern us here. Automation and computer technologies are roughly equivalent (i.e., energic and informational, respectively) but on an intraorganizational (L_{11}) level.

Our attention to "legitimacy" and "technology" was tangential to our main theme, to which we now return. Our simplistic approach to an integrative framework for the study of organizations (L_{11}), their transactional interdependencies (L_{21} and L_{12}), and the connectedness within their environments (L_{22}), gives the following conceptual ingredients: (*1*) units that are mainly formal organizations, and (*2*) relationships between them that are the directed flow[61] of (*3*) energy and information. The enormous and increasing importance of informational transaction has not been matched by conceptual developments in organization theory. The importance of information is frequently cited in a general way, however, especially in the context of organizational change or innovation. Dill has made a cogent argument on the need for more attention to this dimension.[62]

The importance of communication for organizational change has been stressed by Ohlin, March and Simon, Benne, Lippitt, and others.[63] Diversity of informational input has been used to explain the creativity of individuals as well as of social systems.[64] The importance of boundary positions as primary sources of innovative inputs from the environment has been stressed by March and Simon[65] and by Kahn *et al.*[66] James Miller hypothesizes that up to a maximum, which no living system has yet reached, the more energy a system devotes to information processing (as opposed to productive and maintenance activity), the more likely the system is to survive.[67]

Evolution on the biological level is accompanied by improvement in the ability of systems to discover and perform according to contingencies in their environments. The random walk which suffices in a placid-randomized environment must be replaced by stochastic processes under placid-clustered conditions, and by cybernetic processes in disturbed-reactive fields. Among biological/phychological systems, only man appears to have the capacity for the purposeful behavior that may permit adaptation to or control of turbulent environments. There is some question, of course, as to whether man actually *has* the capacity to cope with the turbulence that he has introduced into the environment.

Analogous concepts are equally applicable to the evolution of social systems in general and to formal organizations in particular. The capacity of *any* system for adapting to changing contingencies in its environment is inversely related to its dependence upon instinct, habit, or tradition. Adaptability exists, by definition, to the extent that a system (L_{11}) can survive externally induced (L_{22}) change in its transactional interdependencies (L_{21} and L_{12}); therefore viability equals adaptability.

Hypotheses

Hypothesis 1. Organizational change is largely externally induced.

Any particular change may be adaptive or maladaptive, and it may be one of these in the short run and the other in the long run. There is *no* systematic empirical evidence on the relative influence of internal versus environmental antecedents to organizational change. The empirical task here is to identify organizational changes, and the internal or external origins of each change.

It is crucial to distinguish change on the organizational level from the multitude of changes that may occur in or among subsystems, only some of which give rise to change on the system level. Many social psychologists, for example, study change in individuals and groups *within* organizations, but with no reference to variables of organizational level. Likert's book is one noteworthy exception.[68] The important point is that change on the organizational level is analytically distinct from change on other levels.

Organizational change means any change in the kind or quantity of output. Ideally, output is treated as a function of inputs and of transfer functions (i.e., intra-organizational change is inferred from change in input-output relations). Haberstroh illustrates the use of these general system concepts in the organization context.[69] An excellent discussion of the efficiency and effectiveness of organizations, in an open-systems framework, is given in Katz and Kahn.[70]

However, the input-output functions in diversified industries and the outputs of many service organizations are resistant to objective specification and measurement. An empirical test of this hypothesis, with presently available tools, may have to settle for some set of input and internal change that seems to be reasonably antecedent to output change.

The identification of the origin of change is also beset by difficulties. An input change may indeed have external antecedents, but external events may also be responses to some prior internal change in the focal organization. And internal change may be internally generated, but it may also be the result of an informational input from external sources. Novel informational inputs, as well as novel communication channels, often derive from change in personnel inputs. Increasingly, organizations seek personnel who bring specialized information rather than "manpower" to the organization. The presence of first, second, and higher order causation poses a problem for any empirical test of this hypothesis.

Hypothesis 2. System adaptability (e.g., organizational) is a function of ability to learn and to perform according to changing environmental contingencies.

Adaptability exists, by definition, to the extent that a system can survive externally induced change in its transactional interdependencies in the long run. Diversity in a system's input (L_{21}) and output (L_{12}) interdependencies will increase adaptability. The recent and rapid diversification in major industries illustrates this strategy. Flexible structure (L_{11}, *e.g.*, decentralized decision making) will facilitate adaptation. Beyond this, however, adaptability would seem to be largely a function of a system's perceptual and information-processing capacities.[71] The following variables appear crucial: (*1*) *advance information* of impending externally induced (L_{22}) change in L_{21} or L_{12} transactions; (*2*) *active search* for, and activation of, more advantageous input and output transactions; and (*3*) *available memory store* (L_{11}) of interchangeable input and output components in the environment.

Advance information and active search might be empirically handled with Evan's concept of the role-sets of boundary personnel, along with notions of channel efficiency. For example, overlapping memberships (e.g., on boards) would constitute a particularly efficient channel. Likewise, direct communication between members of separate organizations, while less effective than overlapping memberships, would be a more efficient channel between agencies *A* and *B* than instances where their messages must be mediated by a third agency, *C*. Efficiency of interorganizational communication channels should be positively associated with access to advance information, and be facilitative of search, for example. The members of an organization's informational set may become increasingly differentiated from its energic set. Communication channels to research and marketing firms, universities, governmental agencies and other important information producing and distributing agencies would be expected to increase long-run viability. The third variable, memory store, is probably a function of the efficiency of past and present informational channels, but it involves internal (L_{11}) information processing as well.

Lastly, *any* internal change that improves an organization's transactional advantage (e.g., improved technology) will also be conducive to adaptability. Since organizational innovation is more often imitation than invention,[72] these changes are usually also the product of informational input and can be handled within the same integrative framework.

Summary

The lag between evolution in the real world and evolution in theorists' ability to comprehend it is vast, but hopefully shrinking. It was only a little over one hundred years ago that Darwin identified natural selection as the mechanism of evolutionary process. Despite Darwin's enduring insight, theorists of change, including biologists, have continued to focus largely on internal aspects of systems.

It is our thesis that the selective advantage of one intra- or inter-organizational configuration over another cannot be assessed apart from an understanding of the dynamics of the environment itself. It is the environment which exerts selective pressure. "Survival of the fittest" is a function of the fitness of the environment. The dinosaurs *were* impressive creatures, in their day.

Notes and References

1. Ludwig von Bertalanffy, General System Theory, *General Systems*, 1 (1956), 1-10.
2. F. E. Emery and E. L. Trist, The Causal Texture of Organizational Environments, *Human Relations*, 18 (1965), 21-31.
3. *Ibid.*, 22.
4. I am particularly grateful to Kenneth Boulding for inspiration and to Eugene Litwak, Rosemary Sarri, and Robert Vinter for helpful criticisms. A Special Research Fellowship from the National Institutes of Health has supported my doctoral studies and, therefore, has made possible the development of this paper.
5. The concepts of ideal types of environment, and one of the examples in this paragraph, are from Emery and Trist, *op. cit.*, 24-26.
6. The following illustrations are taken from Emery and Trist, *ibid.*: For random-placid environment see Herbert A. Simon, *Models of Man* (New York: John Wiley, 1957), p. 137; W. Ross Ashby, *Design for a Brain* (2nd ed.; London: Chapman and Hall,

1960), Sec. 15/4; the mathematical concept of random field; and the economic concept of classical market.

For random-clustered environment see Edward C. Tolman and Egon Brunswick, The Organism and the Causal Texture of the Environment, *Psychological Review*, 42 (1935), 43-72; Ashby, *op. cit.*, sec. 15/8; and the economic concept of imperfect competition.

For disturbed-reactive environment see Ashby, *op. cit.*, sec. 7; the concept of "imbrication" from I. Chein, Personality and Typology, *Journal of Social Psychology*, 18 (1943), 89-101; and the concept of oligopoly.

7. Emery and Trist, *op. cit.*, 24.

8. *Ibid.*, 26.

9. *Ibid.*, 24.

10. Amitai Etzioni, New Directions in the Study of Organizations and Society, *Social Research*, 27 (1960), 223-228.

11. Peter M. Blau and Richard Scott, *Formal Organizations* (San Francisco: Chandler, 1962), pp. 194-221.

12. Talcott Parsons, *Structure and Process in Modern Societies* (New York: Free Press, 1960), pp. 63-64.

13. Lloyd E. Ohlin, Conformity in American Society Today, *Social Work*, 3 (1958), 63.

14. Robert C. Hood, Business Organization as a Cross Product of Its Purposes and of Its Environment," in Mason Haire (ed.), *Organizational Theory in Industrial Practice* (New York: John Wiley, 1962), p. 73.

15. Peter F. Drucker, The Big Power of Little Ideas, *Harvard Business Review*, 42 (May 1964), 6-8.

16. John W. Gardner, *Self-Renewal* (New York: Harper & Row, 1963), p. 107.

17. James E. McNulty, Organizational Change in Growing Enterprises, *Administrative Science Quarterly*, 7 (1962), 1-21.

18. Long Range Planning and Cloudy Horizons, *Dun's Review*, 81 (Jan. 1963), 42.

19. Blau and Scott, *op. cit.*, p. 217.

20. Lee Adler, Symbiotic Marketing, *Harvard Business Review*, 44 (November 1966), 59-71.

21. W. R. Dill, Environment as an Influence on Managerial Autonomy, *Administrative Science Quarterly*, 2 (1958), 409-443.

22. James D. Thompson, *Organizations in Action* (New York: McGraw-Hill, 1967), pp. 27-28.

23. Philip Selznick, *TVA and the Grass Roots* (Berkeley: University of California, 1949).

24. V. F. Ridgway, Administration of Manufacturer-Dealer Systems, *Administrative Science Quarterly*, 2 (1957), 464-483.

25. Dill, *op. cit.*

26. Sol Levine and Paul E. White, Exchange as a Conceptual Framework for the Study of Interorganizational Relationships, *Administrative Science Quarterly*, 5 (1961), 583-601.

27. Eugene Litwak and Lydia Hylton, Interorganizational Analysis: A Hypothesis on Coordinating Agencies, *Administrative Science Quarterly*, 6 (1962), 395-420.

28. R. H. Elling and S. Halebsky, Organizational Differentiation and Support: A Conceptual Framework, *Administrative Science Quarterly*, 6 (1961), 185-209.

29. Earl Rubington, Organizational Strain and Key Roles, *Administrative Science Quarterly*, 9 (1965), 350-369.

30. William R. Rosengren, Communication, Organization, and Conduct in the "Therapeutic Milieu," *Administrative Science Quarterly*, 9 (1964), 70-90.
31. Burton R. Clark, Interorganizational Patterns in Education, *Administrative Science Quarterly*, 10 (1965), 224-237.
32. John Maniha and Charles Perrow, The Reluctant Organization and the Aggressive Environment, *Administrative Science Quarterly*, 10 (1965), 238-257.
33. Donald W. Taylor, "Decision Making and Problem Solving," in James G. March (ed.), *Handbook of Organizations* (Chicago: Rand McNally, 1965), pp. 48-82.
34. James G. March and Herbert A. Simon, *Organizations* (New York: John Wiley, 1958), pp. 140-141.
35. David Braybrooke and C. E. Lindblom, *A Strategy of Decision* (Glencoe: The Free Press, 1963), especially ch. 3, 5.
36. Richard M. Cyert and James G. March, *A Behavioral Theory of the Firm* (Englewood Cliffs, N.J.: Prentice-Hall, 1963), p. 100.
37. Shirley Terreberry, "The Evolution of Environments" (mimeographed course paper, 1967), pp. 1-37.
38. J. W. S. Pringle, On the Parallel Between Learning and Evolution, *General Systems*, 1 (1956), 90.
39. Assuming a nonexpanding economy, in the ideal instance.
40. Emery and Trist argue that fates, here, are positively correlated. This writer agrees if an expanding economy is assumed.
41. Arthur L. Stinchcombe, "Social Structure and Organizations," in March (ed.), *op. cit.*, p. 156.
42. Emery and Trist, *op. cit.*, 29.
43. *Ibid.*, 25-26.
44. The author does not agree with Emery and Trist, that *formal* (as distinct from social) organization will emerge in placid-random environments.
45. Clark Kerr, *The Uses of the University* (New York: Harper Torchbooks, 1963).
46. Emile Durkheim, *The Division of Labor in Society*, trans. George Simpson (Glencoe: The Free Press, 1947).
47. Kenneth E. Boulding, "The Economies of Human Conflict," in Elton B. McNeil (ed.), *The Nature of Human Conflict* (Englewood Cliffs, N.J.: Prentice-Hall, 1965), p. 189.
48. William M. Evan, "The Organization-Set: Toward a Theory of Interorganizational Relations," in James D. Thompson (ed.), *Approaches to Organizational Design* (Pittsburgh, Pa.: University of Pittsburgh Press, 1966), pp. 177-180.
49. *Ibid.*, pp. 175-176.
50. *Ibid.*
51. Levine and White, *op. cit.*, 586.
52. Litwak and Hylton, *op. cit.*
53. *Ibid.*, 417.
54. James D. Thompson and William J. McEwen, Organizational Goals and Environment, *American Sociological Review*, 23 (1958), 23-31.
55. *Ibid.*, 23.
56. *Ibid.*, 24.
57. *Ibid.*, 27.
58. *Ibid.*, 25-28.
59. Examples include: Robert Morris and Ollie A. Randall, Planning and Organization of Community Services for the Elderly, *Social Work*, 10 (1965), 96-103; Frank W.

Harris, A Modern Council Point of View, *Social Work,* 9 (1964), 34-41; Harold L. Wilensky and Charles N. Lebeaux, *Industrial Society and Social Welfare* (New York: Russell Sage Foundation, 1958), especially pp. 263-265.

60. Talcott Parsons, "Suggestions for a Sociological Approach to the Theory of Organizations," in Amitai Etzioni (ed.), *Complex Organizations* (New York: Holt, Rinehart, and Winston, 1962), p. 33.

61. Dorwin Cartwright, "The Potential Contribution of Graph Theory to Organization Theory," in Mason Haire (ed.), *Modern Organization Theory* (New York: John Wiley, 1959), pp. 254-271.

62. William R. Dill, "The Impact of Environment in Organizational Development," in Sidney Mailick and Edward H. Van Ness (eds.), *Concepts and Issues in Administrative Behavior* (Englewood Cliffs, N.J.: Prentice-Hall, 1962), pp. 94-109.

63. Ohlin, *op. cit.*, 63; March and Simon, *op. cit.*, pp. 173-183; Kenneth D. Benne, "Deliberate Changing as the Facilitation of Growth," in Warren G. Bennis *et al.* (eds.), *The Planning of Change* (New York: Holt, Rinehart, and Winston, 1962), p. 232; Ronald Lippitt, *The Dynamics of Planned Change* (New York: Harcourt, Brace, and World, 1958), p. 52.

64. For example: Floyd H. Allport, *Theories of Perception and the Concept of Structure* (New York, John Wiley, 1955), p. 76; William F. Ogburn and Meyer F. Nimkoff, *Sociology* (4th ed.; Boston: Houghton Mifflin, 1964), pp. 662-670.

65. March and Simon, *op. cit.*, pp. 165-166, 189.

66. Robert L Kahn *et al., Organizational Stress* (New York: John Wiley, 1964), pp. 101-126.

67. James G. Miller, Toward a General Theory for the Behavioral Sciences, *The American Psychologist*, 10 (1955), 530.

68. Rensis Likert, *New Patterns of Management* (New York: McGraw-Hill, 1961).

69. Chadwick J. Haberstroth, "Organization Design and Systems Analysis," in March (ed.), *op. cit.*, pp. 1171-1211.

70. Daniel Katz and Robert L. Kahn, *The Social Psychology of Organizations* (New York: John Wiley, 1966), especially pp. 149-170.

71. Igor Ansoff speaks of the "wide-open windows of perception" required of tomorrow's firms, and offers a perspective on the future that is fully compatible with that presented here; see The Firm of the Future, *Harvard Business Review*, 43 (September 1965), 162.

72. Theodore Levitt, Innovative Imitation, *Harvard Business Review*, 44 (September 1966), 63-70.

THE MANAGEMENT OF INNOVATION

TOM BURNS
G. M. STALKER

The Analysis of Organizations Under Conditions of Relative Stability and Change

The core of all the twenty studies on which [our] book [*The Management of Innovation*] is based is the description and explanation of what happens when new and unfamiliar tasks are put upon industrial concerns organized for relatively stable conditions. When novelty and unfamiliarity in both market situation and technical information become the accepted order of things, a fundamentally different kind of management system becomes appropriate from that which applies to a relatively stable commercial and technical environment. . . . There is very little I would wish to add or to amend in this section, although, so far as I am able to judge from subsequent uses and references, there must be some wrongly placed emphases.

In the first place, the utility of the notions of "mechanistic" and "organic" management systems resides largely in their being related as dependent variables to the rate of "environmental" change. "Environmental", in this connection, refers to the technological basis of production and to the market situation; indeed, as I have argued elsewhere,[1] . . . the increasing rate of technological change characteristic of the last generation could plausibly be regarded as a function of fundamental changes in the relationship of production to consumption.

If the form of management is properly to be seen as dependent on the situation the concern is trying to meet, it follows that there is no single set of principles for "good organization", an ideal type of management system which can serve as a model to which administrative practice should, or could in time, approximate. It follows also that there is an overriding management task in first interpreting correctly the market and technological situation, in terms of its instability or of the rate at which conditions are changing, and then designing the management system appropriate to the conditions, and making it work. "Direction", as I have labelled this activity, is the distinctive task of managers-in-chief, and is discussed in the final chapters in terms of a critical examination of the role of the managing director; but properly speaking the description and explanation of the interpretative, directive functions of top management belong to the earlier section, since it is these functions that largely determine the effectiveness of the organization as a whole. The examination of the role of the chief executive, that is to say, is logically antecedent to the description and analysis of the organizational problems. . . . For it was failure at this level that produced the characteristic forms of management system encountered in most of the concerns—forms which, from the point of view of their overt constitution and purposes, were clearly inefficient and ineffective, although there are, as

Reprinted by permission of the authors and the publisher, Tavistock Publications Ltd., from *The Management of Innovation*.

we shall see, other points of view from which they may be regarded as serving certain ends and performing certain functions in an entirely efficient manner.

For the individual, much of the importance of the difference between mechanistic and organic systems lies in the extent of his commitment to the working organization. Mechanistic systems (sc. "bureaucracies") define his functions, together with the methods, responsibilities, and powers appropriate to them; in other words, however, this means that boundaries are set. That is to say, in being told what he has to attend to, and how, he is also told what he does not have to bother with, what is not his affair, what is not expected of him, what he can post elsewhere as the responsibility of others. In organic systems, the boundaries of feasible demands on the individual disappear. The greatest stress is placed on his regarding himself as fully implicated in the discharge of any task appearing over his horizon, as involved not merely in the exercise of a special competence but in commitment to the success of the concern's undertakings approximating somewhat to that of the doctor or scientist in the discharge of his professional functions. . . .

Mechanistic and Organic Systems

We are now at the point at which we may set down the outline of the two management systems which represent for us the two polar extremities of the forms which such systems can take when they are adapted to a specific rate of technical and commercial change. The case we have tried to establish from the literature . . . is that the different forms assumed by a working organization do exist objectively and are not merely interpretations offered by observers of different schools.

Both types represent a "rational" form of organization, in that they may both, in our experience, be explicitly and deliberately created and maintained to exploit the human resources of a concern in the most efficient manner feasible in the circumstances of the concern. Not surprisingly, however, each exhibits characteristics which have been hitherto associated with different kinds of interpretation. For it is our contention that empirical findings have usually been classified according to sociological ideology rather than according to the functional specificity of the working organization to its task and the conditions confronting it.

We have tried to argue that these are two formally contrasted forms of management system. These we shall call the mechanistic and organic forms.

A *mechanistic* management system is appropriate to stable conditions. It is characterized by:

(*a*) the specialized differentiation of functional tasks into which the problems and tasks facing the concern as a whole are broken down;

(*b*) the abstract nature of each individual task, which is pursued with techniques and purposes more or less distinct from those of the concern as a whole; i.e., the functionaries tend to pursue the technical improvement of means, rather than the accomplishment of the ends of the concern;

(*c*) the reconciliation, for each level in the hierarchy, of these distinct performances by the immediate superiors, who are also, in turn, responsible for seeing that each is relevant in his own special part of the main task.

(*d*) the precise definition of rights and obligations and technical methods attached to each functional role;

(*e*) the translation of rights and obligations and methods into the responsibilities of a functional position;

(*f*) hierarchic structure of control, authority and communication;

(*g*) a reinforcement of the hierarchic structure by the location of knowledge of actualities exclusively at the top of the hierarchy, where the final reconciliation of distinct tasks and assessment of relevance is made.[2]

(*h*) a tendency for interaction between members of the concern to be vertical, i.e., between superior and subordinate;

(*i*) a tendency for operations and working behaviour to be governed by the instructions and decisions issued by superiors;

(*j*) insistence on loyalty to the concern and obedience to superiors as a condition of membership;

(*k*) a greater importance and prestige attaching to internal (local) than to general (cosmopolitan) knowledge, experience, and skill.

The *organic* form is appropriate to changing conditions, which give rise constantly to fresh problems and unforeseen requirements for action which cannot be broken down or distributed automatically arising from the functional roles defined within a hierarchic structure. It is characterized by:

(*a*) the contributive nature of special knowledge and experience to the common task of the concern;

(*b*) the "realistic" nature of the individual task, which is seen as set by the total situation of the concern;

(*c*) the adjustment and continual re-definition of individual tasks through interaction with others;

(*d*) the shedding of "responsibility" as a limited field of rights, obligations and methods. (Problems may not be posted upwards, downwards or sideways as being someone's else's responsibility);

(*e*) the spread of commitment to the concern beyond any technical definition;

(*f*) a network structure of control, authority, and communication. The sanctions which apply to the individual's conduct in his working role derive more from presumed community of interest with the rest of the working organization in the survival and growth of the firm, and less from a contractual relationship between himself and a non-personal corporation, represented for him by an immediate superior;

(*g*) omniscience no longer imputed to the head of the concern; knowledge about the technical or commercial nature of the here and now task may be located anywhere in the network; this location becoming the *ad hoc* centre of control authority and communication;

(*h*) a lateral rather than a vertical direction of communication through the organization, communication between people of different rank, also, resembling consultation rather than command;

(*i*) a content of communication which consists of information and advice rather than instructions and decisions;

(*j*) commitment to the concern's tasks and to the "technological ethos" of material progress and expansion is more highly valued than loyalty and obedience;

(*k*) importance and prestige attach to affiliations and expertise valid in the industrial and technical and commercial milieux external to the firm.

One important corollary to be attached to this account is that while organic systems are not hierarchic in the same sense as are mechanistic, they remain stratified. Positions are differentiated according to seniority—i.e., greater expertise. The lead in joint decisions is frequently taken by seniors, but it is an essential presumption of the organic system that the lead, i.e. "authority", is taken by whoever shows himself most informed and capable, i.e., the "best authority". The location of authority is settled by consensus.

A second observation is that the area of commitment to the concern—the extent to which the individual yields himself as a resource to be used by the working organization—is far more extensive in organic than in mechanistic systems. Commitment, in fact, is expected to approach that of the professional scientist to his work, and frequently does. One further consequence of this is that it becomes far less feasible to distinguish "informal" from "formal" organization.

Thirdly, the emptying out of significance from the hierarchic command system, by which co-operation is ensured and which serves to monitor the working organization under a mechanistic system, is countered by the development of shared beliefs about the values and goals of the concern. The growth and accretion of institutionalized values, beliefs, and conduct, in the form of commitments, ideology, and manners, around an image of the concern in its industrial and commercial setting make good the loss of formal structure.

Finally, the two forms of system represent a polarity, not a dichotomy; there are, as we have tried to show, intermediate stages between the extremities empirically known to us. Also, the relation of one form to the other is elastic, so that a concern oscillating between relative stability and relative change may also oscillate between the two forms. A concern may (and frequently does) operate with a management system which includes both types.

The organic form, by departing from the familiar clarity and fixity of the hierarchic structure, is often experienced by the individual manager as an uneasy, embarrassed, or chronically anxious quest for knowledge about what he should be doing, or what is expected of him, and similar apprehensiveness about what others are doing. Indeed, as we shall see later, this kind of response is necessary if the organic form of organization is to work effectively. Understandably, such anxiety finds expression in resentment when the apparent confusion besetting him is not explained. In these situations, all managers some of the time, and many managers all the time, yearn for more definition and structure.

On the other hand, some managers recognize a rationale of non-definition, a reasoned basis for the practice of those successful firms in which designation of status, function, and line of responsibility and authority has been vague or even avoided.

The desire for more definition is often in effect a wish to have the limits of one's task more neatly defined—to know what and when one doesn't have to bother about as much as to know what one does have to. It follows that the more definition is given, the more omniscient the management must be, so that no functions are left wholly or partly undischarged, no person is overburdened with undelegated responsibility, or left without the authority to do his job properly. To do this, to have all the separate functions attached to individual roles fitting together and comprehensively, to have communication between persons constantly maintained on a level adequate to the needs of each functional role, requires rules or traditions of behaviour proved over a long time and an equally fixed, stable task. The omniscience which may then be credited to the head of the concern is expressed throughout its body through the lines of command, extending in a clear, explicitly titled hierarchy of officers and subordinates.

The whole mechanistic form is instinct with this twofold principle of definition and dependence which acts as the frame within which action is conceived and carried out. It works, unconsciously, almost in the smallest minutiae of daily activity. "How late is late?" The answer to this question is not to be found in the rule book, but in the superior. Late is when the boss thinks it is late. Is he the kind of man who thinks 8:00 is the time, and 8:01 is late? Does he think that 8:15 is all right occasionally if it is not a regular thing? Does he think that everyone should be allowed a 5-minutes grace after 8:00 but after that they are late?

Settling questions about how a person's job is to be done in this way is nevertheless simple, direct, and economical of effort. . . .

One other feature of mechanistic organization needs emphasis. It is a necessary condition of its operation that the individual "works on his own", functionally isolated; he "knows his job", he is "responsible for seeing it's done". He works at a job which is in a sense artificially abstracted from the realities of the situation the concern is dealing with, the accountant "dealing with the costs side", the works manager "pushing production", and so on. As this works out in practice, the rest of the organization becomes part of the problem situation the individual has to deal with in order to perform successfully; i.e., difficulties and problems arising from work or information which has been handed over the "responsibility barrier" between two jobs or departments are regarded as "really" the responsibility of the person from whom they were received. As a design engineer put in, "When you get designers handing over designs completely to production, it's 'their responsibility' now. And you get tennis games played with the responsibility for anything that goes wrong. What happens is that you're constantly getting unsuspected faults arising from characteristics which you didn't think important in the design. If you get to hear of these through a sales person, or a production person, or somebody to whom the design was handed over to in the dim past, then, instead of being a design problem, it's an annoyance caused by that particular person, who can't do his own job—because you'd thought you were finished with that one, and you're on to something else now."

When the assumptions of the form of organization make for preoccupation with specialized tasks, the chances of career success, or of greater influence, depend rather on the relative importance which may be attached to each special function by the superior whose task it is to reconcile and control a number of them. And, indeed, to press the claims of one's job or department for a bigger share of the firm's resources is in many cases regarded as a mark of initiative, of effectiveness, and even of "loyalty to the firm's interests". The state of affairs thus engendered squares with the role of the superior, the man who can see the wood instead of just the trees, and gives it the reinforcement of the aloof detachment belonging to a court of appeal. The ordinary relationship prevailing between individual managers "in charge of'' different functions is one of rivalry, a rivalry which may be rendered innocuous to the persons involved by personal friendship or the norms of sociability, but which turns discussion about the situations which constitute the real problems of the concern—how to make products more cheaply, how to sell more, how to allocate resources, whether to curtail activity in one sector, whether to risk expansion in another, and so on—into an arena of conflicting interests.

The distinctive feature of the second, organic system is the pervasiveness of the working organization as an institution. In concrete terms, this makes itself felt in a preparedness to combine with others in serving the general aims of the concern. Proportionately to the rate and extent of change, the less can the omniscience appropriate to command organizations be ascribed to the head of the organization; for executives, and even operatives, in a changing firm it is always theirs to reason why. Furthermore, the less definition can be given to status, roles, and modes of communication, the more do the activities of each member of the organization become determined by the real tasks of the firm as he sees them than by instruction and routine. The individual's job ceases to be self-contained; the only way in which "his" job can be done is by his participating continually with others in the solution of problems which are real to the firm, and put in a language of requirements and activities meaningful to them all. Such methods of working put much heavier demands on the individual. . . .

We have endeavoured to stress the appropriateness of each system to its own specific set of conditions. Equally, we desire to avoid the suggestion that either system is superior under all circumstances to the other. In particular, nothing in our experience justifies the assumption that mechanistic systems should be superseded by organic in conditions of stability.[3] The beginning of the administrative wisdom is the awareness that there is no one optimum type of management system.

Notes and References

1. T. Burns, "The Sociology of Industry", in A. T. Welford (ed.) *Society*, London, Routledge & Kegan Paul, 1962 (p. 191).
2. This functional attribute of the head of a concern often takes on a clearly expressive aspect. It is common enough for concerns to instruct all people with whom they deal to address correspondence to the firm (i.e., to its formal head) and for all outgoing letters and orders to be signed by the head of the concern. Similarly, the printed letter heading used by Government departments carries instructions for the replies to be addressed to the Secretary, etc. These instructions are not always taken seriously, either by members of the organization or their correspondents, but in one company this practice was insisted upon and was taken to somewhat unusual lengths; *all* correspondence was delivered to the managing director, who would thereafter distribute excerpts to members of the staff, synthesizing their replies into the letter of reply which he eventually sent. Telephone communication was also controlled by limiting the numbers of extensions, and by monitoring incoming and outgoing calls.
3. A recent instance of this assumption is contained in H. A. Shepard's paper addressed to the Symposium on the Direction of Research Establishments, 1956. "There is much evidence to suggest that the optimal use of human resources in industrial organizations requires a different set of conditions, assumptions, and skills from those traditionally present in industry. Over the past twenty-five years, some new orientations have

emerged from organizational experiments, observations and inventions. The new orientations depart radically from doctrines associated with 'Scientific Management' and traditional bureaucratic patterns.

"The central emphases in this development are as follows:

1. Wide participation in decision-making, rather than centralized decision-making.

2. The face-to-face group, rather than the individual, as the basic unit of organization.

3. Mutual confidence, rather than authority, as the integrative force in organization.

4. The supervisor as the agent for maintaining intragroup and intergroup communication, rather than as the agent of higher authority.

5. Growth of members of the organization to greater responsibility, rather than external control of the member's performance or their tasks."

GENERIC TYPES OF SUBSYSTEMS

DANIEL KATZ
ROBERT L. KAHN

Social organizations like other systems have a through-put or a transformation of the energic input. Those activities concerned with the through-put have been called *production or technical subsystems* (Parsons, 1960). To insure existence beyond a single cycle of productive activity, there must be new materials to be worked on. *Supportive structures* develop in a surviving system to provide a continuing source of production inputs They are of two kinds. One is the extension of the production system into the environment by activities which procure raw materials and dispose of the product. The second type is at the more complex level of maintaining and furthering a favorable environment through relations with other structures in the society—the institutional function, in Parsons' terms.

In addition to the need for production inputs, special attention must be given to the maintenance inputs, i.e., to insuring the availability of the human energy which results in role performance. If the system is to survive, *maintenance substructures* must be elaborated to hold the walls of the social maze in place. Even these would not suffice to insure organizational survival, however. The organization exists in a changing and demanding environment, and it must adapt constantly to the changing environmental demands. *Adaptive structures* develop in organizations to generate appropriate responses to external conditions. Finally, these patterns of behavior need to be coordinated, adjusted, controlled, and directed if the complex substructures are to hold together as a unified system or organization. Hence, *managerial subsystems* are an integral part of permanent elaborated social patterning of behavior.

Thus we can describe the facts of organizational functioning with respect to five basic subsystems: (1) production subsystems concerned with the work that gets done; (2) supportive subsystems of procurement, disposal, and institutional relations; (3) maintenance subsystems for tying people into their functional roles; (4) adaptive subsystems, concerned with organizational change; (5) managerial systems for the direction, adjudication, and control of the many subsystems and activities of the structure.

Production or Technical Subsystems

The production system is concerned with the through-put, the energic or informational transformation whose cycles of activity comprise the major functions of the system. Organizations are commonly classified according to their main productive process, e.g., educational, if concerned with training, political, if concerned with affecting power relations, economic, if concerned with the creation of wealth. . . .

Supportive Subsystems

Supportive subsystems are those which carry on the environmental transactions in procuring the input or disposing of the output or aiding in these processes. They are in part a direct extension of the production activities of the organization in importing the material to be worked on or exporting the finished product. Or they may be indirectly related to the production cycle but supportive of it in maintaining a favorable environment for the operation of the system.

The relating of the system to its larger social environment in establishing its legitimation and support would be an *institutional* function. In general the top echelon of an organization, such as the Board of Trustees, would carry this function and would often have some degree of membership in outside structures. Thus supportive systems concerned with environmental transactions include the specific procurement or disposal structures as well as the more general high level activities of securing favorable relations with larger structures.

Maintenance Subsystems

Maintenance activities are not directed at the material being worked on but at the equipment for getting the work done. In most organizations this equipment consists of patterned human behavior. The arrangement of roles for interrelated performance does not guarantee that people will take or remain in these roles performing their functions. Hence subsystems for recruitment, indoctrination or socialization, rewarding and sanctioning, are found in enduring social structures. These subsystems function to maintain the fabric of interdependent behavior necessary for task accomplishment. They tie people into the system as functioning parts. They are cycles of activity which are tangential to, or criss-cross, the production cycles. Individuals may play both production and maintenance roles, as when members of a college faculty move from their teaching roles to meet as an executive committee to decide on promotions and salary increases for faculty members. In many systems, however, the same individuals do not step from one set of roles to another. The maintenance roles need not be specific to the major differentiating function of the system. The person functioning as an administrator in the maintenance structure is often a generalist who can move from one organization or type of organization to another. Indeed, a director of personnel or training in a given company probably could move more easily and with less strain to a functionally comparable position in another company than to a different subsystem in his own organization.

Whereas the supportive systems of procurement and disposal are concerned with insuring production inputs, i.e., materials and resources for the work of the organization, the maintenance system is concerned with inputs for preserving the system either through appropriate selection of personnel or adequate rewarding of the personnel selected. We have already noted the neglect of the maintenance function in traditional thinking which accepts social structures as objective and fixed in nature as biological relationships. The same neglect characterizes the world of practical action in which attention is centered on the production system and its inputs. Problems of personnel both on the recruitment and morale sides have received belated and inadequate recognition and the position of the director of these operations is generally low in the management hierarchy whether the organization is industrial or governmental.

Reward and sanctioning systems, utilized to maintain role performance, are major maintenance substructures. In social organizations rewards and sanctions are employed with respect to *specific* performances and infractions according to a set of rules. In feudal systems sanctions and rewards tended to be invoked in a more capricious manner. In the small agrarian community punitive actions towards a transgressor were based upon the outraged morality of community members and were not finely attuned to a set of particulars established about the transgressing act.

Social organizations, at least in our culture and era, move toward emphasis upon a reward system rather than a punishment system. To hold members in an organization and to maintain a satisfactory type of role performance means that people's experiences in the system must be rewarding, particularly if they have freedom to move in and out of organizations. Often one set of rewards develops to attract and hold members in a system and another to achieve some optimum level of performance.

In keeping with the relative neglect of maintenance functions is the blindness in most organizational theorizing to a significant characteristic of the reward system, namely its *allocation parameters*, or who gets what and why. The allocation of rewards in most organizations in western nations (and to a greater extent than is realized in communist countries as well) is highly differential between members of various subsystems. The problem is one of keeping people in the organizational system and keeping them motivated to perform when there are conspicuous differences in the amount of return to various subgroups in the organization. Rewards are not only monetary; they also include prestige and status, gratifications from interesting work, identification with group products, and satisfactions from decision making. The distribution of all these types of rewards is a basic dimension for understanding how an organization operates. There is a substantial correlation among the various kinds of reward; the members who are paid the most generally have the highest status, the most interesting jobs, and the opportunity to make decisions. Hence the differentials in rewards to subsystem members are even greater than the differences in monetary return would suggest.

Adaptive Subsystems

Nothing in the production, supportive, and maintenance subsystems would suffice to insure organizational survival in a changing environment. Except for the functions of procurement and disposal, these subsystems face inward; they are concerned with the functioning of the organization as it is rather than with what it might become. The risks of concentrating attention and energies inward are directly proportional to the magnitude and rate of change in the world outside the organization. External changes in taste, in cultural norms and values, in competitive organizations, in economic and political power—all these and many others reach the organization as demands for internal change. To refuse to accede to such demands is to risk the possibility that the transactions of procurement and disposal will be reduced or refused, or that the processes of maintenance will become increasingly difficult. In most formal organizations there arise, therefore, structures which are specifically concerned with sensing relevant changes in the outside world and translating the meaning of those changes for the organization. There may be structures which devote their energies wholly to the anticipation of such changes. All these comprise the adaptive subsystem of the organization and bear such names as product research, market research, long-range planning, research and development, and the like.

Managerial Subsystems

These systems comprise the organized activities for controlling, coordinating, and directing the many subsystems of the structure. They represent another slice of the organizational pattern and are made up of cycles of activities cutting across the structure horizontally to deal with coordination of subsystems and the adjustment of the total system to its environment. The functions of top management require actions affecting large sectors of organizational space, the formulation of rules rather than specific invoking of penalties for the recalcitrant member, or a change in policy to achieve better utilization of the system's resources. The exercise of the management function is observable, however, at all levels of the system. Two major types of managerial subsystems which deserve further description are *regulatory mechanisms* and the *authority structure*.

Our basic model of a social system is a structure which imports energy from the external world, transforms it, and exports a product to the environment which is the source for a reenergizing of the cycle. Substructures may develop which gather and utilize intelligence about the energic transactions. Such devices function to give feedback to the system about its output in relation to its input. Management in modern organizations operates in good part through such *regulatory mechanisms*. When a system operates without a specialized feedback or regulatory mechanism, we shall refer to it as a primitive group rather than a social organization. Voluntary groups, for example, may form from time to time and may carry on some cooperative activity. The degree of accomplishment will be the result of the number of members and their enthusiasm at the moment and will vary greatly from time to time. The group is not guided by any information about its impact upon the world or any intelligence about the contributions of its members. It may not even have a roster of its members and its new chairman may search in vain for the records of what was done under his predecessor, how it was done, and what the outcome was. A voluntary group becomes an organization when it acquires systematic methods for regulating its activities on the basis of information about its functioning. Operationally a voluntary group is identified as an organization when it has a permanent secretariat or some equivalent device for maintaining stability in the offices of secretary and treasurer with respect to membership rolls, finances, and records.

Regulatory mechanisms are highly developed in profit making organizations, and information about the market and the sale of the commodities of the enterprise is constantly used to control the productive activities of the enterprise and its actions with respect to its supply of raw materials. Regulatory mechanisms vary in complexity and sophistication, however, and very primitive mechanisms of regulation may direct the activity of large, complex systems. For example, a medical school may base its admissions upon the number of available microscopes or the size of its laboratories.

The dominant tendency is toward complexity in regulatory mechanisms. Industrial concerns utilize increasingly detailed estimates of economic trends in planning the capture of new markets. A highly significant development in modern industry is the use of electronic computers and automated devices to regulate the activities of the enterprise at two levels. Computers will be used to process all kinds of information about the internal functioning of the organization and about its environment, to guide decisions at the highest echelons about basic policies and procedures—even to help in assigning weights to various factors. Automated devices will be employed within subsystems to provide self-regulation for the performance of certain types of tasks.

The systematic use of information to guide organizational functioning is the sine qua non of an organization. The implications of such regulatory mechanisms are far-reaching. They include the elaboration of the role structure to provide for such a continuing function, and they imply the addition of other structures to coordinate the incoming information with the ongoing activities. The social system of feudalism rested more on status relationships than on highly developed role concepts and relied for stability on a combination of physical force and the mysticism of the masses. Modern role systems, however, need an intelligence function to maintain themselves.

Organizations need not be authoritarian in character, but they must possess an established and definitive form of decision making about organizational matters. The *authority structure* essentially describes the way in which the managerial system is organized with respect to the sources of decision making and its implementation. Decisions are accepted if made in the proper manner, whether by democratic vote or by an edict from duly constituted authority. The essence of authority structure is the acceptance of directives as legitimate, i.e., either the acquiescence or approval by people of rules of the game. The rules may be arrived at through a democratic process or they may be promulgated from above, but in either case they are binding upon the members of the system. They are properties of the system and not of the dominance-submission patterns of individual personalities. We recognize this when we say that a person has exceeded his authority. He has gone beyond the legitimately defined limits of his position. What has obscured this clear theoretical distinction in practice is that authoritarian personalities often select themselves or are selected for positions of power in social systems. Their personality traits may lead them to abuse this legal power in areas where it is difficult to check on their actions. The paradox is that the law enforcement agencies, whether local police, internal revenue agents, immigration authorities, or customs officials, are entrusted with carrying out the rules of the game, but often enjoy a reputation for officiousness or overstepping their authority.

People tend to personalize relationships and often impute personal despotism to the orderly functioning of the social system, confusing the exercise of legal authority with authoritarianism. Since authoritarianism is a bad thing and is the opposite of the desirable qualities of liberty and democracy, there may be rebellion against any rules of the game which the individual does not relish.

Though in some organizations decisions are democratically arrived at, they are abided by until a change is effected through the legitimized channels for change. Or the organization may be authoritarian in character, but again decisions about given types of affairs are made by some appropriate officer. Even in the democratically constructed organization, minor decision making in keeping with lines of policy as determined by majority vote will be entrusted to representatives of the group. Such delegation of power creates a hierarchy of positions within the structure even though the elected official may have to validate his authority from time to time by standing for reelection.

Thus every organization has an *executive system* for carrying out policy or the implementation of administrative decisions. In a democratic structure there is, in addition, a separate *legislative system* with the power vested in the membership to select top executives, to set policy, to choose between alternative policies of the leadership, or to veto policy proposals. In an authoritarian structure a single system may include the *executive* and *legislative* functions, and the top executives do the legislating for the organization. It is also possible for an authoritarian structure to have separate legislative and executive systems, in which an appointed or self-perpetuating board of directors sets policy and a manager and his subordinates execute it. *The essential difference between a democratic and an authoritarian system is not whether executive officers order or consult with those below them but whether the power to legislate on policy is vested in the membership or in the top echelons.*

There is an interpenetration of the authority and reward systems of an organization. The authority structure allocates decision making, and decision making is rewarding in two senses; (1) its exercise is in itself gratifying to the needs of people for participation and autonomy, and (2) it is instrumental in its power potential for achieving other objectives. Hence an authority structure democratically based in a legislative system involving the membership has a built-in reward mechanism not found in an authoritarian system. There are other types of advantages to an authoritarian system but its problems of maintenance differ radically from the democratic system. Organization theorists apart from political scientists have given scant attention to this critical difference between organization forms. In the industrial world the appeal of the unions to workers is often a mystery to industrialists who have failed to grasp the significance of democratic structure and its reward character, even in imperfect manifestation.

Ordinarily the developmental processes by which groups acquire a regulatory mechanism and an authority structure are not independent but interactive. With a regulatory mechanism goes the need for decision making about the uses to which the information will be put. So long as a primitive group can operate in terms of the enthusiasm of its particular adherents at a given time and drop to another level of activity with less motivated followers at another time, it requires only task direction which can be generated within the group itself. But when it moves over to the utilization of information about maintaining some effective ratio of energy input to energy output and some stability in the level of its operations, it needs a more permanent and definitive form of decision making. Thus the authority structure grows in response to the development of a regulatory maintenance mechanism. And conversely, as authority comes to be vested in positions in the group, its exercise is dependent upon information feedback about its functioning. The officers charged with staffing an organization need information about the amount and causes of turnover, and about the kind of people who are lost relative to those who are retained. Some regulatory feedback mechanism is needed to maintain the quantity and quality of personnel which the operations require. The top officers are concerned with the total efficiency of the operations and they will institute cost accounting systems to aid them in the exercise of their authority.

There can be a power structure in primitive groups in terms of the superior personality force of a leader, whether because of physical prowess, mental alertness, or persuasiveness. This is not, however, the same as authority structure in which the order is followed because it comes from the legitimized position in the structure rather than from a certain personality. The soldier salutes the uniform of the superior officer, not the man. The informal group of teenagers on the corner may start as a primitive group with leadership a matter of the interplay of the strongest personalities in the group. After a time a leader may emerge and the group may develop norms about how his legitimate authority should be exercised. It becomes an organization when leaders and followers decide on membership and procedures for admitting novices to membership. This process is one of regulating group functioning through information about its component parts. The gang may, for example, vote to admit Joe Smith because he is a tough fighter, Bill Brown because he has a car, and to restrict other admissions indefinitely in terms of facilities available and activities planned for the future.

The authority structure in feudal and semi-feudal systems is clear and legitimized but is less a matter of role and more a combination of role and status and personality. The noble is obeyed because of his inherited status as a noble which is irretrievably mixed up with him as a person because of the confusion of biological and social inheritance. It is the modern bureaucratic organization, as Max Weber pointed out, which has developed an authority structure of the rational-legal type whereby the rules and prerogatives of authority are quite separated from the person and personality of the wielder of authority. Some structure of authority, some criteria for allocating it, and some rules for its exercise are, however, among the common characteristics of all human organizations.

Reference

Parsons T., 1960, *Structure and Process in Modern Societies*, New York: Free Press.

ORGANIZATIONS IN ACTION

JAMES D. THOMPSON

Variations In Technologies

Clearly, technology is an important variable in understanding the actions of complex organizations. In modern societies the variety of desired outcomes for which specific technologies areavailable seems infinite. A complete but simple typology of technologies which has found order in this variety would be quite helpful. Typologies are available for industrial production (Woodward, 1965) and for mental therapy (Hawkes, 1962) but are not general enough to deal with the range of technologies found in complex organizations. Lacking such a typology, we will simply identify three varieties which are (1) widespread in modern society and (2) sufficiently different to illustrate the propositions we wish to develop.

The Long-linked Technology

A long-linked technology involves serial interdependence in the sense that act Z can be performed only after successful completion of act Y, which in turn rests on act X, and so on. The original symbol of technical rationality, the mass production assembly line, is of this long-linked nature. It approaches instrumental perfection when it produces a single kind of standard product, repetitively and at a constant rate. Production of only one kind of product means that a single technology is required, and this in turn permits the use of clear-cut criteria for the selection of machines and tools, construction of work-flow arrangements, acquisition of raw materials, and selection of human operators. Repetition of the productive process provides experience as a means of eliminating imperfections in the technology; experience can lead to the modification of machines and provide the basis for scheduled preventive maintenance. Repetition means that human motions can also be examined, and through training and practice, energy losses and errors minimized. It is in this setting that the scientific-management movement has perhaps made its greatest contribution.

The constant rate of production means that, once adjusted, the proportions of resources involved can be standardized to the point where each contributes to its capacity; none need be underemployed. This of course makes important contributions to the economic aspect of the technology.

The Mediating Technology

Various organizations have, as a primary function, the linking of clients or customers who are or wish to be interdependent. The commercial bank links depositors and borrowers. The insurance firm links those who would pool common risks. The telephone utility links those who would call and those who would be called. The post office provides a possible linkage of virtually every member of the modern society. The employment agency mediates the supply of labor and the demand for it.

Complexity in the mediating technology comes not from the necessity of having each activity geared to the requirements of the next but rather from the fact that the mediating technology requires operating in *standardized ways*, and *extensively*; e.g., with multiple clients or customers distributed in time and space.

The commercial bank must find and aggregate deposits from diverse depositors; but however diverse the depositors, the transaction must conform to standard terms and to uniform bookkeeping and accounting procedures. It must also find borrowers; but no matter how varied their needs or desires, loans must be made according to standardized criteria and on terms uniformly applied to the category appropriate to the particular borrower. Poor risks who receive favored treatment jeopardize bank solvency. Standardization permits the insurance organization to define categories of risk and hence to sort its customers or potential customers into appropriate aggregate categories; the insured who is not a qualified risk but is so defined upsets the probabilities on which insurance rests. The telephone company became viable only when the telephone became regarded as a necessity, and this did not occur until equipment was standardized to the point where it could be incorporated into one network. Standardization enables the employment agency to aggregate job applicants into categories which can be matched against standardized requests for employees.

Standardization makes possible the operation of the mediating technology over time and through space by assuring each segment of the organization that other segments are operating in compatible ways. It is in such situations that the bureaucratic techniques of categorization and impersonal application of rules have been most beneficial (Weber, 1947; Merton, 1957a).

The Intensive Technology

This third variety we label *intensive* to signify that a variety of techniques is drawn upon in order to achieve a change in some specific object; but the selection, combination, and order of application are determined by feedback from the object itself. When the object is human, this intensive technology is regarded as "therapeutic," but the same technical logic is found also in the construction industry

(Stinchcombe, 1959) and in research where the objects of concern are nonhuman.

The intensive technology is most dramatically illustrated by the general hospital. At any moment an emergency admission may require some combination of dietary, x-ray, laboratory, and housekeeping or hotel services, together with the various medical specialties, pharmaceutical services, occupational therapies, social work services, and spiritual or religious services. Which of these, and when, can be determined only from evidence about the state of the patient.

In the construction industry, the nature of the crafts required and the order in which they can be applied depend on the nature of the object to be constructed and its setting; including, for example, terrain, climate, weather. Organized or team research may draw from a variety of scientific or technical skills, but the particular combination and the order of application depend on the nature of the problem defined.

The development of military combat teams, with a multiplicity of highly skilled capacities to be applied to the requirements of changing circumstances, represents a shift toward the intensive technology in military operations (Janowitz, 1959).

The intensive technology is a custom technology. Its successful employment rests in part on the availability of all the capacities potentially needed, but equally on the appropriate custom combination of selected capacities as required by the individual case or project.

Boundaries of Technical Rationality

Technical rationality, as a system of cause/effect relationships which lead to a desired result, is an abstraction. It is instrumentally perfect when it becomes a closed system of logic. The closed system of logic contains all relevant variables, and only relevant variables. All other influences, or *exogenous variables*, are excluded; and the variables contained in the system vary only to the extent that the experimenter, the manager, or the computer determines they should.

When a technology is put to use, however, there must be not only desired outcomes and knowledge of relevant cause/effect relationships, but also power to control the empirical resources which correspond to the variables in the logical system. A closed system of action corresponding to a closed system of logic would result in instrumental perfection in reality.

The mass production assembly operation and the continuous processing of chemicals are more nearly perfect, in application, than the other two varieties discussed above because they achieve a high degree of control over relevant variables and are relatively free from disturbing influences. Once started, most of the action involved in the long-linked technology is dictated by the internal logic of the technology itself. With the mediating technology, customers or clients intrude to make difficult the standardized activities required by the technology. And with the intensive technology, the specific case defines the component activities and their combination from the larger array of components contained in the abstract technology.

Since technical perfection seems more nearly approachable when the organization has control over all the elements involved,

Proposition 1: Under norms of rationality, organizations seek to seal off their core technologies from environmental influences.

Organizational Rationality

When organizations seek to translate the abstractions called technologies into action, they immediately face problems for which the core technologies do not provide solutions.

Mass production manufacturing technologies are quite specific, *assuming* that certain inputs are provided and finished products are somehow removed from the premises before the productive process is clogged; but mass production technologies do not include variables which provide solutions to either the input- or output-disposal problems. The present technology of medicine may be rather specific if certain tests indicate an appendectomy is in order, if the condition of the patient meets certain criteria, and if certain medical staff, equipment, and medications are present. But medical technology contains no cause/effect statements about bringing sufferers to the attention of medical practitioners, or about the provision of the specified equipment, skills, and medications. The technology of education rests on abstract systems of belief about relationships among teachers, teaching materials, and pupils; but learning theories assume the presence of these variables and proceed from that point.

One or more technologies constitute the core of all purposive organizations. But this technical core is always an incomplete representation of what the organization must do to accomplish desired results. Technical rationality is a necessary component but never alone sufficient to provide *organizational rationality*, which involves acquiring the inputs which are taken for granted by the technology, and dispensing outputs which again are outside the scope of the core technology.

At a minimum, then, organizational rationality involves three major component activities: (1) input activities, (2) technological activities, and (3) output activities. Since these are interdependent, organizational rationality requires that they be appropriately geared to one another. The inputs acquired must be within the scope of the technology, and it must be within the capacity of the organization to dispose of the technological production.

Not only are these component activities interdependent, but both input and output activities are interdependent with environmental elements. Organizational rationality, therefore, never conforms to closed-system logic but demands the logic of an open system. Moreover, since the technological activities are embedded in and interdependent with activities which are open to the environment, the closed system can never be completely attained for the technological component. Yet we have offered the proposition that organizations subject to rationality norms seek to seal off their core technologies from environmental influences. How do we reconcile these two contentions?

Proposition 2: Under norms of rationality, organizations seek to buffer environmental influences by surrounding their technical cores with input and output components.

To maximize productivity of a manufacturing technology, the technical core must be able to operate as if the market will absorb the single kind of product at a continuous rate, and as if inputs flowed continuously, at a steady rate and with specified quality. Conceivably both sets of conditions could occur; realistically they do not. But organizations reveal a variety of devices for approximating these "as if" assumptions, with input and output components meeting fluctuating environments and converting them into steady conditions for the technological core.

Buffering on the input side is illustrated by the stockpiling of materials and supplies acquired in an irregular market, and their steady insertion into the production process. Preventive maintenance, whereby machines or equipment are repaired on a scheduled basis, thus minimizing surprise, is another example of buffering by the input component. The recruitment of dissimilar personnel and their conversion into reliable performers through training or indoctrination is another; it is most dramatically illustrated by basic training or boot camp in military organizations (Dornbusch, 1955).

Buffering on the output side of long-linked technologies usually takes the form of maintaining warehouse inventories and items in transit or in distributor inventories, which permits the technical core to produce at a constant rate, but distribution to fluctuate with market conditions.

Buffering on the input side is an appropriate and important device available to all types of organizations. Buffering on the output side is especially important for mass-manufacturing organizations, but is less feasible when the product is perishable or when the object is inextricably involved in the technological process, as in the therapeutic case.

Buffering of an unsteady environment obviously brings considerable advantages to the technical core, but it does so with costs to the organization. A classic problem in connection with buffering is how to maintain inventories, input or output, sufficient to meet all needs without incurring obsolescence as needs change. Operations research recently has made important contributions toward this problem of "run out versus obsolescence," both of which are costly.

Thus while a fully buffered technological core would enjoy the conditions for maximum technical rationality, organizational rationality may call for compromises between conditions for maximum technical efficiency and the energy required for buffering operations. In an unsteady environment, then, the organization under rationality norms must seek other devices for protecting its technical core.

Proposition 3: Under norms of rationality, organizations seek to smooth out input and output transactions.

Whereas buffering absorbs environmental fluctuations, smoothing or leveling involves attempts to reduce fluctuations in the environment. Utility firms—electric, gas, water, or telephone—may offer inducements to those who use their services during "trough" periods, or charge premiums to those who contribute to "peaking." Retailing organizations faced with seasonal or other fluctuations in demand, may offer inducements in the form of special promotions or sales during slow periods. Transportation organizations such as airlines may offer special reduced fare rates on light days or during slow seasons.

Organizations pointed toward emergencies, such as fire departments, attempt to level the need for their services by activities designed to prevent emergencies, and by emphasis on early detection so that demand is not allowed to grow to the point that would overtax the capacity of the organization. Hospitals accomplish some smoothing through the scheduling of nonemergency admissions.

Although action by the organization may thus reduce fluctuations in demand, complete smoothing of demand is seldom possible. But a core technology interrupted by constant fluctuation and change must settle for a low degree of technical rationality. What other devices do organizations employ to protect core technologies?

Proposition 4: Under norms of rationality, organizations seek to anticipate and adapt to environmental changes which cannot be buffered or leveled.

If environmental fluctuations penetrate the organization and require the technical core to alter its activities, then environmental fluctuations are exogenous variables within the logic of technical rationality. To the extent that environmental fluctuations can be anticipated, however, they can be treated as *constraints* on the technical core within which a closed system of logic can be employed.

The manufacturing firm which can correctly forecast demand for a particular time period can thereby plan or schedule operations of its technical core at a steady rate during that period. Any changes in technical operations due to changes in the environment can be made at the end of the period on the basis of forecasts for the next period.

Organizations often learn that some environmental fluctuations are patterned, and in these cases forecasting and adjustment appear almost automatic. The post office knows, for example, that in large commercial centers large volumes of business mail are posted at the end of the business day, when secretaries leave offices. Recently the post office has attempted to buffer that load by promising rapid treatment of mail posted in special locations during morning hours. Its success in buffering is not known at this writing, but meanwhile the post office schedules its technical activities to meet known daily fluctuations. It can also anticipate heavy demand during November and December, thus allowing its input components lead time in acquiring additional resources.

Banks likewise learn that local conditions and customs result in peak loads at predictable times during the day and week, and can schedule their operations to meet these shifts (Argyris, 1954).

In cases such as these, organizations have amassed sufficient experience to know that fluctuations are patterned with a high degree of regularity or probability; but when environmental fluctuations are the result of combinations of more dynamic factors, anticipation may require something more than the simple projection of previous experience. It is in these situations that forecasting emerges as a specialized and elaborate activity, for which some of the emerging management-science or statistical-decision theories seem especially appropriate.

To the extent that environmental fluctuations are unanticipated they interfere with the orderly operation of the core technology and thereby reduce its performance. When such influences are anticipated and considered as constraints for a particular period of time, the technical core can operate as if it enjoyed a closed system.

Buffering, leveling, and adaptation to anticipated fluctuations are widely used devices for reducing the influence of the environment on the technological cores of organizations. Often they are effective, but there are occasions when these devices are not sufficient to ward off environmental penetration.

Proposition 5: When buffering, leveling, and forecasting do not protect their technical cores from environmental fluctuations, organizations under norms of rationality resort to rationing.

Rationing is most easily seen in organizations pointed toward emergencies, such as hospitals. Even in nonemergency situations hospitals may ration beds to physicians by establishing priority systems for nonemergency admissions. In emergencies, such as community disasters, hospitals may ration pharmaceutical dosages or nursing services by dilution—by assigning a fixed number of nurses to a larger patient population. Mental hospitals, especially state mental hospitals, may ration technical services by employing primarily organic-treatment procedures—electroshock, drugs, insulin—which can be employed more economically than psychoanalytic or *milieu* therapies (Belknap, 1956). Teachers and caseworkers in social welfare organizations may ration effort by accepting only a portion of those seeking service, or if not empowered to exercise such discretion, may concentrate their energies on the more challenging cases or on those which appear most likely to yield satisfactory outcomes (Blau, 1955).

But rationing is not a device reserved for therapeutic organizations. The post office may assign priority to first-class mail, attending to lesser classes only when the priority task is completed. Manufacturers of suddenly popular items may ration allotments to wholesalers or dealers, and if inputs are scarce, may assign priorities to alternative uses of those resources. Libraries may ration book loans, acquisitions, and search efforts (Meier, 1963).

Rationing is an unhappy solution, for its use signifies that the technology is not operating at its maximum. Yet some system of priorities for the allocation of capacity under adverse conditions is essential if a technology is to be instrumentally effective—if action is to be other than random.

The Logic of Organizational Rationality

Core technologies rest on closed systems of logic, but are invariably embedded in a larger organizational rationality which pins the technology to a time and place, and links it with the larger environment through input and output activities. Organizational rationality thus calls for an open-system logic, for when the organization is opened to environmental influences, some of the factors involved in organizational action become *constraints*; for some meaningful period of time they are not variables but fixed conditions to which the organization must adapt. Some of the factors become *contingencies*, which may or may not vary, but are not subject to arbitrary control by the organization.

Organizational rationality therefore is some result of (1) constraints which the organization must face, (2) contingencies which the organization must meet, and (3) variables which the organization can control.

Recapitulation

Perfection in technical rationality requires complete knowledge of cause/effect relations plus control over all of the relevant variables, or closure. Therefore, under norms of rationality (Prop. 1), organizations seek to seal off their core technologies from environmental influences. Since complete closure is impossible (Prop. 2), they seek to buffer environmental influences by surrounding their technical cores with input and output components.

Because buffering does not handle all variations in an unsteady environment, organizations seek to smooth input and output transactions (Prop. 3), and to anticipate and adapt to environmental changes which cannot be buffered or smoothed (Prop. 4), and finally, when buffering, leveling, and forecasting do not protect their technical cores from environmental fluctuations (Prop. 5), organizations resort to rationing.

These are maneuvering devices which provide the organization with some self-control despite interdependence with the environment. But if we are to gain understanding of such maneuvering, we must consider both the direction toward which maneuvering is designed and the nature of the environment in which maneuvering takes place.

References

Argyris, Chris: *Executive Leadership*, New York: Harper & Row, Publishers, Incorporated, 1953.

Belknap, Ivan: *The Human Problems of a State Mental Hospital*, New York: McGraw-Hill Book Company, 1956.

Blau, Peter M.: *The Dynamics of Bureaucracy*, Chicago: The University of Chicago Press, 1955.

Dornbusch, Sanford M.: "The Military Academy as an Assimilating Institution," *Social Forces*, Vol. 33, May, 1955, pp. 316-321.

Hawkes, Robert W.: "Physical Psychiatric Rehabilitation Models Compared", paper presented to the Ohio Valley Sociological Society, 1962.

Janowitz, Morris: "Changing Patterns of Organizational Authority: The Military Establishment," *Administrative Science Quarterly*, Vol. 3, March, 1959, pp. 473-493.

Meir, Richard L.: "Communications Overload," *Administrative Science Quarterly*, Vol 7, March, 1963, pp. 521-544.

Merton, Robert K.: "Bureaucratic Structure and Personality," in Robert K. Merton (Ed.), *Social Theory and Social Structure* (Rev. Ed.), New York: The Free Press of Glencoe, 1957a.

Stinchcombe, Arthur L.: "Bureaucratic and Craft Administration of Production: A Comparative Study," *Administrative Science Quarterly*, Vol. 4, September, 1959, pp. 168-187.

Weber, Max: *The Theory of Social and Economic Organization*, A. M. Henderson and Talcott Parsons (trans.), and Talcott Parsons (Ed.), New York: The Free Press of Glencoe, 1947.

Woodward, Joan: *Industrial Organization: Theory and Practice*, London: Oxford University Press, 1965.

LINKING AN INNOVATIVE SUBSYSTEM INTO THE SYSTEM

ROLF P. LYNTON

> Innovation . . . is not so much the adoption of objects by individuals as it is the acceptance of ideas by (people in) an organization. (Andrews and Greenfield, 1966:81)
>
> Any research process . . . has an inbuilt tendency towards the formation of a relatively closed system, in which self-generated intakes crowd out intakes from the external environment. . . . A major problem is to steer between . . . creative research activities that are irrelevant and . . . relevant research activities that are uncreative. (Miller and Rice, 1967:159-160)

Formal organizational devices for facilitating change in social institutions, particularly institutions in environments characterized by increasing differentiation and complexity, are largely integrative devices. It is on these integrative devices that this paper will concentrate.[1]

Integrative devices provide linkage in two crucial areas: (1) between the institution and its specific publics of consumers and suppliers, as well as its wider public of political and social sanction, which determines the relevance of the institution; and (2) between different parts within the institution, which determines the extent to which the institution operates as a unit.

Both these linkages link subsystems and are commonly themselves subsystems. This paper focuses on systems providing a specified kind of service or material goods which have outgrown the possibility of attaining optimal integration through interpersonal, spontaneous, face-to-face contact, and therefore require formal integrative devices.

In classical organization theory the dominant criterion for this classification was size: a system greater than a given size required formal devices, a smaller system did not. Recent empirical research findings indicate that the degree of differentiation, and therefore the need for integration, correlates much more closely with the degrees of uncertainty in technology and markets than with absolute size (Downs, 1968; Harvey, 1968; Lorsch, 1965). The focus of this paper therefore is on systems (1) that need to cope with high degrees of uncertainty, and (2) that have developed subsystems to develop innovations for the system. In industry, organizations manufacturing electronic apparatus and certain chemicals are examples of such a system; and research and development departments are an example of such a subsystem.

Assessment of Uncertainties

The accuracy with which decision makers in the system assess uncertainties

Reprinted by permission of the author and the publisher from *Administrative Science Quarterly*, vol. 14, no. 3 (Sept. 1969), pp. 398-414.

for the system guides formal differentiation within the system as well as the design of integrating devices. There are two basic models for this assessment. One model treats uncertainties as a succession of discrete stimuli to which the system needs to respond with appropriate innovations. In this model differentiation and integration are functions of the frequency and force of the expected stimuli. It is a model that has affinities with familiar stimulus-response models in learning theory and with the early formulations of an administrator's functions in terms of weight and frequency of decision making. The integrative devices appropriate to this assessment are linkages of minimal complexity and duration. As stimuli for innovative responses increase in frequency, temporary and informal devices may become permanent and formal, but the kinds of devices and their limitations will not change unless the model of assessment changes. The other model treats uncertainties as a continuous general state requiring a continuously varying response from the whole system. This model treats the system and its environment as in continuous interaction in uncertainty and as aiming to achieve and maintain a steady state in and through this interaction. Emery uses the word, "turbulence" to describe the environment in this model (1967:225).

The spontaneous response to a turbulent environment is to reduce the turbulence. The first model aims at reducing the complexity and uncertainty by segmentation or dissociation, which are essentially the defense mechanisms that lead to passive adaptation. The second model aims at establishing hierarchies of goals, which may then serve as guides to behavior, i.e., to allocating attention and other resources to causal strands on the basis of established priorities. Through the development of such codes, the field is no longer perceived as turbulent. Questions about the values themselves, and of the transformation of values into priorities and codes, will not be pursued in this paper, though the later discussion of institutionalized linkages could be analyzed in terms of the values that could emerge from the interactions they encourage (Emery, 1967:225, 229). In the first model, the cost of the responses is a permanent ceiling on the rate of innovation; in the second model, costs occur from the slower rate of innovation due to various rigidities associated with the acceptance and revision of codes.

This paper treats the environment as turbulent and explores the kind of appropriate response by the system, particularly, the design and operation of linkage devices. Figure 1 illustrates the basic two-directional schema for this paper.

Figure 1. Two models of assessing environmental uncertainties and characteristic linkages.

The empirical data to be introduced and analyzed at some length in later sections of the paper show a heavy incidence of failure for *ad hoc* and temporary linkage devices. They refer to situations in which linkages were designed to perform some specific function(s) and failed to do so. Actually an unrecorded kind of failure may be more serious, namely the system rigidities that the introduction of the inadequate linkages reinforced. The basic weakness of the discrete stimulus-innovation model shows up most sharply when the intended linkage *succeeds*. For there is no evidence that the successful integration of two or three subsystems increases the degree of integration of the system as a whole; on the contrary, commonly, a well-integrated subsystem (or a set of subsystems) may become isolated, and then it and the rest of the system become rigid separately, in defense against one another. Katz and Kahn (1966:390) state that "the major error is to disregard the systemic properties of the organization and to confuse individual change with modifications in organizational variables." Very little of the growing literature on innovation and its diffusion has been attentive to this problem. The prevailing focus of attention is on the individual innovator when he adopts an innovation, why, etc. (Rogers, 1962), not on the organizational setting in which innovation takes place. The early sociological role studies may have unwittingly supported this orientation. In the rural economy the typical adopter was an individual farmer rather than a collectivity, such as an organization. Even in later studies the influence of the larger social setting on the farmer-innovator tended to be underestimated. Studies of innovation in educational systems, like schools of various kinds and school districts, either show a lack of available knowledge about the functioning of organizations and communities or suffer from a kind of great-man orientation (Ross, 1958; Carlson, 1964). In anthropological studies too, the properties of a particular innovation and its diffusion across systems and integration within systems have been overemphasized without corresponding attention to the dynamics and functioning of the receiving organization. Gallagher (1963) discussed the power structure in innovation receiving systems, the actual prestige of advocates of the innovation, and other matters influencing if and how an innovation would be integrated into the local organization. But his primary focus too is on the substance of the particular innovation, taking the local system itself as a kind of unmodifiable ground against which the innovation showed up starkly. The currently widespread emphasis on the importance of "dissemination of research findings" seems to continue the popular view that the content or demonstrated efficacy of a particular innovation as such is crucial in determining whether it will be adopted and used effectively. In short, to use an image from Gestalt psychology, specific planned change attempts have most typically been "in figure," occupying the focus of attention, which the organization itself has remained "the ground." That this model commonly persists in the face of growing experience of its inadequacy indicates its long antecedents in history and also the deep reluctance many decision makers seem to feel about making major system changes that may be required to interact effectively with a turbulent environment. They prefer to assess the uncertainty as small and the response to it as routine, whereas it might be more useful to take as a primary target the improvement of system dynamics, specifically the linkage design. To continue the analogy then, this paper treats linkage design as "figure," and innovative needs as "ground."

In Emery's formulation (1966), turbulent environments require the linkage of dissimilar subsystems whose goals correlate positively, i.e., subsystems which are not in competition, cannot take over the role of the other. Therefore linkages between them will tend to maximize cooperation. As Thompson (1967) has shown, such a matrix can take several shapes, but all provide for two aspects: (1) that which links the system to the environment, through which broad social sanctioning is secured and the system is attuned to the needs of the environment and (2) that linkage which enables subsystems to engage in effective joint search for common ground rules, while retaining the degree of privacy, protection, and autonomy they need to carry out their distinctive functions.

The strategic objective then has to be formulated in terms of institutionalization. As institutionalization becomes a prerequisite for achieving a steady state in a turbulent environment, then subsystem goals have to be found and formulated, which accord with system goals and which offer a maximum convergence between its subsystems.

System Differentiation

Effective linkage presupposes appropriate differentiation, which is in turn required by new task complexities. As these occur, subsystems need to be built to deal with primary tasks. Over time, successive levels of differentiation can be established, each reaching primary production systems. The primary task differentiates one subsystem from other subsystems at the same organizational level, and also from subsystems at higher and lower levels of the hierarchy (Lorsch, 1965:151; Lawrence and Lorsch, 1967:213; Miller and Rice, 1967:157; Thompson, 1967).

Appropriate differentiation has three possible dimensions: technology, territory, and time; and Miller (1959) states: "Task performance is impaired if subsystems . . . are differentiated along any other dimension than these." He indicates that at any one organizational level, these three dimensions can have seven possible combinations.

Types of task dependence have been classified in some detail by Herbst (1958), Emery (1958), and Thompson (1967). It is relevant here to consider how, at a given level of differentiation, the subsystems of a larger system are all dependent on supplies, equipment, and services, and are interdependent for the attainment of the goal of the larger system. Emery's (1958) study classifies interdependence into simultaneous or successional, and classifies successional dependence further into cyclic, convergent, or divergent. He also distinguishes between simple and complex dependence and between reciprocal and nonreciprocal dependence. Thompson (1967) presents a simpler typology of interdependence: "pooled," "sequential," and "reciprocal." Lorsch and Lawrence (1968) used Thompson's typology to distinguish between organizations having different degrees of differentiation and using different linkage devices.

While subsystems have in common "an inherent centrifugal tendency" (Parsons, 1956), Miller (1959) noted some particular tendencies associated with differentiation by technology, territory, or time. Differentiation by technology tended to make the preservation of distinctiveness a primary task of the subsystem (for example, demarcation disputes between skilled craftsmen). Differentiation by territory led subsystems to develop a special climate and culture, a particular proficiency. The most complex tendencies were associated with differentiation by time, e.g., tasks with different time cycles or organized on different shifts (Trist, 1963; Lawrence with Lorsch, 1967).

Three of Litwak's (1961) mechanisms of segregation seem to overlap with Miller's for determining points of development at which a shift from one form of structure to another is to be made. His "transferral occupations" arise in the linkage subsystem which this paper examines.

Research versus Operations

Since linkage devices between research and development subsystem(s) and operating subsystem(s) in industrial systems best illustrate the main issues, most of the data for this paper were drawn from studies in industry. Research scientists and operating personnel differ sharply in all three major dimensions of differentiation. In technology, the researcher deals with nonuniform processes, the man in operations with uniform or nonuniform, but programmed, processes (Perrow, 1967); in territory, the two systems are usually kept physically apart, often to avoid conflict (Litwak, 1961); in time, research scientists have longer-range concerns and expect much later gratification from feedback about the results of their work than operating personnel (Lawrence and Lorsch, 1967:35, 36).

The differences are extreme in organizations in which research scientists have great freedom in their choice of problems and procedures. In these cases, the norms and organization of the research department approximate those of an academic environment (Litwak 1961:183). Burns and Stalker (1961:225, 229) maintain that the "prima donna" scientist is actually a more familiar figure in the electronics industry than in the academic world. The characteristic norms of innovative subsystems include: high energy devoted to "novel, significant, focused, internalized, shared goals"; "esprit de corps," "mutual identification with peers"; high autonomy and spontaneity, with freedom for creative experimentation"; and high involvement and commitment (Miles, 1964:655). The researcher's commitment tends to be to the task or to the discipline, whereas the operating personnel's commitment is to the organization; he therefore responds to the sender's recognized research status, whereas operating personnel responds to the level of administrative authority (Smith, 1966:58). He tends to be a younger person than persons of equivalent rank in operations and to have more years of formal education than they (Dalton, 1950). The differentiation between research and operations is marked further by a series of interlocking signs and differences of conduct, for example, different working hours and differences in dress and leisure pursuits (Burns and Stalker, 1961:186).

The differentiation between research and operating subsystems in industry seems then to be institutionalized at all levels: image and self-image (personal), face-to-face relations (interpersonal), organizational structure (inter-subsystem). Moreover, although differentiated groupings tend to be self-perpetuating, special technological factors reinforce this tendency in the case of research and operating subsystems. For research generates further problems for research, and these tend to crowd out problems on which other subsystems would prefer the researchers to work.

"Research institutions have therefore a natural tendency to become increasingly divorced from their (organizational) environments and their boundaries to become increasingly impermeable" (Miller and Rice, 1967:157). Yet, although researchers prefer to work on their own problems, they may need access to data and certainly do need resources from other subsystems. These needs leave important aspects of control and power in the hands of other kinds of people and other kinds of subsystems. In short, technological factors inherent in the research process exaggerate the centrifugal tendencies of research subsystems (Havelock, 1967:23-24), and feedback loops that tend to develop between individuals in subsystems and restrict communication in self-confirming, stabilizing ways are especially tight in this case (Miles, 1964:644). In such sharply separated subsystems, members have even greater difficulty than usual in understanding the language of the members of other subsystems (Burns and Stalker, 1961:155, 174; Kahn *et al.*, 1964:133; Kast and Rosenzweig, 1962:325-326), for each perceives and internalizes those aspects of any new situation that relate specifically to the activities and goals of his subsystem (Dearborn and Simon, 1958:149-144; Barnes, 1960:3-4). In these circumstances, misunderstandings are a common occurrence and tensions are normal. In an atmosphere of tension, joint decision processes between research and operating subsystems then tend to be characterized by bargaining rather than problem solving (Pondy, 1967:319). Some of the characteristics of this bargaining are "careful rationing of information and its deliberate distortion; rigid, formal, circumscribed relations; (and) suspicion, hostility and disassociation" among the subsystems (Pondy, 1967:319; Burns and Stalker, 1961:192, 194; Kahn *et al.*, 1964:134; Litterer, 1963:405-407; Chandler, 1963:154). Shepard (1956) summarized the differences in outlook between the researcher and the operations man along seven dimensions: Table 1.

TABLE 1. Researcher vs. Operations Man: Differential Perceptions of Seven Items.*

	Researcher	Operations man
Research	Future-oriented, perhaps distant future	Focused on present, or just beyond
Identification of researcher	His profession	The company
Research results	Published achievements	Guarded secrets
Research budget	Based on research requirements	Based on company needs
Authority for research	Shared among scientists	Delegated by management
Organization of research	Project groups	Functional groups
Complexity of research management	Desirable fulfillment of managerial competence	Undesirable regression into poor administrative practice

* After Shepard (1956).

These rigidities and negative attitudes provide the potential for conflict. Joan Woodward found that "hostility between research and production personnel . . . probably exaggerated in turn the differentiation based on task differences. This was a noticeable feature of all the large batch and unit production firms studied" (1965:149-151). Studies in a variety of settings show that conflict and tension add strong impetus to the centrifugal tendencies of differentiation. In this atmosphere the parties each have a set to expect conflict and therefore may perceive conflict even when none exists (Pondy, 1967:319). This separation involves high cost. Miller (1959) found that the higher the degree of tension, the smaller the energy directly invested in the pursuit of the objectives of subsystems or of those of the system as a whole (see also Hermann, 1963).

Hypotheses

It is now possible to focus more systematically on the main thesis of this paper. In a turbulent environment, institutions must innovate to survive. Some institutions have differentiated subsystems with the primary task of working out innovative responses to the turbulent environment for the whole system. This task is inherently different in technology, territory, and time from the tasks of other subsystems. Adoption of the innovative products of the subsystem by other subsystems is essential to the effective response of the system to its environment; therefore, innovative and operational subsystems need to be appropriately linked.

On the assumptions that the decision makers of a system are in control of the system's response and that they act rationally, the degree of innovation and the mechanisms of differentiation and of integration depend on the decision makers' assessment of the changing environment. Down's (1968) study explores some personality factors and develops a concept of "sunk costs" to deal with various patterns of disposing of resources in the system and the tendencies these patterns induce over time. Using assessment for this totality, even without examining its components, may at least indicate that important complexities may be worth studying in this connection and are not to be obscured by the more familiar label "perception."

Assessment, as used in this paper, is a function of the decision makers' joint preference for the goal of the institution after taking into account the costs of innovation. It is therefore both how the decision makers assess the environment and the terms in which they rationally explain the innovation and the mechanisms that they institute for it. In this model the decision makers' dominant assessment of environmental requirements for change is the independent variable, and differentiation and linkage devices are dependent variables.

Four major assessments are possible, each of which can lead to a hypothesis. They are ordered here in their historical sequence which also corresponds to ascending degrees of system change. Relating these situations and hypotheses to the two models shown in Figure 1, Hypotheses 2 and 3 restate the first model, and hypothesis 4 the second.

1. The decision makers see "nothing," "no need to change," therefore any need for change that actually arises will be met by *ad hoc* and informal arrangements, e.g., by individuals adjusting their roles.

Hypothesis 1. If, in a turbulent environment, decision makers assess the need for change as negligible, system differentiation and linkage will then be minimal and unorganized, and the effects on system structure will be negligible.

2. The decision makers assess the need to change as temporary, and will organize to meet it by temporary measures, such as meetings and temporary allocations of resources. In short, they will treat it as a project.

Hypothesis 2. If, in a turbulent environment, decision makers assess the need for change as temporary, they will tend to expect the ratio of benefits and costs to be most favorable if they institute temporary differentiation and linkages; the effects of innovation on system structure will then be small and unpredictable.

3. The decision makers assess the need for change as frequent, but specific, and differentiate a permanent subsystem to deal with these specific changes, while the institution as a whole will proceed as before.

Hypothesis 3. If, in a turbulent environment, decision makers assess the need for change as frequent and specific: (a) they will formally differentiate an innovative subsystem, but limit its linkages to specific purposes and (b) when this kind of device and procedure is found to be ineffective, additional system changes will tend to take the form of further differentiation of innovative subsystems, not of changing the linkage devices and procedures.

4. The decision makers assess turbulence in the environment as a continuous state, which calls for sensitive, multifaceted, often unpredictable, and general innovative responses from the system as a whole. Differentiation and integration are major then foci of attention—for system design and preventive maintenance. Subsystems become sharply differentiated and deliberately linked on a permanent basis, and innovation affects the whole institution to a major extent.

Hypothesis 4. If, in a turbulent environment, decision makers assess the need for change as continuous and major, they will tend to differentiate innovative subsystems clearly and integrate them closely into the rest of the system; the effects on the system as a whole will then be major.

The rest of the paper examines the linkage mechanisms characteristic for these four situations and hypotheses.

Need for Change Assessed as Negligible

Situations in which responses within the normal range of adaptation of the system as currently constituted and of the individuals in it can cope with changes in the environment are outside the scope of this paper. Its proper scope begins only when the integrative needs exceed normal adaptation. This commonly occurs imperceptibly as a system grows. If such a discrepancy occurs and persists unattended, unplanned linkage devices find their way into the system's routine workings. In society at large, these unplanned mechanisms are most widely diffused in the form of new norms through literature, art, folklore, mythology, beliefs, mores, orientations, "small talk," etiquette, and through institutional practices of many kinds (Thayer, 1968:241). This list, certainly from folklore onwards, could be applied to any institution. In industry, "management's attempts toward integration may just happen over time, arise as temporary expedients, or emerge as a solution to a crisis situation" (Jasinsky, 1964:329).

At some stage there is an innovator, perhaps a scientist, or a workman. The initiative for informal attempts on linkage usually lies with this innovator. The point here is that, for application, the innovation requires the involvement of people who are different from the innovative person, and who will perceive him as a stranger or agitator (Inkeles, 1951:38-135; Katz and Lazarsfeld, 1955:162-208). Such informal personal linkage makes it possible to appreciate the roots from which formal differentiation and linkage devices commonly grow. Figure 2 illustrates the position of the informal direct linker in an undifferentiated system.

**UNATTACHED
LINKERS**

**LINKERS ATTACHED
TO INNOVATING OR
OPERATING GROUPS**

Figure 2. Informal direct linkers in undifferentiated system. (I = innovator, O = operator, solid circle = formal boundary, broken circle = informal boundary, arrow = informal contact.)

**LINKER ATTACHED
TO BOTH INNOVATIVE
AND OPERATING GROUPS**

Figure 3. Informal third-party linkers in undifferentiated system. (L = linker, I = innovator, O = operator, solid circle = informal boundary, arrow = informal contact.)

Kahn and his colleagues (1964:125-136) found that innovative activity was associated "significantly and positively with both the degree of role conflict (p «0.01) and the amount of tension that the role occupant experienced on the job (p «0.05)." The innovator's interpersonal conflicts were "fought out around his proposals for innovation and vary in intensity according to the orientation of decision makers towards innovative functions." His intra-role conflicts arose from his characteristic impatience with uniform and routine procedures and from the lack of trust he felt "in (his) role senders, irrespective of the degree of conflict (p «0.06)." He "had significantly less communication than others with their role senders (p «0.02)," was also more self-confident in the face of role conflict than persons in uniform work (p «0.02), was more highly involved than others in his job (p «0.05), and attached more importance to his job relative to other areas of life than people in less innovative roles (p «0.05).

The emergence and enthusiasm of such an innovator in the system certainly expands the system's capacity for adaptation, but the cost of informal linkage increases as the expanded limits in turn prove to be too narrow (Burns and Stalker, 1961). Where the main force of innovative activity is concentrated in an energetic scientist-entrepreneur, the linkage problems may overwhelm him.

Linkage may be attempted by an informal third party, most commonly a draughtsman, engineer, sales agent, or purchasing agent. Litwak (1961) calls their role a "transferral occupation." The studies of Burns and Stalker (1961:177) and Woodward (1965:138) are replete with cases in which managers either attach draughtsmen and engineers to development or to production, in the hope that they will "just get along" with their colleagues within the confines of normal bureaucratic rules, or leave them unattached to find their own place in the organization. Figure 3 illustrates the position of the informal third party in such an undifferentiated system.

Kahn and his colleagues conclude that "concentrating the functions of organizational liaison on a very few positions . . . risks much in a few hands, forces a search for champions to fill the crucial positions, and is likely to create inter-organization struggle to insure that their interests will be well represented by the overworked representative" (1964:392-393). The concepts of marginality and tolerated deviance occur again and again in the literature concerning linkage and, along with them, the thought that these marginal men need bases from which to work effectively (Woodward, 1965:142).

Need for Change Assessed as Temporary and Infrequent

The logical response to needs assessed as temporary is to devise correspondingly temporary linkages, a particular type of what Matthew Miles (1964) terms "temporary systems." This paper deals only with situations where this assessment in fact is mistaken, since situations of turbulence are assumed to require permanent linkage devices of a pervasive kind. The situation here differs from that examined in the preceding section, in that (1) the decision makers do see the need for a response beyond the routine capacity of the system; and (2) linkage is made a formal occupation, albeit a temporary one. Formality means more security for the linker at the cost of more constraint. Whereas in the informal situation, the choice of attempting linkage activities, and the manner and timing, were largely the linker's, now the decision makers are likely to play a significant part in initiating, designing and controlling the linkage activities to conform to their assessment. The decision makers' direct interest makes the linker(s) *their* representative. This, in reverse, can give the linker(s) access to possible power and coercion over the people and groups involved in the problem. Figure 4 illustrates formal temporary linkers in a system with no innovative subsystem.

Linkage devices for this situation include temporarily freeing a staff member from his usual activities in order "to deal with the situation," *ad hoc* meetings of people involved in a change, calling in outside consultants, and sending some staff member(s) for training. The first three usually have overtones of "troubleshooting" and of latent coercion by decision makers and their representatives. The question here is whether these overtones promote effective linkage, deter it, or make no difference. The Lawrence and Lorsch (1967) study of within-system linkers found that access to coercive power was not associated with effective linkage. In two high-performing (innovative) companies the linkers were seen as very competent, and the subsystem managers ascribed their influence over decisions to this competence. The linkers in four low-performing (non-innovative) companies on the other hand, were accorded an important voice in decisions "because of the formal

DIRECT LINKAGE   INDIRECT LINKAGE

Figure 4. Formal temporary linkers in system with no innovation subsystem. (L = linker, D = decision makers, l = innovator, O = operator, solid circle = formal boundary, broken circle = informal boundary, arrow = informal contact.)

Figure 5. Linkages between innovative subsystem and other subsystems.

authority given them by top management and their close reporting relationship to top managers'' (Lawrence and Lorsch, 1967:65-66).

Linkage activities in the lower-performing companies appeared to have many aspects characteristic of bargaining. Some linkers in this situation tried to avoid personal contact and preferred to resolve problems through formal memoranda. Similarly Strauss (1962:182) found that linkers tended to expect that people in affected departments would not change their minds.

Resort to authority and coercion can be very tempting: forcing people to make the specific changes required seems quick and easily controllable, that is, inexpensive. Since the need is specific, it does not seem necessary that people should change their minds or appreciate the change. Many studies report *ad hoc* meetings that are so overshadowed by the latent power of absent decision makers, that joint decisions are avoided on the grounds that top management will make its own decision anyway (Lawrence and Lorsch, 1967:66; Burns and Stalker, 1961; Woodward, 1965). These meetings then serve either ritualistic purposes only or become rather elaborate and ill-constituted mechanisms for exchanging information. The ineffective use of time is itself costly, but the indirect costs of such coercion are likely to be higher still. For in a turbulent environment needs for change recur, and meeting these needs by coercion, open or implied, increases resistance to future changes and decreases initiative by people required to direct the changes.

Many decision makers who assess the need for change as temporary seek to reduce the costs of internal disturbance by contracting for temporary assistance from outside the system. Consultants are seen as offering the advantages, not so much of expertise beyond that of employees in the system, but of the outsider free of the normative and interpersonal constraints of the system, and free also of the need to carry on simultaneously their usual activities. Consultants clearly *are* temporary. In their turn, consultants who conceive of their task as consisting of diagnosis and prescription may thereby support the assessment of the decision makers that the need for change is temporary and specific, and call only for a response equally temporary and specific.

Another means of dealing with linkage in this setting is to change some of the staff members who are important in the linkage process. This may be done by replacing personnel who have been unable to cope with the needs for change by others who are "better at getting on with people." The replacement may be temporary or permanent, depending on the frequency and importance of new linkages and alternative dispositions of staff resources. Changing the staff may also be attempted through training, particularly training in attitudes and interpersonal and organizational skills. The studies of Miles and others of innovation in educational systems indicate that changes of this kind call for *additional* linkage—that between the temporary training system and the parent system. The success of action decisions taken in the temporary system depends not only on the quality of these decisions, but also on the sophistication with which members have been able to anticipate the strategic problems they will encounter upon their return (Miles, 1964:484). Miles (1964:643) reported that in one three-day conference of a management team devoted to the improvement of operations in a chemical plant, the members agreed on a list of 47 action decisions, specified deadlines, and identified the persons responsible for ensuring action. When the consultant pointed to the need for some mechanism to guide implementation and cope with new problems, the top manager declared that implementation could easily be accomplished "through the regular line organization"; yet it was clear that the inability of the line organization to cope with these problems had necessitated the conference.

The probable usefulness of training, as of any other temporary devices for dealing with change, is enhanced if the decision makers of the system themselves take part in the temporary system, for studies show that recommendations are then more likely to be accepted (Miles, 1964). But this participation of decision makers also seems to ensure that any action recommendations will be moderate. This is merely another way of saying that meeting the realistic needs of the system is at variance with the constraints of normal system operations. That is the dilemma with which decision makers in these situations seem unable to cope.

Need for Change Perceived as Frequent, But Specific

When decision makers assess the need for change as frequent but still discrete, then the costs of setting up a formal subsystem with the primary task of designing innovations for the system as a whole are seen as justified. But the change is still conceived as an addition to the system, not as a reshaping of the system as a whole for innovation.

The input for the new subsystem may be proposed by the decision makers, by others in the system, or by members in the new subsystem. The output of the new subsystem is expected to be innovative ideas which the rest of the system will then decide to use or not to use. The task of the subsystem is conceived as terminating with communicating the ideas clearly enough for decision makers to understand and so make their decisions rationally. Linkage mechanisms are then conceived as bridges across the gap that is recognized as existing between the differentiated innovative subsystem and other subsystems. Figure 5 illustrates this concept of linkage as bridging the gap between subsystems.

In their study of Scottish engineering units, Burns and Stalker (1961:194-198) described three situations of this type in different companies. In each, a newcomer was brought in to head a new, innovative subsystem. For each system, successful innovation was "quite essential" for survival as an "independent business with its own capacity to compete with others and to expand." In each case, the innovative subsystem was unable to get innovative ideas accepted, and its manager resigned.

Case 1: A new chief development engineer was brought in on the explicit understanding "that he should take over an increasing share of the general management, i.e., of production as well as of design," and so he himself would be an important linkage of the development subsystem with other subsystems. In fact, he was confined by decision makers to acting as a consultant, supplying technical information at the stage of negotiations for contracts with customers. At a critical point in his endeavors to extend his authority beyond the design department, he proposed a plan for reorganizing the system. He was immediately offered a rise in salary and a new title, but no significant organizational change. He resigned.

Case 2: To render it independent of obsolescent products and methods, an established company brought in an industrial scientist to take charge of the laboratory group. His understanding was that he would "take over the whole technical side and be responsible for technical development." After two years the scientist regarded this venture as "wholly unsuccessful". . . . Everything I've put up has been blocked . . . none accepted. It's been their view that whether or not such and such a development takes place is just not my affair; this is the manufacturer's concern . . . and similarly the question of how something is to be developed and produced." Prior to the scientist's resignation, after three years, interaction between him and the managing director in the adjoining office had ceased altogether.

Case 3: Following the Second World War, the directors of the third company decided to engage an industrial scientist as head of the research and development unit to do exploratory work among recent innovations and possible markets. The new research and technical manager was quickly effective in extending the firm's range of materials and processes along traditional lines, and in increasing technical sales. But these very successes, then, locked him into short-term activities with operating subsystems. When a major opportunity occurred for developing substitute plastic materials, he was not given the resources to explore it. Instead the scientist was appointed manager of a new department in addition to continuing as head of the research and development unit. (Development work then became "virtually impossible," while production in the new department was held back by traditional inappropriate practices.) So he too resigned.

Although the newcomer was placed formally on the same level as the departmental and functional managers immediately below the managing director, the role allowed him in practice added to the existing structure and was external to it: he was not permitted to infringe on the control exercised by established members of management. As a result, he was forced to act in a consultant, advisory role, while members of the established hierarchy retained the decision making and control functions. That is, the innovative subsystem had been appended, and no allowance had been made for altering the fields of control in the system structure. This happens, conclude Burns and Stalker (1961:199), "when a special person or organized group of persons is designated as the agent of change and the existing organization is relegated to the role of spectator or patient."

The issue of significant structural change tends to be evaded in two ways. First, difficulties in effecting changes are ascribed to personal conflicts. Given the view of decision makers that an innovative subsystem is an addition, they then see any conflict as arising from the newcomers' personal interest in acquiring more control than they need. Factors of status and power develop and find expressions in increasingly devious and intractable ways, until system weaknesses are translated wholly into personal terms. Then, since experiences like these, being painful, are likely to be repressed rather than examined, disentangled and shared, this personal focus will tend to perpetuate the structure of the system.

The second way in which the significant system changes are evaded is by faulty system responses to difficulties that the subsystem has in effecting linkage. Although the difficulties really originate in the inadequate design and operation of linkage mechanism, decision makers respond by instituting further changes in the innovative subsystem itself. One change is to assign members of the innovative subsystem additional responsibilities in operating subsystems. Such a combination of roles does not prevent failure (Burns and Stalker, 1961; Havelock, 1964:25; Lawrence and Lorsch, 1967), although Palz and Andrews (1966) consistently reported that scientists and engineers in industrial research and development departments who participated in management and knowledge dissemination were more effective and productive also as scientists, as judged by publications and by peer ratings of their scientific excellence and overall usefulness. There may be a cause-and-effect confusion here which only further empirical study can clarify: does such scientific productivity tend to lead to effective participation in the system? Or, does effective and acknowledged membership in the general system tend to promote scientific productivity? Another possibility is suggested by Sieber's (1966) study of the organization of educational research: that some functions may be combined effectively and profitably, as in the Pelz and Andrews (1966) study, while others, such as research and services, tend to combine badly. Kahn's (1964:393) study suggests that roles may also be effectively occupied in rotation.

A second change following linkage difficulties is to leave scientists alone to get on with their science. This is done by freeing them explicitly from the linking task in which they have failed and by establishing an additional group of a different kind of scientist specifically for the linking task. But without further structural change in the whole system, these different scientists are bound to fail at linkage in their turn; then the same process may be repeated, and yet another group may be entrusted with the linkage task. In time, several additional subsystems may get interposed in this manner between the original innovative subsystem and the operating system. Each of these subsystems has small-step linking tasks to the subsystem on either side of it in a lengthening chain of innovative subsystems. Burns and Stalker (1961:157-158) found that some organizations had separate departments for "pure" and "basic" research, and for "design" and "development," although the subsystems in each pair were "almost indistinguishable." Other studies (Kast and Rosenzweig, 1962; Quinn and Mueller, 1963) point to a similar proliferation of scientists and engineering specialists. This process fails to establish the required linkages to the operating system and at the same time makes the necessary system development more complicated and costly. The tendency to proliferate innovative subsystems in attempting to deal with linkage difficulties can be expected to be reinforced by the personal and professional inclinations of both researchers and operating men described in an earlier section of this paper.

The following hypothesis may be worth examining: In situations of stress between innovative and other subsystems, scientists will seek to safeguard their autonomy of work by proposing that the linkage function be carried out by new subsystems that are oriented more to application and less to science. Operating men support the same tendency when they overestimate the value, and underestimate the cost, of further differentiation in the innovative subsystem, following their erroneous impression that an up-to-date system consists of a multiplicity of subsystems.

All this elaboration of the system leaves the major difficulty untouched and is costly. The direct costs of coordinating go up with every differentiation of subsystems, and indirect costs may be even greater, including the creation of jobs, groups, and even departments of highly paid personnel whose survival in the system depends on the perpetuation of their subsystems. These costs are incurred in the attempt of decision makers to escape the problems of reshaping the system for continuous change.

Need for Change Assessed as Continuous

The data for this section of the paper are drawn predominantly from four major field studies in industry to which frequent reference has already been made (Lorsch, 1965; Lawrence and Lorsch, 1967; Burns and Stalker, 1961; Woodward, 1965). All are published in the 1960's, three since 1965. Two present British data, two American. All contain comparison of linkage mechanisms in similar contexts of technology and uncertain environments. But linkage mechanisms effective in some systems seem to be ineffective in others.

The attempt in this section is to analyze the successes and failures in linkages, so that some common factors can be established. The overall issue is institutionalizing linkage mechanisms so that they function as permanent parts of a system that is continuously and flexibly engaged in change; that is, a system that is functioning effectively in a turbulent environment.

The analysis will be in terms of four dimensions: differentiation of linkage mechanisms, the relation of such a mechanism to the subsystems it links, its norms of operation, and its congruence with system structure.

Differentiation

The studies showed effective linkage mechanisms to be formally organized on a permanent basis; for example, engineering department, product management meeting, research and development committee, goal team. The effective linkage mechanisms consisted of people from the different subsystems to be linked; that is, the linkage mechanisms were cross-functional in composition and represented a particular type of differentiation.

The differentiation of effective mechanisms was clear both *vis à vis* the subsystems to be linked and *vis à vis* the decision makers for the whole system. Regarding the first, Lawrence and Lorsch found differentiation to be effective "to the degree to which managers in all the departments felt that they had influence over decisions'' (1967:56). As to the second, they found the influence of effective linkage mechanisms to be ''centered at the operating level, neither higher nor lower than where the decisions could be effectively reached and implemented'' (1967:56).

Figure 6 illustrates effective and ineffective differentiation in these terms. Lorsch (1965:122) listed the differences between effective differentiation in one company and ineffective differentiation in another as follows:

EFFECTIVE DIFFERENTIATION

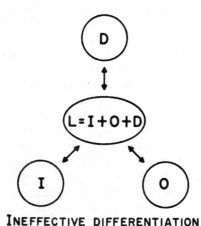

INEFFECTIVE DIFFERENTIATION

Figure 6. Differentiation of linkage mechanism from subsystems and from decision makers. (D = decision makers, L = linker, I = innovator, O = operator, solid circle = formal boundary.)

Effective Mechanism	*Ineffective Mechanism*
Limited attendance to four functional members from the subsystems	Large, included superiors and subordinates
Set out to solve problems and resolve conflict	Set out primarily to exchange information
Did not involve decision makers	Dropped any difficult problems or asked decision makers to solve them

Linkage Mechanism in Relation to
Innovative and Operating Subsystems

Effective linkage mechanisms were equidistant between the subsystems they were to link. Lawrence and Lorsch (1967:59) examined this distance in terms of four ''orientations'': to goals, time, interpersonal relations, and the structure of the linkage mechanism. Linkage mechanisms in high-performance company A were equidistant on all four dimensions, in low-performance company A on only one.

The mechanisms of the other four companies they studied were equidistant on two dimensions.

A second kind of position factor relates the membership of the linkage mechanism with different hierarchical positions in the subsystems. According to Lawrence and Lorsch, a high-level production manager usually has sufficiently specialized knowledge of production processes to consider innovations proposed by scientists and can reach effective decisions about them in a joint meeting. On the other hand, scientific research and development is so specialized that the production manager's peer for linkage is a scientist actually working on the specific problem, or his immediate superior. And the corresponding peer in sales is likely to be a middle manager. The key linkers, whom Lawrence and Lorsch called "integrators," were at different hierarchical levels within their various subsystems and in the system as a whole. Where linkage mechanisms were effective, these hierarchical differences of members outside the linkage subsystem were relinquished upon entry into the linkage subsystem and neither blocked the decision making process nor reduced the acceptability of its results to other subsystems (1967:55-56). The differences in effectiveness related to "the degree to which these key integrators (were) seen by others in his organization as having the most important voice in decisions" (1967:62). In other words, while subsystems may have been formally represented at meetings by their managers, the major activities in and out of formal meetings were those of the various key linkers. Burns and Stalker (1961:88-9) found that the word "committee" captured the essential organizational equality of the members, irrespective of their status outside. In the companies they studied, they found linkage invariably associated with this equality. Effective linkage mechanisms "were indeed devices for abrogating for the length of each meeting the distribution of authority, information, and technical competence pictured in the hierarchic structure of the organization." They saw this abrogation as addressing appropriately the uncertainties in requirements for which the normal management structure was not appropriate (see also Lawrence and Lorsch, 1967:67, ff).

A third position factor is indicated by the reward system. Effective linkage seems to be associated with the extent to which linkers feel evaluated and rewarded according to the overall performance of the subsystems linked. According to Lawrence and Lorsch (1967:67, ff), it was important that linkers "had an incentive for effective integrative activities over and above the supervisory, planning and other functions" they performed within their own subsystems. Similarly, the goal team in Lorsch's (1965:122) study felt responsible for profits in their whole market area, so that each member "should be committed to the decisions we reach as a group."

Operating Norms of Linkage Mechanism

Operating norms relating to two aspects seem to be of particular importance: conflict resolution and flexibility. Lawrence and Lorsch (1967:73-77) list six factors in conflict resolution. According to them, linkage was effective to "the degree of openness with which conflicts were aired and hammered out in departmental meetings." . . .

Flexibility appears to be the second essential norm for the operation of an effective linkage mechanism, with kind and degree of flexibility determined by the functional needs of the mechanisms and the particular situations with which it is dealing at any time. Burns and Stalker (1961:87-89) described the flexible operation of a new research and development committee. It began as "a large, comprehensive affair" but was reduced in size when it became unprofitable to conduct the meetings in a language that shop-floor supervisors could understand readily. Therefore the large meeting was changed. A small professional committee dealt with ongoing projects, and regular foremen's meetings were used to keep the supervisors routinely informed about the committee's work. In short, the hierarchical structure was used as a communication system for this as for other routine matters. However, the committee meetings were expanded to their earlier size whenever a major design change was developed for one of the two main products of the company. Smith mentions a similar flexibility around the question of inviting system decision makers to meetings concerned with linkage (in Bright, 1962:49; see also Thompson, 1966:139-143).

Congruence with System Structure

Lorsch (1965:147) found the locus of formal authority congruent with the norms of conflict resolution: "The level with the authority within each subsystem about scientific transfer was also the level that the norms indicated should resolve differences between subsystems." This congruence existed with both ineffective and effective linkage mechanisms. The effective linkage system had fewer hierarchical levels than the ineffective, as would be expected from other research findings: in a turbulent environment a flatter system structure is associated with higher system performance.

In a turbulent environment, effective linkage mechanisms seem to have structures and operating norms that also characterize the whole system of which they are a part, and the system as a whole reflects more closely the structures and norms characteristic of innovative subsystems than those of traditional operating subsystems.

Discussion and Conclusion

This paper has been concerned with effective linkages in systems relating to turbulent environments. For these systems the problems of effective linkage are particularly difficult and particularly important (Lawrence and Lorsch, 1967:137).

Lawrence and Lorsch (1967) showed a direct relationship between degrees of turbulence, differentiation, and complexity of linkage mechanisms. The mechanisms were least differentiated and complex in the organization belonging to the relatively stable and undifferentiated container industry, more numerous and more complex in the moderately unstable and differentiated food organization, and most clearly differentiated and complex in the highly unstable plastics industry. Each of these high-performing organizations used a different combination of linkage devices (Lawrence and Lorsch, 1967:138, Table IV-1).

For systems in turbulent environments the design, development and operation of linkage mechanisms of appropriate complexity is costly. Decision makers will seek to avoid this investment. Even if they assess the environmental needs correctly, they are inclined to underestimate the response that would be effective and the costs involved in the response. Misjudgment of these costs is frequent among innovators who start their own organizations. As the organization grows, innovators often continue to assume that they can stretch linkage by personal contacts over ever greater numbers of people and finally to a new generation of decision makers and managers. Burns and Stalker (1961:92-94) described this personal pattern of attempted linkage. Characteristically, it results in people left "loose" to find their own way to get done whatever they see as necessary; in continuous definitions and redefinitions of tasks and groups "through a perpetual sequence of encounters" with laboratory chiefs, design engineers, and others "to see the job through"; and in increasing personal costs from "nervous preoccupation with the hazards of social navigation in the structure and with the relative validity of their own claims to authority, information and technical expertise." In one company these disruptive effects were counterbalanced by a general awareness of common purpose and of excitement at the tasks, and by the generally attractive atmosphere in the system. Joan Woodward's study (1965:196) compared the attempts of two other organizations, with similar technology and management structure, to establish a formal linkage mechanism. One organization, less than ten years old, with roles and functions not yet clearly established, persisted and designed an innovative system that fit the formal mechanism closely. The other organization was thirty years old and, the author concluded, too rigid to accept the innovation.

That the development of effective linkage mechanisms is associated with major changes in the system as a whole seems borne out by studies of organizations in a wide variety of settings. From a study of ten cases of organizational development in various settings, Buchanan (1967) established a list of 33 issues arising in each. The one issue that distinguished the seven most successful organizations conspicuously from the three unsuccessful ones was the linkage between the innovative subsystem and the rest of the system. "In two of the three unsuccessful cases, changes were initiated and progress was being made, only to come to a halt because of action by management. . . . Steps taken to accomplish linkage were not effective" (Buchanan 1967:62). In the successful cases, linkage between people at several levels of the system was established either as part of the change-induction plan or by steps taken early in the program. The linkage was in the form of working in small teams on operating problems or in the form of involving members in large numbers and at several levels during the early stages of identifying the linkage task (Buchanan, 1967:62). The successful organizations differed in the model they used for innovating, in the manner in which the model was introduced into the system, the location of the innovative subsystem in the system, and the time at which various levels of decision makers were involved. They were similar, on the other hand, in the following five aspects (Buchanan 1967:64):

1. They differentiated the innovative subsystem sharply and formally.
2. In the models they used they found a basis for establishing goals for improvement.
3. The models focused on problem-solving processes.
4. The models led to changes in the kind, distribution, and amount of power.
5. The models emphasized norms and skills that facilitated collaboration and problem solving rather than negotiation and bargaining.

It seems that as long as the model in its initial conception allows for these five dimensions, the system can develop the appropriate mechanisms for its singular circumstances and needs. In fact, working out its own distinctively appropriate pattern seems to be essential to effectiveness. The freedom to make changes, and the constraint in using this freedom, seem to stem from two sources. One is the shifting technological and informational needs of the system and the ways in which these can be met, given the resources of the system and the particular environment with which it interacts. The other source is the emotions of the people actually involved in the changes, which the linkage mechanisms are to mediate. Uncertainties from both sources have to be reflected in the openness of linkage mechanisms to further change; that is, their flexibility.

The emotional uncertainties seem the more complex. Sofer (1961) analyzed the emotional demands on linkage mechanisms that occurred in three very different organizations. He found that "the organization undertakes an emotional division of labor in attitudes towards innovators in just the same way it distributes any other organizational task" (Sofer, 1961:159). Some members will be for the new venture, others against it. "The relationship (of the innovative subsystem) with colleagues will be uneasy. There occur outbreaks of reciprocal paranoia as well as euphoria." When people in the innovative subsystem get discouraged and uncertain about whether they can perform the innovative task, they tend to withdraw and to create barriers rather than linkages. Sofer noted some of the mechanisms by which innovators tend to drain off internal tension. They called attention to the limitations under which decision makers expected them to succeed, their "rigidity," "short-sightedness," "intolerance" and "conservatism," their unwillingness to collaborate, their wish to see the innovation fail. "All parties will precipitate test cases. These test cases are variously used by all concerned to illustrate those aspects of the total situation that are most favorable to their rationale of the moment" (Sofer 1961:160). Sofer traced the system of defense by which people in the innovative subsystems sought to protect themselves and to explain their reluctance to devise, use and strengthen linkage mechanisms (1961:160-162). The strains in the rest of the system and the ways people express them then tend in turn to isolate the new subsystem further (Burns and Stalker, 1961:171).

In studies of innovation in educational systems, Miles (1964) described how this progressive deterioration of linkage mechanisms made the innovators' fears come true. Support for the innovative subsystem withered, recruitment into it became more difficult, reports of innovative achievements came to lack credibility. Soon the subsystem faced problems of sheer survival (Miles, 1964:654). Under these circumstances intergroup conflict and hostility are very likely to occur, and opposing coalitions develop, with each group magnifying its virtues and the opponents' faults. Such conflict often produced high solidarity *within* the groups. The innovative subsystem, being usually the less powerful, tends to develop substitute satisfactions, like fantasies that some day the others will learn to appreciate them.

Two general conclusions follow. One is that linkage mechanisms need to be flexible and also strong to withstand such strains and such uncertainties. This usually means that they need to be differentiated clearly, be known to have the support of the system's decision makers, and remain highly functional over time. Chin developed the concept of "intersystem" to describe the linkage mechanisms between two subsystems. "The intersystem model exaggerates the virtues of autonomy and the limited nature of interdependence of the interactions between the two connected systems" (Bennis *et al.*, 1964:201-214). The inter-system allows linkage to be rooted in another system, and to offer those "marginal" people who do the linking a base from which to operate and in which to gain and regain perspective and strength.

The second conclusion is simply a forceful reminder that coordination is a heavy cost. This cost may be profitably incurred if, (1) a primary task is clearly differentiated that requires organizational differentiation and, (2) if the new subsystem is maximally autonomous, so that its connections with other subsystems are minimal. In short, the only justification for linkage mechanisms is strict functional interdependence (Kahn *et al.*, 1964:394; Quinn and Mueller, 1963:51). Even if these criteria are rigidly applied, the number of systems that need to design and operate linkage mechanisms will surely increase as more and more decision makers come to recognize the turbulence of the environment.

References

Andrews, John H. M., and T. Barr Greenfield. 'Organizational themes relevant to change in schools." Ontario Journal of Educational Research, 8:81-99. 1966.

Barnes, Louis B. Organizational Systems and Engineering Groups: A Comparative Study of Two Technical Groups in Industry. Boston: Graduate School of Business Administration, Harvard University. 1960.

Bennis, Warren G., Kenneth D. Benne, and Robert Chin. The Planning of Change: Readings in the Applied Behavioral Sciences. New York: Holt, Rinehart & Winston. 1964.

Bright, James R. (ed.). Technological Planning on the Corporate Level (Proceedings of a Conference sponsored by The Associates of the Harvard Business School). Boston: Graduate School of Business Administration, Harvard University. 1962.

————. Research, Development and Technological Innovation: An Introduction. Homewood, Illinois: Irwin. 1964.

Buchanan, Paul C. "The concept of organization development, or self-renewal, as a form of social change." In Goodwin Watson (ed.), Concepts for Social Change: 1-9. Washington D. C. National Training Laboratories. 1967.

Burns, Tom, and G. M. Stalker. The Management of Innovation. London: Tavistock. 1961.

Carlson, R. O. "School superintendents and the adoption of modern math: a social structure profile." In Matthew B. Miles (ed.), Innovation in Education: 329-342. New York: Teachers College, Columbia University. 1964.

Chandler, Alfred D., Jr. Strategy and Structure: Chapters in the History of the Industrial Enterprise. Cambridge: M.I.T. Press. 1963.

Churchman, C. W., and A. H. Scheinblatt. "The researcher and the manager: a dialectic of implementation." Management Science, II (February 1965):B-75. 1965.

Dalton, Melville. "Conflicts between staff and line managerial officers." American Sociological Review, XV (June 1950):342-351. 1950.

Dearborn, Dewitt C., and Herbert A. Simon. "Selective perception: a note on the departmental identification of executives." Sociometry, XXI:140-144. 1958.

Downs, Anthony. Inside Bureaucracy. New York: Little, Brown. 1967.

Emery, F. E. "The next thirty years: concepts, methods and anticipations." Human Relations, XX:199-238. 1967.

Gallagher, A. "Characteristics of socio-technical systems." Document 527. London: Tavistock Institute of Human Relations. 1959.

————. The Role of the Advocate and Directed Change. Symposium paper. Lincoln, Nebraska. 1963.

Harvey, Edward. "Technology and the structure of organizations." American Sociological Review, XXXIII (April 1968) 247-259. 1968.

Havelock, Ronald G. Dissemination and Translation Roles in Education and Other Fields. UCEA Career Development Seminar. Eugene, Oregon. 1967.

Havelock, Ronald G., and Kenneth Benne. An Exploratory Study of Knowledge Utilization. Ann Arbor: Institute for Social Research, University of Michigan. 1964.

Herbst, P. G. "Task structure and work relations." Document 528. London: Tavistock Institute of Human Relations. 1959.

Hermann, Charles F. "Some consequences of crisis which limit the viability of organizations." Administrative Science Quarterly, 8 (June 1963):61-82. 1963.

Hirschman, A. O., and C. E. Lindblom. "Economic development, research and development, policymaking: some convergent views." Behavioral Science, 7:211-222. 1962.

Inkeles, Alex. Public Opinion in Soviet Russia. Cambridge, Mass.: Harvard University Press. 1951.

Jasinski, Frank J. "Adapting organization to new technology." In Joseph A. Litterer (ed.), Organizations: Structure and Behavior. New York: Wiley. 1963.

Kahn, Robert L., Donald M. Wofe, Robert P. Quinn, and J. Diedrick Snoek. Organizational Stress: Studies in Role Conflict and Ambiguity. New York: Wiley. 1964.

Kast, Fremont E., and James E. Rosenzweig (eds.). Science, Technology, and Management. New York: McGraw-Hill. 1962.

Katz, Daniel, and Robert L. Kahn. The Social Psychology of Organizations. New York: Wiley. 1966.

Katz, Elihu, and Paul F. Lazarsfeld. Personal Influence. Glencoe, Ill.: Free Press. 1955.

Lawrence, Paul R., and Jay W. Lorsch. Organization and Environment: Managing Differentiation and Integration. Boston: School of Business Administration, Harvard University. 1967.

Litterer, Joseph A. (ed.). Organizations: Structure and Behavior. New York: Wiley. 1963.

Litwak, Eugene. "Models of bureaucracy which permit conflict." The American Journal of Sociology, LXVII (September 1961):177-184. 1961.

Lorsch, Jay W. Product Innovation and Organization. New York: Macmillan. 1965.

Lorsch, Jay W., and Paul R. Lawrence. Environmental Factors and Organizational Integration. Paper prepared for 63rd Annual Meeting of the American Sociological Association, August 27, 1968, Boston, Mass. 1968.

Miles, B. Matthew (ed.). Innovation in Education. New York: Teachers College, Columbia University. 1964.

Miller, Eric J. "Part III: internal differentiation and problems of management." Human Relations, XII: 261-270. 1959.

Miller, E. J., and A. K. Rice. Systems of Organization. London: Tavistock. 1967.

Parsons, Talcott. "Suggestions for a sociological approach to the theory of organizations—I." Administrative Science Quarterly, 1:63-85. 1956.

Pelz, Donald C., and Frank M. Andrews. Scientists in Organizations. New York: Wiley. 1966.

Perrow, Charles. "A framework for the comparative analysis of organizations." American Sociological Review, XXXII (April 1967):194-208. 1967.

Pondy, Louis R. "Organizational conflict: concepts and models." Administrative Science Quarterly, 12 (September 1967):296-320. 1967.

Quinn, James Brian, and James A. Mueller. "Transferring research results to operations." Harvard Business Review, XLI (January 1963):49-66. 1963.

Rice, A. K. Productivity and Social Organization: The Ahmedabad Experiment. London: Tavistock. 1958.

Rodgers, Everett M. Diffusion of Innovations. New York: Free Press. 1962.

Ross, D. H. (ed.) Administration for Adaptability. New York: Metropolitan School Study Council. 1958.

Selznick, P. Leadership in Administration. New York: Row Peterson. 1957.

Shepard, Herbert A. "Nine dilemmas in industrial research." Administrative Science Quarterly, 1 (December):293-309. 1956.

Sieber, Sam D. The Organization of Educational Research in the United States. New York: Columbia University. 1966.

Smith, Alfred G. Communication and Status: The Dynamics of a Research Center. Eugene, Oregon: Center for the Advanced Study of Educational Administration, University of Oregon. 1966.

Sofer, Cyril. The Organization from Within: A Comparative Study of Social Institutions Based on a Sociotherapeutic Approach. London: Tavistock. 1961.

Strauss, George. "Tactics of lateral relationship: the purchasing agent." Administrative Science Quarterly, 7 (September):161-186. 1962.

Thayer, Lee. Communication and Communication Systems: In Organization, Management and Interpersonal Relations. Homewood, Ill.: Irwin. 1968.

Thompson, James D. Organizations in Action. New York: McGraw-Hill. 1967.

Thompson, Victor A. "Bureaucracy and innovation." Administrative Science Quarterly, 10 (June:1-20). 1965.

Trist, E. L., and G. W. Higgin, H. Murray, A. B. Pollock. Organizational Choice. London: Tavistock. 1963.

Watson, Goodwin (ed.). Change in School Systems. Washington, D. C.: NTL, NEA. 1967.

Woodward, Joan. Industrial Organization: Theory and Practice. London: Oxford University Press. 1965.

PART TWO

Individual Learning and Socialization

In the preceding part the emphasis was on the manner in which environmental contingencies affect the structure of an organization. In this part, the focus is on how individuals adapt to the world within which they must function. Organizations learn to survive by developing different patterns of accommodation to the world in which they function. In this part, the focus shifts from the organization to the individual, but the basic idea of environmental adaptation is the same. The readings in this part illustrate how individuals respond to circumstances in their environment and develop different modes of adaptation to both society and the organization in which they work.

The theoretical framework used here is learning theory. Learning theory is a set of concepts which helps us to understand how relatively stable behavior patterns of individuals develop. Organizations are identified not by characteristics such as geographic location, or other demographic factors, but rather by the degree to which individuals engage in some relatively continuous, stable system of interaction. If individuals interact over time, and if this interaction is fairly persistent, then we may attach the label "organization" to that system of behavior. Of interest here is the manner in which these behavior patterns develop, emerge, and stabilize. Thus, the focus on learning theory.

In the first selection, Hamner deals with two of the basic learning-theory approaches to understanding behavior. He describes the difference between classical conditioning and operant conditioning. Classical conditioning occurs when an individual relates certain cues to one another so that ultimately several different cues may be capable of eliciting a particular response. For example, in the classic experiment by Pavlov, he first caused a dog to salivate by presenting it with food; later, he rang a bell at the same time food was presented. Eventually the dog salivated at the sound of the bell.

In operant conditioning, reinforcement is a critical construct. When behavior is reinforced, the likelihood of it occurring again in response to a particular cue changes. If behavior is positively reinforced, the probability of occurrence of the behavior is increased, but if behavior is negatively reinforced, the likelihood that this response will occur again is decreased. Hamner also provides guidelines useful to the manager or the administrator in using these concepts in a practical operational

83

context. The second article in this part describes the striking success of reinforcement principles in a recent application at Emery Air Freight.

How and why do these concepts apply to the larger issues with which we are concerned here? It is obvious enough that an individual is constantly exposed to a wide range of stimuli and reinforcement in his life experiences. Over a period of time, the manner in which he responds to these stimuli represents a mode of accommodation or adaptation that may be considered as part of the individual's personality. Socialization is a process by which a society inculcates values, norms, ideals, and beliefs to its members, and may be understood in terms of learning theory. From the time an individual is born, he experiences needs, or tensions, that in one way or another, are reinforced. In childhood, one learns over a period of time how to interact with parents who represent authority figures. This is the beginning, Presthus argues, of learning to accommodate to organizations. Interaction with parents represents one's early experience with authority figures. In later life, authority figures are individuals who may be teachers, organizational superiors, or political figures. However, there are different ways in which individuals learn to interact with such authority figures.

Presthus presents some general stereotypes of individuals in organizations, and he defines a behavior pattern that is characterized by each type. The *upward-mobile* may be analogous to the organization man. He is satisfied with his organizational commitment, desires the rewards and status associated with being in the organization, and seeks to satisfy those in higher positions in order to obtain the rewards of the organization. Such an individual may be relatively easy to manage. He is likely to comply with directives simply because compliance is an internalized response for him. The *indifferent* withdraws from the organization. He is there simply because he probably has no alternative. It is difficult, if not impossible, for him to find satisfaction in the organization, but he must work in order to live. The *ambivalent* is likely to be a professional. He is a person highly committed to his own work, rather than to the organization in which he conducts it. In a sense, one can infer from Presthus' types that the ambivalent will be the most difficult to manage and the most difficult person from whom to obtain high levels of organizational commitment. Yet it is possible also that ambivalents may be agents of change or highly competent individuals with whom the organization must come to terms.

If these general modes of accommodation described by Presthus have any usefulness at all, they suggest that organizations are faced with the problem of integrating individuals who come to them with very different points of view about operating within the system. Moreover, different types of organization may be characterized by different proportions of individual types. The bureaucratic organization, it would seem, is more likely to be filled with upward-mobiles and indifferents than with ambivalents. In flexible organizations, which must confront a turbulent environment, it is likely that the ambivalent or highly skilled professional will be found in larger proportions than either the upward-mobile or the indifferent. All this suggests very different managerial problems in dealing with the human resources in the different organizational structures.

Organizations generally face the problem of selecting members from a wide range of backgrounds and experience, a fact which suggests also that members must be selected from a pool of individuals who already have different personality orientations, or patterns of accommodation. Socialization continues within an organization, however. Individuals are subjected to various cues and reinforcements once they become members. People "learn the ropes," which means that they become aware of the values, activities, and behavior required for successful and effective accommodation in the long run. This is the point made by Schein: the organization plays a significant part in shaping the attitudes, values, and beliefs of an individual. Thus, the individual's accommodation pattern prior to joining an organization is affected and perhaps reinforced by the kinds of contingencies that exist within the structure, once he has become a member.

Obviously, the point of view that one brings to an organization will significantly affect the manner in which he reacts to the contingencies in the organizational setting. The upward-mobile may react favorably to a system of rewards which provides high pay-offs, perhaps in increased status, income, or prestige, for loyalty and commitment. The indifferent, on the other hand, may well view the reward system as a manipulative attempt to control his life; thus, his alienation from the organization will only be increased. The ambivalent, viewing the authority system as a nuisance, may interpret the organizational reinforcement mechanism substantially differently than intended, causing problems for upwardly-mobile administrators.

The point of this part can be summarized easily: Individuals are subject to stimuli and reinforcement in their day-to-day experiences in an organization. These contingencies shape their behavior and cause the development of fairly consistent patterns of performance.

The contention that individuals respond to the reward system has the most significant implications for the manager. It is very possible that some individuals may view rewards differently than the manager does. For example, a manager may feel that he is reinforcing effective work behavior using an existing compensation system. He may, at the appropriate time of the year, give an employee a salary increase, comfortable in the conviction that the raise is an appropriate reward for good performance by the subordinate. Suppose, however, that the salary increase is approximately 6 percent, and the cost of living increase in that particular year is 4 percent. The individual may evaluate the increased effort that he has put forth over the year and decide that the 2 percent salary increase was not worth the 10 percent additional work required to obtain it.

Thus, while the manager believes the situation may be positively reinforcing, the individual for whom the reinforcement is intended does not have the same perception. It is this problem with which managers must deal if they intend to use reinforcement to affect performance. Reinforcements must be perceived as rewards or sanctions in order to be effective.

As we will see in part 5, the linkage between performance and reward may be difficult to establish because of the nature of the system itself; in the case of a highly integrated system such as an assembly line, for example, it may be virtually impossible to segregate the contribution of any one individual. In part 5 we will examine some alternative methods of job design, compensation, and training which can serve to facilitate the performance-reward link. We will examine more closely why the organizational system—the environment in which an individual works—must be supportive of the performance desired.

REINFORCEMENT THEORY AND CONTINGENCY MANAGEMENT IN ORGANIZATIONAL SETTINGS

W. CLAY HAMNER

Traditionally management has been defined as the process of getting things done through other people. The succinctness of this definition is misleading in that, while it may be easy to say *what* a manager does, it is difficult to describe the determinants of behavior, i.e. to tell *how* the behavior of the manager influences the behavior of the employee toward accomplishment of a task. Human behavior in organizational settings has always been a phenomenon of interest and concern. However, it has only been in recent years that a concerted effort has been made by social scientists to describe the principles of reinforcement and their implications for describing the determinants of behavior as they relate to the theory and practice of management (e.g. see Nord, 1969; Wiard, 1972; Whyte, 1972; Jablonsky and DeVries, 1972; Hersey and Blanchard, 1972; and Behling, Schriesheim, and Tolliver, in press).[1]

Organizational leaders must resort to environmental changes as a means of influencing behavior. Reinforcement principles are the most useful method for this purpose because they indicate to the leader how he might proceed in designing or modifying the work environment in order to effect specific changes in behavior (Scott and Cummings, 1973). A reinforcement approach to management does not consist of a bag of tricks to be applied indiscriminately for the purpose of coercing unwilling people (Michael & Meyerson, 1962). Unfortunately, many people who think of Skinnerian applications (Skinner, 1969) in the field of management and personnel think of manipulation and adverse control over employees. Increased knowledge available today of the positive aspects of conditioning as applied to worker performance should help to dispel these notions.

The purpose of this paper is to describe the determinants of behavior as seen from a reinforcement theory point of view, and to describe how the management of the contingencies of reinforcement in organizational settings is a key to successful management. Hopefully, this paper will enable the manager to understand how his behavior affects the behavior of his subordinates and to see that in most cases the failure or success of the worker at the performance of a task is a direct function of the manager's own behavior. Since a large portion of the manager's time is spent in the process of modifying behavior patterns and shaping them so that they will be more goal oriented, it is appropriate that this paper begin by describing the processes and principles that govern behavior.

Learning as a Prerequisite for Behavior

Learning is such a common phenomenon that we tend to fail to recognize its occurrence. Nevertheless, one of the major premises of reinforcement theory is that all behavior is learned—a worker's skill, a supervisor's attitude and a secretary's manners. The importance of learning in organizational settings is asserted by Costello and Zalkind when they conclude:

Every aspect of human behavior is responsive to learning experiences. Knowledge, language, and skills, of course; but also attitudes, value systems, and personality characteristics. All the individual's activities in the organization—his loyalties, awareness of organizational goals, job performance, even his safety record have been learned in the largest sense of that term (1963, p. 205).

There seems to be general agreement among social scientists that learning can be defined as *a relatively permanent change in behavior potentiality that results from reinforced practice or experience*. Note that this definition states that there is change in behavior potentiality and not necessarily in behavior itself. The reason for this distinction rests on the fact that we can observe other people responding to their environments, see the consequences which accrue to them, and be vicariously conditioned. For example, a boy can watch his older sister burn her hand on a hot stove and "learn" that pain is the result of touching a hot stove. This definition therefore allows us to account for "no-trial" learning. Bandura (1969) describes this as imitative learning and says that while behavior can be *acquired* by observing, reading, or other vicarious methods, *"performance* of observationally learned responses will depend to a great extent upon the nature of the reinforcing consequences to the model or to the observer" (p. 128).

Luthans (1973, p. 362) says that we need to consider the following points when we define the learning process:

1. Learning involves a change, though not necessarily an improvement, in behavior. Learning generally has the connotation of improved performance, but under this definition bad habits, prejudices, stereotypes, and work restrictions are learned.

2. The change in behavior must be relatively permanent in order to be considered learning. This qualification rules out behavioral changes resulting from fatigue or temporary adaptations as learning.

3. Some form of practice or experience is necessary for learning to occur.

4. Finally, practice or experience must be reinforced in order for learning to occur. If reinforcement does not accompany the practice or experience, the behavior will eventually disappear.

From this discussion, we can conclude that learning is the acquisition of knowledge, and performance is the translation of knowledge into practice. The primary effect of reinforcement is to strengthen and intensify certain aspects of ensuing behavior. Behavior that has become highly differentiated (shaped) can be understood and accounted for only in terms of the history of reinforcement of that behavior (Morse, 1966). Reinforcement generates a reproducible behavior process in time. A response occurs and is followed by a reinforcer, and further responses occur with a characteristic temporal patterning. When a response is reinforced it subsequently occurs more frequently than before it was reinforced. Reinforcement may be assumed to have a characteristic and reproducible effect on a particular behavior, and usually it will enhance and intensify that behavior (Skinner, 1938; 1953).

Two Basic Learning Processes

Before discussing in any detail exactly how the general laws or principles of reinforcement can be used to predict and influence behavior, we must differentiate between two types of behavior. One kind is known as *voluntary* or *operant* behavior, and the other is known as *reflex* or *respondent* behavior. Respondent behavior takes in all responses of human beings that are *elicited* by special stimulus changes in the environment. An example would be when a person turns a light on in a dark room (stimulus change), his eyes contract (respondent behavior).

Operant behavior includes an even greater amount of human activity. It takes in all the responses of a person that may at some time be said to have an effect upon or do something to the person's outside world (Keller, 1969). Operant behavior *operates* on this world either directly or indirectly. For example, when a person presses the up button at the elevator entrance to "call" the elevator, he is operating on his environment.

The process of learning or acquiring reflex behavior is different from the processes of learning or acquiring voluntary behavior. The two basic and distinct learning processes are known as *classical conditioning* and *operant conditioning*. It is from studying these two learning processes that much of our knowledge of individual behavior has emerged.

Classical Conditioning[2]

Pavlov (1902) noticed, while studying the automatic reflexes associated with digestion, that his laboratory dog salivated (unconditioned response) not only when food (unconditioned stimulus) was placed in the dog's mouth, but also when other stimuli were presented before food was placed in the dog's mouth. In other words, by presenting a neutral stimulus (ringing of a bell) every time food was presented to the dog, Pavlov was able to get the dog to salivate to the bell alone.

A stimulus which is not a part of a reflex relationship (the bell in Pavlov's experiment) becomes a *conditioned stimulus* for the response by repeated, temporal pairing with an *unconditioned* stimulus (food) which already elicits the response. This new relationship is known as a conditioned reflex, and the pairing procedure is known as classical conditioning.

While it is important to understand that reflex behavior is conditioned by a different process than is voluntary behavior, classical conditioning principles are of little use to the practicing manager. Most of the behavior that is of interest to society does not fit in the paradigm of reflex behavior (Michael and Meyerson, 1962). Nevertheless, the ability to generalize from one stimulus setting to another is very important in human learning and problem solving, and for this reason, knowledge of the classical conditioning process is important.

Operant Conditioning[3]

The basic distinction between classical and operant conditioning procedures is in terms of the *consequences* of the conditioned response. In classical conditioning, the sequence of events is independent of the subject's behavior. In operant conditioning, consequences (rewards and punishments) are made to occur as a consequence of the subject's response or failure to respond. The distinction between these two methods is shown in Figure 1.

In Figure 1, we see that classical conditioning involves a three stage process. In the diagram, let *S* refer to *stimulus* and R to *response*. We see that in stage

Figure 1. Classical vs. operant conditioning

1, the unconditioned stimulus (food) elicits an unconditioned response (salivation). In stage 2, a neutral stimulus (bell) elicits no known response. However, in stage 3, after the ringing of the bell is repeatedly paired with the presence of food, the bell alone becomes a conditioned stimulus and elicits a conditioned response (salivation). The subject has no control over the unconditioned or conditioned response, but is "at the mercy" of his environment and his past conditioning history.

Note however, that for voluntary behavior, the consequence is dependent on the behavior of the individual in a given stimulus setting. Such behavior can be said to "operate" (Skinner, 1969) on the environment, in contrast to behavior which is "respondent" to prior eliciting stimuli (Michael and Meyerson, 1962). Reinforcement is not given every time the stimulus is presented, but is *only* given when the correct response is made. For example, if an employee taking a work break, puts a penny (R) in the soft drink machine (S), nothing happens (consequence). However, if he puts a quarter (R) in the machine (S), he gets the soft drink (consequence). In other words, the employee's behavior is *instrumental* in determining the consequences which accrue to him.

The interrelationships between the three components of (1) *stimulus* or environment, (2) *response* or performance, and (3) consequences or *reinforcements* are known as the *contingencies* of reinforcement. Skinner (1969) says "The class of responses upon which a reinforcer is *contingent* is called an operant, to suggest the action on the environment followed by reinforcements (p. 7)." Operant conditioning presupposes that human beings explore their environment and act upon it. This behavior, randomly emitted at first, can be constructed as an operant by making a reinforcement contingent on a response. Any stimulus present when an operant is reinforced acquires control in the sense that the rate of response for that individual will be higher when it is present. "Such a stimulus does not act as a *goad*; it does not elicit the response (as was the case in classical conditioning of reflex behavior)[4] in the sense of forcing it to occur. It is simply an essential aspect of the occasion upon which response is made and reinforced (Skinner, 1969; p. 7)."

Therefore, an adequate formulation of the interaction between an individual and his environment must always specify three things: (1) the occasion upon which a response occurs, (2) the response itself and (3) the reinforcing consequences. Skinner holds that the consequences determine the likelihood that a given operant will be performed in the future. Thus to change behavior, the consequences of the behavior must be changed, i.e. the contingencies must be rearranged (the ways in which the consequences are related to the behavior) (Behling, *et al*, in press). For Skinner, this behavior generated by a given set of contingencies can be accounted for without appealing to hypothetical inner states (e.g. awareness or expectancies). "If a conspicuous stimulus does not have an effect, it is not because the organism has not attended to it or because some central gatekeeper has screened it out, but because the stimulus plays no important role in the prevailing contingencies (Skinner 1969, p. 8)."

Arrangement of the Contingencies of Reinforcement

In order to *understand* and *interpret* behavior, we must look at the interrelationship among the components of the contingencies of behavior. If one expects to influence behavior, he must also be able to manipulate the consequences of the behavior (Skinner, 1969). Haire (1964) reports the importance of being able to manipulate the consequences when he says,

> Indeed, whether he is conscious of it or not, the superior is bound to be constantly shaping the behavior of his subordinates by the way in which he utilizes the rewards that are at his disposal, and he will inevitably modify the behavior patterns of his work group thereby. For this reason, it is important to see as clearly as possible what is going on, so that the changes can be planned and chosen in advance, rather than simply accepted after the fact.

After appropriate reinforcers that have sufficient incentive value to maintain stable responsiveness have been chosen, the contingencies between specific performances and reinforcing stimuli must be arranged (Bandura, 1969). Employers intuitively use rewards in their attempt to modify and influence behavior, but their efforts often produce limited results because the methods are used improperly, inconsistently, or inefficiently. In many instances considerable rewards are bestowed upon the workers, but they are not made conditional or contingent on the behavior the manager wishes to promote. Also, "long delays often intervene between the occurrence of the desired behavior and its intended consequences; special privileges, activities, and rewards are generally furnished according to fixed time schedules rather than performance requirements; and in many cases, positive reinforcers are inadvertently made contingent upon the wrong type of behavior (Bandura, 1969, pp. 229-230)."

One of the primary reasons that managers fail to "motivate" workers to perform in the desired manner is due to a lack of understanding of the power of the contingencies of reinforcement over the employee and of the manager's role in arranging these contingencies. The laws or principles for arranging the contingencies are not hard to understand, and if students of behavior grasp them firmly, they are powerful managerial tools which can be used to increase supervisory effectiveness.

As we have said, operant conditioning is the process by which behavior is modified by manipulation of the contingencies of the behavior. To understand how this works, we will first look at various *types* (arrangements) of contingencies, and then at various *schedules* of the contingencies available. Rachlin (1970) described the four basic ways available to the manager of arranging the contingencies—*positive reinforcement, avoidance learning, extinction*, and *punishment*. The difference among these types of contingencies depends on the consequence which results from the behavioral act. Positive reinforcement and avoidance learning are methods of strengthening *desired* behavior, and extinction and punishment are methods of weakening *undesired* behavior.

Positive reinforcement. "A positive reinforcer is a stimulus which, when added to a situation, strengthens the probability of an operant response (Skinner, 1953, p. 73)." The reason it strengthens the response is explained by Thorndike's (1911) Law of Effect. This law states simply that behavior which appears to lead to a positive consequence tends to be repeated, while behavior which appears to lead to a negative consequence tends not to be repeated. A positive consequence is called a reward.

Reinforcers, either positive or negative, are classified as either; (1) unconditioned or primary reinforcers, or (2) conditioned or secondary reinforcers. Primary reinforcers such as food, water, and sex are of biological importance in that they are innately rewarding and have effects which are independent of past experiences. Secondary reinforcers such as job advancement, praise, recognition, and money derive their effects from a consistent pairing with other reinforcers (i.e., they are conditioned). Secondary reinforcement, therefore, depends on the individual and his past reinforcement history. What is rewarding to one person may not be rewarding to another. Managers should look for a reward system which has maximal reinforcing consequences to the group he is supervising.

Regardless of whether the positive reinforcer is primary or secondary in nature, once it has been determined that the consequence has reward value to the worker, it can be used to increase the worker's performance. So the *first step* in the successful application of reinforcement procedures is to select reinforcers that are sufficiently powerful and durable to "maintain responsiveness while complex patterns of behavior are being established and strengthened" (Bandura, 1969, p. 225).

The *second step* is to design the contingencies in such a way that the reinforcing events are made contingent upon the desired behavior. This is the rule of reinforcement which is most often violated. Rewards must result from performance, and the greater the degree of performance by an employee, the greater should be his reward.

Money as a reinforcer will be discussed later, but it should be noted that money is not the only reward available. In fact, for unionized employees, the supervisor has virtually no way to tie money to performance. Nevertheless, other forms of rewards, such as recognition, promotion and job assignments, can be made contingent on good performance. Unless a manager is willing to discriminate between employees based on their level of performance, the effectiveness of his power over the employee is nil.

The arrangement of positive reinforcement contingencies can be pictured as follows:

$$\text{Stimulus} \to \text{Desires Response} \to \text{Positive Consequences}$$
$$(S \to R \to R^+)$$

The stimulus is the work environment which leads to a response (some level of performance). If this response leads to positive consequences, then the probability of that response being emitted again increases (Law of Effect). Now, if the behavior is undesired, then the supervisor is conditioning or teaching the employee that undesired behavior will lead to a desired reward. It is important therefore that the reward administered be equal to the performance input of the employee. Homans (1950) labels this as the rule of distributive justice and stated that this reciprocal norm applies in both formal (work) and informal (friendship) relationships. In other words, the employee *exchanges* his services for the rewards of the organization. In order to maintain desired performance, it is important that the manager design the reward system so that the level of reward administered is proportionately contingent on the level of performance emitted.

The *third step* is to design the contingencies in such a way that a reliable procedure for eliciting or inducing the desired response patterns is established; otherwise, if they never occur there will be few opportunities to influence the desired behavior through contingent management. If the behavior that a manager wishes to strengthen is already present, and occurs with some frequency, then contingent applications of incentives can, from the outset, increase and maintain the desired performance patterns at a high level. However, as Bandura (1969) states, "When the initial level of the desired behavior is extremely low, if the criterion for reinforcement is initially set too high, most, if not all, of the person's responses go unrewarded, so that his efforts are gradually extinguished and his motivation diminished (p. 232)."

The nature of the learning process is such that acquiring the new response patterns can be easily established. The principle of operant conditioning says that an operant followed by a positive reinforcement is more likely to occur under similar conditions in the future. Through the process of *generalization*, the more nearly alike the new situation or stimulus is to the original one, the more the old behavior is likely to be emitted in the new environment. For example, if you contract with an electrician to rewire your house, he is able to bring with him enough old behavioral patterns which he generalized to this unfamiliar, but similar, stimulus setting (the house) in order to accomplish the task. He has learned through his past reinforcement history that, when in a new environment, one way to speed up the correct behavior needed to obtain reward is to generalize from similar settings with which he has had experience. Perhaps one reason an employer wants a person with work experience is because the probability of that person emitting the correct behavior is greater and thus the job of managing that person simplified.

Just as generalization is the ability to react to similarities in the environment, *discrimination* is the ability to react to differences in a new environmental setting. Usually when an employee moves from one environment (a job, a city, an office) to another he finds that only certain dimensions of the stimulus conditions change. While all of the responses of the employee in this new setting will not be correct, by skilled use of the procedures of reinforcement currently being discussed, we can bring about the more precise type of stimulus control called discrimination. When we purchase a new car, we do not have to relearn how to drive a car (generalizable stimulus). Instead we need only to learn the difference in the new car and the old car so that we can respond to these differences in order to get reinforced. This procedure is called *discrimination training*. "If in the presence of a stimulus a response is reinforced, and in the absence of this stimulus it is extinguished, the stimulus will control the probability of the response in high degree. Such a stimulus is called a *discriminative stimulus* (Michael and Meyerson, 1962)."

The development of effective discriminative repertoires is important for dealing with many different people on an interpersonal basis. Effective training techniques will allow the supervisor to develop the necessary discriminative repertoires in his new employees (e.g. see Bass and Vaughan, 1966, *Training in Industry: The Management of Learning*).

Using the principles of generalization and discrimination in a well-designed training program allows the manager to accomplish the third goal of eliciting or inducing the desired response patterns. Training is a method of *shaping* desired behavior so that it can be conditioned to come under the control of the reinforcement stimuli. Shaping behavior is necessary when the response to be learned is not currently in the individual's repertoire and when it is a fairly complex behavior. In shaping, we teach a desired response by reinforcing the series of successive steps which lead to the final response. This method is essentially the one your parents used when they first taught you to drive. You were first taught how to adjust the seat and mirror, fasten the seat belt, turn on the lights and windshield wipers, and then how to start the engine. Each time you successfully completed each stage you were positively reinforced by some comment. You then were allowed to practice driving on back roads and in empty lots. By focusing on one of these aspects at a time and reinforcing proper responses, your parents were able to shape your driving behavior until you reached the final stage of being able to drive. After your behavior was shaped, driving other cars or driving in new territories was accomplished successfully by the process of generalization and discrimination. This same process is used with a management trainee who is rotated from department to department for a period of time until he has "learned the ropes." After his managerial behavior has been minimally shaped, he is transferred to a managerial position where, using the principles of generalization and discrimination, he is able to adjust to the contingencies of the work environment.

Avoidance Learning. The second type of contingency arrangement available to the manager is called escape, or avoidance learning. Just as with positive reinforcement, this is a method of strengthening desired behavior. A contingency arrangement in which an individual's performance can terminate an already noxious stimulus is called *escape* learning. When behavior can prevent the onset of a noxious stimulus the procedure is called *avoidance learning.* In both cases, the results is the development and maintenance of the desired operant behavior (Michael and Meyerson, 1962).

An example of this kind of control can be easily found in a work environment. Punctuality of employees is often maintained by avoidance learning. The noxious stimulus is the criticism by the shop steward or office manager for being late. In order to avoid criticism other employees make a special effort to come to work on time. A supervisor begins criticizing a worker for "goofing off." Other workers may intensify their efforts to escape the criticism of the supervisor.

The arrangement of an escape reinforcement contingency can be diagrammed as follows:

$$\text{Noxious Stimulus} \rightarrow \text{Desired Response} \rightarrow \text{Removal of Noxious Stimulus}$$
$$(S^- \rightarrow R \nrightarrow S^-)$$

The distinction between the process of strengthening behavior by means of positive reinforcement techniques and avoidance learning techniques should be noted carefully. In one case, the individual works hard to gain the consequences from the environment which results from good work, and in the second case, the individual works hard to avoid the noxious aspects of the environment itself. In both cases the same behavior is strengthened.

While Skinner (1953) recognizes that avoidance learning techniques can be used to condition desired behavior, he does not advocate their use. Instead a Skinnerian approach to operant conditioning is primarily based on the principles of positive reinforcement.

Extinction. While positive reinforcement and avoidance learning techniques can be used by managers to strengthen desired behavior, extinction and punishment techniques are methods available to managers for reducing undesired behavior. When positive reinforcement for a learned or previously conditioned response is withheld, individuals will continue to exhibit that behavior for an extended period of time. Under repeated nonreinforcement, the behavior decreases and eventually disappears. This decline in response rate as a result of nonrewarded repetition of a task is defined as *extinction.*

The diagram of the arrangement of the contingency of extinction can be shown as follows:

$$(1) \quad \text{Stimulus} \rightarrow \text{Response} \rightarrow \text{Positive Consequences}$$
$$(S \rightarrow R \rightarrow R^+)$$

$$(2) \quad \text{Stimulus} \rightarrow \text{Response} \rightarrow \text{Withholding of Positive Consequences}$$
$$(S \rightarrow R \nrightarrow R^+)$$

(3) Stimulus → Withholding of Response
(S ⇸ R)

The behavior which was previously reinforced because (a) it was desired or (b) by poor reinforcement practices is no longer desired. To extinguish this behavior in a naturally recurring situation, response patterns substained by positive reinforcement (Stage 1) are frequently eliminated (Stage 3) by discontinuing the rewards (Stage 2) that ordinarily produce the behavior. This method when combined with a positive reinforcement method is the procedure of behavior modification recommended by Skinner (1953). It leads to the least negative side effects and when the two methods are used together, it allows the employee to get the rewards he desires and allows the organization to eliminate the undesired behavior.

Punishment. A second method of reducing the frequency of undesired behavior is through the use of punishment. Punishment is the most controverial method of behavior modification, and most of the ethical questions about operant methods of control center around this technique. "One of the principal objections to aversive control stems from the widespread belief that internal, and often unconscious, forces are the major determinant of behavior. From this perspective, punishment may temporarily suppress certain expressions, but the underlying impulses retain their strength and press continuously for discharge through alternative actions (Bandura, 1969, p. 292)." While Skinner (1953) discounts the internal state hypothesis, he recommends that extinction rather than punishment be used to decrease the probability of the occurrence of a particular behavior.

   Punishment is defined as presenting an aversive or noxious consequence contingent upon a response, or removing a positive consequence contingent upon a response. Based on the Law of Effect, as rewards strengthen behavior, punishment weakens it. This process can be shown as follows:

(1) Stimulus → Undesired Behavior →   Noxious Consequence or
$(S \rightarrow R \rightarrow R^-)$ Withholding of Positive
$(\quad$ or ⇸ $R^+)$ Consequence

(2) Stimulus ⇸ Undesired Behavior
(S ⇸ R)

Notice carefully the difference in the withholding of rewards in the punishment process and the withholding of rewards in the extinction process. In the extinction process, we withhold rewards for behavior that has previously been administered the rewards because the behavior was desired. In punishment, we withhold a reward because the behavior is undesired, has never been associated with the reward before, and is in fact a noxious consequence. For example, if your young son began imitating an older neighborhood boy's use of profanity and you thought it was "cute," you might reinforce the behavior by laughing or by calling public attention to it. Soon, the son learns one way to get the recognition he craves is to use profanity—even though he may have no concept of its meaning. As the child reaches an accountable age, you decide that his use of profanity is no longer as cute as it once was. To stop the behavior you can do one of three things: (1) You can withhold the previous recognition you gave the child by ignoring him (extinction), (2) You can give the child a spanking (punishment by noxious consequence), or (3) You can withhold his allowance or refuse to let him watch television (punishment by withholding of positive consequences not previously connected with the act).

It should be noted that method 2 and perhaps method 3 would be considered cruel because of the parent's own inconsistencies. Punishment should rarely be used to extinguish behavior that has previously been reinforced if the person administering the punishment is the same person who previously reinforced the behavior. However, had the parent failed to extinguish the use of profanity prior to sending the child out in society (e.g. school, church), it is possible that the society may punish the child for behavior that the parent is reinforcing or at least tolerating. It is often argued therefore that the failure to use punishment early in the life of a child for socially unacceptable behavior (e.g. stealing, driving at excessive speeds, poor table manners) is more cruel than the punishment itself, simply because the society will withhold rewards or administer adversive consequences for the behavior which the parents should have extinguished.

The use of aversive control is frequently questioned on the assumption that it produces undesirable by-products. In many cases this concern is warranted. Bandura (1969) states that it depends on the circumstances and on the past reinforcement history of the reinforcement agent and the reinforcement target as to whether punishment or extinction should be used. He says:

> Many of the unfavorable effects, however, that are sometimes associated with punishment are not necessarily inherent in the methods themselves but result from the faulty manner in which they are applied. A great deal of human behavior is, in fact, modified and closely regulated by natural aversive contingencies without any ill effects. On the basis of negative consequences people learn to avoid or to protect themselves against hazardous falls, flaming or scalding objects, deafening sounds, and other hurtful stimuli. . . . In instances where certain activities can have injurious effects, aversive contingencies *must* be socially arranged to ensure survival. Punishment is rarely indicted for ineffectiveness or deleterious side effects when used, for example, to teach young children not to insert metal objects into electrical outlets, not to cross busy thoroughfares . . . Certain types of negative sanctions, if applied considerately, can likewise aid in eliminating self-defeating and socially detrimental behavior without creating any special problems (p. 294).

Rules for Using Operant Conditioning Techniques

Several rules concerning the arrangement of the contingencies of reinforcement should be discussed. While these rules have common sense appeal, the research findings indicate that these rules are often violated by managers when they design control systems.

Rule 1. Don't reward all people the same. In other words, differentiate the rewards based on performance as compared to some defined objective or standard. We know that people compare their own performance to that of their peers to determine how well they are doing ("Social Comparison Theory", Festinger, 1954) and they compare their rewards to the rewards of their peers ("Equity Theory", Adams, 1965) in order to determine how to evaluate their rewards. While some managers seem to think that the fairest system of compensation is one where everyone in the same job classification gets the same pay, employees want differentiation so that they know their importance to the organization. Based on social comparison and equity theory assumptions, it can be argued that managers who reward all people the same are encouraging, at best, only average performance. Behavior of high performance workers is being extinguished (ignored) while the behavior of average performance and poor performance workers is being strengthened by positive reinforcement.

Rule 2. Failure to respond has reinforcing consequences. Managers who find the job of differentiating between workers so unpleasant that they fail to respond must recognize that failure to respond modifies behavior. "Indeed, whether he is conscious of it or not, the superior is bound to be constantly shaping the behavior of his subordinates by the way in which he utilizes the rewards that are at his disposal, and he will inevitably modify the behavior of his work group (Haire, 1964)." Managers must be careful that they examine the performance consequence of their non-action as well as their action.

Rule 3. Be sure to tell a person what he can do to get reinforced. By making clear the contingencies of reinforcement to the worker, a manager may be actually increasing the individual freedom of the worker. The employee who has a standard against which to measure his job will have a built-in feedback system which allows him to make judgments about his own work. The awarding of the reinforcement in an organization where the worker's goal is specified will be associated with the performance of the worker and not based on the biases of the supervisor. The assumption is that the supervisor rates the employee accurately (see Scott and Hamner, 1973a) and that he then reinforces the employee based on his ratings (see Scott and Hamner, 1973b). If the supervisor fails to rate accurately or administer rewards based on performance, then the stated goals for the worker will lose stimulus control, and the worker will be forced to search for the "true" contingencies, i.e. what behavior should he perform in order to get rewarded (e.g. ingratiation? loyalty? positive attitude?).

Rule 4. Be sure to tell a person what he is doing wrong. As a general rule, very few people find the act of failing rewarding. One assumption of behavior therefore is that a worker wants to be rewarded in a positive manner. A supervisor should never use extinction or punishment as a sole method for modifying behavior, but if used judiciously in conjunction with other techniques designed to promote more effective response options (Rule 3) such combined procedures can hasten the change process. If the supervisor fails to specify why a reward is being withheld, the employee may associate it with past desired behavior instead of the undesired behavior that the supervisor is trying to extinguish. The supervisor then extinguishes good performance while having no affect on the undesired behavior.

Rules 3 and 4, when used in combination, should allow the manager to control behavior in the best interest of reaching organizational goals. At the same time they should give the employee the clarity he needs to see that his own behavior and not the behavior of the supervisor controls his outcomes.

Rule 5. Don't punish in front of others. The reason for this rule is quite simple. The punishment (e.g. reprimand) should be enough to extinguish the undesired behavior. By administering the punishment in front of the work group, the worker is doubly punished in the sense that he is also put out of face (Goffman, 1959). This additional punishment may lead to negative side-effects in three ways. First, the worker whose self-image is damaged may feel that he must retaliate in order to protect himself. Therefore, the supervisor has actually increased undesired responses. Secondly, the work group may misunderstand the reason for the punishment and through "avoidance learning" may modify their own behavior in ways not intended by the supervisor. Third, the work group is also being punished in the sense that observing a member of their team being reprimanded has noxious or aversive properties for most people. This may result in a decrease in the performance of the total work group.

Rule 6. Make the consequences equal to the behavior. In other words be fair. Don't cheat the worker out of his just rewards. If he is a good worker, tell him. Many supervisors find it very difficult to praise an employee. Others find it very difficult to counsel an employee about what he is doing wrong. When a manager fails to use these reinforcement tools, he is actually reducing his effectiveness. When a worker is overrewarded he may feel guilty (Adams, 1965) and based on the principles of reinforcement, the worker's current level of performance is being conditioned. If his performance level is less than others who get the same reward, he has no reason to increase his output. When a worker is underrewarded, he becomes angry with the system (Adams, 1965). His behavior is being extinguished and the company may be forcing the good employee (underrewarded) to seek employment elsewhere while encouraging the poor employee (overrewarded) to stay.

An Argument for Positive Reinforcement

Most workers enter the work place willingly if not eagerly. They have a sense of right and wrong and have been thoroughly conditioned by their parents and by society. By the time they reach adulthood, it can be assumed that they are mature. For these reasons, it is argued here as well as by others (Skinner, 1953; Wiard, 1972), that the only tool needed for worker motivation is the presence or absence of positive reinforcement. In other words, managers do not, as a general rule, need to use avoidance learning or punishment techniques in order to control behavior.

Whyte (1972) says "positive reinforcers generally are more effective than negative reinforcers in the production and maintenance of behavior" (p. 67). Wiard (1972) points out, "There may be cases where the use of punishment has resulted in improved performance, but they are few and far between. The pitfalls of punishment can be encountered with any indirect approach" (p. 16). However, a positive reinforcement program is geared toward the desired results. It emphasizes what needs to be done, rather than what should not be done. A positive reinforcement program is result oriented, rather than process oriented. A well designed program encourages individual growth and freedom, whereas negative approach (avoidance learning and punishment) encourages immaturity in the individual and therefore eventually in the organization itself.

The reason organizations are ineffective according to Skinner (1969) is because they insist on using avoidance learning or punishment techniques, and because they fail to use a positive reinforcement program in an effective manner. He says:

> The contingencies of positive reinforcement arranged by governmental and religious agencies are primitive, and the agencies continue to lean heavily on the puritanical solution. Economic reinforcement might seem to represent an environmental solution, but it is badly programmed and the results are unsatisfactory for both the employer (since not much is done) and the employee (since work is still work). Education and the management of retardates and psychotics are still largely aversive. In short, as we have seen, the most powerful forces bearing on human behavior are not being effectively used. . . . Men are happy in an environment in which active, productive, and creative behavior is reinforced in effective ways (pp. 63-64).

Schedules of Positive Reinforcement

The previous discussion was primarily concerned with methods of arranging the contingencies of reinforcement in order to modify behavior. Two major points were discussed. First, some type of reinforcement is necessary in order to produce a change in behavior. Second, a combined program of positive reinforcement and extinction are more effective for use in organizations than are programs using punishment and/or avoidance learning techniques. The previous discussion thus tells what causes behavior and why it is important information for the manager, but it does not discuss the several important issues dealing with the scheduling or administering of positive reinforcement.

According to Costello and Zalkind (1963), "The speed with which learning takes place and also how lasting its effects will be is determined by the timing of reinforcement" (p. 193). In other words, the effectiveness of reinforcement varies as a function of the schedule of its administration. A reinforcement schedule is a more-or-less formal specification of the occurrence of a reinforcer in relation to the behavioral sequence to be conditioned, and effectiveness of the reinforcer depends as much upon its scheduling as upon any of its other features (magnitude, quality and degree of association with the behavioral act) (Adam and Scott, 1971).

There are many conceivable arrangements of a positive reinforcement schedule which managers can use to reward his workers (Ferster and Skinner, 1957). Aldis (1961) identifies two basic types of schedules which have the most promise concerning possible worker motivation. These schedules are *continuous* and *partial reinforcement* schedules.

Continuous reinforcement schedule. Under this schedule, every time the correct operant is emitted by the worker, it is followed by a reinforcer. With this schedule, behavior increases very rapidly but when the reinforcer is removed (extinction) performance decreases rapidly. For this reason it is not recommended for use by the manager over a long period of time. It is also difficult or impossible for a manager to reward the employee continuously for emitting desired behavior. Therefore a manager should generally consider using one or more of the partial reinforcement schedules when he administers both financial and nonfinancial rewards.

Partial reinforcement schedules. Partial reinforcement, where reinforcement does not occur after every correct operant, leads to slower learning but stronger retention of a response than total or continuous reinforcement. "In other words, *learning is more permanent when we reward correct behavior only part of the time*" (Bass and Vaughan, 1966, p. 20). This factor is extremely relevant to the observed strong resistance to changes in attitudes, values, norms, and the like.

Ferster and Skinner (1957) have described four basic types of partial reinforcement schedules for operant learning situations. They are:

1. *Fixed interval schedule.* Under this schedule a reinforcer is administered only when the desired response occurs after the passage of a specified period of time since the previous reinforcement. Thus a worker paid on a weekly basis would receive a full pay check every Friday, assuming that the worker was performing minimally acceptable behavior. This method offers the least motivation for hard work among employees (Aldis, 1961). The kind of behavior often observed with fixed-interval schedules is a pause after reinforcement and then an increase in rate of responding until a high rate of performance occurs just as the interval is about to end. Suppose the plant manager visits the shipping department each day at approximately 10:00 A.M. This fixed schedule of supervisory recognition will probably cause performance to be at its highest just prior to the plant manager's visit and then performance will probably steadily decline thereafter and not reach its peak again until the next morning's visit.

2. *Variable internal schedule.* Under this schedule, reinforcement is administered at some variable interval of time around some average. This schedule is not recommended for use with a pay plan (Aldis, 1961), but it is an ideal method to use for administering praise, promotions, and supervisory visits. Since the reinforcers are dispensed unpredictably, variable schedules generate higher rates of response and more stable and consistent performance (Bandura, 1969). Suppose our plant manager visits the shipping department on an *average* of once a day but at randomly selected time intervals, i.e., twice on Monday, once on Tuesday, not on Wednesday, not on Thursday, and twice on Friday, all at different times during the day. Performance will be higher and have less fluctuation than under the fixed interval schedule.

3. *Fixed ratio schedule.* Here a reward is delivered only when a fixed number of desired responses take place. This is essentially the piece-work schedule for pay. The response level here is significantly higher than that obtained under any of the interval (or time-based) schedules.

4. *Variable ratio schedule.* Under this schedule, a reward is delivered only after a number of desired responses with the number of desired responses changing from the occurrence of one reinforcer to the next, around an average. Thus a person working on a 15 to 1 variable ratio schedule might receive reinforcement after ten responses, then twenty responses, then fifteen responses, etc., to an average of one reinforcer per fifteen responses. Gambling is an example of a variable ratio reward schedule. Research evidence reveals that of all the variations in scheduling procedures available, this is the most powerful in sustaining behavior (Jablonsky and

DeVries, 1972). In industry, this plan would be impossible to use as the only plan for scheduling reinforcement. However, Aldis (1961) suggests how this method could be used to supplement other monetary reward schedules:

> Take the annual Christmas bonus as an example. In many instances, this "surprise" gift has become nothing more than a ritualized annual salary supplement which everybody expects. Therefore, its incentive-building value is largely lost. Now suppose that the total bonus were distributed at irregular intervals throughout the year and in small sums dependent upon the amount of work done. Wouldn't the workers find their urge to work increased? (p. 63).

An important point to remember is that to be effective a schedule should always include the specification of a contingency between the behavior desired and the occurrence of a reinforcer. In many cases it may be necessary to use each of the various schedules for administering rewards—for example, base pay on a fixed interval schedule, promotions and raises on a variable interval schedule, recognition of above average performance with a piece-rate plan (fixed ratio) and supplementary bonuses on a variable ratio schedule. The effect of each of the types of reinforcement schedules and the various methods of arranging reinforcement contingencies on worker performance is summarized in Table 1.

TABLE 1. Operant Conditioning Summary

Arrangement of Reinforcement Contingencies	Schedule of Reinforcement Contingencies	Effect on Behavior When Applied to the Individual	Effect on Behavior When Removed from the Individual
	Continuous Reinforcement	Fastest method to establish a new behavior.	Fastest method to extinguish a new behavior.
	Partial Reinforcement	Slowest method to establish a new behavior.	Slowest method to extinguish a new behavior.
	Variable Partial Reinforcement	More consistent response frequencies.	Slower extinction rate.
	Fixed Partial Reinforcement	Less consistent response frequencies.	Faster extinction rate.
Positive Reinforcement ———— Avoidance Reinforcement		Increased frequency over preconditioning level.	Return to preconditioning level.
Punishment ———— Extinction		Decreased frequency over preconditioning level.	Return to preconditioning level.

(Adapted from Behling et al., reprinted with permission of the author from "Present Theories and New Directions in Theories of Work Effort," *Journal Supplement and Abstract Service* of the American Psychological Corporation.)

The necessity for arranging appropriate reinforcement contingencies is dramatically illustrated by several studies in which rewards were shifted from a response-contingent (ratio) to a time-contingent basis (interval). During the period in which rewards were made conditional upon occurrence of the desired behavior, the appropriate response patterns were exhibited at a consistently high level. When the same rewards were given based on time and independent of the worker's behavior, there was a marked drop in the desired behavior. The reinstatement of the performance-contingent reward schedule promptly restored the high level of responsiveness (Lovaas, Berberich, Perloff, and Schaeffer, 1966; Baer, Peterson, and Sherman, 1967). Similar declines in performance were obtained when workers were provided rewards in advance without performance requirements (Ayllen and Azrin, 1965; Bandura and Perloff, 1967).

Aldis (1961) encourages businessmen to recognize the importance of a positive reinforcement program. He also says that experimentation with various schedules of positive reinforcement is the key to reducing job boredom and increasing worker satisfaction. He concludes:

> Most of us fully realize that a large proportion of all workers hold jobs that are boring and repetitive and that these employees are motivated to work not by positive rewards but by various oblique forms of threat. . . . The challenge is to motivate men by positive rewards rather than by negative punishments or threats of punishments. . . . Businessmen should recognize how much their conventional wage and salary systems essentially rely on negative reinforcement.

> Thus the promise of newer methods of wage payments which rely on more immediate rewards, on piece-rate pay, and greater randomization does not lie only in the increase in productivity that might follow. The greater promise is that such experiments may lead to happier workers as well (p. 63).

Management and the Dissemination of Knowledge

Previously we defined *learning* as the acquisition of knowledge (by the process of operant conditioning), and performance as the translation of knowledge into behavior (depending on the consequences). It can be argued therefore that what managers do is disseminate knowledge to those they manage in order to gain the desired level of performance. The question that remains to be answered is "What is knowledge, i.e., what information should one disseminate in order to control behavior?

There are two types of knowledge according to Skinner (1969). *Private knowledge* (Polanyi, 1960; Bridgeman, 1959) is knowledge established through experience with the contingencies of reinforcement. Skinner says "The world which establishes contingencies of reinforcement of the sort studied in an operant analysis is presumably 'what knowledge is about.' A person comes to know that world and how to behave in it in the sense that he acquires behavior which satisfies the contingencies it maintains" (1969, p. 156). The behavior which results from private knowledge is called *contingency-shaped* behavior. This is the knowledge which one must possess in order to perform correctly in order to get rewarded. This knowledge does not assume any awareness on the part of the person but is based entirely on the person's past reinforcement history. A person can "know how" to play golf, for example, as indicated by a series of low scores—yet it is an entirely different thing to be able to tell others how to play golf. A machine operator may be an excellent employee, but make a poor foreman. One reason may be that, while he possesses private knowledge about his job, he is unable to verbalize the contingencies to other people.

Public knowledge, then, is the ability to derive rules from the contingencies, in the form of injunctions or descriptions which specify occasions, responses, and consequences (Skinner, 1969, p. 160). The behavior which results from public knowledge is called *rule-governed* behavior.

The reason the possession of public knowledge is important to the manager is simple. The employee looks to the manager for information about what behavior is required, how to perform the desired behavior, and what the consequences of the desired behavior will be. Before a manager can give correct answers to these questions, he must understand the true contingencies himself, since his business is not in doing, but in telling others how to do. The point is to be able to analyze the contingencies of reinforcement found in the organization and "to formulate rules or laws which make it unnecessary to be exposed to them in order to behave appropriately" (Skinner, 1969, p. 166).

After living in a large city for a long time, a person is able to go from Point A to Point B with little trouble. The knowledge of how to get around in the city was shaped by the past history with the environment. This behavior is an example of contingency-shaped behavior. If a stranger arrives in the same city and desires to go from Point A to Point B he too will have little trouble. He will look at a map of the city, and follow the path specified by the map. This behavior is an example of rule-governed behavior. Whether or not a person will continue to follow the map (rule) in the future is dependent on the consequences of following the map in the past. If the rule specified the correct contingencies, he probably will continue to use the map, but if a person found the map to be in error, then he will probably look to other sources of information (e.g., asking someone with private knowledge). The same thing happens in industry. If a manager is correct in the specification of the rules, i.e., the new worker follows the rules and receives a reward, then the worker will probably follow the other rules specified by the manager. If the manager specifies incorrect rules, then the worker may look to his peers or to other sources for information (e.g., the union steward) and specification of rules which describe behavior that will be rewarded.

There are two kinds of rules the manager can specify to the employee. A command or *mand* is a rule that specifies behavior and consequences of the behavior, where the consequences are arranged by the person giving the command. The specified or implied consequences for failure to act are usually aversive in nature and the judgment of the correctness of the behavior is made by the person giving the command. A foreman who tells the worker to be on time for work is giving the worker a command. The implied consequence is that if the employee fails to report on time, the foreman will take action.

Advice and warnings are called *tacts* and involve rules which specify the reinforcements contingent on prior stimulation from rules, or laws. They specify the same contingencies which would directly shape behavior (private knowledge). The specification of the tact speeds up the conditioning process. If a secretary tells her boss he should take an umbrella when he goes to lunch she is describing a tact. She has no control over the consequences (getting wet) of the behavior (not carrying the umbrella). Instead it is determined by the environment itself (weather). Skinner (1969) says:

> *Go west, young man* is an example of advice (tacting) when the behavior it specifies will be reinforced by certain consequences which do not result from action taken by the advisor. We tend to follow advice because previous behavior in response to similar verbal stimuli has been reinforced. Go west, young man is a command when some consequences of the specified action are arranged by the commander—say, the aversive consequences arranged by an official charged with relocating the inhabitants of a region. When maxims, rules, and laws are advice, the governed behavior is reinforced by consequences which might have shaped the same behavior directly in the absence of the maxims, rules, and laws. When they are commands, they are effective only because special reinforcements have been made contingent upon them. (p. 148).

While a manager must possess public knowledge as well as private knowledge in order to accomplish his task of "getting things done through other people" in keeping with a plea for positive reinforcement and unbiased reward systems, tacting is the method of rule specification recommended. Skinner (1969) recommends that by specifying the contingencies in such a way that the consequences are positive in nature and failure to respond is met with the withholding of a reward rather than by aversive stimuli, "the 'mand' may be replaced by a 'tact' describing conditions under which specific behavior on the part of the listener will be reinforced (p. 158)." Instead of saying "Give me that report" say "I need the report". "The craftsman begins by ordering his apprentice to behave in a given way; but he may later achieve the same effect simply by describing the relation between what the apprentice does and the consequences" (Skinner, 1969, p. 158). Thus, the technique which managers use to direct the employee can make a lot of difference in the acceptance of the rule by the employee. A mand operates from an avoidance learning base while a tact operates from a positive reinforcement base. A tact is more impersonal and gives the employee freedom in that it does not "enjoin anyone to behave in a given way, it simply describes the contingencies under which certain kinds of behavior will have certain kinds of consequences" (Skinner, 1969, p. 158).

Controversies Surrounding an Operant Approach to Management

The reinforcement approach to the study and control of human behavior has met with resistance and criticism, primarily through a lack of understanding of its recommended uses and limitations. Goodman (1964) wrote, "To be candid, I think operant-conditioning is vastly overrated." Henry (1964) said, "Learning theory has two simple points to make and does so with talmudic ingenuity, variability, intricacy, and insistence. They are reinforcement and extinction. What has to be left out. . . . is thought.''

While the criticisms would be too numerous to mention here, an attempt will be made to examine three of the major controversies surrounding an operant approach to the management of people in organizational settings.

1. *The application of operant conditioning techniques ignores the individuality of man.* Ashby (1967) said "now the chief weakness of programmed instruction is that it rewards rote learning, and worse than that—it rewards only those responses which are in agreement with the programme." Proponents of an operant approach to contingency management recognize that a poorly designed program can lead to rigidity in behavior. This is one of the major reasons that they recommend a program of reinforcement which best fits the group or individuals being supervised. It is untrue, however, that behaviorists ignore the individuality of man. Each man is unique based on his past reinforcement history. When personnel psychologists build sophisticated selection models to predict future performance, they are actually trying to identify those applicants who will perform well under the contingencies of that particular organization. That does not mean that a person rejected cannot be motivated, but only that the current reward system of that organization is better suited for another applicant.[5]

In other words, the problem a manager faces is not to design contingencies that will be liked by all men, "but a way of life which will be liked by those who live it" (Skinner, 1969, p. 41). As Hersey and Blanchard (1972) point out, "Positive reinforcement is anything that is rewarding to the individual being reinforced. Reinforcement, therefore, depends on the individual (p. 22)." What is reinforcing to one may not be reinforcing to someone else based on the person's past history of satiation, deprivation and conditioning operations. A manager can do two things to insure that the contingencies of reinforcement are designed to support the individuality of the worker. First, as noted earlier he can strive to hire the worker who desires the rewards offered by the firms; i.e., can the person be happy or satisfied with this firm? Secondly, if it seems that the contingencies are ineffective, the manager can change the contingencies by using a democratic process—letting the employees design their own reward structure, within the limits set by the organization. "Democracy is an effort to solve the problem by letting the people design the contingencies under which they are to live or—to put it another way—by insisting that the designer himself live under the contingencies he designs" (Skinner, 1969, p. 43).

In summary, therefore, it can be concluded that in a voluntary society, where man has freedom to move from one organization to another, operant methods of control should not ignore the individuality of man. Instead man should seek work where his individuality can best be appreciated and industries should select employees who can best be motivated by the contingencies available to them. It should be noted, however, that through the unethical application of conditioning principles, some employers may exploit workers. The overall evidence would seem to indicate that this is not due to the weakness in behavioral theory, but due to the weakness of man himself.

2. *The application of operant conditioning techniques restricts freedom of choice.*

Discussion of the moral implications of behavioral control almost always emphasize the Machiavellian role of change agents and the self-protective maneuvers of controllers. . . . The tendency to exaggerate the powers of behavioral control by psychological methods alone, irrespective of willing cooperation by the client, and the failure to recognize the reciprocal nature of interpersonal control obscure both the ethical issues and the nature of the social influence processes (Bandura, 1969, p. 85).

Kelman (1965) noted that the primary criterion that one might apply in judging the ethical implications of social influence approaches is the degree to which they promote freedom of choice. If individualism is to be guaranteed, it must be tempered by a sense of social obligation by the individual and by the organization.

Bandura (1969) noted that a person is considered free insofar as he can partly influence future events by managing his own behavior. A person in a voluntary society can within limits exert some control over the variables that govern his own choices. Skinner (1969) noted that "Men are happy in an environment in which active, productive, and creative behavior is reinforced in effective ways" (p. 64). One method of effectively reinforcing behavior is by allowing the employee some determination in the design of the reinforcement contingencies. Another method is to design self-control reinforcement systems in which individuals regulate their own activities (Ferster, Nurnberger and Levitt, 1962; Harris, 1969).

While it cannot be denied that reinforcers which are "all too abundant and powerful" (Skinner, 1966) can restrict freedom of choice, it is not true that a behavioral or Skinnerian approach is against freedom of choice; the opposite is true. As Bandura noted, "Contrary to common belief, behavioral approaches not only support a humanistic morality, but because of their relative effectiveness in establishing self-determination these methods hold much greater promise than traditional procedures for enhancement of behavioral freedom and fulfillment of human capabilities" (p. 88).

3. *Operant theory, through its advocacy of an external reward system, ignores the fact that individuals can be motivated by the job itself.* Deci (1971, 1972) among others (Likert, 1967; Vroom and Deci, 1970) criticizes behaviorists for advocating a system of employee motivation that only utilizes externally mediated rewards, i.e., rewards such as money and praise administered by someone other than the employee himself. In so doing, according to Deci, management is attempting to control the employee's behavior so he will do what he is told. The limitations of this method of worker motivation, for Deci, is that it only satisfies man's "lower-order" needs (Maslow, 1943) and does not take into account man's "higher-order" needs for self-esteem and self-actualization. Deci states, "It follows that there are many important motivators of human behavior which are not under the direct control of managers and, therefore, cannot be contingently administered in a system of piece-rate payments" (1972, p. 218).

Deci recommends that we should move away from a method of external control, and toward a system where individuals can be motivated by the job itself. He says that this approach will allow managers to focus on higher-order needs where the rewards are mediated by the person himself (intrinsically motivated). To motivate employees intrinsically, tasks should be designed which are interesting, creative and resourceful, and workers should have some say in decisions which concern them "so they will feel like causal agents in the activities which they engage in" (Deci, 1972, p. 219). Deci concludes his argument against a contingency approach to management by saying:

> . . . It is possible to pay workers and still have them intrinsically motivated. Hence the writer favors the prescription that we concentrate on structuring situations and jobs to arouse intrinsic motivation, rather than trying to structure piece-rate and other contingency payment schemes. Workers would be intrinsically motivated and would seek to satisfy their higher-order needs through effective performance. The noncontingent payments (or salaries) would help to satisfy the workers and keep them on the job, especially if the pay were equitable (Adams, 1965; Pritchard, 1969), (1972, p. 227).

Deci levels criticism at a positive reinforcement contingency approach on the basis of four issues: (1) advocating that external rewards be administered by someone else, (2) ignoring the importance of the task environment, (3) ignoring the importance of internal rewards, and (4) advocating of a contingent payment plan. Deci makes two errors, from a reinforcement theory point of view, when he advocates noncontingent equitable pay plans. First, equity theory (Adams, 1965) assumes that rewards are based on performance. If they weren't, then the pay would be equal, not equitable. Second, and more crucial, is Deci's assumption that a pay plan can be noncontingent. Bandura notes that "all behavior is inevitably controlled, and the operation of psychological laws cannot be suspended by romantic conceptions of human behavior, any more than indignant rejection of the law of gravity as antihumanistic can stop people from falling" (1969, p. 85). Homme and Tosti (1965) made the point that, "either one manages the contingencies or they get managed by accident. Either way there will be contingencies, and they will have their effect" (p. 16): In other words, if managers instituted a pay plan that was "noncontingent," they would in fact be rewarding poor performance and extinguishing good performance (see Rules 1, 2, and 6).

The assertion that a contingency approach advocates that the rewards always be administered by someone else is false. Skinner specifically (1969, p. 158) recommends that manding behavior be replaced by tacting methods for achieving the same effect. Skinner suggested that one safeguard against exploitation is to make sure that the designer of the contingencies never controls. In addition to recommending that the contingencies be so designed that they are controlled by the environment (tacting), operant theorists have advocated self-control processes in which individuals regulate their own behavior by arranging appropriate contingencies for themselves (Ferster, Nurnberger and Leavitt, 1962). Bandura (1969) concluded that:

> The selection of well-defined objectives, both intermediate and ultimate, is an essential aspect of any self-directed program of change. The goals that individuals choose for themselves must be specified in sufficiently detailed behavioral terms to provide adequate guidance for the actions that must be taken daily

to attain desired outcomes. . . . Individuals can, therefore, utilize objective records of behavioral changes as an additional source of reinforcement for their self-controlling behavior (p. 255).

Studies which have explored the effect of self-reinforcement on performance have shown that systems which allowed workers to keep a record of their own output to use as a continuous feedback system and for reinforcement purposes helped the workers to increase their performance (Kolb, Winter and Berlew, 1968; Fox, 1966). Michigan Bell Telephone Company and the Emery Air Freight Corporation are two of several firms which are currently using self-reinforcement programs in order to increase worker motivation and performance. Both programs have been immensely successful (see *Business Week*, December 18, 1971; and December 2, 1972).

It should be noted that even though the individual is determining his own reward in the self-feedback program, the reinforcers are both externally (money, recognition, praise) and internally (self-feedback) mediated. According to Skinner (1957) and Bem (1967) the self-report feedback is a "tact" or description of an internal feeling state. In both cases, the rewards must be contingent on performance for effective control of the behavior to take place.

Deci's recommendation that jobs should be designed so that they are interesting, creative, and resourceful is wholeheartedly supported by proponents of a positive reinforcement program. Skinner (1969) warns managers that too much dependency on force and a poorly designed monetary reward system may actually reduce performance, while designing the task so that it is automatically reinforcing can have positive effects on performance. Skinner says:

The behavior of an employee is important to the employer, who gains when the employee works industriously and carefully. How is he to be induced to do so? The standard answer was once physical force: men worked to avoid punishment or death. The by-products were troublesome, however, and economics is perhaps the first field in which an explicit change was made to positive reinforcement. Most men now work, as we say, 'for money'.

Money is not a natural reinforcer; it must be conditioned as such. Delayed reinforcement, as in a weekly wage, raises a special problem. No one works on Monday morning because he is reinforced by a paycheck on Friday afternoon. The employee who is paid by the week works during the week to avoid losing the standard of living which depends on a weekly system. Rate of work is determined by the supervisor (with or without the pacing stimuli of a production line), and special aversive contingencies maintain quality. The pattern is therefore still aversive. It has often been pointed out that the attitude of the production-line worker toward his work differs conspicuously from that of the craftsman, who is envied by workers and industrial managers alike. One explanation is that the craftsman is reinforced by more than monetary consequences, but another important difference is that when a craftsman spends a week completing a given set object, each of the parts produced during the week is likely to be automatically reinforcing because of its place in the completed object (p. 18).

Skinner (1969) also agrees with Deci that the piece-rate may actually reduce performance in that it is so powerful it is most often misused, and "it is generally opposed by those concerned with the welfare of the worker (and by workers themselves when, for example, they set daily quotas)" (p. 19).

It appears therefore, that critics of operant conditioning methods misunderstand the recommendations of behaviorists in the area of worker motivation. Operant theory does advocate interesting job design and self-reinforcement feedback systems, where possible. It does not advocate force or try to control the employee's behavior by making the employee "do what he is told." It is not against humanistic morality; rather it advocates that workers be rewarded on their performance and not on their needs alone.

While other controversies about operant conditioning could be reviewed, the examination of these three issues should give the reader a flavor of the criticisms which surround the use of a contingency approach to behavioral control.

Ethical Implications for Worker Control

The deliberate use of positive and negative reinforcers often gives rise to ethical concern about harmful effects which may result from such practices. Poorly designed reward structures can interfere with the development of spontaneity and creativity. Reinforcement systems which are deceptive and manipulative are an insult to the integrity of man. The employee should be a willing party to the influence attempt, with both parties benefiting from the relationship.

The question of whether man should try to control human behavior is covered in a classic paper by Rogers and Skinner (1956). The central issue discussed was one of personal values. Rogers contends that "values" emerge from the individual's "freedom of choice," a realm unavailable to science. Skinner, in rebuttal, points out that the scientific view of man does not allow for such exceptions, and that choice and the resulting values are, like all behavior, a function of man's biology and his environment. Since biology and environment lie within the realm of science, "choice" and "value" must be accessible to scientific inquiry. Skinner and Rogers are both concerned with abuse of the power held by scientists, but Skinner is optimistic that good judgment will continue to prevail. Krasner (1964) agrees with Skinner that we should apply scientific means to control behavior, but warns that behavioral control can be horribly misused unless we are constantly alert to what is taking place in society.

Probably few managers deliberately misuse their power to control behavior. Managers should realize that the mismanagement of the contingencies of reinforcement is actually self-defeating. Workers will no longer allow themselves to be pushed around, but instead will insist that the work environment be designed in such a way that they have a chance at a better life. The effective use of a positive reinforcing program is one of the most critical challenges facing modern management.

The first step in the ethical use of behavioral control in organizations is the understanding by managers of the determinants of behavior. Since reinforcement is the single most important concept in the learning process, managers must learn how to design effective reinforcement programs that will encourage creative, productive, satisfied employees. This paper has attempted to outline the knowledge available for this endeavor.

Notes

1. The author is indebted to Professor William E. Scott, Jr., Graduate School of Business, Indiana University for sharing with him his Skinnerian philosophy.
2. Classical conditioning is also known as respondent conditioning and Pavlovian conditioning.
3. Operant conditioning is also known as instrumental conditioning and Skinnerian conditioning.
4. Parentheses added.
5. This is true because the criterion variable is some measure of performance, and performance is directly tied to the reinforcement consequences for the current employees used to derive the selection model.

References

Adam, E. E., and Scott, W. E., The application of behavioral conditioning procedures to the problems of quality control. *Academy of Management Journal*, 1971, 14, 175-193.

Adams, J. S., Inequity in social exchange, in L. Berkowitz (ed.), *Advances in Experimental Psychology*, Academic Press, 1965, 157-189.

Aldis, O., Of pigeons and men, *Harvard Business Review*, 1961, 39, 59-63.

Ayllon, T. and Azrin, N. H., The measurement and reinforcement of behavior of psychotics, *Journal of the Experimental Analysis of Behavior*, 1965, 8, 357-383.

Ashby, Sir Eric, Can education be machine made?, *New Scientist*, February 2, 1967.

Baer, D. M., Peterson, R. F., and Sherman, J. A., The development of imitation by reinforcing behavioral similarity to a model. *Journal of the Experimental Analysis of Behavior*, 1967, 10, 405-416.

Bandura, A. and Perloff, B., The efficacy of self-monitoring reinforcement systems, *Journal of Personality and Social Psychology*, 1967, 7, 111-116.

Bandura, A., *Principles of Behavior Modification*, Holt, Rinehart and Winston, Inc., New York, 1969.

Bass, B. M. and Vaughan, J. A., *Training in Industry: The Management of Learning*, Wadsworth Publishing Company, Belmont, Calif., 1966.

Behling, O., Schriesheim, C. and Tolliver, J., Present theories and new directions in theories of work effort, *Journal Supplement Abstract Service* of the American Psychological Corporation, in press.

Bem, D. J., Self-perception: An alternative interpretation of cognitive dissonance phenomena, *Psychological Review*, 1967, 74, 183-200.

Bridgeman, D. W., *The Way Things Are*, Harvard Press, Cambridge, Mass., 1959.

Costello, T. W. and Zalkind, S. S., *Psychology in Administration*, Prentice-Hall, Inc., Englewood Cliffs, N. J., 1963.

Deci, E. L., The effects of contingent and noncontingent rewards and controls on intrinsic motivation, *Organizational Behavior and Human Performance*, 1972, 8, 217-229.

Deci, E. L., The effects of externally mediated rewards on intrinsic motivation, *Journal of Personality and Social Psychology*, 1971, 18, 105-115.

Festinger, L., A theory of social comparison processes, *Human Relations*, 1954, 7, 117-140.

Ferster, C. B., and Skinner, B. F., *Schedules of Reinforcement*, Appleton-Century-Crofts, New York, 1957.

Ferster, C. B., Nurenberger, J. I., and Levitt, E.B., The control of eating, *Journal of Mathematics*, 1962, 1, 87-109.

Fox, L., The use of efficient study habits, In R. Ulrich, T. Stachnik, and J. Mabry (Eds.), *Control of Human Behavior*, Scott, Foresman, Glenview, Ill., 1966, 85-93.

Goffman, E., *The Presentation of Self in Everyday Life*, Doubleday, New York, 1959.

Goodman, Paul, *Compulsory Mis-education*, Horizon Press, New York, 1964.

Haire, Mason, *Psychology in Management*, 2nd ed., McGraw-Hill, New York, 1964.

Harris, M. B., A self-directed program for weight control: a pilot study, *Journal of Abnormal Psychology*, 1969, 74, 263-270.

Henry, Jules, Review of human behavior: An inventory of scientific findings by Bernard Berelson and Gary A. Steiner, *Scientific American*, July, 1964.

Hersey, P. and Blanchard, K. H., The management of change: Part 2, *Training and Development Journal*, February, 1972, 20-24.

Hilgard, E. R., *Theories of Learning*, 2nd ed., Appleton-Century-Crofts, New York, 1956.

Homme, L. E., and Tosti, D. T., Contingency management and motivation, *Journal of the National Society for Programmed Instruction*, 1965, 4, 14-16.

Jablonsky, S. and DeVries, D., Operant conditioning principles extrapolated to the theory of management, *Organizational Behavior and Human Performance*, 1972, 7, 340-358.

Keller, F. S., *Learning: Reinforcement Theory*, Random House, New York, 1969.

Kelman, H. C., Manipulation of human behavior: An ethical dilemma for the social scientist, *Journal of Social Issues*, 1965, 21, 31-46.

Kolb, D. A., Winter, S. K., and Berlew, D. E., Self-directed change: Two studies, *Journal of Applied Behavioral Science*, 1968, 4, 453-471.

Krasner, L., Behavior control and social responsibility, *American Psychologist*, 1964, 17, 199-204.

Likert, R., *New Patterns of Management*, McGraw-Hill, New York, 1961.

Lovaas, O. I., Berberich, J. P., Perloff, B. F., and Schaeffer, B., Acquisition of imitative speech for schizophrenic children, *Science*, 1966, 151, 705-707.

Luthans, F., *Organizational Behavior*, McGraw-Hill, New York, 1973.

Maslow, A. H., A theory of human motivation, *Psychological Review*, 1943, 50, 370-396.

McGregor, D., *The Human Side of Enterprise*, New York, McGraw-Hill, 1960.

Michael, J. and Meyerson, L., A behavioral approach to counseling and guidance, *Harvard Educational Review*, 1962, 32, 382-402.

Morse, W. H., Intermittent reinforcement, in W. K. Honig, (ed.), *Operant Behavior*, Appleton-Century-Crofts, New York, 1966.

New tool: Reinforcement for good work, *Business Week*, December 18, 1971, 68-69.

Nord, W. R., Beyond the teaching machine: The neglected area of operant conditioning in the theory and practice of management, *Organizational Behavior and Human Performance*, 1969, 375-401.

Pavlov, I. P., *The Work of the Digestive Glands*, (Translated by W. H. Thompson), Charles Griffin, London, 1902.

Polanyi, M., *Personal Knowledge*, Univ. of Chicago Press, 1960.

Rachlin, H., *Modern Behaviorism*, W. H. Freeman and Co., New York, 1970.

Rogers, Carl R., and Skinner, B. F., Some issues concerning the control of human behavior: A symposium, *Science*, 1956, 124, 1057-1066.

Scott, W. E. and Cummings, L. L., *Readings in Organizational Behavior and Human Performance*, Revised Edition, Irwin, Homewood, Ill., 1973.

Scott, W. E., and Hamner, W. Clay, The effects of order and variance in performance on supervisory ratings of workers, Paper presented at the *45th Annual Meeting*, Midwestern Psychological Association, Chicago, 1973.

Scott, W. E. and Hamner, W. Clay, The effect of order and variance in performance on the rewards given workers by supervisory personnel, mimeo, Indiana University, 1973.

Scott, W. E., Activation theory and task design, *Organizational Behavior and Human Performance*, 1966, 1, 3-30.

Skinner, B. F., *The Behavior of Organisms*. New York: Appleton-Century, 1938.

Skinner, B. F., *Walden Two*. New York: The Macmillan Company, 1948.

Skinner, B. F., Are theories of learning necessary? *Psychological Review*, 1950, 57, 193-216.

Skinner, B. F., *Science and Human Behavior*. New York: The Macmillan Company, 1953.

Skinner, B. F., Freedom and the control of men, *American Scholar*, 1956, 25, 47-65.

Skinner, B. F., Some issues concerning the control of human behavior, *Science*, 1956, 124, 1056-1066.

Skinner, B. F., *Verbal Behavior*. New York: Appleton-Century-Crofts, 1957.

Skinner, B. F. Behaviorism at fifty. *Science*, 1963a, 134, 566-602.

Skinner, B. F., Operant behavior. *American Psychologist*, 1963b, 18, 503-515.

Skinner, B. F., *Contingencies of Reinforcement*, Appleton-Century-Crofts, New York, 1969.

Skinner, B. F., *Beyond Freedom and Dignity*, New York: Alfred A. Knopf, 1971.

Thorndike, E. L., *Animal Intelligence*, Macmillan, New York, 1911.

Vroom, V. H., and Deci, E. L., An overview of work motivation, in V. H. Vroom and E. L. Deci (eds.), *Management and Motivation*, Penguin Press, Baltimore, 1970, 9-19.

Wiard, H., Why manage behavior? A case for positive reinforcement, *Human Resource Management*, Summer, 1972, 15-20.

Where Skinner's theories work, *Business Week*, December, 1972, 64-65.

Whyte, W. F., Skinnerian theory in organizations, *Psychology Today*, April, 1972, 67-68, 96, 98, 100.

AT EMERY AIR FREIGHT: POSITIVE REINFORCEMENT BOOSTS PERFORMANCE

At Emery these days, P.R. stands for *positive reinforcement*, not public relations, and the payoffs from applying Skinner's ideas to the motivation of employees exceed the wildest claims ever made by public relations practitioners for the results of their art. One example: Small shipments intended for the same destination fly at lower rates when shipped together in containers rather than separately. By encouraging employees to increase their use of containers (from 45 percent to 95 percent of all possible shipments), Emery has realized an annual saving of $650,000.

"With savings this large we can't afford to worry about charges that we're manipulating our employees," says Edward J. Feeney, Vice-President—System Performance, the man primarily responsible for introducing P.R. at Emery. Continues Feeney: "Actually, the charge that you're manipulating people when you use positive reinforcement—I prefer myself to say that you're shaping their behavior—is a hollow one to start with. People in business manipulate their employees all the time—otherwise they would go bankrupt. The only questions are, how effective are you as a manipulator and what ends do you further with your manipulation? Our end is improved performance, and we've been damned effective in getting it." Feeney emphasizes that his approach and that of Emery's management generally is pragmatic, not doctrinaire. They're sold on the merits of Skinner's ideas, not because of their internal logic or the eloquence with which they are frequently proposed, but because so far at least they have paid off handsomely in each area Emery has seen fit to apply them.

Importance of Performance Audit

Emery has been selective in its application of P.R.; it's a powerful tool that should be employed where it's most needed and where the potential for improvement is the greatest. These are things that Feeney feels strongly can't be left to intuition or guesswork—hence the necessity for a performance audit before you institute P.R. in a given area. Emery doesn't want to be in the position of the corporation that targeted tardiness reduction as the object of a major effort. Before the drive, tardiness averaged 1/2 of 1 percent; after the drive, 1/4 of 1 percent. Big deal! Emery has a different magnitude of payoff in mind.

Take the example of container utilization that we mentioned. Executives at Emery were convinced that containers were being used about 90 percent of the times they could be used. Measurement of the actual usage—a measurement made by the same managers whose guesses had averaged 90 percent—showed that the actual figure was 45 percent, or half the estimate. Feeney saw no reason, given the proper motivational climate, why employees couldn't consistently meet a standard of 95

Reprinted by permission of the publisher from *Organizational Dynamics*, Winter 1973 © 1973 by AMACOM, a division of American Management Associations.

percent and save Emery $650,000 annually—which, of course, subsequently happened.

The performance audit fulfills two primary purposes. First, it indicates the areas in which the biggest potential profit payoffs exist—the areas in which Emery should focus its attention; second, it convinces previously skeptical managers on quantitative grounds that no words can contravene that there is need for substantial improvement.

The performance audit would be justified for the second effect alone—convincing managers that improvement is needed and persuading them to cooperate with a program designed to bring about the improvement. "Most managers genuinely think that operations in their bailiwick are doing well; a performance audit that proves they're not comes as a real and unpleasant surprise," says Feeney.

We also suspect that an unpleasant surprise of some magnitude is necessary to secure the cooperation of a goodly number of managers in implementing a program that, with its concentration on praise and recognition as motivators and the elimination of censure, runs contrary to the beliefs and practices of a working lifetime.

On the other hand, Feeney emphasizes the importance of cushioning the blow if you want to enlist their cooperation. "We structure the performance audit so that the managers are heroes for making the audits, and we reassure them that irrespective of the current level, they will look good if they can improve."

What about the performance standards set as a part of each performance audit? How are they set? What do they signify? Sometimes, as in the case of the customer service department with its goal of customer call-backs within 90 minutes of the initial telephone query, the department had set the goal in advance of the audit study. On study, it appeared reasonable and it was left unchanged. Sometimes there is no standard, and one has to be set on the basis of observation and common sense.

The latter usually indicates the impracticality of setting perfection or 100 percent performance as your standard. For example, the ideal in answering phone calls from customers would be for the customer never to get a busy signal that might lead him to call one of Emery's competitors. The problem is that studies have shown that in any given hour, five minutes, although not the same five minutes, is always going to account for 35 percent of the calls during the hour. Hence, it's much too costly to staff a switchboard with the number of operators necessary to prevent busy signals during those peak five minutes.

Emery has experimented, with a measure of success, with having employees set the standards for their own jobs. It was done in the customer service office in Chicago. The employees set a higher standard: not just giving customers a progress report within 90 minutes, but having *all* the requested answers to customer queries within that time—and they have presently reached this standard, although they fall short of the 90 to 95 percent achieved on progress reports. The problem, as Feeney sees it, is in giving the employees all the data they need to hit on a reasonable standard—a very time-consuming process. Otherwise, employee-set standards either will be unrealistically high or unacceptably low. Either way, both the company and the employee lose out. The standard that is too low deprives the employee of self-satisfaction and the company of work that it is paying for; the standard that is too high, achievable only once in a while by virtue of extraordinary effort or luck, will leave the employee frustrated and embittered. Sooner or later—and it's usually sooner—his performance will revert to a lower level than before he participated in setting the unattainable standard.

Providing Praise and Recognition—Avoiding Censure

In those areas in which Emery uses P.R. as a motivational tool, nothing is left to chance. Each manager receives two elaborate programmed instruction workbooks prepared in-house and geared to the specific work situation at Emery. One deals with recognition and rewards, the other with feedback. Under recognition and rewards, the workbook enumerates no less than 150 kinds, ranging from a smile and a nod of encouragement, to "Let me buy you a coffee," to detailed praise for a job well done.

Of all forms of praise, the most effective, according to Feeney, is praise for the job well done—expressed in quantitative terms. Not "Keep up the fair work, Murray," as shown on TV, or even "Great going, Joe—keep it up," but "Joe, I liked the ingenuity you showed just now getting those crates into that container. You're running pretty consistently at 98 percent of standard. And after watching you, I can understand why."

In bestowing praise and recognition, Emery follows Skinner pretty closely. There is the same emphasis on reinforcing specific behavior; the same insistence that the behavior be reinforced as soon as possible after it has taken place; the same assertion that you reinforce frequently in the beginning to shape the desired behavior, but that as time goes on, maintaining the desired behavior requires progressively less frequent and unpredictable reinforcement. As Skinner wrote, in reference to Emery's application of his ideas, "You don't need to maintain a system of contrived reinforcers indefinitely. People get the impression that I believe we should all get gumdrops whenever we do anything of value. There are many ways of attenuating a system of reinforcement. . . But the main thing is to let noncontrived reinforcers take over."

At the gumdrop stage of P.R., Feeney urges supervisors to supply praise and recognition at least twice a week during the early weeks or months of behavior shaping. It's impractical to require them to provide P.R. more frequently—they are too busy, they would forget, etc. Once the desired behavior has been established, managers have more discretion—the key point being the unpredictability of the reinforcement, not the frequency. Keep P.R. coming on a descending scale of frequency—but keep the employee guessing as to when or whether he's going to be praised or recognized.

At least in the early days of shaping behavior, it's difficult to determine which deserves the most credit for the improvement in performance—providing praise and recognition or withholding censure and criticism. Particularly in these cases where the manager seldom praised before—even when he had good reason—the switchover from censure to praise produces instant, almost miraculous results. Performance improves dramatically, and along with it, employee morale and superior-subordinate relations.

What do you do with the employee when praise, recognition, and feedback don't work? Do you contrive to refrain from criticising his or her work? At what point do you throw in the sponge?

Feeney's general answer was that P.R. worked with nine employees out of ten. On those occasions where it appeared not to be working, investigation usually revealed that below-standard performance was not the employee's fault—factors such as the wrong tools or work overload were responsible. And once they were corrected, the employee responded as positively to praise and recognition as anyone else. He cited several instances, not among the rank-and-file, where a custom-tailored program of P.R. salvaged men who were 30 days short of being fired.

Even with the below-par employee, the manager takes the positive note. He would probably ignore a day or a week in which no improvement took place, preferring to wait for a period of even slight improvement—say from 70 to 75 per cent. Then he might follow-up his praise of the improvement by asking the man what he thought could be done to improve further. Everything he said from there on would be an attempt to solve the problem and provide the manager with additional opportunities for reinforcement.

All in all, we got the impression of a program that failed, on the few occasions when it did, not because of employee resistance, but because of supervisory intransigence—the boss was unable or unwilling to apply it, especially with the so-called problem employee—and a few supervisors have left Emery in consequence.

Feedback is easier to institutionalize than praise and rewards. A written report is a tangible artifact that you can see. But even with feedback you have occasional lapses, Feeney cautions, in any areas where it isn't mandatory. Some managers loathe paperwork; others are too busy to extend the measure of praise and recognition indicated by the feedback or they don't recognize behavior that deserves positive reinforcement. "The biggest problem with the program occurs," adds Feeney "when managers stop asking for feedback and stop offering recognition and rewards because there's been no recognition of their efforts from above—their boss hasn't asked, 'Why didn't I see your performance report?' or extended any reward or recognition himself. In other words, the program breaks down whenever there are no consequences and no positive reinforcement for the manager who is supposed to implement it."

Beyond Gumdrops—Continuous Feedback

Skinner talks about the necessity of letting the noncontrived reinforcers take over in any program of P.R.—which, in our view, explains the crucial importance at Emery, and probably in any industrial setting, of continuous feedback. Emery, in each area where it has utilized P.R., has required each employee to keep a record himself of what he or she has accomplished each and every day. In customer service, for example, each representative ticked off daily on a sheet how long it had taken to reply to each call. It took no special skill to compare this with the standard of 90 minutes. Similar sheets, all relatively simple and all recorded by the employees themselves, were instituted in all departments covered by P.R.

Noncontrived reinforcers they were not. Emery provided the sheets, gave no option on filling them out, and defined the terms and frequency. But we think this is an example of a contrived reinforcer laying the essential groundwork—providing the time framework for noncontrived reinforcers to mature and take over. Let's postulate three basic stages of development: (1) A period in which frequent P.R. by the supervisor plus continuous feedback leads to rapid progress towards the desired behavior; (2) a period in which infrequent P.R. by the boss is accompanied by continuous feedback—itself, of course, a species of P.R.; (3) a period in which the supervisor is only a very occasional source of P.R. and feedback is overwhelmingly the principal source of contrived reinforcement.

Feeney emphasizes the effect of feedback on improved performance. "We found that when we provided daily feedback only one week out of four or one out of five, performance in the periods without feedback reverted to the previous level or was almost as bad." There's no question that feedback is the critical variable in explaining the success of the program, he adds.

What is continuous feedback, and what is its relation to Skinner's requirement that, in any program of P.R., "The main thing is to let noncontrived reinforcers take over"? The noncontrived reinforcer clearly is the conviction on the employee's part that they are doing a good job, a fair day's work. But how are they to know? Part of the answer is observable—they've been busy, the customers have seemed satisfied, maybe the boss has extended P.R. More conclusive, if they're in doubt, they can look at the sheets and see at a glance exactly how they stand in reference to the standard. In other words, the internal or natural reinforcer—the conviction and satisfaction of a job well done—is corroborated and itself powerfully reinforced by the evidence of a sheet on which the work accomplished is compared daily with the standard for the job.

Feeney tells a story that illustrates both the necessity for continuous feedback and the way in which previous consequences determine present behavior. Emery requires any employee who receives a package damaged during shipment from an airline to fill out a fairly time-consuming form. At a certain installation, he pointed out to the boss that without feedback and P.R. the employees wouldn't bother—the reinforcements they got from filling out the form were all negative. The paperwork was time-consuming and boring, they were likely to get some flack from airline representatives who would in their own good time find ways of hitting back, they were taking time from their number one priority—getting the shipment delivered on time. A check revealed that no damage forms were turned in. However, a physical check of cartons received showed several damaged, one with a hole punched in the side, another that looked as if a hand had reached into the top and taken something out, etc. Feeney feels that his colleague, at this point, got the message. The only way around the problem of getting the damage slips filled out was to (1) specify the desired behavior—i.e. set the standard; (2) require the employee to provide continuous feedback—keep daily records on how many cartons were damaged and submit them to his supervisor; and (3) whenever feasible, positively reinforce the behavior—when the feedback showed that it was justified.

Money and Positive Reinforcement

Skinner includes money in his list of positive reinforcers, as long as it is linked to specific behavior. The weekly paycheck doesn't positively reinforce; it's a negative reinforcer. You work to avoid the loss of the standard of living supported by the paycheck. On the other hand, piece-rate payments geared to specific on-the-job behavior are positive reinforcers; so are commissions paid to salesmen. Just as effective, Skinner argues, would be to take a leaf from gambling and introduce a lottery into industry, with each employee getting a weekly lottery ticket that might pay off in a weekly drawing. Here it's paying off unpredictably but in the long run on a determined schedule that provides the positive reinforcement.

Emery does not use money as a positive reinforcer. Several reasons seem to underly the choice. First, Emery has no employees on incentive payments, not even salesmen; there is therefore no built-in necessity to link dollar payments to improved performance. Second, management holds the belief that performing up to standard is what it has a right to expect from each employee in return for his paycheck. The savings achieved through the program have helped to make it possible for Emery to pay as much or more than its competitors, and offer equal or bigger benefits—facts not lost on its employees. Finally, Emery's experience suggests that praise and recognition, especially self-recognition through feedback, are enough. In some areas, employees have consistently performed up to standard for more than three years. The savings for Emery in consequence have been substantial, despite the omission of money as a positive reinforcer.

At first blush this seems surprising. Interestingly, AT&T had a similar experience with a job-enrichment program that also substantially increased employee productivity and performance. In an AT&T experiment with 120 women answering stockholder inquiries, various measures were taken to give employees more responsibility and control over their jobs. The response was uniformly positive, with one exception—a girl who quit because she wasn't getting more money for a more responsible job. She felt that she was worth more to the company and should be paid more. That only one employee out of 120 expected to get paid more as the consequence of a program that improved the value of their services calls for a little explaining. So does the continuing success of P.R. at Emery.

There are several possible explanations. People know a good thing when they see it. The programs at both AT&T and Emery have improved the intrinsic nature of the job as seen by the employees themselves—that's sufficient reward.

Also, many studies have shown that employees have a crude but keen sense of distributive justice on the job. They may do less than what they themselves consider a fair day's work for a large number of reasons, even though they frequently feel guilty about it. On the other hand, they resent and resist any attempt to exact more than their perception of a fair day's work in return for what they are paid. Improve the job—in Emery's case, provide via praise, recognition, and continuous feedback the evidence of a job well done—and eventually you will develop what Skinner would call the natural reinforcer of job satisfaction. This, in turn, guarantees that the employee will want to live up to his own standard of a fair day's work. In other words, part of the success of P.R. at Emery is that the standards set for employees were seen by them as reasonable to begin with. The missing element was any positive incentive to reach them. The weekly paycheck was ineffective—Skinner is correct—it took praise, recognition, and feedback to do the job.

Similarly, at AT&T, job enlargement and job enrichment provided the incentives to improved performance that hitherto were lacking.

A story that Feeney tells illuminates the problem. A Harvard Business School student on a summer assignment with Emery was helping with a performance audit on one of the loading docks. In the process he managed to gain the confidence of a union steward, who told him in so many words that any problems Emery had with the workers were not due to money—they were well paid. The one thing they weren't getting paid was attention. Many of them worked at night with a minimum of supervision and recognition. A situation in which employees feel fairly paid in relation to the work expected of them but in which money is almost the sole recognition received is ripe for improvement via positive reinforcement.

Proof of the Pudding

At present, P.R. is fully operative in three areas at Emery—in sales and sales training, operations, and containerized shipments. The benefits in all three are impressive, and they have been sustained for periods of from three to four years. We can forget about the Hawthorne effect in explaining the success of P.R. at Emery.

In sales training, each salesman completes a programmed instruction course on his own, with plenty of feedback structured into the course to let him know how he is doing. In addition, sales managers apply P.R. in their day-to-day relations with salesmen, and sales reports provide the indispensable feedback. Sales have gained at a more rapid rate since P.R. entered the sales picture, and Feeney feels that it deserves some of the credit for the increased rate.

The relationship between P.R. and improved customer service, part of operations, is undeniable. Before P.R., standards were met only 30 to 40 percent of the time; after P.R., the figure was 90 to 95 percent. Most impressive is the rapidity of the improvement and its staying power. In the first test office, for example, performance skyrocketed from 30 percent of standard to 95 percent in a single day. Staying power? After almost four years, performance in the vast majority of Emery customer service offices still averages 90 to 95 percent.

In containerized shipping operations the story is the same: With P.R., container use jumped from 45 percent to 95 percent—with the increase in 70 percent of the offices coming in a single day.

There were a few cases in which feedback was temporarily interrupted because of managerial changes and other reasons. Whenever this occurred, performance slumped quickly by more than 50 percent, only to return rapidly to the 95 percent level once the feedback was resumed.

All in all, Emery has saved over $3 million in the past three years. No doubt about it: Positive reinforcement pays.

On the basis of this kind of success, Emery has big plans to expand the use of P.R. It's already been extended to overall dock operations. Emery's route drivers are covered and measured on items such as stops per hour and sometimes on shipments brought back versus shipments dispatched. Eventually P.R. will be introduced wherever it's possible to measure work and set quantifiable standards. Feeney and his group will set their priorities, of course, on the basis of what performance audits tell them about the potential for improvement and savings.

When you have scored the kind of success that Emery has you're not quick to innovate. However, thought is being given to the introduction in certain areas of different rewards and schedules, including having the computer acknowledge behavior and even using some kind of financial reward as a positive reinforcer.

What Does Emery Prove?

More precisely, what does Emery prove about the feasability of behavior modification through positive reinforcement? The question must be asked and answered at several levels. At the first and most apparent level, the answer is easy: In those areas in which Emery has used P.R., behavior modification has been instant, dramatic, sustained, and uniformly in the desired direction. There also seems little doubt that P.R. deserves most of the credit for the dramatic improvement in performance.

A few qualifiers are in order. Positive reinforcement so far has been used selectively at Emery in areas where work could be measured and quantifiable standards set if they didn't already exist, and areas where observation showed that the existing level of performance was far below the standard. This last point applies equally to the customer-service representatives and the dock loaders, but is less true for the salesmen—their performance was lower than Emery felt it should be, but not in the same category as the other two employee groups.

Also Emery has yet to arrive at the point where the natural reinforcers—in this case an internally generated sense of job satisfaction—have taken over. After three to four years of P.R., praise and recognition from the boss is applied infrequently and unpredictably, but the other contrived reinforcer, continuous feedback, is still administered daily. In fact, Emery's past experience has been that whenever it stopped providing continuous feedback, performance rapidly reverted to the previous low levels. On the other hand, this experience occurred during the early days of supplying positive reinforcement. Perhaps now Emery could stop providing continuous feedback and maintain the current high levels of performance. We can only guess.

At another level we have to take into account the context in which P.R. has been used at Emery. We have to consider whether or not special conditions exist at Emery that favor the successful application of positive reinforcement. How far are we justified in claiming that what has worked at Emery will work equally well in a different organization with a different product, a different climate, and different problems?

On the basis of the available evidence, we can't go overboard in generalizing from Emery's undeniable success in applying positive reinforcement to solve its performance problems. That Emery has no incentive programs and is therefore spared the complexity and the conflict habitually generated in manufacturing situations where standards, performance, and earning are inextricably linked; that Emery has so far restricted P.R. to areas in which it has been possible to positively reinforce one employee without producing adverse consequences for any other employee; and that Emery, during the period it has applied P.R., has been a rapid growth organization, able to offer far more than the usual opportunities for growth and promotion are factors that provide a partial measure of the conditions, by no means common in organizations, that have fostered an atmosphere conducive to the application of positive reinforcement.

The second condition we mentioned is something Emery has worked at. Feeney emphasized that Emery was careful not to set individuals or groups competing against each other to see which came closest to meeting the standard. Instead, managers were coached to urge employees to think in terms of what they were doing now compared to what they had done in the past. Comments Feeney, "If you set individuals or teams competing against each other, there's only room for one first—but lots of losers. If you want to know the effect of this kind of competition on performance, all you need is to look at what happens at the end of the baseball season to the performance of the team that's 32 games behind."

Whether the conditions we have described are indispensable to the successful application of P.R. or merely helpful we have no way of determining. The problem is lack of evidence. Emery is the only company to date to have applied P.R. on a fairly broad scale over a fairly long period of time. Even with Emery, neither this report nor a previous article in *Business Week* (Dec. 28, 1971) can claim to be the kind of objective in-depth study that's called for. A few other organizations —among them Cole National in Cleveland, Michigan Bell Telephone, and Ford Motor Co.—are in the early stages of experimenting with positive reinforcement, and more organizations are giving serious thought to using positive reinforcement. More than 200 have contacted Feeney since Emery's work with P.R. received public recognition.

Will positive reinforcement work? Feeney believes that the question has already been answered with a resounding affirmative. He cites upwards of 1000 case studies involving mental patients, delinquent children, and problem pupils in which P.R. resulted in dramatic improvement in behavior. The only questions remaining, as he sees it, are questions of methodology and application.

Of course, none of these episodes took place in an industrial setting. Until we have a lot more evidence—both from Emery and from other sources—any conclusions about the use of P.R. in industry have to be tentative.

One last level of consideration. Positive reinforcement as the answer to organizational problems of productivity and performance has a plethora of rivals. A generation of theorists and practitioners has systematically overturned stones in the search for a formula or method for converting low-producing groups or individuals into high-producing ones. A partial enumeration would include job enrichment and job enlargement, organization development in all its varied guises, Theory Y, participative management, team development, the Scanlon Plan, autonomous leadership. We could go on—but we won't. How does P.R. stack up against these other and we think competing approaches to improving productivity and performance?

At this point it's impossible to give a conclusive answer. We have seen the problems with the evidence on the results of positive reinforcement. Similar problems exist with the results of every other technique for improving productivity and performance. There's little objective evidence available, and what evidence there is abounds in caveats—the technique will work under the proper circumstances, the parameters of which are usually not easily apparent.

Take the entire field of organization development. An exhaustive search of the literature on the subject by Professor George Strauss of the University of California Business School at Berkeley turned up exactly three research studies worthy of the name. What did they prove? That under the proper circumstances OD can increase productivity, though perhaps not as much as conventional techniques such as purchasing new equipment, job simplification, and "weeding out" inefficient operators. So far, the search for a sure-fire all purpose formula for turning low-producing groups into high-producing ones appears to be almost as elusive as the search for the philosopher's stone that would turn everything it touched into gold.

Which leads us to what conclusion as to the merits of positive reinforcement relative to its rivals? With the customary caveats, we feel that P.R. has much to recommend it. As an approach, it deserves more recognition and application than it has hitherto received. It suffers from its sponsorship: Positive reinforcement has a bad name with businessmen and with the general public because of its association with Skinner, his alleged totalitarian leanings, his denial of free will, and the inescapable fact that his theory of human behavior is rooted in his experiments with pigeons. People instinctively resent a theory that seems to suggest that they're not much brighter than pigeons and can be controlled in similar ways.

We understand the problem, but it's unfortunate that it has prevented the more extensive application of positive reinforcement. On the basis of what little we can observe, P.R. is easier, less complex, and less expensive to introduce than most of its rivals, while the results are at least as impressive as those achieved by any of them.

Feeney is probably correct: A lot of managers practice positive reinforcement without knowing it. He cites, for example, Vince Lombardi, who provided endless feedback on performance to his players and who after a really bad defeat never uttered a word of criticism in the locker room. True, but until more organizations consciously and systematically apply positive reinforcement, it will never get the recognition that it appears to deserve.

Selected Bibliography

To anyone who wants to review the evidence that positive reinforcement works, Feeney recommends the following books and articles: Schafer and Martin, *Behavioral Therapy* (McGraw-Hill, 1969), Tharp and Wetzel, *Behavior Modifications of the Natural Environment* (Academic Press, 1969), describes in readable prose how positive reinforcement was used with 150 delinquent children to bring about a remarkable behavior change in 135, Ulrich et al., *Control of Human Behavior* (Scott Foresman), a book described by Feeney as important but highly technical and difficult to read. Finally, the June 1969 issue of *Psychology Today* contains an article, "Smiles, Praise, and a Food Basket," that describes the remarkable improvement positive reinforcement induced in a schizophrenic mental patient.

THE ORGANIZATIONAL SOCIETY

ROBERT PRESTHUS

. . . A basic assumption throughout our analysis is that social values and institutions mold individual personality and behavior. This occurs through a process called socialization. Society, in effect, provides a web of values and expectations that determines the individual's character, his ethical beliefs, and his ideas about progress, success, and failure. "Those drives which make for the differences in men's characters, like love and hatred, the lust for power and the yearning for submission—are all products of the social process."[1] Men may, for example, be born with an impulse to dominate others, but social values such as the democratic ideal of equality determine the manner and extent to which this impulse can be gratified. When men choose, they choose within this context of socially determined values. While our society provides a broad scope for individual choices, organizational influences traced here have significantly changed the conditions under which they are made. . . .

Man's susceptability to socialization is in part explained by the individual's long period of biologic and economic immaturity. While lower animals become self-sufficient shortly after birth, western man is dependent for some two decades before he strikes out alone. During this time he is dependent upon those who provide his emotional and physical sustenance. At the same time, it appears that even as a child he becomes conscious of his power. When toilet training, walking, and speech begin, he learns that he can defy his parents in matters that are obviously important to them. Here again we see that biological impulses are always conditioned by cultural patterns that differ from society to society. Even the Oedipus complex, which Freud believed to be instinctive, is now thought by some anthropologists to be culturally specific, the result of a monogamous, patriarchal family structure.

The family and other authority figures measure the individual's "growth" largely in terms of his adjustment to social norms. Such norms include national traditions and mythology, religious beliefs, economic and political values, in fact, the whole cultural web that sustains us throughout life. These norms include the parents' perception of the kinds of skills and attitudes required by children for success in our organized society. As a result, individual personality tends to reflect the social structure. The dominant values of society become a superego controlling the individual through approval and anxiety. As Fromm observes: "Society must tend to mold the character structure of its members in such a way they will want to do what they have to do under the existing circumstances."[2]

As we have seen, the individual's successive experiences with authority figures result in a "self-system," a way of relating himself to the world. This system becomes a framework for accepting or rejecting the vast number of stimuli that impinge upon him. Millions of sensory fibers transmit such stimuli through his nervous system. Certain reflexes become reinforced and linked together, providing the basis

Reprinted with the permission of the author from Robert Presthus, *The Organizational Society* (New York: Vintage Books, 1965).

for habitual patterns of behavior. *Both an individual's perceptions and his behavior become, so to speak, structured.* He develops a time-tested way of organizing reality, and his reactions become stabilized accordingly. This relatively consistent pattern of behavior is commonly defined as "personality." Moreover, the personality continually reinforces itself by a selective process that tends to accept only approved impressions which are in turn incorporated into the existing value system. Conflicting stimuli are rejected, and when an individual rejects all conflicting stimuli, we say that he has a low tolerance for ambiguity. . . .

Patterns of Accommodation: Upward-Mobiles

We now turn to the discrete types of personal accommodation that seem to occur in organizations. Following interpersonal theory, we assume that men behave according to the perceived expectations of a given social situation. Over a period of time such responses become relatively consistent; they are continually reinforced because they meet compelling individual needs for security, recognition, and group acceptance. While such accommodations are always the result of *interaction* between the bureaucratic situation and personality, social and organizational values mainly determine the character of functional (anxiety-reducing) and dysfunctional (anxiety-producing) behavior in a given culture. Personality is worked out in a social and interpersonal context. As Sullivan observes, man gradually develops through his relations with significant others a self-system, a personal style of behavior that rejects anxiety-producing responses in favor of those that insure approval. The bureaucratic situation seems to evoke three kinds of personal accommodation, each associated with one of our three personality types, the upward-mobiles, the indifferents, and the ambivalents. [Here] we shall consider the most significant of these, the *upward-mobiles*. . . .

If social structure alone were responsible for personality and behavior, our discrete types of accommodation would presumably not exist. The organization would evoke very similar accommodations in all of its members. But as we have seen, not only do different patterns of class socialization and consequent differences in perception and reaction to interpersonal situations characterize individuals, but the same pattern of socialization may evoke different responses among those subject to it. This combining of social and psychological theory is validated by the experience of Durkheim who began his classic study of *Suicide* with the intention of isolating the social roots of self-destruction, but who ended with an essentially psychological and individual cause, *anomie*.

With these qualifications in mind, we now turn to an analysis of the values and behavior of the typical "upward-mobile." Although his behavior may at times appear unappealing, we are concerned with it only as a form of accommodation to the bureaucratic environment. Our interest is analytic rather than clinical.

The upward-mobiles are typically distinguished by high morale; their level of job satisfaction is high. Indeed, the process and criteria by which they are selected insures that they will have an unfailing optimism. The reasons for this are clear. They identify strongly with the organization and derive strength from their involvement. Their dividends also include disproportionate shares of the organization's rewards in power, income, and ego reinforcement. As we have seen, subjective inequality is a built-in feature of big organizations and is rationalized on the basis of equality of opportunity. Power is easily justified by those who have it, since it confirms daily their right (achieved in fair competition) to possess it. The upward-mobiles will not, therefore, seriously question a system that has proved its rationality The system remains an internalized article of faith until, as in the case of Arthur Miller's hero in *Death of A Salesman*, the disparity between rhetoric and reality becomes irrepressible. But even then, self-punitive mechanisms may be invoked to preserve the myth: *personal failure* rather than the failure of the system provides a rationalization.

This ability to identify strongly with the system is highly productive in personal terms since it qualifies the upward-mobile for the organization's major rewards. (As we saw earlier, group influence and rank are a function of acceptance of the group's values.) The organization qua organization has meaning for him, evoking loyalty, affirmation, and a constant point of reference. Having accepted its legitimacy and rationality, he can act on the basis of its value premises. The capacity for identification has great strategic value today because social power is rather evenly divided among competing groups. This condition sharpens the organization's conflicts with competitors and puts a premium on loyalty and certainty among its members. The organization tends to resemble a church, which needs champions to endorse its values and to increase its survival power. No dissenters need apply. The demand is for conformity. A rational and sustained attention to business is required; and the heterodoxy possible in a less organized, more secure society becomes a luxury, because it impairs unity.

Since he accepts the larger purposes of the organization, the upward-mobile finds involvement easy. His personality enables him to deal in oversimplification and idealization. He can act without an immaculate cause. He can overlook the contradictions in the routine operations of the organization, as distinct from its official myths. He is able to find certainty and consistency in an organization that is imperfect because it is real. In a sense, he must avoid reality by cultivating the illusion that its actions eventuate in perfect justice. This characteristic of perception calls to mind W. I. Thomas' observation: "If men define situations as real, they are real in their consequences."[3] The organization's values are internalized by the upward-mobile, and thus become premises of action. This psychic act provides him with an operational skill: *the capacity for action despite conflicting alternatives and contradictory aims*.

Here a distinction must be made between the upward-mobile's values and his behavior. His low toleration for ambiguity and his deference toward authority might seem to disqualify him for the versatile role playing that big organizations require. In a democratic society, for example, the upward-mobile must pay homage to democratic expectations of equality and impartiality, even though he knows that some are born to lead and others to follow. However, he can usually assume the appropriate roles whether or not he identifies with the underlying ideals. He manipulates the democratic consensus favoring permissive authority relations and recognizes that "getting along with people" has career utility. Such role playing emphasizes the need for mock behavior in which polite fictions, irony, and banter are used to "get a message across" without disrupting the status relations of those concerned. . . .

Since upward-mobiles often get to the top of the organization and must deal with members at every level, the significance of their own values and behavior is clear. If these are marked by a need to ward off anxiety or to dominate others, organizational relations will be complicated. Since such compelling needs and the security operations they encourage are almost impossible to change, they may prove disastrous for the organization. . . .

This suggests that the capacity to rationalize organizational claims is part of the value equipment of the upward-mobile. He may respect individual dissent and error, but the question is one of *priority*, and in the last analysis he will accept the organization's values. His ability to appraise situations objectively and to act appropriately is bound up with his loyalty to collective values and abstractions. Since he identifies himself with the organization, in a measure ranging from casual opportunism to compulsive surrender, he becomes an instrument of such values. He becomes *the organization* and can thus accept its logical imperatives without much regard for competing individual values. The wrongs inflicted in defense of institutionalized ideals are well known. To some extent they can be explained in terms of the total loyalty that organizations demand and some individuals seek.

In the context of Merton's distinction, the upward-mobile is typically a "local."[4] Unlike the "cosmopolitan" who has a broad disciplinary or national perspective, his interests and aspirations are tied to his own organization. Always loyal, he regards its rules and actions as "the one best way" to handle large numbers of people. If the organization's claims occasionally result in injustice, this is inevitable in an imperfect world. Never doubting the supremacy of collective values, the upward-mobile enthrones administrative, keeping-the-organization-going skills and values. This accounts in part for his ambivalence toward the specialist whose professional norms compete with his loyalty to the organization. In all this, he personifies the "routinization of charisma" whereby organizations have tended historically to become ever more rational and monistic. A man without a "calling," he brings little passion to his work. Rather, he is a "quill-bearing mammal," a dealer in means for whom the paraphernalia of organization outweigh claims of "mission," creed, and party. These tend instead to become instrumental, honorific abstractions used to evoke affirmation and loyalty in the rank and file.

Acceptance of the organization's goals commits the upward-mobile to conformity and to impatience with those who qualify and dissent. As a result, he tends to personalize opposition, finding it difficult to accept as a matter of principle or honest divergence, and attributing it instead to a querulous wish on the dissenter's part to be different for difference's sake. His temperamental affinity for clear-cut causes and decisive action is relevant here. He will not understand those who fail to see what to him is so clearly evident. The fact that his personal values are not always shared will escape or puzzle him. His hostility toward heterodoxv may be sharpened by a natural resentment that others should escape the discipline and sacrifice that ambition has required of him.

The upward-mobile's dislike for controversial causes is functional because organizational claims now cover such matters. Political opinions, patterns of consumption, off-work activity, etc., tend to fall into the bureaucratic net. By honoring conventional values the upward-mobile not only reinforces the standards by which he himself is measured, he also increases the probability that conformity will occur throughout the organization. This phenomenon is clearly apparent in countries such as England where a remarkable social control is achieved through each class's imitation of the one above it. In big organizations a similar mechanism is apparent in the elite's personification of majority values and in the internalization of those values by subordinates. The efficiency and discipline insured by the resulting "upward-looking posture" is incalculable. . . .

Another characteristic of the upward-mobile is his status anxiety, often manifested in a compulsive concern with rank and the symbols of prestige. The term "anxiety" is deliberate since his concern with status and with its derivatives of power and prestige goes beyond mere sensitivity to define a general orientation. Like the search for power, status enchantment is a constant element in the upward-mobile equation. The authoritarian-personality research found, significantly, that such an orientation is common among individuals who seem to find the bureaucratic environment congenial. As we have seen, status differentiation plays a critical role in big organizations. It provides a psychological environment that is conducive to efficiency in operational terms, reinforcing authority, minimizing overt conflict, and structuring interpersonal relations.

Status will be defined here as the prestige or deference attached to the role or position one holds in an organizational hierarchy.[5] Although status is not always conferred according to formal hierarchical role, since some members (such as our "ambivalents") will not accept line or hierarchial definitions of relative status, in the main status and prestige are assigned and rewarded by elites in terms of formal organizational values. . . .

Personal status and organizational discipline are also reinforced by structured patterns of communication. Seniors communicate through a secretary who becomes her master's alter ego and who often exaggerates the status factors inherent in the relationship. The senior rarely visits the subordinate, since this would put him at a psychological disadvantage and reduce his control of the interpersonal situation. Normally the subordinate will come to the senior, and the latter will set the tone of the meeting. Displeasure can be nicely weighted. The tone of voice, the form of address, the length of the meeting, the amount of time the subordinate is required to wait, whether interruptions for phone calls will be permitted—all tend to define the relative status of the participants, and all can be manipulated to obtain desired consequences. The upward-mobile must become extremely sensitive in measuring out and receiving such dispensations. Versatile role-playing is therefore a vital career skill.

The upward-mobile's preoccupation with status is functional because he is anxious to rise, and because a disciplined self-promotion is required to impress those above him with his suitability for bigger things. As the objective relationship between status and achievement becomes more difficult to establish, the collection of unearned status increments is encouraged. Here again the displacement of goals mentioned earlier is to be seen. *The acquisition of status and prestige becomes an end in itself rather than a derivative of some significant achievement.* A common manifestation is the discreet cultivation of prestigeful elders by young upward-mobiles in need of a patron. Such behavior is directly related to the co-optative mechanism which now governs bureaucratic succession. Significantly, it is also similar to the individual's early dependence upon authority-figures, e.g., his mother, his father, his teacher, etc. . . .

[The upward-mobile's] values and behavior include the capacity to identify strongly with the organization, permitting a nice synthesis of personal rewards and organizational goals. A typical form of accommodation is adjustment through power and special efforts to control situations and people. His "security operations" stress efficiency, strength, self-control, and dominance. His most functional value is a deep respect for authority. Not only are his interpersonal relations characterized by considerable sensitivity to authority and to status differences, but his superiors are viewed as nonthreatening models for his own conduct. Meanwhile, his subordinates are regarded with a considerable detachment which permits "universalistic" decisions that meet organizational as opposed to individual needs. Finally, we saw that changing social conditions and values have increased the utility of upward-mobile skills and values, as illustrated by the impact of the big foundations upon academic work and changing patterns of mobility in business and industry.

Patterns of Accommodation: Indifferents

Our second ideal type of accommodation in big organizations is one of indifference or withdrawal. Security, prestige, and power are the values that mediate accommodation, and men act in ways that seem to secure them. Such values have been endorsed by society's authority figures, and since we all hope to gain some measure of security and prestige, the behavior of such figures becomes a model for our own. Although anxiety reduction is probably the main impetus for such emulation, the ways of reducing it vary with the individual and with the situation. The same situation impels different reactions from different people. Status anxiety may push some of us into compulsive success striving, while others displace this need upon other values. The upward-mobile regards organizations as excellent instruments for satisfying his claims, but the indifferent defines them as calculated systems of frustration. He refuses to compete for the rewards they promise.

Indifference is the typical pattern of accommodation for the majority of organization men. The indifferents are found among the great mass of waged and salaried employees who work in the bureaucratic situation. . . . The indifferents are those who have come to terms with their *work environment* by withdrawal and by a redirection of their interests toward off-the-job satisfactions. They have also been alienated by the *work itself*, which has often been downgraded by machine processing and by assembly-line methods. This dual basis for alienation must be recognized. In industrial psychology the main effort has been to compensate for the deadening effect of the work itself by providing a happy work place. Less attention has been given to alienation from the job itself.

We are not speaking here of pathological kinds of alienation, but of modes of accommodation that often seem basically healthy. The typical indifferent has rejected majority values of success and power. While the upward-mobile strives for such values, obtainable today mainly through big organizations, the indifferent seeks that security which the organization can also provide for those who merely "go along." Such security seeking varies in accord with the demands of personality. One individual may have been taught to expect more than life can reasonably offer, and anxiety and frustration follow as his unrealistic claims are discounted. Another may have learned to expect less; he may refuse to accept success values or to compete for them. This role is encouraged by such bureaucratic conditions as hierarchy, oligarchy, and specialization.

The indifferent reaction, then, is the product of both social and organizational influences. But organizational factors seem to outweigh class-induced mobility expectations. However strong such expectations, they rarely survive in an unsympathetic institutional environment. Today, many a potential entrepreneur languishes in some cul-de-sac because the organizational context no longer sustains his aspirations. The resulting accommodation may also reflect personal failures of nerve and energy, bad luck, and so on. But, essentially, indifference is manifested in a psychic withdrawal from the work arena and a transfer of interest to off-work activities. The employee "goes through the motions," paying lip-service to organizational values, but he no longer retains any real interest in the organization or in work for its own sake.

This accommodation may occur in two stages: alienation and indifference. The alienated are those who come into the organization with great expectations. They are determined to climb. But when bureaucratic and personal limitations blunt their hopes, they become alienated. Over a period of time, it seems, this reaction works itself into indifference. On another level, we are dealing with indifference as an *initial* orientation. Such individuals, usually of working or lower-middle-class origin, have been taught not to expect very much. Both socialization and work experience reinforce this perception of their life chances. And both alienation and indifference counter the organization's claims for loyalty, predictability, and hard work. . . .

We have analyzed the behavior of the *indifferent* as a modal type of accommodation. Bureaucratic conditions of work have encouraged indifference in white-collar and professional areas as well as in the blue-collar world. The university environment has been used to document this trend because the writer knows it well, and more importantly because it has traditionally been among the least structured of work environments. Nevertheless, with the exception of a few prestige schools, the universities now have a significant proportion of indifferents in their faculties. This is explained in part by the high expectations of academic men for autonomy, as well as by the personal need for independent work which brought them to the university in the first instance. A major cause is bureaucratic conditions of work and evaluation that undercut professional standards and values.

The typical indifferent tends to reject the organizational bargain which promises authority, status, prestige, and income in exchange for loyalty, hard work, and identification with its values. Instead, he separates his work from the "meaningful" aspects of his life, which latter include recreation and leisure activities. Like the Hormel employee who spoke of "accomplishing something for the day," he is referring to what he plans to do *after* work. If the indifferent remains committed to his work, he will sometimes distinguish between it and the organization. If he is a college instructor, he may assume a "cosmopolitan" view in which his interests, loyalty, and future are seen as bound up with his *profession*, rather than with the particular school in which he happens to practice it.[6]

The indifferent posture also mediates preorganizational influences of class and education that failed to honor success and the repression of unprofitable opinions. The tension between such values and the organization's claims encourages withdrawal, the rejection of majority values, and a refusal to compete for them. In so defining the work bargain the worker often reveals a realistic perception of himself and his life chances.

One result of this mode of accommodation seems to be alienation from political and community affairs. The indifferent tends to reject his company, his union, his political party, and other voluntary organizations. The mass character of society, the power and remoteness of its organizations, and one's resulting feelings of helplessness are among the psychological bases for alienation. The structural conditions of big organization often mean, too, that the organization rejects the indifferent. Oligarchy, for example, breeds alienation by excluding the vast majority of employees from real participation. The need for skilled leaders; the difficulty of getting the word to large numbers of people; the leaders' drive for power and continuity in office; the complexity of decisions; the need and the desire for secrecy in negotiations with other power groups—all restrict active participation. . . .

Patterns of Accommodation: Ambivalents

The small disenchanted minority of whom this mode is characteristic will be set against organizational patterns of authority, status, and small groups. In both personal and organizational terms, the ambivalent's self-system is generally dysfunctional. Creative and anxious, his values conflict with bureaucratic claims for loyalty and adaptability. While the upward-mobile finds the organization congenial, and the indifferent refuses to become engaged, the ambivalent can neither reject its promise of success and power, nor can he play the roles required to compete for them. While upward-mobile anxiety is usually adaptive, ambivalent anxiety tends toward the neurotic.[7] In the bureaucratic situation, the ambivalent individual is a marginal man with limited career chances.

One important qualification is required. Despite his inability to meet bureaucratic demands, the ambivalent type plays a critical social role, namely, that of providing the insight, motivation, and the dialectic that inspire change. The upward-mobile honors the status quo and the indifferent accepts it, but the ambivalent is always sensitive to the need for change. His innovating role is often obscured because the authority, leadership, and money needed to institutionalize change remain in the hands of organizational elites. Nevertheless, few ideals or institutions escape his critical scrutiny. In his view custom is no guarantee of either rationality of legitimacy. This perception is sharpened by his inability to accept charismatic and traditional bases of authority; rationality alone provides a compelling standard. Certain personality traits underlie this critical posture.

The ambivalent personality is typically an introvert, with intense intellectual interests and limited interpersonal facility. Unlike the upward-mobiles, who stress action, objectivity, and easy interpersonal relations,[8] ambivalents are often subjective and withdrawn. Introversion has been found to be related to neurosis; anxiety and depression are common ailments.[9] Ambivalents have high aspirations, complicated by habitual under-rating of their own performance. Compared with extroverts, their intellectual interests are narrow and deep, accuracy and persistence are highly developed, and verbal facility and intelligence are markedly superior.[10]

The ambivalent ordinarily plays a *specialist*, "cosmopolitan" role. He honors theory, knowledge, and skill. Socialization as an independent professional often blinds him to legitimate organizational needs for control and co-ordination. Believing explicitly that both motivation and expertise come from within, he resists bureaucratic rules and supervision. Attempts to impose standards from without are seen as presumptuous and denigrating. As a result, there is always a gap between his self-perception as an independent professional and the galling realization, punctuated daily by the organization's authority and status differentiations, that he is really an employee. His skill authority is not always recognized, even though it is perfectly clear that his technical judgments have been decisive. The managerial facade with which he is confronted confirms his belief that hierarchical authority is often specious. This tension between skill and hierarchical authority is aggravated by the organization's subjective criteria of seniority and obedience. In sum, the bureaucratic situation is inapposite to his personal and professional values.

The heart of the ambivalent reaction is a tenacious self-concern. Most events are perceived by the ambivalent in terms of himself; personal goals are usually primary. His own experiences and skills seem unique; and when his career expectations prove unrealistic, as they often do, he may invoke humanistic themes to buttress his claims for preference. In terms of an earlier distinction, we may regard the ambivalent as an idealistic, independent personality. Unable to achieve distinction on the organization's terms, he may adopt idiosyncratic alternatives, a reaction encouraged by the erosion of qualitative standards. . . .

In view of the compelling status needs, the intellectual orientation, and the marked educational achievement often characteristic of the introverted type, we may assume that our ambivalent is typically of middle-class origin. However, his socialization has apparently not included the respect for success which is crucial for bureaucratic success. "Success," probably the dominant value in our society, is usually defined in terms of competitive, personal achievement, with references that are mainly economic, but that also include almost any other value that can nourish self-esteem. . . .

As we have seen, authority is distributed disproportionately in organizations. It clusters around the top and decreases at an increasing rate as one descends the hierarchy. Its gradations are clearly marked. A specialist with idealistic value preferences, the typical ambivalent will find it difficult to accept the legitimacy of this system. He cannot believe that those who have great authority really merit it in terms of talent, wisdom, or morality. In this context, psychological tests and interviews of managerial employees in several companies found "no relationship between intelligence and aptitude and individual success as defined by their ranks or by their salaries."[11] Such evidence suggests that the ambivalent's judgments are not entirely imaginary. . . .

[The ambivalent's] most important dysfunction is a distorted, fearful perception of authority. The resulting anxiety is a constant handicap in dealing with his superiors. As we have seen, perhaps the most significant item in organizational adjustment and mobility is one's attitude toward authority. Is the authority system perceived as threatening, or as the natural result of size, specialization, and task-oriented relationships? Is authority regarded as a necessary evil or a positive good? Here again the ambivalent is disadvantaged. While the upward-mobile has a close bond with his father and accepts authority easily, the ambivalent tends to view authority figures as threatening, probably because of rejection or dominance by his father but also because authority figures personify conventional values which he resists. . . .

As we have seen, the upward-mobile views those above him as friendly models, while the ambivalent regards them as threatening figures having the power to disadvantage him. His interpersonal relations become difficult both for himself and his superiors, who are much less interested in him than he thinks. They will be embarrassed by his rejection of the friendly patina that colors their relationship. Whether his reaction takes the form of passive resistance, resigned acceptance, or eager submission, the ambivalent is bound to disrupt the desired smoothness. If he assumes an air of submission, the senior may resent the fact that the relationship now rests on hierarchy rather than on commonsense, precedent, or his own wisdom. Submissiveness marks again the ambivalent's inability to accept the need for the kind of nimble role playing which insures that such relations *seem* permissive at the same time they nicely accommodate the authority structure of the situation. Although upward-mobiles learn to play such roles facilely, the ambivalent is often disqualified by self-consciousness and by awkward notions about equality, compounded at the same time by inconsistent needs within himself to reduce anxiety by submission. . . .

Bureaucratic structure may . . . reduce anxiety and conflict by objective definitions of authority and status. But the leveling effects of bureaucratic work also induce status anxiety as men try to find ways to recapture their individuality. The routinization of work evokes intense efforts to personalize one's job. Also relevant is the impulse to compensate for any loss of pride in skill attending the mechanization of many jobs.[13] Bureaucratic structure thus aggravates status anxiety by its specialization and anonymity, encouraging a preoccupation with indexes, however trivial, that can validate minute differentiations in prestige and income. If the ambivalent could accept the status system and his position in it, his anxiety would indeed be eased, but both restrict his discretion in favor of organizational goals. Accommodation is viewed as a surrender of his individualistic values. Not only are the organization's rules and rewards the instruments of authority, but they symbolize an ordered system which challenges his preference for complexity and spontaneity. . . .

We have traced the dysfunctional results of the ambivalent's adjustment to the bureaucratic situation. The most critical item is his fear of authority which often distorts his interpersonal relations. His inability to accept the organization's collective goals, which violate his need for personal autonomy, is also at work. His "tender-minded" view of human relations disqualifies him for the "universalistic" decision making required for success on organizational terms. Since his preferences include a desire for creativity and for a work environment that permits spontaneity and experiment, the structured personal relations, stereotyped procedures, and group decision making of big organization prove stifling. He rejects its systems of authority and status which often seem to rest upon subjective bases rather than upon the objective, professional claims that motivate him. Nor can he easily identify with the small group .

in which he works, for here too the conditions of participation are similar to those of the larger system. If his values did not include prestige and influence, a happier accommodation might be possible; but these again emphasize his ambiguity and his inability to assume the roles required to achieve them. In sum, with the exception of his critical function as the agent of change, the ambivalent type is uniquely unsuited to the bureaucratic situation.

NOTES AND REFERENCES

1. Erich Fromm: *Man for Himself* (New York: Rinehart & Co., Inc.; 1947), p. 241.
2. Fromm, p. 241.
3. W. I. Thomas: *The Child in America: Behavior Problems and Programs* (New York: Alfred A. Knopf, Inc.; 1932), p. 572.
4. Robert K. Merton: *Social Theory and Social Structure*, rev. ed. (Glencoe, Illinois: The Free Press; 1957), pp. 393-5 and Ch. 10; also, A. W. Gouldner: "Cosmopolitans and Locals: Toward an Analysis of Latent Social Roles," *Administrative Science Quarterly*, Vols. 2, 3, pp. 281-306; 444-80.
5. Sociologists define "status" as the *position* an individual occupies in the social hierarchy, but I use it here in its popular connotation. R. LaPiere: *A Theory of Social Control* (New York: McGraw-Hill Book Co.; 1954); K. Davis: "A Conceptual Analysis of Stratification," *American Sociological Review*, Vol. 7, pp. 309-21.
6. A. W. Gouldner: "Cosmopolitans and Locals: Toward an Analysis of Latent Social Roles," *Admin. Sci. Q.*, Vols. 2, 3, pp. 281-306; 444-80.
7. The distinction between adaptive anxiety and neurotic anxiety is widely accepted in psychology. Among others, see K. Horney: *Neurosis and Human Growth* (New York: W. W. Norton & Co., Inc.; 1950); *The Neurotic Personality of our Time* (New York: W. W. Norton & Co., Inc.; 1937); R. May: *The Meaning of Anxiety* (New York: The Ronald Press Co.; 1950); F. Fromm-Reichmann: *An Outline of Psychoanalysis* (New York: Random House; 1955); R. Grinker: *Psychosomatic Research* (New York: W. W. Norton & Co.; 1953); H. S. Sullivan: *Interpersonal Theory of Psychiatry* and *Conceptions of Modern Psychiatry*; Horney: *New Ways in Psychoanalysis* (New York: W. W. Norton & Co.; 1939); M. R. Stein, *et al.: Identity and Anxiety* (Glencoe, Illinois: The Free Press; 1960).
8. H. J. Eysenck: *The Dimensions of Personality* (London: Routledge, Kegan Paul; 1947), p. 160.
9. In a study of 3,083 factory workers, for example, R. Fraser found that about 30 per cent suffered from minor and disabling neuroses, and that this condition was commonly associated with a "decrease in social contacts," a characteristic behavior of introvert types, *The Incidence of Neuroses Among Factory Workers* (London: H.M.S.O. Report No. 90; 1947).
10. Eysenck: op. cit.
11. F. Herzberg, *et al.: The Motivation to Work* (New York: John Wiley & Sons, Inc.; 1959), p. 129.
12. Adorno, *et al.: The Authoritarian Personality* (New York: Harper & Brothers; 1950); B. K. Ruebush: "Interfering and Facilitating Effects of Test Anxiety," *Journal of Abnormal and Social Psychology*, Vol. 60, pp. 205-12.
13. E. L. Trist and K. W. Bamforth: "Some Social Psychological Consequences of the Long-wall Method of Coal-getting," *Human Relations*, Vol. 4, pp. 3-38.

ORGANIZATIONAL SOCIALIZATION
AND THE PROFESSION OF MANAGEMENT

EDGAR H. SCHEIN

Introduction

Ladies and gentlemen, colleagues and friends. There are few times in one's professional life when one has an opportunity, indeed something of a mandate, to pull together one's thoughts about an area of study and to communicate these to others.[1]

I can define my topic of concern best by reviewing very briefly the kinds of issues upon which I have focused my research over the last several years. In one way or another I have been trying to understand what happens to an individual when he enters and accepts membership in an organization. My interest was originally kindled by studies of the civilian and military prisoners of the Communists during the Korean War. I thought I could discern parallels between the kind of indoctrination to which these prisoners were subjected, and some of the indoctrination which goes on in American corporations when college and business school graduates first go to work for them. My research efforts came to be devoted to learning what sorts of attitudes and values students had when they left school, and what happened to these attitudes and values in the first few years of work. To this end I followed several panels of graduates of the Sloan School into their early career.

When these studies were well under way, it suddenly became quite apparent to me that if I wanted to study the impact of an organization on the attitudes and values of its members, I might as well start closer to home. We have a school through which we put some 200 men per year—undergraduates, regular Master's students, Sloan Fellows, and Senior Executives. Studies of our own students and faculty revealed that not only did the student groups differ from each other in various attitude areas, but that they also differed from the faculty.

For example, if one takes a scale built up of items which deal with the relations of government and business, one finds that the Senior Executives in our program are consistently against any form of government intervention, the Sloans are not as extreme, the Master's students are roughly in the middle, and the faculty are in favor of such intervention. A similar line-up of attitudes can be found with respect to labor-management relations, and with respect to cynicism about how one gets ahead in industry. In case you did not guess, the Senior Executives are least cynical and the faculty are most cynical.

We also found that student attitudes change in many areas during school, and that they change away from business attitudes toward the faculty position. However, a recent study of Sloan Fellows, conducted after their graduation, indicated that most of the changes toward the faculty had reversed themselves to a considerable degree

"Organizational Socialization and the Profession of Management," by Edgar H. Schein, from *Industrial Management Review*, Winter 1968, © 1968 by the Industrial Management Review Association; all rights reserved.

within one year, a finding which is not unfamiliar to us in studies of training programs of all sorts.

The different positions of different groups at different stages of their managerial career and the observed changes during school clearly indicate that attitudes and values change several times during the managerial career. It is the process which brings about these changes which I would like to focus on today—a process which the sociologists would call "occupational socialization," but which I would prefer to call "organizational socialization" in order to keep our focus clearly on the setting in which the process occurs.

Organizational socialization is the process of "learning the ropes," the process of being indoctrinated and trained, the process of being taught what is important in an organization or some subunit thereof. This process occurs in school. It occurs again, and perhaps most dramatically, when the graduate enters an organization on his first job. It occurs again when he switches within the organization from one department to another, or from one rank level to another. It occurs all over again if he leaves one organization and enters another. And it occurs again when he goes back to school, and again when he returns to the organization after school.

Indeed, the process is so ubiquitous and we go though it so often during our total career, that it is all too easy to overlook it. Yet it is a process which can make or break a career, and which can make or break organizational systems of manpower planning. The speed and effectiveness of socialization determine employee loyalty, commitment, productivity, and turnover. The basic stability and effectiveness of organizations therefore depends upon their ability to socialize new members.

Let us see whether we can bring the process of socialization to life by describing how it occurs. I hope to show you the power of this process, particularly as it occurs within industrial organizations. Having done this, I would like to explore a major dilemma which I see at the interface between organizations and graduate management schools. Schools socialize their students toward a concept of a profession, organizations socialize their new members to be effective members. Do the two processes of socialization supplement each other or conflict? If they conflict, what can we do about it in organizations and in the schools?

Some Basic Elements of Organizational Socialization

The term socialization has a fairly clear meaning in sociology, but it has been a difficult one to assimilate in the behavioral sciences and in management. To many of my colleagues it implies unnecessary jargon, and to many of my business acquaintances it implies the teaching of socialism—a kiss of death for the concept right there. Yet the concept is most useful because it focuses clearly on the interaction between a stable social system and the new members who enter it. The concept refers to the process by which a new member learns the value system, the norms, and the required behavior patterns of the society, organization, or group which he is entering. It does not include all learning. It includes only the learning of those values, norms, and behavior patterns which, from the organization's point of view or group's point of view, it is necessary for any new member to learn. This is defined as the price of membership.

What are such values, norms, and behavior patterns all about? Usually they involve:

1. The basic *goals* of the organization.
2. The preferred *means* by which these goals should be attained.
3. The basic *responsibilities* of the member in the role which is being granted to him by the organization.
4. The *behavior patterns* which are required for effective performance in the role.
5. A set of rules or principles which pertain to the *maintenance of the identity and integrity* of the organization.

The new member must learn not to drive Chevrolets if he is working for Ford, not to criticize the organization in public, not to wear the wrong kind of clothes or be seen in the wrong kinds of places. If the organization is a school, beyond learning the content of what is taught, the student must accept the value of education, he must try to learn without cheating, he must accept the authority of the faculty and behave appropriately to the student role. He must not be rude in the classroom or openly disrespectful to the professor.

By what processes does the novice learn the required values and norms? The answer to this question depends in part upon the degree of prior socialization. If the novice has correctly anticipated the norms of the organization he is joining, the socialization process merely involves a reaffirmation of these norms through various communication channels, the personal example of key people in the organization, and direct instructions from supervisors, trainers, and informal coaches.

If, however, the novice comes to the organization with values and behavior patterns which are in varying degrees out of line with those expected by the organization, then the socialization process first involves a destructive or unfreezing phase. This phase serves the function of detaching the person from his former values, of proving to him that his present self is worthless from the point of view of the organization and that he must redefine himself in terms of the new roles which he is to be granted.

The extremes of this process can be seen in initiation rites or novitiates for religious orders. When the novice enters his training period, his old self is symbolically destroyed by loss of clothing, name, often his hair, titles and other self-defining equipment. These are replaced with uniforms, new names and titles, and other self-defining equipment consonant with the new role he is being trained for.

It may be comforting to think of activities like this as being characteristic only of primitive tribes of total institutions like military basic training camps, academies, and religious orders. But even a little examination of areas closer to home will reveal the same processes both in our graduate schools and in the business organizations to which our graduates go.

Perhaps the commonest version of the process in school is the imposition of a tight schedule, of an impossibly heavy reading program, and of the assignment of problems which are likely to be too difficult for the student to solve. Whether these techniques are deliberate or not, they serve effectively to remind the student that he is not as smart or capable as he may have thought he was, and therefore, that there are still things to be learned. As our Sloan Fellows tell us every year, the first summer in the program pretty well destroys many aspects of their self-image.

Homework in statistics appears to enjoy a unique status comparable to having one's head shaved and clothes burned.

Studies of medical schools and our own observations of the Sloan program suggest that the work overload on the students leads to the development of a peer culture, a kind of banding together of the students as a defense against the threatening faculty and as a problem-solving device to develop norms of what and how to study. If the group solutions which are developed support the organizational norms, the peer group becomes an effective instrument of socialization. However, from the school's point of view, there is the risk that peer group norms will set up counter-socializing forces and sow the seeds of sabotage, rebellion, or revolution. The positive gains of a supportive peer group generally make it worthwhile to run the risks of rebellion, however, which usually motivates the organization to encourage or actually to facilitate peer group formation.

Many of our Sloan Fellow alumni tell us that one of the most powerful features of the Sloan program is the fact that a group of some 40 men share the same fate of being put through a very tough educational regimen. The peer group ties formed during the year have proven to be one of the most durable end-results of the educational program and, of course, are one of the key supports to the maintaining of some of the values and attitudes learned in school. The power of this kind of socializing force can be appreciated best by pondering a further statement which many alumni have made. They stated that prior to the program they identified themselves primarily with their company. Following the program they identified themselves primarily with the other Sloan Fellows, and such identification has lasted, as far as we can tell, for the rest of their career.

Let me next illustrate the industrial counterpart of these processes. Many of my panel members, when interviewed about the first six months in their new jobs, told stories of what we finally labeled as "upending experiences." Upending experiences are deliberately planned or accidentally created circumstances which dramatically and unequivocally upset or disconfirm some of the major assumptions which the new man holds about himself, his company, or his job.

One class of such experiences is to receive assignments which are so easy or so trivial that they carry the clear message that the new man is not worthy of being given anything important to do. Another class of such experiences is at the other extreme—assignments which are so difficult that failure is a certainty, thus proving unequivocally to the new man that he may not be as smart as he thought he was. Giving work which is clearly for practice only, asking for reports which are then unread or not acted upon, protracted periods of training during which the person observes others work, all have the same upending effect.

The most vivid example came from an engineering company where a supervisor had a conscious and deliberate strategy for dealing with what he considered to be unwarranted arrogance on the part of engineers whom they hired. He asked each new man to examine and diagnose a particular complex circuit, which happened to violate a number of textbook principles but actually worked very well. The new man would usually announce with confidence, even after an invitation to double-check, that the circuit could not possibly work. At this point the manager would demonstrate the circuit, tell the new man that they had been selling it for several years without customer complaint, and demand that the new man figure out why it did work. None of the men so far tested were able to do it, but all of them were thoroughly chastened and came to the manager anxious to learn where their knowledge was inadequate and needed supplementing. According to this manager, it was much easier from this point on to establish a good give-and-take relationship with his new man.

It should be noted that the success of such socializing techniques depends upon two factors which are not always under the control of the organization. The first factor is the initial motivation of the entrant to join the organization. If his motivation is high, as in the case of a fraternity pledge, he will tolerate all kinds of uncomfortable socialization experiences, even to extremes of hell week. If his motivation for membership is low, he may well decide to leave the organization rather than tolerate uncomfortable initiation rites. If he leaves, the socialization process has obviously failed.

The second factor is the degree to which the organization can hold the new member captive during the period of socialization. His motivation is obviously one element here, but one finds organizations using other forces as well. In the case of basic training there are legal forces to remain. In the case of many schools one must pay one's tuition in advance, in other words, invest one's self materially so that leaving the system becomes expensive. In the case of religious orders one must make strong initial psychological commitments in the form of vows and the severing of relationships outside the religious order. The situation is defined as one in which one will lose face or be humiliated if one leaves the organization.

In the case of business organizations the pressures are more subtle but nevertheless identifiable. New members are encouraged to get financially committed by joining pension plans, stock option plans, and/or house purchasing plans which would mean material loss if the person decided to leave. Even more subtle is the reminder by the boss that it takes a year or so to learn any new business; therefore, if you leave, you will have to start all over again. Why not suffer it out with the hope that things will look more rosy once the initiation period is over.

Several of my panel members told me at the end of one year at work that they were quite dissatisfied, but were not sure they should leave because they had invested a year of learning in that company. Usually their boss encouraged them to think about staying. Whether or not such pressures will work depends, of course, on the labor market and other factors not under the control of the organization.

Let me summarize thus far. Organizations socialize their new members by creating a series of events which serve the function of undoing old values so that the person will be prepared to learn the new values. This process of undoing or unfreezing is often unpleasant and therefore requires either strong motivation to endure it or strong organizational forces to make the person endure it. The formation of a peer group of novices is often a solution to the problem of defense against the powerful organization, and, at the same time, can strongly enhance the socialization process if peer group norms support organizational norms.

Let us look next at the positive side of the socialization process. Given some readiness to learn, how does the novice acquire his new learning? The answer is that he acquires it from multiple sources—the official literature of the organization;

the example set by key models in the organization; the instructions given to him directly by his trainer, coach, or boss; the example of peers who have been in the organization longer and thus serve as big brothers; the rewards and punishments which result from his own efforts at problem solving and experimenting with new values and new behavior.

The instructions and guidelines given by senior members of the organization are probably one of the most potent sources. I can illustrate this point best by recalling several incidents from my own socialization into the Sloan School back in 1956. I came here at the invitation of Doug McGregor from a research job. I had no prior teaching experience or knowledge of organizational or managerial matters. Contrary to my expectations, I was told by Doug that knowledge of organizational psychology and management was not important, but that some interest in learning about these matters was.

The first socializing incident occurred in an initial interview with Elting Morison, who was then on our faculty. He said in a completely blunt manner that if I knew what I wanted to do and could go ahead on my own, the Sloan School would be a great place to be. If I wasn't sure and would look to others for guidance, not to bother to come.

The second incident occurred in a conversation with our then Dean, Penn Brooks, a few weeks before the opening of the semester. We were discussing what and how I might teach. Penn said to me that he basically wanted each of his faculty members to find his own approach to management education. I could do whatever I wanted—so long as I did not imitate our sister school up the river. Case discussion leaders need not apply, was the clear message.

The third incident (you see I was a slow learner) occurred a few days later when I was planning my subject in social psychology for our Master's students. I was quite nervous about it and unsure of how to decide what to include in the subject. I went to Doug and innocently asked him to lend me outlines of previous versions of the subject, which had been taught by Alex Bavelas, or at least to give me some advice on what to include and exclude. Doug was very nice and very patient, but also quite firm in his refusal to give me either outlines or advice. He thought there was really no need to rely on history, and expressed confidence that I could probably make up my own mind. I suffered that term but learned a good deal about the value system of the Sloan School, as well as how to organize a subject. I was, in fact, so well socialized by these early experiences that nowadays no one can get me to coordinate anything with anybody else.

Similar kinds of lessons can be learned during the course of training programs, in orientation sessions, and through company literature. But the more subtle kinds of values which the organization holds, which indeed may not even be well understood by the senior people, are often communicated through peers operating as helpful big brothers. They can communicate the subtleties of how the boss wants things done, how higher management feels about things, the kinds of things which are considered heroic in the organization, the kinds of things which are taboo.

Of course, sometimes the values of the immediate group into which a new person is hired are partially out of line with the value system of the organization as a whole. If this is the case, the new person will learn the immediate group's values much more quickly than those of the total organization, often to the chagrin of the higher levels of management. This is best exemplified at the level of hourly workers where fellow employees will have much more socializing power than the boss.

An interesting managerial example of this conflict was provided by one recent graduate who was hired into a group whose purpose was to develop cost reduction systems for a large manufacturing operation. His colleagues on the job, however, showed him how to pad his expense account whenever they traveled together. The end result of this kind of conflict was to accept neither the cost reduction values of the company nor the cost inflation values of the peer group. The man left the company in disgust to start up some businesses of his own.

One of the important functions of organizational socialization is to build commitment and loyalty to the organization. How is this accomplished? One mechanism is to invest much effort and time in the new member and thereby build up expectations of being repaid by loyalty, hard work, and rapid learning. Another mechanism is to get the new member to make a series of small behavioral commitments which can only be justified by him through the acceptance and incorporation of company values. He then becomes his own agent of socialization. Both mechanisms involve the subtle manipulation of guilt.

To illustrate the first mechanism, one of our graduates went to a public relations firm which made it clear to him that he had sufficient knowledge and skill to advance, but that his values and attitudes would have to be evaluated for a couple of years before he would be fully accepted. During the first several months he was frequently invited to join high ranking members of the organization at their luncheon meetings in order to learn more about how they thought about things. He was so flattered by the amount of time they spent on him, that he worked extra hard to learn their values and became highly committed to the organization. He said that he would have felt guilty at the thought of not learning or of leaving the company. Sending people to expensive training programs, giving them extra perquisites, indeed the whole philosophy of paternalism, is built on the assumption that if you invest in the employee he will repay the company with loyalty and hard work. He would feel guilty if he did not.

The second mechanism, that of getting behavioral commitments, was most beautifully illustrated in Communist techniques of coercive persuasion. The Communists made tremendous efforts to elicit a public confession from a prisoner. One of the key functions of such a public confession, even if the prisoner knew he was making a false confession, was that it committed him publicly. Once he made this commitment, he found himself under strong internal and external pressure to justify why he had confessed. For many people it proved easier to justify the confession by coming to believe in their own crimes than to have to face the fact that they were too weak to withstand the captor's pressure.

In organizations, a similar effect can be achieved by promoting a rebellious person into a position of responsibility. The same values which the new member may have criticized and jeered at from his position at the bottom of the hierarchy suddenly look different when he has subordinates of his own whose commitment he must obtain.

Many of my panel members had very strong moral and ethical standards when they first went to work, and these stood up quite well during their first year at work even in the face of less ethical practices by their peers and superiors. But they reported with considerable shock that some of the practices they had condemned in their bosses were quickly adopted by them once they had themselves been promoted and faced the pressures of the new position. As one man put it very poignantly—"my ethical standards changed so gradually over the first five years of work that I hardly noticed it, but it was a great shock to suddenly realize what my feelings had been five years ago and how much they had changed."

Another version of obtaining commitment is to gain the new member's acceptance of very general ideals like "one must work for the good of the company," or "one must meet the competition." Whenever any counter-organizational behavior occurs one can then point out that the ideal is being violated. The engineer who does not come to work on time is reminded that his behavior indicates lack of concern for the good of the company. The employee who wears the wrong kind of clothes, lives in the wrong neighborhood, or associates with the wrong people can be reminded that he is hurting the company image.

One of my panel members on a product research assignment discovered that an additive which was approved by the Food and Drug Administration might in fact be harmful to consumers. He was strongly encouraged to forget about it. His boss told him that it was the F.D.A.'s problem. If the company worried about things like that it might force prices up and thus make it tough to meet the competition.

Many of the upending experiences which new members of organizations endure are justified to them by the unarguable ideal that they should learn how the company really works before expecting a position of real responsibility. Once the new man accepts this ideal it serves to justify all kinds of training and quantities of menial work which others who have been around longer are unwilling to do themselves. This practice is known as "learning the business from the ground up," or "I had to do it when I first joined the company, now it's someone else's turn." There are clear elements of hazing involved not too different from those associated with fraternity initiations and other rites of passage.

The final mechanism to be noted in a socialization process is the transition to full fledged member. The purpose of such transitional events is to help the new member incorporate his new values, attitudes, and norms into his identity so that they become part of him, not merely something to which he pays lip-service. Initiation rites which involve severe tests of the novice serve to prove to him that he is capable of fulfilling the new role—that he now is a man, no longer merely a boy.

Organizations usually signal this transition by giving the new man some important responsibility or a position of power which, if mishandled or misused, could genuinely hurt the organization. With this transition often come titles, symbols of status, extra rights or prerogatives, sharing of confidential information or other things which in one way or another indicate that the new member has earned the trust of the organization. Although such events may not always be visible to the outside observer, they are felt strongly by the new member. He knows when he has finally "been accepted," and feels it when he becomes "identified with the company."

So much for examples of the process of socialization. Let us now look at some of the dilemmas and conflicts which arise within it.

Failures of Socialization—Non-conformity and Over-conformity

Most organizations attach differing amounts of importance to different norms and values. Some are pivotal. Any member of a business organization who does not believe in the value of getting a job done will not survive long. Other pivotal values in most business organizations might be belief in a reasonable profit, belief in the free enterprise system and competition, belief in a hierarchy of authority as a good way to get things done, and so on.

Other values or norms are what may be called relevant. These are norms which it is not absolutely necessary to accept as the price of membership, but which are considered desirable and good to accept. Many of these norms pertain to standards of dress and decorum, not being publicly disloyal to the company, living in the right neighborhood and belonging to the right political party and clubs. In some organizations some of these norms may be pivotal. Organizations vary in this regard. You all know the stereotype of IBM as a company that requires the wearing of white shirts and hats. In some parts of IBM such values are indeed pivotal; in other parts they are only relevant, and in some parts they are quite peripheral. The point is that not all norms to which the new member is exposed are equally important for the organization.

The socialization process operates across the whole range of norms, but the amount of reward and punishment for compliance or non-compliance will vary with the importance of the norm. This variation allows the new member some degrees of freedom in terms of how far to conform and allows the organization some degrees of freedom in how much conformity to demand. The new man can accept none of the values, he can accept only the pivotal values, but carefully remain independent on all those areas not seen as pivotal, or he can accept the whole range of values and norms. He can tune in so completely on what he sees to be the way others are handling themselves that he becomes a carbon-copy and sometimes a caricature of them.

These basic responses to socialization can be labeled as follows:

Type 1. Rebellion: Rejection of all values and norms

Type 2. Creative individualism: Acceptance only of pivotal values and norms; rejection of all others

Type 3. Conformity: Acceptance of all values and norms

Most analyses of conformity deal only with the type 1 and 3 cases, failing to note that both can be viewed as socialization failures. The rebellious individual either is expelled from the organization or turns his energies toward defeating its goals. The conforming individual curbs his creativity and thereby moves the organization toward a sterile form of bureaucracy. The trick for most organizations is to create the type 2 response—acceptance of pivotal values and norms, but rejection of all others, a response which I would like to call "creative individualism."

To remain creatively individualistic in an organization is particularly difficult because of the constant resocialization pressures which come with promotion or lateral transfer. Every time the employee learns part of the value system of the particular group to which he is assigned, he may be laying the groundwork for conflict when he is transferred. The engineer has difficulty accepting the values of the sales department, the staff man has difficulty accepting the high pressure ways of the production department, and the line manager has difficulties accepting the service and helping ethic of a staff group. With each transfer, the forces are great toward either conforming or rebelling. It is difficult to keep focused on what is pivotal and retain one's basic individualism.

Professional Socialization and Organizational Socialization

The issue of how to maintain individualism in the face of organizational socialization pressures brings us to the final and most problematical area of concern. In the traditional professions like medicine, law, and teaching, individualism is supported by a set of professional attitudes which serve to immunize the person against some of the forces of the organization. The questions now to be considered are (1) Is management a profession? (2) If so, do professional attitudes develop in managers? and (3) If so, do these support or conflict with organizational norms and values?

Professionalism can be defined by a number of characteristics:

1. Professional decisions are made by means of general principles, theories, or propositions which are independent of the particular case under consideration. For management this would mean that there are certain principles of how to handle people, money, information, etc., independent of any particular company. The fact that we can and do teach general subjects in these areas would support management's claim as a profession.

2. Professional decisions imply knowledge in a specific area in which the person is expert, not a generalized body of wisdom. The professional is an expert only in his profession, not an expert at everything. He has to license to be a "wise man." Does management fit by this criterion? I will let you decide.

3. The professional's relations with his clients are objective and independent of particular sentiments about them. The doctor or lawyer makes his decisions independent of his liking or disliking of his patients or clients. On this criterion we have a real difficulty since, in the first place, it is very difficult to specify an appropriate single client for a manager, and, in the second place, it is not at all clear that decisions can or should be made independent of sentiments. What is objectively best for the stockholder may conflict with what is best for the enterprise, which, in turn may conflict with what is best for the customer.

4. A professional achieves his status by accomplishment, not by inherent qualities such as birth order, his relationship to people in power, his race, religion, or color. Industry is increasingly moving toward an acceptance of this principle for managerial selection, but in practice the process of organizational socialization may undermine it by rewarding the conformist and rejecting the individualist whose professional orientation may make him look disloyal to the organization.

5. A professional's decisions are assumed to be on behalf of the client and to be independent of self-interest. Clearly this principle is at best equivocal in manager-customer relations, though again one senses that industry is moving closer to accepting the idea.

6. The professional typically relates to a voluntary association of fellow professionals, and accepts only the authority of these colleagues as a sanction on his own

behavior. The manager is least like the professional in this regard, in that he is expected to accept a principle of hierarchical authority. The dilemma is best illustrated by the previous example which I gave of our Sloan Fellow alumni who, after the program, related themselves more to other Sloans than to their company hierarchy. By this criterion they had become truly professionalized.

7. A professional has sometimes been called someone who knows better what is good for his client than the client. The professional's expertness puts the client into a very vulnerable position. This vulnerability has necessitated the development of strong professional codes and ethics which serve to protect the client. Such codes are enforced through the colleague peer group. One sees relatively few attempts to develop codes of ethics for managers or systems of enforcement.

On several bases, then, management is a profession, but on several others it is clearly not yet a profession.

This long description of what is a profession was motivated by the need to make a very crucial point. I believe that management education, particularly in a graduate school like the Sloan School, is increasingly attempting to train professionals, and in this process is socializing the students to a set of professional values which are, in fact, in severe and direct conflict with typical organizational values.

For example, I see us teaching general principles in the behavioral sciences, economics, and quantitative methods. Our applied subjects like marketing, operations management, and finance are also taught as bodies of knowledge governed by general principles which are applicable to a wide variety of situations. Our students are given very broad concepts which apply to the corporation as a whole, and are taught to see the relationship between the corporation, the community, and the society. They are taught to value the long-range health and survival of economic institutions, not the short-range profit of a particular company. They come to appreciate the necessary interrelationships between government, labor, and management rather than to define these as mutually warring camps. They are taught to look at organizations from the perspective of high ranking management, to solve the basic problems of the enterprise rather than the day-to-day practical problems of staff or line management. Finally, they are taught an ethic of pure rationality and emotional neutrality—analyze the problem and make the decisions independent of feelings about people, the product, the company, or the community. All of these are essentially professional values.

Organizations value many of the same things, in principle. But what is valued in principle by the higher ranking and senior people in the organization often is neither supported by their own behavior, nor even valued lower down in the organization. In fact, the value system which the graduates encounter on their first job is in many respects diametrically opposed to the professional values taught in school. The graduate is immediately expected to develop loyalty and concern for a particular company with all of its particular idiosyncrasies. He is expected to recognize the limitation of his general knowledge and to develop the sort of *ad hoc* wisdom which the school has taught him to avoid. He is expected to look to his boss for evaluation rather than to some group of colleagues outside the company.

Whereas the professional training tells him that knowledge is power, the graduate now must learn that knowledge by itself is nothing. It is the ability to sell knowledge to other people which is power. Only by being able to sell an application of knowledge to a highly specific, local situation, can the graduate obtain respect for what he knows. Where his education has taught the graduate principles of how to manage others and to take the corporate point of view, his organizational socialization tries to teach him how to be a good subordinate, how to be influenced, and how to sell ideas from a position of low power.

On the one hand, the organization via its recruiters and senior people tells the graduate that it is counting on him to bring fresh points of view and new techniques to bear on its problems. On the other hand, the man's first boss and peers try to socialize him into their traditional mold.

A man is hired to introduce linear programming into a production department, but once he is there he is told to lay off because if he succeeds he will make the old supervisors and engineers look bad. Another man is hired for his financial analysis skills but is not permitted access to data worth analyzing because the company does not trust him to keep them confidential. A third man is hired into a large group responsible for developing cost reduction programs in a large defense industry, and is told to ignore the fact that the group is overstaffed, inefficient, and willing to pad its expense accounts. A fourth man, hired for his energy and capability, put it this way as an explanation of why he quit to go into private consulting: "They were quite pleased with work that required only two hours per day; I wasn't."

In my panel of 1962 graduates, 73 percent have already left their first job and many are on their third or fourth. In the class of 1963, the percentage is 67, and in the class of 1964, the percentage is 50. Apparently, most of our graduates are unwilling to be socialized into organizations whose values are incompatible with the ones we teach. Yet these organizations are precisely the ones who may need creative individualists most.

What seems to happen in the early stages of the managerial career is either a kind of postponement of professional socialization while organizational socialization takes precedence, or a rebelling by the graduate against organizational socialization. The young man who submits must first learn to be a good apprentice, a good staff man, a good junior analyst, and perhaps a good low level administrator. He must prove his loyalty to the company by accepting this career path with good graces, before he is trusted enough to be given a position of power. If he has not lost his education by then, he can begin to apply some general principles when he achieves such a position of power.

The businessman wants the school to provide both the professional education and the humility which would make organizational socialization smoother. He is not aware that teaching management concepts of the future precludes justifying the practices of today. Some professional schools clearly do set out to train for the needs of the profession as it is designed today. The Sloan School appears to me to reject this concept. Instead we have a faculty which is looking at the professional manager of five, ten, or twenty years from now, and is training its graduates in management techniques which we believe are coming in the future.

Symptomatic of this approach is the fact that in many of our subjects we are highly critical of the management practices of today, and highly committed to re-educating those managers like Sloan Fellows and Senior Executives who come back to study at M.I.T. We get across in a dozen different ways the belief that most organizations of today are obsolete, conservative, constipated, and ignorant of their own problems. Furthermore, I believe that this point of view is what society and the business community demands of a good professional school.

It would be no solution to abandon our own vision of the manager of the future, and I doubt that those of you in the audience from business and industry would really want us to do this. What you probably want is to have your cake and eat it too—you want us to teach our students the management concepts of tomorrow, and you want us to teach them how to put these concepts into deep freeze while they learn the business of today. Then when they have proven themselves worthy of advancement and have achieved a position of some influence, they should magically resurrect their education and put it to work.

Unfortunately, socialization processes are usually too powerful to permit that solution. If you succeed in socializing your young graduates to your organizations, you will probably also succeed in proving to them that their education was pretty worthless and might as well be put on a permanent rather than temporary shelf. We have research evidence that many well educated graduates do learn to be complacent and to play the organizational game. It is not at all clear whether they later ever resurrect their educational arsenal.

What Is to Be Done about This Situation?

I think we need to accept, at the outset, the reality of organizational socialization phenomena. As my colleague, Leo Moore, so aptly put it, organizations like to put their fingerprints on people, and they have every right to do so. By the same token, graduate schools of business have a right and an obligation to pursue professional socialization to the best of their ability. We must find a way to ameliorate the conflicts at the interface, without, however, concluding that either schools or organizations are to blame and should stop what they are doing.

What the Schools Can Do

The schools, our school in particular, can do several concrete things which would help the situation. First, we can insert into our total curriculum more apprenticeship experience which would bring the realities of organizational life home to the student earlier. But such apprenticeship experiences will not become educational unless we combine them with a second idea, that of providing a practicum on how to change organizations. Such a practicum should draw on each of the course specialties and should be specifically designed to teach a student how to translate his professional knowledge into viable action programs at whatever level of the organization he is working.

Ten years ago we would not have known how to do this. Today there is no excuse for not doing it. Whether the field is operations research, sophisticated quantitative marketing, industrial dynamics, organizational psychology or whatever, we must give our students experience in trying to implement their new ideas, and we must teach them how to make the implementation effective. In effect, we must teach our students to become change-agents, whatever their disciplinary specialty turns out to be. We must teach them how to influence their organizations from low positions of power without sacrificing their professional values in the process. We must teach them how to remain creative individualists in the face of strong organizational socialization pressures.

Combined with these two things, we need to do a third thing. We need to become more involved in the student's efforts at career planning and we need to coordinate our activities more closely with the company recruiters and the university placement officers. At the present I suspect that most of our faculty is quite indifferent to the student's struggles to find the right kind of a job. I suspect that this indifference leaves the door wide open to faulty selection on the part of the student, which can only lead, in the end, to an undermining of the education into which we pour so much effort. We need to work harder to insure that our graduates get jobs in which they can further the values and methods we inculcate.

What the Companies Can Do

Companies can do at least two things. First, they can make a genuine effort to become aware of and understand their own organizational socialization practices. I fear very few higher level executives know what is going on at the bottom of their organization where all the high priced talent they call for is actually employed. At the same time, I suspect that it is their own value system which ultimately determines the socialization activities which occur throughout all segments of the organization. Greater awareness and understanding of these practices should make possible more rational choices as to which practices to encourage and which to de-emphasize. The focus should be on pivotal values only, not on peripheral or irrelevant ones.

Second, companies must come to appreciate the delicate problems which exist both for the graduate and for his first boss in the early years of the career when socialization pressures are at the maximum. If more companies appreciated the nature of this dilemma they would recognize the necessity of giving some training to the men who will be the first bosses of the graduates.

I have argued for such training for many years, but still find that most company effort goes into training the graduate rather than his boss. Yet it is the boss who really has the power to create the climate which will lead to rebellion, conformity, or creative individualism. If the companies care whether their new hires use one or the other of these adaptation strategies, they had better start looking at the behavior of the first boss and training him for what the company wants and hopes for. Too many bosses concentrate on teaching too many peripheral values and thus undermine the possibilities for creative individualism and organization improvement.

Conclusion

The essence of management is to understand the forces acting in a situation and to gain control over them. It is high time that some of our managerial knowledge and skill be focused on those forces in the organizational environment which derive from the fact that organizations are social systems who do socialize their new members. If we do not learn to analyze and control the forces of organizational socialization, we are abdicating one of our primary managerial responsibilities. Let us not shrink away from a little bit of social engineering and management in this most important area of the human side of the enterprise.

References

1. Blau, P.M. and Scott, R.W. *Formal Organizations*. San Francisco: Chandler, 1962.
2. Goffman, E. *Asylums*. Garden City, N.Y.: Doubleday Anchor, 1961.
3. Schein, E. H., Schneier, Inge and Barker, C. H. *Coercive Persuasion*. New York: W. W. Norton, 1961.
4. Schein, E. H. "Management Development as a Process of Influence," *Industrial Management Review*, II (1961), 59-77.
5. Schein, E. H. "Forces Which Undermine Management Development," *California Management Review*, Vol. V, Summer, 1963
6. Schein, E. H. "How to Break in the College Graduate," *Harvard Business Review*, Vol. XLII (1964).
7. Schein, E. H. "Training in Industry: Education or Indoctrination," *Industrial Medicine and Surgery*, Vol. XXXIII (1964).
8. Schein, E. H. *Organizational Psychology*. Englewood Cliffs, N.J.: Prentice-Hall, 1965
9. Schein, E. H. "The Problem of Moral Education for the Business Manager," *Industrial Management Review*, VIII (1966), 3-14
10. Schein, E. H. "Attitude Change During Management Education," *Adminstrative Science Quarterly*, XI (1967), 601-628
11. Schein, E. H. "The Wall of Misunderstanding on the first Job," *Journal of College Placement*, February/March, 1967

PART THREE

Individual Behavior
in the Organization

Previously, we have shown that the contingency model has great importance and usefulness in understanding human performance. In this part we will attempt to build on this model to show how past learning affects work performance. The readings in this part are offered as a starting point for developing a greater understanding of the complexity of human behavior. They are divided into three sections, with each section building upon the previous one.

The first section (A) discusses the effects of attitudes on performance. Because attitudes are learned, we see that the learning process both affects and is affected by attitudes. The second section (B) deals with perception of cues from the environment. A person's ability to perceive and respond to his environment is no better than his ability to generalize and discriminate between cues, and—as we see—a person's needs as well as his attitudes play a major role in determining his perceptual processes. The third section (C), on worker motivation, discusses how attitudes, needs, and perceptions affect motivation. The drive state is often blamed when one fails to perform or is praised when he chooses to perform. It is therefore important that we attempt to understand the components of motivation and try to determine why motivation varies among individuals.

The Effect of Attitudes On Individual Performance

An *attitude* can be defined as an individual's predisposition to evaluate an object in a favorable or unfavorable manner. Attitudes consist of three major components: (1) The cognitive component of an attitude is what a person *believes* about an object. It is determined by the information he possesses about that object. (2) The affective component of an attitude is how a person *feels* about the object. It is his emotional reaction to that object. (3) The *behavioral* component of an attitude is what a person *does* about an object. Further, an individual has a need for internal consistency among the three components of an attitude he holds.

Katz describes the importance of understanding the reasons why people hold the attitudes they do. He says that the *intensity*, the *specificity*, and the *linkage* of an attitude to a related value system are important in determining the resistance of the individual to attitude change. To change a subordinate's attitude, a manager must first know the importance of that attitude for the individual.

Mann, in the second reading, states that the need for consistency of an attitude can exert a powerful force in influencing people to behave in various ways. He discusses a number of theories which deal with the problem of inconsistency among attitude components, and how any disturbance in an individual's attitude system sets in motion active attempts to restore consistency. For example, a male chauvinist confronted with unquestionable competence on the part of subordinate women managers will find himself in a state of attitude inconsistency that must ultimately be resolved. Managers are often faced with the problem of attitudes (beliefs and emotions) interfering with the behavior of employees. One of the key interests of many managers is how such attitudes can be changed.

A study reported by Leiberman says that attitudes follow the reinforcement offered by the organization. Since attitudes are learned, the manager seeking to change the attitude of an employee must change the reinforcement contingencies that shaped the old attitude. Leiberman suggests that it is often helpful to give the individual a new role that leads to adopting the new attitude. One of the fundamental postulates of role theory is that a person's attitude will be influenced by the role that he occupies in a social system.

Specific methods of attitude change are discussed in part 7, "Organizational Change and Development." These methods include (1) a program for changing behavior, with the thought that beliefs and emotional states will follow (behavioral modification), and (2) changing beliefs and emotions, with the thought that behavior will follow (organizational development). Both of these methods are based in consistency theory, and are discussed in part 7.

The Perceptual Process and Human Behavior

The administrator frequently bases decisions and actions on his perceptions of those who work for him. Individual employees perceive the reward structure of the organization, make judgments about it, and then determine what form of behavior is appropriate. Yet different individuals can look at the same object or same person, weigh cues differently based upon their own past history, and come up with unique interpretations. What a person believes to be true about his world is, for him, the "truth." *Facts* are determined by the way people interpret information that they receive, and not by any absolute measure. As Leavitt said, "To ignore differences in perception is to ignore a major determinant of behavior."[1]

Perception involves the selecting, organizing, and interpreting of stimuli from the environment, and can be defined as the process whereby incoming cues from the environment are organized. The organization of such cues through the perceptual process serves a most useful function for the individual. He selectively accepts certain cues from the environment and classifies these cues according to his past history of that stimulus setting. This process enables him to screen out unwanted stimuli, and aids him in organizing his world into a consistent whole. As Mason Haire said, "If we make a separation between the physical world outside of us, on the one hand, and the psychological environment, or the world that we see, on the other, we come to see that the order in organization is not in the physical stimulus, but in the observer.''[2] What Haire is saying is that our world is whatever we see it to be. One of the basic assumptions of the individuality of man is that his past history determines the world he sees.

When we meet someone new, we attempt to classify him into a category so that we can predict his behavior. How we classify him will depend upon the situation in which we observe him, his physical and verbal characteristics, our own past history with similar persons, and our own personal and psychological state at the time we perceive him. To aid in perceiving people, we often use certain devices, called perceptual sets, in order to place them into categories for purposes of prediction. Examples of such devices are stereotyping, halo effect, projection, selective perception, and perceptual readiness.

Zalkind and Costello discuss the importance of understanding the nature of the perceptual process in organizational settings. They describe certain biases which may exist in supervisors and in employees that influence how they judge their fellow workers. They discuss in detail the concepts of stereotyping, halo effect, projection, and perceptual defense mechanisms. They also report on how the characteristics of the perceiver and the perceived affect supervisory ratings given the worker. They conclude their article by saying that managers should be aware of perceptual inaccuracies, and attempt to train supervisors in making accurate perceptual ratings.

Leavitt reinforces the point that the world as it is perceived is the world that is important for determining the behavior of the worker, and he discusses also the importance of managers being able to perceive themselves accurately. The manager must understand his own biases and his own perceptual weaknesses before he can judge other people effectively. Moreover, one of the first steps in changing a person's attitude is getting him to understand how he perceives, or what he feels about, objects or other people.

Selective perception is discussed by Dearborn and Simon, who report a study showing that a manager perceives only those aspects of a situation that relate specifically to the activities and goals of his department. For the organization as a whole, however, it is important that managers view problems from the organizational rather than departmental standpoint.

Motivation and Individual Performance

Motivation can be defined as an inner state that activates, energizes, or moves behavior toward goals. When we speak of motivation or ask about the motives of a person, we are really asking *why* he acts, or why he acts the way he does. The concept of motivation implies that people choose the paths of action they follow; to explore motivation is to ask what the driving forces are that make a person choose or fail to choose a particular path. If a manager understands the motivation of his workers, he can channel this "inner state" toward common goals, that is, goals shared by both the individual and the organization.

Understanding motivation lies in understanding the meanings of, and relationships among, need states, drives, and goals. (An individual's perception of the world, and his attitudes about objects and people in that world, incidentally, play an important part in determining his needs and his goals.) According to Abraham Maslow, the *needs* underlying human motivation can be organized on five general levels, from lowest to highest.[3] He regards these needs as *prepotent*; that is, as one need is satisfied, the next need level comes into play. The lowest-level need he calls *physiological* need. This is the need for food, shelter, clothing, relief from pain, and the like. The next level is the need for *safety* or security. Examples include the need for protection from crime, and the need for job security. The third need level he calls *social need*, or the need for belonging. It is the need for friendship, for affection, and for identification with a group or an organization. This is probably the need of most individuals when they enter an organization. The fourth level of need is the need for *self-esteem* or autonomy. The person now wants to be accepted for his accomplishments as well. This need is the need to be independent in thinking and to be respected. It involves such things as recognition, status, and appreciation. The highest level of need, according to Maslow, is the need for *self-actualization*. Maslow defines this as the tendency for a person to become everything that he is capable of becoming.

A *drive* is a psychological condition which moves a person toward satisfying a need. The needs for food and water are translated into hunger and thirst drives. A *motive* is a subset of a drive state which has a clearly defined goal toward which it strives; *goals* fulfill or satisfy the relevant need. Thus a goal can be defined as anything that will reduce the need state—for example, eating food, drinking water, joining a group, finishing a project.

We tend to think that thoughts and actions reflect needs, drives, motives, and goals. Since needs can be fulfilled in many ways, different people set different goals to satisfy the same needs. The incentive programs, job procedures, and hiring practices that make up an effective reward system must be able to meet the needs of the group which it is trying to "motivate to do a good job."

McClelland suggests that many motives are acquired as a product of past experience. As a result of his research on the need for achievement, he has formulated some ideas of what motive acquisition involves, and how it can be effectively promoted in adults. According to McClelland, the vast majority of successful executives and managers rank high on the personality characteristic he labels *n* achievement, regardless of their nationality or social status. He says that the businessman is not motivated by greed and self-interest, as many people believe, but instead, his success and prestige are a function of his high need for achievement. Characteristics of the high achiever include liking situations in which he is personally responsible for finding solutions to problems, and facing moderately tough goals so that calculated risks can be taken to accomplish them. A high *n* achiever, McClelland says, is always a little overextended, complains of overwork, and has more problems than he can deal with. After research in many countries, McClelland has devised a method for developing high *n* achievers.

Hunt and Hill talk about theories of worker or employee motivation. They begin by discussing the Maslow need theory and the Herzberg motivator-hygiene theory in some detail. Herzberg's theory states that certain job characteristics lead to job satisfaction, while different job characteristics lead to job dissatisfaction. Thus, in this theory, the presence of "motivators" or "satisfiers"—such as achievement, recognition, or the work itself—increase the satisfaction of the worker, while the absence of "hygiene" factors—such as job security, good pay, or good working conditions—lead to dissatisfaction. Hunt and Hill criticize both the Maslow and Herzberg theories as being incomplete, and then present an "expectancy" theory, developed by Vroom, which they believe to be the most complete theory of worker motivation. Expectancy theory simply suggests that individuals will choose behavioral alternatives that have the highest probability of yielding outcomes they prefer. Hunt and Hill conclude, on the basis of a good deal of research, that Vroom's model holds greater promise for predicting behavior in organizations than do the other theories they review. They then discuss the importance, in determining worker motivation, of the environment, the reward system, and the perception and attitudes of the workers—components all included in the Vroom model.

Schein takes a slightly different tack. He discusses the importance of designing the workplace and the reward structure in such a way that the individual's needs can be fulfilled. He also discusses the importance of an equitable exchange process for the channeling of worker motivation. The organizational environment, he states, is instrumental in determining whether or not the worker is motivated to accomplish the task. He points out the necessity of reciprocity in the rewards given to the individual for the performance he gives the organization. He also discusses the importance of the "psychological contract" as a major factor in gaining commitment, loyalty, and enthusiasm for the organization.

It may well be that there is no one best way to improve the motivation of the worker, though in all cases worker motivation is directly linked to worker performance and satisfaction. In part 5, "The Effect of the Organizational Environment on Individual and Group Behavior," we give many examples of motivation programs used in various large organizations.

Notes

1. 1972, p. 30.
2. 1956, p. 40.
3. 1943.

The Effect of Attitudes On Individual Performance

THE FUNCTIONAL APPROACH TO THE STUDY OF ATTITUDES

DANIEL KATZ

The study of opinion formation and attitude change is basic to an understanding of the public opinion process even though it should not be equated with this process. The public opinion process is one phase of the influencing of collective decisions, and its investigation involves knowledge of channels of communication, of the power structures of a society, of the character of mass media, of the relation between elites, factions and masses, of the role of formal and informal leaders, of the institutionalized access to officials. But the raw material out of which public opinion develops is to be found in the attitudes of individuals, whether they be followers or leaders and whether these attitudes be at the general level of tendencies to conform to legitimate authority or majority opinion or at the specific level of favoring or opposing the particular aspects of the issue under consideration. The nature of the organization of attitudes within the personality and the processes which account for attitude change are thus critical areas for the understanding of the collective product known as public opinion.

Early Approaches to the Study of Attitude and Opinion

There have been two main streams of thinking with respect to the determination of man's attitudes. The one tradition assumes an irrational model of man: specifically

Reprinted from *The Public Opinion Quarterly*. vol. 24, by permission of the publisher.

it holds that men have very limited powers of reason and reflection, weak capacity to discriminate, only the most primitive self-insight, and very short memories. Whatever mental capacities people do possess are easily overwhelmed by emotional forces and appeals to self-interest and vanity. The early books on the psychology of advertising, with their emphasis on the doctrine of suggestion, exemplify this approach. One expression of this philosophy is in the propagandist's concern with tricks and traps to manipulate the public. A modern form of it appears in *The Hidden Persuaders,* or the use of subliminal and marginal suggestion, or the devices supposedly employed by the "the Madison Avenue boys." Experiments to support this line of thinking started with laboratory demonstrations of the power of hypnotic suggestion and were soon extended to show that people would change their attitudes in an uncritical manner under the influence of the prestige of authority and numbers. For example, individuals would accept or reject the same idea depending upon whether it came from a positive or a negative prestige source.[1]

The second approach is that of the ideologist who invokes a rational model of man. It assumes that the human being has a cerebral cortex, that he seeks understanding, that he consistently attempts to make sense of the world about him, that he possesses discriminating and reasoning powers which will assert themselves over time, and that he is capable of self-criticism and self-insight. It relies heavily upon getting adequate information to people. Our educational system is based upon this rational model. The present emphasis upon the improvement of communication, upon developing more adequate channels of two-way communication, of conferences and institutes, upon bringing people together to interchange ideas, are all indications of the belief in the importance of intelligence and comprehension in the formation and change of men's opinions.

Now either school of thought can point to evidence which supports its assumptions, and can make fairly damaging criticisms of its opponent. Solomon Asch and his colleagues, in attacking the irrational model, have called attention to the biased character of the old experiments on prestige suggestion which gave the subject little opportunity to demonstrate critical thinking.[2] And further exploration of subjects in these stupid situations does indicate that they try to make sense of a nonsensical matter as far as possible. Though the same statement is presented by the experimenter to two groups, the first time as coming from a positive source and the second time as coming from a negative source, it is given a different meaning dependent upon the context in which it appears.[3] Thus the experimental subject does his best to give some rational meaning to the problem. On the other hand, a large body of experimental work indicates that there are many limitations in the rational approach in that people see their world in terms of their own needs, remember what they want to remember, and interpret information on the basis of wishful thinking. H. H. Hyman and P. Sheatsley have demonstrated that these experimental results have direct relevance to information campaigns directed at influencing public opinion.[4] These authors assembled facts about such campaigns and showed conclusively that increasing the flow of information to people does not necessarily increase the knowledge absorbed or produce the attitude changes desired.

The major difficulty with these conflicting approaches is their lack of specification of the conditions under which men do act as the theory would predict. For the facts are that people do act at times as if they had been decorticated and at times with intelligence and comprehension. And people themselves do recognize that on occasion they have behaved blindly, impulsively, and thoughtlessly. A second major difficulty is that the rationality-irrationality dimension is not clearly defined. At the extremes it is easy to point to examples, as in the case of the acceptance of stupid suggestions under emotional stress on the one hand, or brilliant problem solving on the other; but this does not provide adequate guidance for the many cases in the middle of the scale where one attempts to discriminate between rationalization and reason.

Reconciliation of the Conflict in a Functional Approach

The conflict between the rationality and irrationality models was saved from becoming a worthless debate because of the experimentation and research suggested by these models. The findings of this research pointed toward the elements of truth in each approach and gave some indication of the conditions under which each model could make fairly accurate predictions. In general the irrational approach was at its best where the situation imposed heavy restrictions upon search behavior and response alternatives. Where individuals must give quick responses without adequate opportunities to explore the nature of the problem, where there are very few response alternatives available to them, where their own deep emotional needs are aroused, they will in general react much as does the unthinking subject under hypnosis. On the other hand, where the individual can have more adequate commerce with the relevant environmental setting, where he has time to obtain more feedback from his reality testing, and where he has a number of realistic choices, his behavior will reflect the use of his rational faculties.[5] The child will often respond to the directive of the parent not by implicit obedience but by testing out whether or not the parent really meant what he said.

. . . The theory of psychological consonance, or cognitive balance, assumes that man attempts to reduce discrepancies in his beliefs, attitudes, and behavior by appropriate changes in these processes. While the emphasis here is upon consistency or logicality, the theory deals with all dissonances, no matter how produced. Thus they could result from irrational factors of distorted perception and wishful thinking as well as from rational factors of realistic appraisal of a problem and an accurate estimate of its consequences. Moreover, the theory would predict only that the individual will move to reduce dissonance, whether such movement is a good adjustment to the world or leads to the delusional systems of the paranoiac. In a sense, then, this theory would avoid the conflict between the old approaches of the rational and the irrational man by not dealing with the specific antecedent causes of behavior or with the particular ways in which the individual solves his problems.

In addition to the present preoccupation with the development of formal models concerned with cognitive balance and consonance, there is a growing interest in a more comprehensive framework for dealing with the complex variables and for bringing order within the field. . . . Another point of departure is represented by two groups of workers who have organized their theories around the functions which attitudes perform for the personality. Sarnoff, Katz, and McClintock, in taking this functional approach, have given primary attention to the motivational bases of attitudes and the processes of attitude change.[6] The basic assumption of this group is that both attitude formation and attitude change must be understood in terms of the needs they serve and that, as these motivational processes differ, so too will the conditions and techniques for attitude change. Smith, Bruner, and White have also analyzed the different functions which attitudes perform for the personality.[7] Both groups present essentially the same functions, but Smith, Bruner, and White give more attention to perceptual and cognitive processes and Sarnoff, Katz, and McClintock to the specific conditions of attitude change.

The importance of the functional approach is threefold. (1) Many previous studies of attitude change have dealt with factors which are not genuine psychological variables, for example, the effect on group prejudice of contact between two groups, or the exposure of a group of subjects to a communication in the mass media. Now contact serves different psychological functions for the individual and merely knowing that people have seen a movie or watched a television program tells us nothing about the personal values engaged or not engaged by such a presentation. If, however, we can gear our research to the functions attitudes perform, we can develop some generalizations about human behavior. Dealing with nonfunctional variables makes such generalization difficult, if not impossible.

(2) By concerning ourselves with the different functions attitudes can perform we can avoid the great error of oversimplification—the error of attributing a single cause to given types of attitude. It was once popular to ascribe radicalism in economic and political matters to the psychopathology of the insecure and to attribute conservatism to the rigidity of the mentally aged. At the present time it is common practice to see in attitudes of group prejudice the repressed hostilities stemming from childhood frustrations, though Hyman and Sheatsley have pointed out that prejudiced attitudes can serve a normative function of gaining acceptance in one's own group as readily as releasing unconscious hatred.[8] In short, not only are there a number of motivational forces to take into account in considering attitudes and behavior, but the same attitude can have a different motivational basis in different people.

(3) Finally, recognition of the complex motivational sources of behavior can help to remedy the neglect in general theories which lack specification of conditions under which given types of attitude will change. Gestalt theory tells us, for example, that attitudes will change to give better cognitive organization to the psychological field. This theoretical generalization is suggestive, but to carry out significant research we need some middle-level concepts to bridge the gap between a high level of abstraction and particularistic or phenotypical events. We need concepts that will point toward the types of motive and methods of motive satisfaction which are operative in bringing about cognitive reorganization.

Before we attempt a detailed analysis of the four major functions which attitudes can serve, it is appropriate to consider the nature of attitudes, their dimensions, and their relations to other psychological structures and processes.

Nature of Attitudes: Their Dimensions

Attitude is the predisposition of the individual to evaluate some symbol or object or aspect of his world in a favorable or unfavorable manner. Opinion is the verbal expression of an attitude, but attitudes can also be expressed in nonverbal behavior. Attitudes include both the affective, or feeling core of liking or disliking, and the cognitive, or belief, elements which describe the object of the attitude, its characteristics, and its relations to other objects. All attitudes thus include beliefs, but not all beliefs are attitudes. When specific attitudes are organized into a hierarchical structure, they comprise *value systems*. Thus a person may not only hold specific attitudes against deficit spending and unbalanced budgets but may also have a systematic organization of such beliefs and attitudes in the form of a value system of economic conservatism.

The dimensions of attitudes can be stated more precisely if the above distinctions between beliefs and feelings and attitudes and value systems are kept in mind. The *intensity* of an attitude refers to the strength of the *affective* component. In fact, rating scales and even Thurstone scales deal primarily with the intensity of feeling of the individual for or against some social object. The cognitive, or belief, component suggests two additional dimensions, the *specificity* or *generality* of the attitude and the *degree of differentiation* of the beliefs. Differentiation refers to the number of beliefs or cognitive items contained in the attitude, and the general assumption is that the simpler the attitude in cognitive structure the easier it is to change.[9] For simple structures there is no defense in depth, and once a single item of belief has been changed the attitude will change. A rather different dimension of attitude is the *number and strength of its linkages to a related value system*. If an attitude favoring budget balancing by the Federal government is tied in strongly with a value system of economic conservatism, it will be more difficult to change than if it were a fairly isolated attitude of the person. Finally, the relation of the value system to the personality is a consideration of first importance. If an attitude is tied to a value system which is closely related to, or which consists of, the individual's conception of himself, then the appropriate change procedures become more complex. The *centrality* of an attitude refers to its role as part of a value system which is closely related to the individual's self-concept.

An additional aspect of attitudes is not clearly described in most theories, namely, their relation to action or overt behavior. Though behavior related to the attitude has other determinants than the attitude itself, it is also true that some attitudes in themselves have more of what Cartwright calls an action structure than do others.[10] Brewster Smith refers to this dimension as policy orientation[11] and Katz and Stotland speak of it as the action component.[12] For example, while many people have attitudes of approval toward one or the other of the two political parties, these attitudes will differ in their structure with respect to relevant action. One man may be prepared to vote on election day and will know where and when he should vote and will go to the polls no matter what the weather or how great the inconvenience. Another man will only vote if a party worker calls for him in a car. Himmelstrand's work is concerned with all aspects of the relationship between attitude and behavior, but he deals with the action structure of the attitude itself by distinguishing between attitudes where the affect is tied to verbal expression and attitudes where the affect is tied to behavior concerned with more objective referents of the attitude.[13] In the first case an individual derives satisfaction from talking about a problem; in the second case he derives satisfaction from taking some form of concrete action.

Attempts to change attitudes can be directed primarily at the belief component or at the feeling, or affective, component. Rosenberg theorizes that an effective change in one component will result in changes in the other component and presents experimental evidence to confirm this hypothesis.[14] For example, a political candidate will often attempt to win people by making them like him and dislike his opponent, and thus communicate affect rather than ideas. If he is successful, people will not only like him but entertain favorable beliefs about him. Another candidate may deal primarily with ideas and hope that, if he can change people's beliefs about an issue, their feelings will also change.

Four Functions Which Attitudes Perform for the Individual

The major functions which attitudes perform for the personality can be grouped according to their motivational basis as follows:

1. *The instrumental, adjustive, or utilitarian function* upon which Jeremy Bentham and the utilitarians constructed their model of man. A modern expression of this approach can be found in behavioristic learning theory.

2. *The ego-defensive function* in which the person protects himself from acknowledging the basic truths about himself or the harsh realities in his external world. Freudian psychology and neo-Freudian thinking have been preoccupied with this type of motivation and its outcomes.

3. *The value-expressive function* in which the individual derives satisfactions from expressing attitudes appropriate to his personal values and to his concept of himself. This function is central to doctrines of ego psychology which stress the importance of self-expression, self-development, and self-realization.

4. *The knowledge function* based upon the individual's need to give adequate structure to his universe. The search for meaning, the need to understand, the trend toward better organization of perceptions and beliefs to provide clarity and consistency for the individual, are other descriptions of this function. The development of principles about perceptual and cognitive structure have been the contribution of Gestalt psychology.

Stated simply, the functional approach is the attempt to understand the reasons people hold the attitudes they do. The reasons, however, are at the level of psychological motivations and not of the accidents of external events and circumstances. Unless we know the psychological need which is met by the holding of an attitude we are in a poor position to predict when and how it will change. Moreover, the same attitude expressed toward a political candidate may not perform the same function for all the people who express it. And while many attitudes are predominantly in the service of a single type of motivational process, as described above, other attitudes may serve more than one purpose for the individual. A fuller discussion of how attitudes serve the above four functions is in order.

1. The adjustment function. Essentially this function is a recognition of the fact that people strive to maximize the rewards in their external environment and to minimize the penalties. The child develops favorable attitudes toward the objects in his world which are associated with the satisfactions of his needs and unfavorable attitudes toward objects which thwart him or punish him. Attitudes acquired in the service of the adjustment function are either the means for reaching the desired goal or avoiding the undesirable one, or are affective associations based upon experiences in attaining motive satisfactions.[15] The attitudes of the worker favoring a political party which will advance his economic lot are an example of the first type of utilitarian attitude. The pleasant image one has of one's favorite food is an example of the second type of utilitarian attitude.

In general, then, the dynamics of attitude formation with respect to the adjustment function are dependent upon present or past perceptions of the utility of the attitudinal object for the individual. The clarity, consistency, and nearness of rewards and punishments, as they relate to the individual's activities and goals, are important factors in the acquisition of such attitudes. Both attitudes and habits are formed toward specific objects, people, and symbols as they satisfy specific needs. The closer these objects are to actual need satisfaction and the more they are clearly perceived as relevant to need satisfaction, the greater are the probabilities of positive attitude formation. These principles of attitude formation are often observed in the breach rather than the compliance. In industry, management frequently expects to create favorable attitudes toward job performance through programs for making the company more attractive to the worker, such as providing recreational facilities and fringe benefits. Such programs, however, are much more likely to produce favorable attitudes toward the company as a desirable place to work than toward performance on the job. The company benefits and advantages are applied across the board to all employees and are not specifically relevant to increased effort in task performance by the individual worker.

Consistency of reward and punishment also contributes to the clarity of the instrumental object for goal attainment. If a political party bestows recognition and favors on party workers in an unpredictable and inconsistent fashion, it will destroy the favorable evaluation of the importance of working hard for the party among those whose motivation is of the utilitarian sort. But, curiously, while consistency of reward needs to be observed, 100 per cent consistency is not as effective as a pattern which is usually consistent but in which there are some lapses. When animal or human subjects are invariably rewarded for a correct performance, they do not retain their learned responses as well as when the reward is sometimes skipped.[16]

2. The ego-defensive function. People not only seek to make the most of their external world and what if offers, but they also expend a great deal of their energy on living with themselves. The mechanisms by which the individual protects his ego from his own unacceptable impulses and from the knowledge of threatening forces from without, and the methods by which he reduces his anxieties created by such problems, are known as mechanisms of ego defense. . . . They include the devices by which the individual avoids facing either the inner reality of the kind of person he is, or the outer reality of the dangers the world holds for him. They stem basically from internal conflict with its resulting insecurities. In one sense the mechanisms of defense are adaptive in temporarily removing the sharp edges of conflict and in saving the individual from complete disaster. In another sense they are not adaptive in that they handicap the individual in his social adjustments and in obtaining the maximum satisfactions available to him from the world in which he lives. The worker who persistently quarrels with his boss and with his fellow workers, because he is acting out some of his own internal conflicts, may in this manner relieve himself of some of the emotional tensions which beset him. He is not, however, solving his problem of adjusting to his work situation and thus may deprive himself of advancement or even of steady employment.

Defense mechanisms, Miller and Swanson point out, may be classified into two families on the basis of the more or less primitive nature of the devices employed.[17] The first family, more primitive in nature, are more socially handicapping and consist of denial and complete avoidance. The individual in such cases obliterates through withdrawal and denial the realities which confront him. The exaggerated case of such primitive mechanisms is the fantasy world of the paranoiac. The second type of defense is less handicapping and makes for distortion rather than denial. It includes rationalization, projection, and displacement.

Many of our attitudes have the function of defending our self-image. When we cannot admit to ourselves that we have deep feelings of inferiority we may project those feelings onto some convenient minority group and bolster our egos by attitudes of superiority toward this underprivileged group. The formation of such defensive attitudes differs in essential ways from the formation of attitudes which serve the adjustment function. They proceed from within the person, and the objects and situation to which they are attached are merely convenient outlets for their expression. Not all targets are equally satisfactory for a given defense mechanism, but the point is that the attitude is not created by the target but by the individual's emotional conflicts. And when no convenient target exists the individual will create one. Utilitarian attitudes, on the other hand, are formed with specific reference to the nature of the attitudinal object. They are thus appropriate to the nature of the social world to which they are geared. The high school student who values high grades because he wants to be admitted to a good college has a utilitarian attitude appropriate to the situation to which it is related.

All people employ defense mechanisms, but they differ with respect to the extent that they use them and some of their attitudes may be more defensive in function than others. It follows that the techniques and conditions for attitude change will not be the same for ego-defensive as for utilitarian attitudes.

Moreover, though people are ordinarily unaware of their defense mechanisms, especially at the time of employing them, they differ with respect to the amount of insight they may show at some later time about their use of defenses. In some cases they recognize that they have been protecting their egos without knowing the reason why. In other cases they may not even be aware of the devices they have been using to delude themselves.

3. The value-expressive function. While attitudes have the function of preventing the individual from revealing to himself and others his true nature, other attitudes have the function of giving positive expression to his central values and to the type of person he conceives himself to be. A man may consider himself to be an enlightened conservative or an internationalist or a liberal, and will hold attitudes which are the appropriate indication of his central values. Thus we need to take account of the fact that not all behavior has the negative function of reducing the tensions of biological drives or of internal conflicts. Satisfactions also accrue to the person from the expression of attitudes which reflect his cherished beliefs and his self-image. The reward to the person in these instances is not so much a matter of gaining social recognition or monetary rewards as of establishing his self-identity and confirming his notion of the sort of person he sees himself to be. The gratifications obtained from value expression may go beyond the confirmation of self-identity. Just as we find satisfaction in the exercise of our talents and abilities, so we find reward in the expression of any attributes associated with our egos.

Value-expressive attitudes not only give clarity to the self-image but also mold that self-image closer to the heart's desire. The teenager who by dress and speech establishes his identity as similar to his own peer group may appear to the outsider a weakling and a craven conformer. To himself he is asserting his independence of the adult world to which he has rendered childlike subservience and conformity all his life. Very early in the development of the personality the need for clarity of self-image is important—the need to know "who I am." Later it may be even more important to know that in some measure I am the type of person I want to be. Even as adults, however, the clarity and stability of the self-image is of primary significance. Just as the kind, considerate person will cover over his acts of selfishness, so too will the ruthless individualist become confused and embarrassed by his acts of sympathetic compassion. One reason it is difficult to change the character of the adult is that he is not comfortable with the new "me." Group support for such personality change is almost a necessity, as in Alcoholics Anonymous, so that the individual is aware of approval of his new self by people who are like him.

The socialization process during the formative years sets the basic outlines for the individual's self-concept. Parents constantly hold up before the child the model of the good character they want them to be. A good boy eats his spinach, does not hit girls, etc. The candy and the stick are less in evidence in training the child than the constant appeal to his notion of his own character. It is small wonder, then, that children reflect the acceptance of this model by inquiring about the characters of the actors in every drama, whether it be a television play, a political contest, or a war, wanting to know who are the "good guys" and who are the "bad guys." Even as adults we persist in labeling others in the terms of such character images. Joe McCarthy and his cause collapsed in fantastic fashion when the telecast of the Army hearings showed him in the role of the villain attacking the gentle, good man represented by Joseph Welch.

A related but somewhat different process from childhood socialization takes place when individuals enter a new group or organization. The individual will often take over and internalize the values of the group. What accounts, however, for the fact that sometimes this occurs and sometimes it does not? Four factors are probably operative, and some combination of them may be necessary for internalization. (1) The values of the new group may be highly consistent with existing values central to the personality. The girl who enters the nursing profession finds it congenial to consider herself a good nurse because of previous values of the importance of contributing to the welfare of others. (2) The new group may in its ideology have a clear model of what the good group member should be like and may persistently indoctrinate group members in these terms. One of the reasons for the code of conduct for members of the armed forces, devised after the revelations about the conduct of American prisoners in the Korean War, was to attempt to establish a model for what a good soldier does and does not do. (3) The activities of the group in moving toward its goal permit the individual genuine opportunity for participation. To become ego-involved so that he can internalize group values, the new member must find one of two conditions. The group activity open to him must tap his talents and abilities so that his chance to show what he is worth can be tied into the group effort. Or else the activities of the group must give him an active voice in group decisions. His particular talents and abilities may not be tapped but he does have the opportunity to enter into group decisions, and thus his need for self-determination is satisfied. He then identifies with the group in which such opportunities for ego-involvement are available. It is not necessary that opportunities for self-expression and self-determination be of great magnitude in an objective sense, so long as they are important for the psychological economy of the individuals themselves. (4) Finally, the individual may come to see himself as a group member if he can share in the rewards of group activity which includes his own efforts. The worker may not play much of a part in building a ship or make any decisions in the process of building it. Nevertheless, if he and his fellow workers are given a share in every boat they build and a return on the proceeds from the earnings of the ship, they may soon come to identify with the ship-building company and see themselves as builders of ships.

4. The knowledge function. Individuals not only acquire beliefs in the interest of satisfying various specific needs, they also seek knowledge to give meaning to what would otherwise be an unorganized chaotic universe. People need standards or frames of reference for understanding their world, and attitudes help to supply such standards. The problem of understanding, as John Dewey made clear years ago, is one "of introducing (1) *definiteness* and *distinction* and (2) *consistency* and *stability* of meaning into what is otherwise vague and wavering."[18] The definiteness and stability are provided in good measure by the norms of our culture, which give the otherwise perplexed individual ready-made attitudes for comprehending his universe. Walter Lippmann's classical contribution to the study of opinions and attitudes was his description of stereotypes and the way they provided order and clarity for a bewildering set of complexities.[19] The most interesting finding in Herzog's familiar study of the gratifications obtained by housewives in listening to daytime serials was the unsuspected role of information and advice.[20] The stories were liked "because they explained things to the inarticulate listener."

The need to know does not of course imply that people are driven by a thirst for universal knowledge. The American public's appalling lack of political information has been documented many times. In 1956, for example, only 13 per cent of the people in Detroit could correctly name the two United States Senators from the state of Michigan and only 18 per cent knew the name of their own Congressman. People are not avid seekers after knowledge as judged by what the educator or social reformer would desire. But they do want to understand the events which impinge directly on their own life. Moreoever, many of the attitudes they have already acquired give them sufficient basis for interpreting much of what they perceive to be important for them. Our already existing stereotypes, in Lippmann's language, "are an ordered, more or less consistent picture of the world, to which our habits, our tastes, our capacities, our comforts, and our hopes have adjusted themselves. They may not be a complete picture of the world, but they are a picture of a possible world to which we are adapted."[21] It follows that new information will not modify old attitudes unless there is some inadequacy or incompleteness or inconsistency in the existing attitudinal structure as it relates to the perceptions of new situations.

Notes and References

1. Muzater Sherif, *The Psychology of Social Norms*, New York, Harper, 1936.

2. Solomon E. Asch, *Social Psychology*, New York, Prentice-Hall, 1952

3. *Ibid.*, pp. 426-427. The following statement was attributed to its rightful author, John Adams, for some subjects and to Karl Marx for others: "those who hold and those who are without property have ever formed distinct interests in society." When the statement was attributed to Marx, this type of comment appeared: "Marx is stressing the need for redistribution of wealth." When it was attributed to Adams, this comment appeared: "The social division is innate in mankind."

4. Herbert H. Hyman and Paul B. Sheatsley, "Some Reasons Why Information Campaigns Fail," *Public Opinion Quarterly*, Vol. II, 1947, pp. 413-423.

5. William A. Scott points out that in the area of international relations the incompleteness and remoteness of the information and the lack of pressures on the individual to defend his views results in inconsistencies. Inconsistent elements with respect to a system of international beliefs may, however, be consistent with the larger system of the personality. "Rationality and Non-rationality of International Attitudes," *Journal of Conflict Resolution*, Vol. 2, 1958 pp. 9-16.

6. Irving Sarnoff and Daniel Katz, "The Motivational Bases of Attitude Change," *Journal of Abnormal and Social Psychology*, Vol. 49, 1954, pp. 115-124.

7. M. Brewster Smith, Jerome S. Bruner, and Robert W. White, *Opinions and Personality*, New York, Wiley, 1956.

8. Herbert H. Hyman and Paul B. Sheatsley, "The Authoritarian Personality: A Methodological Critique," in Richard Christie and Marie Jahoda, editors, *Studies in the Scope and Method of the Authoritarian Personality*, Glencoe, Ill., Free Press, 1954, pp. 50-122.

9. David Krech and Richard S. Crutchfield, *Theory and Problems of Social Psychology*, New York, McGraw-Hill, 1948, pp. 160-163.

10. Dorwin Cartwright, "Some Principles of Mass Persuasion," *Human Relations*, Vol. 2, 1949, pp. 253-267.

11. M. Brewster Smith, "The Personal Setting of Public Opinions: A Study of Attitudes toward Russia," *Public Opinion Quarterly*, Vol. II, 1947, pp. 507-523.

12. Daniel Katz and Ezra Stotland, "A Preliminary Statement to a Theory of Attitude Structure and Change," in Sigmund Koch, Editor, *Psychology: A Study of a Science*, Vol. 3, New York, McGraw-Hill, 1959, pp. 423-475.

13. See pages 224-250 of this issue of the *Quarterly*.

14. See pages 319-340 of this issue of the *Quarterly*.

15. Katz and Stotland, *op.cit.*, pp. 434-443.

16. William O. Jenkins and Julian C. Stanley, "Partial Reinforcement: A Review and Critique," *Psychological Bulletin*, Vol. 47, 1950, pp. 193-234.

17. Daniel R. Miller and Guy E. Swanson, *Inner Conflict and Defense*, New York, Holt, 1960, pp. 194-288.

18. John Dewey, *How We Think*, New York, Macmillan, 1910.

19. Walter Lippmann, *Public Opinion*, New York, Macmillan, 1922.

20. Herta Herzog, "What Do We Really Know about Daytime Serial Listeners?" in Paul F. Lazarsfeld and Frank N. Stanton, editors, *Radio Research 1942-1943*, New York, Duell &Pearce, 1944, pp. 3-33.

21. Lippmann, *op.cit.*, p. 95.

ATTITUDES

LEON MANN

Attitudes and Consistency Theory

In the examination of the relationship between components of attitudes and between attitudes and behaviour, it was noted that although the person strives to maintain consistency between these elements, apparent contradictions often occur. As well as the internal structure of attitudes there is the question of structure of attitude systems, clusters of attitudes about a set of related social objects which fit together in an interconnected, integrated whole. For example, attitudes toward Soviet Russia, the UN, President Nasser, Israel and war belong together in a closely-knit system. Attitudes toward virginity, pre-marital intercourse, birth control and the contraceptive pill also co-exist in one system. Interest lies in the extent to which there is consistency between attitudes in a cognitive system, what happens if attitudes become inconsistent with one another, and how adjustments are made to restore the system to consistency.

In seeking answers to these questions, a number of theories of "cognitive" consistency will be examined. The reference is not to attitudinal consistency but to the more generic cognitive consistency. This is because of concern with cognition in the broadest sense, the image or map of the world held by the person which includes thoughts, values and actions as well as attitudes about some object or set of events. At the core of cognitive consistency is the need to attain harmony and congruity between cognitions of objects and persons in the environment. Here are some examples of inconsistent cognitions relating to the realm of attitudes. Fred is secretary of the League of Animal Lovers and yet I know that Fred savagely beats his dog; I believe that the Nazi Party should be banned yet I support every appeal held by the Nazi Party; I know that smoking causes lung cancer and yet I smoke four packets of cigarettes a day. Each of these three sets of cognitions is disturbing and tension arousing because their elements do not fit together. How can the world be logical, meaningful and stable if animal lovers beat their dogs, if I support my enemies and if my favourite habit is killing me? These examples are overwrought and far-fetched, but they give some flavour of what is meant by cognitive inconsistency.

Consider a miniature system in which all of the cognitive elements are consistent as far as the person is concerned (see Figure 1). Imagine that you are the person in this example. You like Joe very much, and he admires the same things you admire (the church) and dislikes what you dislike (Fred and socialism). You are pleased that the church is also against socialism and it is satisfying to know that Fred is for socialism because it justifies your dislike of him. This system is harmonious and consistent. Now suppose that you receive information that throws the entire system into turmoil. You learn that Joe is secretly an ardent socialist, or you discover that Joe has been inviting Fred over for drinks, or that Fred really despises socialism, or, worse still, that your church is now in favour of socialism. It is clear that these new bits of information represent cognitions that are inconsistent with the cognitions you already hold and a state of tension and discomfort results. However, it is not likely that matters will be left that way for very long. Modifications will occur in your feelings and beliefs that are directed toward the restoration of consistency or equilibrium. For example, you might start to like Fred and dislike Joe, or become attracted to socialism, or antagonistic toward the church. To a great extent the loci of these changes would depend upon the strength and degree of interrelatedness of each of the attitudes and beliefs. In general, the weaker, more isolated attitudes are the first to change in the move to restore consistency, but reverberations occur right through the system and it is possible for all cognitions to be changed.

Figure 1. Schematic representation of a miniature cognitive system in which the relationships between each of the elements (socialism, church, Fred, and Joe) are consistent. An unbroken line between two elements represents a positive relationship (support, liking, admiration, etc.). A broken line represents a negative relationship (antagonism, disliking, etc.). Arrows indicate direction of the relationship.

The consistency motive can exert a powerful force in attitude systems influencing the person to make various aspects of his cognitive functioning consistent with one another. There are a number of theories which deal with this problem. All of the theoretical models to be discussed deal with changes toward the restoration of consistency, though they often focus on different modes and specify different theoretical determinants of resolution. All models have as their starting point the consistency principle, though the theorists use different terms, *e.g.*, Heider (1958) talks about "balance", Osgood and Tannenbaum (1955) deal with "symmetry", and Festinger (1957) prefers the term "consonance" to designate much the same state of harmony or equilibrium. Although these models have a good deal in common there are also critical differences among them.

Heider's Balance Principle

The earliest and simplest formulation of the consistency principle is found in Heider's (1958) balance theory. He deals with states of balance and imbalance which exist between three elements: the person (P), another person (O), and some object, idea or issue (X). What are the attitudes of two friends, P and O, toward issue X? A balanced state exists when their attitudes toward the issue are similar, *i.e.*, they both like or both dislike the attitude object. If one of them likes X but the other dislikes it, there will be imbalance, and the resultant feelings of strain will induce pressures toward change in the direction of balance. For example, there may be a falling out between the friends, or they might try to persuade each other to adopt a common harmonious attitude toward the issue. Note that there are three relations in this simple triadic system: P's attitude toward O, P's attitude toward X, and O's attitude toward X. In formal terms, a balanced state would exist if all three relations among P, O, and X were positive, or if two were negative and one positive. An example of the former state: the person admires Churchill and loves cigars; he is delighted that Churchill also loves cigars. An example of the latter: President Nasser (in 1956) despised Jordan and hated Israel; he then assumed that Jordan and Israel liked each other. Feather (1956), an Australian psychologist, has extended and applied Heider's balance principle to the study of communication effects. In his research Feather investigates the relationship between four elements in a communication structure: a *source* presents a *message* about an *issue* to a *receiver*. It was found that when subjects are given hypothetical communication situations, they tend to predict outcomes which represent a state of balance between four elements.

Although it offers a promising start for the analysis of cognitive consistency the balance principle is limited in its scope. Consideration of some novel social contexts and relationships reveal the limitations of the balance principle. If two men were both in love with the same woman would they necessarily have positive attitudes toward each other? If you like chickens and chickens like chicken feed, should you also like chicken feed? Perhaps the balance principle's greatest weakness is its failure to specify the exact location and precise magnitude of attitude change that will occur to restore balance and harmony in a system.

Osgood and Tannenbaum's Congruity Principle

This principle is based on the assumption that it is simpler to hold congruent attitudes toward two related objects, such as President Eisenhower and golf, than to have varying attitudes toward them. The congruity principle goes further than the principle of balance because it makes explicit quantitative predictions about what will happen if the two related objects are not in a state of congruity. For example, a person who has a lukewarm attitude toward Eisenhower and is enthusiastic about golf learns that Eisenhower is a golf fanatic. This person will become more favour-able toward Eisenhower and perhaps slightly less enthusiastic about golf, so that the intensities of the two attitudes shift together. Congruity exists when two related objects are evaluated with equal intensity. In the Eisenhower-golf example the person's wishy-washy attitude toward Eisenhower will shift more than his extreme evaluation of golf because highly "polarized" or extreme attitudes change less than moderate ones. Experimental evidence (*e.g.*, Osgood   Tannenbaum, 1955) provides support for the congruity principle although, like the balance principle, there are limitations to the scope of its operation.

Festinger's Dissonance Theory

The most provocative of the consistency principles has been put forward by Festinger (1957) in his theory of cognitive dissonance. If the person has cognitions about himself or his environment that are inconsistent with each other, *i.e.*, if one cognition implies the opposite of the other, a state of cognitive dissonance exists. Here are four cases of cognitive dissonance arising from each of the principal sources of inconsistency.

(a) Logical inconsistency: I believe there will be a man on the moon by 1970; I think it is impossible to get a device to leave earth's atmosphere.

(b) Cultural mores and norms: I believe it is wrong to burp at formal dinners; I burp at formal dinners.

(c) Opinion inconsistent with action: I believe that the League to Clothe Animals is a hare-brained outfit; I support every appeal sponsored by the League.

(d) Past experience: I always feel pain when I am pricked with a needle; I have just been pricked but I feel no pain.

The state of cognitive dissonance is uncomfortable because it arouses psycholog-ical tension and therefore attempts are made to reduce it by changing either or both cognitions or by adding new cognitions. In the examples above I could modify or add cognitions as follows: *(a)* they will no doubt bring the earth closer to the moon; *(b)* I will no longer burp at formal dinners; *(c)* supporting the L.C.A. is good for my income tax deductions; and *(d)* I sometimes feel pain when I am pricked with a needle. The breadth and scope of dissonance theory is best demonstrated by surveying some of the major sources of dissonance that have been studied experi-mentally.

Unforeseen Negative Consequences

The person who discovers after he has made a choice that it has many negative features is plunged into a state of cognitive dissonance; if he has suffered a great deal for his choice the magnitude of dissonance is very great and attempts are made to reduce it by looking for positive features of the choice. Aronson and Mills (1959) induced dissonance in female students by requiring them to undergo a severe initia-tion ceremony before they were allowed to join a discussion group on sex. One group of girls underwent a mild initiation ceremony in the form of an "embar-rassment" test in which they had to read alone a list of sex-related words such as "prostitute", "virgin", and "petting". The other group, however, was put through a much more severe and demanding test in which they had to read aloud twelve obscene words and two vivid descriptions of sexual activity. All subjects were told that they had passed the test and could join the group. For their first "group" meeting the subjects were allowed to listen to a long and dull tape-recorded discussion about secondary sex behaviour in the lower animals. Finally the subjects were asked to indicate how good they thought the discussion was and how much they liked the members of the group. It was found that those subjects who underwent the severe initiation for the privilege of listening to a dull disappointing discussion reported the group and its discussion to be quite interesting. This suggests that the dissonance aroused by the painful embarrassing test was reduced by seeing the cause for which the individual suffered as worthwhile. Girls who underwent the mild initiation ceremony, and therefore suffered less dissonance, were far more critical and negative in their attitudes to the boring group discussion.

Disconfirmed Expectancies

The person may have prepared himself psychologically for an event that never eventuates, and, worse still, may have even made public his predictions about the event. What happens when an important prophecy fails and dissonance is aroused between what was predicted and what actually occurred is described in the classic field study carried out by Festinger, Riecken and Schachter (1956). In the mid-1950s Mrs. Marion Keech, a suburban housewife, began to receive messages from outer space. Americans and Canadians were intrigued because Mrs. Keech claimed that the message foretold an impending flood that would inundate all of North America on December 21. The publicity given to Mrs. Keech and her messages attracted a small following of believers, as well as Festinger, Riecken and Schachter, who infiltrated the group in order to see how Mrs. Keech would react on December 22. On December 20 Mrs. Keech received a message informing her that the group should be ready to receive a visitor who would arrive at midnight to transport all of them on a flying saucer to the safety of outer space. Midnight came, but no visitor arrived, and the predicted flood was less than seven hours away. Gradually despair and confusion descended upon the group, and Mrs. Keech broke down and began to cry bitterly. The messages were read and reread in case some clue had been overlooked. One explanation after another of the visitor's failure to appear was considered and rejected. Then at 4.45 A.M. Mrs. Keech called the group together and announced she had received a message. In the style of an Old Testament prophet she announced that God had saved the world from destruction because the little group, sitting all night long, had spread so much light that it, and not water, was now flooding the Earth.

Mrs. Keech handled the dissonance existing between the drastic prophecy and the mundane reality by providing a rationalization for the discrepancy between the two. But she also had to deal with the widespread publicity she had received in the mass media. One way of reducing dissonance is to seek the support of others; if others provide social support the individual is better able to convince himself that his belief was correct. Mrs. Keech and the believers, who had been rather shy of publicity before the disconfirmation, now became insatiable publicity seekers and carried out active attempts at proselytization in order to swell the numbers of supporters. In case one is tempted to feel smug about Mrs. Keech's disconfirmed expectancy, it is appropriate to point out that social psychologists also suffer the dissonance of disconfirmed expectations. In 1960, Hardyck and Braden (1962) investigated a group of "faithful" evangelists who prophesied a widespread nuclear disaster on August 15. The disaster did not eventuate but neither did the group seek publicity or social support for their beliefs. Other prophets of doom, completely out of touch with reality, apparently suffer little dissonance when their expectancies are disconfirmed. Thomas Beverly, rector of Lilley, in Hertfordshire, England in the late 17th century was totally immune to cognitive dissonance. In 1695 Beverly wrote a book predicting that the world would end in 1697. In 1698 he wrote a second book complaining that the world had ended in 1697 but that nobody had noticed. It is clear that disconfirmed expectancies may lead to a variety of reactions, not all of them directed toward the reduction of dissonance. It seems that the good people of Hertfordshire have a penchant for prophecy. A religious society placed an advertisement in the local newspaper on Monday, December 9, 1968: "The world is definitely coming to an end on Wednesday December 11, at noon precisely. A full report will appear in this newspaper next Friday . . .''.

Forced Compliance and Insufficient Justification

Imagine that you were a subject in an experiment where you spent over an hour performing an extremely boring and tedious task, such as crossing out fives and sevens in columns of digits. Suppose that after this monotonous hour the experimenter offered you one dollar to help him tell a lie about the task to the next subject waiting to take part in the experiment. The lie involved telling the next subject that the task was extremely interesting. If you agreed to do it, would your private attitude toward the boring task be affected by your objectionable behaviour? Festinger and Carlsmith (1959), who carried out such an experiment, assumed that if a person is induced to say or do something opposite to his private attitude (*i.e.*, say that something is interesting when he really believes it is boring), he suffers feelings of dissonance. One way to reduce the dissonance is to bring attitudes toward the task into line with the act, *i.e.*, to start to believe that the task really is quite interesting. But Festinger and Carlsmith were particularly concerned with the effect of the monetary reward offered to induce the dissonant act of lying. They compared attitudes held toward the boring task by two groups of subjects. One group (like youself) was offered one dollar to tell the lie; the other received the fabulous sum of twenty dollars. They argued that if a person received twenty dollars for telling a lie there is very little dissonance between his act and his belief about the task because he can rationalize that twenty dollars is too much to turn down, and he can afford to see the task for what it really was, dull, boring and monotonous; but if he received a mere one dollar for doing something objectionable he can only ease his extreme feelings of dissonance by rationalizing that perhaps the task was quite interesting. Indeed Festinger and Carlsmith found that subjects given twenty dollars to tell the lie showed fewer positive attitudes toward the task than subjects given one dollar.

The dissonance principle leads to the paradoxical postulate that if a person is given only a few inducements for engaging in behaviour that is discrepant with his attitudes, then subsequent dissonance-reducing attitude change will be greater than if a large inducement is offered. This postulate has aroused a considerable amount of controversy and attempts have been made to interpret Festinger and Carlsmith's findings in terms of the suspicion, anxiety, incredulity and resentment that can be aroused when a hard-up college student is offered all of twenty dollars for telling a very small lie.

Unforeseen negative consequences, disconfirmed expectancies and insufficient justification for forced compliance are but three of the sources of inconsistency dealt with by dissonance theory. Exposure to discrepant information and facts that contradict what is already known is another source of inconsistency. . . . It will be seen that, following decisions which involve a choice between two equally prized or despised alternatives, the individual often experiences the discomfort of dissonance. He may attempt to reduce postdecision dissonance by seeking out supportive consonant information about his choice. Alternatively, he may choose to expose himself equally to both dissonant and consonant information if it has utility, but still may be more critical of the dissonant material (Feather, 1963).

Balance, congruity and dissonance are three versions of the consistency principle, sharing the assumption that perceptions, actions and attitudes maintain close and harmonious relationships with one another. Each version emphasizes the structure of attitude elements and how disharmony in the structure leads to a change in the system. Their significance for attitude change is an understanding of how new information which produces a disturbance in the attitude system sets into motion a set of processes, which, in turn, lead to a restoration of consistency and harmony in the system. Balance and congruity are the most limited in their application because they deal with situations in which there is disharmony in cognitions and discrepancies in evaluations of related objects. Dissonance, on the other hand, is much broader in scope; it focuses on discrepancies between elements of knowledge and action as a source of inconsistency, and accordingly has a great deal to say about cognitive processes in general, in addition to attitude change. The consistency principle, although an important factor in attitudinal dynamics, is not universally dominant; high tolerance for ambiguity, immunity to psychological tension and preference for novelty and complexity are factors which sometimes outweigh the need for consistency.

Social Influence: The Attitude Change Process

How is an individual influenced by the attempts of another person or group to change his opinions? Social influence is not a uniform process and does not follow a single principle. Kelman (1961), for example, has distinguished between three traditional approaches to this problem: (a) social influence on judgement and opinion stemming from pressures to conformity, (b) social influence arising from interaction in small primary groups, such as the family and peer group, and (c) social influence stemming from persuasive communications delivered by prestigious sources. The separation of these different origins of influence is important because each has its unique psychological basis and special consequences for attitude change. For Kelman, each of the three approaches corresponds to a unique process of social influence with its own distinct characteristics.

First, in the process labelled *compliance,* the individual accepts influence because he hopes to achieve a favourable reaction from another person or group. In face-to-face situations, where an individual is put under group pressure to adopt an opinion or judgement which is contrary to what he believes, yielding to the influence attempt is based on a desire to conform to the expectations of others in order to receive rewards or avoid punishments. This is an instance of compliance in which the opinion is adopted publicly without actual inner acceptance. As soon as the group releases its pressure on the individual he reverts to his initial opinion. Perhaps the best example of this kind of compliance is the temporary collaboration elicited in POWs of the communist Chinese during the Korean war.

A second influence process is labelled *identification*, and it occurs when an individual adopts the attitudes of a group because his relationship with the person or group is satisfying and forms part of his self-image. The small primary group with which the individual is closely affiliated exerts a special kind of social influence. Many basic attitudes have their source and support in these groups and reflect their norms, values and beliefs. This is normative social influence stemming from reference groups with which the person is closely identified. Family interactions are the source of the earliest and most potent influences on attitudes. Parents transfer to their children their own opinions, prejudices and preferences through the process of identification, the taking on of the attributes of another. Political and religious beliefs, prejudice and voting behaviour are remarkably homogeneous within families. Together with the family, the school stands out as the central and dominant force in the socialization of political and ideological beliefs in the young child. Even during the years at college, group norms influence the development of attitudes toward important public issues, as has been shown in Newcomb's classic Bennington Study (1958). Although such attitudes are the earliest and are often learned with a high degree of emotional involvement, they are maintained only so long as the relationship to parents and peers is rewarding and satisfying. The rewards which come from accepting normative influence, having the "right" attitudes in the group, include status, recognition, support and acceptance. Adhering to group norms also provides reassurance and the satisfaction of knowing that one is not alone in holding an opinion, an important factor in opinions that are deeply rooted in considerations of social definition and reality. The philosopher Santayana (1922) expresses this idea in his pointed aphorism: "Man is a gregarious animal, and much more so in his mind than in his body. He may like to go alone for a walk, but hates to stand alone in his opinions"(p. 174).

The third process of social influence is *internalization*. Attitude-related information is contained in persuasive communications delivered by reliable and trustworthy sources. Influence is accepted because the persuasive inputs fit in with the individual's value system and produce intrinsic satisfaction. The central idea in this approach is that an opinion or attitude becomes accepted because its adoption and expression lead to actual or anticipated feelings of satsifaction and self-approval.

A group of social psychologists at Yale University (Hovland, Janis & Kelley, 1953) has been closely identified with experimental research which investigates the characteristics of an relationships between the communicator, the message transmitted and the audience (recipient) in the attitude-change process. These variables closely parallel the well-known persuasion formula of "who says what to whom and with what effect".

Some of the major findings of the Yale group will be summarized to give an idea of the scope of the work that has been carried out on the persuasion process. The communicator is more likely to induce attitude change if his credibility (*i.e.*, trustworthiness and expertise) is high; if the communicator advocates a great deal of attitude change he will be more successful up to a point than if he advocates a small amount of change. The way in which a persuasive communication is worded, organized and presented is an important determinant of its reception. If there are two sides to an issue, then a two-sided communication in which both pros and cons are mentioned will be more effective than a one-sided communication for it "innoculates" the audience against later counter-propaganda. If, as in a debate, there are two opposing viewpoints to be communicated, the more effective communication is the first one. If the issues are so complex that the audience is not likely to draw the desired conclusion, the communication will be more effective if a conclusion is drawn for them. Emotional appeals that arouse fear or aggression are more effective with low-intelligence, ignorant people than with well-informed people, but they may boomerang and lead to defensive reactions that prevent acceptance of the message. Finally, among an audience, some people are more susceptible to persuasion than others. In general, women are more persuasible than men; social isolates and people who suffer feelings of low self-esteem are also highly persuasible. Passive listening to, or reading of, the communication is not as effective as role playing, *i.e.*, active participation in rehearsing and improvising arguments in support of the desired attitude. People who experience success or receive approval for their role-playing efforts, or for the position they advocate in the role play, are more likely to adopt the new attitude than those who are not rewarded.

The psychology of persuasive communications has antecedents in the art of rhetoric, essentially the art of persuasion, which flourished during the Roman and Greek Empires. The best account of the development of the art is Aristotle's *Rhetoric*. The political speaker is cautioned to advise what appears to be good. He must understand the audience, knowing what provokes anger, admiration and shame. Clarity is preferred, although a sprinkling of metaphors and figures of speech is permissible. The work of the Yale group on the persuasion process has been regarded as a kind of scientific rhetoric because of its similarity to the ancient art of propagating opinion, and because of its basis in scientifically-established principles.

In this brief discussion of social influence on attitude change a distinction was made between three ways in which social interaction produces modification of opinions and beliefs: compliance following direct pressure to conformity, adherence to group norms because of identification, and internalization stemming from the receipt of persuasive communications in a social relationship. In most social influence situations it is not easy to disentangle the three types since they may function co-jointly. The conceptual distinction, however, has implications for the consequences of any attempt to modify attitudes. One of the most bothersome problems in the area of social influence is the short life of some attitude changes. A seemingly impressive modification of opinion dissipates rapidly soon after the influence attempt and the influence agent becomes bewildered by the apparent display of instability. Recognition that social influence entails different motive patterns helps explain the short-lived nature of some changes in attitude and the relative permanence of others. Pressures to compliance and conformity can rarely be sustained for a long time. For example, in prisoner-of-war camps, as soon as control over the individual lapses he reverts to his own private opinion, an opinion that was never really relinquished. Group norms relevant to attitudes are followed only so long as the individual's relationship to the group remains satisfying or the tension of having a unique opinion cannot be tolerated. If the group outlives its usefulness to the individual, or if a hostile, negative relationship between individual and group develops, the norm-oriented opinion is also discarded. Finally, attitude change produced by a credible persuasive communication persists only as long as the values relevant to the attitude are maintained. In line with the cognitive consistency principle, if the attitude or elements of it become inconsistent with fundamental values regarding the issue, it becomes redundant and is rapidly discarded. An example is found in the large swings and fluctuations in attitudes toward the Vietnam War as information regarding the course and consequences of the war became available to the public.

The mass media of radio, television and newspapers, although they can be "switched off" when something unpalatable to belief is presented, also exert a powerful influence on the public. Often this influence is not direct, but is mediated by opinion leaders, key high-status people in the community who are particularly attentive monitors of the mass media, and who interpret and relay information to their circle of friends and colleagues. In what has been called the "two-step flow of communication", information and ideas flow from the mass media to local community and neighbourhood opinion leaders, and from opinion leaders by word of mouth to rank-and-file members of the community. In the area of intergroup attitudes and relations, direct and enforced contact such as is entailed in working and living together is another medium for modifying attitudes. Contacts between members of various groups, such as Aborigines and whites, are most likely to lead to positive attitude change when the contacts are on a basis of equal social status; when cooperative effort is required to perform a joint task, as in the armed services, a ship or a department store; and when the contact is of sufficient duration to enable mutually satisfying experiences to occur.

Perhaps the most dramatic and least-understood form of attitude change is the sudden conversion which follows some unusual, shocking or painful experience. Stagner (1948) has termed this condition of attitude change "trauma", and illustrates its dynamics with reference to the attraction of some Russian leaders to communism. Such instances of sudden conversion, although unusual, merit closer investigation because of the insights they may yield about the process of belief change. Another illustration of the way in which a brief, dramatic experience is capable of undermining resistance to attitude change is provided in studies of emotional role playing and its use in the modification of smoking habits. In an experiment by Janis and Mann (1965), female college students, all of them heavy smokers, were required to play-act the role of a medical patient suffering from the harmful consequences of cigarette smoking. The experimenter, in the role of "physician", gave each "patient" some "bad news"; a supposed X-ray examination had revealed lung cancer and immediate surgery was necessary. During the spontaneous interchange between "physician" and "patient" additional fear-arousing information was introduced about the pain and risk of surgery, post-operative procedures and the smoking-cancer link. The experience was so realistic and disquieting that almost all of the girls quit or drastically modified their smoking habits after the role-play session, and when followed up 18 months later continued to report a significant decrease in smoking behaviour (Mann & Janis, 1968).

Even within the confines of a laboratory it is possible to develop ego-involving real-life situations which trigger off impressive changes in attitudes and behaviour. . . .

References

Aronson, E., and Mills, J., "The Effect of Severity of Initiation on Liking for a Group," *Journal of Abnormal and Social Psychology*, 1959, 59, 177-181.

Feather, N.T., "Cognitive Dissonance, Sensitivity, and Evaluation," *Journal of Abnormal and Social Psychology*, 1963, 66, 157-163.

Feather, N.T., "A Structural Balance Model of Evaluative Behavior," *Human Relations*, 1965, 18, 171-185.

Festinger, L., and Carlsmith, J.M., "Cognitive Consequences of Forced Compliance," *Journal of Abnormal and Social Psychology*, 1959, 58, 203-210.

Festinger, L., Riecken, H., and Schachter, S. *When Prophecy Fails*. Minneapolis: University of Minnesota Press, 1956.

Hardyck, Jane, and Braden, Marcia, "Prophecy Fails Again: A Report of a Failure to Replicate," *Journal of Abnormal and Social Psychology*, 1962, 65, 136-141.

Heider, F. *The Psychology of Interpersonal Relations*. New York: John Wiley & Sons, Inc. 1958.

Hovland, C., Janis, I.L., and Kelley, H. *Communication and Persuasion*. New Haven: Yale University Press, 1953.

Janis, I.L., and Mann, L., "Effectiveness of Emotional Role-Playing in Modifying Smoking Habits and Attitudes," *Journal of Experimental Research in Personality*, 1965, 1, 84-90.

Kelman, H.C., "Processes of Opinion Change," *Public Opinion Quarterly*, 1961, 25, 57-78.

Mann, L., and Janis, I.L., "A Follow-up Study on the Long-Term Effects of Emotional Role-Playing," *Journal of Personality and Social Psychology*, 1968, 8, 339-342.

Newcomb, T.M., "Attitude Development as a Function of Reference Groups: The Bennington Study," In Eleanor E. Maccoby, T.M. Newcomb, and E.L. Hartley (Eds.), *Readings in Social Psychology*, (3rd edn). New York: Holt, Rinehart & Winston, Inc., 1958. 265-275.

Osgood, C.E., and Tannenbaum, P.H., "The Principle of Congruity in the Prediction of Attitude Change," *Psychological Review*, 1955, 62, 42-55.

Santayana, G., *Soliloquies in England and Later Soliloquies*. New York: Charles Scribner's Sons, 1922.

Stagner, R., *Psychology of Personality*, (2nd edn). New York: McGraw-Hill Book Company, 1948.

THE EFFECTS OF CHANGES IN ROLES ON THE ATTITUDES OF ROLE OCCUPANTS

SEYMOUR LIEBERMAN

Problem

One of the fundamental postulates of role theory, as expounded by Newcomb (2), Parsons (3), and other role theorists, is that a person's attitudes will be influenced by the role that he occupies in a social system. Although this proposition appears to be a plausible one, surprisingly little evidence is available that bears directly on it. One source of evidence is found in common folklore. "Johnny is a changed boy since he was made a monitor in school." "She is a different woman since she got married." "You would never recognize him since he became foreman." As much as these expressions smack of the truth, they offer little in the way of systematic or scientific support for the proposition that a person's attitudes are influenced by his role.

Somewhat more scientific, but still not definitive, is the common finding, in many social-psychological studies, that relationships exist between attitudes and roles. In other words, different attitudes are held by people who occupy different roles. For example, Stouffer *et al.* (5) found that commissioned officers are more favorable toward the Army than are enlisted men. The problem here is that the mere existence of a relationship between attitudes and roles does not reveal the cause and effect nature of the relationship found. One interpretation of Stouffer's finding might be that being made a commissioned officer tends to result in a person's becoming pro-Army—i.e. the role a person occupies influences his attitudes. But an equally plausible interpretation might be that being pro-Army tends to result in a person's being made a commissioned officer—i.e. a person's attitudes influence the likelihood of his being selected for a given role. In the absence of longitudinal data, the relationship offers no clear evidence that roles were the "cause" and attitudes the "effect".

The present study was designed to examine the effects of roles on attitudes in a particular field situation. The study is based on longitudinal data obtained in a role-differentiated, hierarchical organization. By taking advantage of natural role changes among personnel in the organization, it was possible to examine people's attitudes both before and after they underwent changes in roles. Therefore, the extent to which changes in roles were followed by changes in attitudes could be determined, and the cause and effect nature of any relationships found would be clear.

Method: Phase 1

The study was part of a larger project carried out in a medium-sized Midwestern company engaged in the production of home appliance equipment. Let us call the company the Rockwell Corporation. At the time that the study was done, Rockwell

Reprinted from *Human Relations*, 1956, by permission of the publisher, Plenum Publishing Corporation.

employed about 4,000 people. This total included about 2,500 factory workers and about 150 first-level foremen. The company was unionized and most of the factory workers belonged to the union local, which was an affiliate of the U.A.W., C.I.O. About 150 factory workers served as stewards in the union, or roughly one steward for every foreman.

The study consisted of a "natural field experiment". The experimental variable was a change in roles, and the experimental period was the period of exposure to the experimental variable. The experimental groups were those employees who underwent changes in roles during this period; the control groups were those employees who did not change roles during this period. The design may be described in terms of a three-step process: "before measurement", "experimental period", and "after measurement".

Before Measurement.

In September and October 1951, attitude questionnaries were filled out by virtually all factory personnel at Rockwell—2,354 workers, 145 stewards, and 151 foremen. The questions dealt for the most part with employees' attitudes and perceptions about the company, the union, and various aspects of the job situation. The respondents were told that the questionnaire was part of an overall survey to determine how employees felt about working conditions at Rockwell.

Experimental Period.

Between October 1951 and July 1952, twenty-three workers were made foremen and thirty-five workers became stewards. Most of the workers who became stewards during that period were elected during the annual steward elections held in May 1952. They replaced stewards who did not choose to run again or who were not re-elected by their constituents. In addition, a few workers replaced stewards who left the steward role for one reason or another throughout the year.

The workers who became foremen were not made foreman at any particular time. Promotions occurred as openings arose in supervisory positions. Some workers replaced foremen who retired or who left the company for other reasons; some replaced foremen who were shifted to other supervisory positions; and some filled newly created supervisory positions.

After Measurement

In December 1952, the same forms that had been filled out by the rank-and-file workers in 1951 were readministered to:

1. The workers who became foremen during the experimental period (N=23).

2. A control group of workers who did not become foremen during the experimental period (N=46).

3. The workers who became stewards during the experimental period (N=35).

4. A control group of workers who did not become stewards during the experimental period (N=35).

Each control group was matched with its parallel experimental group on a number of demographic, attitudinal, and motivational variables. Therefore, any changes in attitudes that occurred in the experimental groups but did not occur in the control groups could not be attributed to initial differences between them.

The employees in these groups were told that the purpose of the following questionnaire was to get up-to-date measures of their attitudes in 1952 and to compare how employees felt that year with the way that they felt the previous year. The groups were told that, instead of studying the entire universe of employees as was the case in 1951, only a sample was being studied this time. They were informed that the sample was chosen in such a way as to represent all kinds of employees at Rockwell—men and women, young and old, etc. The groups gave no indication that they understood the real bases on which they were chosen for the "after" measurement or that the effects of changes in roles were the critical factors being examined. . . .[1]

Results: Phase 1.

The major hypothesis tested in this study was that people who are placed in a role will tend to take on or develop attitudes that are congruent with the expectations associated with that role. Since the foreman role entails being a representative of management, it might be expected that workers who are chosen as foremen will tend to become more favorable toward management. Similarly, since the steward role entails being a representative of the union, it might be expected that workers who are elected as stewards will tend to become more favorable toward the union. Moreover, in so far as the values of management and of the union are in conflict with each other, it might also be expected that workers who are made foremen will become less favorable toward the union and workers who are made stewards will become less favorable toward management.

Four attitudinal areas were examined: 1. attitudes toward management and officials of management; 2. attitudes toward the union and officials of the union; 3. attitudes toward the management-sponsored incentive system; and 4. attitudes toward the union-sponsored seniority system. The incentive system (whereby workers are paid according to the number of pieces they turn out) and the seniority system (whereby workers are promoted according to the seniority principle) are two areas in which conflicts between management and the union at Rockwell have been particularly intense. Furthermore, first-level foremen and stewards both play a part in the administration of these systems, and relevant groups hold expectations about foreman and steward behaviors with respect to these systems. Therefore, we examined the experimental and control groups' attitudes toward these two systems as well as their overall attitudes toward management and the union.

The data tend to support the hypothesis that being placed in the foreman and steward roles will have an impact on the attitudes of the role occupants. . . . Both experimental groups undergo systematic changes in attitudes, in the predicted directions, from the "before" situation to the "after" situation. In the control groups, either no attitude changes occur, or less marked changes occur, from the "before" situation to the "after" situation.

Although a number of the differences are not statistically significant, those which are significant are all in the expected directions, and most of the non-significant differences are also in the expected directions. New foremen, among other things, come to see Rockwell as a better place to work compared with other companies, develop more positive perceptions of top management officers, and become more favorably disposed toward the principle and operation of the incentive system. New stewards come to look upon labor unions in general in a more favorable light, develop more positive perceptions of the top union officers at Rockwell, and come to prefer seniority to ability as a criterion of what should count in moving workers to better jobs. In general, the attitudes of workers who become foremen tend to gravitate in a pro-management direction and the attitudes of workers who become stewards tend to move in a pro-union direction.

A second kind of finding has to do with the relative *amount* of attitude change that takes place among new foremen in contrast to the amount that takes place among new stewards. On the whole, more pronounced and more widespread attitude changes occur among those who are made foremen than among those who are made stewards. . . . The workers who are made foremen undergo significant attitude changes, relative to the workers who are not made foremen, on ten of the sixteen attitudinal items. . . . By contrast, the workers who are made stewards undergo significant attitude changes, relative to the workers who are not made stewards, on only three of the sixteen items. However, for the steward role as well as for the foreman role, most of the differences found between the experimental and control groups still tend to be in the expected directions.

The more pronounced and more widespread attitude changes that occur among new foremen than among new stewards can probably be accounted for in large measure by the kinds of differences that exist between the foreman and steward roles. For one thing, the foreman role represents a relatively permanent position, while many stewards take the steward role as a "one-shot" job and even if they want to run again their constituents may not re-elect them. Secondly, the foreman role is a full-time job, while most stewards spend just a few hours a week in the performance of their steward functions and spend the rest of the time carrying out their regular rank-and-file jobs. Thirdly, a worker who is made a foreman must give up his membership in the union and become a surrogate of management, while a worker who is made a steward retains the union as a reference group and simply takes on new functions and responsibilities as a representative of it. All of these differences suggest that the change from worker to foreman is a more fundamental change in roles than the change from worker to steward. This, in turn, might account to a large extent for the finding that, although attitude changes accompany both changes in roles, they occur more sharply among new foremen than among new stewards.

A third finding has to do with the *kinds* of attitude changes which occur among workers who change roles. As expected, new foremen become more pro-management and new stewards become more pro-union. Somewhat less expected is the finding that new foremen become more anti-union but new stewards do not become more anti-management. Among workers who are made foremen, statistically significant shifts in an anti-union direction occur on four of the eight items dealing with the union and the union-sponsored seniority system. Among workers who are made stewards, there are no statistically significant shifts in either direction on any of the eight items having to do with management and the management-sponsored incentive system.

The finding that new foremen become anti-union but that new stewards do not become anti-management may be related to the fact that workers who become fore-men must relinquish their membership of the union, while workers who become stewards retain their status as employees of management. New foremen, subject to one main set of loyalties and called on to carry out a markedly new set of functions, tend to develop negative attitudes toward the union as well as positive attitudes toward management. New stewards, subject to overlapping group membership, and still dependent on management for their livelihoods, tend to become more favorable toward the union but they do not turn against management, at least not within the relatively limited time period covered by the present research project. Over time, stewards might come to develop somewhat hostile attitudes toward management, but, under the conditions prevailing at Rockwell, there is apparently no tendency for such attitudes to be developed as soon as workers enter the steward role.

Method: Phase 2

One of the questions that may be raised about the results that have been pre-sented up to this point concerns the extent to which the changed attitudes displayed by new foremen and new stewards are internalized by the role occupants. Are the changed attitudes expressed by new foremen and new stewards relatively stable, or are they ephemeral phenomena to be held only as long as they occupy the foreman and steward roles? An unusual set of circumstances at Rockwell enabled the researchers to glean some data on this question.

A short time after the 1952 re-survey, the nation suffered an economic reces-sion. In order to meet the lessening demand for its products, Rockwell, like many other firms, had to cut its work force. This resulted in many rank-and-file workers being laid off and a number of the foremen being returned to non-supervisory jobs. By June 1954, eight of the twenty-three workers who had been promoted to foreman had returned to the worker role and only twelve were still foremen. (The remaining three respondents had voluntarily left Rockwell by this time.)

Over the same period, a number of role changes had also been experienced by the thirty-five workers who had become stewards. Fourteen had returned to the worker role, either because they had not sought re-election by their work groups or because they had failed to win re-election, and only six were still stewards. (The other fifteen respondents, who composed almost half of this group, had either volun-tarily left Rockwell or had been laid off as part of the general reduction in force.)

Once again, in June 1954, the researchers returned to Rockwell to re-administer the questionnaires that the workers had filled out in 1951 and 1952. The instructions to the respondents were substantially the same as those given in 1952—i.e. a sample of employees had been chosen to get up-to-date measures of employees' attitudes toward working conditions at Rockwell and the same groups were selected this time as had been selected last time in order to lend greater stability to the results.

In this phase of the study, the numbers of cases with which we were dealing in the various groups were so small that the data could only be viewed as suggestive, and systematic statistical analysis of the data did not seem to be too meaningful. However, the unusual opportunity to throw some light on an important question sug-gests that a reporting of these results may be worthwhile.

Results: Phase 2

The principal question examined. here was: on those items where a change in roles resulted in a change in attitudes between 1951 and 1952, how are these attitudes influenced by a reverse change in roles between 1952 and 1954?

The most consistent and widespread attitude changes noted between 1951 and 1952 were those that resulted when workers moved into the foreman role. What are the effects of moving out of the foreman role between 1952 and 1954? The data indicate that, in general, most of the "gains" that were observed when workers became foremen are "lost" when they become workers again. . . . The foremen who remain foremen either retain their favorable attitudes toward management or become even more favorable toward management between 1952 and 1954, while the demoted foremen show fairly consistent drops in the direction of re-adopting the attitudes they held when they had been in the worker role. On the whole, the attitudes held by demoted foremen in 1954, after they had left the foreman role, fall roughly to the same levels as they had been in 1951, before they had ever moved into the foreman role.

The results on the effects of moving out of the steward role are less clear-cut. . . . There is no marked tendency for ex-stewards to revert to earlier-held attitudes when they go from the steward role to the worker role. At the same time, it should be recalled that there had not been particularly marked changes in their attitudes when they initially changed from the worker role to the steward role. These findings, then, are consistent with the interpretation offered earlier that the change in roles between worker and steward is less significant than the change in roles between worker and foreman.

A question might be raised about what is represented in the reversal of attitudes found among ex-foremen. Does it represent a positive taking-on of attitudes appropriate for respondents who are re-entering the worker role, or does it constitute a negative, perhaps embittered reaction away from the attitudes they held before being demoted from the foreman role? A definitive answer to this question cannot be arrived at, but it might be suggested that if we were dealing with a situation where a reversion in roles did not constitute such a strong psychological blow to the role occupants (as was probably the case among demoted foremen), then such a marked reversion in attitudes might not have occurred. . . .[2]

Discussion

A role may be defined as a set of behaviors that are expected of people who occupy a certain position in a social system. These expectations consist of shared attitudes or beliefs, held by relevant populations, about what role occupants should and should not do. The theoretical basis for hypothesizing that a role will have effects on role occupants lies in the nature of these expectations. If a role occupant meets these expectations, the "rights" or "rewards" associated with the role will be accorded to him. If he fails to meet these expectations, the "rights" or "rewards" will be withheld from him and "punishments" may be meted out.[3]

A distinction should be made between the effects of roles on people's attitudes and the effects of roles on their actions. How roles affect actions can probably be explained in a fairly direct fashion. Actions are overt and readily enforceable. If a person fails to behave in ways appropriate to his role, this can immediately be seen, and steps may be taken to bring the deviant or non-conformist into line. Role deviants may be evicted from their roles, placed in less rewarding roles, isolated from other members of the group, or banished entirely from the social system.

But attitudes are not as overt as actions. A person may behave in such a way as to reveal his attitudes, but he can—and often does—do much to cover them up. Why, then, should a change in roles lead to a change in actions? A number of explanatory factors might be suggested here. The present discussion will be confined to two factors that are probably generic to a wide variety of situations. One pertains to the influence of reference groups; the other is based on an assumption about people's need to have attitudes internally consistent with their actions.

A change in roles almost invariably involves a change in reference groups. Old reference groups may continue to influence the role occupant, but new ones also come into play. The change in reference groups may involve moving into a completely new group (as when a person gives up membership in one organization and joins another one) or it may simply involve taking on new functions in the same group (as when a person is promoted to a higher position in a hierarchical organization). In both situations, new reference groups will tend to bring about new frames of reference, new self-percepts, and new vested interests, and these in turn will tend to produce new attitudinal orientations.

In addition to a change in reference groups, a change in roles also involves a change in functions and a change in the kinds of behaviors and actions that the role occupant must display if he is to fulfil these functions. A change in actions, let us assume, comes about because these actions are immediately required, clearly visible, and hence socially enforceable. If we further assume a need for people to have attitudes that are internally consistent with their actions, then at least one aspect of the functional significance of a change in attitudes becomes clear. A change in attitudes enables a new role occupant to justify, to make rational, or perhaps simply to rationalize his change in actions. Having attitudes that are consistent with actions helps the role occupant to be "at one" with himself and facilitates his effective performance of the functions he is expected to carry out.

The reference-group principle and the self-consistency principle postulate somewhat different chains of events in accounting for the effects of roles on attitudes and actions. In abbreviated versions, the different chains may be spelled out in the following ways:

1. Reference-group principle: A change in roles involves a change in reference groups . . . which leads to a change in attitudes . . . which leads to a change in actions.

2. Self-consistency principle: A change in roles involves a change in functions . . which leads to a change in actions . . . which leads to a change in attitudes.

In the former chain, a person's attitudes influence his actions; in the latter chain, a person's actions influence his attitudes. Both chains might plausibly account for the results obtained, but whether either chain, both chains, or other chains is or are valid cannot be determined from the data available. A more direct investigation of the underlying mechanisms responsible for the impact of roles on attitudes would appear to be a fruitful area for further research.

But apart from the question of underlying mechanisms, the results lend support to the proposition that a person's attitudes will be influenced by his role. Relatively consistent changes in attitudes were found both among workers who were made foremen and among workers who were made stewards, although these changes were more clear-cut for foremen than for stewards. The more interesting set of results—as far as role theory in general is concerned—would seem to be the data on the effects of entering and leaving the foreman role. It was pointed out earlier that the foreman role, unlike the steward role, is a full-time, relatively permanent position, and moving into this position entails taking on a very new and different set of functions. When workers are made foremen, their attitudes change in a more pro-management and anti-union direction. When they are demoted and move back into the worker role, their attitudes change once again, this time in a more pro-union and anti-management direction. In both instances, the respondents' attitudes seem to be molded by the roles which they occupy at a given time.

The readiness with which the respondents in this study shed one set of attitudes and took on another set of attitudes might suggest either that 1. the attitudes studied do not tap very basic or deep-rooted facets of the respondents' psyches, or 2. the character structures of the respondents are such as not to include very deeply ingrained sets of value orientations. Riesman (4) deals with this problem in his discussion of "other-directedness" vs. "inner-directedness". How much the rapid shifts in attitudes observed here reflect the particular kinds of respondents who underwent changes in roles in the present situation, and how much these shifts reflect the national character of the American population, can only be speculated on at the present time. . . .

Notes

1. Some of the top officials of management and all of the top officers of the union at Rockwell knew about the nature of the follow-up study and the bases on which the experimental and control groups were selected.

2. There were a number of reactions to demotion among the eight ex-foremen, as obtained from informal interviews with these respondents. Some reached inpunitively (i.e., they blamed uncontrollable situational determinants) and did not seem to be bothered by demotion. Others reacted extrapunitively (i.e., they blamed management) or intrapunitively (i.e., they blamed themselves) and appeared to be more disturbed by demotion. One way of testing the hypothesis that attitude reversion is a function of embitterment would be to see if sharper reversion occurs among extrapunitive and intrapunitive respondents. However, the small number of cases does not permit an analysis of this kind to be carried out in the present situation.

3. An earlier discussion of the role concept, with particular reference to its application to the study complex organizations, is found in Jacobson, Charters, and Lieberman (1).

References

1. Jacobson, E., Charters, W. W., Jr., and Lieberman, S. "The Use of the Role Concept in the Study of Complex Organizations." *J. Soc. Issues,* Vol. 7, No. 3, pp. 18-27, 1951.
2. Newcomb, T.M. *Social Psychology.* New York: The Dryden Press, 1950; London: Tavistock Publications, 1952.
3. Parsons, T. *The Social System.* Glencoe, Ill.: The Free Press, 1951; London: Tavistock Publications Ltd., 1951.
4. Riesman, D. *The Lonely Crowd.* New Haven: Yale Univ. Press, 1950.
5. Stouffer, S.A., Suchman, E.A., DeVinney, L. C., Star, S. A., and Williams, R. M., Jr. *The American Soldier: Adjustment During Army Life* (Vol. 1). Princeton University Press, 1949.
6. Walker, H.M., and Lev, J. *Statistical Inference.* New York: Henry Holt and Co., Inc., 1953.

PERCEPTION FROM THE INSIDE LOOKING OUT

HAROLD J. LEAVITT

The major questions [here] are these: How and why do people see things differently? How objective can people be? Do people see only what they want to see?
Or don't want to see? What part do people's personal views of the world play in
the supervisory process?

The Perceptual World

Most of us recognize that the world-as-we-see-it is not necessarily the same
as the world-as-it-"really"-is. Our answer depends on what we heard, not on what
was really said. The housewife buys what she likes best, not what is best. Whether
we feel hot or cold depends on us, not on the thermometer. The same job may
look like a good job to one of us and a sloppy job to another.

To specify the problem, consider the line drawing in figure 1. This is a picture
of a woman. Here are some questions about it: (1) How old is the woman at the
time of the picture? (2) Does she have any outstanding physical characteristics? (3)
Is she "reasonably attractive" or "downright ugly"?

Show the picture to ten other people. Do they all see the same thing? If some
think she looks between twenty and thirty, does anyone think she's over fifty? If

Figure 1. Wife or mother-in-law?

some think she's over fifty, does anyone think she's between twenty and thirty? How does one account for the conflicts? Are the differences simply differences in taste? Or in standards of beauty? Or is each person distorting the "real" world in a different way?

This old psychology-textbook picture is intentionally ambiguous. It can be seen either as an ugly old hag with a long and crooked nose and toothless mouth or as a reasonably attractive young girl with head turned away so that one can barely see one eyelash and part of a nose. More importantly, the picture will be based on the "facts" as they are seen by another viewer.

Incidentally, if the reader still sees only one of the two figures, he is getting a good feeling of what a "need" is. The tension or discomfort that one feels when he thinks he is missing some things others can see or when he feels he hasn't quite closed a gap in his knowledge—that is a need. And it will probably be difficult to concentrate on reading further until he satisfies that unsatisfied need by finding the second face in the picture.

The Influence of Our Needs on Our Perceptions

The hag picture is another demonstration of a commonplace observation, i.e., that people see things differently, that the world is what we make it, that everyone wears his own rose-colored glasses. But consider some additional questions: Whence the rose-colored glasses? Are the glasses always rose-colored? That is, does one always see what he wants to see, or does he see what he is afraid he will see, or both?

These questions are important because the primary issue of "human relations" is to consider ways in which individuals can affect the behavior of other individuals. If it is true that people behave on the basis of the perceived world, then changing behavior in a predetermined direction can be made easier by understanding the individual's present perception of the world. For if there is any common human-relations mistake made by industrial superiors in their relations with subordinates, it is the mistake of assuming that the "real" world is all that counts, that everyone works for the same goals, that the facts speak for themselves.

But if people do act on their perceptions, different people perceive things differently. How, then, is the manager, for example, to know what to expect? What determines how particular people will perceive particular things?

The answer has already been given in the preceding chapters. People's perceptions are determined by their needs. Like the mirrors at amusement parks, we distort the world in relation to our own tensions. Children from poorer homes, when asked to draw a quarter, draw a bigger than actual one. Industrial employees, when asked to describe the people they work with, talk more about their bosses (the people more important to their needs) than about their peers or subordinates, and so on.

But the problem is more complicated than that. People may perceive what is important to their needs, but does this mean people see what they want to see, or what they are afraid to see? Both wishes and fears are important to one's needs. The answer seems to be that we perceive both, but according to certain rules. We magnify a compliment from higher up in the organization but we also magnify a word of disapproval. We dream of blondes, but we also have nightmares. And sometimes we just don't pay attention at all to things that are quite relevant. We forget dentist's appointments; we oversleep when we have examinations coming up; we manage to forget to clean the basement or to call on this particular customer.

Selective Perception

What, then, are the rules of selective perception? The best answer we can give is this one: If one reexamines his memories of the past, he may find that his recall of positive, satisfying things is better than his recall of negative, unpleasant things. He may find it easier to wake early to go fishing than to get to a dentist's appointment. He may look forward, in fact, to doing pleasant, satisfying jobs but may evade mildly disturbing and unpleasant jobs. A senior executive once commented to the author that the biggest problem he encounters with young management people is their tendency to avoid the little unpleasant decisions—like disciplining people or digging through boring and repetitive records or writing unpleasant letters. This executive felt that his younger men would be far more effective if they could learn to deal as promptly with these uncomfortable little decisions as they did with the big ones.

But we can see some sense in this selective remembering if we look for it. There are some advantages to a person in being blind to unpleasantness, even if such blindness cuts down his working effectiveness. Ignoring the unpleasant may represent more than "laziness." It may be a sensible defensive device, psychologically speaking. Thus, most people are able to ignore soft background conversation while working. In effect they are psychologically deaf to a potentially distracting part of the real world. And this defense helps them to concentrate on their work. Similarly, most people manage to ignore the threat of the hydrogen bomb and to go on eating and sleeping as though this dangerous part of the real world were not here. It can even be shown experimentally that words with unpleasant connotations tend to be recognized more slowly when exposed for very brief intervals than words with pleasant connotations.

The strange part of this defensive process, however, is that in order *not* to hear the distracting music or *not* to see the unpleasant words one must first hear and see them. One has to see the word, recognize that it is unpleasant, and reject it almost simultaneously, so that one can say, "No. I didn't see what that word was." Hence the label "defense" attached to this phenomenon—defense against the entry of preselected things mildly disturbing to one's equilibrium. So two of our rules of selective perception become: (1) see what promises to help satisfy needs, and (2) ignore mildly disturbing things.

Suppose, though, that while one is successfully ignoring background talk someone back there starts to shout; or, while one is successfully ignoring the H-bomb, an H-bomb falls on London. At those points, when the unpleasantness becomes intense and dangerous, people stop defending and begin attacking. They stop ignoring the irritation and start directing all their attention to it. This reversal seems to happen suddenly, at some specific threshold. The distant irritation increases to a point at which it becomes so real, so imminent, and so threatening that we reverse our course, discard the blindfold, and preoccupy ourselves completely with the thing previously ignored.

This is the third rule: Pay attention to things that are really dangerous. The whole picture now begins to look like this: *People perceive what they think will help satisfy needs; ignore what is disturbing; and again perceive disturbances that persist and increase. . . .*

This process may not seem entirely logical to an outside observer, but it is quite reasonable psychologically. For this kind of self-imposed psychological blindness helps the person to maintain his equilibrium while moving toward his objectives. An organism lacking this ability to fend off minor threats might well find itself torn apart in its attempt to deal simultaneously with all of them. Or, at least, an individual unable to ignore unpleasant realities might spend so much of his energy dealing with them that he would make little progress toward his major goals. For once a person has learned to perceive a multitude of threats and dangers in his world he needs a system of defense against them. One should add, however, that some individuals may see relatively few things as dangerous and therefore have little need for defense, while for others the world holds dangers at every turn.

. . . [Earlier] we suggested that a person who has encountered a relatively helpful world is likely to perceive more of his environment as potentially helpful. If, however, the world has been mostly frustrating, then more of it, and especially new things in it, will be seen as potentially dangerous. Being dangerous, they must be fended off. But, paradoxically, to be fended off they must first be seen. So to protect himself from more insecurity, the insecure person must first see the things that will provoke insecurity and then manage to deny to himself that he has seen them.

Projections of the Perceived World

The basic point of this [paper]; the point that the world as it is perceived is the world that is behaviorally important, underlies the development of the now generally familiar projective tests. Originally projectives were designed for the diagnosis of aberrations in personality, but . . . they are [also] being used industrially. The same idea also underlies what market researchers now call "motivation research" into consumer attitudes, techniques for discovering people's views of the "facts" of advertising and product design. Consumer research in general can be thought of as an attempt to make a diagnosis of the relevant parts of the consumer's view of the world so that products can be designed to be seen as aids rather than obstacles.

For managerial purposes, the importance of the perceptual world is clear. If one's concern as a supervisor or counselor or committee member is to try to effect some change in the behavior of other people, and if in turn people's present behavior is determined largely by their perceptions of their environments, then it is critical that one seek to understand their perceptions if one is to understand the circumstances under which their behavior might change.

For example, managers assume almost universally that subordinates want promotions. And yet more than one subordinate has been driven into panic and disappointment because he felt psychologically forced to accept a promotion that no one (sometimes even himself) bothered to find out he did not want.

Often assumptions about the perceptions of others are wrong because they are incomplete. One may assume correctly that employees want more money, but he may fail to understand that more money is acceptable only within a certain framework of independence. This is the paternalism problem.

Sometimes the problem is simple lack of sensitivity for other people. Thus a foreman once complained to the writer about how odd people seemed. He said one of his employees had gotten terribly upset "for no reason at all." The foreman had said, "Hey, boy, go over there and pick that up!" The employee got angry. He had said, "Don't call me 'boy'; I have a name!" The foreman couldn't understand why the employee, a Negro, should get angry about a "perfectly reasonable" request like that.

Or again many parents argue for the importance of heredity over environment because their own children seem to be so different from one another. "Our second child," they will say, "was just a completely different person from the first, though we treated them both *exactly* alike." Parents may be truthful in feeling that they treated two children alike, but it is unwise to assume that the children were therefore treated alike. The first child's world did not include the second child; but the second's did include the first. Indeed the evidence is now quite good that certain personality variables are related to the birth order of children in families. First-born children tend to be more affiliative and more dependent than later-born, for example, and generally more susceptible to social pressure. Moreover, for the infant whose slate is relatively blank, the minor marks made by parents may be major marks for the child. Thus many parents pass lightly over the differences between feeding an infant now or ten minutes from now. But the child is not likely to pass over the same thing nearly so lightly. The manager is likely to pay little attention to his criticism of a subordinate's work. But for the subordinate it is a week's food for worry.

One more example. Sales managers often complain of the difficulties they encounter in getting salesmen to make cold calls. The salesman says he was too busy, or there were better prospects, or he had to catch up on some reports. Is he lazy? Or just defending himself—perhaps unconsciously—against a perceived threat? If it is a defensive process, there are two general ways in which the manager can try to shake the salesman loose. He can teach him to feel comfortable about cold calls, or he can change the mild threat to a major one so that it can no longer safely be ignored. But if he chooses the latter course he had better consider the by-products.

Perceiving Oneself

So far we have talked about perceptions of things and other people. But one of the people each of us perceives is himself, as he is, and also as he would like other people to see him. Each of us struts his own act before the world, as it were, in an effort to have other people see us as the kind of person we value.

Quite early in life, we begin to learn what kinds of groups we want to join, what kinds of social classes to aspire to, what kinds of status to achieve. Two of us may have equally intense needs for status and prestige, but if we have grown up in different environments, one of us may seek that status by acting masculine and powerful, or by affecting long hair and a beard. Another may seek to fulfill the same needs by costuming himself in high-style fashions or by donning the pin-striped uniform of the executive.

Teenagers are often painfully awkward as they strive to perfect their own private acts. They seem to feel it terribly important to appear to be what they doubt they really are. Later they become more skilful, either because their acts are better or because their acts are not very far from what the actors really are.

Note that our acts are functional for us. They are performed by both teenagers and adults for good reasons. An act is a way of filling a role. It is also a way of protecting the vulnerable parts of ourselves from real or fancied attack. But our act is effective in performing its functions only if other people accept it. And other people usually accept acts when the gap between our acting selves and their estimate of our "real" selves is small. Other people tend to be reasonably accurate judges, too. So acting problems arise as the distance between act and reality increases.

It is also true that acts are often uncomfortable for the actor. The girl friend happily abandons the courting dance as soon as the wedding is over. But until she has the man tied down and delivered, she must play her version of the coquette, no matter how much worry and fret it requires. Similarly the company executive must act decisively, though privately he may yearn for a chance to weep on someone's shoulder.

But though our acts are functional, they contribute to a social world full of distorted signals. You are trying to tell me that you are strong, worldly, and decisive (and you may be—or you may not), and I am just as busily trying to communicate to you that I am the sagacious, understanding, intellectually stimulating character I would like to be (and may actually be—or may not). We have both been practicing our acts for a long time. So we have both developed clever ways of being convincing, ways that the poor inept adolescent has not even dreamed of. But we have also developed clever ways of spotting the other guy's act.

Our relationship becomes even further confounded by the fact that we read one another's cover stories through our own need-distorted glasses. While you stand there trying to radiate strength and decisiveness, I see you as brash and immature. And you, wanting action and recognition, see my efforts at quiet, pipe-smoking wisdom as dullness and lack of imagination. Looked at this way the wonder is not that we find it so difficult to understand one another, but that we are able to understand one another at all.

The first big problem then is the problem of accuracy, of somehow gaining more accurate information about other people—estimating the discrepancy between the actor and the "real" person. The second problem is to estimate how well our act is working. For surely we are in considerable trouble if the self we want to present to the world is presented so badly, so weakly, so transparently that everyone else is discounting it. We are in a bad way if the people around us are saying: "There is a man who is trying to act decisive and sure of himself, while in fact it is as plain as the nose on your face that he is really unsure of himself, indecisive, anxious."

To the best of this writer's knowledge there is only one general mechanism by which such distortions in relationships can be reduced, and that is the mechanism of *feedback*. If somehow we can develop better ways by which we can learn from other people how our act is getting across, then we can either modify it so that it gets across more fully or we can try to reduce the discrepancy between the act and ourselves, so that it is an easier act to play convincingly. The first course leads to a world of intrigue and gamesmanship; the second, to a simpler, less distorted world.

By this reasoning, other people, if we can get them to provide us with appropriate feedback, can do us considerable service in helping us to bring what we wish to be closer to what we are, and to reduce our uncertainty and anxiety in the process. . . .

In Summary

People see things differently. Even "facts" may be seen quite differently by different people. Relevance to one's needs is the most important determinant of one's personal view of the world. Things that seem to be aids to satisfying one's needs are seen quickly. But things that look like obstacles, if they are not critically threatening, may also be seen quickly, only then to be denied so that they appear not to have been seen at all. By denying obstacles, people "protect" themselves temporarily from them. If they really become dangerous, however, people drop the blinders and face the obstacles.

One of the things we perceive is ourselves and other people. To protect and enhance ourselves, we try to manipulate the picture other people have of us by putting up a front that will make them think we are what we want to be. The problem of our act, and getting it across successfully, depends mostly on our ability to pick up audience reactions accurately. And accurate audience reactions are hard to come by because the audience is acting too.

To ignore differences in perception is to ignore a major determinant of behavior. Yet it is easy to assume unwarrantedly that everyone views the world from the same perspective as the viewer. Time spent trying to reach a common view is not wasted time.

PERCEPTION: IMPLICATIONS FOR ADMINISTRATION

SHELDON S. ZALKIND
TIMOTHY W. COSTELLO

Management practice is being increasingly influenced by behavioral science research in the areas of group dynamics, problem solving and decision making, and motivation. One aspect of behavior which has not been fully or consistently emphasized is the process of perception, particularly the recent work on person perception.

In this paper we shall summarize some of the findings on perception as developed through both laboratory and organizational research and point out some of the administrative and managerial implications. We discuss first some basic factors in the nature of the perceptual process including need and set; second, some research on forming impressions; third, the characteristics of the perceiver and the perceived; fourth, situational and organizational influences on perception; and finally, perceptual influences on interpersonal adjustment.

Nature of the Perceptual Process

What are some of the factors influencing perception? In answering the question it is well to begin by putting aside the attitude of naïve realism, which suggests that our perceptions simply register accurately what is "out there." It is necessary rather to consider what influences distort one's perceptions and judgments of the outside world. Some of the considerations identified in the literature up to the time of Johnson's 1944 review of the research on object perception (where distortion may be even less extreme than in person perception) led him to suggest the following about the perceiver:[1]

Reprinted by permission of the authors and the publisher, *Administrative Science Quarterly*, vol. 7, no. 3 (Sept. 1962), pp. 218-35.

1. He may be influenced by considerations that he may not be able to identify, responding to cues that are below the threshold of his awareness. For example, a judgment as to the size of an object may be influenced by its color even though the perceiver may not be attending to color.

2. When required to form difficult perceptual judgments, he may respond to irrelevant cues to arrive at a judgment. For example, in trying to assess honesty, it has been shown that the other person's smiling or not smiling is used as a cue to judge his honesty.

3. In making abstract or intellectual judgments, he may be influenced by emotional factors—what is liked is perceived as correct.

4. He will weigh perceptual evidence coming from respected (or favored) sources more heavily than that coming from other sources.

5. He may not be able to identify all the factors on which his judgments are based. Even if he is aware of these factors he is not likely to realize how much weight he gives to them.

These considerations do not imply that we respond only to the subtle or irrelevant cues or to emotional factors. We often perceive on the basis of the obvious, but we are quite likely to be responding as well to the less obvious or less objective.

In 1958, Bruner, citing a series of researches, described what he called the "New Look" in perception as one in which personal determinants of the perceptual process were being stressed.[2] Bruner summarized earlier work and showed the importance of such subjective influences as needs, values, cultural background, and interests on the perceptual process. In his concept of "perceptual readiness" he described the importance of the framework or category system that the perceiver himself brings to the perceiving process.

Tapping a different vein of research, Cantril described perceiving as a "transaction" between the perceiver and the perceived, a process of negotiation in which the perceptual end product is a result both of influences within the perceiver and of characteristics of the perceived.[3]

One of the most important of the subjective factors that influence the way we perceive, identified by Bruner and others, is *set*. A study by Kelley illustrated the point.[4] He found that those who were previously led to expect to meet a "warm" person, not only made different judgments about him, but also behaved differently toward him, than those who were expecting a "cold" one. The fact was that they simultaneously were observing the same person in the same situation. Similarly, Strickland indicated the influence of set in determining how closely supervisors feel they must supervise their subordinates.[5] Because of prior expectation one person was trusted more than another and was thought to require less supervision than another, even though performance records were identical.

Forming Impressions of Others

The data on forming impressions is of particular importance in administration. An administrator is confronted many times with the task of forming an impression of another person—a new employee at his desk, a visiting member from the home office, a staff member he has not personally met before. His own values, needs, and expectations will play a part in the impression he forms. Are there other factors that typically operate in this area of administrative life? One of the more obvious influences is the physical appearance of the person being perceived. In a study of this point Mason was able to demonstrate that people agree on what a leader should look like and that there is no relationship between the facial characteristics agreed upon and those possessed by actual leaders.[6] In effect, we have ideas about what leaders look like and we can give examples, but we ignore the many exceptions that statistically cancel out the examples.

In the sometimes casual, always transitory situations in which one must form impressions of others it is a most natural tendency to jump to conclusions and form impressions without adequate evidence. Unfortunately, as Dailey showed, unless such impressions are based on important and relevant data, they are not likely to be accurate.[7] Too often in forming impressions the perceiver does not know what is relevant, important, or predictive of later behavior. Dailey's research furthermore supports the cliché that, accurate or not, first impressions are lasting.

Generalizing from other research in the field, Soskin described four limitations on the ability to form accurate impressions of others.[8] First, the impression is likely to be disproportionately affected by the type of situation or surroundings in which the impression is made and influenced too little by the person perceived. Thus the plush luncheon club in which one first meets a man will dominate the impression of the man himself. Secondly, although impressions are frequently based on a limited sample of the perceived person's behavior, the generalization that the perceiver makes will be sweeping. A third limitation is that the situation may not provide an opportunity for the person perceived to show behavior relevant to the traits about which impressions are formed. Casual conversation or questions, for example, provide few opportunities to demonstrate intelligence or work characteristics, yet the perceiver often draws conclusions about these from an interview. Finally, Soskin agrees with Bruner and Cantril that the impression of the person perceived may be distorted by some highly individualized reaction of the perceiver.

But the pitfalls are not yet all spelled out; it is possible to identify some other distorting influences on the process of forming impressions. Research has brought into sharp focus some typical errors, the more important being stereotyping, halo effect, projection, and perceptual defense.

Stereotyping

The word "stereotyping" was first used by Walter Lippmann in 1922 to describe bias in perceiving peoples. He wrote of "pictures in people's heads," called stereotypes, which guided (distorted) their perceptions of others. The term has long been used to describe judgments made about people on the basis of their ethnic group membership. For example, some say "Herman Schmidt [being German] is industrious." Stereotyping also predisposes judgments in many other areas of interpersonal relations. Stereotypes have developed about many types of groups, and they help to prejudice many of our perceptions about their members. Examples of stereotypes of groups other than those based on ethnic identification are bankers, supervisors, union members, poor people, rich people, and administrators. Many unverified qualities are assigned to people principally because of such group memberships.

In a research demonstration of stereotyping, Haire found that labeling a photograph as that of a management representative caused an impression to be formed of the person, different from that formed when it was labeled as that of a union leader.[9] Management and labor formed different impressions, each seeing his opposite as less dependable than his own group. In addition, each side saw his own group as being better able than the opposite group to understand a point of view different from its own. For example, managers felt that other managers were better able to appreciate labor's point of view. Each had similar stereotypes of his opposite and considered the thinking, emotional characteristics, and interpersonal relations of his opposite as inferior to his own. As Stagner pointed out, "It is plain that unionists perceiving company officials in a stereotyped way are less efficient than would be desirable.[10] Similarly, company executives who see all labor unions as identical are not showing good judgment or discrimination."

One of the troublesome aspects of stereotypes is that they are so widespread. Finding the same stereotypes to be widely held should not tempt one to accept their accuracy. It may only mean that many people are making the same mistake. Allport has demonstrated that there need not be a "kernel of truth" in a widely held stereotype.[11] He has shown that while a prevalent stereotype of Armenians labeled them as dishonest, a credit reporting association gave them credit ratings as good as those given other ethnic groups.

Bruner and Perlmutter found that there is an international stereotype for "businessmen" and "teachers."[12] They indicated that the more widespread one's experience with diverse members of a group, the less their group membership will affect the impression formed.

An additional illustration of stereotyping is provided by Luft.[13] His research suggests that perception of personality adjustment may be influenced by stereotypes, associating adjustment with high income and maladjustment with low income.

Halo Effect

The term halo effect was first used in 1920 to describe a process in which a general impression which is favorable or unfavorable is used by judges to evaluate several specific traits. The "halo" in such case serves as a screen keeping the perceiver from actually seeing the trait he is judging. It has received the most attention because of its effect on rating employee performance. In the rating situation, a supervisor may single out one trait, either good or bad, and use this as the basis for his judgment of all other traits. For example, an excellent attendance record causes judgments of productivity, high quality of work, and so forth. One study in the U. S. Army showed that officers who were liked were judged more intelligent than those who were disliked, even though they had the same scores on intelligence tests.

We examine halo effect here because of its general effect on forming impressions. Bruner and Taguiri suggest that it is likely to be most extreme when we are forming impressions of traits that provide minimal cues in the individual's behavior, when the traits have moral overtones, or when the perceiver must judge traits with which he has had little experience.[14] A rather disturbing conclusion is suggested by Symonds that halo effect is more marked the more we know the acquaintance.[15]

A somewhat different aspect of the halo effect is suggested by the research of Grove and Kerr.[16] They found that knowledge that the company was in receivership caused employees to devalue the higher pay and otherwise superior working conditions of their company as compared to those in a financially secure firm.

Psychologists have noted a tendency in perceivers to link certain traits. They assume, for example, that when a person is aggressive he will also have high energy or that when a person is "warm" he will also be generous and have a good sense of humor. This logical error, as it has been called, is a special form of the halo effect and is best illustrated in the research of Asch.[17] In his study the addition of one trait to a list of traits produced a major change in the impression formed. Knowing that a person was intelligent, skillful, industrious, determined, practical, cautious, and warm led a group to judge him to be also wise, humorous, popular, and imaginative. When warm was replaced by cold, a radically different impression (beyond the difference between warm and cold) was formed. Kelley's research illustrated the same type of error.[18] This tendency is not indiscriminate; with the pair "polite-blunt," less change was found than with the more central traits of "warm-cold."

In evaluating the effect of halo on perceptual distortion, we may take comfort from the work of Wishner, which showed that those traits that correlate more highly with each other are more likely to lead to a halo effect than those that are unrelated.[19]

Projection

A defense mechanism available to everyone is projection, in which one relieves one's feelings of guilt by projecting blame onto someone else. Over the years the projection mechanism has been assigned various meanings. The original use of the term was concerned with the mechanism to defend oneself from unacceptable feelings. There has since been a tendency for the term to be used more broadly, meaning to ascribe or attribute any of one's own characteristics to other people. The projection mechanism concerns us here because it influences the perceptual process. An early study by Murray illustrates its effect.[20] After playing a dramatic game, "Murder," his subjects attributed much more maliciousness to people whose photographs were judged than did a control group which had not played the game. The current emotional state of the perceiver tended to influence his perceptions of others; i.e., frightened perceivers judged people to be frightening. More recently, Feshback and Singer revealed further dynamics of the process.[21] In their study, subjects who had been made fearful judged a stimulus person (presented in a moving picture) as both more fearful and more aggressive than did nonfearful perceivers. These authors were able to demonstrate further that the projection mechanism at work here was reduced when their subjects were encouraged to admit and talk about their fears.

Sears provides an illustration of a somewhat different type of projection and its effect on perception.[22] In his study projection is seeing our own undesirable personality characteristics in other people. He demonstrated that people high in such traits as stinginess, obstinacy, and disorderliness, tended to rate others much higher on these traits than did those who were low in these undesirable characteristics. The tendency to project was particularly marked among subjects who had the least insight into their own personalities.

Research thus suggests that our perceptions may characteristically be distorted by emotions we are experiencing or traits that we possess. Placed in the administrative setting, the research would suggest, for example, that a manager frightened by rumored organizational changes might not only judge others to be more frightened than they were, but also assess various policy decisions as more frightening than they were. Or a general foreman lacking insight into his own incapacity to delegate might be oversensitive to this trait in his superiors.

Perceptual Defense

Another distorting influence, which has been called perceptual defense, has also been demonstrated by Haire and Grunes to be a source of error.[23] In their research they ask, in effect, "Do we put blinders on to defend ourselves from seeing those events which might disturb us?" The concept of perceptual defense offers an excellent description of perceptual distortion at work and demonstrates that when confronted with a fact inconsistent with a stereotype already held by a person, the perceiver is able to distort the data in such a way as to eliminate the inconsistency. Thus, by perceiving inaccurately, he defends himself from having to change his stereotypes.

Characteristics of Perceiver and Perceived

We have thus far been talking largely about influences on the perceptual process without specific regard to the perceiver and his characteristics. Much recent research has tried to identify some characteristics of the perceiver and their influence on the perception of other people.

The Perceiver

A thread that would seem to tie together many current findings is the tendency to use oneself as the norm or standard by which one perceives or judges others. If we examine current research, certain conclusions are suggested:

1. *Knowing oneself makes it easier to see others accurately.* Norman showed that when one is aware of what his own personal characteristics are he makes fewer errors in perceiving others.[24] Weingarten has shown that people with insight are less likely to view the world in black-and-white terms and to give extreme judgments about others.[25]

2. *One's own characteristics affect the characteristics he is likely to see in others.* Secure people (compared to insecure) tend to see others as warm rather than cold, as was shown by Bossom and Maslow.[26] The extent of one's own sociability influences the degree of importance one gives to the sociability of other people when one forms impressions of them.[27] The person with "authoritarian" tendencies is more likely to view others in terms of power and is less sensitive to the psychological or personality characteristics of other people than is a nonauthoritarian.[28] The relatively few categories one uses in describing other people tend to be those one uses in describing oneself.[29] Thus traits which are important to the perceiver will be used more when he forms impressions of others. He has certain constant tendencies, both with regard to using certain categories in judging others and to the amount of weight given to these categories.[30]

3. *The person who accepts himself is more likely to be able to see favorable aspects of other people.*[31] This relates in part to the accuracy of his perceptions.

If the perceiver accepts himself as he is, he widens his range of vision in seeing others; he can look at them and be less likely to be very negative or critical. In those areas in which he is more insecure, he sees more problems in other people.[32] We are more likely to like others who have traits we accept in ourselves and reject those who have the traits which we do not like in ourselves.[33]

4. *Accuracy in perceiving others is not a single skill.* While there have been some variations in the findings, as Gage has shown, some consistent results do occur.[34] The perceiver tends to interpret the feelings others have about him in terms of his feelings towards them.[35] One's ability to perceive others accurately may depend on how sensitive one is to differences between people and also to the norms (outside of oneself) for judging them.[36] Thus, as Taft has shown, the ability to judge others does not seem to be a single skill.[37]

Possibly the results in these four aspects of person perception can be viewed most constructively in connection with earlier points on the process of perception. The administrator (or any other individual) who wishes to perceive someone else accurately must look at the other person, not at himself. The things that he looks at in someone else are influenced by his own traits. But if he knows his own traits, he can be aware that they provide a frame of reference for him. His own traits help to furnish the categories that he will use in perceiving others. His characteristics, needs, and values can partly limit his vision and his awareness of the differences between others. The question one could ask when viewing another is: "Am I looking at him, and forming my impression of his behavior in the situation, or am I just comparing him with myself?"

There is the added problem of being set to observe the personality traits in another which the perceiver does not accept in himself, e.g., being somewhat autocratic. At the same time he may make undue allowances in others for those of his own deficiencies which do not disturb him but might concern some people, e.g., not following prescribed procedures.

The Perceived

Lest we leave the impression that it is only the characteristics of the perceiver that stand between him and others in his efforts to know them, we turn now to some characteristics of the person being perceived which raise problems in perception. It is possible to demonstrate, for example, that the status of the person perceived is a variable influencing judgments about his behavior. Thibaut and Riecken have shown that even though two people behave in identical fashion, status differences between them cause a perceiver to assign different motivations for the behavior.[38] Concerning co-operativeness, they found that high status persons are judged as wanting to co-operate and low status persons as having to co-operate. In turn, more liking is shown for the person of high status than for the person of low status. Presumably, more credit is given when the boss says, "Good morning," to us than when a subordinate says the same thing.

Bruner indicated that we use categories to simplify our perceptual activities. In the administrative situation, status is one type of category, and role provides another. Thus the remarks of Mr. Jones in the sales department are perceived differently from those of Smith in the purchasing department, although both may say the same thing. Also, one who knows Jones's role in the organization will perceive his behavior differently from one who does not know Jones's role. The process of categorizing on the basis of roles is similar to, if not identical with, the stereotyping process described earlier.

Visibility of the traits is also an important variable influencing the accuracy of perception.[39] Visibility will depend, for example, on how free the other person feels to express the trait. It has been demonstrated that we are more accurate in judging people who like us than people who dislike us. The explanation suggested is that most people in our society feel constraint in showing their dislike, and therefore the cues are less visible.

Some traits are not visible simply because they provide few external cues for their presence. Loyalty, for example, as opposed to level of energy, provides few early signs for observation. Even honesty cannot be seen in the situations in which most impressions are formed. As obvious as these comments might be, in forming impressions many of us nevertheless continue to judge the presence of traits which are not really visible. Frequently the practical situation demands judgments, but we should recognize the frail reeds upon which we are leaning and be prepared to observe further and revise our judgments with time and closer acquaintance.

Situational Influences on Perception

Some recent research clearly points to the conclusion that the whole process of interpersonal perception is, at least in part, a function of the *group* (or interpersonal) context in which the perception occurs. Much of the research has important theoretical implications for a psychology of interpersonal relations. In addition, there are some suggestions of value for administrators. It is possible to identify several characteristics of the interpersonal climate which have direct effect on perceptual accuracy. As will be noted, these are characteristics which can be known, and in some cases controlled, in administrative settings.

Bieri provides data for the suggestion that when people are given an opportunity to interact in a friendly situation, they tend to see others as similar to themselves.[40] Applying his suggestion to the administrative situation, we can rationalize as follows: Some difficulties of administrative practice grow out of beliefs that different interest groups in the organization are made up of different types of people. Obviously once we believe that people in other groups are different, we will be predisposed to see the differences. We can thus find, from Bieri's and from Rosenbaum's work, an administrative approach for attacking the problem.[41] If we can produce an interacting situation which is co-operative rather than competitive, the likelihood of seeing other people as similar to ourselves is increased.

Exline's study adds some other characteristics of the social context which may influence perception.[42] Paraphrasing his conclusions to adapt them to the administrative scene, we can suggest that when a committee group is made up of congenial members who are willing to continue work in the same group, their perceptions of the goal-directed behavior of fellow committee members will be more accurate, although observations of purely personal behavior (as distinguished from goal-directed behavior) may be less accurate.[43] The implications for setting up committees and presumably other interacting work groups seem clear: Do not place together those with a past history of major personal clashes. If they must be on the same committee, each must be helped to see that the other is working toward the same goal.

An interesting variation in this area of research is the suggestion from Ex's work that perceptions will be more influenced or swayed by relatively unfamiliar people in the group than by those who are intimates.[44] The concept needs further research, but it provides the interesting suggestion that we may give more credit to strangers for having knowledge, since we do not really know, than we do to our intimates, whose backgrounds and limitations we feel we do know.

The *organization*, and one's place in it, may also be viewed as the context in which perceptions take place. A study by Dearborn and Simon illustrates this point.[45] Their data support the hypothesis that the administrator's perceptions will often be limited to those aspects of a situation which relate specifically to his own department, despite an attempt to influence him away from such selectivity.

Perception of self among populations at different levels in the hierarchy also offers an opportunity to judge the influence of organizational context on perceptual activity. Porter's study of the self-descriptions of managers and line workers indicated that both groups saw themselves in different terms, which corresponded to their positions in the organization's hierarchy.[46] He stated that managers used leadership-type traits (e.g., inventive) to describe themselves, while line workers used follower-type terms (e.g., co-operative). The question of which comes first must be asked: Does the manager see himself this way because of his current position in the organization? Or is this self-picture an expression of a more enduring personal characteristic that helped bring the manager to his present position? This study does not answer that question, but it does suggest to an administrator the need to be aware of the possibly critical relationship between one's hierarchical role and self-perception.

Perceptual Influences on Interpersonal Adjustment

Throughout this paper, we have examined a variety of influences on the perceptual process. There has been at least the inference that the operations of such influences on perception would in turn affect behavior that would follow. Common sense judgment suggests that being able to judge other people accurately facilitates smooth and effective interpersonal adjustments. Nevertheless, the relationship between perception and consequent behavior is itself in need of direct analysis. Two aspects may be identified: (1) the effect of accuracy of perception on subsequent behavior and (2) the effect of the duration of the relationship and the opportunity for experiencing additional cues.

First then, from the applied point of view, we can ask a crucial question: Is there a relationship between accuracy of social perception and adjustment to others? While the question might suggest a quick affirmative answer, research findings are inconsistent. Steiner attempted to resolve some of these inconsistencies by stating that accuracy may have an effect on interaction under the following conditions: when the interacting persons are co-operatively motivated, when the behavior which is accurately perceived is relevant to the activities of these persons, and when members are free to alter their behavior on the basis of their perceptions.[47]

Where the relationship provides opportunity only to form an impression, a large number of subjective factors, i.e., set, stereotypes, projections, etc., operate to create an early impression, which is frequently erroneous. In more enduring relationships a more balanced appraisal may result as increased interaction provides additional cues for judgment. In his study of the acquaintance process, Newcomb showed that while early perception of favorable traits caused attraction to the perceived person, over a four-month period the early cues for judging favorable traits became less influential.[48] With time, a much broader basis was used which included comparisons with others with whom one had established relationships. Such findings suggest that the warnings about perceptual inaccuracies implicit in the earlier sections of this paper apply with more force to the short-term process of impression forming than to relatively extended acquaintance-building relationships. One would thus hope that rating an employee after a year of service would be a more objective performance than appraising him in a selection interview—a hope that would be fulfilled only when the rater had provided himself with opportunities for broadening the cues he used in forming his first impressions.

Summary

Two principal suggestions which increase the probability of more effective administrative action emerge from the research data. One suggestion is that the administrator be continuously aware of the intricacies of the perceptual process and thus be warned to avoid arbitrary and categorical judgments and to seek reliable evidence before judgments are made. A second suggestion grows out of the first: increased accuracy in one's self-perception can make possible the flexibility to seek evidence and to shift position as time provides additional evidence.

Nevertheless, not every effort designed to improve perceptual accuracy will bring about such accuracy. The dangers of too complete reliance on formal training for perceptual accuracy are suggested in a study by Crow.[49] He found that a group of senior medical students were somewhat less accurate in their perceptions of others after a period of training in physician-patient relationships than were an untrained control group. The danger is that a little learning encourages the perceiver to respond with increased sensitivity to individual differences without making it possible for him to gauge the real meaning of the differences he has seen.

Without vigilance to perceive accurately and to minimize as far as possible the subjective approach in perceiving others, effective administration is handicapped. On the other hand, research would not support the conclusion that perceptual distortions will not occur simply because the administrator says he will try to be objective. The administrator or manager will have to work hard to avoid seeing only what he wants to see and to guard against fitting everything into what he is set to see.

We are not yet sure of the ways in which training for perceptual accuracy can best be accomplished, but such training cannot be ignored. In fact, one can say that one of the important tasks of administrative science is to design research to test various training procedures for increasing perceptual accuracy.

Notes and References

1. D. M. Johnson, A Systematic Treatment of Judgment, *Psychological Bulletin*, 42 (1945), 193-224.
2. J. S. Bruner, "Social Psychology and Perception," in E. Maccoby, T. Newcomb, and E. Hartley, eds. *Readings in Social Psychology* (3rd ed.: New York, 1958), pp. 85-94.
3. H. Cantril, Perception and Interpersonal Relations, *American Journal of Psychiatry*, 114 (1957), 119-126.
4. H. H. Kelley, The Warm-Cold Variable in First Impressions of Persons, *Journal of Personality*, 18 (1950), 431-439.
5. L. H. Strickland, Surveillance and Trust, *Journal of Personality*, 26 (1958), 200-215.
6. J. Mason, Judgements of Leadership Based upon Physiognomic Cues, *Journal of Abnormal and Social Psychology*, 54 (1957), 273-274.
7. C. A. Dailey, The Effects of Premature Conclusion upon the Acquisition of Understanding of a Person, *Journal of Psychology*, 33 (1952), 133-152.
8. W. E. Soskin, Influence of Information on Bias in Social Perception, *Journal of Personality*, 22, (1953), 118-127.
9. M. Haire, Role Perceptions in Labor-Management Relations: An Experimental Approach, *Indistrial Labor Relations Review*, 8, (1955), 204-216.
10. R. Stagner, *Psychology of Industrial Conflict* (New York, 1956), p. 35.
11. G. Allport, *Nature of Prejudice* (Cambridge, Mass., 1954).
12. S. Bruner and H. V. Perlmutter, Compatriot and Foreigner: A Study of Impression Formation in Three Countries, *Journal of Abnormal and Social Psychology*, 55 (1957), 253-260.
13. J. Luft, Monetary Value and the Perception of Persons, *Journal of Social Psychology*, 46 (1957), 245-251.
14. J. S. Bruner and A. Taguiri, "The Perception of People," ch. xvii in G. Lindzey, ed., *Handbook of Social Psychology* (Cambridge, Mass., 1954).
15. P. M. Symonds, Notes on Rating, *Journal of Applied Psychology*, 7 (1925), 188-195.
16. B. A. Grove and W. A. Kerr, Specific Evidence on Origin of Halo Effect in Measurement of Morale, *Journal of Social Psychology*, 34 (1951), 165-170.
17. S. Asch, Forming Impressions of Persons, *Journal of Abnormal and Social Psychology*, 60 (1946), 258-290.
18. Kelley, *op.cit.*
19. J.Wishner, Reanalysis of "Impressions of Personality," *Psychology Review*, 67 (1960), 96-112.
20. H. A. Murray, The Effect of Fear upon Estimates of the Maliciousness of Other Personalities, *Journal of Social Psychology*, 4, (1933), 310-329.
21. S. Feshback and R. D. Singer, The Effects of Fear Arousal upon Social Perception, *Journal of Abnormal and Social Psychology*, 55, (1957), 283-288.
22. R. R. Sears, Experimental Studies of Perception, 1. Attribution of Traits, *Journal of Social Psychology*, 7 (1936), 151-163.
23. M. Haire and W. F. Grunes, Perceptual Defenses: Processes Protecting an Original Perception of Another Personality, *Human Relations*, 3, (1958), 403-412.
24. R. D. Norman, The Interrelationships among Acceptance-Rejection, Self-Other Identity, Insight into Self, and Realistic Perception of others, *Journal of Social Psychology*, 37, (1953), 205-235.

25. E. Weingarten, A Study of Selective Perception in Clinical Judgment, *Journal of Personality,* 17 (1949), 369-400.
26. J. Bossom and A. H. Maslow, Security of Judges as a Factor in Impressions of Warmth in Others, *Journal of Abnormal and Social Psychology,* 55 (1957), 147-148.
27. D. T. Benedetti and J. G. Hill, A Determiner of the Centrality of a Trait in Impression Formation, *Journal of Abnormal and Social Psychology,* 60 (1960), 278-279.
28. E. E. Jones, Authoritarianism as a Determinant of First-Impressions Formation, *Journal of Personality,* 23 (1954), 107-127.
29. A. H. Hastorf, S. A. Richardson, and S. M. Dornbusch, "The Problem of Relevance in the Study of Person Perception," in R. Taguiri and L. Petrullo, *Person Perception and Interpersonal Behavior* (Stanford, Calif. 1958).
30. L. J. Cronbach, Processes Affecting Scores on "Understanding of Others" and "Assumed Similarity," *Psychology Bulletin,* 52 (1955), 177-193.
31. K. T. Omwake, The Relation between Acceptance of Self and Acceptance of Others Shown by Three Personality Inventories, *Journal of Consulting Psychology,* 18 (1954), 443-446.
32. Weingarten, *op. cit.*
33. R. M. Lundy, W. Katovsky, R. L. Cromwell, and D. J. Shoemaker, Self Acceptability and Descriptions of Sociometric Choices, *Journal of Abnormal and Social Psychology,* 51 (1955), 260-262.
34. N. L. Gage, Accuracy of Social Perception and Effectiveness in Interpersonal Relationships, *Journal of Personality,* 22 (1953), 128-141.
35. R. Taguiri, J. S. Bruner, and R. Blake, On the Relation between Feelings and Perceptions of Feelings among Members of Small Groups," in Maccoby *et al., Readings in Social Psychology, op. cit.*
36. U. Bronfenbrenner, J. Harding, and M. Gallway, "The Measurement of Skill in Social Perception," in H. L. McClelland, D.C. Baldwin, U. Bronfenbrenner, and F.L. Strodtbeck, eds., *Talent and Society* (Princeton, N. J., 1958), pp. 29-111.
37. R. Taft, The Ability to Judge People, *Psychological Bulletin,* 52 (1955), 1-21.
38. J. W. Thibaut and H. W. Riecken, Some Determinants and Consequences of the Perception of Social Causality, *Journal of Personality,* 24 (1955), 113-133.
39. Bruner and Taguiri, *op. cit.*
40. J. Bieri, Change in Interpersonal Perception Following Interaction, *Journal of Abnormal and Social Psychology,* 48 (1953), 61-66.
41. J. E. Rosenbaum, Social Perception and the Motivational Structure of Interpersonal Relations, *Journal of Abnormal Psychology,* 59 (1959), 130-133.
42. R. V. Exline, Interrelations among Two Dimensions of Sociometric Status, Group Congeniality and Accuracy of Social Perception, *Sociometry,* 23 (1960), 85-101.
43. R. V. Exline, Group Climate as a Factor in the Relevance and Accuracy of Social Perception, *Journal of Abnormal and Social Psychology,* 55 (1957), 382-388.
44. J. Ex, The Nature of the Relation between Two Persons and the Degree of Their Influence on Each Other, *Acta Psychologica,* 17 (1960), 39-54.
45. D. C. Dearborn and H. A. Simon, Selective Perception. A Note on the Departmental Identifications of Executives, *Sociometry,* 21 (1958), 140-144.
46. L. W. Porter, Differential Self-Perceptions of Management Personnel and Line Workers, *Journal of Applied Psychology,* 42 (1958), 105-109.
47. J. Steiner, Interpersonal Behavior as Influenced by Accuracy of Social Perception, *Psychological Review,* 62 (1955), 168-275.

48. T. M. Newcomb, The Perception of Interpersonal Attraction, *American Psychologist*, 11 (1956), 575-586, and *The Acquaintance Process* (New York, 1961).

49. W. J. Crow, Effect of Training on Interpersonal Perception, *Journal of Abnormal and Social Psychology*, 55 (1957), 355-359.

SELECTIVE PERCEPTION

DEWITT C. DEARBORN
HERBERT A. SIMON

An important proposition in organization theory asserts that each executive will perceive those aspects of the situation that relate specifically to the activities and goals of his department (2, Ch. 5, 10). The proposition is frequently supported by anecdotes of executives and observers in organizations, but little evidence of a systematic kind is available to test it. It is the purpose of this note to supply some such evidence.

The proposition we are considering is not peculiarly organizational. It is simply an application to organizational phenomena of a generalization that is central to any explanation of selective perception: Presented with a complex stimulus, the subject perceives in it what he is "ready" to perceive; the more complex or ambiguous the stimulus, the more the perception is determined by what is already "in" the subject and the less by what is in the stimulus (1, pp. 132-133).

Cognitive and motivational mechanisms mingle in the selective process, and it may be of some use to assess their relative contributions. We might suppose either: (1) selective attention to a part of a stimulus reflects a deliberate ignoring of the remainder as irrelevant to the subject's goals and motives, or (2) selective attention is a learned response stemming from some past history of reinforcement. In the latter case we might still be at some pains to determine the nature of the reinforcement, but by creating a situation from which any immediate motivation for selectivity is removed, we should be able to separate the second mechanism from the first. The situation in which we obtained our data meets this condition, and hence our data provide evidence for internalization of the selective processes.

Method of the Study

A group of 23 executives, all employed by a single large manufacturing concern and enrolled in a company sponsored executive training program, was asked to read

Reprinted by permission of the authors and the publisher, the American Sociological Association, from *Sociometry*, vol. 21 (1958), pp. 140-43.

a standard case that is widely used in instruction in business policy in business schools. The case, Castengo Steel Company described the organization and activities of a company of moderate size specializing in the manufacture of seamless steel tubes, as of the end of World War II. The case, which is about 10,000 words in length, contains a wealth of descriptive material about the company and its industry and the recent history of both (up to 1945), but little evaluation. It is deliberately written to hold closely to concrete facts and to leave as much as possible of the burden of interpretation to the reader.

When the executives appeared at a class to discuss the case, but before they had discussed it, they were asked by the instructor to write a brief statement of what they considered to be the most important problem facing the Castengo Steel Company—the problem a new company president should deal with first. Prior to this session, the group had discussed other cases, being reminded from time to time by the instructor that they were to assume the role of the top executive of the company in considering its problems.

The executives were a relatively homogeneous group in terms of status, being drawn from perhaps three levels of the company organization. They were in the range usually called "middle management," representing such positions as superintendent of a department in a large factory, product manager responsible for profitability of one of the ten product groups manufactured by the company, and works physician for a large factory. In terms of departmental affiliation, they fell in four groups:

Sales (6) Five product managers or assistant product managers, and one field sales supervisor.

Production (5): Three department superintendents, one assistant factory manager, and one construction engineer.

Accounting (4): An assistant chief accountant, and three accounting supervisors —for a budget division and two factory departments.

Miscellaneous (8): Two members of the legal department, two in research and development, and one each from public relations, industrial relations, medical and purchasing.

The Data

. . . We tested our hypothesis by determining whether there was a significant relation between the "most important problem" mentioned and the departmental affiliation of the mentioner. In the cases of executives who mentioned more than one problem, we counted all those they mentioned. We compared (1) the executives who mentioned "sales," "marketing," or "distribution" with those who did not; (2) the executives who mentioned "clarifying the organization" or some equivalent with those who did not; (3) the executives who mentioned "human relations," "employee relations" or "teamwork" with those who did not. The findings are summarized in the Table.

The difference between the percentages of sales executives (83%) and other executives (29%) who mentioned sales as the most important problem is significant at the 5 per cent level. Three of the five nonsales executives, moreover, who mentioned sales were in the accounting department, and all of these were in positions

Department	Total number of executives	Number who mentioned		
		Sales	"Clarify organization"	Human relations
Sales	6	5	1	0
Production	5	1	4	0
Accounting	4	3	0	0
Miscellaneous	8	1	3	3
Totals	23	10	8	3

that involved analysis of product profitability. This accounting activity was, in fact, receiving considerable emphasis in the company at the time of the case discussion and the accounting executives had frequent and close contacts with the product managers in the sales department. If we combine sales and accounting executives, we find that 8 out of 10 of these mentioned sales as the most important problem; while only 2 of the remaining 13 executives did.

Organization problems (other than marketing organization) were mentioned by four out of five production executives, the two executives in research and development, and the factory physician, but by only one sales executive and no accounting executives. The difference between the percentage for production executives (80%) and other executives (22%) is also significant at the 5 per cent level. Examination of the Castengo case shows that the main issue discussed in the case that relates to manufacturing is the problem of poorly defined relations among the factory manager, the metallurgist, and the company president. The presence of the metallurgist in the situation may help to explain the sensitivity of the two research and development executives (both of whom were concerned with metallurgy) to this particular problem area.

It is easy to conjecture why the public relations, industrial relations, and medical executives should all have mentioned some aspect of human relations, and why one of the two legal department executives should have mentioned the board of directors.

Conclusion

We have presented data on the selective perceptions of industrial executives exposed to case material that support the hypothesis that each executive will perceive those aspects of a situation that relate specifically to the activities and goals of his department. Since the situation is one in which the executives were motivated to look at the problem from a company-wide rather than a departmental viewpoint, the data indicate further that the criteria of selection have become internalized. Finally, the method for obtaining that we have used holds considerable promise as a projective device for eliciting the attitudes and perceptions of executives.

References

1. Bruner, J. S., "On Perceptual Readiness," *Psychological Review*, 1957, 64, 123-152
2. Simon, H. A., *Administrative Behavior*, New York: Macmillan, 1947.

Section C

Motivation And Individual Performance

TOWARD A THEORY
OF MOTIVE ACQUISITION

DAVID C. McCLELLAND

Too little is known about the processes of personality change at relatively complex levels. The empirical study of the problem has been hampered by both practical and theoretical difficulties. On the practical side it is very expensive both in time and effort to set up systematically controlled educational programs designed to develop some complex personality characteristic like a motive, and to follow the effects of the education over a number of years. It also presents ethical problems since it is not always clear that it is as proper to teach a person a new motive as it is a new skill like learning to play the piano. For both reasons, most of what we know about personality change has come from studying psychotherapy where both ethical and practical difficulties are overcome by the pressing need to help someone in real trouble. Yet, this source of information leaves much to be desired: It has so far proven difficult to identify and systematically vary the "inputs" in psychotherapy and to measure their specific effects on subsequent behavior, except in very general ways (cf. Rogers & Dymond, 1954).

On the theoretical side, the dominant views of personality formation suggest anyway that acquisition or change of any complex characteristic like a motive in adulthood would be extremely difficult. Both behavior theory and psychoanalysis agree that stable personality characteristics like motives are laid down in childhood. Behavior theory arrives at this conclusion by arguing that social motives are learned by close association with reduction in certain basic biological drives like hunger, thirst, and physical discomfort which loom much larger in childhood than adulthood. Psychoanalysis, for its part, pictures adult motives as stable resolutions of basic con-

From *American Psychologist*, vol. 20 (1965), pp. 321-33. Copyright 1965 by the American Psychological Association. Reprinted by permission.

flicts occurring in early childhood. Neither theory would provide much support for the notion that motives could be developed in adulthood without somehow recreating the childhood conditions under which they were originally formed. Furthermore, psychologists have been hard put to it to find objective evidence that even prolonged, serious, and expensive attempts to introduce personality change through psychotherapy have really proven successful (Eysenck, 1952). What hope is there that a program to introduce personality change would end up producing a big enough effect to study?

Despite these difficulties a program of research has been under way for some time which is attempting to develop the achievement motive in adults. It was undertaken in an attempt to fill some of the gaps in our knowledge about personality change or the acquisition of complex human characteristics. Working with n Achievement has proved to have some important advantages for this type of research: The practical and ethical problems do not loom especially large because previous research (McClelland, 1961) has demonstrated the importance of high n Achievement for entrepreneurial behavior and it is easy to find businessmen, particularly in underdeveloped countries, who are interested in trying any means of improving their entrepreneurial performance. Furthermore, a great deal is known about the origins of n Achievement in childhood and its specific effects on behavior so that educational programs can be systematically planned and their effects evaluated in terms of this knowledge. Pilot attempts to develop n Achievement have gradually led to the formulation of some theoretical notions of what motive acquisition involves and how it can be effectively promoted in adults. These notions have been summarized in the form of 12 propositions which it is the ultimate purpose of the research program to test. The propositions are anchored so far as possible in experiences with pilot courses, in supporting research findings from other studies, and in theory.

Before the propositions are presented, it is necessary to explain more of the theoretical and practical background on which they are based. To begin with, some basis for believing that motives could be acquired in adulthood had to be found in view of the widespread pessimism on the subject among theoretically oriented psychologists. Oddly enough we were encouraged by the successful efforts of two quite different groups of "change agents"—operant conditioners and missionaries. Both groups have been "naive" in the sense of being unimpressed by or ignorant of the state of psychological knowledge in the field. The operant conditioners have not been encumbered by any elaborate theoretical apparatus; they do not believe motives exist anyway, and continue demonstrating vigorously that if you want a person to make a response, all you have to do is elicit it and reward it (cf. Bandura & Walters, 1963, pp. 238 ff.). They retain a simple faith in the infinite plasticity of human behavior in which one response is just like any other and any one can be "shaped up" (strengthened by reward)—presumably even an "achievement" response as produced by a subject in a fantasy test. In fact, it was the naive optimism of one such researcher (Burris, 1958) that had a lot to do with getting the present research under way. He undertook a counseling program in which an attempt to elicit and reinforce achievement-related fantasies proved to be successful in motivating college students to get better grades. Like operant conditioners, the missionaries have gone ahead changing people because they have believed it possible. While the evidence is not scientifically impeccable, common-sense observation yields dozens of cases of adults whose motivational structure has seemed to be quite radically and permanently altered by the educational efforts of Communist Party, Mormon, or other devout missionaries.

A man from Mars might be led to observe that personality change appears to be very difficult for those who think it is very difficult, if not impossible, and much easier for those who think it can be done. He would certainly be oversimplifying the picture, but at the very least his observation suggests that some theoretical revision is desirable in the prevailing views of social motives which link them so decisively to early childhood. Such a revision has been attempted in connection with the research on n Achievement (McClelland, Atkinson, Clark & Lowell, 1953) and while it has not been widely accepted (cf. Berelson & Steiner, 1964), it needs to be briefly summarized here to provide a theoretical underpinning for the attempts at motive change to be described. It starts with the proposition that all motives are learned, that not even biological discomforts (as from hunger) or pleasures (as from sexual stimulation) are "urges" or "drives" until they are linked to cues that can signify their presence or absence. In time clusters of expectancies or associations grow up around affective experiences, not all of which are connected by any means with biological needs (McClelland et al., 1953, Ch. 2), which we label motives. More formally, motives are "affectively toned associative networks" arranged in a hierarchy of strength or importance within a given individual. Obviously, the definition fits closely the operations used to measure a motive: "an affectively toned associative cluster" is exactly what is coded in a subject's fantasies to obtain an n Achievement score. The strength of the motive (its position in the individual's hierarchy of motives) is measured essentially by counting the number of associations belonging to this cluster as compared to others that an individual produces in a given number of opportunities. If one thinks of a motive as an associative network, it is easier to imagine how one might go about changing it: The problem becomes one of moving its position up on the hierarchy by increasing its salience compared to other clusters. It should be possible to accomplish this end by such tactics as: (a) setting up the network—discovering what associations, for example, exist in the achievement area and then extending, strengthening, or otherwise "improving" the network they form; (b) conceptualizing the network—forming a clear and conscious construct that labels the network; (c) tying the network to as many cues as possible in everyday life, especially those preceding and following action, to insure that the network will be regularly rearoused once formed; and (d) working out the relation of the network to superordinate associative clusters, like the self-concept, so that these dominant schemata do not block the train of achievement thoughts—for example, through a chain of interfering associations (e.g., "I am not really the achieving type").

This very brief summary is not intended as a full exposition of the theoretical viewpoint underlying the research, but it should suffice to give a rough idea of how the motive was conceived that we set out to change. This concept helped define the goals of the techniques of change, such as reducing the effects of associative interference from superordinate associate clusters. But what about the techniques themselves? What could we do that would produce effective learning of this sort? Broadly speaking, there are four types of empirical information to draw on. From the animal learning experiments, we know that such factors as repetition, optimal time intervals between stimulus, response, and reward, and the schedule of rewards are very important for effective learning. From human learning experiments, we know that such factors as distribution of practice, repetitions, meaningfulness, and recitation are important. From experiences with psychotherapy (cf. Rogers, 1961), we learn that warmth, honesty, non-directiveness, and the ability to recode associations in line with psychoanalytic or other personality theories are important. And, from the attitude-change research literature, we learn that such variables as presenting one side or two, using reason or prestige to support an argument, or affiliating with a new reference group are crucial for developing new attitudes (cf. Hovland, Janis, & Kelley, 1953). Despite the fact that many of these variables seem limited in application to the learning situation in which they were studied, we have tried to make use of information from all these sources in designing our "motive acquisition" program and in finding support for the general propositions that have emerged from our study so far. For our purpose has been above all to produce an effect large enough to be measured. Thus we have tried to profit by all that is known about how to facilitate learning or produce personality or attitude change. For, if we could not obtain a substantial effect with all factors working to produce it, there would be no point to studying the effects of each factor taken one at a time. Such a strategy also has the practical advantage that we are in the position of doing our best to "deliver the goods" to our course participants since they were giving us their time and attention to take part in a largely untried educational experience.[1]

Our overall research strategy, therefore, is "subtractive" rather than "additive." After we have demonstrated a substantial effect with some 10-12 factors working to produce it, our plan is to subtract that part of the program that deals with each of the factors to discover if there is a significant decline in the effect. It should also be possible to omit several factors in various combinations to get at interactional effects. This will obviously require giving a fairly large number of courses in a standard institutional setting for the same kinds of businessmen with follow-up evaluation of their performance extending over a number of years. So obviously it will be some time before each of the factors incorporated into the propositions which follow can be properly evaluated so far as its effect on producing motive change is concerned.

The overall research strategy also determined the way the attempts to develop the achievement motive have been organized. That is to say, in order to process enough subjects to permit testing the effectiveness of various "inputs" in a reasonable number of years, the training had to be both of *short duration* (lasting 1-3 weeks) and *designed for groups* rather than for individuals as in person-to-person counseling. Fortunately these requirements coincide with normal practice in providing short courses for business executives. To conform further with that practice, the training has usually also been *residential* and *voluntary*. The design problems introduced by the last characteristic we have tried to handle in the usual ways by putting half the volunteers on a waiting list or giving them a different, technique-oriented course, etc. So far we have given the course to develop n Achievement in some form or another some eight times to over 140 managers or teachers of management in groups of 9-25 in the United States, Mexico, and India. For the most part the course has been offered by a group of 2-4 consultant psychologists either to executives in a single company as a company training program, or to executives from several different companies as a self-improvement program, or as part of the program of an institute or school devoted to training managers. The theoretical propositions which follow have evolved gradually from these pilot attempts to be effective in developing n Achievement among businessmen of various cultural backgrounds.

The first step in a motive development program is to create confidence that it will work. Our initial efforts in this area were dictated by the simple practical consideration that we had to "sell" our course or nobody would take it. We were not in the position of an animal psychologist who can order a dozen rats, or an academic psychologist who has captive subjects in his classes, or even a psychotherapist who has sick people knocking at his door every day. So we explained to all who would listen that we had every reason to believe from previous research that high n Achievement is related to effective entrepreneurship and that therefore business executives could expect to profit from taking a course designed to understand and develop this important human characteristic. What started as a necessity led to the first proposition dealing with how to bring about motive change.

Proposition 1. The more reasons an individual has in advance to believe that he can, will, or should develop a motive, the more educational attempts designed to develop that motive are likely to succeed. The empirical support for this proposition from other studies is quite impressive. It consists of (a) the prestige-suggestion studies showing that people will believe or do what prestigeful sources suggest (cf. Hovland et al., 1953); (b) the so-called "Hawthorne effect" showing that people who feel they are especially selected to show an effect will tend to show it (Roethlisberger & Dickson, 1947); (c) the "Hello-Goodbye" effect in psychotherapy showing that patients who merely have contact with a prestigeful medical authority improve significantly over waiting list controls and almost as much as those who get prolonged therapy (Frank, 1961); (d) the "experimenter bias" studies which show that subjects will often do what an experimenter wants them to do, even though neither he nor they know he is trying to influence them (Rosenthal, 1963); (e) the goal-setting studies which show that setting goals for a person particularly in the name of prestigeful authorities like "science" or "research" improves performance (Kausler, 1959; Mierke, 1955); (f) the parent-child interaction studies which show that parents who set higher standards of excellence for their sons are more likely to have sons with high n Achievement (Rosen & D'Andrade, 1959). The common factor in all these studies seems to be that goals are being set for the individual by sources he respects—goals which imply that his behavior should change for a variety of reasons and that it *can* change. In common-sense terms, belief in the possibility and desirability of change are tremendously influential in changing a person.

So we have used a variety of means to create this belief: the authority of research findings on the relationship of n Achievement to entrepreneurial success, the suggestive power of membership in an experimental group designed to show an effect, the prestige of a great university, our own genuine enthusiasm for the course and our conviction that it would work, as expressed privately and in public speeches. In short, we were trying to make every use possible of what is sometimes regarded as an "error" in such research—namely, the Hawthorne effect, experimenter bias, etc., because we believe it to be one of the most powerful sources of change.

Why? What is the effect on the person, theoretically speaking, of all this goal setting for him? Its primary function is probably to arouse what exists of an associative network in the achievement area for each person affected. That is, many studies have shown that talk of achievement or affiliation or power tends to increase the frequency with which individuals think about achievement or affiliation or power (cf. Atkinson, 1958). And the stronger the talk, the more the relevant associative networks are aroused (McClelland et al., 1953). Such an arousal has several possible effects which would facilitate learning: (*a*) It elicits what exists in the person of a "response" thus making it easier to strengthen that response in subsequent learning. (*b*) It creates a discrepancy between a goal (a "Soll-lage" in Heckhausen's—1963—theory of motivation) and a present state ("Ist-lage") which represents a cognitive dissonance the person tries to reduce (cf. Festinger, 1957); in common-sense terms he has an image clearly presented to him of something he is not but should be. (*c*) It tends to block out by simple interference other associations which would inhibit change—such as, "I'm too old to learn," "I never learned much from going to school anyway," "What do these academics know about everyday life?" or "I hope they don't get personal about all this."

After the course has been "sold" sufficiently to get a group together for training, the first step in the course itself is to present the research findings in some detail on exactly how n Achievement is related to certain types of successful entrepreneurial performance. That is, the argument of *The Achieving Society* (McClelland, 1961) is presented carefully with tables, charts, and diagrams, usually in lecture form at the outset and with the help of an educational TV film entitled the *Need to Achieve*. This is followed by discussion to clear up any ambiguities that remain in their minds as far as the central argument is concerned. It is especially necessary to stress that not all high achievement is caused by high n Achievement—that we have no evidence that high n Achievement is an essential ingredient in success as a research scientist, professional, accountant, office or personnel manager, etc.; that, on the contrary, it seems rather narrowly related to entrepreneurial, sales, or promotional success, and therefore should be of particular interest to them because they hold jobs which either have or could have an entrepreneurial component. We rationalize this activity in terms of the following proposition.

Proposition 2. The more an individual perceives that developing a motive is consistent with the demands of reality (and reason), the more educational attempts designed to develop that motive are likely to succeed. In a century in which psychologists and social theorists have been impressed by the power of unreason, it is well to remember that research has shown that rational arguments do sway opinions, particularly among the doubtful or the uncommitted (cf. Hovland et al., 1953). Reality in the form of legal, military, or housing rules does modify white prejudice against Negroes (cf. Berelson & Steiner, 1964, p. 512). In being surprised at Asch's discovery that many people will go along with a group in calling a shorter line longer than it is, we sometimes forget that under most conditions their judgments conform with reality. The associative network which organizes "reality"—which places the person correctly in time, place, space, family, job, etc.—is one of the most dominant in the personality. It is the last to go in psychosis. It should be of great assistance to tie any proposed change in an associative network in with this dominant schema in such a way as to make the change consistent with reality demands or *"reasonable"* extensions of them. The word "reasonable" here simply means extensions arrived at by the thought processes of proof, logic, etc., which in adults have achieved a certain dominance of their own.

The next step in the course is to teach the participants the n Achievement coding system. By this time, they are a little confused anyway as to exactly what we mean by the term. So we tell them they can find out for themselves by learning to code stories written by others or by themselves. They take the test for n Achievement before this session and then find out what their own score is by scoring this record. However, we point out that if they think their score is too low, that can be easily remedied, since we teach them how to code and how to write stories saturated with n Achievement; in fact, that is one of the basic purposes of the course: to teach them to think constantly in n Achievement terms. Another aspect of the learning is discriminating achievement thinking from thinking in terms of power or affiliation. So usually the elements of these other two coding schemes are also taught.

Proposition 3. The more thoroughly an individual develops and clearly conceptualizes the associative network defining the motive, the more likely he is to develop the motive. The original empirical support for this proposition came from the radical behaviorist Skinnerian viewpoint: If the associative responses are the motive (by definition), to strengthen them one should elicit them and reinforce them, as one would shape up any response by reinforcement (cf. Skinner, 1953). But, support for this proposition also derives from other sources, particularly the "set" experiments. For decades laboratory psychologists have known that one of the easiest and most effective ways to change behavior is to change the subject's set. If he is responding to stimulus words with the names of animals, tell him to respond with the names of vegetables, or with words meaning the opposite, and he changes his behavior immediately and efficiently without a mistake. At a more complex level Orne (1962) had pointed out how powerful a set like "This is an experiment" can be. He points out that if you were to go up to a stranger and say something like "Lie down!" he would in all probability either laugh or escape as soon as possible. But, if you say "This is an experiment! Lie down!" more often than not, if there are other supporting cues, the person will do so. Orne has demonstrated how subjects will perform nonsensical and fatiguing tasks for very long periods of time under the set that "this is an experiment." At an even more complex level, sociolologists have demonstrated often how quickly a person will change his behavior as he adopts a new role set (as a parent, a teacher, a public official, etc.). In all these cases an associative network exists usually with a label conveniently attached which we call set and which, when it is aroused or becomes salient, proceeds to control behavior very effectively. The purpose of this part of our course is to give the subjects a set or a carefully worked out associative network with appropriate words or labels to describe all its various aspects (the coding labels for parts of the n Achievement scoring system like Ga+, I+, etc.; cf. Atkinson, 1958). The power of words on controlling behavior has also been well documented (cf. Brown, 1958).

It is important to stress that it is not just the label (n Achievement) which is taught. The person must be able to produce easily and often the new associative network itself. It is here that our research comes closest to traditional therapy which could be understood as the prolonged and laborious formation of new associative networks to replace anxiety-laden ones. That is, the person over time comes to form a new associative network covering his relations, for example, to his father and mother, which still later he may label an "unresolved Oedipus complex." When cues arise that formerly would have produced anxiety-laden associations, they now evoke this new complex instead, blocking out the "bad" associations by associative interference. But all therapists, whether freudian or Rogerian, insist that the person must learn to produce these associations in their new form, that teaching the label is not enough. In fact, this is probably why so-called directive therapy is ineffective: It tries to substitute new constructs ("You should become an achiever") for old neurotic or ineffective ones ("rather than being such a slob") without changing the associative networks which underlie these surface labels. A change in set such as "Respond with names of vegetables" will not work unless the person has a whole associative network which defines the meaning of the set. The relation of this argument is obvious both to Kelly's (1955) insistence on the importance of personal constructs and to the general semanticists' complaints about the neurotic effects of mislabeling or overabstraction (Korzybsky, 1941).

But, theoretically speaking, why should a change in set as an associative network be so influential in controlling thought and action? The explanation lies in part in its symbolic character. Learned acts have limited influence because they often depend on reality supports (as in typewriting), but learned thoughts (symbolic acts) can occur any time, any place, in any connection, and be applied to whatever the person is doing. They are more generalizable. Acts can also be inhibited more easily than thoughts. Isak Dinesen tells the story of the oracle who told the king he would get his wish so long as he never thought of the left eye of a camel. Needless to say, the king did not get his wish, but he could easily have obeyed her prohibition if it had been to avoid *looking* at the left eye of a camel. Thoughts once acquired gain more control over thoughts and actions than acquired acts do because they are harder to inhibit. But why do they gain control over actions? Are not thoughts substitutes for actions? Cannot a man learn to think achievement thoughts and still not act like an achiever in any way? The question is taken up again under the next proposition, but it is well to remember here that thoughts are symbolic acts and that practice of symbolic acts facilitates performing the real acts (cf. Hovland, 1951, p. 644).

The next step in the course is to tie thought to action. Research has shown that individuals high in n Achievement tend to act in certain ways. For example, they prefer work situations where there is a challenge (moderate risk), concrete feedback on how well they are doing, and opportunity to take personal responsibility for achieving the work goals. The participants in the course are therefore introduced to a "work" situation in the form of a business game in which they will have an opportunity to show these characteristics in action or more specifically to develop them through practice and through observing others play it. The game is designed to mimic real life: They must order parts to make certain objects (e.g., a Tinker Toy model bridge) after having estimated how many they think they can construct in the time allotted. They have a real chance to take over, plan the whole game, learn from how well they are doing (use of feedback), and show a paper profit or loss at the end. While they are surprised often that they would have to display their real action characteristics in this way in public, they usually get emotionally involved in observing how they behave under pressure of a more or less "real" work situation.

Proposition 4. The more an individual can link the newly developed network to related actions, the more the change in both thought and action is likely to occur and endure. The evidence for the importance of action for producing change consists of such diverse findings as (*a*) the importance of recitation for human learning, (*b*) the repeated finding that overt commitment and participation in action changes attitudes effectively (cf. Berelson & Steiner, 1964, p. 576), and (*c*) early studies by Carr (cf. McGeoch & Irion, 1952) showing that simply to expose an organism to what is to be learned (e.g., trundling a rat through a maze) is nowhere near as effective as letting him explore it for himself in action.

Theoretically, the action is represented in the associative network by what associations precede, accompany, and follow it. So including the acts in what is learned *enlarges* the associative network or the achievement construct to include action. Thus, the number of cues likely to trip off the n Achievement network is increased. In commonsense terms, whenever he works he now evaluates what he is doing in achievement terms, and whenever he thinks about achievement he tends to think of its action consequences.

So far the course instruction has remained fairly abstract and removed from the everyday experiences of businessmen. So, the next step is to apply what has been learned to everyday business activities through the medium of the well-known case-study method popularized by the Harvard Business School. Actual examples of the development of the careers or firms of business leaders or entrepreneurs are written up in disguised form and assigned for discussion to the participants. Ordinarily, the instructor is not interested in illustrating "good" or "bad" managerial behavior—that is left to participants to discuss—but in our use of the material, we do try to label the various types of behavior as illustrating either n Achievement and various aspects of the achievement sequence (instrumental activity, blocks, etc.), or n Power, n Affiliation, etc. The participants are also encouraged to bring in examples of managerial behavior from their own experience to evaluate in motivational terms.

Proposition 5. The more an individual can link the newly conceptualized association-action complex (or motive) to events in his everyday life, the more likely the motive complex is to influence his thoughts and actions in situations outside the training experience. The transfer-of-training research literature is not very explicit on this point, though it seems self-evident. Certainly, this is the proposition that underlies the practice of most therapy when it involves working through or clarifying, usually in terms of a new, partially formed construct system, old memories, events from the last 24 hours, dreams, and hopes of the future. Again, theoretically, this should serve to enlarge and clarify the associative network and increase the number of cues in everyday life which will rearouse it. The principle of symbolic practice can also be invoked to support its effectiveness in promoting transfer outside the learning experience.

For some time most course participants have been wondering what all this has to do with them personally. That is to say, the material is introduced as something that ought to be of interest to them. But, sooner or later, they must confront the issue as to what meaning n Achievement has in their own personal lives. We do not force this choice on them nor do we think we are brainwashing them to believe in n Achievement. We believe and we tell them we believe in the "obstinate audience" (cf. Bauer, 1964), in the ultimate capacity of people to resist persuasion or to do in the end what they really want to do. In fact, we had one case in an early session of a man who at this point decided he was not an achievement-minded person and did not want to become one. He subsequently retired and became a chicken farmer to the relief of the business in which he had been an ineffective manager. We respected that decision and mention it in the course as a good example of honest self-evaluation. Nevertheless, we do provide them with all kinds of information as to their own achievement-related behavior in the fantasy tests, in the business game, in occasional group dynamics session—and ample opportunity and encouragement to think through what this information implies so far as their self-concept is concerned and their responsibilities to their jobs. Various devices such as the "Who am I?" test, silent group meditation, or individual counseling have been introduced to facilitate this self-confrontation.

Proposition 6. The more an individual can perceive and experience the newly conceptualized motive as an improvement in the self-image, the more the motive is likely to influence his future thoughts and actions. Evidence on the importance of the ego or the self-image on controlling behavior has been summarized by Allport (1943). In recent years, Rogers and his group (Rogers, 1961; Rogers & Dymond, 1954) have measured improvement in psychotherapy largely in terms of improvement of the self-concept in relation to the ideal self. Indirect evidence of the importance of the self-schema comes from the discussion over whether a person can be made to do things under hypnosis that are inconsistent with his self-concept or values. All investigators agree that the hypnotist can be most successful in getting the subject to do what might normally be a disapproved action if he makes the subject perceive the action as consistent with his self-image or values (cf. Berelson & Steiner, 1963, p. 124).

The same logic supports this proposition. It seems unlikely that a newly formed associative network like n Achievement could persist and influence behavior much unless it had somehow "come to terms" with the pervasive superordinate network of associations defining the self. The logic is the same as for Proposition 2 dealing with the reality construct system. The n Achievement associations must come to be experienced as related to or consistent with the ideal self-image; otherwise associations from the self-system will constantly block thoughts of achievement. The person might be thinking, for example: "I am not that kind of person; achievement means judging people in terms of how well they perform and I don't like to hurt people's feelings."

Closely allied to the self-system is a whole series of networks only half conscious (i.e., correctly labeled) summarizing the values by which the person lives which derive from his culture and social milieu. These values can also interfere if they are inconsistent with n Achievement as a newly acquired way of thinking. Therefore, it has been customary at this point in the course to introduce a value analysis of the participants' culture based on an analysis of children's stories, myths, popular religion, comparative attitude surveys, customs, etc., more or less in line with traditional, cultural anthropological practice (cf. Benedict, 1946; McClelland,

1964). For example, in America we have to work through the problem of how being achievement oriented seems to interfere with being popular or liked by others which is highly valued by Americans. In Mexico a central issue is the highly valued "male dominance" pattern reflected in the patriarchal family and in the *macho* complex (being extremely masculine). Since data show that dominant fathers have sons with low n Achievement and authoritarian bosses do not encourage n Achievement in their top executives (Andrews, 1965), there is obviously a problem here to be worked through if n Achievement is to survive among thoughts centered on dominance. The problem is not only rationally discussed. It is acted out in role-playing sessions where Mexicans try, and often to their own surprise fail, to act like the democratic father with high standards in the classic Rosen and D'Andrade (1959) study on parental behavior which develops high n Achievement. Any technique is used which will serve to draw attention to possible conflicts between n Achievement and popular or traditional cultural values. In the end it may come to discussing parts of the *Bhagavad Gita* in India, or the *Koran* in Arab countries, that seem to oppose achievement striving or entrepreneurial behavior.

Proposition 7. The more an individual can perceive and experience the newly conceptualized motive as an improvement on prevailing cultural values, the more the motive is likely to influence his future thoughts and actions. The cultural anthropologists for years have argued how important it is to understand one's own cultural values to overcome prejudices, adopt more flexible attitudes, etc., but there is little hard evidence that doing so changes a person's behavior. What exists comes indirectly from studies that show prejudice can be decreased a little by information about ethnic groups (Berelson & Steiner, 1963, p. 517), or that repeatedly show an unconscious link between attitudes and the reference group (or subculture to which one belongs—a link which presumably can be broken more easily by full information about it, especially when coupled with role-playing new attitudes (cf. Berelson & Steiner, 1963, pp. 566 ff.).

The theoretical explanation of this presumed effect is the same as for Proposition 2 and 6. The newly learned associative complex to influence thought and action effectively must somehow be adjusted to three superordinate networks that may set off regularly interfering associations—namely, the networks associated with reality, the self, and the social reference group or subculture.

The course normally ends with each participant preparing a written document outlining his goals and life plans for the next 2 years. These plans may or may not include references to the achievement motive; they can be very tentative, but they are supposed to be quite specific and realistic; that is to say, they should represent moderate levels of aspiration following the practice established in learning about n Achievement of choosing the moderately risky or challenging alternative. The purpose of this document is in part to formulate for oneself the practical implications of the course before leaving it, but even more to provide a basis for the evaluation of their progress in the months after the course. For it is explained to the participants that they are to regard themselves as "in training" for the next 2 years, that 10-14 days is obviously too short a time to do more than conceive a new way of life: It represents the residential portion of the training only. Our role over the next 2 years will be to remind them every 6 months of the tasks they have set themselves by sending them a questionnaire to fill out which will serve to rearouse many of the issues discussed in the course and to give them information on how far they have progressed toward achieving their goals.

Proposition 8. The more an individual commits himself to achieving concrete goals in life related to the newly formed motive, the more the motive is likely to influence his future thoughts and actions.

Proposition 9. The more an individual keeps a record of his progress toward achieving goals to which he is committed, the more the newly formed motive is likely to influence his future thoughts and actions. These propositions are both related to what was called "pacing" in early studies of the psychology of work. That is, committing oneself to a specific goal and then comparing one's performance to that goal has been found to facilitate learning (cf. Kausler, 1959), though most studies of levels of aspiration have dealt with goal setting as a result rather than as a "cause" of performance. At any rate, the beneficial effect of concrete feedback on learning has been amply demonstrated by psychologists from Thorndike to Skinner. Among humans the feedback on performance is especially effective if they have high n Achievement (French, 1958), a fact which makes the relevance of our request for feedback obvious to the course participants.

The theoretical justification for these propositions is that in this way we are managing to keep the newly acquired associative network salient over the next 2 years. We are providing cues that will regularly rearouse it since he knows he is still part of an experimental training group which is supposed to show a certain type of behavior (Proposition 1 again). If the complex is rearoused sufficiently often back in the real world, we believe it is more likely to influence thought and action than if it is not aroused.

As described so far the course appears to be devoted almost wholly to cognitive learning. Yet this is only part of the story. The "teachers" are all clinically oriented psychologists who also try to practice whatever has been learned about the type of human relationship that most facilitates emotional learning. Both for practical and theoretical reasons this relationship is structured as warm, honest, and nonevaluative, somewhat in the manner described by Rogers (1961) and recommended by distinguished therapists from St. Ignatius[2] to Freud. That is to say, we insist that the only kind of change that can last or mean anything is what the person decides on and works out by himself, that we are there not to criticize his past behavior or direct his future choices, but to provide him with all sorts of information and emotional support that will help him in his self-confrontation. Since we recognize that self-study may be quite difficult and unsettling, we try to create an optimistic relaxed atmosphere in which the person is warmly encouraged in his efforts and given the opportunity for personal counseling if he asks for it.

Proposition 10. Changes in motives are more likely to occur in an interpersonal atmosphere in which the individual feels warmly but honestly supported and respected by others as a person capable of guiding and directing his own future behavior. Despite the widespread belief in this proposition among therapists (except for operant conditioners), one of the few studies that directly supports it has been conducted by Ends and Page (1957) who found that an objective learning-theory approach was less successful in treating chronic alcoholics than a person-oriented, client-centered approach. Rogers (1961) also summarizes other evidence that therapists who are warmer, more empathic, and genuine are more successful in their work. Hovland et al. (1953) report that the less manipulative the intent of a communicator, the greater the tendency to accept his conclusions. There is also the direct evidence that parents of boys with high n Achievement are warmer, more encouraging and less directive (fathers only) than parents of boys with low n Achievement (Rosen & D'Andrade, 1959). We tried to model ourselves after those parents on the theory that what is associated with high n Achievement in children might be most likely to encourage its development in adulthood. This does not mean permissiveness or promiscuous reinforcement of all kinds of behavior; it also means setting high standards as the parents of the boys with high n Achievement did but having the relaxed faith that the participants can achieve them.

The theoretical justification for this proposition can take two lines: Either one argues that this degree of challenge to the self-schema produces anxiety which needs to be reduced by warm support of the person for effective learning to take place, or one interprets the warmth as a form of direct reinforcement for change following the operant-conditioning model. Perhaps both factors are operating. Certainly there is ample evidence to support the view that anxiety interferes with learning (cf. Sarason, 1960) and that reward shapes behavior (cf. Bandura & Walters, 1963, pp. 283 ff.).

One other characteristic of the course leads to two further propositions. Efforts are made so far as possible to define it as an "experience apart," "an opportunity for self-study," or even a "spiritual retreat" (though that term can be used more acceptably in India than in the United States). So far as possible it is held in an isolated resort hotel or a hostel where there will be few distractions from the outside world and few other guests. This permits an atmosphere of total concentration on the objectives of the course including much informal talk outside the sessions about Ga+, Ga−, I+, and other categories in the coding definition. It still comes as a surprise to us to hear these terms suddenly in an informal group of participants talking away in Spanish or Telugu. The effect of this retreat from everyday life into a special and specially labeled experience appears to be twofold: It dramatizes or increases the salience of the new associative network and it tends to create a new reference group.

Proposition 11. Changes in motives are more likely to occur the more the setting dramatizes the importance of self-study and lifts it out of the routine of everyday life. So far as we know there is no scientific evidence to support this proposition, though again if one regards Jesuits as successful examples of personality change, the Order has frequently followed the advice of St. Ignatius to the effect that "the progress made in the Exercizes will be greater, the more the exercitant withdraws from all friends and acquaintances, and from all worldly cares." Theory supports the proposition in two respects: Removing the person from everyday routine (*a*) should decrease interfering associations (to say nothing of interfering appointments and social obligations), and (*b*) should heighten the salience of the experience by contrast with everyday life and make it harder to handle with the usual defenses ("just one more course," etc.). That is to say, the network of achievement-related associations can be more strongly and distinctly aroused in contrast to everyday life, making cognitive dissonance greater and therefore more in need of reduction by new learning. By the same token we have found that the dramatic quality of the experience cannot be sustained very long in a 12-18-hour-a-day schedule without a new routine attitude developing. Thus, we have found that a period somewhere between 6 to 14 days is optimal for this kind of "spiritual retreat." St. Ignatius sets an outside limit of 30 days, but this is when the schedule is less intensive (as ours has sometimes been), consisting of only a few hours a day over a longer period.

Proposition 12. Changes in motives are more likely to occur and persist if the new motive is a sign of membership in a new reference group. No principle of change has stronger empirical or historical support than this one. Endless studies have shown that people's opinions, attitudes, and beliefs are a function of their reference group and that different attitudes are likely to arise and be sustained primarily when the person moves into or affiliates with a new reference group (cf. Berelson & Steiner, 1963, pp. 580 ff.). Many theorists argue that the success of groups like Alcoholics Anonymous depends on the effectiveness with which the group is organized so that each person demonstrates his membership in it by "saving" another alcoholic. Political experience has demonstrated that membership in small groups like Communist or Nazi Party cells is one of the most effective ways to sustain changed attitudes and behavior.

Our course attempts to achieve this result (*a*) by the group experience in isolation—creating the feeling of alumni who all went through it together; (*b*) by certain signs of identification with the group, particularly the language of the coding system, but also including a certificate of membership; and (*c*) by arranging where possible to have participants come from the same community so that they can form a "cell" when they return that will serve as an immediate reference group to prevent gradual undermining of the new network by other pressures.

In theoretical terms a reference group should be effective because its members constantly provide cues to each other to rearouse the associative network, because they will also reward each other for achievement-related thoughts and acts, and because this constant mutual stimulation, and reinforcement, plus the labeling of the group, will prevent assimilation of the network to bigger, older, and stronger networks (such as those associated with traditional cultural values).

In summary, we have described an influence process which may be conceived in terms of "input," "intervening," and "output" variables as in Table 1. The propositions relate variables in Column A via their effect on the intervening variables in Column B to as yet loosely specified behavior in Column C, which may be taken as evidence that "development" of n Achievement has "really" taken place. The problems involved in evaluation of effects are as great and as complicated as those involved in designing the treatment, but they cannot be spelled out here, partly for lack of space, partly because we are in an even earlier stage of examining and classifying the effects of our training 1 and 2 years later preparatory to conceptualizing more clearly what happens. It will have to suffice to point out that we plan extensive comparisons over a 2-year period of the behaviors of our trained subjects compared with matched controls along the lines suggested in Column C.

What the table does is to give a brief overall view of how we conceptualize the educational or treatment process. What is particularly important is that the propositions refer to *operationally defined* and *separable* treatment variables. Thus, after having demonstrated hopefully a large effect of the total program, we can subtract a variable and see how much that decreases the impact of the course. That is to say, the course is designed so that it could go ahead perfectly reasonably with very

TABLE 1. Variables Conceived as Entering into the Motive Change Process

A. Input or independent variables	B. Intervening variables	C. Output or dependent variables
1. Goal setting for the person (P1, P11)	Arousal of associative network (salience)	Duration and/or extensiveness of changes in:
2. Acquisition of n Achievement associative network (P2, P3, P4, P5)	Experiencing and labeling the associative network	1. n Achievement associative network
3. Relating new network to superordinate networks	Variety of cues to which network is linked	2. Related actions: use of feedback, moderate risk taking, etc.
reality (P2)	Interfering associations assimilated or bypassed by reproductive interference	3. Innovations (job improvements)
the self (P6)		4. Use of time and money
cultural values (P7)		5. Entrepreneurial success as defined by nature of job held and its rewards
4. Personal goal setting (P8)		
5. Knowledge of progress (P3, P4, P9)		
6. Personal warmth and support (P10)	Positive affect associated with network	
7. Support of reference group (P11, P12)		

Note.—P1, P11, etc. refer to the numbered propositions in the text.

little advanced goal setting (P1), with an objective rather than a warm personal atmosphere (P11), without the business game tying thought to action (P9), without learning to code n Achievement and write achievement-related stories (P3), without cultural value analysis (P7), or an isolated residential setting (P1, P11, P12). The study units are designed in a way that they can be omitted without destroying the viability of the treatment which has never been true of other studies of the psychotherapeutic process (cf. Rogers & Dymond, 1954).

But is there any basis for thinking the program works in practice? As yet, not enough time has elapsed to enable us to collect much data on long-term changes in personality and business activity. However, we do know that businessmen can learn to write stories scoring high in n Achievement, that they retain this skill over 1 year or 2, and that they like the course—but the same kinds of things can be said about many unevaluated management training courses. In two instances we have more objective data. Three courses were given to some 34 men from the Bombay area in early 1963. It proved possible to develop a crude but objective and reliable coding system to record whether each one had shown *unusual* entrepreneurial activity in the 2 years prior to the course or in the 2 years after course. "Unusual" here means essentially an unusual promotion or salary raise or starting a new business venture of some kind. Of the 30 on whom information was available in 1965, 27% had been unusually active before the course, 67% after the course ($x^2 = 11.2$, $p \ll .01$). In a control group chosen at random from those who applied for the course in 1963, out of 11 on whom information has so far been obtained, 18% were active before 1963, 27% since 1963.

In a second case, four courses were given throughout 1964 to a total of 52 small businessmen from the small city of Kakinada in Andhra Pradesh, India. Of these men, 25% had been unusually active in the 2-year period before the course, and 65% were unusually active immediately afterwards ($x^2 = 17.1$, $p \ll .01$). More control data and more refined measures are needed, but it looks very much as if, in India at least, we will be dealing with a spontaneous "activation" rate of only 25%—35% among entrepreneurs. Thus we have a distinct advantage over psychotherapists who are trying to demonstrate an improvement over a two-thirds spontaneous recovery rate. Our own data suggest that we will be unlikely to get an improvement or "activation" rate much above the two-thirds level commonly reported in therapy studies. That is, about one-third of the people in our courses have remained relatively unaffected. Nevertheless the two-thirds activated after the course represent a doubling of the normal rate of unusual entrepreneurial activity—no mean achievement in the light of the current pessimism among psychologists as to their ability to induce lasting personality change among adults.

One case will illustrate how the course seems to affect people in practice. A short time after participating in one of our courses in India, a 47-year-old businessman rather suddenly and dramatically decided to quit his excellent job and go into the construction business on his own in a big way. A man with some means of his own, he had had a very successful career as employee-relations manager for a large oil firm. His job involved adjusting management-employee difficulties, negotiating union contracts, etc. He was well-to-do, well thought of in his company, and admired in the community, but he was restless because he found his job increasingly boring. At the time of the course his original n Achievement score was not very high and he was thinking of retiring and living in England where his son was studying. In an interview, 8 months later, he said the course had served not so much to "motivate" him but to "crystallize" a lot of ideas he had vaguely or half consciously picked up about work and achievement all through his life. It provided him with a new language (he still talked in terms of standards of excellence, blocks, moderate risk, goal anticipation, etc.), a new construct which served to organize those ideas and explain to him why he was bored with his job, despite his obvious success. He decided he wanted to be an n-Achievement-oriented person, that he would be unhappy in retirement, and that he should take a risk, quit his job, and start in business on his own. He acted on his decision and in 6 months had drawn plans and raised over $1,000,000 to build the tallest building in his large city to be called the "Everest Apartments." He is extremely happy in his new activity because it means selling, promoting, trying to wangle scarce materials, etc. His first building is partway up and he is planning two more.

Even a case as dramatic as this one does not prove that the course produced the effect, despite his repeated use of the constructs he had learned, but what is especially interesting about it is that he described what had happened to him in exactly the terms the theory requires. He spoke not about a new motive force but about how existing ideas had been crystallized into a new associative network, and it is this new network which *is* the new "motivating" force according to the theory.

How generalizable are the propositions? They have purposely been stated generally so that some term like "attitude" or "personality characteristic" could be substituted for the term "motive" throughout, because we believe the propositions will hold for other personality variables. In fact, most of the supporting experimental evidence cited comes from attempts to change other characteristics. Nevertheless, the propositions should hold best more narrowly for motives and especially the achievement motive. One of the biggest difficulties in the way of testing them more generally is that not nearly as much is known about other human characteristics or their specific relevance for success in a certain type of work. For example, next to nothing is known about the need for power, its relation to success, let us say, in politics or bargaining situations, and its origins and course of development in the life history of individuals. It is precisely the knowledge we have about such matters for the achievement motive that puts us in a position to shape it for limited, socially and individually desirable ends. In the future, it seems to us, research in psychotherapy ought to follow a similar course. That is to say, rather than developing "all purpose" treatments, good for any person and any purpose, it should aim to develop specific treatments or educational programs built on laboriously accumulated detailed knowledge of the characteristic to be changed. It is in the spirit that the present research program in motive acquisition has been designed and is being tested out.

Notes

1. Parenthetically, we have found several times that our stated desire to evaluate the effectiveness of our course created doubts in the minds of our sponsors that they did not feel about many popular courses for managers that no one has ever evaluated or plans to evaluate. An attitude of inquiry is not always an asset in education. It suggests one is not sure of his ground.
2. In his famous spiritual exercises which have played a key role in producing and sustaining personality change in the Jesuit Order, St. Ignatius states: "The director of the Exercizes ought not to urge the exercitant more to poverty or any promise than to the contrary, nor to one state of life or way of living more than another . . . [while it is proper to urge people outside the Exercizes] the director of the Exercizes . . . without leaning to one side or the other, should permit the Creator to deal directly with the creature, and the creature directly with his Creator and Lord."

References

Allport, G. W. The ego in contemporary psychology. *Psychological Review*, 1943, 50, 451-478.

Andrews, J. D. W. The achievement motive in two types of organizations. *Journal of Personality and Social Psychology*, 1965, in press.

Atkinson, J. W. (Ed.) *Motives in fantasy, action and society.* Princeton, N. J.: Van Nostrand, 1958.

Bandura, A., & Walters, R. H. *Social learning and personality development.* New York: Holt, Rinehart & Winston, 1963.

Bauer, R. A. The obstinate audience: The influence process from the point of view of social communication. *American Psychologist*, 1964, 19, 310-329.

Benedict, Ruth. *The chrysanthemum and the sword.* Boston: Houghton Mifflin, 1946.

Berelson, B., & Steiner, G. A. *Human Behavior: An inventory of scientific findings.* New York: Harcourt, Brace, 1964.

Brown, R. W. *Words and things.* Glencoe, Ill.: Free Press, 1958.

Burris, R. W. The effect of counseling on achievement motivation. Unpublished doctoral dissertation, University of Indiana, 1958.

Ends, E. J., & Page, C. W. A study of three types of group psychotherapy with hospitalized male inebriates *Quarterly Journal on Alcohol,* 1957, 18, 263-277.

Eysenck, H. J. The effects of psychotherapy: An evaluation. *Journal of Consulting Psychology,* 1952, 16, 319-324.

Festinger, L. *A theory of cognitive dissonance.* New York: Harper & Row, 1957.

Frank, J. *Persuasion and healing.* Baltimore: Johns Hopkins Press, 1961.

French, E. G. Effects of the interaction of motivation and feedback on task performance. In J. W. Atkinson (Ed.), *Motives in fantasy, action and society.* Princeton, N. J.: Van Nostrand, 1958. Pp. 400-408.

Heckhausen, H. Eine Rahmentheorie der Motivation in zehn Thesen. *Zeitschrift für experimentelle und angewandte Psychologie,* 1963, X/4, 604-626.

Hovland, C. I. Human learning and retention. In S. S. Stevens (Ed.), *Handbook of experimental psychology.* New York: Wiley, 1951.

Hovland, C. I., Janis, I. L., & Kelley, H. H. *Communication and persuasion: Psychological studies of opinion change.* New Haven: Yale Univer. Press, 1953.

Kausler, D. H. Aspiration level as a determinant of performance. *Journal of Personality,* 1959, 27, 346-351.

Kelley, G. A. *The psychology of personal constructs.* New York: Norton, 1955.

Korzybski, A. *Science and sanity.* Lancaster, Pa.: Science Press, 1941.

McClelland, D. C. *The achieving society.* Princeton, N. J.: Van Nostrand, 1961.

McClelland, D. C. *The roots of consciousness.* Princeton, N. J.: Van Nostrand, 1964.

McClelland, D. C., Atkinson, J. W., Clark, R. A., & Lowell, E. L. *The achievement motive.* New York: Appleton-Century, 1953.

McGeoch, J. A., & Irion, A. L. *The psychology of human learning.* (2nd ed.) New York: Longmans, Green, 1952.

Mierke, K. *Wille und Leistung.* Göttingan: Verlag für Psychologie, 1955.

Orne, M. On the social psychology of the psychological experiment: With particular reference, to demand characteristics and their implications. *American Psychologist,* 1962, 17, 776-783.

Roethlisberger, F. J., & Dickson, W. J. *Management and the worker.* Cambridge: Harvard Univer. Press, 1947.

Rogers, C. R. *On becoming a person.* Boston: Houghton Mifflin, 1961.

Rogers, C.R., & Dymond, R. F. (Eds.) *Psychotherapy and personality change.* Chicago: Univer. Press, 1954.

Rosen, B. C., & D'Andrade, R. G. The psychosocial origins of achievement motivation. *Sociometry,* 1959, 22, 185-218.

Rosenthal, R. On the social psychology of the psychological experiment: The experimenter's hypothesis as unintended determinant of experimental results. *American Scientist,* 1963, 51, 268-283.

Sarason, I. Empirical findings and theoretical problems. 1960, 57, 403-416.

THE NEW LOOK IN MOTIVATION THEORY
FOR ORGANIZATIONAL RESEARCH

J. G. HUNT
J. W. HILL

During the last few years the treatment of motivation with respect to industrial and other formal organizations has more often than not been in terms of models by Maslow or Herzberg.[1] Where theories are apparently so thoroughly accepted one naturally assumes a fairly substantial amount of data leading to empirical verification. However, as we shall show, there is relatively little empirical evidence concerning Maslow's theory; and while there are many studies bearing on Herzberg's theory, it remains controversial. After comparing these two approaches and reviewing their present status, we will describe a newer motivation theory developed by Vroom, which is similar to those developed by Atkinson et al. and Edwards in experimental psychology, and Peak, Rosenberg, and Fishbein in social psychology.[2] It is our contention, on both theoretical and empirical grounds, that Vroom's theory, more than Maslow's or Herzberg's, is in line with the thinking of contemporary psychologists and industrial sociologists and is the best yet developed for organizational use.

The Maslow Model

Maslow's theory hypothesizes five broad classes of needs arranged in hierarchical levels of prepotency so that when one need level is satisfied, the next level is activated. The levels are: (1) physiological needs; (2) security or safety needs; (3) social, belonging, or membership needs; (4) esteem needs further subdivided into esteem of others and self-esteem including autonomy; and (5) self-actualization or self-fulfillment needs.

The original papers present very little empirical evidence in support of the theory and no research at all that tests the model in its entirety. Indeed, Maslow argues that the theory is primarily a framework for future research. He also discusses at length some of the limitations of the model and readily admits that these needs may be unconscious rather than conscious. While Maslow discusses his model and its limitations in detail, a widely publicized paper by McGregor gives the impression that the model can be accepted without question and also that it is fairly easy to apply.[3] In truth, the model is difficult to test, which is probably why there are so few empirical studies to either prove or refute the theory.

Porter provides the most empirical data concerning the model.[4] At the conscious level he measures all except the physiological needs. His samples are based only on managers, but they cover different managerial levels in a wide range of business organizations in the United States and thirteen other countries. Porter's studies have

Reproduced by permission of the Society for Applied Anthropology from *Human Organization*, vol. 28, no. 2 (1969).

a number of interesting findings, but here we are primarily concerned with two: (1) in the United States and Britain (but not in the other twelve countries) there tends to be a hierarchical satisfaction of needs as Maslow hypothesizes; and (2) regardless of country or managerial level there is a tendency for those needs which managers feel are most important to be least satisfied.

A study by Beer of female clerks provides additional data concerning the model.[5] He examines the relationship between participative and considerate or human relations-oriented supervisory leadership styles and satisfaction of needs. He also goes one step further and argues that need satisfaction, as such, does not necessarily lead to motivation. Rather, motivation results only from need satisfaction which occurs in the process of task-oriented work. He reasons that a participative leadership style should meet this condition since it presumably allows for the satisfaction of the higher order needs (self-actualization, autonomy, and esteem). Beer found that workers forced to arrange needs in a hierarchy (as required by his ranking method) tend to arrange them as predicted by Maslow. He also found that self-actualization, autonomy, and social needs were most important while esteem and security needs were least important, although his method (unlike Porter's) did not allow a consideration of the relationship between importance and need satisfaction. Interestingly enough, there was no significant relationship between need satisfaction and Beer's measure of motivation nor between any of the leadership style dimensions and motivation. There were, however, significant relationships between leadership style dimensions and need satisfaction. Beer concludes that the model has questionable usefulness for a theory of industrial motivation although it may provide a fairly reliable measurement of the a priori needs of industrial workers.

We have found only three studies that systematically consider the Maslow theory in terms of performance.[6]

The first of these, by Clark, attempts to fit a number of empirical studies conducted for different purposes into a framework which provides for progressive activation and satisfaction of needs at each of the hierarchical levels. The findings are used to make predictions concerning productivity, absenteeism, and turnover as each need level is activated and then satisfied. While the article does not explicitly test the Maslow model, it is highly suggestive in terms of hypotheses for future research that might relate the theory to work group performance.

A second study, by Lawler and Porter, correlates satisfaction of managers' needs (except physiological) with rankings of their performance by superiors and peers. All correlations are significant but low, ranging from .16 to .30. Lawler and Porter conclude that satisfaction of higher order needs is more closely related to performance than satisfaction of lower order needs. However, the differences are not very great and they are not tested for significance. For example, correlations of superior ratings for the lower order security and social needs are .21 and .23 while for the higher order esteem, autonomy, and self-actualization needs they are .24, .18, and .30. Peer correlations are similar. Thus, unlike Lawler and Porter, we conclude that in this study the correlations for lower order needs are about the same as for higher order needs.

A more recent Porter and Lawler investigation seems to provide additional support for their earlier findings by showing that higher order needs accounted for more relationships significant at the .01 level than lower order needs. However, they do not report correlations between these needs and performance and so we cannot evaluate their conclusion as we did for their earlier study.

The Herzberg Model

A second frequently mentioned motivational model is that proposed by Herzberg and his associates in 1959.[7] They used a semistructured interview technique to get respondents to recall events experienced at work which resulted in a marked improvement or a marked reduction in their job satisfaction. Interviewees were also asked, among other things, how their feelings of satisfaction or dissatisfaction affected their work performance, personal relationships, and well-being. Content analysis of the interviews suggested that certain job characteristics led to job satisfaction, while *different* job characteristics led to job dissatisfaction. For instance, job achievement was related to satisfaction while working conditions were related to dissatisfaction. Poor conditions led to dissatisfaction, but good conditions did not necessarily lead to satisfaction. Thus, satisfaction and dissatisfaction are not simple opposites. Hence a two-factor theory of satisfaction is needed.

The job content characteristics which produced satisfaction were called "motivators" by Herzberg and his associates because they satisfied the individual's need for self-actualization at work. The job environment characteristics which led to dissatisfaction were called "hygienes" because they were work-supporting or contextual rather than task-determined and hence were analogous to the "preventative" or "environmental" factors recognized in medicine. According to this dichotomy, motivators include achievement, recognition, advancement, possibility of growth, responsibility, and work itself. Hygienes, on the other hand, include salary; interpersonal relations with superiors, subordinates, and peers; technical supervision; company policy and administration; personal life; working conditions; status; and job security.

There is considerable empirical evidence for this theory. Herzberg himself, in a summary of research through early 1966, includes 10 studies of 17 populations which used essentially the same method as his original study.[8] In addition, he reviews 20 more studies which used a variety of methodologies to test the two-factor theory. Of the studies included in his review, those using his critical incident method generally confirm the theory. Those using other methods give less clear results, which Herzberg acknowledges but attempts to dismiss for methodological reasons. At least nine other studies, most of which have appeared since Herzberg's 1966 review, raise even more doubts about the theory.[9]

While it is beyond the scope of the present article to consider these studies in detail, they raise serious questions as to whether the factors leading to satisfaction and dissatisfaction are really different from each other. A number of the studies show that certain job dimensions appear to be more important for *both* satisfaction and dissatisfaction. Dunnette, Campbell, and Hakel for example, conclude from these and also from their own studies that Herzberg is shackled to his method and that achievement, recognition, and responsibility seem important for both satisfaction *and* dissatisfaction while such dimensions as security, salary, and working conditions are less important.[10] They also raise by implication an issue concerning Herzberg's methodology which deserves further comment. That is, if data are analyzed in terms of percentage differences between groups, one result is obtained; if they are analyzed in terms of ranks within groups, another result occurs. The first type of analysis is appropriate for identifying factors which account for differences between events (as Herzberg did in his original hypothesis). The second type of analysis is appropriate if we want to know the most important factors within the event categories (which is what Herzberg claims he was doing). Analyzing the findings of Dunnette and his colleagues by the first method, we confirm Herzberg's theory; but if we rank the findings within categories, as Dunnette et al. also did, we find no confirmation. If we want to know whether "achievement" is important in job satisfaction we must look at its relative rank among other factors mentioned in the events leading to satisfaction, not whether it is mentioned a greater percentage of the time in satisfying events than in dissatisfying events. This distinction in analytical methods was discussed several years ago by Viteles and even earlier by Kornhauser.[11]

We conclude that any meaningful discussion of Herzberg's theory must recognize recent negative evidence even though the model seems to make a great deal of intuitive sense. Much the same can be said of Maslow's theory.

Figure 1. Maslow's need-priority model compared with Herzberg's motivation-hygiene model. (Adapted from K. Davis, *Human Relations at Work*, New York: McGraw-Hill, 1967, p. 37.)

Further Considerations in Using the Maslow and Herzberg Theories

Putting aside for the moment the empirical considerations presented by the two models, it is instructive to compare them at the conceptual level suggested in Figure 1. While the figure shows obvious similarities between the Maslow and Herzberg models, there are important differences as well. Where Maslow assumes that any need can be a motivator if it is relatively unsatisfied, Herzberg argues that only the higher order needs serve as motivators and that a worker can have unsatisfied needs in both the hygiene and motivator areas simultaneously. One might argue that the reason higher order needs are motivators is that lower order needs have essentially been satisfied. However, Herzberg presents some evidence that even in relatively low level blue-collar and service jobs, where presumably lower order needs are less well-satisfied, the higher order needs are still the only ones seen by the workers as motivators.[12]

Another important consideration is the relationship of these models to the accomplishment of organizational objectives. Even if there were unequivocal empirical support for the theories, there is need to translate the findings into usable incentives for promoting such objectives as superior performance, lower turnover, lower absenteeism, etc. If not, they are of little use to industrial organizations. As indicated earlier, there is relatively little evidence empirically relating Maslow's model to performance, or even to psychological well-being. Furthermore, the one Lawler and Porter study seems to show that satisfaction of higher and lower order needs are about equally related to performance, although their later investigation suggests that the former are more strongly related to performance than the latter. But we cannot tell for sure because correlations and differences between correlations are not reported.

Similarly, although Herzberg asked his respondents for effects of job events on their performance, he reports only two studies which attempt to measure performance independent of the respondent's estimate. These seem to show the performance is favorably influenced as more "motivators" are provided in the job.[13] However, insufficient data are presented to permit evaluation of the adequacy of the experimental design and performance measures. A study by Friedlander and Walton that considered employee turnover used a modification of Herzberg's technique and found that employees' reasons for staying on the job were different than their reasons for leaving.[14] The reasons for staying would be called "motivators" while those for leaving were "hygiene" factors.

We conclude that Herzberg's two-factor theory *may* be related to turnover and performance; but present studies are subject to serious criticisms. And we could find only two empirical investigations which related Maslow's model to any of these outputs.

In addition, it should be noted that neither model adequately handles the theoretical problem of some kind of linkage by which individual need satisfaction is related to the achievement of organizational objectives. Given the present formulation, it is entirely possible that there can be need satisfaction which is *not necessarily* directed toward the accomplishment of organizational goals. For example, an important organizational objective might be increased production, but workers might conceivably receive more need satisfaction from turning out a higher quality product at a sacrifice in quantity. They might also be meeting their social needs through identification with a work group with strong sanctions against "rate busting."

Finally, neither of these theories as they stand can really handle the problem of individual differences in motivation. Maslow, for example, explains that his model may not hold for persons with particular experiences. His theory is therefore non-predictive because data that do not support it can be interpreted in terms of individual differences in previous need gratification leading to greater or lesser prepotency of a given need-category.[15] Herzberg, in similar fashion, describes seven types of people differentiated by the extent to which they are motivator or hygiene seekers, or some combination of the two, although he never relates these differences empirically to actual job performance. We turn then to a model which explicitly recognizes these issues and appears to offer great potential for understanding motivation in organizations.

The Vroom Model

Brayfield and Crockett as long ago as 1955 suggested an explicit theoretical linkage between satisfaction, motivation and the organizational goal of productivity. They said:

> It makes sense to us to assume that individuals are motivated to achieve certain environmental goals and that the achievement of these goals results in satisfaction. Productivity is seldom a goal in itself but is more commonly a means to goal attainment. Therefore, . . . we might expect high satisfaction and high productivity to occur together when productivity is perceived as a path to certain important goals and when these goals are achieved.[16]

Georgopoulas, Mahoney, and Jones provide some early empirical support for this notion in their test of the "path-goal hypothesis."[17] Essentially, they argue that an individual's motivation to produce at a given level depends upon his particular needs as reflected in the goals toward which he is moving *and* his perception of the relative usefulness of productivity behavior as a path to attainment of these goals. They qualify this, however, by saying that the need must be sufficiently high, no other economical paths must be available to the individual, and there must be a lack of restraining practices.

More recently, Vroom has developed a motivational model which extends the above concepts and is also related to earlier work of experimental and social psychologists.[18] He defines motivation as a "process governing choices, made by persons or lower organisms, among alternative forms of voluntary activity."[19] The concept is incorporated in Figure 2, which depicts Vroom's model graphically. Here, the individual is shown as a role occupant faced with a set of alternative "first-level outcomes." His preference choice among these first-level outcomes is determined by their expected relationship to possible "second-level outcomes."

Two concepts are introduced to explain the precise method of determining preferences for these first-level outcomes. These concepts are *valence* and *instrumentality*. Valence refers to the strength of an individual's desire for a particular out-

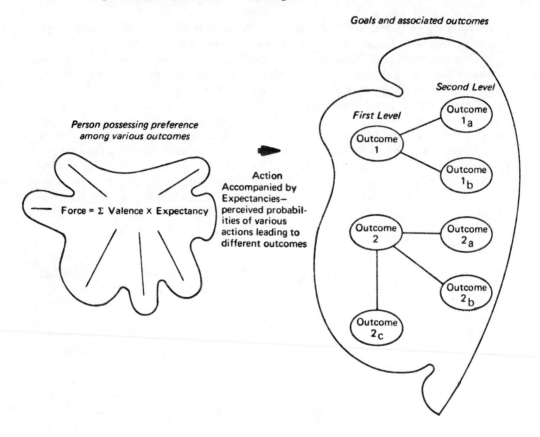

Figure 2. Vroom's motivational model. (Adapted from M. D. Dunnette, "The Motives of Industrial Managers," *Organizational Behavior and Human Performance*, vol. 2, New York: Academic Press, 1967, p. 178.)

come. Instrumentality indicates an individual's perception of the relationship between a first-level outcome and a second-level outcome or, in other words, the extent to which a first-level outcome is seen as leading to the accomplishment of a second-level outcome.

Valence is measured by instructing workers to rank important individual goals in order of their desirability, or they may rate goals on Likert-type scales. Instrumentality can be measured by rating scales which involve perceived differences in the direction and strength of relationships between various first- and second-level outcomes. Important goals of industrial workers often cited in the empirical behavioral science literature are promotion, pay, pleasant working conditions, and job security. The goals can be ranked by individual workers in terms of their desirability. The resulting scores are measures of valence. In addition, each individual can be instructed to indicate on an appropriate scale the likelihood that a certain job behavior, e.g., high productivity, will lead to each of the four goals described. This score is the instrumental relationship between productivity and a specified goal.

Obviously there are alternative methods of measurement available for the concepts; we will leave these for a more detailed discussion later.

Vroom expresses the valence of a first-level outcome to a person "as a monotonically increasing function of an algebraic sum of the products of the valences of all [second-level] outcomes and his conceptions of its instrumentality for the attainment of the [second-level] outcomes."[20]

For example, assume that an individual desires promotion and feels that superior performance is a very strong factor in achieving that goal. His first-level outcomes are then superior, average, or poor performance. His second-level outcome is promotion. The first-level outcome of high performance thus acquires a positive valence by virtue of its expected relationship to the preferred second-level outcome of promotion. Assuming no negative second-level outcomes associated with high performance and no other first-level outcomes that contribute to promotion, we expect motivation toward superior performance because promotion is important and superior performance is seen as instrumental in its accomplishment. Or, to put it in Vroom's terms, performance varies directly with the product of the valence of the reward (promotion) and the perceived instrumentality of performance for the attainment of the reward.

An additional concept in Vroom's theory is *expectancy*. This is a belief concerning the likelihood that a particular action or effort will be followed by a particular first-level outcome and can be expressed as a subjective probability ranging from 0 to 1. Expectancy differs from instrumentality in that it relates *efforts* to first-level outcomes where instrumentality relates first- and second-level outcomes to each other. Vroom ties this concept to his previous one by stating, "the force on a person to perform an [action] is a monotonically increasing function of the algebraic sum of the products of the valences of all [first-level] outcomes and the strength of his expectancies that the [action] will be followed by the attainment of these outcomes."[21] "Force" here is similar to our concept of motivation.

This motivational model, unlike those discussed earlier, emphasizes individual differences in motivation and makes possible the examination of very explicit relationships between motivation and the accomplishment of organizational goals, whatever these goals may be. Thus, instead of assuming that satisfaction of a specific need is likely to influence organizational objectives in a certain way, we can find out how important to the employees are the various second-level outcomes (worker goals), the instrumentality of various first-level outcomes (organizational objectives) for their attainment, and the expectancies that are held with respect to the employees' ability to influence the first-level outcomes.

Empirical Tests of Vroom's Model

Vroom has already shown how his model can integrate many of the empirical findings in the literature on motivation in organizations.[22] However, because it is a relatively recent development, empirical tests of the model itself are just beginning to appear. Here we shall consider four such investigations.

In the first study, Vroom is concerned with predicting the organizational choices of graduating college students on the basis of their instrumentality-goal index scores.[23] These scores reflect the extent to which membership in an organization was perceived by the student as being related to the acquisition of desired goals.

According to the theory, the chosen organization should be the one with the highest instrumentality-goal index. Ratings were used to obtain preferences for 15 different goals and the extent to which these goals could be attained through membership in three different organizations. These two ratings were thus measures of the valences of second-level outcomes and the instrumentality of organizational membership for attainment of these outcomes, respectively. The instrumentality-goal index was the correlation between these two measures. But Vroom's theory also involves consideration of expectancy, i.e., how probable is it that the student can become a member of a particular organization. The choice is not his alone but depends upon whether he is acceptable to the organization. A rough measure of expectancy in this study was whether or not the student had received an offer by the organization. If he had received an offer, expectancy would be high; if not, it would be low. The results show that, considering only organizations from which offers of employment were actually recieved, 76 percent of the students chose the organization with the highest instrumentality-goal index score. The evidence thus strongly supports Vroom's theory.

The next study, by Galbraith and Cummings, utilizes the model to predict the productivity of operative workers.[24] Graphic rating scales were used to measure the instrumentality of performance for five goals—money, fringe benefits, promotion, supervisor's support, and group acceptance. Similar ratings were used for measuring the desirability of each of the goals for the worker. The authors anticipated that a worker's expectation that he could produce at a high level would have a probability of one because the jobs were independent and productivity was a function of the worker's own effort independent of other human or machine pacing. Figure 3 outlines the research design.

g = Desirability of a particular outcome (rating)
I = Instrumentality of production for particular outcomes (rating of relationship)
E = Expectancy (=1 here because worker sets own pace and is assumed to be capable of high productivity)
V = (Valence) the sum of the cross products of instrumentality and g
F = (Force) expectancy times the valence of productivity
Productivity = Objective measures of amount of production in relation to the production standard.

Figure 3. Individual goals and productivity as measured by Vroom's model in one industrial plant. (Based on data from J. Galbraith and L. L. Cummings, "An Empirical Investigation . . . of Task Performance . . . ," *Organizational Behavior and Human Performance*, vol. 2, New York: Academic Press, 1967, p. 178.)

Multiple regression analysis showed that productivity was significantly related positively to the instrumentality-goal interactions for supervisor support and money, and there was an almost significant ($p \ll 10$) relationship with group acceptance. The other factors did not approach significance and the authors explain this lack of significance in terms of the situational context. That is, fringe benefits were dependent not so much on productivity as on a union/management contract, and promotion was based primarily on seniority. Thus the instrumentality of productivity for the attainment of these goals was low and the model would predict no relationship. The Galbraith and Cummings study thus supports Vroom's contention that motivation is related to productivity in those situations where the acquisition of desired goals is dependent upon the individual's production and not when desired outcomes are contingent on other factors.

A third study is that of Hill relating a model similar to Vroom's to behavior in a utility company.[25] Hill's model is based upon Edward's subjective expected utility maximization theory of decision making.[26] Here one given a choice between alternatives A and/or B will select that alternative which maximizes his subjective expected utility or expected value. If the outcomes associated with action A are more desirable than those associated with B, and their probability of occurrence is greater than or equal to those associated with B, then an individual will choose behavior A over behavior B. The basic concepts are subjective expectation and subjective utility or valence. Expectation and utility are multiplicatively related and can be measured by the same techniques used to test Vroom's theory. Where a relationship is found between Subjective Expected Utility (S.E.U.) and overt behavior, it can be interpreted as support for Vroom.

The behavior considered in Hill's study is that of job bidding. This behavior is encountered in organizations that post descriptions of job openings on employee bulletin boards and encourage qualified employees to "bid" (apply) for them. Here records were kept of the number of bids made over a three-year period by groups of semi-skilled electrical repairmen matched in learning ability, seniority in grade, and age. The men were asked about the consequences of bidding and not bidding on the next higher grade job, and rated the consequence on a seven-point scale of desirability and a similar scale of probability of occurrence. Bidders were those who had bid three or more times during that time.

Fourteen different S.E.U. indices were computed from interview data to determine the relative validity of each in predicting bidding behavior. Typical of these indices were: (1) the sums of the cross products of expectation and utility for the positive consequences of bidding ($\sum \overset{+}{S.E.U.}$); (2) the same score for the negative consequences of bidding ($\sum \overset{-}{S.E.U.}$); and (3) the cross products of the *mean* expectation and utility scores for positive and negative consequences ($\sum \dfrac{\overset{+}{S.E.U.}}{N}, \sum \dfrac{\overset{-}{S.E.U.}}{N}$). In addition to these S.E.U. indices, two traditional attitudinal and motivational measures were used. Semantic Differential scales measured each subject's respective evaluation of bidding and the next higher grade job and each subject's Need for Achievement was obtained.[27]

It was hypothesized that: (1) there would be a positive correlation between the S.E.U. indices and bidding; and (2) the S.E.U. indices would be more highly related to bidding behavior than the traditional measures.

We do not discuss relationships for all of the indices here but do consider results for one of the more comprehensive indices and those from multiple regression analysis. This index is the algebraic sum of the cross products of the positive and negative consequences of bidding minus the same score for not bidding for each individual. The correlation of this index with bidding was .26, p«.05 for a one-tailed test. The correlations between the two Semantic Differential scales and bidding were -.09 and -.25, respectively. Neither of these is significant for a one-tailed test predicting a positive correlation. The correlation between Need for Achievement and bidding was a nonsignificant .17. A multiple regression analysis determined the relative contribution of the S.E.U. indices to the prediction of bidding. A variable was selected for analysis on the basis of its relationship to the criterion and its intercorrelation with the other predictors. The multiple correlation for bidding and seven selected variables was .61, p«.05. This correlation included for S.E.U. indices, all of which had higher beta weights than the Semantic Differentials or Need for Achievement. Thus, these variables accounted for more variance in the criterion than did the traditional attitudinal and motivational measures. Both hypotheses were therefore confirmed. This study adds support to the usefulness of this type of model in the study of motivation.

Finally, Lawler and Porter report a study that attempts to relate managerial attitudes to job performance rankings by superiors and peers.[28] In it, 154 managers from five different organizations completed questionnaires concerning seven kinds of rewards, and their expectations that different kinds of behavior would lead to these rewards. The expectations and the ratings of the importance of instrumentality and valence, respectively, were combined multiplicatively to yield multiple correlations which were significantly related to supervisor and peer rankings of the manager's effort to perform his job well. The correlations were higher with effort to perform the job than with the rankings of job performance. Lawler and Porter predicted this result because they reasoned that job performance is influenced by variables other than motivation—e.g., by ability and role perceptions. Of course, Vroom's model is not a behavioral theory but one of motivation only. Motivation is not going to improve performance if ability is low or role perceptions are inaccurate. Vroom's model explains how goals influence effort and that is exactly the relationship found by Lawler and Porter.

Conclusion

Taken together, the four studies discussed in the previous section seem to show that Vroom's model holds great promise for predicting behavior in organizations. There still remain some unanswered questions. We do not know all of the goals that have positive valence in a work situation. We do not know how much of a difference in force is necessary before one kind of outcome is chosen over another. Nor do we know what combination of measures yields the best prediction in a given situation. The answers to these and other questions await further research.

One more point should perhaps be made concerning the four studies and their measurement of Vroom's concepts. While it is true that all of them used subjective measures, the model can in fact be tested with more objective devices. Instrumentality can be inferred from organization practices, expectations can be manipulated by instructions, and goals can be inferred from observed approach and avoidance behaviors. Of course, all of these techniques require assumptions concerning their relationship to the worker's subjective perceptions of the situation; but the model is certainly not bound to the methods of measurement used so far. Vroom specifies in considerable detail the different kinds of techniques that might be used to test his model.[29]

More work must be done before we can make any statements concerning the overall validity of Vroom's model. But the vigor of his formulation, the relative ease of making the concepts operational, and the model's emphasis on individual differences show considerable promise. We are also encouraged by the results of relatively sophisticated studies testing the theory. We believe it is time for those interested in organizational behavior to take a more thoroughly scientific look at this very complex subject of industrial motivation, and Vroom's model seems a big step in that direction.

Notes and References

1. A. H. Maslow, *Motivation and Personality*, New York: Harper, 1954; "A Theory of Human Motivation," *Psychological Review*, vol. 50, 1943, pp. 370-396; *Eupsychian Management*, Homewood, Ill.: Irwin-Dorsey, 1965; F. Herzberg, B. Mausner, and B. B. Snyderman, *The Motivation to Work*, New York: Wiley, 1959; F. Herzberg, *Work and the Nature of Man*, Cleveland: World Publishing, 1966, pp. 130-131; V. H. Vroom, *Work and Motivation*, New York: Wiley, 1964.

2. J. W. Atkinson, J. R. Bastian, R. W. Earl, and G. H. Litwin, "The Achievement Motive, Goal Setting, and Probability Preferences," *Journal of Abnormal and Social Psychology*, vol. 60, 1960, pp. 27-36; W. Edwards, "Behavioral Decision Theory," *Annual Review of Psychology*, Palo Alto: Annual Reviews Inc., 1961, pp. 473-499; H. Peak, "Attitude and Motivation," *Nebraska Symposium on Motivation*, Lincoln: University of Nebraska, 1955, pp. 148-184; M. Rosenberg, "Cognitive Structure and Attitudinal Affect," *Journal of Abnormal and Social Psychology*, vol. 53, 1956, pp. 367-372; M. Fishbein, "An Operational Definition of Belief and Attitude," *Human Relations*, vol. 15, 1962, pp. 35-43.

3. D. McGregor, "Adventure in Thought and Action," *Proceedings of the Fifth Anniversary Convocation of the School of Industrial Management, Massachusetts Institute of Technology*, Cambridge, Mass.: M.I.T., 1957, pp. 23-30.

4. L. W. Porter, *Organizational Patterns of Managerial Job Attitudes*, New York: American Foundation for Management Research, 1964. See also M. Haire, E. Ghiselli, and L. W. Porter, *Managerial Thinking: An International Study*, New York: Wiley, 1966, especially Chaps. 4 and 5.

5. M. Beer, *Leadership, Employee Needs, and Motivation*, Columbus: Bureau of Business Research, Ohio State, 1966.

6. J. V. Clark, "Motivation in Work Groups: A Tentative View," *Human Organization*,

vol. 19, 1960, pp. 199-208; E. E. Lawler and L. W. Porter, "The effect of Performance on Job Satisfaction," *Industrial Relations,* vol. 7, no. 1, 1967, pp. 20-28; L. W. Porter and E. E. Lawler, *Managerial Attitudes and Performance,* Homewood, Ill.: Irwin-Dorsey, 1968, pp. 148, 150.

7. Herzberg, Mausner, and Snyderman, op. cit.

8. Herzberg, op. cit., Chaps. 7 and 8. See also K. Davis, *Human Relations at Work,* 3d ed., New York: McGraw-Hill, 1967, pp. 32-36; R. J. Burke, "Are Herzberg's Motivators and Hygienes Undimensional?" *Journal of Applied Psychology,* vol. 50, 1966, pp. 317-321.

9. For a review of six of these studies as well as a report on their own similar findings, see M. D. Dunnette, J. P. Campbell, and M. D. Hakel, "Factors Contributing to Job Satisfaction and Job Dissatisfaction in Six Occupational Groups," *Organizational Behavior and Human Performance,* vol. 2, 1967, pp. 143-174. See also C. L. Hulin and P. A. Smith, "An Empirical Investigation of Two Implications of the Two-Factor Theory of Job Satisfaction," *Journal of Applied Psychology,* vol. 51, 1967, pp. 396-402; C.A. Lindsay, E. Marks, and L. Gorlow, "The Herzberg Theory: A Critique and Reformulation," *Journal of Applied Psychology,* vol. 51, 1967, pp. 330-339. This latter study and one by J. R. Hinrichs and L.A. Mischkind, "Empirical and Theoretical Limitations of the Two-Factor Hypothesis of Job Satisfaction," *Journal of Applied Psychology,* vol. 51, 1967, pp. 191-200, are especially useful for suggesting possible reformulations and extensions of the theory which may help overcome some of the objections voiced in the studies mentioned above.

10. Dunnette, Campbell, and Hakel, op. cit., pp. 169-173.

11. M. S. Viteles, *Motivation and Morale in Industry,* New York: Norton, 1953, Chap. 14; A. Kornhauser, "Psychological Studies of Employee Attitudes," *Journal of Consulting Psychology,* vol. 8, 1944, pp. 127-143.

12. Herzberg, op. cit, Chaps. 7-9.

13. Herzberg, op. cit., Chap. 8.

14. F. Friedlander and E. Walton, "Positive and Negative Motivations Toward Work," *Administrative Science Quarterly,* vol. 9, 1964, pp. 194-207.

15. It should be noted that the Porter and Lawler research reported above extends the Maslow model by providing an explicit linkage between need satisfaction and performance and also implicitly recognizes individual motivational differences. To do these things, their research makes use of the Vroomian concepts discussed in the next section.

16. A. H. Brayfield and W. H. Crockett, "Employee Attitudes and Employee Performance," *Psychological Bulletin,* vol. 52, 1955, p. 416.

17. B. S. Georgopoulas, G. M. Mahoney, and N. W. Jones, "A Path-Goal Approach to Productivity," *Journal of Applied Psychology,* vol. 41, 1957, pp. 345-353.

18. This section is based especaiily on discussions in Vroom, op. cit., Chaps. 2 and 7. See also J. Galbraith and L. L. Cummings, "An Empirical Investigation of the Motivational Determinants of Task Performance: Interactive Effects between Instrumentality—Valence and Motivation—Ability," *Organizational Behavior and Human Performance,* vol. 2, 1967, pp. 237-257.

19. Vroom, op. cit., p. 6.

20. Vroom, op. cit., p. 17.

21. Vroom, op. cit., p. 18.

22. Vroom, op. cit.

23. V. H. Vroom, "Organizational Choice: A Study of Pre- and Postdecision Processes," *Organizational Behavior and Human Performance*, vol. 1, 1966, pp. 212-225.

24. Galbraith and Cummings, op. cit., pp. 237-257.

25. J. W. Hill, "An Application of Decision Theory to Complex Industrial Behavior," unpublished dissertation, Detroit: Wayne State University, 1965.

26. Edwards, op. cit., pp. 473-499.

27. For discussions of these measures, see C. Osgood, G. Suci, and P. Tannenbaum, *The Measurement of Meaning*, Urbana: University of Illinois, 1957; A. L. Edwards, *Personal Preference Schedule Manual*, New York: Psychological Corporation, 1959.

28. E. E. Lawler and L. W. Porter, "Antecedent Attitudes of Effective Managerial Performance," *Organizational Behavior and Human Performance*, vol. 2, 1967, pp. 122-142.

29. Vroom, *Work and Motivation*, op. cit., Chap. 2.

THE PSYCHOLOGICAL CONTRACT

EDGAR H. SCHEIN

I would like to underline the importance of the psychological contract as a major variable of analysis. It is my central hypothesis that whether a person is working effectively, whether he generates commitment, loyalty, and enthusiasm for the organization and its goals, and whether he obtains satisfaction from his work, depends to a large measure on two conditions: (1) the degree to which his own expectations of what the organization will provide him and what he owes the organization match what the organization's expectations are of what it will give and get; (2) assuming there is agreement on expectations, what actually is to be exchanged—money in exchange for time at work; social-need satisfaction and security in exchange for work and loyalty; opportunities for self-actualization and challenging work in exchange for high productivity, quality work, and creative effort in the service of organizational goals; or various combinations of these and other things.

Ultimately the relationship between the individual and the organization is interactive, unfolding through mutual influence and mutual bargaining to establish a workable psychological contract. We cannot understand the psychological dynamics if we look only to the individual's motivations or only to organizational conditions and practices. The two interact in a complex fashion, requiring us to develop theories and research approaches which can deal with systems and interdependent phenomena.[1]

Furthermore, we must develop concepts which can deal with the *process* by

From Edgar H. Schein, *Organizational Psychology*, 2nd. ed., © 1970, pp. 77-79. Reprinted by permission of Prentice-Hall, Inc., Englewood Cliffs, New Jersey.

which the psychological contract is initially negotiated between individual and organization, and the *process* by which it is renegotiated during the employee's organizational career. For example, *organizational socialization* is one such concept, referring to the fact that organizations have goals, norms, values, preferred ways of doing things which are usually taught systematically, though not necessarily overtly, to all new members.[2] Some of the norms can be thought of as *pivotal*, in the sense that adherence to them is a requirement of continued membership in the organization. For a manager it is required that he believe in the validity of the free enterprise system; for a professor, that he accept the canons of research and scholarship. Other organizational norms are *peripheral*, in the sense that it is desirable for members to possess them but not essential. For example, for a manager it may be desirable from the point of view of the organization that he be a man, have certain political views, wear the right kind of clothes, use only the company products, and so on. For a professor, it may be desirable that he like to teach, be willing to help in the administration of the university, spend most of his time on campus rather than on consulting trips, and so on. Violation of these norms does not cause loss of membership, however, if the pivotal norms are adhered to.

In thinking about the adjustment of the individual to the organization, we can identify three types of possible adjustments, based on which sets of norms are adhered to. Acceptance of *neither* the pivotal nor peripheral norms can be thought of as *"active rebellion"* and is likely to lead to voluntary or involuntary loss of membership. Acceptance of *both* pivotal and peripheral norms can be thought of as *"conformity"* and is likely to lead to the loyal but uncreative "organization man" or "bureaucrat." Acceptance of pivotal norms but rejection of peripheral norms can be thought of as *"creative individualism,"* in the sense that the person still works on behalf of those norms of the organization that are pivotal, but retains his sense of identity and exercises creativity in helping the organization to achieve its goals.

Such creativity can be thought of either in terms of new products and new solutions to organizational problems, or in terms of "role innovation," inventing new ways to do a job.[3] Thus, a professor can be creative by finding some new scientific law or he can be "role innovative" by developing new ways of teaching; a manager can invent a new financial control system or he can invent new ways of relating to managers in other departments which improve the overall effectiveness of the organization.

From the point of view of the organization, it is desirable to create conditions which make it possible for members to be creative individualists rather than conformists or rebels. From the point of view of society, it is desirable to have an educational system which predisposes people to want to be creative individualists. If one views schools and colleges as organizations which socialize students as well as educate them, the organizational question becomes, what kind of school organization creates conditions for students to develop a creative individualistic orientation?

Managers of organizations, whether they be of businesses or schools, must become aware not only of the complexities of human motivation, but of the dynamic processes which occur as the person enters into and pursues a career within an organization. Just as the manner in which a person is selected, trained, and assigned influences his image of the organization, so the manner in which he is managed will influence this image. A manager must be aware of the interaction between these various organizational systems and must think integratively about them. For example, if he plans to manage people in a way that will challenge them and provide them with opportunities to use all their potential, he must be careful that the manner in which they are selected, tested, trained, and assigned to their jobs does not undermine the very motivations he wishes to draw on. What this means in practice is that all those members of the organization who are responsible for the various functions should, together, think through carefully the consequences of the various approaches, and coordinate their activities to accomplish whatever shared goals they have.

Notes and References

1. In some experimental studies which attempted to test directly the relationship of feelings of equity in the psychological contract to productivity on a task, Adams showed that subjects who feel they are being overpaid for their level of ability will produce more than subjects who feel they are being fairly paid relative to their level of ability. The interpretation is that if the organization gives more than it gets, in the eyes of the subject, he will work harder to make the relationship more just. J.S. Adams and W.B. Rosenbaum, "The Relationship of Worker Productivity to Cognitive Dissonance about Wage Inequities," *Journal of Applied Psychology* 46 (1962): 161-64.
2. E.H. Schein, "Organizational Socialization and the Profession of Management," Third Douglas McGregor Address, *Industrial Management Review* 9 (1968): 1-15.
3. E. H. Schein, "Occupational Socialization in the Professions: The Case of Role Innovation," *Technology Review* (October-November 1970): 32-38.

PART FOUR

Group Behavior
and Intergroup Conflict
in the Organization

We now examine how group behavior, both within and between groups or departments, plays a major part in determining the effectiveness of the organization itself. As we discuss the group as a unit of behavior, it will become apparent that individual goals, group goals, and organizational goals are often not compatible. We then examine how conflict arises, causing many forms of dysfunctional behavior to emerge. Again, just as with the individual, the contingencies of the group and the organization must be examined in order to determine why this conflict has taken place, and how a manager can go about resolving or managing it.

Determinants of Group Behavior

A *group* can be defined as two or more people who (1) interact with one another, (2) are psychologically aware of one another, (3) perceive themselves to be a member of the group, and (4) work toward a common goal. The key words here are *interaction, awareness*, and *goal*. In other words, some degree of inter-dependence determines group membership. Much like the individuals discussed by Schein in his article, "Organizational Socialization and the Profession of Management," groups develop *norms, interaction patterns* and *role expectations* for the behavior of individual members. Groups enable individuals to have an outlet for their affiliation needs. They also enable members to develop a sense of identity or self-esteem and help them gain status. Primarily, however, groups are established to accomplish a task. Modern technology is such that individuals alone cannot accomplish as much as groups of individuals working together.

In every organization there are *formal* groups—that is, groups to which a member is assigned as a part of his work role—and *informal* groups, or friendship groups, which develop on the basis of mutual attraction. In both types of groups the individual's attitudes, perceptions, judgments, and goals are important in determining the groups' effectiveness. For this reason a great deal of group effort is spent socializing the new member when he enters.

There are basically six properties of groups which determine their structure and which can be used to measure group effectiveness in reaching goals. The first property is *status*, defined as social ranking. Within a group, the status of each individual is based on his importance to the group and his influence on group members. As group members gravitate toward one another in striving for common goals, the interaction becomes stabilized in a pattern of reciprocities manifested in a hierarchical status ranking of individual members.

Just as individuals have status within the group, various groups have status within the organization. For example, staff departments often have higher status in the organization than do line departments, even though line-department members may feel they are doing the real work.

The second group property is *cohesiveness*, defined as the positive mutual attraction of the group and its members. The more cohesive the group, the more likely the group's goals will be accepted by the members of the group, and therefore the more likely the group will reach its goals.

The third group property is *size*. Research has found that performance quality and productivity are positively correlated with the group size, under most circumstances. The exception is decision-making, where a decision is reached faster in a smaller group.

The fourth group property is *goal*, defined as a successful level of performance—in the group's terms. A group's goal can be either pro- or anti-organizational. For example, a work group can decide to meet organizational goals, or it can decide to restrict output to maintain group identity and power base.

The fifth group property is *communication pattern*. Communication channels among individuals in a group influence their interaction and the functioning of the group as a whole. Research presented in several of the readings in this part shows that this property has a great deal to do with the satisfaction of group members and their willingness to accept group goals.

The sixth and perhaps most important property is *leadership style*, defined as interpersonal *influence* directed through the communication process toward a specific goal or goals. Contingencies of reinforcement are a primary tool available to the group leader for influencing group members.

The selections in this part explore the first five properties of group structure that determine group effectiveness. Because leadership is perhaps the most important property, it is treated in a separate part (part 6). Here, we consider the formation of groups, the structural characteristics of groups, and the social relationships in groups as they affect goal attainment within the organization.

McGinnies discusses various group terms and distinguishes between various types of groups. He then reports on the effect that various properties of the group have on task performance. From this reading, managers can gain knowledge which will aid them in structuring groups so that they can increase their potential effectiveness. McGinnies concludes that the primary tool available to the manager for influencing group task performance is the incentive arrangement, or the contingencies of reinforcement.

Shaw says that people join groups in order to fulfill a need state. He examines the question: If a person wants to join a particular group, what attraction does the specific group have for him and what is it about him that attracts the group? Shaw concludes by saying, ''it appears that interpersonal attraction is a function of the degree to which the person expects affiliation with the others to be rewarding. The difficult task is to identify the many sources of reinforcement in interpersonal relationships."

Kolasa notes several ways in which a group can influence its members. He then goes on to discuss several of the properties of groups which are significant for determining the output of the group and the satisfaction of its members with the group itself.

Social exchange is a relationship in which the parties mutually reward one another. When a person in an exchange relationship gets more or less reward than he deserves, we have what Adams defines as *inequity*. Adams offers a detailed discussion of how equitable and inequitable situations can occur, and the effect that they have on the motivation and behavior of individuals within groups.

Basically, this theory suggests that the manager knows that rewards should be contingent on performance and also that the payoff is evaluated in terms of whether or not the recipient feels that it is equitable, compared to what he believes he deserves or to what he feels others have gotten.

Katz explains how informal work groups form in complex organizations, and the various positive and negative effects that they can have on organizational structure and goal accomplishment.

For instance, the Hawthorne studies demonstrate how group pressures to produce at certain levels can be more influential than production quotas. Katz points out that workers in groups have "status," which is accorded to them by others. An individual may react to a manager's directive in terms of whether or not it will increase or decrease his status position in the group.

Intergroup Conflict in the Organization

Conflict arises primarily because of different goals, or because of disagreement about the best or correct solution to a problem. There are many kinds of conflict. Some types of conflict are constructive; others are dysfunctional. There are four basic types of conflict in an organization. The first type is *issue* conflict, which generally results from disagreement between two groups on the basis of differences in organizational viewpoint. For example, a sales department may want to ease credit restrictions because of pressure from the marketing vice president to increase sales. The credit department, however, feels pressure from the comptroller to keep credit losses to a minimum. Interdepartmental conflict will result.

The second type of conflict is *interpersonal*. This is conflict between two people based on personal differences. It may have originally started as an issue conflict and then, over a period of time, developed into a personality conflict.

A third type of conflict is called *role* conflict. This occurs when an individual has incompatible or overloading pressure from two or more sources. If a manufacturing vice president asks a plant manager to increase output of Product X, for example, and the sales force is asking for more of product Y, the plant manager is in a state of role conflict; that is, incompatible demands are being made upon him.

The fourth type of conflict is *intrapersonal*, wherein a person's values and beliefs are incompatible with his behavior. For example, an employee whose religious faith forbids him to work on Sunday learns that he must work on Sunday or lose his job. He is in a state of intrapersonal conflict in that his behavior (working on Sunday) will be in direct conflict with his belief that working on Sunday is wrong.

In the past, all conflict within organizations has been viewed as dysfunctional. Conflict can, however, be a first step in making organizational changes that may lead to more effective organizational functioning.

Litterer discusses the causes and utility of conflict. He shows that some of the causes of conflict are imbedded in the characteristics and structure of the organization, and hence are to some degree inescapable. He concludes that managers should learn to manage inescapable conflict and make it work.

Pondy discusses conflict within and between organizations. He reviews three conceptual models of major classes of conflict, taking up where Litterer left off in discussing the dysfunctional and functional aspects of conflict. Pondy shows how equilibrium, or stability, can be established in a conflict situation. He says the main way a manager can reduce conflict is to rearrange the contingencies of reinforcement so that efforts in the direction of conflict reduction and equilibrium are positively rewarded.

Another method of dealing effectively with conflict is the exercise of control and authority over the individuals in conflict. Frequently, questions of organizational control focus on the relations among units, departments, or groups within an organization, rather than upon individuals. For example, when two units conflict over how scarce resources are allocated, an effective managerial tactic may be to introduce some sort of participative mechanism, by which both units can influence the final decision. Some organization development strategies (see part 7) are aimed primarily at conflict reduction. Groups, confrontation strategies, or simple organization redesign may be intended to create a situation in which one can live with problems intrinsic to the character of the "system."

Hickson et al. argue that differential power among organizational units is the basis of organizational control. Drawing upon the work of such organization theorists as March, Thompson, Lawrence, Lorsch, and Perrow, the Hickson group argues that all organizations, just as all individuals and all groups, are limited in their power to determine what they do, and are interdependent with other units. One of the results of such limits and interdependencies is conflict, growing out of unequal power and dependencies among various departments in the organization. Hickson et al. discuss how different individual units gain power within the organization, and the functional and dysfunctional results.

This jockeying for power, with resultant interpersonal and interunit conflict, can often create structural arrangements that are difficult to change. The Hickson et al. article not only gives insight into potential causes of conflict between organizations, but also offers an understanding of the bases of power needed by leaders to direct and control.

Finally, as Walton and Dutton make clear, dealing with conflict is not an easy task. Many factors must be considered when seeking to remove the causes of conflict. For example, the nature of the task could be such (as with an assembly line) that restructuring the jobs is not a feasible solution. In some jobs, the performance criteria are vague, as we have noted in part 1. When this is the case, individuals and groups may legitimately disagree on what criteria should be used to assess performance.

When interest groups press contrary positions, conflict is likely. Walton and Dutton suggest several conflict resolution strategies, ranging from a change in structure (see part 1) to third-party intervention (see part 7).

BEHAVIOR IN SMALL GROUPS

ELLIOTT McGINNIES

In considering the manner in which perceptions and judgments are influenced by social variables, particularly in a group setting, we focused our attention on the individual. But the group itself is also a legitimate object of study, and there is evidence that the products of group interaction cannot necessarily be predicted from the performance of the individuals outside the group situation. Experiments on group behavior frequently are designed to permit observation of the effects of social interaction on all of the members, not just the effects on one person selected for study. Both the composition and the behavior history of a group are determinants of its effective stimuli for the individual members. The group also determines the nature and pattern of the reinforcements the members receive in the course of their interactions with one another. Group composition and other salient features of the situation can be manipulated in the social-psychological laboratory, and we shall examine some of the studies of small groups in which this has been done.

Primary and Secondary Groups

Group influences are most apparent in face-to-face situations where communication between individuals is immediate and direct. But everyone reveals his past history of interaction in groups, even when he is alone. The behaviors that have been acquired in group situations become habitual, so that in a real sense each of us is the product of a number of social groups. To be sure, the behavior of some persons seems to reflect group influence more than the behavior of others; that is, they

From *Social Behavior: A Functional Analysis*, by Elliott McGinnies. Houghton Mifflin Company, 1970. Reprinted by permission of the publishers.

behave more in accordance with the prevailing norms of their society. The striking differences that can be observed among individuals in matters of opinion and attitude can be traced to affiliation with different groups and consequent differences in histories of social reinforcement.

Individuals seek different kinds of group memberships depending upon their particular habits and attitudes. These behavioral dispositions, in turn, have derived from earlier social interactions, the most important of which involved the family. Parents are not only the most important stimulus figures for the child, they also provide the reinforcements that shape his behavior. Behavior acquired at this early stage, with minor changes, frequently characterizes the individual for the rest of his life. Certainly most of our important attitudes dealing with such matters as religion, morals, and political philosophy are learned in the family. A group such as the family, where the members have intimate and immediate access to one another, is called a *primary group*. A group in which the members, due to geographical or other circumstances, may only occasionally engage in face-to-face interaction, is called a *secondary group*. This is a classic distinction derived from German sociology, in which the terms *Gemeinschaft* and *Gesellschaft* are used to distinguish between a smaller community and a larger society.

The distinction between a primary and a secondary group is sometimes tenuous and arbitrary. As the children in a family grow older, they increasingly interact with individuals outside this primary group. They join with their peers to form new primary groups, in which the members share interests relating to politics, education, religion, work, or recreation, to mention just a few possibilities. These primary groups may, in turn, be parts of a larger, secondary group, such as a political party or a church organization. The resources of secondary groups generally exceed those of primary groups, and membership in a secondary group frequently enables the individual to extend his behavior repertoire in ways that cannot be supported by a smaller, primary group. Joining a political party, for example, provides one with a greater opportunity to effect social change than he would have when acting either entirely by himself or in concert with others in a small group. The members of a political group are held together not just by certain commonalities of interest and intent but also by long-term expectancies of reward for their efforts.

Reference Groups

The term reference group is sometimes used to denote that primary or secondary group from which an individual has acquired certain attitudes or certain behavior patterns. Because most persons belong to a number of different groups, both primary and secondary, i.e., the family, church, labor union, fraternal or civic organization, their behavior often can be understood in terms of those groups in which it was acquired. What happens when different groups reinforce incompatible behaviors? Consider a college freshman who comes from a family where drinking alcoholic beverages is disapproved but who joins a fraternity in which a certain amount of alcohol consumption is not only tolerated but encouraged. He may behave discriminatively by drinking when with his companions and abstaining when at home. In this manner, he is positively reinforced for his behavior in both groups. Or he may attempt to demonstrate his newfound independence and striving for maturity by drinking both in college and at home. Inasmuch as he will experience aversive consequences in the home situation, we must assume that his behavior is controlled more by the immediate consequences of drinking than by his family's reactions. What he does when not in the presence of either his family or his fraternity brothers will depend upon which of these two reference groups has more effectively reinforced his behavior of drinking or not drinking.

An illustration of the role of reference groups in social behavior is provided by some observations made at Bennington College in the 1930's by Theodore Newcomb. Questionnaires measuring political-economic progressivism were given to members of the student body each year to determine how these attitudes might change over four years of college experience. A steady decrease in conservatism, with a concomitant increase in progressivism, was found in students as they advanced from the freshman through the senior years. For example, significant differences existed among these four groups in support for the conservative Republican presidential candidate of 1936, Alfred Landon. Sixty-two per cent of the freshmen, 43 per cent of the sophomores, 15 per cent of the juniors, and 15 per cent of the seniors favored Landon. Interestingly, 66 per cent of the parents of the students favored Landon, a figure most closely approximating that of the freshmen. It was apparent that political-economic attitudes became increasingly divorced from parental attitudes as the students proceeded from freshman class to senior class. An additional finding was that the more popular students scored more often as progressives than as conservatives on the attitude measure (Newcomb, 1943).

Charters and Newcomb (1958) asked students from a large psychology class who had identified themselves as members of the Roman Catholic Church to participate in an experiment ostensibly designed to construct an attitude scale. The students were divided into two groups. Members of a control group were given no special instructions other than to respond to the items on the scale. The members of the experimental group, however, were reminded of their membership in the Catholic Church, after which they discussed certain basic assumptions of the Church. Follwing this procedure, which was designed to emphasize their religious affiliation, they responded to the items on the attitude scale. Certain items were worded so that they could be answered not only from a Catholic point of view but from other points of view as well. It was found that the students in the experimental group, for whom membership in the Catholic Church had been made salient, responded to the critical items in a more orthodox Catholic fashion than did the students in the control group.

Both of the experiments just cited demonstrate that behavior often can be predicted from information about a person's history of affiliation with different social groups. An individual can be said to behave in accordance with his identification with certain reference groups which are important and significant to him. Or he can be said to have adopted a typical performance, or *role*, that is appropriate to the group situation in which he finds himself. Although the concepts of role and reference group are useful as descriptive devices, it will suit our purposes better to view the behavior as reflecting an acquired capacity of the individual to make discriminations that maximize his chances of being positively reinforced in a particular social situation. Consider the Bennington students studied by Newcomb. Many of the freshmen undoubtedly found themselves in a conflict situation. Certain verbal responses (attitudes) that had been positively reinforced within the family failed to evoke similar approval from those they recognized as campus leaders. As they progressed from freshman class to senior class standing, these students must occasionally have made utterances on political and economic issues that were not in accord with the attitudes they had acquired in their families. These utterances, we may assume, were promptly reinforced, and the probability that they would be repeated was thus increased. Because the sources of reinforcement were fellow students, including upperclassmen with more liberal attitudes, the attitudes of the freshmen were gradually modified in the direction of conformity to those prevailing in the college community.

The results obtained by Charters and Newcomb may be explained in a similar manner if we are willing to make several additional assumptions. The verbal habits in this situation were probably acquired in large part through prior education in Catholic ideology. Why did those subjects for whom membership in the Catholic Church was made salient respond in a more typically Catholic fashion than those who were not reminded of this particular group affiliation? The simplest explanation of this is that the instructions altered the stimulus characteristics of the situation so as to make the s^Ds similar to those associated with previously reinforced, pro-Catholic verbalizations. In other words, if I am reminded of the fact that I am a Catholic in a group of fellow Catholics and then am asked to respond to questions that allow for doctrinal interpretation, I will tend to make those responses that have been reinforced in similar situations in the past. In short, my behavior will generalize to this new situation. If, on the other hand, I am not made aware of the special nature of the group, then my behavior is controlled by a different set of stimuli, and I will not necessarily emit characteristically Catholic responses. Identifying a group as having certain properties relevant to an individual's attitudes gives a unique structure to the situation and highlights the discriminative stimuli to which he will respond. The *behavior most likely to occur in a new situation is that which has a history of positive reinforcement in similar prior situations*.

Even the selectivity of perception may in some instances be attributed to the influence of reference groups. As Shibutani (1961) points out, a prostitute and a social worker walking through a slum area probably notice different things. Differences in taste concerning art, music, and decor reflect the influence of the social groups to which one has belonged. These groups provided the occasions on which certain behaviors were learned and from which responses will generalize to new situations that contain some of the same stimulus elements.

Audience Effects on Task Performance

Floyd Allport (1920) has taken the position that an individual's motivational state is altered in the context of a group. The effect on behavior is generally one of enhancement, or *social facilitation*. Allport studied groups composed of three to five students at Harvard and Radcliffe colleges. The task of all the subjects in the groups was to write associations to stimulus words such as "building" and "laboratory." Their responses were compared with those of other subjects who formed associations working alone instead of in a group. The results, according to Allport, showed that the presence of a coworking group had the effect of speeding up the process of free association. To be sure, individual differences were manifested; some subjects were distracted in the group situation and were less productive of verbal associations. In general, however, Allport's experiment revealed the operation of a subtle social influence on behavior that had traditionally been studied only with single individuals. In work groups, this facilitation effect is sometimes manifested as greater quantity but poorer quality of output.

Social Facilitation

We may consider it an established principle, then, that being in a group has unique stimulus value for the individual. Can the group situation be shown to influence behavior more complex than that involving simple discriminations or judgments? For example, do individuals perform skilled tasks better alone or in a group? An early attempt to answer this question was made by Travis (1925), who trained twenty-two college undergraduates to perform fairly skillfully on a pursuit rotor. This device resembles a phonograph turntable near the edge of which is mounted a small metal disc about the size of a nickel. The subject's task is to keep a flexible pointer in contact with this target while the turntable revolves at 60 R.P.M. After the students had practiced on this task until their performances had reached a stable level, they were asked to do the same thing in front of a small "audience" consisting of other students. The average time on target for the subjects when performing before their peers was somewhat longer than when they had performed alone, indicating an apparent group influence on accuracy in a simple task involving motor skill. Other early demonstrations of this sort included the discovery that individuals solved simple multiplication problems more rapidly and produced more associations to words when in the presence of passive spectators than when working alone (Dashiell, 1930).

Taylor and Faust (1952) also obtained evidence that the performance of individuals in a group may be superior in some respects to their individual efforts. They recorded the number of questions asked as well as the time required by individuals alone and in groups to guess the correct answer in a game of Twenty Questions. The groups, composed of either two or four individuals, required on the average fewer questions and less time to solve the problems than did individuals. Size of the group, within these limits, was not an important variable. The authors point out, however, that in terms of man-minutes required for solution, the performance of individuals was superior to that of groups and the performance of groups of two was superior to that of groups of four. Two persons, however, did not solve a given problem in less than half the time required by one person, as would be necessary to demonstrate group superiority. These experimental results suggest that the performance of individuals in a group is indeed likely to be different from their performance alone, but not necessarily more efficient.

A vigilance problem. More recently, Bergum and Lehr (1963) recorded the performances of twenty National Guard trainees who were required to sit in isolated booths and observe a panel on which twenty red lights were mounted in a circle. The lights were lit up in sequence, and this circular pattern was repeated every five seconds. During an hour, however, there were twenty-four instances of a light failing to go on in its proper sequence. It was the task of the subjects to monitor the display and press a button whenever such an interruption in the sequence occurred. After twenty minutes of training, followed by a ten-minute rest, the subjects performed alone on this vigilance task for two hours and fifteen minutes. Twenty additional subjects, similarly trained, were told that from time to time during the test period their booths would be visited by a Lieutenant Colonel or a Master Sergeant. Four such visits were actually made to each subject. The mean performance of these "supervised" subjects was then compared with that of the "unsupervised" subjects over five successive twenty-seven minute intervals.

As a result of fatigue, the performance of both the groups deteriorated with time. But the subjects who were subjected to unannounced visits by their superiors maintained a distinctly higher level of performance than those who monitored the light panel unsupervised. The occasional visits by a military superior placed these subjects on a variable interval schedule of reinforcement, and their performances—aside from fatigue decrement—were typical of those found with this type of schedule.

Decision-making. A different type of task, devised by Banta and Nelson (1964), required college students to judge the reactions of a hypothetical individual to a list of attitude statements after first being told the person's reaction to five similar statements. Dyads (two-person groups) were formed to work on this task, and the partners were told that they must agree on a decision, then record their action by pressing a signal button. A light was flashed by the experimenter whenever the decision favored by a previously designated member of each pair was adopted. Control groups performed the same task under noncontingent reinforcement. The probability that the reinforced partner would have his opinions reported out of the dyad rose with successive trials. The nonreinforced subjects, on the other hand, made fewer and fewer proposals for a solution, and their partners began to dominate the decision-making process. This experimental result has its counterpart in committee processes, where those members whose proposals are consistently adopted are often seen to play an increasingly dominant role in the group's deliberations. Nonreinforcement, through repeated failure to have their suggestions acted on by the group, causes some individuals to virtually withdraw from debate in favor of those whose contributions are rewarded. As we shall see later in this chapter, it is possible by selective manipulation of the reinforcement contingencies to encourage the performance of the more reticent members of a group and to depress that of the more aggressive individuals.

Social Inhibition

Social interaction may also have an inhibiting rather than a facilitating effect. Allport (1920) reported, for example, that individuals who free associated to words in the presence of others gave more common and fewer uncommon responses. Idiosyncratic associations, in other words, seem to be inhibited, or suppressed, in a group situation. This observation is consistent with the findings of Sherif (1966) and Asch (1952). These investigators, as you will recall, observed a trend toward development of a group norm in situations where individuals reported their perceptions of either the movement of a point of light or the length of a line. The giving of more "common" associations to stimulus words in a group situation reveals the operation of a similar movement toward established norms. The general principle that seems to emerge from these experiments is that individual behavior in a group situation is modified in accordance with the particular stimulus features that characterize the group. Differences in the prior experiences of the individual group members determine whether task performance will be facilitated or inhibited in any single case.

Zajonc (1966) has argued that a distinction should be made between situations where individuals are performing tasks in the mere *presence of others* and those where several persons are *simultaneously engaged in* the same activity. We might add a third category, where a task can be solved only through the *joint or combined efforts* of several individuals. This last situation involves a special sort of social interaction, called cooperation, and may be deferred for later discussion. Consider for a moment just those situations where a person performs in the company of others or where several persons perform simultaneously but independently. Although we have focused our attention on results that indicated a *facilitation effect* in both of these instances, several investigators have reported just the opposite. Pessin (1933) found that subjects who memorized lists of nonsense syllables in the presence of spectators required more repetitions and made more errors than when they learned equivalent materials alone. Previously, Husband (1931) had reported that finger-maze learning was slower in the presence of an observer. As we have already noted, there is evidence that both the quality and orginality of performance may suffer in a group situation. Apparently, a social context for individual task performance does not provide unalloyed advantages.

Learning vs. performance. Zajonc (1966), after reviewing this general problem, suggests that "learning is impaired and performance facilitated by the presence of an audience" (p. 14). *Learning,* Zajonc points out, refers to the acquisition of new responses, while *performance* refers to the emission of previously learned responses. He argues that in any learning situation the subject tends at first to make a great many incorrect responses. When performing a previously learned task, however, an individual emits more correct than incorrect responses. An audience has the effect of enhancing the emission of *dominant responses,* and these are predominantly incorrect during learning and predominantly correct during performance.

Although Zajonc offers an explanation of this effect in terms of increased motivation and arousal in the presence of an audience, let us suggest an alternative interpretation. First, as pointed out, individuals tend to make a great many errors during learning. As a consequence of previous experiences in performing before a group, the individual comes to anticipate reactions of disparagement when he commits blunders. He is likely to generalize this expectancy to a learning situation in which other persons are present. In other words, his behavior is controlled not only by stimuli representing the task but also by stimuli provided by the audience; and the latter have been the occasions for ridicule contingent upon the commission of blunders. Consequently, every error he makes during learning serves as a conditioned stimulus for the anxiety occasioned by public disparagement, whether or not such a reaction is actually forthcoming from the present audience. Because he makes more incorrect than correct responses during the early phases of learning, the emotional reactions that have been conditioned to public ineptness interfere with both his attention and his coordination. The individual, therefore, does not acquire new response patterns as readily when he is in a situation that has the potentiality of becoming aversive whenever he makes a mistake.

Consider, on the other hand, the behavior of a person who is engaged before an audience in a previously learned, well-practiced task. If he has any degree of competence in the task, he will make more correct than incorrect responses. Previous experience has taught him that a competent performance will earn the plaudits of onlookers. Insofar as the correct responses are already within his repertoire, he will be reinforced by the sheer presence of an audience whenever they occur. Incorrect responses, although they will be more aversive in the presence of a group, will occur less frequently, and the attendant emotional reactions will not be as disruptive of the total performance as those that would occur during learning under similar circumstances. Whether or not the presence of others facilitates or inhibits performance, then, is seen to depend upon the overall level of task competence that the individual has attained. His operant level of correct responses must exceed that of incorrect responses in order for reinforcing consequences to occur more frequently than aversive consequences. We need not look far in everyday experience to find examples of this principle. The amateur performer in any field—entertainment, sports, public speaking—finds his behavior progressively deteriorating as soon as he commences to fumble and blunder before an audience. The task that was incompletely mastered when practiced alone becomes a nightmare in the presence of a group, the very existence of which is aversive when one performs inadequately. To the skilled professional, on the other hand, an audience serves as an additional source of reinforcement, adding to the satisfaction that the performer experiences when he practices competently alone.

Reasoning from everyday observation, however, is not an adequate substitute for experimental data. Fortunately, several studies have been reported that bear upon the adequacy of this analysis. Cottrell, Rittle, and Wack (1967) examined both the difficulty of the task and the degree of competence of their subjects in relation to speed of learning either alone or in the presence of an audience. Their subjects were 102 male undergraduates confronted with the task of learning lists of paired associates. This is a situation in which the subject views pairs of words, presented one pair at a time on a memory drum. On successive trials, he must try to name correctly the *second* word of each pair upon presentation of the first word. Items typical of such pairs would be *barren-fruitless, avid-grouchy,* and *desert-leading.* These particular pairs, in fact, were part of a difficult list used by these investigators. The difficulty lies in the fact that there are few within-pair associations and many strong associations between members of different pairs, for example, *barren, arid,* and *desert.* This means that a subject is apt to respond to the first word of a pair with its associate from another pair. In an easier task, the words in each pair had strong associations, and there were few associations between members of different pairs. Thus, the correct responses in the case of pairs such as *adept-skillful* and *barren-fruitless* would be learned more readily than those in the pairs previously mentioned.

The subjects were divided into slow, medium, and fast learners on the basis of the number of trials required for them to learn a practice list. The numbers of errors they made in learning the test lists were then computed as a function of the presence and the absence of a two-person audience watching the subject attentively while he learned. When the subjects learned the easy lists, it apparently made little difference whether the two observers were present or not. Nor did differences in learning skill of the subjects appear to affect their reactions markedly in the presence of an audience. In the case of the difficult list, however, the presence of an audience had the effect of causing the less able learners to commit more errors. The fast learners made slightly fewer errors when their performance was being observed.

Attentive vs. inattentive audiences. Zajonc's view that the mere presence of other persons increases the subject's "motivation" to perform suggests that it should make little difference whether or not the audience members are attending to what the subject is doing. If, as we have suggested, the potential of other individuals as agents of reinforcement is critical in their effect upon a performer, then it should matter whether they are merely physically present or are present as spectators. Cottrell and his colleagues (1968) examined the possibility that subjects engaged in a recognition task would perform differently in the presence of an audience and in the presence of others who did not constitute an audience. Forty-five male college sutdents first practiced pronouncing ten nonsense words like *afworbu* and *biwonji*. Two words were assigned to each of five training frequencies: 1, 2, 5, 10, and 25. Thus, the subjects read and repeated some of the words twenty-five times and others only once. This procedure established certain of these new verbal habits as more dominant than others. Dominant responses, remember, have been found to occur more readily than weaker responses in the presence of an audience.

The subjects were then assigned to one of three test conditions. They attempted to recognize the words they had just practiced when the words were projected at very short durations on a screen seven feet away. Some of the subjects did this alone, others were observed by two spectators, and still others performed in the presence of two *blindfolded* individuals, who were ostensibly becoming dark-adapted for another experiment. Out of 160 flashes on the screen, 120 constituted pseudo-recognition trials; that is, the stimulus was one of the training words but presented in a reversed position and thereby rendered unreadable. Inasmuch as the subjects were instructed to guess on every trial, the experimenters could determine the extent to which they would emit responses that had been made more or less dominant during training. And they could relate these differences to the particular conditions in which the subjects found themselves.

The data revealed that the presence of an audience enhances the emission of dominant responses in preference to subordinate responses. The mere presence of other persons, however, produces no such effect upon performance; that is, the subjects guessed as many of the high frequency training words when alone as they did in the presence of two blindfolded students. In reconsidering these and related findings, Cottrell (1968) suggests what amounts to a reinforcement interpretation. He observes that if performance before an audience usually results in positive or negative outcomes for the individual, he will come to anticipate such outcomes when placed in an audience situation. Although Cottrell goes further and speaks of a learned source of drive, it is not necessary to do so. The nonsense words that were practiced less frequently by the subjects may be viewed as having the status of potentially "incorrect" responses during the guessing phase, while those that were frequently practiced are analogous to "correct" responses. As we have previously suggested, an audience provides cues for the emission of performances having the greatest likelihood of being positively reinforced. Responses that are most likely to be correct ordinarily are those that have been practiced most frequently. Individuals who are present but are not able to observe what one is doing do not provide the same cues to potential consequences as an audience does. Performance in these circumstances is not likely to differ from performance when alone. This analysis proceeds from a consideration of the individual's history of reinforcement in situations similar to the one in which he now finds himself. No inferences about drive states are needed, and none are made. We can make fairly accurate predictions about how an individual will perform if we know something about his level of skill, his past experience in similar situations, and the nature of the occasion on which he is currently being required to demonstrate his proficiency.

The Role of Incentives

One way of facilitating task performance is to offer incentives for increased competence. The most generally effective incentive seems to be money, but money will serve this function only in situations where its potential as a reinforcer will not be offset by other, aversive consequences. An experiment conducted in the late 1920's (Roethlisberger and Dickson, 1947) illustrates this point. As one of a series of studies done at Western Electric's Hawthorne plant in Chicago, the experiment involved workers who attached and soldered banks of wires to a telephone switchboard component. Fourteen workers and one observer were placed in a special room, and various wage incentives were introduced in an attempt by the management to discover which ones would most facilitate production.

Taken at face value, this experiment would seem to represent a straightforward manipulation of amount of anticipated monetary reinforcement to discover the effect on productivity. The results, however, were disappointing. Level of productivity remained relatively constant despite variations in the wage incentives that were offered. The apparent explanation for this failure to increase production through wage incentives is one of those that seems obvious after the fact. Each worker feared that if output were increased, management would maintain its current level of expenses by decreasing the payment for each unit produced. Management did not, of course, threaten any such readjustment of incentives in the event of an increase in output, but the workers apparently assumed that this might happen. Olmstead (1959) summarizes the situation in the vernacular of the participants: "A good guy won't be a chiseler: he'll do his share and not expect others to 'carry' him (except in certain circumstances). Thirdly, he won't be a squealer; he will protect the group code against outside interference. Finally, he won't put on airs or be a snob, that is, he will manifest in his non-work behavior his 'democratic' submission to group ideals" (p. 29).

This classic study illustrates the danger of attempting to define a reinforcer independent of its effects upon behavior. Money, in this instance, was rendered ineffective as an incentive because of the way in which the workers interpreted the situation. This interpretation was reinforced by the group, and deviant behavior by an individual member in the form of increased productivity would probably have had aversive consequences to that individual. In fact, Coch and French (1948) observed a clothespresser who was "scapegoated" by her coworkers because her efficiency rating had climbed above the average for the group.

References

Aiken, E. G. Interaction process analysis changes accompanying operant conditioning of verbal frequency in small groups. *Perceptual and Motor Skills*, 1965a, 21, 52-54.

Aiken, E. G. Changes in interpersonal descriptions accompanying the operant conditioning of verbal frequency in groups. *Journal of Verbal Learning and Verbal Behavior*, 1965b, 4, 243-247.

Allport, F. H. The influence of the group upon association and thought. *Journal of Experimental Psychology*, 1920, 3, 159-182.

Allport, F. H. *Social psychology.* Boston: Houghton Mifflin, 1924.

Altman, I., and Haythorn, W. W. The ecology of isolated groups. *Behavioral Science*, 1967, 12, 169-182.

Altman, I., and McGinnies, E. Interpersonal perception and communication in discussion groups of varied attitudinal composition. *Journal of Abnormal and Social Psychology*, 1960, 60, 390-395.

Asch, S. E. Effects of group pressure upon the modification and distortion of judgments. In G. E. Swanson, T. M. Newcomb, and E. L. Hartley (Eds.), *Readings in social psychology* (rev. ed.). New York: Holt, Rinehart and Winston, 1952.

Azrin, N. H., and Lindsley, O. R. The reinforcement of cooperation between children. *Journal of Abnormal and Social Psychology*, 1956, 52, 100-102. Copyright 1956 by the American Psychological Association. Data in Table 6.1 of this book reprinted by permission.

Bales, R. F. *Interaction process analysis.* Reading, Mass.: Addison-Wesley, 1950.

Banta, T. J., and Nelson, C. Experimental analysis of resource location in problem solving groups. *Sociometry*, 1964, 27, 488-501.

Bavelas, A. Communication patterns in task oriented groups. *Journal of the Acoustical Society of America*, 1950, 22, 725-730.

Bavelas, A., Hastorf, R. H., Gross, A. E., and Kite, W. R. Experiments on the alteration of group structure. *Journal of Experimental Social Psychology*, 1965, 1, 55-70.

Bergum, B.O., and Lehr, D. J. Effects of authoritarianism on vigilance performance. *Journal of Applied Psychology*, 1963, 47, 75-77.

Brown, J. F. *Psychology and the social order.* New York: McGraw-Hill, 1936.

Burgess, R. L. Communication networks: An experimental reevaluation. *Journal of Experimental Social Psychology*, 1968, 4, 324-337.

Butler, D. C., and Miller, N. "Power to reinforce" as a determinant of communication. *Psychological Reports*, 1965a, 16, 705-709.

Butler, D. C., and Miller, N. Power to reward and punish in social interaction. *Journal of Experimental Social Psychology*, 1965b, 1, 311-322.

Charters, W. W., and Newcomb, T. M. Some attitudinal effects of experimentally increased salience of a membership group. In E. E. Maccoby, T. M. Newcomb, and E. L. Hartley (Eds.), *Readings in social psychology* (3rd ed.). New York: Holt, Rinehart and Winston, 1958, pp. 276-280.

Cieutat, J. J. Surreptitious modification of verbal behavior during class discussion, *Psychological Reports*, 1959, 5, 648.

Coch, L., and French, J. R. P., Jr. Overcoming resistance to change. *Human Relations,* 1948, 1, 512-532.

Cohen, D. J. Justin and his peers: An experimental analysis of a child's social world. *Child Development,* 1962, 23, 697-717.

Collins, B. E., Davis, H. L., Myers, J. G., and Silk, A. J. An experimental study of reinforcement and participant satisfaction. *Journal of Abnormal and Social Psychology,* 1964, 68, 463-467.

Cottrell, N. B. Performance in the presence of other human beings: Mere presence, audience, and affiliation effects. In E.C. Simmel, R. A. Hoppe, and G. A. Milton (Eds.), *Social facilitation and imitative behavior.* Boston: Allyn and Bacon, 1968.

Cottrell, N. B., Rittle, R. H., and Wack, D. L. Presence of an audience and list type (competitional or noncompetitional) as joint determinants of performance in paired associates learning. *Journal of Personality,* 1967, 35, 425-434.

Cottrell, N. B., Sekerak, G. J., Wack, D. L., and Rittle, R. H. Social facilitation of dominant responses by the presence of an audience and the mere presence of others. *Journal of Personality and Social Psychology,* 1968, 9, 245-250.

Dashiell, J. F. An experimental analysis of some group effects. *Journal of Abnormal and Social Psychology,* 1930, 25, 190-199.

Deutsch, M. An experimental study of the effects of cooperation and competition upon group process. *Human Relations,* 1949, 2, 129-152, 199-231.

Deutsch, M. Field theory in social psychology. In G. Lindzey and E. Aronson (Eds.), *Handbook of social psychology* 2nd ed.). Reading, Mass.: Addison-Wesley, 1968

Gerwirtz, J. L., and Baer, D. M. The effect of brief social deprivation on behaviors for a social reinforcer. *Journal of Abnormal and Social Psychology,* 1958, 56, 49-56.

Hare, A. P., and Bales, R. F. Seating position and small group interaction. *Sociometry,* 1963, 25, 480-486.

Haythorn, W. W. Project Argus: A program of isolation and confinement research. *Naval Research Reviews,* December 1967, 1-8.

Haythorn, W. W., and Altman, I. Together in isolation. *Trans-Action,* January/February 1967.

Heise, G. A., and Miller, G. A. Problem solving by small groups using various communication nets. *Journal of Abnormal and Social Psychology,* 1951, 46, 327-336.

Heyns, R. W., and Lippitt, R. Systematic observational techniques. In G. Lindzey (Ed.), *Handbook of social psychology* 2nd ed.). Reading, Mass.: Addison-Wesley, 1968.

Husband, R. W. Analysis of methods in human maze learning. *Journal of Genetic Psychology,* 1931, 39, 258-277.

Kelley, H. H., and Thibaut, J. W. Experimental studies of group problem solving and process. In G. Lindzey (Ed.), *Handbook of social psychology.* Vol. 2. Reading, Mass.: Addison-Wesley, 1954.

Kelley, H. H., Thibaut, J. W., Radloff, R., and Mundy, D. The development of cooperation in a "minimal social situation." *Psychological Monographs,* 1962, 76, No. 19.

Krech, D., and Crutchfield, R. S. *Theory and problems of social psychology.* New York: McGraw-Hill, 1948.

Leavitt, H. J. Some effects of certain communication patterns on group performance. *Journal of Abnormal and Social Psychology,* 1951, 46, 38-50.

Levin, G., and Shapiro, D. The operant conditioning of conversation. *Journal of the Experimental Analysis of Behavior,* 1962, 5, 309-316.

Lewin, K. *Field theory in social science.* New York: Harper and Row, 1951.

McGinnies, E., and Altman, I. Discussion as a function of attitudes and content of a persuasive communication. *Journal of Applied Psychology,* 1959, 43, 53-59.

McGrath, J. E., and Altman, I. *Small Group research*. New York: Holt, Rinehart and Winston, 1966.

McNair, D. M. Reinforcement of verbal behavior. *Journal of Experimental Psychology*, 1957, 53, 40-46.

Newcomb, T. M. *Personality and social change*. New York: Dryden Press, 1943.

Oakes, W. F. Reinforcement of Bales' categories in group discussion. *Psychological Reports*, 1962a, 11, 427-435.

Oakes, W. F. Effectivness of signal light reinforcers given various meanings on participation in group discussion. *Psychological Reports*, 1962b, 11, 469-470.

Oakes, W. F., Droge, A. E., and August, B. Reinforcement effects on participation in group discussion. *Psychological Reports*, 1960, 7, 503-514.

Oakes, W. F., Droge, A. E., and August, B. Reinforcement effects on conclusions reached in group discussions. *Psychological Reports*, 1961, 9, 27-34.

Olmstead, M. S. *The small group*. New York: Random House, 1959.

Pessin, J. The comparative effects of social and mechanical stimulation on memorizing. *American Journal of Psychology*, 1933, 45, 263-270.

Rabinowitz, L., Kelley, H. H., and Rosenblatt, R. M. Effects of different types of interdependence and response conditions in the minimal social situation. *Journal of Experimental Social Psychology*, 1966, 2, 169-197.

Roethlisberger, F. J., and Dickson, W. J. *Management and the worker*. Cambridge, Mass.: Harvard University Press, 1947.

Rosenberg, S. The maintenance of a learned response in controlled interpersonal conditions. *Sociometry*, 1959, 22, 124-138.

Rosenberg, S. Cooperative behavior in dyads as a function of reinforcement parameters. *Journal of Abnormal and Social Psychology*, 1960, 60, 318-333.

Rosenberg, S. Influence and reward in structured two-person interactions. *Journal of Abnormal and Social Psychology*, 1963, 67, 379-387.

Rosenberg, S., and Hall, R. L. The effects of different social feedback conditions upon performance in dyadic teams. *Journal of Abnormal and Social Psychology*, 1958, 57, 271-277.

Shapiro, D. The reinforcement of disagreement in a small group. *Behavior Research and Therapy*, 1963, 1, 267-272.

Shaw, M. E. Communication networks. In L. Berkowitz (Ed.), *Advances in experimental psychology*. Vol. I. New York: Academic Press, 1964.

Shepherd, C. R. *Small groups: Some sociological perspectives*. San Francisco: Chandler, 1964.

Sherif, M. *The psychology of social norms*. New York: Harper and Row Torchbooks, 1966. Originally published in the *Archives of Psychology*, 1935, No. 187, under the title "A study of some social factors in perception."

Shibutani, S. *Society and personality*. Englewood Cliffs, N. J.: Prentice-Hall, 1961.

Sidowski, J. B. Reward and punishment in a minimal social situation. *Journal of Experimental Psychology*, 1957, 54, 318-326.

Sidowski, J. B., Wyckoff, L. B., and Tabory, L. The influence of reinforcement and punishment in a minimal social situation. *Journal of Abnormal and Social Psychology*, 1956, 52, 115-119.

Steinzor, B. The spatial factor in face-to-face discussion groups. *Journal of Abnormal and Social Psychology*, 1950, 45, 552-555.

Taylor, D. W., and Faust, W. L. Twenty questions: Efficiency in problem solving as a function of size of group. *Journal of Experimental Psychology*, 1952, 44, 360-368.

Travis, L. E. The effect of a small audience upon eye-hand coordination. *Journal of Abnormal and Social Psychology*, 1925, 20, 142-146.

Tsai, L. T. Cited in O. Koehler, Team arbeit bei ratten. *Orion*, 1953, 8, 5.

Ward, C. D. Seating arrangement and leadership emergence in small discussion groups. *Jour nal of Social Psychology*, 1968, 74, 83-90.

Zajonc, R. B. *Social psychology: An experimental approach*. Belmont, Calif.: Wadsworth, 1966.

WHY PEOPLE JOIN GROUPS

MARVIN E. SHAW

If we assume that people join groups voluntarily, the first question that must be asked then is, Why do people join groups? The question can, of course, be answered at many levels. At the most general level, we may say that people join groups because the group meets some individual need. There are some tasks that can be accomplished only by groups, there may exist a personal need for affiliation, etc. In fact, a number of theorists have proposed theories of interpersonal attraction based upon the notion of reinforcement. Thibaut and Kelley (1959) formulated the concepts of *comparison level* (CL) and *comparison levels for alternatives* (CLalt). According to this theory, the comparison level is the standard which an individual uses to evaluate an interpersonal relationship. If the rewards and costs which accrue from the relationship are above the CL, the relationship is evaluated favorably; if they are below the CL, the relationship is evaluated unfavorably. The CLalt is the standard the individual uses to determine whether to enter into a new relationship or to remain in an already existing one. If the net reward-cost outcome is above that expected from other available relationships, the individual will enter into or continue the relationship; if below available alternatives, he will not enter (or continue) the relationship. Clearly, this theory assumes that the individual establishes and maintains an interpersonal relationship because of the rewards that accrue from it.

A similar theory was proposed by Newcomb (1956), who equated attraction and repulsion to another person with positive or negative attitudes toward that person. These attitudes are established according to reinforcement principles, and hence the individual is attracted or repulsed, depending upon the rewards or punishments that derive from his relationship with another. We will have more to say about these theories after we have discussed some of the relevant research findings.

General explanations have a certain appeal because they seem intuitively correct. But it is not enough to offer general explanations. One may well ask, What are the needs that are satisfied by group membership? What constitute rewards and punishments? The next level of explanation is represented by Cartwright and Zander's (1960) statement that the group itself may be the object of need or the group may simply be the means for satisfying some need that lies outside the group. When these two general classes are examined more closely, it becomes evident that each of them can be analyzed into several smaller classes, which in turn can be subdivided even further. Sources of need satisfaction residing in the group include at least (1) attraction to the members of the group (interpersonal attraction), (2) attraction to the activities of the group, (3) attraction to the goals of the group (i.e., the goals of the group are valued by the individual), and (4) group membership per se. Needs outside the group that may be satisfied through group membership include at least (1) attraction to others outside the group and (2) attraction to goals outside the group. Let us examine these factors in greater detail.

Interpersonal Attraction

The variables influencing the attraction of one person to another have probably been studied more extensively than any other determinant of group formation. The early studies tended to consider secondary determinants, such as propinquity (Festinger, 1953a) and interaction (Bovard, 1956; Palmore, 1955). However, these variables merely provide the opportunity for the operation of primary variables, such as attitude similarity, value congruence, personality characteristics, and the like. Nevertheless, it is instructive to consider some of the environmental factors that make it possible for other variables to exert their effects on interpersonal attraction.

Proximity, Contact, and Interaction

Investigations of environmental and group process variables as determinants of group formation and interpersonal attraction are usually discussed under one of three headings: proximity, contact, or interaction. These factors are closely related and represent varying degrees of association rather than unique variables. In general, *proximity* has been used to refer to the physical distance between individuals, *contact* to situations in which individuals are likely to be in each other's presence frequently, and *interaction* to situations in which the behavior of each person influences the other.

In a number of field studies the physical distance between individuals has been found to be related to affiliation. The classical study of the formation of friendships in a student housing complex (Festinger, Schachter, & Back, 1950) clearly revealed the role of proximity in the establishment of interpersonal relationships. Married couples were assigned to housing by the university housing office in order of application, without regard to college major, classification, or other variables that might influence the formation of friendships. Festinger et al. found that such relationships were determined largely by proximity. Persons living next door to each other most frequently became friends. Couples who occupied corner units or end units which faced the street frequently became social isolates. The results of other investigations agree in showing a positive relationship between attraction and proximity; e.g., Maissonneuve, Palmade, and Fourment (1952) observed that propinquity and liking choices were related in boarding school classes; Byrne and Buehler (1955) found that seat neighbors in college classes were more likely to become acquainted; and Sommer (1959) noted that persons who sat near each other in the cafeteria of a large mental hospital interacted more than persons in more distant positions. It is clear, then, that proximity contributes to group formation.

There has been considerable interest in the degree to which contact between minority groups affects the relationships between such groups. Many investigations reveal that contact results in more favorable attitudes toward members of minority groups and an increased willingness to affiliate with them. During World War II, Stouffer, Suchman, DeVinney, Star, and Williams (1949) observed that the degree to which white soldiers thought it was a good idea to have Negroes in the company varied directly with the amount of contact they had had with Negroes. Results consistent with this finding have been obtained in a variety of settings. Deutsch and Collins (1951) compared black-white relations in a housing project in which black and white families were assigned to buildings in segregated areas with those in an integrated apartment house. They found there were more frequent and more intimate interpersonal relations among blacks and whites in the integrated project than in the segregated one. Furthermore, they were able to demonstrate that this difference did not exist prior to residence in the housing projects. Similarly, Jahoda (1961) found a considerable reduction in preferences for residential segregation following black-white contact as neighbors or on the job, and Harding and Hogrefe (1952) found that white persons who had worked with Negroes on an equal basis were more willing to do so again than those who had not.

It has already been suggested that proximity, contact, and interaction probably are not primary determinants of attraction; i.e., proximity makes it possible for individuals to come into contact and interact with each other, and such interaction makes it possible for them to learn about characteristics of others that make them attractive (e.g., their physical attractiveness, their attitudes, etc.). This interpretation is supported by evidence that proximity and interaction do not always lead to increased attraction. Festinger (1953a) described a housing project in which few group memberships existed among residents. In this project, the residents felt they were forced to live in the project because of a housing shortage, and their attitudes toward fellow residents were quite negative. Gundlach (1956) reported similar negative attitudes on the part of white women workers who had been assigned to work with Negroes with similar educations and backgrounds. Experimental studies in which interaction provided no evidence concerning the characteristics of others also yielded generally negative results, i.e., no relationship between amount of interaction and liking (Stotland & Cottrell, 1962; Stotland, Cottrell, & Laing, 1960).

If we are correct in believing that proximity and interaction merely provide the opportunity for individuals to learn about the characteristics of others that make them attractive, it is important to know what these other characteristics are and to explore just how they function to determine attractiveness.

Physical Attractiveness

Probably the most obvious source of attraction between two persons is sheer physical attractiveness. When a person exemplifies the physical characteristics which contribute to the perception of beauty or handsomeness (in a given culture), others are prone to be attracted to him and to want to associate with him. The importance of physical attractiveness in dating behavior, for example, has been demonstrated by Walster, Aronson, Abrahams, and Rottman (1966). They conducted a field study in which subjects were randomly paired at a "computer dance." They found that, regardless of a subject's own attractiveness, how much he liked his partner, how much he wanted to date her again, and how often he actually asked her out again were a function of her physical attractiveness. Scores on the Minnesota Multiphasic Personality Inventory, the Minnesota Counseling Inventory, Berger's (1952) Scale of Self-acceptance, the Minnesota Scholastic Aptitude test, and high school percentile rank—all were found to be unrelated to how much the partner wanted to continue the interaction. A recent study by Schlosser (1969) also demonstrated that physical attractiveness is a determinant of interpersonal attraction, even when the physically attractive other behaves in a way which interferes with attainment of a common goal.

Similarity

It has been proposed by a number of writers that individuals are attracted to those who are similar to themselves. For example, Newcomb (1956) suggested that it is more likely that an interaction will be rewarding when the two interactors are similar, since one of the rewards deriving from interaction is social support for one's attitudes, beliefs, and opinions. Heider (1958) also theorized that similarity should produce interpersonal attraction. It is important to remember, however, that similarity is not a general quality. It is appropriate to consider similarity only with respect to specified characteristics (see Cronbach & Gleser, 1953). Hence, it is reasonable to expect that interpersonal attraction is related to similarity with respect to those characteristics which are judged important by the persons involved in the interaction. The variable most widely investigated within this general category of significant characteristics is probably *attitude similarity*. For instance, Newcomb (1961) invited students to live in a house rent-free in exchange for serving as research subjects. Seventeen men were selected for each of two years. At the time they moved into the house, no one knew any other member of the group. The men completed a series of attitude and value inventories and also estimated the attitudes of others in the group. Initially, proximity of room assignments was the primary determinant of attraction. Later, attraction was found to be a function of perceived similarity of attitudes.

The effects of attitude similarity on interpersonal attraction have been studied extensively by Byrne and his associates. In an initial study, Byrne (1961) followed Newcomb in assuming that reciprocal rewards and punishments are important determinants of attraction and that perceived similarity-dissimilarity is rewarding-punishing. Byrne devised the following technique for examining the similarity-attraction hypothesis, using twenty-six issues ranging from such relatively important things as integration, God, and premarital sexual relations to such relatively unimportant things as western movies and television programs. Subjects were asked to express their attitudes on these issues on a 7-point rating scale and to indicate how important each item was to them. Two weeks later subjects were falsely informed that the scale had been given as part of a study of interpersonal prediction, that students in another class had taken the same test, and that they were now to be given each other's test with the name removed in the hope that they could learn about one another from this information. Actually, fake scales were made up to represent four conditions: the other's attitudes were (1) the same as those expressed by the subject, (2) exactly opposite to those expressed by the subject, (3) the same on important issues but opposite on unimportant issues, and (4) the same on unimportant but opposite on important issues. The subjects then indicated how well they liked the other person and how much they would enjoy working with him. Attraction was significantly higher when the other person's attitudes were similar than when they were dissimilar according to both measures. Importance of issues had a significant effect only for the liking ratings. Using essentially the same technique, Byrne and Nelson (1964, 1965b) systematically varied both attitude similarity and topic importance, and found only similarity to be related to attraction. However, in a subsequent study, Byrne, London, and Griffitt (1968) demonstrated that importance significantly influenced attraction when topics heterogeneous in importance are associated with one other person.

Several subsequent studies by Byrne and his coworkers have consistently found attitude similarity to be a determinant of attraction (Byrne & Griffitt, 1966; Byrne & Nelson, 1965a; Byrne, Nelson, & Reeves, 1966; Byrne & Rhamey, 1965). The study by Byrne and Rhamey probably illustrates the relationship between attraction and attitude similarity most clearly. They required 180 subjects to read questionnaires purportedly filled out by an anonymous stranger and to evaluate him on a number of variables, including attraction. The stranger's responses agreed with those of the subject on 100 percent, 67 percent, 33 percent, or none of the items. Subjects were also given information about the stranger's evaluation of them, which was positive, neutral, or negative. [From the] attraction scores . . . [it was] quite evident that attraction is a positive, increasing function of the proportion of attitudes that are similar to those expressed by the subject. The effects are most strongly operative in the neutral evaluation condition, which suggests that evaluation by the other person also influences one's attraction to him.

That attitude similarity may not always be positively related to attraction has been shown by Novak and Lerner (1968). Forty-eight males and forty-eight females evaluated a "partner" who held either similar or dissimilar attitudes and who was described as either normal or emotionally disturbed. Subjects were less willing to interact with an emotionally disturbed person when he held similar attitudes than when he held dissimilar attitudes.

Similarity with respect to other characteristics has also been shown to be a determinant of attraction. *Similarity of personality* as a determinant of attraction was studied by Griffitt (1966), using the Byrne technique of evaluation of a stranger on the basis of his responses to a self-concept inventory. When the self-descriptions of the subject and those of the stranger agreed on 33 percent of the tiems, the mean attraction score was 8.76 as compared with a mean score of 11.61 when there was 100 percent agreement. Byrne, Griffitt, and Stefanik (1967) had 151 subjects examine the responses of strangers to a repression-sensitization scale. The stranger had responded as the subject did on 25 percent, 50 percent, or 80 percent of the items. The subjects then rated the stranger's attractiveness; mean attraction scores were 6.17, 8.29, and 9.70 for the three degrees of response agreement, respectively. The evidence therefore indicates that similarity of personality characteristics is also positively related to interpersonal attraction. This conclusion is supported by Izard

(1960a, 1960b), who found that friends were more alike on personality profiles than were random pairs.

There is evidence to suggest, however, that mere similarity may not always be a determinant of attractiveness. Rychlak (1965) examined the effects of similarity and compatibility of needs upon preferences for interpersonal role relationships. Similarity was based upon two persons having the same need (e.g., both have a need for dominance), compatibility upon two persons having complementary needs (e.g., one has a need for nuturance and the other a need for succorance), and incompatibility upon one person's having a need that is inconsistent with that of the other (e.g., one has a need for order and the other a need for change). After participation in two small group problems, subjects selected most and least preferred coworkers for the roles of boss, employee, and neighbor. Rychlak's findings supported the hypothesis that need compatibility is a determinant of attraction, whereas need similarity and need incompatibility are not related to attraction. A study by Jellison and Zeisset (1969) indicated that the degree to which trait similarity is related to attractiveness depends upon the desirability of the trait and also upon the degree to which the trait is common in the general population. When a desirable trait is shared by another, the other is more attractive when the shared trait is uncommon in the general population than when it is common; however, when the shared trait is undesirable, the other person is more attractive when the trait is common than when it is uncommon. A. R. Cohen (1956) found similarity of ego defenses to be related to attraction, whereas similarity based on projection preferences had the opposite effect.

These studies demonstrate that similarity of certain personality characteristics is related to interpersonal attraction, at least under some conditions. However, it should be evident that the similarity of personality traits must be perceived by the individual in order for it to influence his attraction to the other person. The relation between perceived or assumed similarity and interpersonal attraction was investigated many years ago by Fiedler, Warrington, and Blaisdell (1952). Members and pledges of a college fraternity sorted seventy-six statements descriptive of personality traits four times: (1) describing self, (2) describing how one would ideally like to be, (3) predicting how one's best-liked fellow group member would describe himself, and (4) predicting how one's least-liked fellow group member would describe himself. There was no correlation between real similarity (descriptions of self) and choices of best-liked or least-liked group member. However, subjects perceived persons whom they liked best as more similar to their ideal self and as more similar to themselves than others whom they liked least. A later study by Fiedler, Hutchings, and Dodge (1959) yielded similar findings.

Economic similarity has been shown to be a determinant of attractiveness by Byrne, Clore, and Worchel (1966). High and low economic status subjects evaluated strangers on the basis of responses to economic items dealing with spending money. Ratings of attractiveness were higher when the stranger's responses indicated an economic status similar to that of the subject.

Similarity of race and similarity of sex as determinants of attraction were investigated by Smith, Williams, and Willis (1967). White and black subjects rated a stimulus person on acceptability as a friend. The stimulus person was described as to race, sex, and belief congruence relative to the subject. Race and sex were found to be related to attractiveness, but neither was as strong as belief congruence. Since the investigators' manipulation of belief congruence was essentially the same as the variations used in the studies of attitude similarity-dissimilarity, their findings support earlier studies concerning the importance of attitude similarity as a determinant of attraction.

The *perceived ability* of others also appears to be a determinant of the degree to which an individual desires to affiliate with another. Gilchrist (1952) demonstrated that subjects in a problem-solving situation prefer to work with individuals who have been successful previously in solving problems. This effect was verified in a subsequent study by Shaw and Gilchrist (1955). These studies also showed that although successful persons were initially chosen by both previously successful and previously unsuccessful persons, there was an increasing tendency (over time) for unsuccessful persons to shift to choices of other unsuccessful persons for affiliation. There is some suggestion, then, that similarity of perceived ability may also be a determinant of attraction. Zander and Havelin (1960) reported results consistent with this interpretation; subjects preferred to associate with others having similar ability.

In summary, the degree to which one person is attracted to another has been shown to be due to physical attractiveness of the other person, the degree to which the two persons are similar with respect to a variety of characteristics, and the perceived ability of the other person. Similarity has been studied far more extensively than other determinants of attractiveness and the evidence is highly consistent: Attraction is a function of attitude similarity, belief congruence, personality similarity, race similarity, sex similarity, and economic similarity. It is also evident that under some circumstances similarity of characteristics may lead to reduced attraction, e.g., when the other person is seen as emotionally disturbed or when needs are the characteristics under consideration. In the latter case, need compatibility appears to be the important factor. The implicit assumption in the foregoing discussion is, of course, that attraction between two persons will influence the formation of groups with these persons as members. Undoubtedly, there are many other determinants of interpersonal attraction that we have not considered here.

Group Activities

An individual may be attracted to a group because he enjoys the things the group members do. A person may join a bridge club, not because he enjoys playing bridge (although he might enjoy it), but because he finds the social activities pleasant. A person may join the Kiwanis Club merely because he enjoys meetings and civic activities, although, of course, he may be in agreement with the goals of the club. One could cite many examples of this kind of attraction to the activities of a group, but data from controlled studies are scarce.

Perhaps the most convincing evidence was provided by Sherif and Sherif (1953), who studied group formation in summer camps for boys. They were able to demonstrate, among other things, that boys who were interested in the same activities tended to form groups. Related evidence has also been provided by Thibaut (1950). He found that the attractiveness of the activities in a group affected the attractiveness of group membership. Thus, although the empirical evidence is not extensive, it generally supports the proposition that group activities constitute one source of attraction to the group.

Group Goals

In many ways it is difficult to separate the activities of a group from its goals, and an individual may be attracted to a group because he both enjoys its activities and values its goals or purposes. For example, a person may join a group formed for the purpose of raising funds to support the local church because he enjoys fundraising activities and because he believes it is good to support the church. On the other hand, a person who very much disliked soliciting funds might join this group if he valued highly the goal of church support. It is improbable, however, that a person who enjoyed the activities in a particular group would join it if he negatively valued the group's goals and purposes. .

The role of group goals in group formation has been demonstrated most clearly in the investigations of group relations by Sherif and Sherif (1953). After initially establishing intergroup hostility and tension through a series of ingenious manipulations, they attempted to reestablish harmony and integration. In the initial stages of the study, members of a boys' summer camp were formed into two groups on the basis of selected activities. For approximately five days, situations were arranged in which it seemed that one group interfered with or frustrated the other group. For example, following an athletic victory by one group (the Bull Dogs) over the other (the Red Devils), both were invited to attend a party in the mess hall with the stated purpose of reducing intergroup conflict. However, it was arranged so that the Red Devils got to the mess hall first and found ice cream and cake on a table. Half of the refreshments were battered and broken whereas the other half were in good condition. The Red Devils were told to serve themselves and leave the Bull Dogs their share. Without comment, they chose the good half and carried it to their table. The reaction of the Bull Dogs to this treatment was predictable: They called the Red Devils "pigs," "bums," etc., and generally derogated them. When the intergroup conflict created by procedures of this sort had been firmly established, Sherif and Sherif attempted to reduce the conflict and to rearrange group boundaries by introducing common "supraordinate" goals. The most effective of these was a campwide softball game in which a team of best players from both groups were elected by the boys from the entire camp to compete with a team coming from a neighboring camp. Although the supraordinate goal approach did not completely eliminate the hostilities produced by the earlier manipulations, there was a significant reduction in the amount of hostility and tension and some realignment of group boundaries.

The results of this extensive series of studies demonstrate two ways in which attraction to group goals can contribute to group formation. In the early stages of group development, the conflict between groups led to increased group cohesiveness. One element of this cohesiveness was the "common enemy." Or to say it another way, one of the goals of the Bull Dogs was to get even with the Red Devils. More significant, perhaps, is the demonstration that a common group goal can produce new group memberships.

The effects that being in a common predicament has on group attraction are also demonstrated by a study of the consequences of shared stress on interpersonal liking (Latane, Eckman, & Joy, 1966). The investigators proposed that people who are undergoing stress together do something for one another that serves to reduce the stress, thus positively reinforcing each other. Female subjects were assigned to either an experimental condition in which they shared an electric shock or a condition in which each received the same shock but not together. It was found that ratings of liking for the other person were significantly greater in the shared condition, but only when subjects were firstborns. The treatment in such a study is certainly rather weak, and perhaps it is surprising that it had any effect at all. To the extent that it did, however, the results support the hypothesis that attraction to goals constitutes one basis for group attraction.

Group Membership

It has also been proposed that membership in a group per se may be rewarding to an individual, quite apart from the particular individuals who are members of the group, the group activities, or the pruposes of the group. The results reported by Latane et al. and discussed above might be interpreted as supporting this proposition. It was suggested many years ago that there exists an "affiliation want" (Trotter, 1920), which is one of four instincts that govern man's life. Later theorists have denied the instinctual nature of the need for affiliation, but nevertheless posit such a need as playing an important role in social groupings (McClelland, Atkinson, Clark, & Lowell, 1953; Schachter, 1959). Schachter proposed that one of the functions of affiliation is to reduce anxiety, and his research generally supported this view. Research by others also agrees with this hypothesis. Pepitone and Kleiner (1957) varied the amount of threat experienced by group members and found that high threat yielded greater increases in attraction to the group than low threat. In a second study (Kleiner, 1960) it was found that reduction of threat increased the attractiveness of a confederate who played the role of group member.

Another reason for need affiliation was suggested by Singer and Schockley (1965), namely, that people affiliate in order to compare abilities (cf. Festinger, 1954). Thirty-nine female students were randomly assigned to either a condition in which they had knowledge concerning their performance on an experimental task or one in which they did not have this information. All subjects were then given a choice of waiting for the next part of the study alone or with others. Those who had no knowledge of their performance chose to affiliate significantly more than did those who had such information (6 of 8 versus 2 of 22).

The strongest support for the existence of a need for affiliation is provided by a series of investigations which attempted to show that the need for affiliation can be manipulated through deprivation in the same manner as a physiological need such as hunger.

Gewirtz and Baer (1958b) invited children, aged from three years ten months to five years three months, to play a game using toys. In a deprivation condition, the subject was deprived of social contact for twenty minutes before playing the game. When the child arrived at the laboratory, a familiar adult appeared and announced that the toy was broken but was being repaired. He was given plausible assurance that the toy would be repaired in a few minutes and, since the experimenter did not want the child to miss his turn, he was to wait. The adult then left him alone in a relatively barren room for the twenty-minute period. In the control (non-deprivation) condition, the child began the game immediately upon arrival at the laboratory. Each child played a game which required him to drop marbles into holes in the toy. After a four-minute period to establish a base-line rate, the experimenter dispensed social reinforcements according to a predetermined schedule immediately after the subject had dropped a marble into the least preferred hole (as determined during the base-line period). Reinforcements were verbal expressions of approval such as "good," "fine," "good one," etc. The reinforcements increased the rate of dropping marbles in the nonpreferred hole significantly more in the deprivation condition than in the nondeprivation condition, but only when the experimenter was a member of the opposite sex. In a follow-up study (Gewirtz & Baer, 1958a), a satiation condition was added in which the experimenter maintained a steady stream of conversation with the subject for twenty minutes before the game was started. The effects of reinforcement were significantly greater in the deprivation than in the nondeprivation condition, and greater in the nondeprivation than in the satiation condition. Both boys and girls served as subjects, but only a female experimenter was used. The opposite-sex effect observed in the first study was not found.

Gewirtz and Baer concluded that social deprivation enhances the effectiveness of a social reinforcer, thus supporting the hypothesis that there exists a need for affiliation. However, Walters and Karal (1960) were unable to replicate these findings with college students. Obviously, there is some question whether a twenty-minute period of deprivation is sufficient to arouse the need for affiliation in adults. In a second study (Walters & Ray, 1960), it was found that anxious isolated subjects differed in their response to deprivation whereas nonanxious subjects did not. These investigators concluded that the results reported by Gewirtz and Baer were due to anxiety aroused in the isolated subjects. On the other hand, Stevenson and Cruse (1961) found that social reinforcements were effective in changing behavior, and Stevenson and Odom (1962) demonstrated that the enhanced effects of social reinforcements after social deprivation could not be accounted for in terms of general deprivation. Thus, although there are some conflicting findings, the bulk of the evidence supports the hypothesis that need for affiliation can be manipulated in a manner similar to the manipulation of physiological needs, and that such manipulation has similar effects on responses to reinforcers.

Instrumental Effects of Group Membership

It is perhaps unnecessary to note that an individual may join a group in order to achieve some goal outside the group. A young man may join a college fraternity as a means of meeting young ladies who are members of college sororities. In this case, the source of attraction to the group resides in the person(s) of others who are not members of the group; that is, the joiner is attracted to persons outside the group whom he believes he can affiliate with more readily if he becomes a member of the group in question. It is also obvious that a person may join a group because he believes this will be instrumental in the achievement of goals outside the group. For example, a businessman may join a civic club because he believes that such membership will "be good for business." It is not always easy to separate attraction to others outside the group and attraction to goals outside the group. Therefore, we will examine the general proposition that the sources of reinforcement attainable from group membership may reside outside the group itself.

A number of studies have shown that a group may be perceived as a means to an end outside the group. In a study of labor unions Rose (1952) found that members of local unions report that the major benefits from membership are higher wages and greater job security. However, since attainment of such benefits is a major goal of labor union, this finding could just as easily be interpreted in terms of attraction to group goals. A more direct bit of evidence was provided by Willerman and Swanson (1953) in their study of college sororities. They found that one important reason for joining a sorority was the increased prestige in the college community that can be achieved through sorority membership. A similar study of reasons for belonging to a business organization demonstrated that goals outside the group, such as need for recognition and autonomy, were important factors in the desire to remain in the organization (Ross & Zander, 1957). Although not extensive, the empirical data thus support the hypothesis that individuals sometimes join groups to achieve goals that lie outside the group. Group membership is seen as instrumental in achieving these outside goals.

So, why do people join groups? After reviewing the multitude of factors related to group formation and membership, we find that the answer still seems to be: because the group is perceived as a means of satisfying some individual need or needs. But we have identified and examined some of the things about group membership that are perceived as sources of need satisfaction. For example, Newcomb (1956) has shown how similarity may affect attraction via generalization. It is more likely that an individual will receive reward from another person if that other person is similar to persons who have been rewarding in the past. The effects of need complementarity also may be interpreted in terms of reinforcements. If one person has a need to be dominant and the other a need to be submissive, affiliation will lead to need satisfaction for both. The effects of perceived success of the other person, group activities, group goals, and group instrumentality also may be seen as due to the fact that they satisfy individual needs. Thibaut and Kelley's (1959) analysis of attraction in terms of rewards and costs relative to comparison levels also shows how need satisfaction may be related to such factors as personal success of the other and attitude similarity. For example, the successful person is undoubtedly seen as possessing abilities that will help the group achieve its goals or that may be useful in helping the individual achieve individual goals. In either case, the successful person is seen as contributing to the satisfaction of personal needs, if one affiliates with him. In like manner, the effects of attitude similarity can be shown to be due to the expectation of need satisfaction. One of the rewards or benefits deriving from association with others is the validation of beliefs and attitudes; one may certainly expect validation if the other person holds similar attitudes. Therefore, it appears that interpersonal attraction is a function of the degree to which the person expects affiliation with the other to be rewarding. The difficult task is to identify the many sources of reinforcement in interpersonal relationships.

References

Berger, E. The relation between expressed acceptance of self and expressed acceptance of others. *Journal of Abnormal and Social Psychology,* 1952, 47, 778-782.

Bovard, E. W. Conformity to social norms and attraction to the group. *Science,* 1953, 118, 598-599.

Byrne, D., & Buehler, J. A. A note on the influence of propinquity upon acquaintanceships. *Journal of Abnormal and Social Psychology,* 1955, 51, 147-148.

Byrne, D., Clore, J. L., Jr. & Worchel, P. Effect of economic similarity-dissimilarity on interpersonal attraction. *Journal of Personality and Social Psychology,* 1966, 4, 220-224.

Byrne, D., & Griffitt, W. A developmental investigation of the law of attraction. *Journal of Personality and Social Psychology,* 1966, 4, 699-702.

Byrne, D., Griffitt, W., & Stefaniak, D. Attraction and similarity of personality characterisitcs. *Journal of Personality and Social Psychology,* 1967, 5, 82-90.

Byrne, D., London, O., & Griffitt, W. The effect of topic importance and attitude similarity-dissimilarity on attraction in an intrastranger design. *Psychonomic Science,* 1968, II, 303-304.

Byrne, D., & Nelson, D. Attraction as a function of attitude similarity-dissimilarity: The effect of topic importance. *Psychonomic Science,* 1964, I, 93-94.

Byrne, D., & Nelson, D. Attraction as a linear function of proportion of positive reinforcements. *Journal of Personality and Social Psychology,* 1965a, I, 659-663.

Byrne, D., & Nelson, D. The effect of topic importance and attitude similarity-dissimilarity on attraction in a multi-stranger design. *Psychonomic Science,* 1965b, 3, 449-450.

Byrne, D., Nelson, D., & Reeves, K. Effects of consensual validation and invalidation on attraction as a function of verifiability. *Journal of Experimental Social Psychology,* 1966, 2, 98-107.

Byrne, D., & Rhamey, R. Magnitude of positive and negative reinforcements as a determinant of attraction. *Journal of Personality and Social Psychology,* 1965, 2, 885-889.

Cartwright, D., & Zander, A. (Eds.) *Group dynamics: Research and theory.* (3d ed.) Evanston, Ill.: Row, Peterson, 1960.

Cohen, A. R Experimental effects of ego-defense preference on interpersonal relations. *Journal of Abnormal and Social Psychology,* 1956, 52, 19-27.

Cronbach, L. J., & Cleser, G. C. Assessing similarity between profiles. *Psychological Bulletin,* 1953, 50, 456-473.

Deutsch, M., & Collins, M. E. *Interracial housing: A psychological evaluation of a social experiment.* Minneapolis: University of Minnesota Press, 1951.

Festinger, L. A theory of social comparison processes. *Human Relations,* 1954, 7, 117-140.

Festinger, L. Group attraction and membership. In D. Cartwright and A. Zander (Eds.), *Group dynamics: Research and theory.* Evanston, Ill.: Row, Peterson, 1953. Pp. 92-101.

Festinger, L. Schachter, S., & Back, K. W. *Social pressure in informal groups.* New York: Harper, 1950.

Fiedler, F. E., Hutchings, E. B., & Dodge, J. S. Quasi-therapeutic relations in small college and military groups. *Psychological Monographs,* 1959, 73, no. 473.

Fiedler, F. E., Warrington, W. G., & Blaisdell, F. J. Unconscious attitudes as correlates of sociometric choice in a social group. *Journal of Abnormal and Social Psychology,* 1952, 47, 790-796.

Gewirtz, J. L., & Baer, D. M. Deprivation and satiation of social reinforcers as drive conditions. *Journal of Abnormal and Social Psychology,* 1958a, 57, 165-172

Gewirtz, J. L., & Baer, D. M. The effect of brief social deprivation on behaviors for a social reinforcer. *Journal of Abnormal and Social Psychology,* 1958b, 56, 49-56.

Gilchrist, J. C. The formation of social groups under conditions of success and failure. *Journal of Abnormal and Social Psychology,* 1952, 47, 194-187.

Griffitt, W. Interpersonal attraction as a function of self concept and personality similarity-dissimilarity. *Journal of Personality and Social Psychology,* 1966, 4, 581-584.

Gundlach, R. H. Effects of on-the-job experiences with Negroes upon racial attitudes of white workers in union shops. *Psychological Reports,* 1956, 2, 67-77.

Harding, J., & Hogrefe, R. Attitudes of white department store employees toward Negro coworkers. *Journal of Social Issues,* 1952, 8, 18-28.

Heider, F. *The psychology of interpersonal relations.* New York: Wiley, 1958.

Izard, C. E. Personality similarity and friendship. *Journal of Abnormal and Social Psychology,* 1950a, 61, 47-51.

Izard, C. E. Personality similarity, positive affect, and interpersonal attraction. *Journal of Abnormal and Social Psychology,* 1960b, 61, 484-485.

Jahoda, M. Race relations and mental health. In UNESCO, *Race and sicence.* New York: Columbia, 1961.

Jellison, J. M., & Zeisset, P. J. Attraction as a function of the commonality and desirability of a trait shared with another. *Journal of Personality and Social Psychology,* 1969, II, 115-120.

Kleiner, R. J. The effect of threat reduction upon interpersonal attractiveness. *Journal of Personality,* 1960, 28, 145-155.

Latane, B., Eckman, J., & Joy, V. Shared stress and interpersonal attraction. *Journal of Experimental Social Psychology,* 1966, I, 80-94.

McClelland, D. C., Atkinson, J. W., Clark, R. A., & Lowell, E. L. *The achievement motive.* New York: Appleton-Century-Crofts, 1953.

Maissonneuve, J., Palmade, G., & Fourment, C. Selective choices and propinquity. *Sociometry,* 1952, 15, 1350140.

Newcomb, T. M. The prediction of interpersonal attraction. *American Psychologist,* 1956, II, 575-586.

Newcomb, T. M. *The acquaintance process.* New York: Holt, 1961.

Novak, D. W., & Lerner, M. J. Rejection as a consequence of perceived similarity. *Journal of Personality and Social Psychology,* 1968, 9, 147-152.

Palmore, E. B. The introduction of Negroes into white departments. *Human Organization,* 1955, 14, 27-28.

Pepitone, A., & Kleiner, R. J. The effects of threat and frustration on group cohesiveness. *Journal of Abnormal and Social Psychology,* 1957, 54, 192-199.

Rose, A. *Union solidarity.* Minneapolis: University of Minnesota Press, 1952.

Ross, I., & Zander, A. Need satisfaction and employee turnover. *Personnel Psychology,* 1957, 10, 327-338.

Rychlak, J. F. The similarity, compatibility, or incompatibility of needs in interpersonal selection. *Journal of Personality and Social Psychology,* 1965, 2, 334-340.

Schachter, S. *The psychology of affiliation.* Stanford, Calif.: Stanford University Press, 1959.

Schlosser, M. Liking as a function of physical attractiveness and task performance. Unpublished master's thesis, University of Florida, Gainesville, 1969.

Shaw, M. E., & Gilchrist, J. C. Repetitive task failure and sociometric choice. *Journal of Abnormal and Social Psychology,* 1955, 50, 29-32.

Sherif, M., & Sherif, C. W. *Groups in harmony and tension.* New York: Harper & Row, 1953.

Singer, J. E., & Schockley, V. L. Ability and affiliation. *Journal of Personality and Social Psychology,* 1965, 1, 95-100.

Smith, C. R., Williams, L., & Willis, R. H. Race, sex, and belief as determinants of friendship acceptance. *Journal of Personality and Social Psychology,* 1967, 5, 127-137.

Sommer, R. Studies in personal space. *Sociometry,* 1959, 22, 247-260.

Stevenson, H. W., & Cruse, D. B. The effectiveness of social reinforcement with normal and feebleminded children. *Journal of Personality,* 1961, 29, 124-135.

Stevenson, H. W., & Odom, R. D. The effectiveness of social reinforcement following two conditions of social deprivation. *Journal of Abnormal and Social Psychology,* 1962, 65, 429-431.

Stotland, E., & Cottrell, N. B. Similarity of performance as influenced by interaction, self-esteem, and birth order. *Journal of Abnormal and Social Psychology,* 1962, 64, 183-191.

Stotland, E., Cottrell, N. B., & Laing, G. Group interaction and perceived similarity of members. *Journal of Abnormal and Social Psychology,* 1960, 61, 335-340.

Stouffer, S. A., Suchman, E. A., DeVinney, L. C., Star, S. A. & Williams, R. M., Jr. *The American soldier: Adjustment during army life.* Vol. 1. Princeton, N. J.: Princeton, 1949.

Thibaut, J. W. An experimental study of the cohesiveness of underprivileged groups. *Human Relations,* 1950, 3, 251-278.

Thibaut, J. W., & Kelley, H. H. *The social psychology of groups.* New York: Wiley, 1959.

Trotter, W. *Instincts of the herd in peace and war.* (rev. ed.) London: Allen, 1920.

Walster, E., Aronson, V., Abrahams, D., & Rottman, L. Importance of physical attractiveness in dating behavior. *Journal of Personality and Social Psychology,* 1966, 4, 508-516.

Walters, R. H., & Karal, P. Social deprivation and verbal behavior. *Journal of Personality,* 1960, 28, 89-107.

Walters, R. H., & Ray, E. Anxiety, social isolation, and reinforcer effectiveness. *Journal of Personality,* 1960, 28, 358-367.

Willerman, B., & Swanson, L. Group prestige in voluntary organizations. *Human Relations,* 1953, 6, 57-77.

Zander, A., & Havelin, A. Social comparison and interpersonal attraction. *Human Relations,* 1960, 13, 21-32.

SOCIAL INFLUENCE OF GROUPS

BLAIR J. KOLASA

Social Influence

The influence of the group on its members can take place in many ways. Often there are well-known and accepted norms to follow, but where the standards are not very clear the actions of the individual members are affected still more by their view of the patterns of behavior exhibited by others in the group. Even definite criteria are followed, however, because of the real or implied pressures of the social group. What is of greater importance, however, is that the mere presence of other people affects the performance of a person.

In an early and well-known experiment, Sherif (1936) asked subjects in a darkened room to estimate the extent and direction of movement of a tiny pinpoint of light. (The light really did not move although people ordinarily perceived movement—a phenomenon known as the *autokinetic effect*). Individual estimates were very close together when made in a group and did not diverge significantly when the subjects were later asked to make estimates while alone. When Sherif started with subjects making estimates when no other members were present, the estimates were quite divergent. When later gathered into a group, the estimates of individuals began to converge and, while they were very close, these were not as close as the nearly identical estimates given by members of the group that started out together as a group. The earlier individual experiences clearly played a role even though the group influences were more significant.

A closer look at the influence processes in a group setting reveals the role of already familiar social concepts such as norms in the specific context of interaction in groups.

Group Norms

Norms [are of course] very important in human affairs; this is no less true when we look more closely into the functioning of groups. The rules of behavior that are important for the functioning of the group become even more important when the group or the task becomes larger. Some guidelines are necessary to help the group reach a goal, although, as Thibaut and Kelley (1959) point out, the norm structure can become so complex that it interferes with the effective functioning of the group. In this situation it is likely that more attention is paid to the following of the rules to the letter than to the fulfillment of the functions those rules were intended to serve originally. Norms may be described in various ways, depending on the focus of attention. There may be a concentration on the processes at work in the social situation or on the effects of the functioning of norms. Looking at norms as sanctions emphasizes their role as a process; common behavior of group members is an immediate effect, and the support of group activity may be regarded as an only slightly more distant effect.

Real or imagined pressures to conform to the norms of the group often have been described by casual observers of the social scene. There is some general opinion that the very notion of conformity is antagonistic to individual fulfillment and, eventually, the attainment of societal well-being. Indeed it might, but such superficial pronouncements overlook the positive and sometimes necessary aspects of conformity to group norms. Cartwright and Zander (1960, p. 159) point out that pressures for conformity can help the group accomplish its goals by providing information on "reality" to its members so that the group can maintain itself. These social pressures can provide stability and information for both individual members and the total group in the common pursuit of functional goals.

The influence of the group toward conformity can be demonstrated in many ways. An early experiment by Asch (1952) indicated that even simple tasks could be altered by group pressures. Asch had members of a small group make judgments in the presence of each other. The subjects were to match a criterion line with one of three lines presented along with it; this was a task so simple that a large number of subjects given the choices earlier made virtually no mistakes. The experimental group itself was composed of individuals who were unaware of the fact that some of the other members were instructed by the experimenter to give incorrect answers occasionally. The naive subjects, when faced with unanimous choices by the other members, often gave the same incorrect choices. This did not occur with some subjects and even those who did conform did not always do so; the number of incorrect choices, however, was quite high. Asch varied the experiment by changing the number in the group and in the majority. A majority of three was found to be as influential as any larger ones (up to 16 were tried). If one other person was present who supported the naive subject, this was enough to reduce the influence of the majority or even eliminate it entirely.

The Asch experiment called for very simple judgments—ones where there should have been little doubt as to outcome. If the group influence was strong with respect to easy judgments of lengths of lines, it should not be too surprising to find strong group influences in more common social situations where the "correct" choices are less easy to find than are the group guidelines.

Other experimenters have confirmed the basic results of Asch's study (Rosenberg, 1961). Milgram (1964) also found that naive subjects administered more pain to other subjects under the social pressure of a group (accomplices of the experimenter) than they would on their own initiative.

Some individuals find it easier to conform than do others; the differences between the independent and the submissive undoubtedly are based in personality factors. Steiner and Johnson (1963) confirm the generally accepted guess that authoritarians are more conforming than are nonauthoritarians. The authors found an easy acceptance of the decisions of a respected group of peers. When strong needs for social approval are considered in addition to the authoritarian pattern, subjects who are highly motivated with respect to this factor are more likely to agree with expressed opinions of their peers (Stickland and Crowne, 1962).

Other variables play a role too, however. Older subjects are less likely to conform (DiVesta and Cox, 1960). The same authors found also that females and those with less intellectual ability showed more conformity. Milgram (1964) supported the latter point in finding that college graduates conformed less than those in lower educational brackets.

There is substantial evidence to support a statement that when an individual takes a stand publicly, he is more likely to be influenced by group norms than when he arrives at a conclusion in private. Raven (1959) found greater pressure to conform to the group norm when the individual either had to communicate his opinion or where possibility of rejection for nonconformity existed. Kelley and Volkart (1952) found similar results when they presented a critical speech to a group of boy scouts. Half the group was told that the results of a later questionnaire about the speech would be made public while the other half was assured that their responses would not be disclosed. Those boy scouts who were told their questionnaires would be made public tended to agree more with the speaker.

Cohesiveness

The perceptions of the bonds between individuals are important aspects of group functioning. There is even some doubt as to whether there will be any unifying adherence to group norms without cohesiveness, the condition defined as "that group property which is inferred from the number and strength of mutual positive attitudes among the members of a group" (Lott, 1961 p. 279).

It might be expected that the influence a group will exert upon its members will be related to the cohesiveness of the group, that is, the greater the cohesiveness the greater the influence. Festinger et al. (1950) found this to be the case. The same authors described the basis for the influence as being in the attractiveness of the group for its members. Individuals may want to belong to the group for several reasons—the group may be the mediator for certain goals that are important for members, being a member of the group may have certain attractions in itself, or people may want to belong to the group simply because they like the other members.

Since norms involve criteria for behavior, they tend to reduce any anxiety about what is "right" or proper. The more homogeneous the group, the more consistent the criteria are likely to be; this, in turn, makes the group more cohesive, and so on, in a reinforcing cycle. The more the values of the group are shared, the more cohesive the group is likely to be. The "tightly knit group" means a greater sharing of values and more identification with group perspectives.

Cohesiveness of the group will be greater if changes in the membership of the group occur less or not at all (Lasswell and Kaplan, 1950). A few new members may not be resisted or may even be welcomed by the existing membership; when there is a chance of the intrusion of a large number of new participants, there is less likely to be acceptance of the new members. The newcomers, on the other hand, may come into the new situation with trepidation or feelings of inferiority (Shils, 1950). Cohesiveness may be enhanced in many different ways or through the use of many different techniques. It has been characteristic of many "in" groups that their existence has been furthered by the use of secret symbols, passwords, or any mystical arrangements that unify them and set them apart from others.

Cohesiveness of a group influences communications within it and, at the same time, communications have some effect on cohesiveness. Festinger and Thibaut

(1951) found that where there was a wide range of opinion in decision-making groups, there was a tendency for communications to be directed to those members who were at the extremes of the range of opinions. There are more communications to the deviate from group norms, since these are attempts to bring him "back into the fold." The attempts are made partly because the deviate may represent a threat to the existence and stability of the group. Because of this threat, there is, in addition, hostility often expressed toward the nonconformist, the rejection being particularly strong in high-cohesiveness groups (Schachter, 1951).

Lott (1961) suggests that a more cohesive group has a higher level of communication between the members. There is also some suggestion that cohesiveness will increase if communication among members of a group increases, particularly if there are visible rewards in this procedure for the various members. This may be similar to the point that Homans (1950) has indicated, that interaction between members of a group and attractiveness were directly related. This would mean that interaction and communication would bring increased liking of other members and vice versa.

As might be expected, a cohesive group is more likely to arise in a situation calling for cooperative activity and is likely to be more effective in performance than is one where competition occurs internally. Klein (1956) has indicated that compatibility of members and similarity in characteristics of individuals lead to more effective collaboration and performance. He indicates that the badly organized group is no better than one that is composed of members in competition with one another where individuals hinder others in attainment of a goal. There is also more likelihood of communication of hostile feelings, criticism, withholding of information, and less communication in a poorly organized group. What communication does occur may be largely irrelevant or unrelated to the task.

Group discussions of problems to be faced and procedures to be followed is probably more effective in carrying out group performance than is any individual educational effort.

Competition

A competitive atmosphere involving groups may play an important role in their functioning in many practical situations. It may be commonly believed, especially in industrial concerns, that competition between individuals and groups within the company is of value in stimulating higher performance. Whether this is so or not is important to determine.

Some contribution to an understanding of the effects of competition and cooperation on individual and group performance is gained through a reading of results of a basic experiment by Mintz (1951). Mintz arranged metal cones in a bottle with an opening just large enough for the cones to be withdrawn one at a time. Water was introduced into the jar from below in the experiment while the subjects were instructed to withdraw the cones without getting them wet. There were two experimental conditions; in one a reward was promised to the person who retrieved his cone without getting it wet; a fine was paid if the cone was dampened by the rising water. The second experimental variation indicated that a similar group of students succeeded in cooperating and getting their cones out within a short period of time. There were no "traffic jams" under the cooperative pattern of behavior while the reward-and-fine conditions produced blockage and nonadaptive behavior over half the time. The experimenter obtained this result with no more than the threat of a mild fear of failure or the payment of a 10 cent fine.

Another of the earlier experimental studies of competition versus cooperation was done by Deutsch (1949). His subjects performed tasks ranging from simple puzzles to more complex problems of human relations. On most tasks the cooperative groups produced at a higher level than did the competitive groups, perhaps because of greater coordination in the cooperative teams. An added feature was a friendlier spirit among the cooperators. A later attempt by Jones and Vroom (1964) to isolate key factors in a similar situation led to the conclusion that the more effective performance of cooperative groups was the result of an effective division of labor. Performance was likely to be adversely affected when members had strong preferences for a particular task. This was true in cooperative as well as competitive groups.

These results and those of other researchers give some indication of the influence of group norms and the resulting cohesiveness on the performance of the members' conformity to norms. Hammond and Goldman (1961, p. 60) phrase it in terms of "noncompetition (being) more favorable to the group process."

Participation

In one way or another, various group studies have buttressed the view that a significant factor contributing to the effectiveness of the group is that of participation by the members in its functioning. Several research studies, particularly in industry, have indicated the importance of this factor.

The "Hawthorne studies" represent one of the most significant conceptual influences in the area of organizational behavior, particularly in an industrial setting. While the experiments focused on the influence of the group on productivity of workers, the deeper implications for a general theory of human behavior and the applications of it in an administrative framework have had great impact on organizational theorists and practitioners. These studies, begun in the 1920's in the Hawthorne plant of the Western Electric Company, have been discussed by many, including Roethlisberger and Dickson (1947) and Homans (1950).

The original interest of the experimenters in this series of studies was in the effects of environmental factors on work performance. They varied the level of illumination, for instance, and related this to measures of output, using small groups of workers selected from the general work force as subjects placed in specially prepared test facilities. During the course of the experiments, the investigators recognized that variables other than those with which they were concerned were playing a very important role in the final output. It was the recognition of the social factors contribution to performance for which these studies became justly famous. The girls who were selected for the test room experience participated in the planning of the experiment, and their views were taken into account throughout. The girls felt "it was fun" and, even though the number of observers was greater and their attention higher in the test situation than in the ordinary work environment, the girls felt no sense of anxiety because of tight control. The group developed leadership and common purpose; the work situation became a very cohesive one, where, when individuals may not have felt up to par, the other members of the group "carried" them. In short, there emerged an effectively functioning social group in a warm relationship with its supervisors. What about the original dependent variable—work output? There need not be any concern on this score by those who concentrated only on production. Output progressed to consistently higher levels without stress on the individuals and, of course, while this could not continue indefinitely, the workers were highly motivated to show increasing improvement.

This was in distinct contrast to the situation the workers said existed in their original work stations. It was also distinctly different from the situation existing in another work group that was observed without any of the preliminary discussion or participation by the workers in the new investigation. Even though there was a wage incentive system in this group, which should have provided some increase in output and wages, production figures remained remarkably constant over a period of time. Work procedures and the resulting output were influenced by the shared attitudes and values of the group; the work group set norms which maintained a ceiling on output. Those workers who exceeded the ceiling were given evidence of social disapproval, verbally or physically. Output was not exceedingly low, however, since the group norms included a floor for production, below which employees could not fall without being called a "chiseler" or something similar.

This work unit proved to be less cohesive than the original experimental one. While there was a common set of values and sentiments, the main group was characterized by a set of cliques, each with limited interests. Relationships with supervisors were less friendly and more formal than in the cohesive participating group. Workers felt more closely supervised when, in reality, there was less overall supervision in the regular work situation than in the test group. Both groups seemed to be organized; the difference arose from the fact that the test group was organized in cooperation with management for a common purpose while the second informal work group was organized in opposition to management. In both cases, however, an analysis of the informal group clearly indicated the strong influence of social factors on individual and group performance.

Another well-known study of the importance of participation in the functioning of groups was done at the Harwood Manufacturing Corporation by Coch and French (1948). While the study focused on the change process and the specific techniques possible in the overcoming of resistance to change, the techniques used and the results illustrate several aspects of group dynamics. The experiment was conducted at a time when the factory was involved in a style change that necessitated a revision of work roles and procedures. The investigators arranged to have matched groups of employees exposed to three degrees of participation in determining the new work assignments. One group had virtually no participation in the process; they were assigned tasks from the very beginning. The second group participated indirectly through a group of representatives selected from the original group. The final variation involved complete participation in the determining of programs and assignments in the changeover. After the changeover, the no-participation group showed little or no improvement in their performance. Resistance was notable among the members of the production crew, and many examples of hostility and aggression between workers and supervisors were common. The group that participated through representatives worked well with the supervisor or staff man and showed a substantial increase in performance, particularly in the second week after the change. The total participation group adapted to the change very rapidly and progressed to levels that were significantly higher than their earlier performance. The emotional tone of the group was very good; there was excellent cooperation between individuals in the group and the supervisor, and no aggression was evident.

At the end of the month, the no-participation group had made no progress and were assigned to new jobs somewhere else in the factory. When they were reassembled after a few months and permitted to participate in still another change, this group operated at the same high levels that earlier participation groups achieved, a level that, again, was significantly higher than the positions reached where they were not permitted to participate. The experimenters felt that such participation leads to higher morale or better labor-management relations in addition to higher production. The entire management of the company felt that the practical results were very valuable, over and above any of the theoretical additions this study has made to concepts of group processes and intergroup relations generally.

It may be, however, that, while there is a strong motivational basis for individual participation, the strength of this factor may not be uniform for all individuals. Vroom (1959) related personality with group participation and performance. He found the highest satisfaction in the job and the best performance in those individuals who had a high need for independence. Individuals who are highly dependent and were authoritarian-oriented were affected less by the opportunity to participate and showed no relationship between felt participation and job performance. This study indicates that, while participation is related to performance and is important in group functioning, we should also look to variations in individuals in terms of the need for participation.

Broader situational and demographic variables are not, of course, without their influence on the interaction within the small group. A series of studies on an important small group in the legal area, the jury, has indicated several avenues of influence from outside the immediate group situation. Strodtbeck, James, and Hawkins (1958) determined the influence of socioeconomic status and occupation on the interaction in the mock jury. It was found that those individuals who participated more were most often chosen as foreman. Men participated in jury deliberations much more frequently than did women, and there was much more activity from those individuals in higher socioeconomic brackets.

Group Problem Solving

One of the aspects of group functioning that has attracted considerable interest down through the years is that of group problem solving. The basic question has been whether the product of the intellectual functioning of a group is superior to that of a group of individuals functioning separately.

In one of the earliest studies on the question of group versus individual problem solving, Allport (1920) found a difference in favor of the group because a greater variety of ideas arose in that social setting. Lorge and Solomon (1960) replicated an earlier study by Shaw (1932) and found (as Shaw did) that, generally, groups were superior to individuals. Level of aspiration was a significant factor; no individual without aspiration was able to solve the problem, while groups were not affected as strongly. Argyle (1957) agreed in terms of superiority of the group. He isolated two factors in the process, namely, the improvement of judgment through prior judgment and the superiority achieved through a combination of individual judgments. Group problem solving increased the number of alternatives available and stimulated activity toward a typical solution to identify blind alleys that individuals might find themselves in if they pursue the task alone.

It is safe to say that most of the studies in this area report a superiority of group over individual approaches although at least one (Moore and Anderson, 1954) does not. It may be that the source of disagreement lies mainly in the conditions surrounding the task and in the individuals who are subjects. The preponderance of expert opinion, however, is in favor of superiority of the group in problem-solving performance.

There has been further interest in a specific variant of group problem solving known popularly as "brainstorming" where the focus is on unrestricted and uninhibited associative responses by members of an assembled group. The group is under instructions to be unconcerned about the logic or validity of an idea and to respond with as many as possible.

Results of experiments in this area have been somewhat controversial. Osborn (1957), among others, has noted evidence for a greater variety and creativity in group solutions under the brainstorming instructions to provide ideas without concern for their value or logic. Taylor et al. (1958) indicate that this has not been true in their experience. The latter findings may represent, however, an inability of the individuals in the group to rid themselves of limiting attitudes; other situational and relational factors also may be playing an inhibiting role.

Structural Factors

Simple physical factors affect social relationships of individuals. In a small group situation they may play an even greater role than in broad social interaction, since the more immediate psychological factors have a tendency to be highlighted in the more proximate influences of the small group.

Size

The number of individuals in a group can, at least at a casual initial impression, determine much of the activity of the group. It would seem logical that the greater the number of individuals interacting, the less intimate their relationships would be. The sheer volume of interactions then necessary would tend to make any concerted action much more difficult. The role of the leader would, however, be much more significant in a group of larger size.

What the "proper" number of individuals in the group may be could depend upon the circumstances in which the group operates, particularly the purpose or function. Sargent and Williamson (1958) indicate, after a survey of the field, that a fact-finding group is probably most effective when it is composed of about 14 members. An executive or action-taking group functions best at a size of approximately seven members. The validity of these figures is reinforced by information from many legislative bodies that indicates memberships in the two different types of functioning groups as hovering close to the figures given.

An experimental study (Bales and Borgatta, 1955) of the effect of size on the interaction within the group provides some empirical results. The experimenters varied group size from two up to seven and recorded observations in the 12 categories of the Bales Interaction Analysis procedure. The overall results indicate, not surprisingly, that each member is faced with the greater number of individuals with whom to interact as size increases and the amount of time available to talk to others then is reduced per capita. When specific types of interaction are considered in the increase in size, the following actions also increase: showing solidarity, releasing tension, and giving suggestion. The following activities show a decrease with size: showing agreement, asking for opinion, and showing tension. These patterns of initiated behavior probably show the increased pressure on the individuals for activities that will further the functioning of the group despite the increase in size.

Berelson and Steiner (1964) conclude that even-numbered groups show more disagreement than odd-numbered groups because of the possibility for subgroups of equal size to be pitted against each other. They further state that the "perfect" group size is five, where, if subgroups develop, a minority group of two permits participation and individual development in support of a position while a majority of three is not completely overwhelming yet strong enough to prevail.

Simmel was one of the first researchers to point out the characteristics of two-person and three-person groups and to discuss the differences between them. Three-person groups quickly break down into two subgroups, that is, two persons team up as a majority against the remaining member. This division may not be an active or aggressive one, however, since the minority of one may simply be a less interested or even apathetic member of the group. It is more stable than a two-man group in the sense of accomplishment of purpose by the majority but unstable in that it breaks down very quickly into subgroups of two and one. The group of two is less stable because there is a great deal of tension in the evenly balanced person-to-person situation. There is, however, a recognition of the need for understanding, tolerance, and the avoidance of disagreement. The husband-wife group is a good example, and many of the characteristics of their situation can apply generally to all groups of two.

These findings have given rise to the statements of small group researchers that the dyad (two-person group) is more stable than the triad (three-person group). This may be only a newer and more precise way of stating the old maxim "two is company and three is a crowd."

Placement

Interaction between individuals and groups often is affected by their location with respect to each other. It might be expected that individuals who do not interact do not get to know each other. The converse, however, is not so readily guessed, that is, that those who do interact are more likely to be attracted to each other (Homans, 1950).

Festinger et al. (1950) compared sociometric choices with the physical distance between individuals and found a high relationship. Individuals living closest were chosen more often and, as the distances between persons increased, choices between them became less frequent. This study was conducted in a housing project where even minor distances such as a few feet were significant; people whose front doors face each other directly are more likely to interact with greater frequency than when they are located in other ways.

Further evidence of the impact of physical placement on primary relationships is presented by Whyte (1956) in *The Organization Man*. No demographic variables such as occupation, background, religion, or education could explain the "web of friendship" that existed in the example of suburbia studied. The basis for primary social relationships turned out to be propinquity—groups at social events were composed of those who lived in the same geographic area. Whyte also noted, among other factors, the link between centrality of location and popularity. The more introverted could remain so by locating in peripheral areas.

There is much more to the patterning of groups than physical placement, of course. Similarities of interest, status, and life style are apt to be just as important as location, and perhaps even more so. The author recalls, from several years as a "participant observer" in a planned and cohesive community, that friendship groups were frequently structured along occupational lines. Just as important seemed to be the memberships of the wives in social or charitable organizations. Despite the overlapping that inevitably occurs in any complex social relationship, the common thread between individuals was most often a shared set of values and status.

Communication in Groups

Communication is a basic aspect of the interaction in groups of individuals. Whether on a person-to-person basis or on a level involving a greater number in the network, communication serves to provide information and is a prime vehicle for influencing others. Of all aspects of communication that might be of special interest in a group setting, those relating to the direction of transmission and the arrangements of networks are probably of greatest pertinence for discussion.

Direction of Communication

Communication may proceed only one-way or the information may be transmitted back and forth; that is, two-way communication may take place. A speaker may simply lecture to an audience or a boss may not permit any questioning of his position by subordinates. In those situations, the communication is pretty much limited to one-way. Certainly, subtle cues may be transmitted by the audience back to the speaker but, for all practical purposes, the direction is unilateral. In two-way communication the channels are utilized in both directions. Statements and questions are made back and forth.

Each type of communication has its own characteristics which may determine the usefulness of procedure. Leavitt (1964, p. 143), long an active researcher in this area, has summarized the findings of experiments on direction of communication. Two-way may be slower than one-way communication, but it is more accurate. Senders in the two-way process may have more anxiety or feel under attack because receivers communicate their feelings. At the same time, the receivers feel more sure of themselves since they get a better idea of whether they are correct in their judgments. Two-way communication appears more disorderly and less efficient to an outside observer, but it works better.

The implications for a communicator in any type of organization are striking. An administrator in business or a teacher in an educational setting may feel that a one-way communication system is mandatory to preserve order and promote efficiency in the organization. While "giving orders" has been a traditional pattern of behavior in many business or school situations, there is some doubt that, apart from reducing the anxiety of "boss" or "teacher," it is an effective means of promoting organizational welfare.

Communication Networks

The structuring of communication channels between individuals in a group influences the interaction of its members and the functioning of the group as a whole. Research on communication networks was stimulated by some original work by Bavelas (1948) but was expanded upon by others, notably Leavitt (1951) and Guetzkow and Simon (1955). The experiments on the effects of communication networks, while very basic and spartan as precise experiments must be, can provide valuable information for an understanding of the functioning of communications in groups placed in various institutional settings. Small group communication networks can be structured in the patterns shown in Figure 1. All are patterns of communication involving individuals in groups of five and, while still other patterns of communication are possible (a "chain" of individuals, for example), the patterns in Figure 1 are sufficient for describing salient features of experiments in small group communication nets.

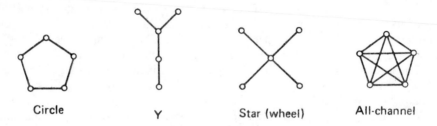

Circle   Y   Star (wheel)   All-channel

Figure 1. Some communication networks in groups (Leavitt, H. 1951).

Those who would wish to transfer behavioral information to an applied setting would undoubtedly have greatest interest in the relationships between communication networks and performance of the group. Questions such as "which network is most efficient?" might be asked. The difficulty in answering comes in the further specification of effectiveness; speed or accuracy may be the prime consideration. In addition, the nature of the task, the order of presentation, or other conditions play a role, and there are other factors that have an additional influence on performance, if only indirectly. Motivation and morale can show some relationships with type of communication network and, as has been pointed out repeatedly, these factors can influence the performance of a group or individual.

Leavitt (1964) summarized his work and that of others in a comparison of networks operating under various conditions. The "star" network will be faster than the "circle," at least in the initial stages of organization if not throughout the entire handling of the task. The star will provide a great deal of satisfaction for the member in the central position; the others in the network are likely to be considerably less satisfied in the outcome of the task. Of possible greater importance is the difference between the star and the circle in terms of having to cope with new tasks once the networks have been organized and the earlier tasks completed. With new tasks that call for a change in approach or method of problem solving, the circle shows that it can cope much better with the changed conditions. Undoubtedly the superiority in problem solving in new situations is a result of the opportunity for greater participation by circle members in the problem-solving task. The centrality of the star network seems to be the basis for the continuing errors made in new problems.

Satisfaction in the outcome is higher in the circle networks where everyone participates in all aspects of the decision making. Morale in a group where the members are allowed to participate is much higher than in one in which few get the opportunity to play a role. Satisfaction is high, of course, for the member who occupies the central position in the star, but the peripheral members' morale is usually much lower than that of those in the circle.

With some reservations, based on the fact of limited applications to "real" situations, Leavitt (1964, pp. 236-237) suggests that "good" networks are those that are equalitarian in nature, that is, where individuals have many neighbors or equal access to at least two direct channels in the group. The reader is reminded to consider these findings in connection with the earlier considerations of one-way and two-way communications.

References

Allport, F. (1920). The influence of the group upon association and thought. *Journal of Experimental Psychology*, 3, 159-182.

Argyle, M. (1957). Social pressure in public and private situations. *Journal of Abnormal and Social Psychology*, 54, 172-175.

Asch, S. (1952) *Social psychology*. Englewood Cliffs, N.J.: Prentice-Hall.

Bales, R. (1951). *Interaction process analysis: a method for the study of small groups*. Cambridge, Mass.: Addison-Wesley.

Bales, R., and Borgatta, E. (1955). Size of group as a factor in the interaction profile. In Hare, A. et al. (eds.) *Small groups: studies in social interaction*. New York: Knopf, 395-413.

Bavelas, A. (1948). A mathematical model for group structures. *Applied Anthropology*, 7, 16-30.

Bennett, E. (1955). Discussion, decision, commitment, and consensus in "group decisions." *Human Relations*, 8, 251-274.

Berelson, B. and Steiner, G. (1964). *Human behavior*. New York: Harcourt, Brace and World.

Browne, C. (1951). Study of executive leadership in business; sociometric pattern. *Journal of Applied Psychology*, 35, 34-37.

Burgess, E. (1926). The family a unity of interacting personalities. *Family* 7, 3-9.

Cartwright, D. and Zander, A. eds. (1960). *Group dynamics: research and theory* (2nd ed.). New York: Harper & Row.

Chapple, E. (1940). Measuring human relations: an introduction to the study of the interaction of individuals. *Genetic Psychology Monograph*, 22, 1-147.

Coch, L. and French, J. (1948). Overcoming resistance to change. *Human Relations,* 1, 512-534.

Cooley, C. (1909). *Social organization.* New York: Scribner's.

Dalton, M. (1959). *Men who manage.* New York: Wiley.

Deutsch, M. (1949). An experimental study of the effects of cooperation and competition upon group processes. *Human Relations,* 2, 199-231.

DiVesta, F. and Cox, L. (1960). Some dispositional correlates of conformity behavior. *The Journal of Social Psychology,* 52, 259-268.

Festinger, L. (1950). Laboratory experiments: the role of group belongingness. In Miller, J. (ed.). *Experiments in social process.* New York: McGraw-Hill, 31-46.

Festinger, L., Schachter, S., and Back, K. (1950). *Social pressures in informal groups: a study of a housing project.* New York: Harper.

Festinger, L. and Thibaut, J. (1951). Interpersonal communication in small groups. *Journal of Abnormal and Social Psychology,* 46, 92-99.

Gouldner, A. and Gouldner, H. (1963). *Modern sociology.* New York: Harcourt, Brace and World.

Guetzkow, H. and Simon, H. (1955). The impact of certain communication nets upon organization and performance in task-oriented groups. *Management Science,* 1, 233-250.

Hammond, L. and Goldman, M. (1961). Competition and non-competition and its relationship to individual and group productivity. *Sociometry,* 24, 46-60.

Heyns, R. and Lippitt, R. (1954). Systematic observational techniques. In Lindzey, G. (ed.). *Handbook of Social Psychology,* Chap. 10. Reading, Mass.: Addison-Wesley.

Hollander, E. and Webb, W. (1955). Leadership, followership and friendship: an analysis of peer nominations. *Journal of Abnormal and Social Psychology,* 50, 163-167.

Homans, G. (1950). *The human group.* New York: Harcourt, Brace and World.

Horsfall, A. and Arensberg, C. (1949). Teamwork and productivity in a shoe factory. *Human Organization,* 8, 13-25.

Jacobs, J. (1945). The application of sociometry to industry. *Sociometry,* 8, 181-198.

Jennings, H. (1937). Structure of leadership-development and sphere of influence. *Sociometry,* 1, 99-143.

Jones, S. and Vroom, V. (1964). Division of labor and performance under cooperative and competitive conditions. *Journal of Abnormal and Social Psychology,* 68, 313-320.

Kelley, H. and Volkhart, E. (1952). The resistance to change of group-anchored attitudes. *American Sociological Review,* 17, 453-465.

Kerstetter, L. and Sargent, J. (1940). Re-assignment therapy in the classroom. *Sociometry,* 3, 292-306.

Klein, J. (1956). *The study of groups.* London: Routledge.

Krech, D., Crutchfield, R., and Ballachey, E. (1962). *Individual in society.* New York: McGraw-Hill.

Lasswell, H. and Kaplan, A. (1950). *Power and society: a framework for political inquiry.* New Haven, Conn.: Yale University Press.

Leavitt, H. (1951). Some effects of certain communication patterns on group performance. *The Journal of Abnormal and Social Psychology,* 46, 38-50.

Leavitt, H. (1964). *Managerial psychology.* Chicago: University of Chicago Press.

Lorge, I. and Solomon, H. (1960). Group and individual performance in problem solving related to previous exposure to problem, level of aspiration, and group size. *Behavioral Science,* 5, 28-38.

Lott, B. (1961). Group cohesiveness: a learning phenomenon. *The Journal of Social Psychology,* 55, 275-286.

McGregor, D. (1960). *The human side of enterprise.* New York: McGraw-Hill.

Menzel, A. and Katz, E. (1956). Social relations and innovation in the medical profession: the epidemiology of a new drug. *Public Opinion Quarterly,* 19, 337-352.

Milgram, S. (1964). Group pressure and action against a person. *Journal of Abnormal and Social Psychology,* 69, 137-143.

Mintz, A (1951). Nonadaptive group behavior. *The Journal of Abnormal and Social Psychology,* 46, 150-159.

Moore, O. and Anderson, S. (1954). Search behavior in individual and group problem solving. *American Sociological Review,* 19, 702-714.

Moreno, J. L. (1934). *Who shall survive?* Washington: Nervous and Mental Disease Publishing Co.

Osborn, A. (1957). *Applied imagination.* New York: Scribner's.

Raven, B. (1959). Social influence on opinions and the communication of related content. *Journal of Abnormal and Social Psychology,* 58, 119-128.

Roethlisberger, F. and Dickson, W. (1939). *Management and the worker.* Cambridge, Mass.: Harvard University Press.

Rosenberg, L. (1961). Group size, prior experience, and conformity. *Journal of Abnormal and Social Psychology,* 63, 436-437.

Sargent, S. and Williamson, R. (1958). *Social psychology.* New York: Ronald.

Schachter, S. (1951). Deviation, rejection, and communication. *Journal of Abnormal and Social Psychology,* 46, 190-207.

Schein, E. (1965). *Organizational psychology.* Englewood Cliffs, N.J.: Prentice-Hall.

Shaw, M. (1932). A comparison of individuals and small groups in the rational solution of complex problems. *American Journal of Psychology,* 44, 491-504.

Sherif, M. (1936). *The psychology of social norms.* New York: Harper.

Sherif, M. and Sherif, C. (1956). *An outline of social psychology* (rev. ed.). New York: Harper.

Shils, E. (1950). Primary groups in the American army. In Merton, R. and Lazarsfeld, P. (eds). *Continuities in social research: studies in the scope and method of "the American soldier."* New York: Free Press.

Speroff, B. and Kerr, W. (1952). Steel mill "hot strip" accidents and interpersonal desirability values. *Journal of Clinical Psychology,* 8, 89-91.

Steiner, I. and Johnson, H. (1963). Authoritarianism and conformity. *Sociometry,* 26, 21-34.

Strickland, B. and Crowne, D. (1962). Conformity under conditions of simulated group pressure as a function of the need for social approval. *The Journal of Social Psychology,* 58, 171-181.

Strodtbeck, F., James, R. and Hawkins, C. (1958). Social status in jury deliberations. In Maccoby, E., Newcomb, T., and Hartley, E. (eds). *Readings in social psychology,* (3rd ed.). New York: Holt.

Taylor, D., Berry, P., and Block, C. (1958). Does group participation when using brainstorming facilitate or inhibit creative thinking? *Administrative Science Quarterly,* 3, 23-47.

Thelen, H. (1963). *Dynamics of groups at work.* Chicago: University of Chicago Press.

Thibaut, J. and Kelley, H. (1959). *The social psychology of groups.* New York: Wiley.

Tönnies, F. (1st ed., 1887). *Gemeinshaft and gesellschaft* (Loomis, C., trans.) (1940). *Fundamental concepts of sociology.* New York: American Book Co.

Van Zelst, R. (1952). Validation of a sociometric regrouping procedure. *Journal of Abnormal and Social Psychology,* 47, 299-301.

Vroom, V. (1959). Some personality determinants of the effects of participation. *Journal of Abnormal and Social Psychology,* 59, 322-327.

Whyte, W. (1956). *The organization man*. New York: Simon & Schuster.

Williams, S. and Leavitt, H. (1947). Group opinion as a prediction of military leadership. *Journal of Consulting Psychology*, 11, 283-291.

Zeleny, L. (1941). Status: its measurements and control in education. *Sociometry*, 4, 193-204.

INEQUITY IN SOCIAL EXCHANGE

J. STACY ADAMS

Introduction

Philosophers, political scientists, politicians, jurists, and economists traditionally have been the ones concerned with the just distribution of wealth, power, goods, and services in society. Social psychologists and their brethren, with the notable exceptions of Blau (1964), Homans (1961), and Thibaut and Kelley (1959), have displayed remarkably little professional interest in this, despite the fact that the process of exchange is almost continual in human interactions. They have, of course, studied social behavior involving reciprocal, as distinguished from unilateral, transactions, but their sights have been focused on the amount and content of communications; attitudinal, affective, motivational, perceptual, and behavioral changes; changes in group structure, leadership, and so on, rather than on exchange proper. Yet, the process of exchange appears to have characteristics peculiar to itself and to generate affect, motivation, and behavior that cannot be predicted unless exchange processes are understood.

A distinguishing characteristic of exchange processes is that their resultants have the potentiality of being perceived as just or unjust. But what are the consequences of outcomes being perceived as meeting or not meeting the norms of justice? Nearly all the attention given to this question has been to establish a relationship between perceived injustice and dissatisfaction (Homans, 1950, 1953, 1961; Jaques, 1956, 1961a; Patchen, 1959, 1961; Stouffer *et al.*, 1949; Vroom, 1964; Zaleznik *et al.*, 1958). Not surprisingly, this has been accomplished with success. Does a man treated unfairly simply express dissatisfaction? Are there not other consequences of unfair exchanges? What behavior is predictable? These questions and related ones are a principal concern of this paper.

Rather than simply present a theory from which the behavior of persons engaged in a social exchange may be deduced, the plan of this chapter is to present first in chronological order two major concepts relating to the perception of justice and

Reprinted by permission of the author and the publisher, Academic Press, Inc., from *Advances in Experimental Psychology*, L. Berkowitz, ed. (1965).

injustice. First is the concept of relative deprivation and the complementary concept of relative gratification, developed by Stouffer and his associates (1949). Homans' highly elaborated concept of distributive justice (1961) will be discussed next. These will then be integrated into a theory of inequity from which it will be possible to specify the antecedents and consequences of injustice in human exchanges.

Relative Deprivation

Following World War II, the publication of the first *American Soldier* volume by Stouffer and his colleagues (1949) excited interest among sociologists and social psychologists. The effect was at least in part due to the introduction of a new concept, relative deprivation, used by the authors to explain what were seemingly paradoxical findings. According to Merton and Kitt (1950), the formal status of the concept was that of an intervening variable which explained the observed relationship between an independent variable, such as education level or rate of promotion, and a dependent variable, such as satisfaction with some aspect of Army life.

Relative deprivation was not formally defined by the authors, however, nor by Merton and Kitt (1950), who analyzed in great detail the implication of the concept for sociological theory in general and for reference group theory in particular. The essential meaning of the concept may be inferred from two illustrations of its use by the authors of *The American Soldier*. Despite the objective fact that soldiers with a high school education had better opportunities for advancement in the Army, high school graduates were not as satisfied with their status and jobs as were less educated men. This apparent paradox is explained by assuming that the better-educated men had higher levels of aspiration, partly based on what would be realistic status expectations in civilian life, and that they were, therefore, relatively deprived of status and less satisfied with the status they achieved. It may be noted that the validity of this explanation depends upon showing that level of aspiration is greater than status achieved among high school graduates as contrasted to soldiers with less education. While this is not demonstrated by the authors, it appears to be a credible assumption. It is the relative deprivation, then, that accounts for less satisfaction among better-educated men.

A second illustrative use of relative deprivation is made by the authors of *The American Soldier* in accounting for the puzzling fact that Army Air Corps men were less satisfied with promotion opportunities than were men in the Military Police, even though objective opportunities for mobility were vastly greater in the Air Corps. Relative deprivation is invoked to explain the anomaly as follows: The high promotion rate in the Air Corps induces high expectations of mobility; lower-ranking and low-mobile men, compared to high-ranking and high-mobile men, feel deprived in the face of their expectations and express dissatisfaction. Among military policemen, on the other hand, expectations of promotion are low, and the fate of most policemen is quite similar: namely, low rank. In sum, there is a discrepancy between expectation and achievement among Air Corps enlisted men and little or no discrepancy between expectation and achievement among men in the Military Police. The discrepancy results in dissatisfaction with mobility. Or more precisely, the assumed existence of a discrepancy between expectation and achievement is held to account for the empirical observation that men were less satisfied in one branch than in the other.

Spector (1956), in an experiment directly related to these findings by Stouffer *et al.*, varied perceived probability of promotion and fulfillment and tested the hypothesis that "*on failing to achieve* an attractive goal, an individual's morale will be higher if the probability of achieving the goal had been perceived to be low than if it had been perceived to be high" (p. 52). He found that the high expectations-nonpromotion group had lower morale and was less satisfied with the promotion system than was the low expectations-nonpromotion group, thus corroborating experimentally the military survey findings. Comparable findings have been made by Gebhard (1949).

The effects of relative deprivation (the unfair violation of expectations) upon sociometric choices are clearly shown in an experiment designed by Thibaut (1950) to learn about the conditions that affect group cohesiveness. Underprivileged boys from camps and settlement houses in the Boston area participated in the experiment in groups of 10 to 12 boys, all of whom had known, played, and lived with one another for some time. After filling out a questionnaire in which they were asked to rank the four boys they would most like to have on their team to play games if their groups were to be divided, the boys in each group were split into two teams of five or six. Thibaut formed each team so that each boy would have about an equal number of preferred and of nonpreferred partners and so that each team would be composed of approximately the same number of popular, or *central,* and less popular, or *peripheral,* boys in terms of sociometric choices received. Although there were several experimental conditions in his study, only one of them concerns us here. This is the condition in which each set of two teams played four games and one of the pairs was given consistently an inferior, menial, uninteresting, or unpleasant role during the series of games. These were the *low-status* teams (called "unsuccessful low-status" by Thibaut).

Following the last game, each boy answered a questionnaire in which he was again asked to order his preferences for teammates. A general finding was that a boy tended to shift his sociometric choices after the games to boys who had actually been teammates. Of greater interest here is the fact that low-status *central* boys were more likely to display such shifts than were low-status *peripheral* boys. The former were popular boys, presumably aware of their status among their fellows, who were forced to assume low-status roles in violation of the roles they would customarily play. The role of the low-status peripheral boys, on the other hand, were more or less a confirmation of their relatively low popularity among their friends. Compared to the peripheral boys, then, the central boys were relatively deprived, and they manifested their greater dissatisfaction with their fate by shifting to a greater extent their sociometric choices from central boys on the opposing team to boys on their own team. Thibaut also reports evidence that the low-status central boys displayed exceptional hostility to members of the opposing (high-status) teams and that all low-status boys keenly felt the injustice of their fate.

These findings are of especial interest because they cannot be accounted for simply on the hypothesis that abuse or minority group membership will result in withdrawal and increased cohesiveness. Such a hypothesis would have required that low-status peripheral and central boys show the same behavior. But, as noted, central boys were more likely to shift their sociometric choices and to display overt hostility to opponents. They were the ones who suffered the greater relative deprivation.

The studies that have been described form an interesting set. In the data from the surveys by Stouffer *et al.* (1949), there is no empirical evidence of relative deprivation. None of the soldiers or airmen were asked, for example, if specific expectations were violated or, more directly, if they felt relatively deprived with respect to status. Relative deprivation was used, ex post facto, to explain anomalous findings. The concept had no existential character; it was a hypothetical construct—rather than an intervening variable, as Merton and Kitt classified it (1950). The Spector (1956) experiment, by manipulating expectations of promotions and achievement, created a condition of relative deprivation. Thus, operationally, relative deprivation took on the status of a variable, an independent variable, variations in which were related to variations in "morale." In another laboratory experiment, Thibaut (1950) created conditions of relative deprivation, which were not any the less real for having been created unintentionally by his manipulations of group status and group success. In this respect his experiment is analogous to Spector's. But the nature of his experimental task allowed a very broad range of behavior to be displayed spontaneously. As a result there was direct evidence of feelings of injustice in reaction to the manipulation of relative deprivation, as well as of dissatisfaction, hostility, withdrawal, and changes in sociometric choices. Thus, proceeding from the military surveys to the Thibaut experiment, a useful construct emerges, receives experimental support, and its meaning becomes elaborated.

Bearing this and the survey and experimental data described earlier in mind, there emerge certain conclusions. First, it seems that manifest dissatisfaction and other behavior are responses to acutely felt injustice, rather than directly to relative deprivation. Relative deprivation is a condition occurring naturalistically or an experimental manipulation which elicits feelings of injustice. In turn, feelings of injustice trigger expressions of dissatisfaction and, in addition, the kind of behavior exhibited by Thibaut's juvenile subjects. Injustice, then, may be said to mediate the effects of relative deprivation. A second conclusion is that what is just is based upon relatively strong expectations, such as that educational achievement will be correlated with job status achievement and that one will be promoted at about the same rate as one's fellows, or that the role one plays in one situation—in laboratory games—will be in line and with the role one usually assumes—in the settlement house or camp.

Thirdly, it is clear that a comparative process is inherent in the development of expectations and the perception of injustice, as implied by the term *relative* deprivation. Well-educated men felt unfairly treated in comparison to the treatment they would have received in civilian life or in comparison to the treatment civilians did receive. Injustice was suffered by unpromoted or less-mobile airmen in relation to the general mobility of men in the Air Corps, whereas there was no such felt injustice among low-mobile military policemen when they compared their rate of promotion to the low promotion rate prevalent in the Military Police.

A particularly felicitous additional example of the process of comparison and its importance is provided by Sayles (1958). He notes that ". . . foundries are often hot spots, highly aggressive in seeking fulfillment of their demands where they are part of larger manufacturing organizations. However, when the plant is entirely devoted to the foundry operation, they are relatively weak and inactive" (p. 104). Foundry workers are highly paid to compensate for the unpleasant work conditions and the high physical exertion required and because of a short labor supply in this skill area. Other workers, however, rank foundry operators quite low and look down on them, according to Sayles. Thus, when foundry employees are present for purposes of comparison, other workers feel relatively deprived as regards earnings, and the resulting dissatisfaction may take hostile forms. Conversely, the foundry workers, being the butt of the despisement of others, may react by being unusually assertive and demanding.

Finally, it may be noted, if it is not obvious, that felt injustice is a response to a *discrepancy* between what is perceived to be and what is perceived should be. In the illustrative cases taken from *The American Soldier* and from the Spector and Thibaut experiments, it is a response to a discrepancy between an achievement and an expectation of achievement.

Distributive Justice

The existence of relative deprivation necessarily raises the question of distributive justice, or of the fair share-out of rewards; for, as noted earlier, deprivation is perceived relationally. The concept is not new, having been explored by political philosophers and others from the time of Aristotle. In the hands of Homans (1950, 1953, 1961) and of his colleagues (Zaleznik *et al.*, 1958), the concept of distributive justice has taken on the articulated character of what may be more properly called a theory. As fully developed by Homans (1961), it is a theory employing quasi-economic terms. According to him, distributive justice among men who are in an exchange relationship with one another obtains when the profits of each are proportional to their investments. Profit consists of that which is received up in the exchange, such as foregoing the rewards obtainable in another exchange, or a burden assumed as a specific function of the exchange, such as a risk, which would include not only potential real loss but the psychological discomfort of uncertainty as well. Investments in an exchange are the relevant attributes that are brought by a party to the exchange. They include, for example, skill, effort, education, training, experience, age, sex and ethnic background.

Schematically, for a dyad consisting of A and B, distributive justice between them is realized when :

$$\frac{\text{A's rewards less A's costs}}{\text{A's investments}} = \frac{\text{B's rewards less B's costs}}{\text{B's investments}}$$

When an inequality between the proportions exists, the participants to the exchange will experience a feeling of injustice and one or the other party will experience deprivation. The party specifically experiencing relative deprivation is the one for whom the ratio of profits to investments is the smaller.

Making explicit that it is the relation between *ratios* of profits to investments that results in felt justice or injustice is a distinct contribution that takes us beyond the concept of relative deprivation. To be sure, an individual may feel deprived, but he feels deprived not merely because his rewards or profits are less than he expected or felt was fair. Many men, when comparing their rewards to those of another, will perceive that their rewards are smaller, and yet they will not feel that this state of affairs is unjust. The reason is that persons obtaining the higher rewards are perceived as deserving them. That is, their rewards are greater because their investments are greater. Thus, for example, if being of the male sex is perceived as a higher investment than being of the female sex, a woman operator earning less than a man doing the same work will not feel unjustly treated. The proportionality of profits to investments is comparable for the woman and for the man. Similarly, a young instructor usually does not feel that his rewards, low as they may be, compare unfairly with those of an associate professor in his department. As Homans notes, "Justice is a curious mixture of equality within inequality" (1961, p. 244).

The theory of distributive justice also addresses itself to the case of two or more persons, each of whom receives his rewards from a third party: an employer, for example. In such an instance, each of the persons is in an exchange with the employer, as in the simple dyadic situation discussed; but, in addition, each man will expect that the employer will maintain a fair ratio of rewards to investments between himself and other men. This, of course, is the perennial dilemma of employers, and it almost defies a perfect solution, though it is capable of better solutions than are often developed. One difficulty with finding neat solutions is that A's perception of his rewards, costs, and investments are not necessarily identical with B's perception of A's situation. To complicate matters, two persons, though they might agree as to what their investments are, may disagree as to the weight each investment should be given. Should age count more than sex? Should education be given as much weight as job experience? The psychometrics of this have not yet received much attention.

The relationship of distributive justice to satisfaction is treated only briefly by Homans, but it is nevertheless the subject of a formal theoretical proposition. If a state of injustice exists and it is to a man's disadvantage—that is, the man experiences deprivation—he will "display the emotional behavior we call anger" (Homans, 1961, p. 75). Here Homans is overly influenced by Skinnerian rhetoric. He means, plainly, that dissatisfaction will be felt or expressed. If, on the other hand, distributive justice fails of realization and is, to an observer at least, to a man's advantage, he will feel guilty. This aspect of the proposition is more novel and is substantiated by observations by Jaques (1956, 1961a) and by laboratory experiments by Adams (1963a) that will be discussed later. Homans also implies that the thresholds for displaying dissatisfaction and guilt are different when he remarks that ". . . he (the guilty man) is less apt to make a prominent display of his guilt than of his anger" (1961, p. 76). This suggestion, also made by Adams (1963a) and deducible from observations made by Jaques (1956), implies that distributive justice must fail of realization to a greater extent when it is favorable to an individual before he reacts than when it is to his disadvantage.

. Others have stated formal propositions that obviously refer to the same phenomena as encompassed by the theory of distributive justice. The propositions listed by two writers are especially noteworthy because they were expressed in terms similar to those of Homans. Sayles (1958, p. 98), discussing the manifestation of dissatisfaction in industrial work groups, surmised that factory workers "compute" the fairness of their wages as follows:

$$\frac{\text{Our importance in the plant}}{\text{Any other group's importance}} = \frac{\text{Our earnings}}{\text{Their earnings}}$$

When the equality obtains, satisfaction is experienced. An inequality between the ratios causes pressures for redress, accompanied by dissatisfaction. "Importance in the plant" may be taken as equivalent to the perceived investments of group members, including skills and type of work performed, length of service, and such. This is made explicit in his model of the "economic world of the worker in his work group." According to this analysis, men are portrayed as comparing their jobs to other jobs and asking the questions, "Are these higher paying jobs actually more skilled than our own?" and "Do we earn *enough more* than the lower rated jobs to compensate for the skill difference?" (Sayles, 1958, p. 105). The term "earnings" is, of course, comparable to Homans' rewards but is a less comprehensive term, excluding other outcomes such as intrinsic job rewards. It also subsumes less than the concept of profit or net reward, since it makes no provision for negative outcomes or costs, such as unfavorable work conditions or tyrannical supervision. Nevertheless, it is clear that Sayles conceives of justice as being a function of the perceived equality of ratios of investments and of rewards.

Using the terms of Festinger's theory of cognitive dissonance (1957), Patchen postulates that workers making wage comparisons make a cognitive relation of the following type (1961, p. 9):

$$\frac{\text{My pay}}{\text{His (their) pay}} \quad \text{compared to} \quad \frac{\text{My position on dimensions related to pay}}{\text{His (their) position on dimensions related to pay}}$$

This formulation is similar to Sayles' but more explicit, for dimensions related to pay are specified as being attributes such as skill, education, and seniority. These are clearly the same as Homans' investments. Patchen differs somewhat from Homans in his conceptualization, however, in that he also includes job interest among his "dimensions" related to pay. This is not so much an investment as it is a reward, either with positive or negative valence. When, according to Patchen, an inequality results from the comparison of the two proportions, cognitive dissonance is experienced. In turn, dissatisfaction is manifested. However, dissonance and the attendant dissatisfaction are not necessarily a bad state of affairs from the point of view of the individual. Patchen points this out in an interesting departure from dissonance theory. Although consonant comparisons may be satisfying, they provide no basis for mobility aspirations, whereas dissonant comparisons unfavorable to the person permit a man to think that he is more deserving, that he merits higher pay or status. In effect, then, Patchen suggests that the motivation to attain consonance may be dominated by achievement motivation, and that under these circumstances dissatisfaction resulting from dissonant comparisons may be tolerated. Parenthetically, it may be pointed out that the pitting of these two motivations may partially explain why researchers have been unable to replicate some experiments that offered support for dissonance predictions (see Conlon, 1965, for example).

Relative deprivation and distributive justice, as theoretical concepts, specify some of the conditions that arouse perceptions of injustice and, complementarily, the conditions that lead men to feel that their relations with others are just. But they fail to specify theoretically what are the consequences of felt injustice, other than dissatisfaction. To be sure, Sayles (1958) mentions the use of grievance procedures and strikes to force redress, Homans (1961) cites a study by Clark (1958) in which a female employee reported slowing her pace of work as a means of establishing a more just relation with a co-worker, and Patchen (1961) gives evidence of dissonance reduction when wage comparisons are dissonant. However, these are more or less anecdotal and are not an articulated part of a theory. Men do not simply become dissatisfied with conditions they perceive to be unjust. They usually do something about them. In what follows, then, a theory will be developed that will specify both the antecedents of perceived injustice and its consequences. It is not a new theory. There are already too many "little" theories in social psychology. Rather, it builds upon the work previously described, and, in addition, derives a number of major propositions from Festinger's theory of cognitive dissonance (1957).

Inequity

In what follows it is hoped that a fairly comprehensive theory of inequity will be elaborated. The term *inequity* is used instead of *injustice* first, because the author has used this term before (Adams and Rosenbaum, 1962; Adams, 1963a,b, 1965; Adams and Jacobsen, 1964), second, to avoid the confusion of the many connotative meanings associated with the term *justice,* and third, to emphasize that the primary concern is with the causes and consequences of the absence of equity in human exchange relationships. In developing the theory, major variables affecting perceptions of inequity in an exchange will be described. A formal definition of inequity will then be proposed. From this point the effects of inequity upon behavior and cognitive processes will be discussed and research giving evidence of the effects will be presented. For heuristic purposes employee-employer exchanges will be a focus because such relations are within the experience of almost everyone and constitute a significant aspect of human intercourse. Moreover, much empirical research relating to inequity has been undertaken in business and industrial spheres or in simulated employment situations. It should be evident, however, that the theoretical notions offered are quite as relevant to any social situation in which an exchange takes place, explicitly or implicitly, whether between teammates, teacher and student, lovers, child and parent, patient and therapist, or opponents or even enemies, for between all there are expectations of what is fair exchange.

Antecedents of Inequity

Whenever two individuals exchange anything, there is the possibility that one or both of them will feel that the exchange was inequitable. Such is frequently the case when a man exchanges his services for pay. On the man's side of the exchange are his education, intelligence, experience, training, skill, seniority, age, sex, ethnic background, social status, and, of course, the effort he expends on the job. Under special circumstances other attributes will be relevant. These may be personal appearance or attractiveness, health, possession of certain tools, the characteristics of one's spouse, and so on. They are what a man perceives as his contributions to the exchange, for which he expects a just return. As noted earlier, these are the same as Homans' (1961) investments. A man brings them into an exchange, and henceforth they will be referred to as his *inputs*. These inputs, let us emphasize, are *as perceived by their contributor* and are not necessarily isomorphic with those perceived by the other party to the exchange. This suggests two conceptually distinct characteristics of inputs, *recognition* and *relevance*.

The possessor of an attribute, or the other party to the exchange, or both, may recognize the existence of the attribute in the possessor. If either the possessor or both members of the exchange recognize its existence, the attribute has the potentiality of being an input. If only the nonpossessor recognizes its existence, it cannot be considered psychologically an input so far as the possessor is concerned. Whether or not an attribute having the potential of being an input is in fact an input is contingent upon the possessor's perception of its relevance to the exchange. If he perceives it to be relevant, if he expects a just return for it, it is an input. Problems of inequity arise if only the possessor of the attribute considers it relevant to the exchange, or if the other party to the exchange considers it irrelevant and acts accordingly. Thus, unless prohibited from doing so by contract terms, an employer may consider seniority irrelevant in granting promotions, thinking it wiser to consider merit alone, whereas the employee may believe that seniority is highly relevant. In consequence, the employee may feel that injustice has been done. Conversely, the employer who is compelled to use seniority rather than merit as a promotion criterion may well feel that he has been forced into an inequitable exchange. In a personal communication Crozier (1960) made a relevant observation. Paris-born bank clerks worked side by side with clerks who did identical work and earned identical wages but who were born in the provinces. The Parisians were dissatisfied with their wages, for they considered that a Parisian upbringing was an input deserving recognition. The bank management, although recognizing that place of birth distinguished the two groups, did not, of course, consider birthplace relevant in the exchange of services for pay.

The principal inputs that have been listed vary in type and in their degree of relationship to one another. Some variables such as age are clearly continuous; others, such as sex and ethnicity, are not. Some are intercorrelated: seniority and age, for example. Sex, on the other hand, is largely independent of the other variables, with the possible exception of education and some kinds of effort. Although these intercorrelations, or the lack of them, exist in a state of nature, it is probable that the individual cognitively treats all input variables as independent. Thus, for example, if he were assessing the sum of his inputs, he might well "score" age and seniority separately. It is as if he thought, "I am older and have been with Acme longer than Joe," without taking account of the fact that the two attributes are correlated. This excursion into the "black box" should not imply, as Homans (1961) seems to imply, that men assess various components of an exchange on an ordinal scale. If the work of Jaques on equitable payment (1956, 1961a) is taken at face value, there is reason to believe in this respect that men employ interval and ratio scales, or that, at the very least, they are capable of making quite fine ordinal discriminations.

On the other side of an exchange are an individual's receipts. These *outcomes*, as they will be termed, include in an employee-employer exchange pay, rewards intrinsic to the job, satisfying supervision, seniority benefits, fringe benefits, job status and status symbols, and a variety of formally and informally sanctioned perquisites, such as the right of a higher-status person to park his car in a privileged location. These are examples of positively valent outcomes. But outcomes may have negative valence. Poor working conditions, monotony, fate uncertainty, and the many "dissatisfiers" listed by Herzberg *et al.* (1959) are no less "received" than, say, wages and are negatively valent. They would be avoided, rather than approached, if it were possible. As in the case of job inputs, job outcomes are often intercorrelated. For example, greater pay and higher job status are likely to go hand-in-hand.

In other than employee-employer exchanges, though they are not precluded from these exchanges, relevant positive outcomes for one or both parties may consist of affection, love, formal courtesies, expressions of friendship, fair value (as in merchandise), and reliability (as part of the purchase of a service). Insult, rudeness, and rejection are the other side of the coin. It may be noted that in a vast array of social relations reciprocity is a functional element of the relation. What is in fact referred to by reciprocity is equality of exchange. The infinitive "to reciprocate" is commonly used to denote an obligation to give someone equal, positively valent outcomes in return for outcomes received. When a housewife says, "John, we must have the Browns over, to reciprocate," she means to maintain a social relationship by reestablishing a parity in the outcomes of the two families. In this connection, it can be observed that reciprocation is usually "in kind." That is, there is a deliberate effort to match outcomes, to give equal value for value received. People who undershoot or overshoot the mark are called "cheapskates" or "uppish" and pretentious, respectively.

In a manner analogous to inputs, outcomes are *as perceived*, and, again, they should be characterized in terms of recognition and relevance. If the recipient or both the recipient and giver of an outcome in an exchange recognize its existence, it has the potentiality of being an outcome psychologically. If the recipient considers it relevant to the exchange and it has some marginal utility for him, it *is* an outcome. Not infrequently the giver may give or yield something which, though of some cost to him, is either irrelevant or of no marginal utility to the recipient. An employer may give an employee a carpet for his office in lieu, say, of a salary increment and find that the employee is dissatisfied, perhaps because in the subculture of that office a rug has no meaning, no psychological utility. Conversely, a salary increment may be inadequate, if formalized status recognition was what was wanted and what had greater utility. Or, in another context, the gift of a toy to a child may be effectively irrelevant as reciprocation for a demonstration of affection on his part is he seeks affection. Fortunately, in the process of socialization, through the reinforcing behavior of others and of the "verbal community" (Skinner, 1957), the human organism learns not only what is appropriate reciprocation, but he learns also to assess the marginal utility of a variety of outcomes to others. In the absence of this ability, interpersonal relations would be chaotic, if not impossible. An idea of the problems that would exist may be had by observing travelers in a foreign culture. Appropriate or relevant reciprocation of outcomes is difficult, even in such mundane exchanges as tipping for services.

In classifying some variables as inputs and others as outcomes, it is not implied that they are independent, except conceptually. Inputs and outcomes are, in fact, intercorrelated, but imperfectly so. Indeed, it is because they are imperfectly correlated that there need be concern with inequity. There exist normative expectations of what constitute "fair" correlations between inputs and outcomes. The expectations are formed—learned—during the process of socialization, at home, at school, at work. They are based by observation of the correlations obtaining for a reference person or group—a co-worker or a colleague, a relative or neighbor, a group of co-workers, a craft group, an industry-wide pattern. A bank clerk, for example, may determine whether her outcomes and inputs are fairly correlated, in balance so to speak, by comparing them with the ratio of the outcomes to the inputs of other female clerks in her section. The sole punch-press operator in a manufacturing plant may base his judgment on what he believes are the inputs and outcomes of other operators in the community or region. For a particular professor the relevant reference group may be professors in the same discipline and of the same academic "vintage." While it is clearly important to be able to specify theoretically the appropriate reference person or group, this will not be done here, as the task is beyond the scope of the paper and is discussed by others (e.g., Festinger, 1954; Hyman, 1942; Merton and Kitt, 1950; Patchen, 1961). For present purposes, it will be assumed that the reference person or group will be one comparable to the comparer on one or more attributes. This is usually a co-worker in industrial situations, according to Livernash (1953), but, as Sayles (1958) points out, this generalization requires verification, as plausible as it may appear.

When the normative expectations of the person making social comparisons are violated, when he finds that his outcomes and inputs are not in balance in relation to those of others, feelings of inequity result. But before a formal definition of inequity is offered, two terms of reference will be introduced to facilitate later discussion, *Person* and *Other*. *Person* is any individual for whom equity or inequity exists. *Other* is any individual with whom Person is in an exchange relationship, or with whom Person compares himself when both he and Other are in an exchange relationship with a third party, such as an employer, or with third parties who are considered by Person as being comparable, such as employers in a particular industry or geographic location. Other is usually a different individual, but may be Person in another job or in another social role. Thus, Other might be Person in a job he held previously, in which case he might compare his present and past outcomes and inputs and determine whether or not the exchange with his employer, present or past, was equitable. The terms Person and Other may also refer to groups rather than to individuals, as when a class of jobs (e.g., toolmakers) is out of line with another class (e.g., lathe operators), or when the circumstances of one ethnic group are incongruous with those of another. In such cases, it is convenient to deal with the class as a whole rather than with individual members of the class.

Definition of Inequity

Inequity exists for Person whenever he perceives that the ratio of his outcomes to inputs and the ratio of Other's outcomes to Other's inputs are unequal. This may happen either (a) when he and Other are in a direct exchange relationship or (b) when both are in an exchange relationship with a third party and Person compares himself to Other. The values of outcomes and inputs are, of course, as perceived by Person. Schematically, inequality is experienced when either

$$\frac{O_p}{I_p} < \frac{O_a}{I_a} \quad \text{or} \quad \frac{O_p}{I_p} > \frac{O_a}{I_a},$$

Where $O = \Sigma_{oi}$, $I = \Sigma_{oi}$ and p and a are subscripts denoting Person and Other, respectively. A condition of equity exists when

$$\frac{O_p}{I_p} = \frac{O_a}{I_a}.$$

The outcomes and inputs in each of the ratios are conceived as being the sum of such outcomes and inputs as are perceived to be relevant to a particular exchange. Furthermore, each sum is conceived of as a weighted sum, on the assumption that individuals probably do not weight elemental outcomes or inputs equally. The work of Herzberg *et al.* (1959) on job "satisfiers" and "dissatisfiers" implies strongly that different outcomes, as they are labeled here, have widely varying utilities, negative as well as positive. It also appears reasonable to assume that inputs as diverse as seniority, skill, effort, and sex are not weighted equally. Zaleznik *et al.* (1958), in attempting to test some predictions from distributive justice theory in an industrial corporation, gave equal weight to five factors which correspond to inputs as defined here—age, seniority, education, ethnicity, and sex—but were unable to sustain their hypotheses. In retrospect, they believe (Zaleznik *et al.*, 1958) that weighting these inputs equally may have represented an inadequate assumption of the manner in which their respondents summed their inputs.

From the definition of inequity it follows that inequity results for Person not only when he is, so to speak, relatively underpaid, but also when he is relatively overpaid. Person, will, for example, feel inequity exists not only when his effort is high and his pay low, while Other's effort and pay are high, but also when his effort is low and his pay high, while Other's effort and pay are low. This proposition receives direct support from experiments by Adams and Rosenbaum (1962), Adams (1963a), and Adams and Jacobsen (1964) in which subjects were inequitably overpaid. It receives some support also from an observation by Thibaut (1950) that subjects in whose favor the experimenter discriminated displayed "guilty smirks" and "sheepishness." The magnitude of the inequity experienced will be a monotomically increasing function of the size of the discrepancy between the ratios of outcomes to inputs. The discrepancy will be zero, and equity will exist, under two circumstances: first, when Person's and Other's outcomes are equal and their inputs are equal. This would be the case, for example, when Person perceived that Other's wages, job, and working conditions were the same as his and that Other was equal to him on such relevant dimensions as sex, skill, seniority, education, age, effort expended, physical fitness, and risk incurred (risk of personal injury, of being fired for errors committed, for instance). Secondly, the ratios will be equal when Person perceives that Other's outcomes are higher (or lower) than his and that Other's inputs are correspondingly higher (or lower). A subordinate who compares himself to his supervisor or work group leader typically does not feel that he is unjustly treated by the company that employs them both, because the supervisor's greater monetary compensation, better working conditions, and more interesting, more varied job are matched on the input side of the ratio by more education, wider range of skills, greater responsibility and personal risk, more maturity and experience, and longer service.

Although there is no direct, reliable evidence on this point, it is probable, as Homans (1961) conjectured, that the thresholds for inequity are different (in absolute terms from a base of equity) in cases of under- and overreward. The threshold would be higher presumably in cases of overreward, for a certain amount of incongruity in these cases can be acceptably rationalized as "good fortune" without attendant discomfort. In his work on pay differentials, Jaques (1961b) notes that in instances of undercompensation, British workers paid 10% less than the equitable level show "an active sense of grievance, complaints or the desire to complain, and, if no redress is given, an active desire to change jobs, or to take action . . ." (p. 26). In cases of overcompensation, he observes that at the 10 to 15% level above equity "there is a strong sense of receiving preferential treatment, which may harden into bravado, with underlying feelings of unease . . ." (p. 26). He states further, "The results suggest that it is not necessarily the case that each one is simply out to get as much as he can for his work. There appear to be equally strong desires that each one should earn the right amount—a fair and reasonable amount relative to others" (p. 26).

In the preceding discussion, Person has been the focus of attention. It should be clear, however, that when Person and Other are in an exchange interaction, Other will suffer inequity if Person does, but the nature of his experience will be opposite to Person, it will be favorable to Other, and vice versa. This will hold provided Person's and Other's perceptions of outcomes and inputs are equivalent and provided that the outcome-input ratio discrepancy attains threshold level. When Person and Other are not engaged in an exchange with one another but stand in an exchange relationship with a third party, Other may or may not experience inequity when Person does. Given the prerequisites mentioned above, he will experience inequity if he compares himself to Person with respect to the same question as induces Person to use Other as a referent (e.g., "Am I being paid fairly?").

Consequences of Inequity

Although there can be little doubt that inequity results in dissatisfaction, in an unpleasant emotional state, be it anger or guilt, there will be other effects. A major purpose of this paper is to specify these in terms that permit specific predictions to be made. Before turning to this task, two general postulates are presented, closely following propositions from cognitive dissonance theory (Festinger, 1957). First, the presence of inequity in Person creates tension in him. The tension is proportional to the magnitude of inequity present. Second, the tension created in Person will motivate him to eliminate or reduce it. The strength of the motivation is proportional to the tension created. In short, the presence of inequity will motivate Person to achieve equity or to reduce inequity, and the strength of motivation to do so will vary directly with the magnitude of inequity experienced. From these postulates and from the theory of cognitive dissonance (Festinger, 1957; Brehm and Cohen, 1962), means of reducing inequity will be derived and presented. As each method of reduction is discussed, evidence demonstrating usage of the method will be presented. Some of the evidence is experimental; some of it is the result of field studies, either of a survey or observational character.

1. Person Altering His Inputs. Person may vary his inputs, either increasing them or decreasing them, depending on whether the inequity is advantageous or disadvantageous. Increasing inputs will reduce felt inequity, if

$$\frac{O_p}{I_p} > \frac{O_a}{I_a}$$

conversely, decreasing inputs will be effective, if

$$\frac{O_p}{I_p} < \frac{O_a}{I_a} .$$

In the former instance, Person might increase either his productivity or the quality of his work, provided that it is possible, which is not always the case. In the second instance, Person might engage in "production restriction," for example. Whether Person does, or can, reduce inequity by altering his inputs is partially contingent upon whether relevant inputs are susceptible to change. Sex, age, seniority, and ethnicity are not modifiable. Education and skill are more easily altered, but changing these requires time. Varying inputs will also be a function of Person's perception of the principal "cause" of the inequity. If the discrepancy between outcome-input ratios is primarily a function of his inputs being at variance with those of Other, Person is more likely to alter them than if the discrepancy is largely a result of differences in outcomes. Additionally, it is postulated that given equal opportunity to alter inputs and outcomes, Person will be more likely to lower his inputs when

$$\frac{O_p}{I_p} < \frac{O_a}{I_a}$$

than he is to increase his inputs when

$$\frac{O_p}{I_p} > \frac{O_a}{I_a} .$$

This is derived from two assumptions: first, the assumption stated earlier that the threshold for the perception of inequity is higher when Person is overrewarded than when he is underrewarded; secondly, the assumption that Person is motivated to minimize his costs and to maximize his gains. By the second assumption, Person will reduce inequity, insofar as possible, in a manner that will yield him the largest outcomes.

Altering certain inputs has the corollary effect of altering the outcomes of Other. A change in the quality and amount of work performed, for instance, will usually affect the outcomes of Other. When this is the case, the effect of both changes will operate in the same direction in the service of inequity reduction. It follows, therefore, that *less* a change in inputs is required to eliminate inequity than if the change had no effect on Other's outcomes. Inputs, a change in which would have no or very little impact on Other's outcomes, are attributes such as education, age, and seniority—at least to the extent that they are uncorrelated with performance. . . .

Person Altering His Outcomes. Person may vary his outcomes, either decreasing or increasing them, depending on whether the inequity is advantageous or disadvantageous to him. Increasing outcomes will reduce inequity, if

$$\frac{O_p}{I_p} < \frac{O_a}{I_a}$$

conversely, decreasing outcomes will serve the same function, if

$$\frac{O_p}{I_p} > \frac{O_a}{I_a}.$$

Of these two possibilities, the second is far less likely, and there is no good evidence of the use of this means of reducing inequity, though some may be available in the clinical literature. There are, however, data bearing on attempts to increase outcomes, data other than those related to wage increase demands in union-management negotiations, probably only a part of which are directly traceable to wage inequities. . . .

Person Distorting His Inputs and Outcomes Cognitively. Person may cognitively distort his inputs and outcomes, the direction of the distortion being the same as if he had actually altered his inputs and outcomes, as discussed above. Since most individuals are heavily influenced by reality, substantial distortion is generally difficult. It is pretty difficult to distort to oneself, to change one's cognitions about the fact, for example, that one has a BA degree, that one has been an accountant for seven years, and that one's salary is $700 per month. However, it is possible, within limits, to alter the utility of these. For example, State College is a small backwoods school with no reputation, or, alternatively, State College has one of the best business schools in the state and the dean is an adviser to the Bureau of the Budget. Or, one can consider the fact that $700 per month will buy all of the essential things of life and a few luxuries, or, conversely, that it will never permit one to purchase a Wyeth oil painting or an Aston Martin DB5. There is ample evidence in the psychological literature, especially that related to cognitive dissonance theory, that individuals do modify or rearrange their cognitions in an effort to reduce perceived incongruities (for a review, see Brehm and Cohen, 1962). Since it has been postulated that the experience of inequity is equivalent to the experience of dissonance, it is reasonable to believe that cognitive distortion may be adopted as a means of reducing inequity. In a variety of work situations, for example in paced production line jobs, actually altering one's inputs and outcomes may be difficult; as a consequence these may be cognitively changed in relatively subtle ways.

Although not a cognitive change in inputs and outcomes per se, related methods of reducing inequity are for Person to alter the *importance* and the *relevance* of his inputs and outcomes. If, for example, age were a relevant input, its relative importance could be changed to bring about less perceived inequity. Person could convince himself that age was either more or less important than he thought originally. In terms of the statement made earlier that net inputs (and outcomes) were a weighted sum of inputs, changing the importance of inputs would be equivalent to changing the weights associated with them. Altering the relevance of inputs and outcomes is conceived of as more of an all-or-none process: Present ones are made irrelevant or new ones are made relevant. For instance, if Person perceived that the discrepancy between his and Other's outcome-input ratios were principally a result of his outcomes being too low, he might become "aware" of one or more outcomes he had not recognized as being relevant before, perhaps that his job had variety absent from Other's job. Obviously, importance and relevance of inputs and outcomes are not completely independent. An outcome suddenly perceived as being relevant automatically assumes some importance; conversely, one that is made irrelevant in the service of inequity reduction assumes an importance of zero. Nevertheless, the psychological processes appear to be different and it is useful, therefore, to keep them conceptually distinct. . . .

Person Leaving the Field. Leaving the field may take any of several ways of severing social relationships. Quitting a job, obtaining a transfer, and absenteeism are common forms of leaving the field in an employment situation. These are fairly radical means of coping with inequity. The probability of using them is assumed to increase with magnitude of inequity and to decrease with the availability of other means. . . .

Person Acting on Other. In the face of injustice, Person may attempt to alter or cognitively distort Other's inputs and outcomes, or try to force Other to leave the field. These means of reducing inequity vary in the ease of their use. Getting Other to accept greater outcomes, which was a possible interpretation of some of the findings by Leventhal *et al.* (1964), would obviously be easier than the opposite. Similarly, inducing Other to lower his inputs may be easier than the reverse. For example, all other things being equal, such as work group cohesiveness and the needs and ability of an individual worker, it is probably easier to induce a "rate buster" to lower his inputs than to get a laggard to increase them. The direction of the change attempted in the inputs and outcomes of Other is the reverse of the change that Person would make in his own inputs and outcomes, whether the change be actual or cognitive. By way of illustration, if Person experienced feelings of inequity because he lacked job experience compared to Other, he could try to induce Other to decrease a relevant input instead of increasing his own inputs. . . .

Person Changing the Object of His Comparison. Person may change Other with whom he compares himself when he experiences inequity and he and Other stand in an exchange relationship with a third party. This mode is limited to the relationship specified; it is not applicable when Person and Other are in a direct exchange. Changing the object of comparison in the latter situation would reduce to severing the relationship.

The resolution of inequity by changing comparison object is undoubtedly difficult of accomplishment, particularly if Person has been comparing himself to Other for some time. Person would need to be able to make himself noncomparable to Other on one or more dimensions. For instance, if Other, whose outcome-input ratio was previously equal to Person's received a salary increase without any apparent increment in inputs, Person could try to reduce the resulting feeling of inequity by conceiving of Other as belonging now to a different organizational level. But this would likely meet with little success, at least in this culture. A cognitive change of this sort would be extremely unstable, unless it were accompanied by changes in the perception of Other's inputs: for instance, that Other had assumed greater responsibility when his salary was increased. But this involves a process of inequity reduction already referred to. . . .

Choice among Modes of Inequity Reduction. Although reference has been made previously to conditions that may affect the use of one or another method of reducing inequity, there is need for a general statement of conditions that will govern the adoption of one method over another. Given the existence of inequity, any of the means of reduction described earlier are potentially available to Person. He may alter or attempt to alter any of the four terms in the inequality formula or change his cognitions about any of them, or he may leave the field and change his comparison Other, but it is improbable that each of the methods are equally available to him *psychologically* (no reference is made to environmental constraints that may affect the availability of methods), as the work of Steiner and his colleagues on alternative methods of dissonance reduction suggests (Steiner, 1960; Steiner and Johnson, 1964; Steiner and Peters, 1958; Steiner and Rogers, 1963).

Set forth below are some propositions about conditions determining the choice of modes by person. As will be noted, the propositions are not all independent of one another, and each should be prefaced by the condition, *ceteris paribus*.

(a) Person will maximize positively valent outcomes and the valence of outcomes.

(b) He will minimize increasing inputs that are effortful and costly to change.

(c) He will resist real and cognitive changes in inputs that are central to his self-concept and to his self-esteem. To the extent that any of Person's outcomes are related to his self-concept and to his self-esteem, this proposition is extended to cover his outcomes.

(d) He will be more resistant to changing cognitions about his own outcomes and inputs than to changing his cognitions about Other's outcomes and inputs.

(e) Leaving the field will be resorted to only when the magnitude of inequity experienced is high and other means of reducing it are unavailable. Partial withdrawal, such as absenteeism, will occur more frequently and under conditions of lower inequity.

(*f*) Person will be highly resistant to changing the object of his comparisons, Other, once it has stabilized over time and, in effect, has become an anchor.

These propositions are, admittedly, fairly crude, but they permit, nevertheless, a degree of prediction not available otherwise. In the resolution of a particular injustice, two or more of the processes proposed may be pitted one against the other. To propose which would be dominant is not possible at this stage of the development of the theory. One might propose that protection of self-esteem would dominate maximization of outcomes, but it would be conjecture in the absence of evidence.

Conclusion

Dissatisfaction is both so commonplace and such an irritant, particularly in industrial and other large organizations, that it has been the subject of widespread research (see Vroom, 1964, for a . . . thorough review). Despite prima facie evidence that feelings of injustice underlay a significant proportion of cases of dissatisfaction, thorough behavioral analyses of injustice were not made until recently. In the classic Hawthorne studies (Roethlisberger and Dickson, 1939), there was ample evidence that much of the dissatisfaction observed among Western Electric Company employees was precipitated by felt injustice. Describing complaints, the authors referred frequently to reports by workers that wages were not in keeping with seniority, that rates were too low, that ability was not rewarded, and the like, as distinguished from reports that, for example, equipment was not working and that the workshop was hot. They stated that "no physical or logical operations exist which can be agreed upon as defining them" (p. 259), and they sought "personal or social situations" (p. 269) that would explain the complaints parsimoniously. Yet, the notion of injustice was not advanced as an explanatory concept.

It is not contended here, of course, that all dissatisfaction and low morale are related to a person's suffering injustice in social exchanges. But it should be clear from the research described that a significant portion of cases can be usefully explained by invoking injustice as an explanatory concept. More importantly, much more than dissatisfaction may be predicted once the concept of injustice is analyzed theoretically. . . .

The need for much additional research notwithstanding, the theoretical analyses that have been made of injustice in social exchanges should result not only in a better general understanding of the phenomenon, but should lead to a degree of social control not previously possible. The experience of injustice need not be an accepted fact of life.

References

Adams, J. S. (1961). Wage inequities in a clerical task. Unpublished study. General Electric Company, New York.

Adams J. S. (1963a). Toward an understanding of inequity. *J. abnorm. soc. Psychol.* 67, 422-436.

Adams, J. S. (1936b). Wage inequities, productivity, and work quality. *Industr. Relat.* 3, 9-16.

Adams, J. S. (1965). Etudes expérimentales en matière d'inégalités de salaires, de productivité et de qualité du travail. *Synopsis* 7, 25-34.

Adams, J. S., and Jacobsen, Patricia R. (1964). Effects of wage inequities on work quality. *J. abnorm. soc. Psychol.* 69, 19-25.

Adams, J. S., and Rosenbaum, W. B. (1962). The relationship of worker productivity to cognitive dissonance about wage inequities. *J. appl. Psychol.* 46, 161-164.

Arrowood, A. J. (1961). Some effects on productivity of justified and unjustified levels of reward under public and private conditions. Unpublished doctoral disseration (Dep. Psychol.), Univer. of Minnesota.

Blau, P. (1964). *Exchange and power in social life.* New York: Wiley.

Bramel, D. (1962). A dissonance theory approach to defensive projection. *J. abnorm. soc. Psychol.* 64, 121-129.

Brehm, J. W., and Cohen, A. R. (1962). *Explorations in cognitive dissonance.* New York: Wiley.

Clark, J. V. (1958). A preliminary investigation of some unconscious assumptions affecting labor efficiency in eight supermarkets. Unpublished doctoral dissertation (Grad. Sch. Business Admin.), Harvard Univer.

Conlon, Elizabeth T. (1965). Performance as determined by expectation of success and failure. Unpublished doctoral dissertation (Dep. Social Psychol.), Columbia Univer.

Crozier, M. (1960). Personal communication to the author.

Festinger, L. (1954). A theory of social comparison processes. *Hum. Relat.* 7, 117-140.

Festinger, L. (1957). *A theory of cognitive dissonance.* Evanston, Ill.: Row, Peterson.

Gebhard, Mildred E. (1949). Changes in the attractiveness of activities: the effect of expectation preceding performance. *J. exp. Psychol.* 39, 404-413.

Herzberg, F., Mausner, B., and Snyderman, Barbara B. (1959). *The motivation to work.* New York: Wiley.

Homans, G. C. (1950). *The human group.* New York: Harcourt, Brace.

Homans, G. C. (1963). Status among clerical workers. *Hum. Organiz.* 12, 5-10.

Homans, G. C. (1961). *Social behavior: its elementary forms.* New York: Harcourt, Brace.

Hyman, H. (1942). The psychology on status. *Arch. Psychol.* 38, No. 269.

Jaques, E. (1956). *Measurement of responsibility.* London: Tavistock.

Jaques, E. (1961a). *Equitable payment.* New York: Wiley.

Jaques, E. (1961b). An objective approach to pay differentials. *Time Motion Study* 10, 25-28.

Leventhal, G., Reilly, Ellen, and Lehrer, P. (1964). Change in reward as a determinant of satisfaction and reward expectancy. Paper read at West. Psychol. Assoc. Portland, Ore.

Livernash, E. R. (1953). Job evaluation. In W. S. Woytinsky *et al.* (Eds.), *Employment and wages in the United States.* New York: Twentieth Century Fund, pp. 427-435.

Merton, R. K., and Kitt, Alice S. (1950). Contributions to the theory of reference group behavior. In *Continuities in social research.* R. K. Merton and P. F. Lazarsfeld (Eds.), Glencoe, Ill.: Free Press, pp. 40-105.

Newcomb, T. M. (1943). *Personality and social change: attitude formation in a student community.* New York: Dryden.

Patchen, M. (1959). Study of work and life satisfaction, Report No. II: Absences and attitudes toward work experience. Inst. for Social Res., Ann Arbor, Mich.

Patchen, M. (1961). *The choice of wage comparison.* Englewood Cliffs, N.J.: Prentice-Hall.

Pilisuk, M. (1962). Cognitive balance and self-relevant attitudes. *J. abnorm. soc. Psychol.* 65, 95-103.

Roethlisberger, F. J., and Dickson, W. J. (1939). *Management and the worker.* Cambridge, Mass.: Harvard Univer. Press.

Sayles, L. R. (1958). *Behavior of industrial work groups: prediction and control.* New York: Wiley.

Skinner, B. F. (1957). *Verbal behavior.* New York: Appleton.

Spector, A. J. (1956). Expectations, fulfillment, and morale. *J. abnorm. soc. Psychol.* 52, 51-56.

Steiner, I. D. (1960). Sex differences in the resolution of A-B-X conflicts. *J. Pers.* 28, 118-128.

Steiner, I. D. and Johnson, H. H. (1964). Relationships among dissonance reducing responses. *J. abnorm. soc. Psychol.* 68, 38-44.

Steiner, I. D., and Peters, S. C. (1958). Conformity and the A-B-X model. *J. Pers.* 26, 229-242.

Steiner, I. D., and Rogers, E. D. (1963). Alternative responses to dissonance. *J. abnorm. soc. Psychol.* 66, 128-136.

Stouffer, S. A., Suchman, E. A., DeVinney, L. C., Starr, Shirley A., and Williams R. M., Jr. (1949). *The American soldier: adjustment during army life.* Vol. 1. Princeton, N. J.: Princeton Univer. Press.

Thibaut, J. (1950). An experimental study of the cohesiveness of underprivileged groups. *Hum. Relat.* 3, 251-278.

Thibaut, J. W., and Kelley, H. H. (1959). *The social psychology of groups.* New York: Wiley.

Vroom, V. H. (1964). *Work and motivation.* New York: Wiley.

Weick, K. E. (1964). Reduction of cognitive dissonance through task enhancement and effort expenditure. *J. abnorm. soc. Psychol.* 66, 533-539.

Zaleznik, A., Christensen, C. R., and Roethlisberger, F. J. (1958). The motivation, productivity, and satisfaction of workers. A prediction study (Grad. Sch. Business Admin.) Harvard Univer.

EXPLAINING INFORMAL WORK GROUPS IN COMPLEX ORGANIZATIONS: THE CASE FOR AUTONOMY IN STRUCTURE

FRED E. KATZ

A generation after the Hawthorne studies, no one questions the existence of informal groups in complex organizations. Numerous studies have documented their existence, especially among employees in the lowest ranks. But the task remains

Reprinted by permission of the author and the publisher from *Administrative Science Quarterly*, vol. 10, no. 2 (Sept. 1965), pp. 204-21.

of developing an adequate *conceptual* explanation of how persons in the lowest ranks, with their limited career prospects in their work and slight opportunity for advancement, are incorporated into work organizations on a relatively permanent basis. Stated differently, how can one account for the integration of organizations that include a large number of persons who are largely disenfranchised from the organization's reward system? How can one account for the apparent collaboration, if not loyalty, of persons who, since the time of Marx, have been described as being alienated from their work?[1] A brief, though oversimplified answer is that workers need work and factories need workers. One can hardly argue with this statement. Yet, the economic interdependence of workers and factories does not clarify the nature of the structural arrangement under which the interdependence is worked out.

The proposed answer to the question of how workers are incorporated into complex organizations has two aspects: (1) Workers have considerable autonomy within the confines of the organization. Even when their work is prescribed in exact detail, the work role tends to be defined narrowly. This leaves a considerable portion of the worker's life within the work organization *undefined*. (2) Workers tend to use this autonomy to bring their working-class culture into the organization, even though this is alien to the bureaucratic ethos of the higher echelons of the organization. This produces continuity between the workman's outside life and his participation in the work setting—a setting to which he has very limited allegiance.[2] This continuity in turn, promotes worker's integration into work organizations. After a general presentation of this perspective, it is illustrated through a detailed review of one of Donald Roy's case studies of factory workers. No attempt will be made to assess the degree of fit of this perspective to particular types of industries.

The guiding perspective is that the culture of informal work groups is a manifestation of autonomy within the confines of the organization, and that autonomy is an aspect of organizational structure that needs systematic study. Autonomy is defined as independence from external control. Here, it means that the activities of workers within the organization are not fully controlled by the organization. This leaves room for development of informal patterns of various sorts—those that lessen boredom of workers, those that help get work done, as well as those that are alienative to the organization. I shall attempt to view autonomy as an aspect of the very structure of organizations, as spheres of independence which are delegated by the organization. Direct and indirect delegation of autonomy suggest themselves. The first refers to specific rules that delimit an area of autonomy. For example, a rule specifying that the foreman can decide who will work the night shift indicates a sphere in which the foreman has autonomy, one in which he exercises discretion. By contrast indirect delegation of autonomy results from the absence of rules; in a sphere where no clear rules exist, autonomy exists by default. Both direct and indirect delegation of autonomy promotes spheres of activity that are not closely controlled by the organization. The present thesis is that the resulting autonomous behavior needs to be considered as an aspect of organizational structure, not merely as deviance. This paper will mainly examine autonomy based on indirect delegation, since this seems to characterize informal patterns among workers.

Worker autonomy can be regarded as part of the barter arrangement between workers and the organization, where limited affiliation with the organization is exchanged for a degree of autonomy. The arrangement has important adaptive functions for both parties. For the organization it is a way of promoting the affiliation of some of its employees with the organization, while at the same time excluding them from certain vital spheres of organizational activity. For workers it permits continuation of the working-class style of life and provides ties of sociability in a context that in many ways is alien to the workman's culture. In short, the autonomy appears to have adaptive and pattern-maintenance functions for the workers, and adaptive and goal-attainment functions for the organization. It must be noted that worker autonomy, although enacted *in* the work organization is essentially *external* to his work role. This contrasts with the autonomy pattern for white collar workers, that is, all those who—from the lowliest clerk to the president—make up the administrative hierarchy. They have greater autonomy *within* their work role, but their role is more broadly defined than that of the worker.[3] In a sense the white-collar worker takes his work role *outside* the organization; the blue-collar worker brings his non-work role *into* the organization.

This use of the term "autonomy" covers part of the same ground that is now covered by the term "informal organization"; but I hope it will eliminate some of the difficulties that exist in the way informal organization is now distinguished from formal organization. Simon and his colleagues summarize the existing distinction.[4] Formal organization is defined as "a planned system of cooperative effort in which each participant has a recognized role to play and duties or tasks to perform."[5] Informal organization is defined as "the whole pattern of actual behavior—the way members of the organization really do behave—insofar as these actual behaviors do not coincide with the formal plan."[6] One reason for questioning this distinction is that it has led to research strategies that appear to have produced a self-fulfilling prophecy by inadvertently reiterating the contention that informal patterns deviate from the planned system, without subjecting this contention to critical analysis. It comes about somewhat as follows: The official rules do not prescribe informal behavior patterns; therefore, informal behavior must be discovered through direct, detailed investigation—usually by direct observation of ongoing behavior. Direct observation is very likely to emphasize actual behavior rather than abstract rules, collaboration on the local level rather than collaboration with the total organization, innovation and departure from rules rather than compliance. All these artifacts of the research process are conducive to perpetuating the initial contention that informal patterns deviate from the planned system. As a result, despite evidence that informal patterns may be very firmly established within an organization,[7] the view persists that informal patterns lack legitimacy and permanence. If the behavior patterns that are relevant to formal structure were subjected to detailed observational scrutiny, one might well discover a picture far closer to so-called informal patterns than we now have.[8]

The definition of formal organization focuses on a planned system, and the definition of informal organization on actual behavior. This is a weak distinction, theoretically. Actual behavior is undoubtedly relevant to planned systems; and system characteristics, even planned ones, are relevant to actual behavior. The distinction seems to need refocusing to enable orderly analysis of structure and ongoing behavior. I would suggest the following perspective: Organizational structure includes relatively controlled and relatively autonomous spheres. The controlled sphere is based on direct specification of behavior; the autonomous sphere is based on both direct and indirect specification of behavior. Direct specification of behavior approximates the formal organization concept; but it allows spheres of autonomy as well as spheres of controlled activity. The indirect specification of behavior approximates the traditional informal organization, but under comparable conceptual footing with the planned formal system.

The writings of Chester Barnard illustrate that autonomous and controlled behavior coexist within organizations and that the executive must fuse them together.[9] He notes that autonomy among personnel is not necessarily a disaster to executive control but may, in fact, be an asset to administrative processes. He suggests that the executive must rely on the "willingness to serve"[10] of those under his command; he must recognize that there is a "zone of indifference"[11] in which persons are prepared to accept orders, and beyond which they are prone to oppose orders. Informal patterns, in Barnard's view of the executive, are not divisive forces, but instead, are "expansion of the means of communication with reduction in the necessity for formal decisions, the minimizing of undesirable influences, and the promotion of desirable influences concordant with the scheme of formal responsibilities."[12] From Barnard's perspective both formal and informal patterns can be harnessed in the service of a "co-operating system." But it seems that the real point is not the blending of formally and informally organized behavior, but the blending of controlled and autonomous behaviors that exist within organizations. Barnard's model of the organization is suffused with autonomy patterns that can serve the whole organization; some of these patterns proceed from direct official specification of behavior and some come from indirect specification.

The Worker's Place in the Organization

Workers are here viewed as being permitted to develop relatively autonomous subcultures and subsystems of social interaction in their day-to-day routines. The autonomous patterns diverge from the officially prescribed patterns, but are very much in line with the workman's style of life and culture outside the organization. The culture of the working-class man is in many ways alien to the decorum and demeanor expected of white-collar members of the organization. In the routinized work of the white-collar worker there is no room for the sudden display of anger of the working-class male; in the face-the-public white-collar worker there is little scope for the pervasive sexual allusions of the working-class male. Yet within the working clique inside the organization the workman can enact the culture patterns of his life outside the organization. He can, for example, indulge freely in what is perhaps the workman's major form of creative mental activity: verbal play, imaginative exploits, and the romanticism on the theme of sex.[13] Indeed, the workman has a large sphere of verbal freedom, since much of what he says "doesn't count," so far as his work is concerned. Unlike the white-collar worker, whose work consists of a world of words, written and spoken, the worker is basically measured by the contributions of his hands. Therefore, his verbal jostlings, such as the razzing of the lowest person on the prestige totem pole, are not considered part of his job. There is every indication (as is shown in the review of the study by Donald Roy), that the content of the verbal banter contains reference to the work-man's niche in the social order and the conditions of his social existence.[14] These are also reflected in patterns of practical jokes and prankish physical contact, which are characteristic of the workman's culture, but taboo in the culture of the white-collar worker.[15]

By contrast, the white-collar workers, whether senior executive or junior administrators, have a broad affinity for the organizational style of behavior. They are likely to be members of the middle or upper class, where they have learned the demeanor and proprieties of manner they will be expected to exercise in their position in the organization.[16] There is little abrupt discontinuity, for instance, between the style of dress and speech of their social class and that associated with the bureaucratic style of behavior. Stated differently, they can carry over elements of their external life into the organization and apply them to their job without having to make fundamental adjustments in their general style of behavior; although this does not mean that they have nothing to learn in their work. The organization-man thesis makes the same point in converse terms: The work habits and interests of the white-collar worker spill over into his family and community life. For the white-collar worker, the organization is less clearly differentiated from the culture of his private world than it is from the private world of the worker; the organization is not the enemy camp. The blue-collar worker, on the other hand, is eager to leave his work behind him as he leaves the gates of the factory.[17]

How does autonomy in the role of white-collar worker differ from that of the worker? Briefly stated, white-collar workers have greater autonomy *in their task-related activities* than does the blue-collar worker: the time clock; the regimentation involved in feeding a machine and gearing one's work to the pace of a machine, of doing one's work exclusively at the location of a particular machine—these apply to the blue-collar worker to a far larger extent than to the white-collar worker. For the latter, work is defined more broadly than it is for the blue-collar worker, requiring a more diffuse commitment. This means that for the white-collar worker a broad range of activities and personal attributes are defined as relevant to work, from personal grooming to getting along with others. Organizing a Little League baseball team, the fate of the local community chest drive, and participation in college alumni affairs—a good organization man's allegiance to the organization and his style of work include taking part in these activities after working hours and communicating these interests to his work peers. It is difficult to assess which activities are regarded as clearly *external* to his work role. On the other hand, the worker's tasks are defined more narrowly, leaving scope for activity that is defined as *external* to his work, but enacted while he is at his place of work.

The limited bases for the worker's *allegiance* to the work organization are given tacit recognition not only in the worker being excluded from administrative decision making, but also in his being allowed to bring into the work setting working-class culture patterns and to fashion them into relatively autonomous subcultures. In short, the worker's external affiliations; i.e., with the working-class style of life, are permitted to intrude into the organization that employs him. This can be viewed as part of the exchange (in addition to monetary pay) for limited forms of reward and participation that the worker is allowed by the employing organization. In view of the differentiation between worker subculture and bureaucratic culture, the worker's immersion in working-class patterns may serve to perpetuate his disenfranchisement from the administrative sphere, resulting in a vicious cycle.

The pattern pictured thus far of workers in relation to factory is chiefly characteristic of the modern western world. A contrasting example exists in the Japanese pattern, where the worker is expected to make a lifetime commitment to one firm.[18] The worker does not expect to leave his initial place of employment—the idea of moving to a better job seems highly incongruous. The firm does not intend to dismiss employees, no matter how uneconomical this may prove to be. In this arrangement the worker's affiliation with the firm is a relatively complete one, and there appears to be little external autonomy.

Enactment of Worker Autonomy: An Example

The empirical study of workers in factories has been a favorite of sociologists and social psychologists. The focus of many of these studies is on what actually goes on in work settings. Among the most eloquently descriptive studies of the culture and interaction patterns of workers are those by Donald F. Roy. One of his studies, his "Banana Time," will therefore be examined at some length.[19] Roy describes a small work group of men engaged in exceedingly simple manual work operating a punch press—it took about fifteen minutes to learn the job. Roy himself participated, and his description bears the mark of intimate immersion in the field situation while, at the same time, bringing to it keen observational skills. He describes how he attempted, during the early days of work, to meet the problems of great boredom by inventing little games. He partly succeeded. After a while he noticed that the banterings and "kidding" by the workers around him were not purely haphazard, but actually served a similar function as his games; they, too, reduced boredom. Following this insight he made systematic studies and discovered *patterns* among the bantering and joking.

> What I saw at first, before I began to observe, was occasional flurries of horse play so simple and unvarying in pattern and so childish in quality that they made no strong bid for attention. For example, Ike would regularly switch off the power at Sammy's machine whenever Sammy made a trip to the lavatory or the drinking fountain. Correlatively, Sammy invariably fell victim to the plot by making an attempt to operate his clicking hammer after returning to the shop. And, as the simple pattern went, this blind stumbling into the trap was always followed by indignation and reproach from Sammy, smirking satisfaction from Ike, and mild paternal scolding from George. My interest in this procedure was at first confined to wondering when Ike would weary of his tedious joke or when Sammy would learn to check his power switch before trying the hammer.
>
> But, as I began to pay closer attention, as I began to develop familiarity with the communication system, the disconnected became connected, the nonsense made sense, the obscure became clear, and the silly actually funny. And, as the content of the interaction took on more and more meaning, the interaction began to reveal structure.[20]

Roy discovered that the day's routine was broken by activities other than those formally instituted (by the company) or "idiosyncratically developed disjunctions," but were an "ordered series of informal interactions." He describes many forms of interruption that took place and the patterning involved in them. One of these was "peach time," when one worker, Sammy, provided a peach and shared it. His beneficiaries greeted his contribution with disgruntlement and complaints about the quality of the peach. "Banana time" followed.

> Banana time followed peach time by approximately an hour. Sammy again provided the refreshments, namely, one banana. There was, however, no four-way sharing of Sammy's banana. Ike would gulp it down by himself after surreptitiously extracting it from Sammy's lunch box, kept on a shelf behind Sammy's work station. Each morning, after making the snatch, Ike would call out, "Banana time!" and proceed to down his prize, while Sammy made futile protests and denunciations. George would join in with mild remonstrances, sometimes scolding Sammy for making so much fuss. The banana was one which Sammy brought for his own consumption at lunch time; he never did get to eat his banana, but kept bringing one for his lunch. At first this daily theft startled and amazed me. Then I grew to look forward to the daily seizure and the verbal interaction that followed.[21]

In addition to peach time and banana time there was coffee time, fish time, coke time, lunch time, and window-opening time. Each of them was marked by a distinctive pattern of interaction. In addition to these patterned times, Roy notes themes in verbal interplay.

> The themes had become standardized in their repetition . . . topics of conversation ranged in quality from an extreme of nonsensical chatter to another extreme of serious discourse. Unlike the times, these themes flowed one into the other in no particular sequence of predictability. Serious conversation could suddenly melt into horse play, and vice versa. In the middle of a serious discussion on the high cost of living, Ike might drop a weight behind the easily startled Sammy, or hit him over the head with a dusty paper sack. Interaction would immediately drop to a low comedy exchange of slaps, threats, guffaws, and disapprobations. . . .[22]

In this verbal interplay exaggeration was a common feature. For instance, one of the men had received one hundred dollars from his son; from that day he was seen as a man with a sizable, steady income—a man ready to retire. Roy, after having admitted that he owned two acres of land, became a large landowner, and his farm became populated with horses, cows, pigs, and chickens. Sexuality also came in for a large share of regular and inventive verbal play.

Roy's article is perhaps a culmination in a series of research findings that, since the days of the Hawthorne studies, have pointed to the demise of the economic man without, however, completing the task of making social organization the focus of analysis. The early studies, in their opposition to the economic-man thesis, pointed out that the individual was not guided only by his own monetary self-interest. Indeed, he could be guided against his own self-interest by his worker peer group; the individual worker might actually lose income by following the output control patterns of his peers. It was emphasized that there was a "group factor" in work situations; but an individualistic, social psychological focus was retained for this group factor. In the Hawthorne studies there was much concern with changes in attitude toward work; the meaning of work was considered a basic factor in individuals' performance; and work groups were considered in molding the meaning and attitudes for members of the group.[23] Roy's interpretation of his findings is similarly social psychological. It is that the informal patterns serve primarily to provide job satisfaction by relieving *boredom*. Along with many students of industrial relations in the last thirty years, he notes the existence of relatively distinct subgroups that have relatively distinct culture and interaction patterns, and that are separate from the formal structure in the factory. Yet, the basic interpretation is in individualistic, psychological terminology: it relieves boredom. Even if one accepts the psychological perspective, one must question whether routine, repetitive work is necessarily conducive to boredom. For example, Chinoy's study of automobile assembly-line workers suggests that workers' response to routine, repetitive work is perhaps better characterized by irritation over lack of control over one's work than by boredom.[24] To realize that routine, repetitive activity does not necessarily lead to boredom, one should allow for the influence of culture. The researcher may be exaggerating the activistic theme of Western societies. The Jicarilla Apache, for example, "have an infinite capacity for not being bored. They can sit for hours on end and apparently do nothing; they certainly don't intellectualize about doing nothing."[25]

The focus of the present paper suggests attention to what seems to be a basic feature in the social organization of the work situation, the autonomy enjoyed by the work group.[26] It does this on Roy's evidence that *considerable structuring of the work situation is done by the workers themselves*. What, then, is the content of the autonomous group culture? As Roy describes it, the work situation includes a great variety of behaviors that are not directly connected with *work*. Many of these fit Simmel's description of play forms of social reality.[27] Subjects that are of serious concern, such as economic security, sexual virility, health and death, submission to the authority of other men, family loyalty, and status aspirations, are examined in a context where they are stripped of their serious content. But the manner in which attention is paid to these subjects is particularly important. Flitting from one topic to another—from the deeply serious to the comic, from the immediately practical to the remotely romantic—indicates the decided irrelevance of the practical, concrete reality in which each of the subjects is embedded. Perhaps it is because members are simultaneously engaged in serious work that they feel free to treat other concerns so detachedly. Roy's group appears to be a veritable haven for the enactment of play forms. Elements of life that are largely beyond the control of the individual are exposed and, in a fashion, are dealt with. All this is most clearly evident in the verbal themes. In addition to play forms, it may well be that the various social interaction patterns—the "razzing" of Sammy, the paternalism of George—are reiterations of serious realities in the larger social context in which the men find themselves. It is noteworthy that it is Sammy, the newest immigrant (all three men are immigrants) who is the scapegoat; it is George, the only Gentile, who quietly occupies the superior status; it is the Negro handyman who is the object of sterotypical banter about uncontrolled sexuality.

These elements, whether they are fairly explicit reiterations or play forms of the workman's life outside the factory, are continuities between life outside the factory and life inside the factory and therefore are important for understanding the nature of the bond between the worker and the organization in which he is employed. Work peers participate in a common culture, which relies heavily on their common fate both within and *outside* the organization. In their commonality they retain a fundamental alienation from the white-collar ranks in the organization. This appears to be demonstrated in Chinoy's findings of workers' widespread lack of interest in becoming foremen or white-collar workers.[28] It is also supported by Walker and Guest's study of assembly-line workers. They found largely favorable reaction by workers to their immediate job, but intense dissatisfaction with the factory as a whole.[29] Although there is a lack of affiliation with the white-collar ranks of the organization, the worker *does* form bonds within the organization—with his own work peers.[30] For the organization, this dual relationship provides an uneasy truce without lessening the fundamental internal antithesis, and manifests itself in problems of morale and communications. At the same time the structure of the situation—the existence of two cultures—assures the continuity of the basic antithesis.

Roy points out that the group had developed a "full-blown socio-cultural system." The group was to a considerable extent a separate and distinct system, one in which the members had active, at times even creative, participation—in sharp contrast to their minimal participation in the larger organization. But it does not seem that *work* was at all a major focus of this sociocultural system! If one accepts this point, one gains a tool for reconciling the dilemma as to whether factory workers are strongly alienated from their work.[31] It appears that work is *one of a variety* of topics around which Roy's group had developed behavioral patterns, but work was by no means the central point of attention of this "full-blown sociocultural system."

The contention that work is not a central feature of Roy's work group differs considerably from traditional explanations of informal groups. Although no claim is made about the representativeness of the Roy group, it must be understood that the sort of data he presented has traditionally been interpreted largely in terms of its relevance to *work*. Statements to the effect that informal activities give meaning to dull, routine factory work[32] and that "work output is a function of the degree of work satisfaction, which in turn depends upon the informal social patterns of the work group"[33] are typical examples. These statements provide a social-psychological explanation of the group's mediating effect between the individual and his work, but they are hardly adequate in providing a structural explanation of the place of informal groups in a complex organization.

In addition to the social-psychological interpretations, there are well-documented studies—by Roy and others—which show production control and worker collusion against management by informal groups of workers.[34] Here there can be no doubt that informal patterns are relevant to work. But it is not certain, even here, that informal groups exist primarily for the worker's control over work or whether the explanation should not be reversed: that control over work exists because of the presence of informal groups which, in turn, exist because of the worker's relative autonomy.

In summary, it is suggested that Roy's work group exhibits a rich sociocultural system that is made possible by substantial worker autonomy. The autonomy exists by default; worker's roles are narrowly defined, leaving a considerable sphere of undefined action within the confines of the organization. The content of worker's sociocultural system is made up of a variety of elements from the culture and social context of workers outside the factory. These elements manifest themselves as direct reiterations as well as play forms of the reality. They provide continuity between the workman's life outside the factory and his participation within the factory.

In using the Roy study to illustrate autonomy patterns among informal groups, certain cautionary statements must be made. The group Roy studied may be atypical in the small amount of managerial supervision and in the degree of isolation from the rest of the factory, which might allow a disproportionately high degree of autonomy, as compared with other work groups. One can only answer that this requires investigation; it has not been demonstrated at this time. Also, worker autonomy structure is evident in other studies, as implied, for example, in Gouldner's conception of the managerial "indulgency pattern" toward workers,[35] and Bensman and Gerver's study of "deviancy in maintaining the social system" in a factory.[36] In addition, autonomy patterns among employees who are operating on higher echelons than laborers have been explored by Chester Barnard[37] and in the various writings of Peter Blau;[38] but these are outside the scope of the present paper.[39]

Note on the Theory of Integration of Complex Organizations

Complex organizations must have ways of procuring and integrating the services of a variety of participants. On a common-sense level one can see the process of procurement and integration accomplished most readily in organizations that have coercive means at their disposal. Prisons can force inmates to peel potatoes. But organizations that do not have coercion at their disposal provide a problem for the analyst. There can be little doubt that most complex organizations do, in fact, solve the problem. How is it accomplished?

The concern of this paper has been the integration of a particular segment of the membership of complex organizations, namely blue-collar workers in factories. The particular issue, here, is how these persons are recruited and integrated into the organization, which offers them few of the rewards that it can bestow. The answer is that a federalistic type of solution exists: Workers are permitted ample separation from the total organization and, to a considerable extent, their integration into the larger system is left to them. Informal work group cultures are the concrete structures that make up the solution.

The separation of workers from the employing organization provides workers with flexibility and options as to the degree of alienation from the whole organization. At the same time, the separation gives the organization freedom to adopt means and goals that are disparate, if not alien, to those of the workers. The federalistic balance of autonomy for the blue-collar workers as against the white-collar staff allows flexibility to both sides; but it is also a potential source of divergence and conflict, which finds nurture in the separate subcultures.

In contrast to the form of integration suggested here, other writings have shown much concern with models of organization that dwell on lessening internal differentiation. Workers and the white-collar staff are seen as diverging in interest and this divergence can *and needs to be* lessened if the organization is to operate effectively.[40] These writings differ from the present essay both in theoretical and practical focus. On the theoretical side, the present exposition is based strongly on the view that autonomy can be viewed as a structural principle of organizations, which can have positive or negative consequences for the operation of organizations. Structured autonomy manifests itself in internal divergencies, but these are not necessarily disruptive and maladaptive for the whole organization or any part of it. As to practical goals, many writers, notably Whyte and Argyris,[41] are concerned with the problem of improving human relations in industrial concerns. The practical focus here is not on improving social relationships in complex organizations; it is on the problem of improving the analytic theory of complex organizations. I do not claim that this is a more worthy or pressing problem than that of improving human relationships in complex organizations, merely that it *is* a problem. . . .

Notes and References

1. For a survey and research application of the the the theme of worker alienation, see Robert Blauner, *Alienation and Freedom: The Factory Worker and His Industry* (Chicago: University of Chicago, 1964).

2. For a summary of the literature on the limited commitment of workers to the complex organizations in which they work, as well to work itself, see Chris Argyris, *Integrating the individual and the Organization* (New York: John Wiley, 1964). In Pt. IV the author provides a summary of the debate as to whether the worker is alienated. Argyris' book is addressed to the same general issue as the present paper, but his approach differs in that it focuses on the issue—a very important one—of developing organizational patterns so that there is congruence between the psychological needs of members and the administrative requirements of the organization. The present paper, in contrast, attempts to remain entirely on the level of social structure. See, also, R. Dubin, "Industrial Workers' World: A Study of the 'Central Life Interests' of Industrial Workers," in Erwin O. Smigel (ed.), *Work and Leisure* (New Haven: College and University Press, 1963), pp. 53-72.

3. This viewpoint is more fully developed in Fred E. Katz, "The School As a Complex Organization," *Harvard Educational Review*, 34 (Summer, 1964).

4. Herbert A. Simon, Donald W. Smithburg, and Victor Thompson, *Public Administration* (New York: Alfred Knopf, 1962).

5. *Ibid.*, p. 5.

6. *Ibid.*, p. 87.

7. Fritz J. Roethlisberger and William J. Dickson, *Management and the Worker* (Cambridge: Harvard University, 1939). This classic report is still one of the most complete studies of informal groups. See also Peter M. Blau. "Structural Effects," *American Sociological Review*, 25 (1960), 178-193; also his *The Dynamics of Bureaucracy* (Chicago: University of Chicago, 1955).

8. Indeed, Blau's work comes close to providing just such a picture; see Blau, *The Dynamics of Bureaucracy, op. cit.*

9. Chester I. Barnard, *The Functions of the Executive* (Cambridge: Harvard University, 1938).

10. *Ibid.,* 83 ff.

11. *Ibid.,* 167 ff.

12. *Ibid.,* p. 227.

13. I am not suggesting that middle and upper class males do not engage in this form of mental sport, but I do suggest that for the working-class male it is a *major* creative outlet, and much less so for the middle and upper classes.

14. S. M. Miller and Frank Riessman suggest that the "factory 'horseplay,' the ritualistic kidding" are partly an expression of the working-class theme of person centeredness; see their "The Working-Class Subculture," in A. B. Shostak and W. Gomberg (eds.), *Blue Collar World* (Englewood Cliffs, N. J.: Prentice-Hall, 1964), pp. 24-35.

15. Participating in physical contact—be it fighting, prankish shoving, or contact sports—are chiefly characteristic of male preadult culture. Presumably it is only at the low socioeconomic levels that this pattern continues into adulthood. It is not clear whether similar continuities exist in *preadult* and adult female culture among working-class women.

16. It makes little difference whether they are members of the middle or upper class or use these classes as a reference group to guide their behavior.

17. Robert Blauner "Occupational Differences in Work Satisfaction," in R. L. Simpson and I. H. Simpson (eds.) *Social Organization and Behavior* (New York: John Wiley, 1964), pp. 287-292.

18. James C. Abegglen, *The Japanese Factory: Aspects of Its Social Organization* (New York: Free Press, 1960). Opinion differs as to whether Abegglen's formulation about life-long commitment applies to blue-collar workers in large factories. (I am indebted to the editors for this insight.)

19. Donald F. Roy, " 'Banana Time,' Job Satisfaction and Informal Interaction," *Human Organization,* 18 (1960), 158-168.

20. *Ibid.,* p. 161.

21. *Ibid.,* p. 162.

22. *Ibid.,* p. 163.

23. Fritz J. Roethlisberger and William J. Dickson, *op. cit.,* and Edward Gross, *Work and Society* (New York: Thomas Crowell, 1958), ch. xiv.

24. Ely Chinoy, *Automobile Workers and the American Dream* (Garden City, N. Y.: Doubleday, 1955).

25. Personal communication from H. Clyde Wilson.

26. Focus on autonomy structure does not altogether avoid the pitfall of potentially over-emphasizing one set of structures and one set of functions, just as social-psychological studies have done. But it should serve to broaden the existing basis of analysis.

27. K. H. Wolff (ed. and transl.), *The Sociology of George Simmel* (New York: Free Press, 1950).

28. Ely Chinoy, *op. cit.*; see especially, ch. v. See also, E. W. Bakke, *The Unemployed Worker* (New Haven: Yale University, 1940); and poll conducted by *Fortune* (May, 1947), both cited by Chinoy. Chinoy's explanation of the lack of desire for promotion is that workers have become so discouraged in the course of their work careers that they have given up. He notes that workers are reacting to "the limited opportunities available, to the uncertainties stemming from the informal procedures by which fore-

men were chosen, and to the nature of the foreman's job itself . . ." (p. 49). This explanation is not irreconcilable with the one offered here. The young factory worker, who does have visions of advancement, is presumably not sufficiently knowledgeable about the culture wall between himself and the administrative bureaucrat.

29. Charles R. Walker and Robert H. Guest, *The Man on the Assembly Line* (Cambridge, Mass.: Harvard University, 1952); see, for example, pp. 139-140

30. Dubin's studies suggest, however, that workers' friendship bonds with work peers are less important than bonds with peers outside the work setting; see Robert Dubin, *op. cit.*

31. Argyris, *op. cit.*, believes that workers are strongly alienated; Walker and Guest, *op. cit.*, note that workers they studied were relatively contented doing simple, repetitive work.

32. Edward Gross, *op. cit.*, p. 526.

33. Reinhard Bendix and Lloyd H. Fisher, "The Perspectives of Elton Mayo," in Amitai Etzioni, (ed.), *Complex Organizations: A Sociological Reader* (New York: Holt, Rinehart, and Winston, 1961), p. 119.

34. See, Donald Roy "Efficiency and 'The Fix': Informal Intergroup Relations in a Piecework Machine Shop," in S. M. Lipset and N. J. Smelser (ed.), *Sociology: The Progress of a Decade* (Englewood Cliffs, N. J.: Prentice-Hall, 1961), pp. 378-390; also his "Quota Restriction and Goldbricking in a Machine Shop," *American Journal of Sociology,* 57 (March, 1952), 427-442.

35. Alvin W. Gouldner, *Wildcat Strike* (Yellow Springs, Ohio: Antioch Press, 1954).

36. Joseph Bensman and Israel Gerver, "Crime and Punishment in the Factory: The Function of Deviancy in Maintaining the Social System," *American Sociological Review,* 28 (August, 1963), 588-598.

37. Chester Barnard, *op. cit.*

38. Peter M. Blau, "Structural Effects," *op. cit.,* and *The Dynamics of Bureaucracy, op. cit.*

39. A broader formulation of autonomy structure has been attempted in Fred E. Katz, *op. cit.*

40. Argyris, *op. cit.,* and other writings by the same author. See also the writings of W. F. Whyte; for example, *Patterns of Industrial Peace* (New York: Harper and Row, 1951) and *Money and Motivation* (New York: Harper and Row, 1955).

41. *Ibid.*

CONFLICT IN ORGANIZATION: A RE-EXAMINATION

JOSEPH A. LITTERER

The prevalence of conflict in organizations is only too apparent, not only from our personal experiences but also from literature of organizational studies.[1] All schools of thought on organizations have recognized that conflict exists. They have differed in how they looked at it. The writers of classical organization theory viewed conflict as undesirable, detrimental to the organization. Ideally it should not exist. Their prescription was simple. Eliminate it. This could be done by adequate job definition, detailed specification of relationships among positions, careful selection of people to fill positions, and thorough training of people once they had been assigned.[2]

This view of the classic organization writers paralleled the view of others on the handling of tension within people. A fundamental position of many who analyzed individual behavior was that individuals were motivated by a desire for tension reduction. The prescription in both therapy and organizational design therefore was to take steps or make arrangements which would reduce tension within individuals. More recently it has become accepted that tension is normal, even desirable, with the thought growing that "healthy" personalities actually seek to increase tension.[3]

This shift in thinking about personality has both a parallel and an impact on the thinking about conflict in organizations. If tension is not only acceptable but useful in individuals, then one source of individual tension, organizational conflict, may also be not only acceptable but useful. That, within certain bounds, conflict is acceptable and useful is the conclusion reached by a number of recent authors.[4] We therefore bring conflict from the role of a condemned, to that of a considered, variable.

While doubtless some forms and certain degrees of conflict are dysfunctional or "unhealthy," other types, to certain degrees, are useful. The questions then are

Reprinted by permission of the author and publisher from *Academy of Management Journal* (Sept. 1966).

how much conflict is functional and where are the limits beyond which it becomes dysfunctional. The problem before us is therefore much more complex than previously. At one time the ideal amount of conflict was zero and the common decision was "eliminate it." Now the questions are what are the limits within which conflict is useful and how does one manage conflict.

Functions and Variables

The theme of this paper is to examine what is involved in managing conflict in organizations, given that it has both functional and dysfunctional potentialities. To reduce this to a manageable task, many important things will be excluded. We will not consider intrapersonal conflicts or conflicts between a person's self concept and the role which he occupies. Further, we will not even begin to explore the almost completely untapped area concerned with determining the type and degree of conflict which is functional and that which is dysfunctional. Our approach instead will be from the point of view of examining what conflict is and identifying the organizational elements that produce it. If we are to manage conflict within reasonable boundaries, it is to these elements that we have to look to find the levers and handles with which to do the job.

Functions of Conflict

Although the detrimental effects of conflict have been frequently cited, the advantages of conflict have received but scant attention. A number of different functions of conflict in organizations have been identified and discussed in the literature. Perhaps one of the most important cited by a number of investigators[5] is that conflict initiates a search for some way to resolve or ameliorate the conflict and therefore leads to *innovation* and *change*. It should also be noted at the same time that conflict not only leads to a search for change but it also makes change more acceptable, even desirable.

Closely related with the above is the observation that a conflict energizes people to activity, sometimes just to reduce the conflict and its concurrent displeasures, at other times because the conflict gives a zest to certain activities.

Conflict within an organization can be an essential portion of a cybernetic system. It often occurs at the point at which some other systems within the organization are functioning inadequately and therefore calls attention to these problem areas and generates a serach for solutions or improvements. Conflicts often leads to shifts or reallocations of existing or future rewards or resources, thereby fundamentally changing important aspects of the organization. Budget allocation and unions-management conflicts are among many widely recognized.

It should be pointed out that conflicts between units or people on one level in an organization will often keep them from effectively confronting units or people at different hierarchal levels. A manager at one level may have far more influence over subordinates if they are competing with each other than if they unite to work against him, as we are reminded by the old political adage "divide and conquer." We should not fail to recognize, however, that this also occurs in reverse, that subordinates may often achieve considerable autonomy when the superiors are in conflict and therefore have neither the time nor the energy to expend in dominating those at a lower level.

There are doubtless other functions that conflict serves in organizations. The point is, however, not to compile a list but to say that conflict can be of use to organizations and that some of these uses are of great importance.

Definition of Conflict

Let us examine the organization elements which cause interperson, person-unit and interunit conflict. First, conflict is a battle or clash involving two people or more in opposition to each other. From our point of view, it is an inter-personal or interunit event and involves a particular type of interaction. The roots of this particular type of interaction reveal most about conflict. Conflict occurs when one sees the prospect of relative deprivation resulting from the actions of or in interacting with the other. For example, to some people, having to take orders from a person whom they think to be in lower status would result in their losing some of their own status and hence they would be deprived. However, the loss can be relative since conflict can occur when both parties are gaining but one or both feel that the other may gain more. Then one or both may perceive the outcome as a second-best position.

Our definition of conflict, then, is that conflict is a *type of behavior which occurs* when two or more parties are in opposition or in battle *as a result* of a perceived relative deprivation from the activities of or interacting with another person or group.

Four Conflict Situations

The organizational causes of conflict are numerous. The particular organizational elements which lead to conflict do not bring this result about directly. Instead they create conditions which affect the perception and motivation of organizational members in such a way that conflict results. There are then a set of intervening variables which transform structural forms into behavioral outputs. The many organizational structures which produce conflict seem to feed four principal types of intervening variables or organizational situations. These are win-lose situations (or competition over position), competition over resources or work arrangements, status incongruencies, and perpetual differences.

Win-Lose Situations

This intervening variable develops when two people or two units have goals which cannot exist simultaneously. Surprisingly, organizations set up many circumstances which lead to this condition. This is commonly witnessed in inspection situations. The inspector is hired to find errors but errors are someone else's output. Therefore every time the inspector finds an error justifying his position's existence and opening the opportunity for praise and reward, someone else is losing. The latter's output is shown to be inadequate and his rewards are endangered. Formal inspection positions such as those of quality control inspectors come to mind most readily, but it should be recognized that many staff positions have inspection components which produce in part the conflict so frequently noted among line and staff positions. Accounting is one type of staff work with large inspection components.[6]

Inspection is one type of win-lose situation. There are others not so obvious, however. Not long ago a major airline was faced with considerable conflict between two of its managers at a western city. Upon investigation it was found that the Sales Manager, in order to increase his sales volume, wanted to provide certain services for customers. These, however, would be provided by the employees and from the budgets of the Ramp and Services Manager. There was considerable effort to decentralize and promote as much autonomy for individual managers as possible and handsome bonus systems were set up on certain standards of individual managerial performance. If the Sales Manager could increase his sales he would have many advantages. Conversely, if the Ramp Services Manager could keep his costs down he too would have many rewards coming to him. Hence the problem, and the conflict; the Sales Manager could not get his bonus unless the Ramp Services Manager were to forego some of his own. This condition, although not always clearly recognized, exists in many organizations where reward systems are based upon individual performances which are not independent but are very much interdependent.

Competition over Means Utilization

In this area, conflict occurs not over goals which may be similar, but stems from the fact that there are differing ideas as to what means are appropriate or who will have the means. French has shown that conflicts over the means to goal accomplishment are more disruptive of group cohesiveness than conflicts over differing goals.[7]

Another common source of conflict involves shared dependence on limited resources and scheduling problems.[8] Those that center on budgetary decisions, allocation of capital resources and the efforts made by certain departments to assure themselves that adequate supplies of scarce personnel are provided by the personnel department are recognized and common.

Scheduling problems are often not as clearly recognized and are perhaps more common. A common situation is cited by Whyte in a plant where a group of women workers was asked to participate in establishing new work norms.[9] As might be expected from previous studies, the standards they established were actually above those the industrial engineering department would have provided. However, worker-set performance standards 30-50 percent over engineering standards, instead of being a satisfactory situation, created numerous problems. The department following this one faced an avalanche of material which created considerable pressure. Departments preceding this one were placed under considerable pressure to produce more. Employees in these and other departments hearing of the high earnings in the initial department complained about inequities. The engineering department felt humiliated at having so badly misjudged workable standards. Management at several levels, seeing all these events, felt that somehow things were out of control and that their position was being eroded.

Status Incongruency

An often neglected but extremely pervasive influence on behavior stems from the fact that people want to know where they stand relative to others, that is, what their status is. This might not be too much of an issue if there were but one standard for evaluating a person. But actually there are numerous status hierarchies and one's position is never the same on them all. Further, it is often changing.

One set of status problems in industry arises from the impact of changing technology. Men who entered companies years ago and rose slowly through the ranks often feel that seniority and age justify fairly high status positions. However, they may find themselves superseded by younger men moved into higher level positions because their more recent technical training better fits them to cope with modern business problems. Working for someone younger than themselves and with less seniority, these men feel their status has been eroded and often accept this with little grace.

There are many other things, however, which create status incongruencies. For example, it is generally felt that those who give orders or initiate action for others have higher status than those who receive the orders or have work initiated for them. Work-flow relationships can often cause difficulties, however. Whyte in his study of the restaurant industry found situations where waitresses or other women could initiate activities for men by transmitting orders to them.[10] In other situations cooks would have work initiated by runners. In each case, it appeared that low-status people were initiating work for those of higher status, in opposition to normal expectation, and much conflict arose.

Perceptual Differences

It has long been recognized that people who look at things differently often come into conflict. In organizations, people see things differently for a variety of reasons, among them locational factors. It is frequently observed that people in different functional departments will tend to have different views of what is good for the company and how things are to be done. The classic conflicts between marketing and production over such things as delivery times, quality and lengths of production runs are well known. People in these departments not only perform different types of work but also interact with different publics. Marketing people interact most frequently with people outside the company, customers and competitors; those in manufacturing interact mostly with other departments within the company or with the union. These differences in systemic linkages and activities lead to differences in perception of considerable magnitude.[11]

Hierarchal location also has an impact. The problems seen by the first line supervisor, faced with the enormous pressures of day-to-day operations, are quite different from those of the managers two and three levels above whose time perspectives are greater and whose pressures take a different form and come from different quarters. The manager looking at a long-range development may not want certain relationships established with the union. But the foreman, faced with the fact that he must meet a shipping date at the end of the month, may be much more prone to accept a short-term solution and worry about the future some other time.[12]

This scarcely exhausts all the intervening variables. Looking at the four, however, one can begin to understand which types of situations might be useful, that is, functional and which might lead to dysfunctional consequences.

Functional versus Dysfunctional

As pointed out earlier, conflict often leads to innovation. Innovation usually offers some way of resolving differences so that both parties gain more in the new arrangement than they lose.

With this in mind, it is fairly easy to see that incompatible goals are very difficult to resolve, in fact, often impossible. Often even mediation is impossible and the only thing that can take care of them is arbitration.[13] The other solution is to remove completely the element causing the incompatible goals. Such a solution was described by Argyris when a plant manager tried to find some way of assigning charges for a shipment of inferior products returned by a customer. The competition among the various foremen was fierce, each trying to avoid having the charges assigned to his unit. In the end the plant manager had to assign them to general plant overhead.[14]

Incompatible means leading to conflict can be reduced or eliminated by a search for another means set more acceptable to all parties concerned. This source of conflict seems to lead to creative resolutions far more frequently than any of the other types and therefore can most likely lead to invention and adaptation. This idea of finding or creating a third ground for resolving differences was an aspect of creativity that concerned Mary Parker Follett.[15]

Status incongruencies can be energizers in the sense that they may awaken a person to the fact that his performance and his background need improvement in order to secure a position more compatible with the status he would like to occupy. Not so much the source of innovation, this can be a source of motivation. On the other hand, status incongruency can produce a destructive form of conflict leading to long and bitter hostility rather than changes in individual talents or performance or advancement.

In almost any organization and certainly in large organizations, it is impossible for anyone to observe all the things which are relevant to the organization; hence, different perceptions are sure to exist. Such differences, when they culminate in broadening the view of the opposing parties or when they bring problems to the attention of higher individuals in the organization, may be very valuable in detecting serious breakdowns in the overall functioning of an organization. The problem, of course, is to keep these perceptions from becoming rigid and the conflicts from becoming fixed. This can be greatly facilitated in many ways, such as planned position rotation, training programs, committees and the like.

This has been an all too brief examination of how the intervening variables can be used to determine which are sources of useful conflict and how conflict can be managed in an organization. We still have one important topic to consider, the actions or programs to be taken to manage conflict.

Managing Conflict Situations

Three basic strategies have been proposed for handling conflict situations.[16]

Making the System Work

Let us consider the situation where people find themselves in what they deem to be a situation of status incongruency. One solution would be to work with the individuals to get them to accept that: Age is going to keep them from certain types of positions, or that if they are not going to work to learn new technologies, they cannot expect to get promoted and so on. The system essentially stays the same but some of the elements in it are modified to make the current arrangements more workable.

Developing Additional Machinery

An alternate to modifying some of the elements in the system is to alter the system by adding or replacing elements. For example, when conflicts develop because a low-status person is initiating action for one of higher status, the conflicts can be reduced in part by creating a buffer. Whyte described a situation where runners were to write an order on a slip of paper and place it on a hook from which the cooks could take it, thereby making the interaction less direct.[17] This reduction led to less conflict.

Changing Institutional Structure to Eliminate the Cause of the Conflict

Sometimes even modifying the system is not sufficient to reduce conflict and a major change is required in the organization, such as creating new positions or departments. For example, with the conflicts between the cook and runner, one solution proposed was to have the information on orders related to the cook by a supervisor rather than by the runner. Even though this would require the creation of a special new supervisory position, the initiation of work would then be more in line with the usual expectations of status differences.

These three events in sequence constitute an overall mechanism for reducing conflict in organizations. We first try to make the system work, then try to develop additional machinery and when all else fails restructure the basic system.[18] To go from one event to another as a "natural" process can be wasteful and unnecessary. Our previous analysis showed that some situations can be corrected only by the latter step and others by only the last two. Hence, by analyzing the source of conflict, it is possible to choose the appropriate strategy in this sequence.

Conclusion

The intent of this paper was to explore conflict in organizations. It is not a single, simple, but a very complex, cluster of events. While it has detrimental effects, it can also have very useful consequences. The assumption that conflict was universally detrimental was consistent with earlier organizational models, given their basic concern with stable organizations and goal maximization. The functional possibilities of conflict became apparent in examining a system model of organizations, for here conflict's role as a control and innovation element can be considered.

This paper has examined only those portions of conflict most directly concerned with the questions of what use is conflict and how can it be managed. Even in this area, there are critical questions of how much conflict is useful and what forms of conflict are most useful. It has been shown that different organization arrangements produce different competitive situations, and that the effect of conflict depends to a considerable degree on the nature of the conflict.

It is concluded that conflict is a manageable organizational event producing both functional and dysfunctional effects. Conflict in this light is almost completely unexplored as a topic and therefore is one on which much constructive work can be expended.

Notes and References

1. See for example: Chris Argyris, *The Impact of Budgets on People* (New York: The Controllers Institute Research Foundation, 1952), Alvin Gouldner, *Patterns of Industrial Bureaucracy* (Glencoe: The Free Press, 1954); Melville Dalton, *Men Who Manage* (New York: John Wiley & Sons, 1959); Peter Blau, *The Dynamics of Bureaucracy* (Chicago: University of Chicago Press, 1955).

2. With varying degrees of explicitness these points are made by many writers. See for example Frederick W. Taylor, *Scientific Management* (New York: Harper & Brothers, 1947); L. Urwick, *The Elements of Administration* (New York, Harper & Brothers, 1943); James Mooney, *Principles of Organization* (New York: Harper & Brothers, 1947).

3. See for example, Gordon W. Allport, "The Trend in Motivational Theory," *American Journal of Orthopsychiatry*, Vol. 23, (1953) pp. 107-119; Viktor E. Frankl, *From Death Camp to Existentialism* (Boston: Beacon Press, 1949); and William Wolf, "Wider Horizons in Psychotherapy," *American Journal of Psychotherapy*, Vol. 16, No. 1, January 1963, pp. 124-149.

4. Dalton, *op. cit.;* Kenneth Boulding, *Conflict Management and Organizations* (Ann Arbor: Foundation for Research on Human Behavior, 1961), p. 1 and Chris Argyris, *Integrating the Individual and the Organization* (New York, John Wiley & Sons, 1964), particularly Chapter 1.

5. Dalton, *op. cit.;* Peter Blau and William R. Scott, *Formal Organizations* (San Francisco: Chandler Publishing Company, 1962); James G. March and Herbert A. Simon, *Organizations* (New York, John Wiley & Sons, 1959).

6. March and Simon, *op. cit.*, p. 122.

7. John R. P. French, Jr., "The Disruption and Cohesion of Groups," *The Journal of Abnormal and Social Psychology*, Vol. 36, (1941), pp. 361-377.

8. March and Simon, *op. cit.*, p. 122.

9. William Foote Whyte, *Money and Motivation* (New York: Harper & Brothers, 1955).

10. William Foote Whyte, *Human Relations in the Restaurant Industry* (New York: Harper & Brothers, 1948).

11. See for example, DeWitt C. Dearborn and Herbert A. Simon, "Selective Perception: A Note on Departmental Identification of Executives," *Sociometry, Vol. 21*, (1958) pp. 140-144.

12. For an interesting discussion of this point see Norman H. Martin, "Differential Decisions in the Management of an Industrial Plant," *Journal of Business*, Vol. 29, (1956) pp. 249-260.

13. Bernard M. Bass, *Organizational Psychology* (New York: Allyn and Bacon, 1965), p. 336.

14. Argyris, *op. cit.*, (1952).
15. Metcalf and Urwick (eds.), *Dynamic Administration* (New York: Harper & Brothers, 1941).
16. Daniel Katz, "Approaches to Managing Conflict," in *Conflict Management and Organizations* (Ann Arbor: Foundation for research on Human Behavior, 1961).
17. Whyte, (1948), *op. cit.* See also Elias Porter, "The Parable of the Spindle," *Harvard Business Review* (May-June, 1962).
18. There is a close parallel between the strategy sequence for conflict reduction proposed by Katz and the innovation process discussed by March and Simon, *op. cit.*

ORGANIZATIONAL CONFLICT: CONCEPTS AND MODELS

LOUIS R. PONDY

There is a large and growing body of literature on the subject of organizational conflict. The concept of conflict has been treated as a general social phenomenon, with implications for the understanding of conflict within and between organizations.[1] It has also assumed various roles of some importance in attempts at general theories of management and organizational behavior.[2] Finally, conflict has recently been the focus of numerous empirical studies of organization.[3]

Slowly crystallizing out of this research are three conceptual models designed to deal with the major classes of conflict phenomena in organizations.[4]

1. *Bargaining model.* This is designed to deal with conflict among interest groups in competition for scarce resources. This model is particularly appropriate for the analysis of labor-management relations, budgeting processes, and staff-line conflicts.

2. *Bureaucratic model.* This is applicable to the analysis of superior-subordinate conflicts or, in general, conflicts along the vertical dimension of a hierarchy. This model is primarily concerned with the problems caused by institutional attempts to control behavior and the organization's reaction to such control.

3. *Systems model.* This is directed at lateral conflict, or conflict among the parties to a functional relationship. Analysis of the problems of coordination is the special province of this model.

Running as common threads through each of these models are several implicit orientations. The most important of these orientations follow:

1. Each conflict relationship is made up of a sequence of interlocking conflict episodes; each episode exhibits a sequence or pattern of development, and the conflict relationship can be characterized by stable patterns that appear across the se-

Reprinted by permission of the author and the publisher from *Administrative Science Quarterly*, vol. 12, no. 2 (Sept. 1967), pp. 296-320.

quence of episodes. This orientation forms the basis for a working definition of conflict.

2. Conflict may be functional as well as dysfunctional for the individual and the organization; it may have its roots either within the individual or in the organizational context; therefore, the desirability of conflict resolution needs to be approached with caution.

3. Conflict is intimately tied up with the stability of the organization, not merely in the usual sense that conflict is a threat to stability, but in a much more complex fashion; that is, conflict is a key variable in the feedback loops that characterize organizational behavior. These orientations are discussed before the conceptual models are elaborated.

A Working Definition of Conflict

The term "conflict" has been used at one time or another in the literature to describe: (*1*) *antecedent conditions* (for example, scarcity of resources, policy differences) of conflictful behavior, (*2*) *affective states* (e.g., stress, tension, hostility, anxiety, etc.) of the individuals involved, (*3*) cognitive states of individuals, i.e., their perception or awareness of conflictful situations, and (*4*) conflictful behavior, ranging from passive resistance to overt aggression. Attempts to decide which of these classes—conditions, attitude, cognition, or behavior—is really conflict is likely to result in an empty controversy. The problem is not to choose among these alternative conceptual definitions, since each may be a relevant stage in the development of a conflict episode, but to try to clarify their relationships.

Conflict can be more readily understood if it is considered a dynamic process. A conflict relationship between two or more individuals in an organization can be analyzed as a sequence of conflict episodes. Each conflict episode begins with conditions characterized by certain conflict potentials. The parties to the relationship may not become aware of any basis of conflict, and they may not develop hostile affections for one another. Depending on a number of factors, their behavior may show a variety of conflictful traits. Each episode or encounter leaves an aftermath that affects the course of succeeding episodes. The entire relationship can then be characterized by certain stable aspects of conditions, affect, perception, and behavior. It can also be characterized by trends in any of these characteristics.

This is roughly analogous to defining a "decision" to include activities preliminary to and following choice, as well as the choice itself. In the same sense that a decision can be thought of as a process of gradual commitment to a course of action, a conflict episode can be thought of as a gradual escalation to a state of disorder. If choice is the climax of a decision, then by analogy, open war or aggression is the climax of a conflict episode.

This does not mean that every conflict episode necessarily passes through every stage to open aggression. A potential conflict may never be perceived by the parties to the conflict, or if perceived, the conflict may be resolved before hostilities break out. Several other alternative courses of development are possible. Both Coleman and Aubert make these points clearly in their treatments of the dynamics of conflict.[5]

Just as some decisions become programmed or routinized, conflict management in an organization also becomes programmed or institutionalized sometimes. In fact, the institutionalization of means for dealing with recurrent conflict is one of the important aspects in any treatment of the topic. An organization's success hinges to a great extent on its ability to set up and operate appropriate mechanisms for dealing with a variety of conflict phenomena.

Five stages of a conflict episode are identified: (*1*) latent conflict (conditions), (*2*) perceived conflict (cognition), (*3*) felt conflict (affect), (*4*) manifest conflict (behavior), and (*5*) conflict aftermath (conditions). The elaboration of each of these stages of a conflict episode will provide the substance for a working definition. Which specific reactions take place at each state of a conflict episode, and why, are the central questions to be answered in a theory of conflict. Only the framework within which those questions can be systematically investigated is developed here.

Latent Conflict

A search of the literature has produced a long list of underlying sources of organizational conflict. These are condensed into three basic types of latent conflict: (*1*) competition for scarce resources, (*2*) drives for autonomy, and (*3*) divergence of subunit goals. Later in the paper each of these fundamental types of latent conflict is paired with one of the three conceptual models. Briefly, competition forms the basis for conflict when the aggregated demands of participants for resources exceed the resources available to the organization; autonomy needs form the basis of conflict when one party either seeks to exercise control over some activity that another party regards as his own province or seeks to insulate itself from such control; goal divergence is the source of conflict when two parties who must cooperate on some joint activity are unable to reach a consensus on concerted action. Two or more types of latent conflict may, of course, be present simultaneously.

An important form of latent conflict, which appears to be omitted from this list, is role conflict. The role conflict model treats the organization as a collection of role sets, each composed of the focal person and his role senders. Conflict is said to occur when the focal person receives incompatible role demands or expectations from the persons in his role set.[6] This model has the drawback that it treats the focal person as merely a passive receiver rather than as an active participant in the relationship. It is argued here, that the role conflict model does not postulate a distinct type of latent conflict. Instead, it defines a conceptual relationship, the role set, which may be useful for the analysis of all three forms of latent conflict described.

Perceived Conflict

Conflict may sometimes be perceived when no conditions of latent conflict exist, and latent conflict conditions may be present in a relationship without any of the participants perceiving the conflict.

The case in which conflict is perceived when no latent conflict exists can be handled by the so-called "semantic model" of conflict.[7] According to this explanation, conflict is said to result from the parties' misunderstanding of each others' true position. It is argued that such conflict can be resolved by improving communications between the parties. This model has been the basis of a wide variety of management techniques aimed at improving interpersonal relations. Of course, if the parties' true positions *are* in opposition, then more open communication may only exacerbate the conflict.

The more important case, that some latent conflicts fail to reach the level of awareness also requires explanation. Two important mechanisms that limit perception of conflict are the suppression mechanism and the attention-focus mechanism.[8] Individuals tend to block conflicts that are only mildly threatening out of awareness.[9] Conflicts become strong threats, and therefore must be acknowledged, when the conflicts relate to values central to the individual's personality. The suppression mechanism is applicable more to conflicts related to personal than to organizational values. The attention-focus mechanism, however, is related more to organizational behavior than to personal values. Organizations are characteristically faced with more conflicts than can be dealt with given available time and capacities. The normal reaction is to focus attention on only a few of these, and these tend to be the conflicts for which short-run, routine solutions are available. For organizations successfully to confront the less programmed conflicts, it is frequently necessary to set up separate subunits specifically to deal with such conflicts.

Felt Conflict

There is an important distinction between perceiving conflict and feeling conflict. A may be aware that B and A are in serious disagreement over some policy, but it may not make A tense or anxious, and it may have no effect whatsoever on A's affection towards B. The personalization of conflict is the mechanism which causes most students of organization to be concerned with the dysfunctions of conflict. There are two common explanations for the personalization of conflict.

One explanation is that the inconsistent demands of efficient organization and individual growth create anxieties within the individual.[10] Anxieties may also result from identity crises or from extra-organizational pressures. Individuals need to vent these anxieties in order to maintain internal equilibrium. Organizational conflicts of the three latent types described earlier provide defensible excuses for displacing these anxieties against suitable targets. This is essentially the so-called "tension-model."[11]

A second explanation is that conflict becomes personalized when the whole personality of the individual is involved in the relationship. Hostile feelings are most common in the intimate relations that characterize total institutions, such as monasteries, residential colleges, and families.[12] In order to dissipate accumulated hostilities, total institutions require certain safety-valve institutions such as athletic activities or norms that legitimize solitude and withdrawal, such as the noncommunication norms prevalent in religious orders.

Thus, felt conflict may arise from sources independent of the three types of latent conflict, but latent conflicts may provide appropriate targets (perhaps symbolic ones) for undirected tensions.

Manifest Conflict

By manifest conflict is meant any of several varieties of conflictful behavior. The most obvious of these is open aggression, but such physical and verbal violence is usually strongly proscribed by organizational norms. Except for prison riots, political revolutions, and extreme labor unrest, violence as a form of manifest conflict in organizations is rare. The motivations toward violence may remain, but they tend to be expressed in less violent form. Dalton has documented the covert attempts to sabotage or block an opponent's plans through aggressive and defensive coalitions.[13] Mechanic has described the tactics of conflict used by lower-level participants, such as apathy or rigid adherence to the rules, to resist mistreatment by the upper levels of the hierarchy.[14]

How can one decide when a certain behavior or pattern of behavior is conflictful? One important factor is that the behavior must be interpreted in the context in which it takes place. If A does not interact with B, it may be either because A and B are not related in any organizational sense, or because A has withdrawn from a too stressful relationship, or because A is deliberately frustrating B by withdrawing support, or simply because A is drawn away from the relationship by other competing demands upon his time. In other words, knowledge of the organizational requirements and of the expectations and motives of the participants appears to be necessary to characterize the behavior as conflictful. This suggests that behavior should be defined to be conflictful if, and only if, some or all of the participants perceive it to be conflictful.

Should the term manifest conflict be reserved for behavior which, in the eyes of the actor, is deliberately and consciously designed to frustrate another in the pursuit of his (the other's) overt or covert goals? But what of behavior which is not *intended* to frustrate, but does? Should not that behavior also be called conflictful? The most useful definition of manifest conflict seems to be that behavior which, in the mind of the actor, frustrates the goals of at least some of the other participants. In other words, a member of the organization is said to engage in conflictful behavior if he consciously, but not necessarily deliberately, blocks another member's goal achievement. He may engage in such behavior *deliberately* to frustrate another, or he may do so in spite of the fact that he frustrates another. To define manifest conflict in this way is to say that the following question is important: "Under what conditions will a party to a relationship *knowingly* frustrate another party to the relationship? Suppose A unknowingly blocks B's goals. This is not conflictful behavior. But suppose B informs A that he perceives A's behavior to be conflictful; if then A acknowledges the message and *persists* in the behavior, it is an instance of manifest conflict.

The interface between perceived conflict and manifest conflict and the interface between felt conflict and manifest conflict are the pressure points where most conflict resolution programs are applied. The object of such programs is to prevent conflicts which have reached the level of awareness or the level of affect from erupting into noncooperative behavior. The availability of appropriate and effective administrative devices is a major factor in determining whether conflict becomes manifest. The collective bargaining apparatus of labor-management disputes and budgeting systems for internal resource allocation are administrative devices for the resolution of interest-group conflicts. Evan and Scott have described due process or appeal systems for resolving superior-subordinate conflicts.[5] Mechanisms for resolving lateral conflicts among the parties to a functional relationship are relatively undeveloped. Transfer-pricing systems constitute one of the few exceptions. Much more common are organizational arrangements designed to *prevent* lateral conflicts, e.g., plans, schedules, and job descriptions, which define and delimit subunit responsibilities. Another alternative is to reduce the interdependence between conflicting subunits by introducing buffers, such as inventories, which reduce the need for sales and production departments in a business firm to act in perfect accord.

The mere availability of such administrative devices is not sufficient to prevent conflict from becoming manifest. If the parties to a relationship do not value the relationship, or if conflict is strategic in the pursuit goals, then conflictful behavior is likely. Furthermore, once conflict breaks out on some specific issue, then the conflict frequently widens and the initial specific conflict precipitates more general and more personal conflicts which had been suppressed in the interest of preserving the stability of the relationship.[16]

Conflict Aftermath

Each conflict episode is but one of a sequence of such episodes that constitute the relationships among organization participants.[17] If the conflict is genuinely resolved to the satisfaction of all participants, the basis for a more cooperative relationship may be laid; or the participants, in their drive for a more ordered relationship may focus on latent conflicts not previously perceived and dealt with. On the other hand, if the conflict is merely suppressed but not resolved, the latent conditions of conflict may be aggravated and explode in more serious form until they are rectified or until the relationship dissolves. This legacy of a conflict episode is here called "conflict aftermath."[18]

However, the organization is not a closed system. The environment in which it is imbedded may become more benevolent and alleviate the conditions of latent conflict, for example, by making more resources available to the organization. But a more malevolent environment may precipitate new crises. The development of each conflict episode is determined by a complex combination of the effects of preceding episodes and the environmental milieu. The main ideas of this view of the dynamics of conflict are summarized in Figure 1.

Functions and Dysfunctions of Conflict

Few students of social and organizational behavior have treated conflict as a neutral phenomenon to be studied primarily because of scientific curiosity about its nature and form, its causes, and its effects. Most frequently the study of conflict has been motivated by a desire to resolve it and to minimize its deleterious effects on the psychological health of organizational participants and the efficiency of organization performance. Although Kahn and others pay lip service to the opinion that, "one might well make a case for interpreting some conflict as essential for the continued development of mature and competent human beings," the overriding bias of their report is with the "personal costs of excessive emotional strain," and, they state, "the fact that common reactions to conflict and its associated tensions are often dysfunctional for the organization as an on-going social system and self-defeating for the person in the long run."[19] Boulding recognizes that some optimum level of conflict and associated personal stress and tension are necessary for progress and productivity, but he portrays conflict primarily as a personal and social cost.[20] Baritz argues that Elton Mayo has treated conflict as "an evil, a symptom of the lack of social skills," and its alleged opposite, cooperation, as "symptomatic of

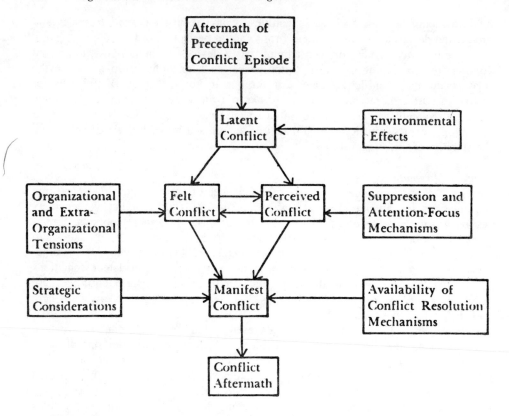

Figure 1. The dynamics of a conflict episode.

health.''[21] Even as dispassionate a theory of organization as that of March and Simon defines conflict conceptually as a *''breakdown* in the standard mechanisms of decision making''; i.e., as a malfunction of the system.[22]

It has become fashionable to say that conflict may be either functional or dysfunctional and is not necessarily either one. What this palliative leaves implicit is that the effects of conflict must be evaluated relative to some set of values. The argument with those who seek uniformly to abolish conflict is not so much with their *a priori* assertion that conflict is undesirable, as it is with their failure to make explicit the value system on which their assertion rests.

For the purposes of this research, the effects of organizational conflict on individual welfare are not of concern. Conflict may threaten the emotional well-being of individual persons; it may also be a positive factor in personal character development; but this research is not addressed to these questions. Intra-individual conflict is of concern only in so far as it has implications for organizational performance. With respect to organizational values, *productivity,* measured in both quantitative and qualitative terms, is valued; other things being equal, an organization is ''better'' if it produces more, if it is more innovative, and if its output meets higher standards of quality than other organizations. *Stability* is also valued. An organization improves if it can increase its cohesiveness and solvency, other things being equal. Finally *adaptability* is valued. Other things being equal, organizations that can learn and improve performance and that can adapt to changing internal and environmental pressures are preferred to those that cannot. In this view, therefore, to say that conflict is functional or dysfunctional is to say that it facilitates or inhibits the organization's productivity, stability, or adaptability.

Clearly, these values are not entirely compatible. An organization may have to sacrifice quality of output for quantity of output; if it pursues policies and actions that guarantee stability, it may inhibit its adaptive abilities. It is argued here that a given conflict episode or relationship may have beneficial or deleterious effects on productivity, stability, and adaptability. Since these values are incompatible, conflict may be simultaneously functional and dysfunctional for the organization.

A detailed examination of the functional and dysfunctional effects of conflict is more effectively made in the context of the three conceptual models. Underlying that analysis is the notion that conflict disturbs the "equilibrium" of the organization, and that the reaction of the organization to disequilibrium is the mechanism by which conflict affects productivity, stability, and adaptability.

Conflict and Equilibrium

One way of viewing an organization is to think of each participant as making contributions, such as work, capital, and raw materials, in return for certain inducements, such as salary, interest, and finished goods. The organization is said to be in "equilibrium" if inducements exceed contributions (subjectively valued) for every participant, and in "disequilibrium" if contributions exceed inducements for some or all of the participants. Participants will be motivated to restore equilibrium either by leaving the organization for greener pastures, when the disequilibrium is said to be "unstable," or by attempting to achieve a favorable balance between inducements and contributions within the organization, when it is considered "stable." Since changing organizational affiliation frequently involves sizable costs, disequilibria tend to be stable.

If we assume conflict to be a cost of participation, this inducements-contributions balance theory may help in understanding organizational reactions to conflict. It suggests that the perception of conflict by the participants will motivate them to reduce conflict either by withdrawing from the relationship, or by resolving the conflict within the context of the relationship, or by securing increased inducements to compensate for the conflict.

The assumption that conflict creates a disequilibrium is implicit in nearly all studies of organizational conflict. For example, March and Simon assume that "where conflict is perceived, motivation to reduce conflict is generated," and conscious efforts to resolve conflict are made.[23] Not all treatments of the subject make this assumption, however. Harrison White attacks the March-Simon assumption of the disequilibrium of conflict as "naive."[24] He bases his assertion on his observation of chronic, continuous, high-level conflict in administrative settings. This, of course, raises the question, "Under what conditions *does* conflict represent a disequilibrium?"

To say that (perceived) conflict represents a state of disequilibrium and generates pressures for conflict resolution, is to say three things: (*1*) that perceived conflict is a cost of participation; (*2*) that the conflict disturbs the inducements-contributions balance; and (*3*) that organization members react to perceptions of conflict by attempting to resolve the conflict, *in preference to* (although this is not made explicit in the March-Simon treatment) other reactions such as withdrawing from the relationship or attempting to gain added inducements to compensate for the conflict.

1. *Conflict as a cost.* Conflict is not necessarily a cost for the individual. Some participants may actually enjoy the "heat of battle." As Hans Hoffman argues, "The unique function of man is to live in close creative touch with chaos and thereby experience the birth of order."[25]

Conflict may also be instrumental in the achievement of other goals. One of the tactics of successful executives in the modern business enterprise is to create confusion as a cover for the expansion of their particular empire.[26] or, as Sorensen observes, deliberately to create dissent and competition among one's subordinates in order to ensure that he will be brought into the relationship as an arbiter at critical times, as Franklin D. Roosevelt did.[27] Or, conflict with an out-group may be desirable to maintain stability within the in-group.

In general, however, conflict can be expected to be negatively valued; particularly if conflict becomes manifest, and subunit goals and actions are blocked and frustrated. Latency or perception of conflict should be treated as a cost, only if harmony and uniformity are highly valued. Tolerance of divergence is not generally a value widely shared in contemporary organizations, and under these conditions latent and perceived conflict are also likely to be treated as costly.

2. *Conflict as a source of disequilibrium.* White's observation of *chronic* conflict creates doubt as to whether conflict represents a disequilibrium.[28] He argues that if conflict *were* an unstable state for the system, then only transient conflict or conflict over shifting foci would be observable. Even if organizational participants treat conflict as a cost, they may still endure intense, chronic conflict, if there are compensating inducements from the organization in the form of high salary, opportunities for advancement, and others. To say that a participant will endure chronic conflict is not to deny that he will be motivated to reduce it; it is merely to say that if the organization member is unsuccessful in reducing conflict, he may still continue to participate if the inducements offered to him exceed the contributions he makes in return. Although conflict may be one of several sources of disequilibrium, it is neither a necessary nor a sufficient condition of disequilibrium. But, as will be shown, equilibrium nevertheless plays an important role in organizational reactions to conflict.[29]

3. *Resolution pressures a necessary consequence of conflict.* If conflicts are relatively small, and the inducements and contributions remain in equilibrium, then the participants are likely to try to resolve the conflict within the context of the existing relationship.[30] On the other hand, when contributions exceed inducements, or when conflict is intense enough to destroy the inducements-contributions balance and there is no prospect for the re-establishment of equilibrium, then conflict is likely

to be reduced by dissolving the relationship. Temporary imbalances, of course, may be tolerated; i.e., the relationship will not dissolve if the participants perceive the conflicts to be resolvable in the near future.

What is the effect of conflict on the interaction rate among participants? It depends on the stability of the relationship. If the participants receive inducements in sufficient amounts to balance contributions, then perception of conflict is likely to generate pressures for *increased* interaction, and the content of the interaction is likely to deal with resolution procedures. On the other hand, if conflict represents a cost to the participant and this cost is not compensated by added inducements, then conflict is likely to lead to *decreased* interaction or withdrawal from the relationship.

To summarize, conflict is frequently, but not always, negatively valued by organization members. To the extent that conflict *is* valued negatively, minor conflicts generate pressures towards resolution without altering the relationship; and major conflicts generate pressures to alter the form of the relationship or to dissolve it altogether. If inducements for participation are sufficiently high, there is the possibility of chronic conflict in the context of a stable relationship.

Three Conceptual Models of Organizational Conflict

As Ephron points out, only a very abstract model is likely to be applicable to the study of all organizational conflict phenomena.[31] To be useful in the analysis of real situations, a general theoretical framework must at least fit several broad classes of conflict, some or all of which may occur within the same organization. This suggests that different ways of abstracting or conceptualizing a given organization are required, depending on what phenomena are to be studied. The three models of organization described at the beginning of this paper are the basis of the general theory of conflict presented here.

Bargaining Model

A reasonable measure of the potential conflict among a set of interest groups is the discrepancy between aggregated demands of the competing parties and the available resources. Attempts at conflict resolution usually center around attempting either to increase the pool of available resources or to decrease the demands of the parties to the conflict. Because market mechanisms or elaborate administrative mechanisms have usually evolved to guarantee orderly allocation of scarce resources, bargaining conflicts rarely escalate to the manifest level, except as strategic maneuvers.[32] Walton and McKersie describe such conflicts as complex relationships which involve both integrative (cooperative) and distributive (competitive) subprocesses.[33] Each party to the conflict has an interest in making the total resources as large as possible, but also in securing as large a share of them as possible for itself. The integrative subprocess is largely concerned with joint problem solving, and the distributive subprocess with strategic bargaining. A major element of strategy in strategic bargaining is that of attitudinal structuring, whereby each party attempts to secure the moral backing of relevant third parties, (for example, the public or the government).

An important characteristic of interest-group conflicts is that negotiation is frequently done by representatives who face the dual problems of (*1*) securing consensus for the negotiated solution among respective group members, and (*2*) compromising between the demands for flexibility by his opposite number and the demands for rigidity by his own group.[34] The level of perceived conflict will increase as the deadline for a solution approaches; and interest-group conflicts are invariably characterized by deadline prsssures.

Most of Walton and McKersie's framework has been developed and applied within the context of labor-management relations. But the interest-group model is not limited to this sphere of activity. Pondy has described the process of capital budgeting as a process of conflict resolution among departments competing for investment funds.[35] Wildavsky has described government budgeting as a political process involving the paraphernalia of bargaining among legislative and executive interest groups.[36] Just as past labor agreements set precedents for current labor agreements, budgeting is an incremental process that builds on the residues of previous budgetary conflicts. But, whereas the visible procedures of bargaining are an accepted part of labor-management relations, there are strong pressures in budgeting (particularly *business* budgeting) to conceal the bargaining that goes on and to attempt to cloak all decisions in the guise of rationality.[37]

Bureaucratic Model

The bureaucratic model (roughly equivalent to Ephron's "political" model) is appropriate for the analysis of conflicts along the *vertical* dimension of a hierarchy, that is, conflicts among the parties to an authority relation. Vertical conflicts in an organization usually arise because superiors attempt to control the behavior of subordinates, and subordinates resist such control. The authority relation is defined by the set of subordinate activities over which the subordinate has surrendered to a superior the legitimacy to exercise discretion.[38] The potential for conflict is thus present when the superior and subordinate have different expectations about the zone of indifference. The subordinate is likely to perceive conflict when the superior attempts to exercise control over activities outside the zone of indifference; and the superior perceives conflict when his attempts at control are thwarted. Superiors are likely to interpret subordinate resistance as due to resentment of the exercise of *personal* power. A typical bureaucratic reaction to subordinate resistance is therefore the substitution of impersonal rules for personal control. As numerous students of bureaucracy are quick to point out, however, the unanticipated reaction to rules is more conflict, not less. The usual reasoning goes as follows: The imposition of rules defines the authority relation more clearly and robs the subordinate of the autonomy provided by ambiguity. Replacing supervision with control by rules invariably narrows the subordinate's freedom of action, makes his behavior more predictable to others, and thus weakens his power position in the organization. Control over the conditions of one's own existence, if not over others', is highly valued in organizations, particularly in large organizations. The subordinate therefore perceives himself to be threatened by and in conflict with his superiors, who are attempting to decrease his autonomy.

But why should autonomy be so important? What is the drawback to being subject to a benevolent autocrat? The answer, of course, is that autocrats seldom are or seldom remain benevolent. There is no assurance that the superior's (the organization's) goals, interests, or needs will be compatible with those of the subordinate, especially when: (*1*) organizations are so large that the leaders cannot identify personally with the rank and file; (*2*) responsibilities are delegated to organizational subunits, and subunit goals, values, etc. become differentiated from those of the hierarchy; and (*3*) procedures are formalized, and the organization leaders tend to treat rank and file members as mere instrumentalities or executors of the procedures.

In short, numerous factors influence goals and values along the vertical dimension of an organization; therefore, because subordinates to an authority relation can not rely on superiors to identify with their goals, autonomy becomes important. This leads to resistance by subordinates to attempts by superiors to control them, which in turn generates pressures toward routinization of activities and the institution of impersonal rules. This may lead to relatively predictable, conflict-free behavior, but behavior which is rigid and largely immune to personal persuasion. It is ironic that these very factors provide the potential for conflict when the organization must adapt to a changing environment. Rigidity of behavior, which minimizes conflict in a stable environment, is a major source of conflict when adaptability is required.

Research on leadership and on role conflict also provides important insights into vertical conflict. Whereas bureaucratic developments have sought to minimize conflict by altering the *fact* of supervision (for example, the use of impersonal rules and emphasis on procedure), leadership developments have sought to alter the *style* of supervision (for example, Likert's "linking pin" proposal and the various techniques of participative management).[39] Instead of minimizing dependence and increasing autonomy, leadership theorists have proposed minimizing conflict by using personal persuasion and group pressures to bring subordinate goals more closely into line with the legitimate goals of the organization. They have prescribed solutions which decrease autonomy and increase dependence. By heightening the individual's involvement in the organization's activities, they have actually provided the basis for the intense personal conflict that characterizes intimate relations.[40]

Both the bureaucratic and the leadership approaches to vertical conflict, as discussed here, take the superior-subordinate dyad as the unit of analysis. The role-conflict approach opens up the possibility of examining the conflicts faced by a man-in-the-middle between the demands of his subordinates and the demands of his superiors. Blau and Scott have suggested that effective leadership can occur only on alternate levels of a hierarchy.[41] The "man-in-the-middle" must align himself with the interests of either his superior or his subordinate, and in so doing he alienates the other. Of the three conceptual models of conflict, the bureaucratic model has probably received the most attention from researchers from a wide variety of disciplines. Partly because of this diversity, and partly because of the ease with which researchers identify with values of efficiency or democracy, this model is the least straightforward of the three.

Systems Model

The systems model, like Ephron's "administrative" model, derives largely from the March-Simon treatment of organizational conflict.[42] It is appropriate for the analysis of conflicts among the parties to a functional relationship. Or to use Walton's terminology, the systems model is concerned with "lateral" conflicts or conflicts among persons at the same hierarchial level.[43] Whereas the authority-structure model is about problems of control, and the interest-group model is about problems of competition, the systems model is about problems of coordination.

The dyad is taken as the basic building block of the conceptual system. Consider two individuals, each occupying some formal position in an organization and playing some formal role with respect to the other. For example, *A* is the production manager and *B* the marketing manager of the *XYZ* company. The production manager's position is defined by the responsibility to use resources at his disposal (for example, raw materials, workers, machines) to manufacture specified products within certain constraints of quantity, quality, cost, time, and perhaps procedure. The marketing manager's position is defined by the responsibility to use resources at his disposal (for example, promotional media, salesmen, salable goods) to market and sell the company's products within certain constraints of product mix, cost, profitability, customer satisfaction, and so on. The constraints under which each manager operates and the resources at his disposal may be set for him by himself, by the other manager, or by someone else either in or outside of the company. The role of each with respect to the other is specified by the set of directions, requests, information, and goods which he minimally must or maximally may give to or receive from the other manager. The roles may also specify instances of and procedures for joint selection of product mix, schedules, and so on. These *formal* specifications of position and role are frequently described in written job descriptions, but may also form part of a set of unwritten, stable, widely shared expectations legitimized by the appropriate hierarchial authorities. If certain responsibilities and activities are exercised without legitimization, that is, without the conscious, deliberate recognition and approval of the appropriate authorities, then they constitute *informal* positions and roles. Such expectations may still be widely shared, and are not necessarily illegitimate, i.e., specifically proscribed by the hierarchial authorities.

The fundamental source of conflict in such a system arises out of the pressures toward suboptimization. Assume first that the organization is goal-oriented rather than procedure-oriented. The subunits in a goal-oriented system will, for various reasons, have different sets of active goals,[44] or different preference orderings for the same set of goals. If in turn, two subunits having differentiated goals are functionally interdependent, then conditions exist for conflict. Important types of interdependence matter are: (*1*) common usage of some service or facility, (*2*) sequences of work or information flow prescribed by task or hierarchy, and (*3*) rules of unanimity or consensus about joint activity.

Two ways of reducing conflict in lateral relationships, if it be desirable to do so, therefore, are to reduce goal differentiation by modified incentive systems, or by proper selection, training, or assignment procedures; and to reduce functional interdependence. Functional interdependence is reduced by (*1*) reducing dependence on common resources; (*2*) loosening up schedules or introducing buffers, such as inventories or contingency funds; and (*3*) reducing pressures for consensus. These techniques of preventing conflict may be costly in both direct and indirect costs. Interpersonal friction is one of the costs of "running a tight ship."

If the parties to the conflict are flexible in their demands and desires,[45] the conflict is likely to be perceived only as a transient disturbance. Furthermore, the conflict may not be perceived, if alternative relationships for satisfying needs are available. This is one of the persuasive arguments for building in redundant channels of work and information flow.

Some relationships may be traditionally conflictful (e.g., administration-faculty, sales-production, and others). The parties to such a relationship have a set to expect conflict, and therefore may perceive conflict when none exists.

As to the forms of manifested conflict, it is extremely unlikely that any violent or aggressive actions will occur. First, strongly held norms proscribe such behavior. Secondly, the reaction of other parties to the relationship is likely to be that of withdrawing all cooperation. A much more common reaction to perceived conflict is the adoption of a joint decision process characterized by bargaining rather than problem solving. Walton, Dutton, and Fitch have described some of the characteristics of a bargaining style: careful rationing of information and its deliberate distortion; rigid, formal, and circumscribed relations; suspicion, hostility, and disassociation among the subunits.[46] These rigidities and negative attitudes, of course, provide the potential for conflict over other issues in future episodes of the relationship.

Summary

It has been argued that conflict within an organization can be best understood as a dynamic process underlying a wide variety of organizational behaviors. The term conflict refers neither to its antecedent conditions, nor individual awareness of it, nor certain affective states, nor its overt manifestations, nor its residues of feeling, precedent, or structure, but to all of these taken together as the history of a conflict episode.

Conflict is not necessarily bad or good, but must be evaluated in terms of its individual and organizational functions and dysfunctions. In general, conflict generates pressures to reduce conflict, but chronic conflict persists and is endured under certain conditions, and consciously created and managed by the politically astute administrator.

Conflict resolution techniques may be applied at any of several pressure points. Their effectiveness and appropriateness depends on the nature of the conflict and on the administrator's philosophy of management. The tension model leads to creation of safety-valve institutions and the semantic model to the promotion of open communication. Although these may be perfectly appropriate for certain forms of imagined conflict, their application to real conflict may only exacerbate the conflict.

A general theory of conflict has been elaborated in the context of each of three conceptual models: (*1*) a bargaining model, which deals with interest groups in competition for resources; (*2*) a bureaucratic model, which deals with authority relations and the need to control; and (*3*) a systems model, which deals with functional relations and the need to coordinate.

Notes and References

1. Jessie Bernard, T. H. Pear, Raymond Aron, and Robert C. Angell, *The Nature of Conflict* (Paris: UNESCO, 1957); Kenneth Boulding, *Conflict and Defense* (New York: Harper, 1962); Lewis Coser, *The Functions of Social Conflict* (Glencoe, Ill.: Free Press, 1956); Kurt Lewin, *Resolving Social Conflict* (New York: Harper, 1948); Anatol Rapaport, *Fights, Games, and Debates* (Ann Arbor: University of Michigan, 1960); Thomas C. Schelling, *The Strategy of Conflict* (Cambridge, Mass.: Harvard Univ., 1961); Muzafer Sherif and Carolyn Sherif, *Groups in Harmony and Tension* (Norman, Okla.: University of Oklahoma, 1953): Georg Simmel, *Conflict*, trans. Kurt H. Wolff (Glencoe, Ill.: Free Press, 1955).

2. Bernard M. Bass, *Organizational Psychology* (Boston, Mass.: Allyn and Bacon, 1965); Theodore Caplow, *Principles of Organization* (New York: Harcourt, Brace, and World, 1964); Eliot D. Chapple and Leonard F. Sayles, *The Measure of Management* (New York: Macmillan, 1961), Michel Crozier, *The Bureaucratic Phenomenon* (Glencoe, Ill.: Free Press, 1964); Richard M. Cyert and James G. March, *A Behavioral Theory of the Firm* (Englewood Cliffs, N. J.: Prentice-Hall, 1963); Alvin W. Gouldner, *Patterns of Industrial Bureaucracy* (Glencoe, Ill.: Free Press, 1954); Harold J. Leavitt, *Managerial Psychology* (Chicago: University of Chicago, 1964); James G. March and Herbert A. Simon, *Organizations* (New York: Wiley, 1958); Philip Selznick, *TVA and the Grass Roots* (Berkeley: University of California, 1949); Victor Thompson, *Modern Organization* (New York: Knopf, 1961).

3. Joseph L. Bower, The Role of Conflict in Economic Decision-making Groups, *Quarterly Journal of Economics*, 79 (May 1965), 253-257; Melville Dalton, *Men Who Manage* (New York: Wiley, 1959); J. M. Dutton and R. E. Walton, "Interdepartmental Conflict and Cooperation: A Study of Two Contrasting Cases," dittoed, Purdue University, October 1964; William Evan, Superior-Subordinate Conflict in Research Organizations, *Administrative Science Quarterly*, 10 (June 1965), 52-64; Robert L. Kahn, *et al.*, *Studies in Organizational Stress* (New York: Wiley, 1964); L. R. Pondy, Budgeting and Inter-Group Conflict in Organizations, *Pittsburgh Business Review*, 34 (April 1964), 1-3; R. E. Walton, J. M. Dutton, and H. G. Fitch, *A Study of Conflict in the Process, Structure, and Attitudes of Lateral Relationships* (Institute Paper No. 93; Lafayette, Ind.: Purdue University, November 1964); Harrison White, Management Conflict and Sociometric Structure, *American Journal of Sociology*, 67 (September 1961), 185-199; Mayer N. Zald, Power Balance and Staff Conflict in Correctional Institutions, *Administrative Science Quarterly*, 7 (June 1962), 22-49.

4. The following conceptualization draws heavily on a paper by Lawrence R. Ephron, Group Conflict in Organizations: A critical Appraisal of Recent Theories, *Berkeley Journal of Sociology*, 6 (Spring 1961), 53-72.

5. James S. Coleman, *Community Conflict* (Glencoe, Ill.: Free Press, 1957); Vilhelm Aubert, Competition and Dissensus: Two Types of Conflict and Conflict Resolution, *Journal of Conflict Resolution*, 7 (March 1963), 26-42.

6. Kahn, *et al.*, *op. cit.*, pp. 11-35.

7. Bernard, Pear, Aron, and Angell, *op. cit.*

8. These two mechanisms are instances of what Cyert and March, *op. cit.*, pp. 117-118, call the "quasi-resolution" of conflict.

9. Leavitt, *op. cit.*, pp. 53-72.

10. Chris Argyris, *Personality and Organization: The Conflict Between the System and the Individual* (New York: Harper, 1957).

11. Bernard, Pear, Aron, and Angell, *op. cit.*
12. It should be emphasized that members of total institutions characteristically experience both strong positive *and* negative feelings for one another and toward the institution. It may be argued that this ambivalence of feeling is a primary cause of anxiety. See Coser, *op. cit.,* pp. 61-65; and Amitai Etzioni and W. R. Taber, Scope, Pervasiveness, and Tension Management in Complex Organizations, *Social Research,* 30 (Summer 1963) 220-238.
13. Dalton, *op. cit.*
14. David Mechanic, "Sources of Power of Lower Participants in Complex Organizations," in W. W. Cooper, H. J. Leavitt, and M. W. Shelly (eds.), *New Perspectives in Organization Research* (New York: Wiley, 1964), pp. 136-149.
15. Evan, *op. cit.;* William G. Scott, *The Management of Conflict: Appeals Systems in Organizations* (Homewood, Ill.: Irwin, 1965). It is useful to interpret recent developments in leadership and supervision (e.g., participative management, Theory Y, linking-pin functions) as devices for preventing superior-subordinate conflicts from arising, thus, hopefully, avoiding the problem of developing appeals systems in the first place.
16. See Coleman, *op. cit.,* pp. 9-11, for an excellent analysis of this mechanism. A chemical analogue of this situation is the supersaturated solution, from which a large amount of chemical salts can be precipitated by the introduction of a single crystal.
17. The sequential dependence of conflict episodes also plays a major role in the analysis of role conflicts by Kahn, *et al., op. cit.,* pp. 11-35. Pondy, *op. cit.* has used the concept of "budget residues" to explain how precedents set in budgetary bargains guide and constrain succeeding budget proceedings.
18. Aubert, *op. cit.*
19. Kahn, *et al., op. cit.,* p. 65.
20. Boulding, *op. cit.,* pp. 305-307.
21. Loren Baritz, *The Servants of Power* (Middletown, Conn.: Wesleyan University, 1960). p. 203.
22. March and Simon, *op. cit.,* p. 112, italics mine. At least one author, however, argues that a "harmony bias" permeates the entire March-Simon volume. It is argued that what March and Simon call conflicts are mere "frictions" and "differences that are not within a community of interests are ignored." See Sherman Krupp, *Pattern in Organization Analysis* (New York: Holt, Rinehart and Winston, 1961), pp. 140-167.
23. March and Simon, *op. cit.,* pp. 115, 129.
24. Harrison White, *op. cit.*
25. Quoted in H. J. Leavitt and L. R. Pondy. *Readings in Managerial Psychology* (Chicago: University of Chicago, 1964), p. 58.
26. Dalton, *op. cit.*
27. Theodore Sorensen, *Decision Making in the White House* (New York: Columbia University, 1963), p. 15. This latter tactic, of course, is predicated and the fact that, *for the subordinates,* conflict is indeed a cost!
28. Harrison White, *op. cit.*
29. Conflict may actually be a source of equilibrium and stability, as Coser, *op. cit.,* p. 159, points out. A multiplicity of conflicts internal to a group, Coser argues, may breed solidarity, provided that the conflicts do not divide the group along the same axis, because the multiplicity of coalitions and associations provide a web of affiliation for the exchange of dissenting viewpoints. The essence of his argument is that some conflict is inevitable, and that it is better to foster frequent minor conflicts of interest,

344   *Organizational Behavior and Management*

and thereby gradually adjust the system, and so forestall the accumulation of latent antagonisms which might eventually disrupt the organization. Frequent minor conflicts also serve to keep the antagonists accurately informed of each other's relative strength, thereby preventing a serious miscalculation of the chances of a successful major conflagration and promoting the continual and gradual readjustment of structure to coincide with true relative power.

30. For example, labor unions, while they wish to win the economic conflict with management, have no interest in seeing the relationship destroyed altogether. They may, however, choose to threaten such disruptive conflict as a matter of strategy.

31. Ephron, *op. cit.*, p. 55.

32. However, the Negro demonstrations of the 1960's and the labor riots of the early twentieth century testify to the futility of managing interest-group conflicts when mechanisms for resolution are not available or when the parties in power refuse to create such mechanisms.

33. R. E. Walton and R. B. McKersie, *A Behavioral Theory of Labor Negotiations* (New York: McGraw-Hill, 1965).

34. These two negotiator problems are termed "factional conflict" and "boundary conflict" by Walton and McKersie, *op. cit.*, p. 283 ff.

35. Pondy, *op. cit.*

36. Aaron Wildavsky, *The Politics of the Budgetary Process* (Boston: Little, Brown, 1964).

37. March and Simon, *op. cit.*, p. 131.

38. This set of activities is usually called the "zone of indifference" or "zone of acceptance." See Chester Barnard, *The Functions of the Executive* (Cambridge, Mass.: Harvard University, 1960), pp. 168-170, and Herbert A. Simon, *Administrative Behavior* (New York: Macmillan, 1960), pp. 11-13.

39. Rensis Likert, *New Patterns of Management* (New York: McGraw-Hill, 1961); See, for example, Chris Argyris, *Interpersonal Competence and Organizational Effectiveness* (Homewood, Ill.: Dorsey, 1962), or Douglas McGregor, *The Human Side of Enterprise* (New York: McGraw-Hill, 1960).

40. Coser, *op. cit.*, pp. 67-72.

41. Peter Blau and Richard Scott, *Formal Organizations* (San Francisco: Chandler, 1962), pp. 162-163.

42. March and Simon, *op. cit.*, pp. 112-135.

43. R. E. Walton, "Theory of Conflict in Lateral Organizational Relationships," (Institute Paper No. 85; Lafayette, Ind.: Purdue University, November 1964).

44. Following Simon, we treat a goal as any criterion of decision. Thus, both purposes and constraints are taken to be goals. See Herbert A. Simon, On the Concept of Organizational Goal, *Administrative Science Quarterly*, 9 (June 1964), 1-22.

45. Such flexibility is one of the characteristics of a problem-solving relationship. Conversely, a bargaining relationship is characterized by rigidity of demands and desires.

46. Walton, Dutton, and Fitch, *op. cit.*

A STRATEGIC CONTINGENCIES' THEORY
OF INTRAORGANIZATIONAL POWER

D. J. HICKSON
C. R. HININGS
C. A. LEE
R. E. SCHNECK
J. M. PENNINGS

Typically, research designs have treated power as the independent variable. Power has been used in community studies to explain decisions on community programs, on resource allocation, and on voting behavior: in small groups it has been used to explain decision making; and it has been used in studies of work organizations to explain morale and alienation. But within work organizations, power itself has not been explained. This paper sets forth a theoretical explanation of power as the dependent variable with the aim of developing empirically testable hypotheses that will explain differential power among subunits in complex work organizations.

The problems of studying power are well known from the cogent reviews by March (1955, 1966) and Wrong (1968). These problems led March (1966: 70) to ask if power was just a term used to mask our ignorance, and to conclude pessimistically that the power of the concept of power "depends on the kind of system we are confronting."

Part of March's (1966) pessimism can be attributed to the problems inherent in community studies. When the unit of analysis is the community, the governmental, political, economic, recreational, and other units which make up the community do not necessarily interact and may even be oriented outside the supposed boundaries of the community. However, the subunits of a work organization are mutually related in the interdependent activities of a single identifiable social system. The perspective of the present paper is due in particular to the encouraging studies of subunits by Lawrence and Lorsch (1967a, 1967b) and begins with their (1967a: 3) definition of an organization as "a system of interrelated behaviors of people who are performing a task that has been differentiated into several distinct subsystems."

Previous studies of power in work organizations have tended to focus on the individual and to neglect subunit or departmental power. This neglect led Perrow (1970: 84) to state: "Part of the problem, I suspect, stems from the persistent attempt to define power in terms of individuals and as a social-psychological phenomenon. . . . Even sociological studies tend to measure power by asking about an individual. . . . I am not at all clear about the matter, but I think the term takes on different meanings when the unit, or power-holder, is a *formal group* in an *open system* with *multiple goals,* and the system is assumed to reflect a political-domination model of organization, rather than only a cooperative model. . . . The fact that after a cursory search I can find only a single study that asks survey questions regarding

Reprinted by permission of the author and the publisher from *Administrative Science Quarterly*, vol. 16, no. 2 (June 1971), pp. 216-27.

the power of functional *groups* strikes me as odd. Have we conceptualized power in such a way as to exclude this well-known phenomenon?''

The concept of power used here follows Emerson (1962) and takes power as a property of the social relationship, not of the actor. Since the context of the relationship is a formal organization, this approach moves away from an overpersonalized conceptualization and operationalization of power toward structural sources. Such an approach has been taken only briefly by Dubin (1963) in his discussion of power, and incidentally by Lawrence and Lorsch (1967b) when reporting power data. Most research has focused on the vertical superior-subordinate relationship, as in a multitude of leadership studies. This approach is exemplified by the extensive work of Tannenbaum (1968) and his colleagues, in which the distribution of perceived power was displayed on control graphs. The focus was on the vertical differentiation of perceived power, that is, the exercise of power by managers who by changing their behavior could vary the distribution and the total amount of perceived power.

By contrast, when organizations are conceived as interdepartmental systems, the division of labor becomes the ultimate source of intraorganizational power, and power is explained by variables that are elements of each subunit's task, its functioning, and its links with the activities of other subunits. Insofar as this approach differs from previous studies by treating power as the dependent variable, by taking subunits of work organizations as the subjects of analysis, and by attempting a multivariate explanation, it may avoid some of the previous pitfalls.

Elements of a Theory

Thompson (1967: 13) took from Cyert and March (1963) a viewpoint which he hailed as a newer tradition: ''A newer tradition enables us to conceive of the organization as an open system, indeterminate and faced with uncertainty, but subject to criteria of rationality and hence needing certainty . . . we suggest that organizations cope with uncertainty by creating certain parts specifically to deal with it, specializing other parts in operating under conditions of certainty, or near certainty.''

Thus organizations are conceived of as interdepartmental systems in which a major task element is coping with uncertainty. The task is divided and allotted to the sub-systems, the division of labor creating an interdependency among them. Imbalance of this reciprocal interdependence (Thompson, 1967) among the parts gives rise to power relations. The essence of an organization is limitation of the autonomy of all its members or parts, since all are subject to power from the others; for subunits, unlike individuals, are not free to make a decision to participate, as March and Simon (1958) put it, nor to decide whether or not to come together in political relationships. They must. They exist to do so. Crozier (1964: 47) stressed in his discussion of power ''the necessity for the members of the different groups to live together; the fact that each group's privileges depend to quite a large extent on the existence of other group's privileges.'' The groups use differential power to function within the system rather than to destroy it.

If dependency in a social relation is the reverse of power (Emerson, 1962), then the crucial unanswered question in organizations is: what factors function to vary dependency, and so to vary power? Emerson (1962: 32) proposed that "the dependence of actor A upon actor B is (*1*) directly proportional to A's motivational investment in goals mediated by B, and (2) inversely proportional to the availability of those goals to A outside of the A—B relation." In organizations, subunit B will have more power than other subunits to the extent that (*1*) B has the capacity to fulfill the requirements of the other subunits and (2) B monopolizes this ability. If a central problem facing modern organizations is uncertainty, then B's power in the organization will be partially determined by the extent to which B copes with uncertainties for other subunits, and by the extent to which B's coping activities are available elsewhere.

Thus, intraorganizational dependency can be associated with two contributing variables: (*1*) the degree to which a subunit copes with uncertainty for other subunits, and (2) the extent to which a subunit's coping activities are substitutable. But if coping with uncertainty, and substitutability, are to be in some way related to power, there is a necessary assumption of some degree of task interconnection among subunits. By definition, organization requires a minimum link. Therefore, a third variable, centrality, refers to the varying degree above such a minimum with which the activities of a subunit are linked with those of other subunits.

Before these three variables can be combined in a theory of power, it is necessary to examine their definition and possible operationalization, and to define power in this context.

Power

Hinings *et al.* (1967: 62) compared power to concepts such as bureaucracy or alienation or social class, which are difficult to understand because they tend to be treated as "large-scale unitary concepts." Their many meanings need disentangling. With the concept of power, this has not yet been accomplished (Cartwright, 1965), but two conceptualizations are commonly employed: (*1*) power as coercion, and (2) power as determination of behavior.

Power as coercive force was a comparatively early conceptualization among sociologists (Weber, 1947; Bierstedt, 1950). Later, Blau (1964) emphasized the imposition of will despite resistance.

However, coercion is only one among the several bases of power listed by French and Raven (1959) and applied across organizations by Etzioni (1961); that is, coercion is a means of power, but is not an adequate definition of power. If the direction of dependence in a relationship is determined by an imbalance of power bases, power itself has to be defined separately from these bases. Adopting Dahl's (1957) concept of power, as many others have done (March, 1955); Bennis *et al.*, 1958; Emerson, 1962; Harsanyi, 1962; Van Doorn, 1962; Dahlstrom, 1966; Wrong, 1968; Tannenbaum, 1968; Luhmann, 1969), power is defined as the determination of the behavior of one social unit by another.

If power is the determination of A's behavior by B, irrespective of whether one, any, or all the types of bases are involved, then authority will here be regarded as that part of power which is legitimate or normatively expected by some selection of role definers. Authority may be either more or less than power. For subunits it might be represented by the formally specified range of activities they are officially required to undertake and, therefore, to decide upon.

Discrepancies between authority and power may reflect time lag. Perrow (1970) explored the discrepancy between respondent's perceptions of power and of what power should be. Perhaps views on a preferred power distribution precede changes in the exercise of power, which in turn precede changes in expectations of power, that is in its legitimate authority content. Perhaps today's authority hierarchy is partly a fossilized impression of yesterday's power ranking. However this may be, it is certainly desirable to include in any research not only data on perceived power and on preferred power, but also on positional power, or authority, and on participation, or exercised power (Clark [ed.], 1968).

Kaplan (1964) succinctly described three dimensions of power. The weight of power is defined in terms of the degree to which B affects the probability of A behaving in a certain way, that is, determination of behavior in the sense adopted here. The other dimensions are domain and scope. Domain is the number of A's, persons or collectivities, whose behavior is determined; scope is the range of behaviors of each A that are determined. For subunit power within an organization, domain might be the number of other subunits affected by the issues, scope the range of decision issues affected, and weight the degree to which a given subunit affects the decision process on the issues. In published research such distinctions are rarely made. Power consists of the sweeping undifferentiated perceptions of respondents when asked to rank individuals or classes of persons, such as supervisors, on influence. Yet at the same time the complexity of power in organizations is recognized. If it is taken for granted that, say, marketing has most to do with sales matters, that accounting has most to do with finance matters, supervisors with supervisory matters, and so on, then the validity of forcing respondents to generalize single opinions across an unstated range of possibilities is questionable.

To avoid these generalized opinions, data collected over a range of decision topics or issues are desirable. Such issues should in principle include all recognized problem areas in the organization, in each of which more than one subunit is involved. Examples might be marketing strategies, obtaining equipment, personnel training, and capital budgeting.

Some suggested subvariables and indicators of power and of the independent variables are summarized in Table 1. These are intended to include both individual perceptions of power in the form of questionnaire responses and data of a somewhat less subjective kind on participation in decision processes and on formal position in the organization.

It is now possible to examine coping with uncertainty, substitutability and centrality.

Uncertainty and Coping with Uncertainty

Uncertainty may be defined as a lack of information about future events, so that alternatives and their outcomes are unpredictable. Organizations deal with environmentally derived uncertainties in the sources and composition of inputs, with uncertainties in the processing of throughputs, and again with environmental uncertainties in the disposal of outputs. They must have means to deal with these uncertainties for adequate task performance. Such ability is here called coping.

In his study of the French tobacco manufacturing industry, Crozier (1964: 164) suggested that power is related to "the kind of uncertainty upon which depends

TABLE 1. Variables and Operationalizable Subvariables

Power (weight, domain, scope)	*Coping with uncertainty*, classified as:
Positional power (authority)	By prevention (forestalling uncertainty)
Participation power	By information (forecasting)
Perceived power	By absorption (action after the event)
Preferred power	
Uncertainty	*Substitutability*
Variability of organizational inputs	Availability of alternatives
Feedback on subunit performance;	Replaceability of personnel
Speed	
Specificity	*Centrality*
Structuring of subunit activities	Pervasiveness of workflows
	Immediacy of workflows

the life of the organization.'' March and Simon (1958) had earlier made the same point, and Perrow (1961) had discussed the shifting domination of different groups in organizations following the shifting uncertainties of resources and the routinization of skills. From studies of industrial firms, Perrow (1970) tentatively thought that power might be due to uncertainty absorption, as March and Simon (1958) call it. Lawrence and Lorsch (1967b) found that marketing had more influence than production in both container-manufacturing and food-processing firms, apparently because of its involvement in (uncertain) innovation and with customers.

Crozier (1964) proposed a strategic model of organizations as systems in which groups strive for power, but his discussion did not clarify how uncertainty could relate positively to power. Uncertainty itself does not give power: coping gives power. If organizations allocate to their various subunits task areas that vary in uncertainty, then those subunits that cope most effectively with the most uncertainty should have most power within the organization, since coping by a subunit reduces the impact of uncertainty on other activities in the organization, a shock absorber function. Coping may be by prevention, for example, a subunit prevents sales fluctuations by securing firm orders; or by information, for example, a subunit forecasts sales fluctuations; or by absorption, for example, a drop in sales is swiftly countered by novel selling methods (Table 1). By coping, the subunit provides pseudo certainty for the other subunits by controlling what are otherwise contingencies for other activities. This coping confers power through the dependencies created.

Thus organizations do not necessarily aim to avoid uncertainty nor to reduce its absolute level, as Cyert and March (1963) appear to have assumed, but to cope with it. If a subunit can cope, the level of uncertainty encountered can be increased by moving into fresh sectors of the environment, attempting fresh outputs, or utilizing fresh technologies.

Operationally, raw uncertainty and coping will be difficult to disentangle, though theoretically the distinctions are clear. For all units, uncertainty is in the raw situation which would exist without the activities of the other relevant subunits, for example, the uncertainty that would face production units if the sales subunit were not there to forecast and/or to obtain a smooth flow of orders. Uncertainty might be indicated by the variability of those inputs to the organization which are taken by the subunit. For instance, a production subunit may face variability in raw materials and engineering may face variability in equipment performance. Lawrence and Lorsch (1967a) attempted categorizations of this kind. In addition, they (1967a: 14) gave a lead with "the time span of definitive feedback from the environment." This time span might be treated as a secondary indicator of uncertainty, making the assumption that the less the feedback to a subunit on the results of what it is doing, and the less specific the feedback, the more likely the subunit is to be working in a vague, unknown, unpredictable task area. Both speed and specificity of feedback are suggested variables in Table 1.

Furthermore, the copious literature on bureaucratic or mechanistic structures versus more organic and less defined structures could be taken to imply that routinized or highly structured subunits, for example, as conceptualized and measured by Pugh *et al.* (1968), will have stable homogeneous activities and be less likely to face uncertainty. This assumption would require empirical testing before structuring of activities could be used as an indicator of uncertainty, but it is tentatively included in Table 1.

In principle, coping with uncertainty might be directly measured by the difference between the uncertainty of those inputs taken by a subunit and the certainty with which it performs its activities nonetheless. This would indicate the degree of shock absorption.

The relation of coping with uncertainty to power can be expressed by the following hypothesis:

Hypothesis 1. The more a subunit copes with uncertainty, the greater its power within the organization.

The hypothesis is in a form which ignores any effects of centrality and substitutability.

Substitutability

Concepts relating to the availability of alternatives pervade the literature on power. In economics theory the degree of competition is taken as a measure of the extent to which alternatives are available from other organizations, it being implied that the power of an organization over other organizations and customers is a function of the amount of competition present. The same point was the second part of Emerson's (1962) power-dependency scheme in social relations, and the second requirement or determinant in Blau's (1964) model of a power relationship.

Yet only Mechanic (1962) and Dubin (1957, 1963) have discussed such concepts as explanations of organizational power. Mechanic's (1962: 358) hypothesis 4 stated: "Other factors remaining constant, a person difficult to replace will have greater power than a person easily replaceable." Dubin (1957) stressed the very similar notion of exclusiveness, which as developed later (Dubin, 1963: 21), means that: "For any given level of functional importance in an organization, the power residing in a functionary is inversely proportional to the number of other functionaries in the organization capable of performing the function." Supporting this empirically, Lipset *et al.* (1956) suggested that oligarchy may occur in trade unions because of the official's monopoly of political and negotiating skills.

The concept being used is represented here by the term substitutability, which can, for subunits, be defined as the ability of the organization to obtain alternative performance for the activities of a subunit, and can be stated as a hypothesis for predicting the power of a subunit as follows:

Hypothesis 2. The lower the substitutability of the activities of a subunit, the greater its power within the organization.

Thus a purchasing department would have its power reduced if all of its activities could be done by hired materials agents, as would a personnel department if it were partially substituted by selection consultants or by line managers finding their staff themselves. Similarly, a department may hold on to power by retaining information the release of which would enable others to do what it does.

The obvious problem in operationalization is establishing that alternative means of performing activities exist, and if they do, whether they could feasibly be used. Even if agents or consultants exist locally, or if corporation headquarters could provide services, would it really be practicable for the organization to dispense with its own subunit? Much easier to obtain are data on replaceability of subunit personnel such as length of training required for new recruits and ease of hiring, which can be regarded as secondary indicators of the substitutability of a subunit, as indicated in Table 1.

Centrality

Given a view of organizations as systems of interdependent roles and activities, then the centrality of a subunit is the degree to which its activities are interlinked into the system. By definition, no subunit of an organization can score zero centrality. Without a minimum of centrality, coping with uncertainty and substitutability cannot affect power; above the minimum, additional increments of centrality further differentiate subunit power. It is the degree to which the subunit is an interdependent component, as Thompson (1967: 54) put it, distinguishing between pooled, sequential, and reciprocal interdependence patterns. Blau and Scott (1962) made an analogous distinction between parallel and interdependent specialization. Woodward (1965: 126) also introduced a concept of this kind into her discussion of the critical function in each of unit, large batch and mass, and process production: "there seemed to be one function that was central and critical in that it had the greatest effect on success and survival."

Within the overall concept of centrality, there are inconsistencies which indicate that more than one constitutive concept is being used. At the present stage of conceptualization their identification must be very tentative. First, there is the idea that the activities of a subunit are central if they are connected with many other activities in the organization. This workflow pervasiveness may be defined as the degree to which the workflows of a subunit connect with the workflows of other subunits. It describes the extent of task interactions between subunits, and for all subunits in an organization it would be operationalized as the flowchart of a complete systems analysis. For example, the integrative subsystems studied by Lawrence and Lorsch (1967a: 30), "whose members had the function of integrating the sales-research and the production-research subsystems" and which had structural and cultural characteristics intermediate between them, were presumably high on workflow pervasiveness because everything they did connected with the workflows of these several other subsystems. Research subsystems, however, may have been low on this variable if they fed work only to a single integrative, or production, subsystem.

Secondly, the activities of a subunit are central if they are essential in the sense that their cessation would quickly and substantially impede the primary workflow of the organization. This workflow immediacy is defined as the speed and severity with which the workflows of a subunit affect the final outputs of the organization. Zald (1962) and Clark (1956) used a similar idea when they explained differential power among institution staff and education faculty by the close relation of their activities to organization goals.

The pervasiveness and immediacy of the workflows of a subunit are not necessarily closely related, and may empirically show a low correlation. A finance department may well have pervasive connections with all other subunits through the budgeting system, but if its activities ceased it would be some time before the effects were felt in, say, the production output of a factory; a production department controlling a stage midway in the sequence of an automated process, however, could have high workflow immediacy though not high pervasiveness.

The two main centrality hypotheses can therefore be stated as follows:

Hypothesis 3a. The higher the pervasiveness of the workflows of a subunit, the greater its power within the organization.

Hypothesis 3b. The higher the immediacy of the workflows of a subunit, the greater its power within the organization.

Control of Contingencies

Hypotheses relating power to coping with uncertainty, substitutability, and the subvariables of centrality have been stated in a simple single-variable form. Yet it follows from the view of subunits as interdependent parts of organizational systems that the hypotheses in this form are misleading. While each hypothesis may be empirically upheld, it is also hypothesized that this cannot be so without some values of both the other main independent variables. For example, when a marketing department copes with a volatile market by forecasting and by switching sales staff around to ensure stable orders, it acquires power only because the forecast and the orders are linked to the workflow of production, which depends on them. But even then power would be limited by the availability of a successful local marketing agency which could be hired by the organization, and the fact that salesmen were low skilled and easily replaceable.

To explain this interrelationship, the concept of control of contingencies is introduced. It represents organizational interdependence; subunits control contingencies for one another's activities and draw power from the dependencies thereby created. As a hypothesis:

Hypothesis 4. The more contingencies are controlled by a subunit, the greater its power within the organization.

A contingency is a requirement of the activities of one subunit which is affected by the activities of another subunit. What makes such a contingency strategic, in the sense that it is related to power, can be deduced from the preceding hypotheses.

The independent variables are each necessary but not sufficient conditions for control of strategic contingencies, but together they determine the variation in interdependence between subunits. Thus contingencies controlled by a subunit as a consequence of its coping with uncertainty do not become strategic, that is, affect power, in the organization without some (unknown) values of substitutability and centrality. A strategic contingencies theory of power is therefore proposed and is illustrated by the diagram in Figure 1.

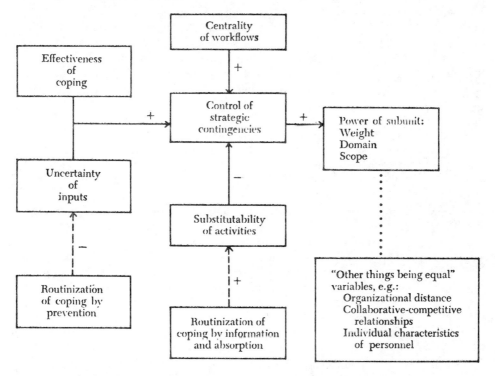

⟶ Direct relationship with power; ------- indirect relationship with power; ....
relationship with power other than by control of contingencies.

Figure 1. The strategic contingencies theory and routinization.

In terms of exchange theory, as developed by Blau (1964), subunits can be seen to be exchanging control of strategic contingencies one for the other under the normative regulation of an encompassing social system, and acquiring power in the system through the exchange. The research task is to elucidate what combinations of values of the independent variables summarized in hypotheses 1-3 allow hypothesis 4 to hold. Ultimately and ideally the aim would be to discover not merely the weightings of each in the total effect upon power, but how these variables should be operationally interrelated to obtain the best predictions. More of one and less of another may leave the resulting power unchanged. Suppose an engineering subunit has power because it quickly absorbs uncertainty by repairing breakdowns which interfere with the different workflows for each of several organization outputs. It is moderately central and nonsubstitutable. A change in organization policy bringing in a new technology with a single workflow leading to a single output would raise engineering's centrality, since a single breakdown would immediately stop everything, but simultaneously the uncertainty might be reduced by a maintenance program which all but eliminates the possibility of such an occurrence.

Though three main factors are hypothesized, which must change if power is to change, it is not assumed that all subunits will act in accord with the theory to increase their power. This has to be demonstrated. There is the obvious possibility of a cumulative reaction in which a subunit's power is used to preserve or increase the uncertainty it can cope with, or its centrality, or to prevent substitution, thereby increasing its power, and so on. Nor is it argued that power or authority are intentionally allocated in terms of the theory, although the theory is open to such an inference.

Routinization

Most studies that refer to uncertainty contrast it with routinization, the prior prescription of recurrent task activities. Crozier (1964) held that the power of the maintenance personnel in the tobacco plants was due to all other tasks being routinized. A relative decline in the power of general medical personnel in hospitals during this century is thought to be due to the routinization of some tasks, which previously presented uncertainties which could be coped with only by a physician, and the transfer of these tasks to relatively routinized subunits, such as inoculation programs, mass X-ray facilities, and so on (Perrow, 1965; Gordon and Becker, 1964). Crozier (1964: 165) crystallized the presumed effects of routinization; "But the expert's success is constantly self-defeating. The rationalization process gives him power, but the end results of rationalization curtail his power. As soon as a field is well covered, as soon as the first intuitions and innovations can be translated into rules and programs, the expert's power disappears."

The strategic contingencies' theory as developed in Figure 1 clarifies this. It suggests that research has been hampered by a confusion of two kinds of routinization, both of which are negatively related to power but in different ways. Routinization may be (*a*) of coping by prevention, which prevents the occurrence of uncertainty; and (*b*) of coping by information or absorption which define how the uncertainty which does occur shall be coped with.

Preventive routinization reduces or removes the uncertainty itself, for example, planned maintenance, which maintenance in Crozier's (1964) tobacco factories would have resisted; inoculation or X-ray programs; and long-term supply contracts, so that the sales staff no longer have to contend with unstable demand. Such routinization removes the opportunity for power, and it is this which is self-defeating (Crozier, 1964: 165) if the expert takes his techniques to a point when they begin not only to cope but to routinely diminish the uncertainty coped with. Thus reducing the uncertainty is not the same as reducing the impact of uncertainty. According to the hypothesis, a sales department which transmits steady orders despite a volatile market has high power; a sales department which reduces the uncertainty itself by long-term tied contracts has low power.

Routinization of coping by information and absorption is embodied in job descriptions and task instructions prescribing how to obtain information and to respond to uncertainty. For maintenance personnel, it lays down how to repair the machine; for physicians, it lays down a standard procedure for examining patients and sequences of remedies for each diagnosis. How does this affect power, since it does not eliminate the uncertainty itself, as preventive routinization does? What it does is increase substitutability. The means of coping become more visible and possible substitutes more obvious, even if those substitutes are unskilled personnel from another subunit who can follow a standard procedure but could not have acquired the previously unexpressed skills.

There is probably some link between the two kinds of routinization. Once preventive routinization is accomplished, other coping routinization more easily follows, as indeed it follows any reduction of uncertainty.

Studies of Subunit Power

Testing of Hypotheses on Earlier Work
The utility of the strategic contingencies theory should be tested on published work, but it is difficult to do this adequately, since most studies stress only one possibility. For example, Crozier (1964) and Thompson (1967) stressed uncertainty, Dubin (1963) stressed exclusiveness of function, and Woodward (1965) spoke of the critical function.

The difficulty is also due to the lack of data. For example, among several studies in which inferences about environmental uncertainty are drawn, only Lawrence and Lorsch (1967b) presented data. They combine executive's questionnaire responses on departmental clarity of job requirements, time span of definitive feedback on departmental success in performance, and uncertainty of cause and effect in the department's functional area.

Lawrence and Lorsch (1967b: 127) found that in two food-processing organizations, research was most influential, then marketing, excluding the field selling unit, and then production. However, influence, or perceived power as it is called here, was rated on the single issue of product innovation and not across a range of issues as suggested earlier in this paper; validity therefore rests on the assumption of equal potential involvement of each function in this one issue. Would research still be most influential if the issues included equipment purchase, or capital budgeting, or personnel training? Even so, on influence over product innovation, an uncertainty hypothesis could be said to fit neatly, since the subunits were ordered on perceived uncertainty of subenvironment exactly as they were on influence.

But uncertainty alone would not explain power in the other firms studied. Although in six plastics firms, coordinating sections or integrating units were perceived as having more influence than functional subunits because "integration itself was the most problematic job" (Lawrence and Lorsch 1967b: 62), it was also a central job in terms of workflow pervasiveness.

Furthermore, in two container manufacturing organizations, although the market subenvironment was seen as the least uncertain, the sales subunit was perceived as the most influential (Lawrence and Lorsch 1967b: 111). An explanation must be sought in the contingencies that the sales subunit controls for production and for research. In this industry, outputs must fit varying customer requirements for containers. Scheduling for production departments and design problems for research departments are therefore completely subject to the contingencies of orders brought in by the sales department. Sales has not only the opportunity to cope with such uncertainty as may exist over customer requirements, it is highly central; for its activities connect it directly to both the other departments—workflow pervasiveness —and if it ceased work production of containers would stop—workflow immediacy. The effects of centrality are probably bolstered by nonsubstitutability, since the sales subunit develops a necessary particularized knowledge of customer requirements. Production and research are, therefore, comparatively powerless in face of the strategic contingencies controlled by the sales subunit.

In short, only a sensitive balancing of all three factors can explain the patterns of contingencies from which power strategically flows.

This is plain also in Crozier's (1964) insightful study of small French tobacco-manufacturing plants. Crozier (1964: 109) had the impression that the maintenance engineers were powerful because "machine stoppages are the only major happenings that cannot be predicted"; therefore the engineers had (Crozier, 1964: 154) "control over the last source of uncertainty remaining in a completely routinized organizational system." But this is not enough for power. Had it been possible to contract maintenance work to consulting engineers, for example, then programs of preventive maintenance might have been introduced, and preventive routinization would have removed much of the uncertainty. However, it is likely that union agreements ensured that the plant engineers were nonsubstitutable. In addition, in these small organizations without specialist control and service departments, the maintenance section's work linked it to all production subunits, that is, to almost every other subunit in the plant. So workflow pervasiveness was high, as was workflow immediacy, since cessation of maintenance activities would quickly have stopped tobacco outputs. The control of strategic contingencies which gave power to the engineers has to be explained on all counts and not by uncertainty alone.

Crozier's (1964) study is a warning against the facile inference that a power distribution fitting the strategic contingencies theory is necessarily efficient, or rational, or functional for an organization; for the power of the engineers to thwart the introduction of programmed maintenance was presumably neither efficient, rational, nor functional.

A challenge to the analysis made is presented by Goldner's (1970) description of a case where there was programmed maintenance and yet the maintenance section held power over production. Goldner (1970) attributed the power of the maintenance subunit to knowing how to install and operate such programs, to coping with breakdowns as in the Crozier (1964) cases, and to knowing how to cope with a critical problem of parts supplies. The strategic contingencies theory accords with his interpretation so long as knowing how to install a program takes effect as coping with uncertainty and not yet as preventive routinization which stops breakdowns. This is where an unknown time element enters to allow for changes in the variables specified and in any associated variables not yet defined. For a time, knowing the answer to an uncertainty does confer power, but the analyses of routinization derived from the theory, as shown in Figure 1, suggests that if this becomes successful preventive routinization, it takes a negative effect upon power. The net result for power in Goldner's (1970) case would then be from the interplay of the opposed effects of activities some of which are preventively routinized, thus decreasing power, and some of which continue to be nonroutine, thus increasing power.

On the other hand, Goldner's (1970) description of the powerful industrial relations subunit in the same plant clearly supports the strategic contingencies theory by showing that coping with uncertainty, centrality, and substitutability had the effect predicted here. The industrial relations subunit exploited uncertainty over the supply and cost of personnel, which arose from possible strikes and pay increases, by (Goldner, 1970: 104) "use of the union as an outside threat." It coped effectively by its nonroutinized knowledge of union officials and of contract interpretation; and its activities were centrally linked to those of other subunits by the necessity for uniform practice on wages and employment. Industrial relations staff developed nonsubstitutable interpersonal and bargaining skills.

There are no means of assessing whether the univariate stress on uncertainty in the handful of other relevant studies is justified. Perrow (1970) explained the greater perceived power of sales as against production, finance, and research, in most of 12 industrial firms, by the concept of uncertainty absorption (March and Simon, 1958). Sales was strategic with respect to the environment. Is the one case where it came second to production the only case where it was also substitutable? Or not central?

White (1961) and Landsberger (1961) both suggested that power shifts over periods of time to follow the locus of uncertainty. Both studied engineering factories. From the histories of three firms, Landsberger (1961) deduced that when money was scarce and uncertain, accounting was powerful; when raw materials were short, purchasing was powerful; and, conversely, when demand was insatiable sales were weakened. In the Tennessee Valley Authority, a nonmanufacturing organization, Selznick (1949) attributed the eventual power of the agricultural relations department to its ability to cope with the uncertain environmental threat represented by the Farm Bureau.

Yet while these earlier studies emphasized uncertainty in one way or another, others called attention to substitutability and probably also to centrality. Again the implication is that contingencies are not strategically controlled without some combination of all three basic variables. For example, the engineers described by Strauss (1962, 1964) appeared to have more power than purchasing agents because the latter were substitutable, that is, the engineers can set specifications for what was to be bought even though the purchasing agents considered this their own responsibility. Thompson (1956: 300) attributed variations in perceived power within and between two U.S. Air Force wings to the changing "technical requirements of operations," which may have indicated changing centralities and substitutabilities.

In the absence of data, consideration of further different kinds of organization must remain pure speculation, for example, the power of surgical units in hospitals, the power of buyers in stores, the power of science faculties in universities.

Other Variables Affecting Power

In order that it can be testable, the strategic contingencies theory errs on the side of simplicity. Any theory must start with a finite number of variables and presume continual development by their alteration or deletion, or by the addition of new variables. As stated, the theory uses only those variables hypothesized to affect power by their contribution to the control of contingencies exercised by a subunit. Other possible explanations of power are not considered. This in itself is an assumption of the greater explanatory force of the theory. Blalock :1961: 8) put the problem clearly: "The dilemma of the scientist is to select models that are at the same time simple enough to permit him to think with the aid of the model but also sufficiently realistic that the simplifications required do not lead to predictions that are highly inaccurate."

In recognition of this, Figure 1 includes several "other things being equal" variables as they are called, that may affect power, but are assumed to do so in other ways than by control of contingencies. One such range of possible relevant variables is qualities of interdepartmental relationships, such as competitiveness versus collaborativeness (Dutton and Walton, 1966). Does the power exercised relate to the style of the relationship through which the power runs? Another possibility is pinpointed by Stymne (1968: 88): "A unit's influence has its roots partly in its strategical importance to the company and partly in nonfunctional circumstances such as tradition, or control over someone in top management through, for example, family relationship." The tradition is the status which may accrue to a particular function because chief executives have typically reached the top through it. Many case studies highlight the personal links of subunits with top personnel (Dalton, 1959; Gouldner, 1955). The notion might be entitled the organizational distance of the subunit, a variant of social distance.

Finally, but perhaps most important, individual differences must be accepted, that is, differences in the intelligence, skills, ages, sexes, or personality factors such as dominance, assertiveness, and risk-taking propensity, of personnel in the various subunits.

Conclusion

The concept of work organizations as interdepartmental systems leads to a strategic contingencies theory explaining differential subunit power by dependence on contingencies ensuing from varying combinations of coping with uncertainty, substitutability, and centrality. It should be stressed that the theory is not in any sense static. As the goals, outputs, technologies, and markets of organizations change so, for each subunit, the values of the independent variables change, and patterns of power change.

Many problems are unresolved. For example, does the theory implicitly assume perfect knowledge by each subunit of the contingencies inherent for it in the activities of the others? Does a workflow of information affect power differently to a workflow of things? But with the encouragement of the improved analysis given of the few existing studies, data can be collected and analyzed, hopefully in ways which will afford a direct test.

References

Bennis, Warren G., N. Berkowitz, M. Affinito, and M. Malone. "Authority, power and the ability to influence." Human Relations, 11: 143-156. 1958.

Bierstedt, Robert. "An analysis of social power." American Sociological Review, 15: 730-736. 1950.

Blalock, Hubert M. Causal Inferences in Nonexperimental Research. Chapel Hill: University of North Carolina Press. 1961.

Blau, Peter. Exchange and Power in Social Life. New York: Wiley. 1964.

Blau, Peter, and W. Richard Scott. Formal Organizations: A Comparative Approach. London: Routledge and Kegan Paul. 1962.

Cartwright, Darwin. "Influence, leadership, control." In James G. March (ed.), Handbook of Organizations: 1-47. Chicago: Rand McNally. 1965.

Clark, Burton R. "Organizational adaptation and precarious values: a case study." American Sociological Review, 21: 327-336. 1956.

Clark, Terry N. (ed.) Community Structure Analyses. San Francisco: Chandler. 1968.

Crozier, Michel. The Bureaucratic Phenomenon. London: Tavistock. 1964.

Cyert, Richard M., and James G. March. A Behavioral Theory of the Firm. Englewood Cliffs, N. J.: Prentice-Hall. 1963.

Dahl, Robert A. "The concept of power." Behavioral Science, 2: 201-215. 1957.

Dahlstrom, E. "Exchange, influence, and power." Acta Sociologica, 9: 237-284. 1966.

Dalton, Melville. Men Who Manage. New York: Wiley. 1959.

Dubin, Robert. "Power and union-management relations." Administrative Science Quarterly, 2: 60-81. 1957.

———."Power, function, and organization." Pacific Sociological Review, 6: 16-24. 1963.

Dutton, John M., and Richard E. Walton. "Interdepartmental conflict and cooperation: two contrasting studies." Human Organization, 25: 207-220. 1966.

Emerson, R. E. "Power-dependence relations." American Sociological Review, 27: 31-41. 1967.

Etzioni, Amitai. A Comparative Analysis of Complex Organizations. New York: Free Press. 1961.

French, John R. P., and Bertram Raven. "The bases of social power." In D. Cartwright (ed.); Studies in Social Power: 150-167. Ann Arbor: University of Michigan. 1959.

Goldner, Fred H. "The division of labor: process and power." In Mayer N. Zald (ed.), Power in Organizations: 97-143. Nashville: Vanderbilt University Press. 1970.

Gordon, Gerald, and Selwyn Becker. "Changes in medical practice bring shifts in the patterns of power." The Modern Hospital (February): 89-91, 154-156. 1964.

Gouldner, Alvin W. Wildcat Strike. London: Routledge. 1955.

Harsanyi, John C. "Measurement of social power, opportunity costs, and the theory of two-person bargaining games." Behavioral Science, 7: 67-80. 1962.

Hinings, Christopher R., Derek S. Pugh, David J. Hickson, and Christopher Turner. "An approach to the study of bureaucracy." Sociology, 1: 61-72. 1967.

Kaplan, Abraham. "Power in perspective." In Robert L. Kahn and Elise Boulding (eds.), Power and Conflict in Organizations: 11-32. London: Tavistock. 1964.

Landsberger, Henry A. "The horizontal dimension in bureaucracy." Administrative Science Quarterly, 6: 299-332. 1961.

Lawrence, Paul R., and Jay W. Lorsch. "Differentiation and integration in complex organizations." Administrative Science Quarterly, 12: 1-47. 1967a.

———. Organization and Environment. Cambridge: Division of Research, Graduate School of Business Administration, Harvard University. 1967.

Lipset, Seymour M., Martin A. Trow, and James A. Coleman. Union Democracy. Glencoe, Ill.: Free Press. 1956.

Luhmann, Niklaus. "Klassische theorie der macht." Zeitschrift fur Politik, 16: 149-170.

March, James G. "An introduction to the theory and measurement of influence." American Political Science Review, 49: 431-450. 1955.

———. "The power of power." In David Easton (ed.), Varieties of Political Theory: 39-70. Englewood Cliffs. N. J.: Prentice-Hall. 1966.

March, James G., and Herbert A. Simon. Organizations. New York: Wiley. 1958.

Mechanic, David. "Sources of power of lower participants in complex organizations." Administrative Science Quarterly, 7: 349-364. 1962.

Perrow, Charles. "The analysis of goals in complex organizations." American Sociological Review, 26: 854-866. 1961.

———. "Hospitals: technology, structure, and goals." In James G. March (ed.), Handbook of Organizations: 910-971. Chicago: Rand McNally. 1965.

———. "Departmental power and perspectives in industrial firms." In Mayer N. Zald (ed.), Power in Organizations: 59-89. Nashville: Vanderbilt University Press. 1970.

Pugh, Derek S., David J. Hickson, Christopher R. Hinings, and Christopher Turner, "Dimensions of organization structure." Administrative Science Quarterly, 13: 65-105. 1968.

Selznick, Philip. T.V.A. and the Grass Roots. Berkeley: University of California Press. 1949.

Strauss, George. "Tactics of lateral relationship: the purchasing agent." Administrative Science Quarterly, 7: 161-186. 1962.

———. "Work-flow frictions, interfunctional rivalry, and professionalism." Human Organization, 23: 137-150. 1964.

Stymne, Bengt. "Interdepartmental communication and intraorganizational strain." Acta Sociologica, 11: 82-100. 1968.

Tannenbaum, Arnold S. Control in Organizations. New York: McGraw-Hill. 1968.

Thompson, James D. "Authority and power in 'identical' organizations." American Journal of Sociology, 62: 290-301. 1956.

———. Organizations in Action. New York: McGraw-Hill. 1967.

Van Doorn, Jaques A. A. "Sociology and the problem of power." Sociologica Neerlandica, 1: 3-47. 1962.

Weber, Max. The Theory of Social and Economic Organization. Glencoe, Ill.: Free Press. 1947.

White, Harrison. "Management conflict and sociometric structure." American Journal of Sociology, 67: 185-199. 1961.

Woodward, Joan. Industrial Organization: Theory and Practice. London: Oxford University Press. 1965.

Wrong, Dennis H. "Some problems in defining social power." American Journal of Sociology, 73, 673-681. 1968.

Zald, Mayer, N. "Organizational control structures in five correctional institutions." American Journal of Sociology, 68: 335-345. 1962.

THE MANAGEMENT OF INTERDEPARTMENTAL CONFLICT: A MODEL AND REVIEW

RICHARD E. WALTON
JOHN M. DUTTON

Horizontal interactions are seldom shown on the organizational chart, but trans-actions along this dimension are often at least as important as vertical interactions (Simpson, 1959; Landsberger, 1961; Burns and Stalker, 1961). This paper presents a general model of interdepartmental conflict and its management, together with a review of the relevant literature. The model includes five sets of related variables: antecedents to conflict, attributes of the lateral relationship, management of the inter-face, consequences of the relationship, and responses of higher executives. Figure 1 shows the general relationship among these sets of variables.

The general model is postulated as applicable to all lateral relations between any two organizational units (departments, divisions, sections, and so on) that engage in any type of transaction, including joint decision making, exchanging information, providing expertise or advice, and auditing or inspecting.

Antecedents to Interunit Conflict and Collaboration

Manifest conflict results largely from factors which originate outside the par-ticular lateral relationship under consideration or which antedate the relationship. Hypotheses and models that use external factors to predict lateral relations have been advanced by March and Simon (1958), Thompson (1961), Caplow (1964), Lawrence and Lorsch (1967a, b,) and Pondy (1967). The present model describes nine major types of antecedents: mutual dependence, asymmetries, rewards, organizational dif-ferentiation, role dissatisfaction, ambiguities, common resources, communication obstacles, and personal skills and traits.

Mutual Task Dependence

Mutual task dependence is the key variable in the relevance of the interunit conflict model in general and the impact of the postulated conflict antecedents in particular. Task dependence is the extent to which two units depend upon each other for assistance, information, compliance, or other coordinative acts in the performance of their respective tasks. It is assumed here that dependence is mutual and can range from low to high. Asymmetry in the interdependence is treated later.

According to Miller (1959), the more performance of one unit depends on the performance of all other units, the more likely is the system to perform without external control. Other studies, however, Dutton and Walton (1966), for example, indicate that task interdependence not only provides an incentive for collaboration,

Reprinted by permission of the author and the publisher from *Administrative Science Quarterly*, vol. 14, no. 1 (March 1969), pp. 73-84.

Figure 1. General model of interunit conflict.

but also presents an occasion for conflict and the means for bargaining over inter-departmental issues. A related factor, task overload, has similarly mixed potential for conflict and collaboration. Overload conditions may intensify the problem of scarce resources and lead to bargaining; may increase tension, frustration, and aggression; and may decrease the time available for the social interactions that would enable the units to contain their conflict. On the other hand, overload may place a premium on mutual assistance. The net directional effects of high task interdependence and overload are therefore uncertain.

Other implications of the extent of mutual task dependence are more predictable. High task interdependence and overload tend to heighten the intensity of either interunit antagonisms or friendliness, increase the magnitude of the consequences of unit conflict for organizational performance, and contribute to the difficulty of changing an ongoing pattern.

Task-related Asymmetries

Symmetrical interdependence and symmetrical patterns of initiation between units promote collaboration; asymmetrical interdependence leads to conflict. For example, in a study by Dalton (1959), a staff group resented the asymmetries in their relationship with line groups. The staff group had to understand the problems of the line groups, had to get along with them, promote their ideas, and justify their existence; but none of these relations were reciprocal requirements imposed on the line groups. Strauss (1962) reported that asymmetrical high dependence of purchasing agents on another group led them to make more attempts to influence the terms of requisitions they received and thereby force interaction to flow both ways.

The adverse effects of asymmetrical conditions are sometimes related to the fact that one unit has little incentive to coordinate. The more dependent unit may try to increase the incentive of the more independent unit to cooperate by interfering with their task performance. The assumption is that once the independent unit is made aware of their need for the cooperation of the dependent unit (i.e., to desist from interfering acts), they will behave more cooperatively (supply the assistance necessary). This tactic may indeed achieve its purpose, and the conflict-interference elicits a retaliatory response.

Conflict is also produced by differences in the way units are ranked along various dimensions of organizational status, namely direction of initiation of action, prestige, power, and knowledge. Seiler (1963) studied in an organization in which it was generally agreed that research had more prestige than engineering and engineering had more prestige than production. When the sequential pattern of initiation and influence followed this status ordering, it was accepted. However, where a lower-status industrial engineering group needed to direct the higher-status research group to carry out routine tests, the result was a breakdown in relationships between the departments.

Inconsistency between the distribution of knowledge among departments and the lateral influence patterns are also a source of conflict. Lawrence and Lorsch (1967a) advanced the idea that the more the influence of each unit is consistent with key competitive factors, the more effectively will interunit issues be resolved. They noted that in container firms, customer delivery and product quality were crucial for competitive success; therefore, sales and production were required to have the most influence in the resolution of interunit conflict. By contrast, in the food industry, where market expertise and food science were essential, sales and research were required to be the more influential. Landsberger (1961) also found that the locus of power among three plants in the same industry was affected by their different market positions.

Zald (1962) in a study of correctional institutions offered a power-balance proposition about the effect of relative power: assuming task interdependence and divergent values among three units (teachers, cottage parents, and social service workers), conflict is most likely to occur between units that are unable to control the situation and those perceived as being in control. He found that the patterns of conflict among these three units were generally consistent with predictions based on this power-balance hypothesis.

Performance Criteria and Rewards

Interunit conflict results when each of the interdependent departments has responsibility for only one side of a dilemma embedded in organizational tasks. Dutton and Walton (1966) noted that the preference of production units for long, economical runs conflicted with the preference of sales units for quick delivery to good customers. Dalton (1959) observed that staff units valued change, because that was one way they proved their worth; whereas line units valued stability, because change reflected unfavorably upon them or inconvenienced them. Also, staff units were strongly committed to preserving the integrity of control and rule systems, whereas line personnel believed they could be more effective by flexible reinterpretation of control and incentive schemes, and by ignoring many discipline and safety violations. A study by Strauss (1962) showed that engineers preferred to order brand items, whereas purchasing agents sought specifications suitable for several vendors. Similar instances abound. Landsberger (1961) postulated several basic dilemmas which probably underlie many interdepartmental differences: flexibility versus stability; criteria for short-run versus long-run performance; emphasis on measurable results versus attention to intangible results; maximizing organizational goals versus responding to other societal needs.

Although the dilemmas may be inherent in the total task, the reward system designed by management can serve either to sharpen or to blunt their divisive effective: the more the evaluations and rewards of higher management emphasize the separate performance of each department rather than their combined performance, the more conflict.

Close, one-to-one supervisory styles have generally been assumed to promote more conflict among peers than general supervision in which the superior also deals with subordinates as a group (Likert 1961). One might speculate that group supervisory patterns are taken to indicate emphasis on group rather than individual performance criteria; and that group patterns allow the supervisor to observe the process and to reward cooperative acts.

Organizational Differentiation

Litwak (1961) postulated that uniform tasks require a bureaucratic type of organization, characterized by impersonality of relations, prior specification of job authority, emphasis on hierarchical authority, separation of policy and administration, and emphasis on general rules and specialization; whereas nonuniform tasks require a human-relations organization with the contrasting characteristics. In contemporary society, most large-scale organizations have to deal with both uniform and nonuniform tasks, and must combine these contradictory forms of social relations into a professional model. Litwak regards the inclusions of these contradictory forms as a source of organizational conflict.

Lawrence and Lorsch (1967a) emphasized the effects of differentiation. Where each unit (such as research, sales, or production) performs a different type of task and copes with a different segment of the environment, the units will develop significant internal differences. Such units may differ from each other (*a*) in the degree of structure, that is, tightness of rules, narrowness of span of supervisory control, frequency and specificity of performance review; and in the orientation of its members; (*b*) toward the environment, such as new scientific knowledge versus customer problems and market opportunities versus costs of raw materials and processing; (*c*) toward time, such as planning time perspective; and (*d*) toward other people, such as, openness and permissiveness of interpersonal relationships. Lawrence and Lorsch measured these differences in six plastics organizations with the results shown in Table 1.

Lawrence and Lorsch believe this fourfold differentiation is largely a response to the degree of uncertainty in the environments of the different departments. They

TABLE 1. Differences Related to Environment of Departments

Departments	Orientation toward environment	Orientation toward time	Degreee of formality in departmental structure	Permissiveness versus directiveness in orientation toward others
Applied research	Techno-economic	Long	Medium	Medium
Sales	Market	Short	High	Low
Production	Techno-economic	Short	High	High

* After Lawrence and Lorsch (1967).

use a notion of optimum degree of differentiation, which depends upon the task environments. Thus, either overdifferentiation or underdifferentiation has implications for the coordinative processes. Although greater differentiation apparently results in more *potential* for conflict, these authors do not assume that more manifest conflict will automatically result. In their study of six plastics organizations, the degree of integration did not, in fact, vary strictly with the degree of differentiation.

Role Dissatisfaction

Role dissatisfaction, stemming from a variety of sources, can be a source of conflict. Blocking status aspirations in purchasing agents (Strauss, 1962) and in staff members (Dalton, 1959) led to conflict with other units. In these cases, professionals felt they lacked recognition and opportunities for advancement. Similarly, White (1961) stated that members might feel that the growth of their units and its external status did not meet their needs, and therefore might enter another unit or withdraw from contacts which were painful reminders of the lack of status. Where one unit informally reports on the activities of another unit, resentment can occur, as with staff units reporting to management on production irregularities (Dalton, 1959). Argyris (1964) and Dalton (1959) both argued that role dissatisfaction and conflict followed where one unit with the same or less status set standards for another.

Where there is role dissatisfaction, ambiguities in the definition of work responsibilities further increase the likelihood of interunit conflict. Landsberger (1961) pointed out that ambiguities tempted the dissatisfied unit to engage in offensive maneuvers so as to improve its lot, and thus induced other units to engage in defensive maneuvers.

Role dissatisfaction and ambiguity are related to more basic organizational variables, including growth rate, organizational level, and hierarchical differences. Organizational growth appears to have offsetting consequences. Slower rates of organizational growth and of opportunities for promotion increase role dissatisfaction, but are also accompanied by fewer ambiguities. Interfaces higher in the organization are more likely to be marked by conflict to redefine departmental responsibilities. At the higher levels, jurisdictional boundaries are less clear (Pondy, 1967), and the participants perceive more opportunity to achieve some restructuring. Steep and heavily emphasized hierarchical differences in status, power, and rewards were seen by

Thompson (1961) as responsible for some lateral conflict, because these factors tended to activate and to legitimate individual aspiration for increased status and power and tended to lead to increased upward orientation toward the desires of one's superiors, rather than to problem orientation and increased horizontal coordination.

Ambiguities

In addition to its interaction with role dissatisfaction, ambiguity contributes to interunit conflict in several other ways. Difficulty in assigning credit or blame between two departments increases the likelihood of conflict between units. Dalton (1959) attributed part of the staff-line conflict he observed to the fact that although improvements required collaboration between line and staff units, it was later difficult to assess the contribution of each unit. Similarly, disputes resulted between production and sales units, when it could not be determined which department made a mistake (Dutton and Walton, 1966).

Low routinization and uncertainty of means to goals increase the potential for interunit conflict. This proposition is supported by Zald (1962) in his study of interunit conflict in five correctional institutions. Similarly, ambiguity in the criteria used to evaluate the performance of a unit may also create tension, frustration, and conflict (Kahn, Wolfe, *et al.*, 1964). Organization planning, which includes clarity of rule definition, correlated positively with measures of lateral coordination and problem solving in a study of ten hospitals by Georgopoulas and Mann (1962).

Dependence on Common Resources

Conflict potential exists when two units depend upon a common pool of scarce organizational resources, such as, physical space, equipment, manpower, operating funds, capital funds, central staff resources, and centralized services (e.g., typing and drafting). If the two units have interdependent tasks, the competition for scarce resources will tend to decrease interunit problem solving and coordination. Also, if competition for scarce resources is not mediated by some third unit and they must agree on their allocation, they will come into direct conflict.

Communication Obstacles

Semantic difficulties can impede communications essential for cooperation. Strauss (1964) observed that differences in training of purchasing agents and engineers contributed to their conflicts. March and Simon (1958) stated that organizational channeling of information introduced bias.

Common experience reduces communication barriers and provides common referents. Miller (1959) proposed that the less units know about each other's job, the less collaboration and that lack of knowledge can lead to unreasonable interunit demands through ignorance. Cozer (1956) argued that accommodation is especially dependent on knowledge of the power of the other unit.

Personal Skills and Traits

Walton and McKersie (1965), reviewing experimental studies, found that certain personality attributes, such as high authoritarianism, high dogmatism, and low self-esteem, increased conflict behavior. Kahn *et al.* (1964: 256) found that in objective role conflict persons who scored lower on neurotic anxiety scales tended to depart more from "cordial, congenial, trusting, respecting, and understanding relations," and introverts tended to lose their confidence, trust, and respect for work associates more than extroverts.

Most interunit relationships are mixed-motive situations, which require high behavioral flexibility to manage optimally. A person with a narrower range of behavioral skills is less likely to exploit the integrative potential fully in an interunit relationship. He may either engage in bargaining to the exclusion of collaborative problem solving, or withdraw or become passive (Walton and McKersie, 1966) found that personal dissimilarities, such as, background, values, education, age, social patterns lowered the probability of interpersonal rapport between unit representatives, and in turn decreased the amount of collaboration between their respective units. Personal status incongruities between departmental representatives, that is, the degree to which they differed in rank orderings in various status dimensions (such as length of service, age, education, ethnicity, esteem in eyes of superiors, pay and so on) increase the tendency for conflict (Dutton and Walton, 1966).

Personal satisfaction with the internal climate of one's unit decreases the likelihood that a member will initiate interunit conflict. Seiler (1963) observed that in one firm, constructive handling of interdepartmental differences occurred in part because the members of each department derived social satisfaction from their work associates, had high job interest and good opportunities for promotions, and were not in conflict with each other.

Interdepartmental Relationship

Tactics of Conflict and Indicators of Collaboration
The literature on interdepartmental relations has been most vivid in its description of manifest conflict and collaboration processes. Dalton (1959) observed that staff units were encouraged by top management to monitor and report on the activities of line units, and the line units retaliated by resisting the ideas of the staff units and discouraging their promotions. He also observed power struggles between line units and documented the conflict tactics of coalitions, distortion of information, and misappropriation of resources.

Strauss (1962) observed the tactics of purchasing agents who wished to increase their authority and influence over decisions shared with engineering and production. The purchasing agents made restrictive rules for the other units, evaded their rules, relied on personal contacts and persuasion to subvert the other units, and altered organization structure.

Focusing on positive relations, Georgopoulos and Mann (1962) used coordination as their broadest concept, which included "the extent to which the various interdependent parts of an organization function each according to the needs and requirements of the other parts of the total system. In a study of ten hospitals, they found that over-all coordination correlated positively with (*a*) shared expectations, (*b*) absence of intraorganizational tension, (*c*) awareness of problems and solving of problems, and (*d*) ease of communication.

System Characteristics of an Interunit Relationship

Attempting to incorporate aspects of the approaches just described, Walton (1966) developed a theory which also explains the system dynamics of conflict and collaboration in the interunit relationship. Three components of the relationship are considered: (*a*) exchange of information in the joint decision process, (*b*) structure of interunit interactions and decision making, and (*c*) attitudes toward the other unit. Two opposite types of relationships, "integrative" and "distributive," are postulated as frequently encountered systems of interunit behavior (see Table 2). This particular model now appears to be most applicable to lateral relations where the dominant transaction at the interface is joint decision making; where there is relative symmetry in interdependency; and where the transactions required are relatively frequent and important.

TABLE 2. Components and Characteristics of Contrasting Types of Lateral Relationships.

Component	Type of lateral relationship	
	Integrative	Distributive
Form of joint decision process	Problem-solving: free exchange of information, conscientious accuracy in transmitting information	Bargaining: careful rationing, and deliberate distortion of information.
Structure of interaction and framework of decision	Flexible, informal, open	Rigid, formal, circumscribed.
Attitudes toward other unit	Positive attitudes: trust, friendliness, inclusion of other unit.	Negative attitudes: suspicion, hostility, dissociation from other unit.

* After Walton (1966).

In the most general sense, the chain of assumptions underlying Walton's systems theory of lateral relationships (and explaining the distributive syndrome, in particular) is as follows: First, an antecedent, say goal competition between participants engaged in joint decision making, induces the units to engage in concealment and distortion tactics in their exchange of information, such that joint decision making takes on the character of bargaining. Second, in order to ration and distort information effectively and systematically, a unit will attempt to place limitations on the interactions and other behavior of their counterpart in order to make them more predictable and keep them within certain boundaries. Third, the way information is handled (concealment, distortion, etc.) and the way interactions are patterned (circumscribed, rigid, etc.) results in suspicion and hostility. Furthermore, these negative attitudes have a feedback effect which tend to reinforce the same interaction structure and information-handling pattern.

Regardless of the antecedents, the theory hypothesizes that the conflict relationship will become fixed as a result of: the tendency to generalize a conflictful orientation to the many areas of interunit decision making, the self-reinforcing nature of the various elements of a relationship pattern, the reciprocal nature of a conflictful orientation between units, and the tendency toward socialization and institutionalization of these orientations within a unit.

The individual propositions contained in the model are generally supported by a review of the relevant literature in experimental social psychology (Walton, 1966). The hypothesized variation of attributes of a relationship are also generally supported by a comparative field study of production-sales relationships in six plants (Walton, Dutton, and Fitch, 1966). The hypothesized dominant cause-effect relationships among process, structure, and attitude are anecdotally supported in a comparison of two plants (Dutton and Walton, 1966).

The theory suggests that the total lateral relationship is influenced or determined by contextual factors operating first upon the way the parties exchange information, with the effects on interaction structure and interunit trust as subsequent reactions. However, although the process of exchanging information may be the most frequent determinant, it is not exclusively the point of entry in the lateral relationship. For instance, personality and status may first influence attitudes such as trust and friendliness in which case the pattern of information exchange and interaction structure are a secondary reaction.

Management of the Interface

The relationship between units is largely a function of the conflict potential inherent in the factors already discussed; but it is also subject to control by the participants, their effectiveness depending upon how much conscious effort they invest in management of the interface and the appropriateness of the techniques they use.

Interface conflict will be managed best where the attention devoted to interface management corresponds to the degree of differentiation between departments. Lawrence and Lorsch (1967a) compared integrative devices used by three high-performing organizations selected from industries with high, medium, and low differentiation. The most differentiated firm had the most elaborate array of interface management techniques, including a separate integrative department with the primary purpose of coordinating the basic functional units, permanent teams consisting of representatives of members from functional units together with the integrative department, direct contact across hierarchies at all levels, procedures for appeal to a common superior, and a coordination system involving written communications. As expected, when all three organizations were compared, the same rank order obtained for the differentiation scores as for the degree of elaboration of integrative devices. Explicit conflict-resolution mechanisms can be overelaborate, however. For example, a formal coordinative unit was used between slightly differentiated units in a *low*-performing unit. Lawrence and Lorsch concluded that the units were not sufficiently differentiated to justify the coordinative unit, and the result was that the superfluous unit added noise to the system, actually decreasing coordination.

In their comparison of six plastics firms, Lawrence and Lorsch found that three factors promoted effective resolution of interdepartmental conflict and thus high organizational performance. First, where there is a separate coordinating person or unit, the coordinating unit will be most effective if its degree of structure and the goal, time, and interpersonal orientations of its personnel are intermediate between those of the units linked. Second, where there is a separate coordinating unit, conflict resolution will be more effective if its personnel have relatively high influence based on perceived expertise, and if they are evaluated and rewarded on over-all performance measures embracing the activities of the several departments. Third, interunit cooperation will be more effectively achieved and over-all organizational performance will be higher to the extent that managers openly confront differences rather than smooth them over or force decisions. The more subtle aspects of confrontation are discussed by Schmidt and Tannenbaum (1960) and Walton (1968), who analyze the advantages and risks of confronting differences, the timing and skill required, as well as the conditions under which confrontation is most appropriate.

Seiler (1963) also observed techniques for management of interunit conflict. A department may keep its own records, so as to reduce requests for information and thus avoid distasteful contact; a junior member may be assigned as the liaison person, where his presence will not arouse status conflict; and inventories may be introduced to reduce scheduling interdependence.

Consequences of Interunit Conflict

The manifest characteristics of interunit conflict include: a competitive orientation, bargaining and restrictions on information, circumscribed interaction patterns, and antagonistic feelings. To determine whether the conflict has an adverse effect on organizational performance, one must assess the consequences of these characteristics. Whether a competitive orientation is in fact energizing or debilitating for members of the unit will depend in part on the personalities of the participants. For some, competition is motivating and arouses energies not otherwise available for organizational tasks; for others conflict is a major threat. Whether competitive energy will contribute to over-all performance depends upon whether a unit can improve its performance without interfering with the performance of another unit.

Another factor governing the motivational effect of conflict is the degree of symmetry in tactics between units. Crozier (1961) reported that managers who were not able to retaliate when conflict was initiated responded by withdrawing commitment from their job. Seiler (1963) postulated that internal social stability, value sharing between units, and a legitimate authority hierarchy between units were important in influencing whether interunit competition would result in destructive conflict.

According to Strauss (1964), the competitive orientation that accompanies conflict behavior may also contribute to a system of checks and balances, increase the availability of new ideas to compete with established ones, and decrease the type of collusion among middle managers, deprives higher-level top management of information.

It seems reasonable to assume that the more important the interdependence, the more a restriction on interunit information becomes damaging. When a lateral relationship involves joint decision making, each unit can bias the decisions in its own favor by controlling information relevant to these decisions. Even minor concealment or distortion can be of great importance, if the decisions are key ones.

The structural attributes of a conflictful relationship are not necessarily variable in the lateral relationship, as for example, the number of liaison contacts between departments, which may be specified by higher authorities. Whether a structural attribute has a positive or an adverse effect on over-all performance depends on factors other than structure. For example, in a conflictful pattern more problems are referred to the superiors. On the one hand, referral may overload a superior; on the other, a superior may find himself more informed about operations and subordinates. Similarly, referral of problems requiring new policy may also be organizationally useful. Also, the inability of a decision-making pair to change decision rules or apply them flexibly may result in decisions that are not innovative. However, given the larger network of task relationships in which the pair is embedded, the inflexibility may produce a degree of predictability, which is valuable for some other reason.

Channeling all interunit interactions through a few liaison persons in a conflict syndrome often reduces over-all performance; for where other persons are either affected by an interunit decision or have potentially relevant information or opinions, ignoring their contribution decreases the quality of the decisions and lowers the commitment to decisions.

Apart from their influence on the quality of decisions, the attributes of an interunit relationship may impinge upon coordinative activities. For example, a tendency to avoid contact can result in implementation that lacks coordination. The seriousness of the effect of conflict in decreasing the rate of interaction between the units therefore depends in part upon how much coordination is required to implement joint decisions.

Conflict relationships involve sterotyping and include *attitudes* of low friendliness, low trust, and low respect. Such attitudes indirectly affect performance. For example, low trust limits the flow of relevant task information and decreases coordinative interactions. Furthermore, some persons experience psychological strain when other persons dislike or distrust them. Dalton (1959: 95) reported that staff men were shocked by the need to engage in conflict that required them to use their interpersonal skills as much as their academic skills. The stress of this interpersonal or intergroup climate may result in higher turnover or withdrawal from interdepartmental relations.

A positive by-product of interunit rivalry is more unit cohesion, which contributes to cooperation within the unit. Each unit may become more receptive to directives from their own hierarchy; but sometimes the centralization of control within the unit causes frustration in subordinates (Seiler, 1963). Competition may serve as a useful training device. Managers' insight into how the respective goals of interdependent units contribute to over-all goals may be sharpened. Negotiating and policymaking skills of prospective top managers may be increased, and tolerance of unavoidable conflict may be developed.

Some of the postulated relationships between attributes of a conflictful syndrome and consequences for over-all performance are shown in Table 3. Each of the relationships is subject to limiting conditions, some of which were noted earlier. The point being made is that conclusions about the effect of a generally competitive or conflictful relationship can only be made on the basis of an analysis of the specific components of the pattern together with an analysis of the task. Comparative field data are needed to evaluate the validity of the concept of an optimum degree of competitiveness and rivalry. The optimum might be expected to vary, depending upon the type of interunit interdependence, the type of work of each unit, and the personalities of unit representatives.

TABLE 3. Consequences of Interunit Conflict

Attributes of conflictful lateral relationships	Illustrative consequences
Competition in general	Motivates or debilitates Provides checks and balances
Concealment and distortion	Lowers quality of decisions
Channeled interunit contacts	Enhances stability in the system
Rigidity, formality in decision procedures	Enhances stability in the system Lowers adaptability to change
Appeals to superiors for decisions	Provides more contact for superiors May increase or decrease quality of decisions
Decreased rate of interunit interaction	Hinders coordination and implementation of tasks
Low trust, suspicion, hostility	Psychological strain and turnover of personnel or decrease in individual performance.

Responses of Higher Executives

Response Tendencies of Executives

The response of executives refers to how superiors react to information about subordinate organizational units; that is, to low performance and attributes of the interunit relationship itself. Here "low performance" means inadequate productivity, low adaptability, or inability of the units to conserve their human and other resources.

A manager's response is a combination of his habitual patterns, emotional reactions, and deliberate responses. This idiosyncratic element in the system of interunit conflict shown in Figure 1 is a major problem in developing a general explanatory or predictive model of the total system. For the same reason, however, it is an opportunity for improving the interunit relationship. Several automatic responses to low performance can be noted for illustration. If the joint performance of two units is considered inadequate, higher executives may place particular emphasis on observable, short-run measures of performance for each subunit. Thus, poor performance, whatever its source, may lead to the very rewards, controls, and styles of supervision here shown to be antecedents to conflict. If the relationships hypothesized are valid, reinforcing feedback will lead to more interunit conflict and still lower performance. White (1961) reported that higher executives who were dissatisfied with the performance of subordinate units frequently responded by reorganizing the units. The feelings of status depreciation or power deprivation and the ambiguity which frequently follow a reorganization may increase the potential for conflict.

Executive Responses in Relation to Model

The model has implications both for determining what needs changing and for developing a strategy for achieving the change. Executive responses can either reinforce and intensify a conflict pattern, or create pressures to change it. Much depends upon how sophisticated a diagnostic model the manager uses. Ideally he would take into account all the valid implications of a model of the antecedents, dynamics, and consequences of conflict.

The model as a diagnostic tool. Cause-and-effect relationships can be traced back through the model as follows:

1. Are there manifestations of conflict or low collaboration in the lateral relationship? If not, this interunit conflict model is not relevant. If so, determine the particular aspects of the relationship processes that are impinging upon performance; for instance, distortion of information, infrequent interaction, and lack of mutual assistance.

2. Are these dysfunctional elements of the conflict process inherent in a competitive interunit relationship? If not, determine how the management activities at the interface are inadequate, and whether these can be modified by suggesting or requiring changes in them. If they are, determine what particular contextual variables are responsible for the competitive orientation; for example, scarce resources, competitive reward system, asymmetrical task interdependence, or personalities of key liaison personnel.

3. Which of the contextual factors that create the interunit conflict are not inherent in the technology or are not essential parts of the administrative apparatus? Determine which of these might be modified to have a significant influence on the relationship.

An exhaustive treatment of the factors which are instrumental in altering a conflictful interunit relationship and which executives can modify would review the entire model. Instead, only a few relevant executive responses that have been treated in the literature are considered.

Thompson (1960) identified three areas of executive response: First, "Within limits, administrative allocations (of rewards, status symbols, resources, etc.) determine the relative deprivation experienced by organizational members, and thereby control potential conflict inherent in modern technologies'' (392). Second, ''To the extent that recruitment and selection procedures limit or maintain it within manageable pattern, the organization can manage the potential conflict in latent role diversity'' (394). By latent role diversity, Thompson means differences in socioeconomic status, ethnic background, and so on. Third, ''By varying the distinctiveness of the organization, the proportion of members exposed, and the frequency and regularity of their exposure, the organization gains a measure of control over conflict stemming from potential reactions to competing pressures'' (396). Here he is referring to organizational conflict induced by ideas or pressures from the organization's environment.

Landsberger (1961) states that horizontal differences in authority can be more strongly supported by organizational logic, and need be less dependent on arbitrary fiat than vertical authority. On the other hand, differences in lateral authority are less obvious and are less likely to be stated explicitly, and therefore tend toward conflict. Consequently, one executive response is to make explicit rules allocating final authority for decisions on interunit activities, so as to depersonalize the order. A related response is for higher executives to develop rules to cover an increasing proportion of interunit transactions, and thereby confine decisions to exceptional situations, a practice noted by both Brown (1960) and Landsberger (1961).

Pondy (1967) refers to other devices which are not only available to those who manage the interface, but which can also be included in the executive response repertory: reducing dependence on common resources, transfer pricing between units, loosening schedules, or introducing buffer inventories. Litwak (1961) suggests many ''mechanisms or segregation,'' used to reduce the conflict generated by contradictory social forms which modern organizations must incorporate, including stricter role separation between those for whom affect and those for whom strict objectivity is important; physical separation, such as moving the research facility away from the production facility; and transferral occupations, such as engineers who maintain involvement with a product from research to production stages.

Implications of the model for change of strategy. Ideally, higher executives would develop a strategy for modifying the level of interunit conflict and collaboration which not only acts on the problem diagnosed, but also takes into account the self-perpetuating characteristics of conflict relationships. The analysis of the dynamics of lateral relationship not only underscored the self-reinforcing tendencies of conflictful patterns, and attitudes between units; it is also stressed the reciprocal and regenerative tendencies of conflictful approaches to the interface.

These self-reinforcing, regenerative and reciprocal tendencies lead to persistence of a conflict process; therefore, higher management needs to engage in activities designed to replace existing patterns. Blake, Shepard and Mouton (1964), and Walton (1968) have outlined theories and techniques of third-party consulting interventions. The underlying assumption is that the units must find a new culture in which to view and understand each other. Various techniques of re-education can be used to change intergroup perceptions based on stereotypes, misunderstanding the intention of others, and past history of hostile relations. Thus, whether higher executives conclude that basic contextual factors or techniques for interface management need to be modified, change effort will be effective only if it includes some interventions which help change the existing pattern.

Conclusions

Several features of the model of interunit conflict deserve emphasis: First, no a priori assumption is made that interunit conflict should be reduced. Second, the model recognizes a large number of potential determinants of conflict and conflict-reinforcement syndromes. Third, the model incorporates contextual and structural factors emphasized by sociologists and economists, as well as interpersonal interaction phenomena studied by social psychologists. These approaches are integrated in the explanatory model and in the action implications of the model. Fourth, the model of the internal dynamics of the relationship particularly throws light on the problems of unfreezing the existing patterns. Fifth, the ability to manage interunit conflict is shown to require sophistication in executive response.

References

Argyris, Chris. Integrating the Individual and the Organization. New York: Wiley. 1964.

Blake, R. R., and H. A. Shephard, and J. S. Mouton. Intergroup Conflict in Organizations. Ann Arbor: Foundation for Research on Human Behavior. 1964.

Brown, Wilfred. Explorations in Management. London: Tavistock. 1960.

Burns, T., and G. M. Stalker. The Management of Innovation. London: Tavistock. 1961.

Caplow, T. Principles of Organization. New York: Harcourt, Brace and World. 1964.

Cozer, L. A. The Functions of Social Conflict. Glencoe, Illinois: Free Press. 1956.

Crozier, Michel. "Human relations at the management level in a bureaucratic system of organization." Human Organization, 20: 51-64, 1961.

Dalton, M. Men Who Manage. New York: Wiley. 1959.

Dutton, J. M., and R. E. Walton. "Interdepartmental conflict and cooperation: two contrasting studies." Human Organization, 25: 207-220. 1966.

Georgopoulos, B., and F. Mann. The Community General Hospital. New York: Macmillan. 1962.

Kahn, R. L., D. M. Wolfe, R. P. Quinn, J. D. Snoek, and R. A. Rosenthal. Organizational Stress: Studies in Role Conflict and Ambiguity. New York: Wiley. 1964.

Landsberger, H. A. "The horizontal dimension in a bureaucracy." Administrative Science Quarterly, 6: 298-333. 1961.

Lawrence, P. R., and J. W. Lorsch. Organization and Environment. Boston: Division of Research, Graduate School of Business Administration, Harvard University. 1967a.

————. "Differentiation and integration in complex organizations." Administrative Science Quarterly, 12: 1-47. 1967b.

Likert, R. New Patterns of Management. New York: McGraw-Hill. 1961.

Litwak, E. "Models of bureaucracy which permit conflict." American Journal of Sociology, 67: 177-184. 1961.

March, J. G., and H. A. Simon. Organizations. New York: Wiley. 1958.

Miller, E. J. "Technology, territory and time." Human Relations, 12: 243-272. 1959.

Pondy, L. R. "Organizational conflict: concepts and models." Administrative Science Quarterly, 12: 296-320. 1967.

Schmidt, W., and R. Tannenbaum. "The management of differences." Harvard Business Review, 38 (November-December): 107-115. 1960.

Seiler, J. A. "Diagnosing interdepartmental conflict." Harvard Business Review, 41 (September-October): 121-132. 1963.

Simpson, R. L. "Vertical and horizontal communication in formal organization." Administrative Science Quarterly, 4: 188-196. 1959.

Strauss, G. "Tactics of lateral relationship: the purchasing agent." Administrative Science Quarterly, 7: 161-186. 1962.

———. "Work-flow frictions, interfunctional rivalry, and professionalism: a case study of purchasing agents." Human Organization, 23: 137-149. 1964.

Thompson, J. D. "Organizational management of conflict." Administrative Science Quarterly, 4: 389-409. 1960.

Thompson, V. A. Modern Organization. New York: Alfred A. Knopf. 1961.

Walton, R. E. "Theory of conflict in lateral organizational relationships." In J. R. Lawrence (ed.), Operational Research and the Social Sciences: 409-428. London: Tavistock. 1966.

———. "Interpersonal confrontation and basic third-party roles." Journal of Applied Behavioral Sciences. 1968.

Walton, R. E., J. M. Dutton, and H. G. Fitch. "A study of conflict in the process, structure, and attitudes of lateral relationships." In Haberstroh and Rubenstein (eds.), Some Theories of Organization. Revised edition: 444-465. Homewood, Illinois: Irwin. 1966.

Walton, R. E., and R. B. McKersie. A Behavioral Theory of Labor Negotiations. New York: McGraw-Hill. 1965.

———. "Behavioral dilemmas in mixed-motive decision making." Behavioral Science, 11: 370-384. 1966.

White, J. "Management conflict and social structure." American Journal of Sociology, 67: 185-191. 1961.

Zald, M. N. "Power balance and staff conflict in correctional institutions." Administrative Science Quarterly, 7: 22-49. 1962.

PART FIVE

The Effect of the Organizational Environment on Individual and Group Behavior

In part 2 we showed that behavior patterns can be understood in terms of reinforcement associated with behavior, but one cannot assume that in every case reinforcements are knowingly and explicitly administered by other people. Behavior is also patterned by reinforcements implicit in the organizational setting in which it occurs.

The activity of a person is limited, for example, by the physical space and conditions in which he functions; his decisions are limited by the amount of authority he has. Assigning a person to a job, in effect, designates both a work space and a level of decision-making authority. Behavior within these limits is acceptable; deviation may be sanctioned.

The organizational setting may influence and reinforce behavior in many ways, and it may often be precisely the undesirable behavior which is system-reinforced. Redesigning the system or the task may prove much more effective than pleading with an individual to change his behavior.

Among the factors which may influence and shape the behavior of individuals in organizations are (1) the nature of the work, (2) the physical location of the job, (3) rules and policies, (4) performance evaluation systems, (5) compensation practices. The readings in this part are chosen to give the reader some understanding of how structural factors affect attitudes and performance, and—it is hoped—some insight into effective structuring for effective performance.

The *nature of an individual's work assignment* can affect his attitudes and performance. Sayles and Strauss treat this point extensively. Assembly lines, for instance, are relatively repetitive and routine, with a controlled work pace. The work of various individuals is highly interdependent and any one person has little or no control over what he does or when he does it. Boredom, fatigue, and high levels of dissatisfaction are often present because harder work is unlikely to lead to greater productivity. At best, the worker may be able to minimize scrap losses. While this certainly may represent cost saving, significant increases in performance levels are unlikely. If more output is needed, the whole line must speed up.

In nonroutine work assignments, an individual has greater control over the work pace. This greater freedom is usually associated with high levels of satisfaction because increases in effort are likely to lead to improved performance. The individual may also have some discretion over the kind of work he is doing. In essence, the job controls the person less, and he controls the job more.

The *physical location* of the work assignment determines, in part, the nature and intensity of interaction patterns. *Where* an individual works is a determinant of *whom* he works with. People located close to each other will interact more frequently, increasing group cohesiveness. It was shown by Kolasa in part 3 that cohesiveness may affect attitudes and behavior. A work group located at a site far removed from the home office, for example, may well feel left out, or individuals in a geographically dispersed organization may feel less organizational commitment than individuals in close geographic proximity. Frequent geographical moves on behalf of an organization may prevent an employee from developing long-term social contacts in a community. This limits his social interaction mostly to others in the same organization. Such limitations could contribute to a closer identification with the organization than with external groups.

Rules and policies specify action to be taken. They define what to do, when to do it, and the general range of discretion in decision-making. In general, rules and policies are applicable to all who hold a particular job, or work within a particular group. Rules and policies are highly impersonal but are important for work planning and scheduling, since individuals in various parts of the organization base their expectations of others upon them. Rules and policies of course describe contingency relationships; they attempt to specify behavior which will be punished or rewarded.

Formal *authority structure* defines status and rights of decision. Formal role definition, specifying authority and responsibility, is associated with a position, rather than an individual, and are vested in who holds the position. These rights transfer to new incumbents. Thus, the authority structure is a stable characteristic of the organization over time. When a formal job description allows an individual the right to allocate resources and make decisions about their use, it gives him an important base of power. He may use it to extract compliance within the bounds of the psychological contract. Thus, formal role definition is an important systemic property.

The behavior of individuals is strongly influenced by the *performance evaluation system*, which is intended as a formal means of monitoring performance. Ridgway notes that, in general, quantitative measures are meant to be performance *indicators*, judged and assessed in light of many other factors. It is often true, however, that a manager relies primarily on these measures in the evaluation of individual performance. Once an organization unit has determined that certain assessment factors are to be used as a basis for rewards and sanctions, and ultimately in personnel decisions, individuals in the organization learn to work toward the achievement of the measure, sometimes disregarding the manner in which the level of achievement is obtained.

For example, if cost savings are used as an assessment factor, a department head may forego needed maintenance to keep his operating costs at a minimum. While this decision may result in a better performance measure for him, he may incur excessive costs for the organization in the long run; that is, the equipment on which the maintenance should have been performed may need replacement sooner than otherwise necessary, for example. By this time, however, the manager may have been promoted. Just as a student learns to be grade-conscious in taking exams, perhaps at the expense of true learning, so organization members may learn to meet their performance measures rather than focus on the intended purpose of the measures. If performance evauation is to be effective, reward must be associated with behavior patterns which result in desirable outcomes. As Nord notes, "If you want a certain result and it does not occur, you had better change the reinforcement contingencies to increase its probable occurrence."

Finally, the *compensation system*, and the manner in which it is used, must be considered a structural factor affecting performance. It is often mistakenly assumed that the compensation system itself can positively or negatively reinforce behavior. Compensation often does *not* have a positive reinforcing effect, simply because there is relatively little relationship between increased performance and increased compensation. In many instances, compensation increases are viewed as systems rewards; that is discussed by Katz and Kahn. Payments of this type may help acquire and keep good people, but they are not likely to affect level of achievement.

To make compensation an *instrumental* reward, as defined by Katz and Kahn, is extremely difficult. Compensation is paid at fixed intervals. Yet work activities go on continuously, so specific behavior which a manager might wish to reinforce may occur at other intervals than when payments are made. It seems impossible to develop a compensation system which can be flexible enough for a manager to use to reinforce behavior when it occurs. In addition, the amount of compensation associated with performance increases may be relatively small. An employee may well find the increased effort not worth the money. Compensation *does* have a reinforcing effect when its level or amount of increase is an indicator of status or rank in an organization. High value may be placed on relatively small, modest increments in pay—if they are larger than those given to others. Thus, even small pay increases may be reinforcing if they are perceived as general social reinforcements, or status indicators.

The selection by Nord more fully extends learning theory from the standpoint of application, discussing in further detail the ways in which the work setting conditions behavior and suggesting alternative ways of designing structural factors to improve performance.

In summary, this part focuses on the effects of the procedural and structural system on the members of an organization. These systemic factors, recognized or not, are likely to be significant conditions of behavior, imposing constraints, providing guidelines, and otherwise setting conditions which influence behavior patterns.

Alteration of structural factors may be difficult, costly, and difficult to perceive as a need, but the system must be congruent with effective performance for the latter to occur. This problem of organization change is the subject of part 7.

BEYOND THE TEACHING MACHINE:
OPERANT CONDITIONING IN MANAGEMENT

WALTER R. NORD

The work of B. F. Skinner and the operant conditioners has been neglected in management and organizational literature. The present paper is an attempt to eliminate this lacuna. When most students of management and personnel think of Skinner's work, they begin and end with programmed instruction. Skinner's ideas, however, have far greater implications for the design and operation of social systems and organizations than just the teaching machine. These additional ideas could be of great practical value.

While neglecting conditioning, writers in the administrative, management, and personnel literature have given extensive attention to the work of other behavioral scientists. McGregor and Maslow are perhaps the behavioral scientists best known to practitioners and students in the area of business and management. Since the major concern of managers of human resources is the prediction and control of the behavior of organizational participants, it is curious to find that people with such a need are extremely conversant with McGregor and Maslow and totally ignorant of Skinner. This condition is not surprising since leading scholars in the field, of what might be termed the applied behavioral sciences, have turned out book after book, article after article, and anthology after anthology with scarcely a mention of Skinner's contributions to the design of social systems. While many writers who deal with the social psychology of organizations are guilty of the omission, this paper will focus primarily on the popular positions of Douglas McGregor, Abraham Maslow, and Frederick Herzberg to aid in exposition.

Almost every book in the field devotes considerable attention to Maslow and McGregor. These men have certainly contributed ideas which are easily understood and "make sense" to practitioners. Also, many practitioners have implemented some of these ideas successfully. However, the belief in the Maslow-McGregor creed is not based on a great deal of evidence. This conclusion is not mine alone, but in fact closely parallels Maslow's (1965) own thoughts. He wrote:

> After all, if we take the whole thing from McGregor's point of view of a contrast between a Theory X view of human nature, a good deal of the evidence upon which he bases his conclusions comes from my researches and my papers on motivations, self-actualization, et cetera. But I of all people should know just how shaky this foundation is as a final foundation. My work on motivations came from the clinic, from a study of neurotic people. The carry-over of this theory to the industrial situation has some support from industrial studies, but certainly I would like to see a lot more studies of this kind before feeling finally convinced that this carry-over from the study of neurosis to the study of labor in factories is legitimate. The same thing is true of my studies of self-actualizing

Reprinted from *Organizational Behavior and Human Performance*, vol. 4, no. 4 (November 1969), pp. 375-401. Copyright © 1970 Academic Press, Inc. Printed in U.S.A.

people—there is only this one study of mine available. There were many things wrong with the sampling, so many in fact that it must be considered to be, in the classical sense anyway, a bad or poor or inadequate experiment. I am quite willing to concede this—as a matter of fact, I am eager to concede it—because I'm a little worried about this stuff which I consider to be tentative being swallowed whole by all sorts of enthusiastic people, who really should be a little more tentative in the way that I am (p. 55-56).

By contrast, the work of Skinner (1953) and his followers has been supported by millions of observations made on animals at all levels of the phylogenetic scale, including man. Over a wide variety of situations, behavior has been reliably predicted and controlled by operant and classical conditioning techniques.

Why then have the applied behavioral sciences followed the McGregor-Maslow approach and ignored Skinner? Several reasons can be suggested. First is the metaphysical issue. Modern Americans, especially of the managerial class, prefer to think of themselves and others as being self-actualizing creatures operating near the top of Maslow's need-hierarchy, rather than as animals being controlled and even "manipulated" by their environment. McGregor (1960) developed his argument in terms of Maslow's hierarchy. Skinner's position is unattractive in the same way the Corpernican theory was unattractive. Second, Skinner's work and stimulus response psychology in general appear too limited to allow application to complex social situations. Certainly, this point has much merit. The application of *S-R* theory poses a terribly complex engineering problem, perhaps an insoluble one in some areas. Nevertheless, the designs of some experimental social systems, which will be discussed later in this paper, demonstrate the feasibility of the practical application of Skinnerian psychology to systems design. A third possible reason for the acceptance of the McGregor and Maslow school and rejection of Skinner may stem from the fact that the two approaches have considerable, although generally unrecognized overlap. As will be shown below, McGregor gave primary importance to the environment as the determinant of individual behavior. Similarly, although not as directly, so does Maslow's hierarchy of needs. The major issue between Skinner and McGregor-Maslow has to do with their models of man. Skinner focuses on man being totally shaped by his environment. Maslow-McGregor see man as having an essence or intrinsic nature which is only congruent with certain environments. The evidence for any one set of metaphysical assumptions is no better than for almost any other set. Empirically, little has been found which helps in choosing between Skinner's and McGregor's assumptions. Further, since most managers are concerned mainly with behavior, the sets of assumptions are of limited importance. It should be noted, however, that if McGregor's writings were stripped of Maslow's model of man, his conclusions on the descriptive and proscriptive levels would remain unchanged. Such a revision would also make McGregor's ideas almost identical with Skinner's. With more attention to contingencies of reinforcement and a broader view of the possibilities of administering reinforcement, the two sets of ideas as they apply to prediction and control of action would be virtually indistinguishable.

The remainder of this paper will be devoted to three areas. First, the similarities and differences between McGregor and Skinner will be discussed. Then, a summary of the Skinnerian position will be presented. Finally, the potential of the Skinnerian approach for modern organizations will be presented with supporting evidence from social systems in which it has already been applied.

McGregor and Skinner Compared

The importance of environmental factors in determining behavior is the crucial and dominant similarity between Skinner and McGregor. As will be shown below, environmental determination of behavior is central to both men.

McGregor (1960) gave central importance to environmental factors in determining how a person behaves. For example, he saw employee behavior as a consequence of organizational factors which are influenced by managerial strategy. In a sense, Theory X management leads to people behaving in a way which confirms Theory X assumptions, almost as a self-fulfilling prophecy. In addition, McGregor's statement of Theory Y assumptions places stress on "proper conditions," rewards and punishments, and other environmental factors. Further, he recognized the importance of immediate feedback in changing behavior. Also, he noted that failure to achieve results is often due to inappropriate methods of control. These are the very terms a behaviorist such as Skinner uses in discussing human actions. Finally, McGregor (1966) noted stimulus-response psychology as a possible model for considering organizational behavior. However, he discarded the reinforcement approach because it did not permit intrinsic rewards to be dealt with. Such a view not only lead him to discard a model which describes, by his own admission, important behaviors, but is based on an incomplete view of reinforcement.

McGregor's basic arguments could have been based on Skinner rather than Maslow. The major difference would be the assumption of fewer givens about human nature. In view of this similarity one need not choose either Skinner or McGregor. Rather, there is considerable overlap in that both focus on changing the environmental conditions to produce changes in behavior. Further, both writers place substantial emphasis on the goals of prediction and control. Both are quire explicit in suggesting that we often get undesired results because we use inappropriate methods of control. In fact, the emphasis that McGregor's (1960) first chapter gives to the role of environment in controlling behavior seems to place him clearly in the behavioral camp.

Certainly there are important differences between Skinner and McGregor as well as the marked similarities noted above. For example, McGregor's (1960) use of Maslow's hierarchy of needs implies a series of inborn needs as a focus of the causal factors of behavior whereas Skinner (1953) views environmental factors as the causes of behavior. This difference does not, however, suggest an unresolvable conflict on the applied level. Skinner too allows for satiation on certain reinforcers which will be subject to species' and individual differences. Proceeding from this premise, Skinner focuses on the environmental control of behavior in a more rigorous and specific fashion than did McGregor. For example, McGregor (1960) advocated an agricultural approach to development which emphasizes the provision of the conditions for behavioral change as a management responsibility. He noted in a general way that features of the organization, such as a boss, will influence behavioral change. He added that the change would not be permanent unless the organizational environment reinforced the desired behavior pattern. Such a general approach is an assumed basis for Skinner, who proceeds to focus on the types of reinforcement, the details of the administration of reinforcement, and the outcomes which can be expected from the administration of various types of reinforcement. Thus, changes in behavior which are predicted and achieved by Skinnerian methods can be viewed as empirical support for the work of McGregor.

There are other commonalities in the thinking of the two men. Both assume that there are a wide number of desirable responses available to a person which he does not make, because the responses are not rewarded in the environment. Both suggest that many undesired responses are repeated because they are rewarded. Both are clearly advocating a search for alternatives to controlling behavior which will be more effective in developing desired responses.

At this same level of analysis, there seems to be one major difference which revolves around the issue of self-control. However, this difference may be more apparent than real. Skinner (1953) wrote "It appears, therefore, that society is responsible for the larger part of the behavior of self-control. If this is correct, little ultimate control remains with the individual (p. 240)." Continuing on self-control, Skinner adds: "But it is also behavior; and we account for it in terms of other variables in the environment and history of the individual. It is these variables which provide the ultimate control (p. 240)."

In apparent contrast, McGregor (1960) stated: "Theory *Y* assumes that people will exercise self-direction and self-control in the achievement of organizational objectives *to the degree that they are committed to those objectives* (p. 56)." Seemingly this statement contradicts Skinner in placing the locus of control inside the individual. However, this conflict is reduced a few sentences later when McGregor (1960) added "Managerial policies and practices materially affect this degree of commitment (p. 56)." Thus, both writers, Skinner far more unequivocally than McGregor, see the external environment as the primary factor in self-control. While McGregor polemicized against control by authority, he was not arguing that man is "free." Perhaps the more humanistic tone of McGregor's writing or his specific attention to managerial problems faced in business is responsible for his high esteem among students of management relative to that accorded Skinner. While metaphorically there is great difference, substantively there is little. It would seem, however, that metaphors have led practitioners and students of applied behavioral science to overlook some valuable data and some creative management possibilities.

One major substantive difference between the two approaches exists: it involves intrinsic rewards. McGregor (1966) saw a dichotomy in the effects of intrinsic and extrinsic rewards, noting research which has shown intrinsic ones to be more effective. He concludes the "mechanical" view (reinforcement theory) is inadequate, because it does not explain the superior outcomes of the use of "intrinsic" over "extrinsic" rewards. Here, as will be discussed in more detail later in connection with Herzberg, the problem is McGregor's failure to consider scheduling of reinforcement. "Intrinsic" rewards in existing organizations may be more effective because they occur on a more appropriate schedule for sustaining behavior than do "extrinsic" rewards. Intrinsic rewards are given by the environment for task completion or a similar achievement, and often occur on a ratio schedule. The implications of this crucial fact will be discussed shortly in considering Skinner's emphasis on the scheduling of rewards. For the present, it is suggested that McGregor gave little attention to reinforcement schedules and made a qualitative distinction between external and internal rewards. He seems to agree with Skinner that achievement, task completion, and control of the environment are reinforcers in themselves. Skinner's work suggests, however, that these rewards have the same consequences as "extrinsic" rewards, if they are given on the same schedule.

By way of summary to this point, it appears that more humanistic social scientists have been preferred by managers to behaviorists such as Skinner in their efforts to improve the management of human resources. Perhaps the oversight has been due to the congruence between their values and the metaphysics of people such as McGregor and Maslow. The differences between McGregor and Skinner do not appear to involve open conflict.

To the extent the two approaches agree, the major criterion in employing them would seem to be the degree to which they aid in predicting and controlling behavior toward organizational goals. The work of Skinner and his followers has much to offer in terms of the above criterion. In particular, McGregor's followers might find Skinner's work an asset in implementing Theory *Y*. The remainder of this paper will develop some of the major points of the Skinnerian approach and seek to explore their potential for industrial use.

Conditioning—A Synthesis for Organizational Behavior

The behavioral psychology of Skinner assumes, like Theory *Y*, that rate of behavior is dependent on the external conditions in which the behavior takes place. Like Theory *X*, it stresses the importance of the administration of rewards and punishments. Unlike Theory *X*, Skinnerian psychology places emphasis on rewards. Like Theory *Y* it emphasizes the role of interdependence between people in a social relationship and thus views the administration of rewards and punishments as an exchange. For those who are unfamiliar with the work of Skinner and his followers, a brief summary follows. Like any summary of an extensive body of work, this review omits a lot of important material. A more detailed, yet simple, introduction to conditioning can be found in Bijou and Baer (1961) and Skinner (1953). Extensions of this work by social exchange theorists such as Homans (1961) suggest that the conditioning model can be extended to a systems approach, contrary to McGregor's (1966) belief.

Generally, conditioned responses can be divided into two classes. Each class is acquired in a different fashion. The first class, generally known as respondent or classically conditioned behavior, describes the responses which are controlled by prior stimulation. These responses, generally thought of as being involuntary or reflexive, are usually made by the "smooth muscles." Common ones are salivation and emotional responses. Initially, the presentation of an unconditioned stimulus will elicit a specific response. For example, food placed on one's tongue will generally cause salivation. If a bell is sounded and then food is placed on the tongue, and this process is repeated several times, the sound of the bell by itself will elicit salivation. By this process, stimuli which previously did not control behavior such as the bell, can become a source of behavior control. Many of our likes and dislikes, our anxieties, our feelings of patriotism, and other emotions can be thought of as such involuntary responses. The implications of emotional responses are of major importance to the management of human resources and more will be said about them later. However, the second class of responses, the operants, are of even greater importance.

The rate of operant responses are influenced by events which follow them. These events are considered to be the consequences of behavior. The responses, generally thought to be voluntary, are usually made by striped muscles. All that is necessary for the development of an operant response is that the desired response has a probability of occurring which is greater than zero for the individual involved. Most rapid conditioning results when the desired response is "reinforced" immediately (preferably about one-half second after the response). In other words, the desired response is followed directly by some consequence. In simple terms, if the outcome is pleasing to the individual, the probability of his repeating the response is apt to be increased. If the consequence is displeasing to the individual, the probability of his repeating the response is apt to be decreased. The process of inducing such change (usually an increase) in the response rate, is called operant conditioning. In general, the frequency of a behavior is said to be a function of its consequences.

The above description of operant conditioning is greatly simplified. The additional considerations which follow will only partially rectify this state. One crucial factor has to do with the frequency with which a given consequence follows a response. There are several possible patterns. Most obviously, the consequence can be continuous (for example, it follows the response every time the response is made). Alternatively a consequence might follow only some of the responses. There are two basic ways in which such partial reinforcement can be administered. First, the consequence can be made contingent on a certain number of responses. Two sub-patterns are possible. Every nth response may be reinforced or an average of 1/n of the responses may be reinforced in a random pattern. These two related patterns are called ratio schedules. The former is known as a fixed ratio and the latter is known as a variable ratio. Ratio schedules tend to generate a high rate of response, with the variable ratio schedule leading to a more durable response than both the fixed-ratio and continuous patterns. A second technique of partial reinforcement can be designed where the consequence follows the response only after a certain amount of time has elapsed. The first response made after a specified interval is then reinforced, but all other responses produce neutral stimulus outcomes. This pattern can also be either fixed or variable. Generally, interval schedules develop responses which are quite long lasting when reinforcement is no longer given, but do not yield as rapid a response rate as ratio schedules do. Obviously, mixed patterns of ratio and interval schedules can also be designed.

A second consideration about operant conditioning which deserves brief mention is the concept of a response hierarchy. All the responses which an individual could make under a given set of conditions can be placed in order according to probability that they will be made. In this view, there are two basic strategies for getting an individual to make the desired response. First, one could attempt to reduce the probability of all the more probable responses. Second, one could attempt to increase the probability of the desired response. Of course, some combination of these two approaches may often be used.

Strategies for changing the probability of a response can be implemented by punishment, extinction, and positive reinforcement. Generally punishment and extinction are used to decrease the occurrence of a response, whereas positive reinforcement is used to increase its probability. An understanding of these three operations in behavior control is important, not only for knowing how to use them, but chiefly because of the unanticipated consequences of their side-effects.

Punishment is the most widely used technique in our society for behavior control. Perhaps, as Reese (1966) said, the widespread use of punishment is due to the immediate effects it has in stopping or preventing the undesired response. In this sense, the punisher is reinforced for punishing. Also, many of us seem to be influenced by some notion of what Homans (1961) called distributive justice. In order to reestablish what we believe to be equity, we may often be led to punish another person. This ancient assumption of ". . . an eye for an eye . . ." has been widely practiced in man's quest for equity and behavior control.

Whatever the reason for punishing, it can be done in two ways, both of which have unfortunate side-effects. First, punishment can be administered in the form of some aversive stimulus such as physical pain or social disapproval. Secondly, it can be administered by withdrawing a desired stimulus. The immediate effect is often the rapid drop in frequency of the punished response. The full effects, unfortunately, are often not clearly recognized. Many of these consequences are crucial for managers of organizations.

Punishment may be an inefficient technique for controlling behavior for a number of reasons. First, the probability of the response may be reduced only when the threat of punishment is perceived to exist. Thus, when the punishing agent is away, the undesired response may occur at its initial rate. Secondly, punishment only serves to reduce the probability of the one response. This outcome does not necessarily produce the desired response, unless that response is the next most probable one in the response hierarchy. Really, what punishment does is to get the individual to do something other than what he has been punished for. A third effect, is that the punishment may interfere with the response being made under desired circumstances. For example, if an organizational member attempts an innovation which is met with punishment by his superiors because they did not feel he had the authority to take the step, it is quite possible that his creative behavior will be reduced even in those areas where his superiors expect him to innovate.

In addition to these effects there are some other important by-products of punishment. Punishment may result in a person making responses which are incompatible with the punished response. Psychological tension, often manifested in emotional behavior such as fear or anxiety, is often the result. Secondly, punishment may lead to avoidance and dislike of the punishing agent. This effect can be especially important to managers who are attempting to build open, helping relationships with subordinates. The roles of punishing agent and helper are often incompatible. Many line-staff conflicts in organizations undoubtedly can be explained in these terms. Finally, punishment may generate counter-aggression. Either through a modeling effect or a justice effect, the punished person may respond with aggressive responses towards the punishing agent or towards some other stimulus.

The second technique for behavior change, commonly called extinction, also focuses primarily on reducing the probability of a response. Extinction arises from repeated trials where the response is followed by a neutral stimulus. This technique generates fewer by-products than punishment. However, like punishment, it does not lead to the desired response being developed. Furthermore, to the extent that one has built up an expectation of a reward for a certain response, a neutral consequence may be perceived as punishing. Thus, extinction may have some advantages over punishment, but has many of the same limitations.

Positive reinforcement is the final technique for changing behavior. Under conditions of positive reinforcement, the response produces a consequence that results in an increase in the frequency of the response. It is commonly stated that such a consequence is rewarding, pleasing, or drive reducing for the individual. The operant conditioners, however, avoid such inferences and define positive reinforcers, as stimuli which increase the probability of a preceding response. Positive reinforcement is efficient for several reasons. First, it increases the probable occurrence of the desired response. The process involves rewarding approximations to the direct response itself immediately after it is made. The desired behavior is being directly developed as opposed to successive suppression of undesired acts. Secondly, the adverse emotional responses associated with punishment and extinction are apt to be reduced and in fact favorable emotions may be developed. Since people tend to develop positive affect to others who reward them, the "trainer" is apt to become positively valenced in the eyes of the "learner."

By way of summary, Skinner's (1953) approach suggested that the control of behavior change involves a reduction in the probability of the most prepotent response and/or an increase in the probability of some desired response. Punishment and extinction may be used. These means can only reduce the probability of the unwanted response being made. Also, they may have undesired side-effects. The third technique, positive reinforcement, has the important advantage of developing the desired response rather than merely reducing the chances of an undesired one. Also, positive reinforcement is apt to produce favorable rather than unfavorable "side-effects" on organizational relationships.

This approach seems to suggest that both or neither Theory *X* and Theory *Y* assumptions are useful. This section suggested that conditioning may be both Theory *X* and Theory *Y*. Perhaps since the operant view does not make either set of assumptions, it is neither Theory *X* nor Theory *Y*. Operant conditioning is consistent with Theory *Y* in suggesting that the limits on human beings are a function of the organizational setting, but like Theory *X*, implies something about human nature; namely that deprivation or threat of some sort of deprivation is a precondition for behavior to be controlled. From the managerial perspective, however, the nomonological question is of little significance. The important thing to managers is behavior and the major point of this approach is that behavior is a function of its consequences. Good management is that which leads to the desired behavior by organizational members. Management must see to it that the consequences of behavior are such as to increase the frequency of desired behavior and decrease the frequency of undesired behaviors. The question becomes, how can managers develop a social system which provides the appropriate consequences? In many ways the answer to this question is similar to what Theory *Y* advocates have suggested. However, there are some new possibilities.

Applications of Conditioning in Organizations

The potential uses of the Skinnerian framework for social systems are increasing rapidly. The approach has far more applicability to complex social systems than has often been recognized. McGregor's rejection of the stimulus-response or the reward-punishment approach as inadequate for management because it does not allow for a systems approach is quite inconsistent with this general trend and his own environmentally based approach. Recent work in the field of behavioral control has begun to refute McGregor's position. The Skinnerian view can be and has been used to redesign social systems.

The most complete redesign was envisioned by Skinner (1948) in his novel, *Walden Two*. In this book, Skinner developed a society based on the use of positive reinforcement and experimental ethics geared to the goal of competition of a coordinated social unit with its environment. In other words, the system is designed to reward behaviors which are functional for the whole society. Social change is introduced on the basis of empirical data. As a result of the success of this system, man is enabled to pursue those activities which are rewarding in themselves. Although the book is a novel, it can be a valuable stimulus for thought about the design of social organization.

In addition, Skinner (1954) has taken a fresh look at teaching and learning in conventional educational systems. He noted that the school system depends heavily on aversive control or punishment. The use of low marks and ridicule have merely been substituted for the "stick." The teacher, in Skinner's view, is an out of date reinforcing mechanism. He suggested the need to examine the reinforcers which are available in the system and to apply them in a manner which is consistent with what is known about learning. For example, control over the environment itself may be rewarding. Perhaps grades reinforce the wrong behavior and are administered on a rather poor schedule. It would seem that a search for new reinforcers and better reinforcement schedules is appropriate for all modern organizations.

These speculations suggest the potential for great advances. *Walden Two* is in many ways an ideal society but has been a source of horror to many readers. The thoughts about changes in teaching methods are also a subject of controversy. However, the environment can be designed to aid in the attainment of desired ends. People resist the idea that they can be controlled by their environment. This resistance does not change the fact that they are under such control. Recently, evidence has begun to accumulate that the Skinnerian approach can be employed to design social systems.

Much of this evidence was collected in settings far removed from modern work organizations. The reader's initial response is apt to be, "What relevance do these studies have to my organization?" Obviously, the relationship is not direct. However, if, as the operant approach maintains, the conditioning process describes the acquisition and maintenance of behavior, the same principles can be applied to any social organization. The problem of application becomes merely that of engineering. The gains may well be limited only by an administrator's ingenuity and resources.

Much of the evidence comes from studies of hospitalized mental patients and autistic children, although some has been based on normal lower class children.

A few examples from these studies will serve to document the great potential of the conditioning methods for social systems. Allyon and Azrin (1965) observed mental patients' behavior to determine what activities they engaged in when they had a chance. They then made tokens contingent on certain responses such as work on hospital tasks. These tokens could be exchanged for the activities the patients preferred to engage in. The results of this approach were amazing. In one experiment five schizophrenics and three mental defectives served as Ss. They did jobs regularly and adequately when tokens were given for the job. Such performance was reported to be in sharp contrast to the erratic and inconsistent behavior characteristic of such patients. When the tokens were no longer contingent on the work, the performance dropped almost to zero. In a second experiment, a whole ward of 44 patients served as Ss. A similar procedure was followed and 11 classes of tasks observed. When tokens were contingent upon the desired responses, the group spent an average of 45 hours on the tasks daily. When tokens were not contingent on responses, almost no time was spent on the tasks. The implications seem rather clear. When desired behavior is rewarded, it will be emitted, when it is not rewarded, it will not be emitted.

A great deal of related work has been reported. Allyon (1966) and Wolf, Risley, and Mees (1966) have shown how a reinforcement procedure can be effective in controlling the behavior of a psychotic patient and of an autistic child respectively. These are but a few of the many studies in a growing body of evidence.

More important for present purposes are the application of this approach in more complex social situations. The work of Hamblin *et al.* (1967) shows some of the interesting possibilities of the conditioning approach for school classes and aggressive children. A token system was used to shape desired behavior. Through the application of the conditioning approach to the school system, gains may be made in educating children from deprived backgrounds. Two examples will illustrate these possibilities.

The first example comes from a recent newspaper story. A record shop owner in a Negro area of Chicago reported seeing the report card of a Negro boy. The owner thought the boy was bright, but the report card showed mostly unsatisfactory performance. He told the boy he would give him $5 worth of free records if he got all "excellents" on the next report card. Ten weeks later the boy returned with such a card to collect his reward. The owner reported that similar offers to other children had a remarkable effect in getting them to study and do their homework. The anecdote demonstrates what everyone knows anyway: people will work for rewards. It also suggests the converse: people will not work if rewards do not exist. The problems of education in the ghetto and motivation to work in general, may be overcome by appropriate reinforcement. Further support for this statement comes from the work of Montrose Wolf.

Wolf (1966) ran a school for children, most of whom were sixth graders, in a lower class Negro area of Kansas City. The children attended this school for several hours after school each day and on Saturday. Rewards were given in the form of tickets which could be saved and turned in for different kinds of things like toys, food, movies, shopping trips, and other activities. Tickets were made contingent on academic performance within the remedial school itself, and on performance in the regular school system. The results were remarkable. The average regular school grade of the students was raised to C from D. The results on standard achievement tests showed the remedial group progressed over twice as much in one year as they had done the previous year. They showed twice as much progress as a control group. Other gains were also noted. Wolf reported that a severe punishment was not to let the children attend school. They expressed strong discontent when school was not held because of a holiday. He further noted that when reading was no longer rewarded with tickets, the students still continued to read more than before the training. Arithmetic and English did not maintain these increments. Thus, to some extent, reading appeared to be intrinsicly rewarding.

A final point concerns the transferability of skills learned in such a school to society at large. Will the tasks that are not rewarding in themselves be continued? The answer is probably not, unless other rewards are provided. The task then becomes to develop skills and behavior which society itself will reward. If this method is applied to develop behavior which is rewarded by society, the behavior is apt to be maintained. The same argument holds for organizational behavior. It will be fruitless to develop behavior which is not rewarded in the organization.

In summary, evidence has been presented to show the relevance of the Skinnerian approach to complex social systems. Certainly the evidence is only suggestive of future possibilities. The rest of this paper attempts to suggest some of these implications for organizational management.

Management Through Positive Reinforcement

The implications of the systematic use of positive reinforcement for management range over many traditional areas. Some of the more important areas include training and personnel development, compensation and alternative rewards, supervision and leadership, job design, organizational design, and organizational change.

Training and Personnel Development

The area of training has been the first to benefit from the application of conditioning principles with the use of programmed learning and the teaching machine. An example of future potential comes from the Northern Systems Company Training Method for assembly line work. In this system, the program objectives are broken down into subobjectives. The training employs a lattice which provides objective relationships between functions and objectives, indicates critical evaluation points, and presents a visual display of go-no-go functions. Progress through various steps is reinforced by rewards. To quote from a statement of the training method ". . . the trainee gains satisfaction only by demonstrated performance at the tool stations. Second, he quickly perceives that correct behaviors obtain for him the satisfaction of his needs, and that incorrect behaviors do not (p. 20)." Correct performance includes not only job skills, but also the performance of social interaction which is necessary in a factory setting. The skills taught are designed to allow for high mobility in the industrial world. The Northern System's method develops behavior which the economic and social system will normally reinforce and has been successful in training people in a wide variety of skills. Its potential in training such groups as the "hard-core" unemployed seems to be limited only by the resources and creativity of program designers.

The Skinnerian approach seems to have potential for all areas of personnel development, not only for highly programmed tasks. Reinforcement theory may be useful in the development of such behaviors as creativity. The work of Maltzman, Simon, Raskin, and Licht (1960) demonstrated this possibility. After a series of experiments employing a standard experimental training procedure with free association materials, these investigators concluded that a highly reliable increase in uncommon responses could be produced through the use of reinforcement. The similarity of their results to those of operant experiments with respect to the persistance of the responses and the effect of repetitions, led them to conclude that originality is a form of operant behavior. Positive reinforcement increased the rate at which original responses were emitted.

Support is also available for the efficacy of operant conditioning to more conventional personnel and leadership development. Three such contributions are discussed below. The first concerns the organizational environment as a shaper of behavior of which Fleishman's (1967) study is a case in point. He found that human relations training programs were only effective in producing on-the-job changes if the organizational climate was supportive of the content of the program. More generally it would appear that industrial behavior is a function of its consequences. Those responses which are rewarded will persist: those responses which are not rewarded or are punished will decrease in frequency. If the organizational environment does not reward responses developed in a training program, the program will be, at best, a total waste of time and money. As Sykes (1962) has shown, at worst, such a program may be highly disruptive. A second implication of operant conditioning concerns the content of personnel development programs in the area of human relations. If, as Homans (1961) and others have suggested, social interaction is also influenced by the same operant principles, then people in interaction are constantly "shaping" or conditioning each other. The behavior of a subordinate is to some degree developed by his boss and vice-versa. What more sensible, practical point could be taught to organizational members than that they are teaching their fellow participants to behave in a certain manner? What more practical, sensible set of principles could be taught than that, due to latent dysfunctions generated, punishment and extinction procedures are less efficient ways to influence behavior than positive reinforcement? Clearly, the behavioral scientists who have contributed so greatly to organizational practice and personnel development have not put enough emphasis on these simple principles. The third implication for personnel development is added recognition that annual merit interviews and salary increments are very inefficient development techniques. The rewards or punishments are so delayed that they can be expected to have little feedback value for the employees involved. More frequent appraisals and distribution of rewards are apt to be far more effective, especially to the degree that they are related to specific tasks or units of work.

Job Design

Recently, behavioral scientists have emphasized the social psychological factors which need to be attended to in job design. McGregor and others have suggested job enlargement. Herzberg (1968) has argued that job enlargement just allows an individual to do a greater variety of boring jobs and suggests that "job enrichment" is needed. For present purposes, job enlargement and job enrichment will be lumped together. Both of these approaches are consistent with the conditioning view if two differences can be resolved. First, the definitions of motivation must be translated into common terms. Second, reinforcers operating in the newly designed jobs must be delineated and tested to see if the reinforcers postulated in the newly designed jobs are really responsible for behavioral changes or if there are other reinforcers operating.

With respect to the definitions of motivation, the two approaches are really similar in viewing the rate of behavior as the crucial factor. The major differences exist on the conceptual level. Both job enlargement and job enrichment are attempts to increase motivation. Conceptually, McGregor and Herzberg tend to view motivation as some internal state. The conditioning approach does not postulate internal states but rather deals with the manipulation of environmental factors which influence the rate of behavior. Actually, some combination of the two approaches may be most useful theoretically as Vinacke (1962) has suggested. However, if both approaches are viewed only at the operational level, it is quite probable that rates of behavior could be agreed on as an acceptable criterion. Certainly from the practitioners viewpoint, behavior is the crucial variable. When a manager talks about a motivated worker, he often means one who frequently makes desired responses at a high rate without external prompting from the boss. The traditional view of motivation as an inner-drive is of limited practical and theoretical value.

If both approaches could agree on the behavioral criterion, at least on an operational level, the operant approach could be employed to help resolve some practical and theoretical problems suggested by the work of McGregor and Herzberg. Since, generally speaking, the external conditions are most easily manipulated in an organization, attention can be focused on designing an environment which increases the frequency of the wanted responses. As a result, practitioners and students of organization could deal with motivation without searching for man's essence. We can avoid the metaphysical assumptions of Maslow and McGregor until they are better documented. The issue of a two-factor theory of motivation proposed by Herzberg which recently has been severely challenged by Lindsay, Marks, and Gorlow (1967) and Hulin and Smith (1967) among others can also be avoided. Attention can be confined to developing systems which produce high rates of desired behavior. Thus the conceptual differences about motivation do not cause unresolvable conflict at the present time.

The second area of difference between McGregor-Herzberg and the operant explanation of the effects of job enrichment stems from the failure of Herzberg and McGregor to recognize the great variety of possible rewards available in job design. The Skinnerian approach leads to the development of a more comprehensive discussion of the rewards from enriched or enlarged jobs. In terms of the operant approach, both job enrichment and job enlargement are apt to lead to what would generally be called greater motivation or what we will call higher rates of desired behavior. McGregor and Herzberg suggest feelings of achievement and responsibility explain these results. The reinforcement approach leads to a search for specific rewards in these newly designed jobs.

Job enlargement can be viewed simply as increasing the variety of tasks a person does. Recent research on self-stimulation and sensory deprivation has suggested that stimulation itself is reinforcing, especially when one has been deprived of it. The increased variety of tasks due to job enlargement may thus be intrinsically rewarding due to a host of reinforcers in the work itself rather than to any greater feeling of responsibility or achievement. These feelings may be a cause of greater productivity or merely correlates of the receipt of these intrinsic rewards from stimulation. The evidence is not clear, but the effects of job enlargement can at least be partially explained in operant terms.

Some additional support from this idea comes from Schultz's (1964) work on spontaneous alternation of behavior. Schultz suggested that spontaneous alternation of human behavior is facilitated 1) when responses are not reinforced and/or are not subjected to knowledge of correctness, 2) by the amount of prior exercise of one response alternative, and 3) by a short intertrial interval. Low feedback and reinforcement, short intervals between responses, and the frequent repetition of one response are all characteristic of many jobs which need enlargement. Merely making different responses may be rewarding to a worker, thereby explaining some of the benefits noted from job enlargement. It has also been noted that people create variation for themselves in performing monotonous tasks. For example, ritualized social interaction in the form of social "games" is a form of such alternation workers developed noted by Roy (1964).

By way of summary, much of the current work on job enlargement and enrichment has attributed the effects to feelings of achievement or responsibility, without taking into account numerous other possible reinforcers which may be more basic. Further research to determine the efficacy of these various possibilities is needed before definite conclusions can be drawn. Do the feelings of achievement or responsibility operate as reinforcers in an operant manner? Do these feelings come from other more basic rewards as task variety? Present data does not permit answers to these questions.

With respect to the benefits noted from job enrichment, an operant model may provide further insights. Herzberg. (1968) maintained that some jobs can not be "enriched" or made more motivating in themselves. It is the contention of this paper that it is not the tasks which are the problem, but it is the reinforcement schedules. For example, what could be more boring, have less potential for achievement and realization of Herzberg's satisfiers, than the game of bingo. Yet people will sit for hours at bingo, often under punishing conditions (since the house takes in more than it pays out) and place tokens on numbers. Similar behavior is exhibited at slot-machines and other gambling devices. Most operational definitions of motivation would agree that these players are highly motivated. The reason is clear from the operant viewpoint. The reinforcement schedule employed in games of chance, the variable ratio schedule, is a very powerful device for maintaining a rapid rate of response. With respect to job design, the important requirement is that rewards follow performance on an effective schedule.

The type of rewards Herzberg (1968) called satisfiers may be important motivators because they are distributed on a variable ratio schedule. Herzberg's data does not rule out this explanation. Take achievement, for example. If a person is doing a job from which it is possible to get a feeling of achievement, there must be a reasonably large probability that a person will not succeed on the task. Often times, this condition means that some noncontinuous schedule or reinforcement is operating. An individual will succeed only on some variable ratio schedule. In addition, successful completion of the task is often the most important reward. The reward is, of course, immediate. A similar statement could be made about tasks which are said to yield intrinsic satisfaction, such as crossword puzzles or enriched jobs. Thus the factors Herzberg called motivators may derive their potency from the manner in which the rewards are administered. The task is immediately and positively reinforced by the environment on a variable ratio schedule. Often the schedule is one which rewards a very small fraction of a large number of responses. Since behavior is a function of its consequences, if jobs can be designed to reinforce desired behavior in the appropriate manner, "motivated" workers are apt to result. Some of Herzberg's results may be explained without resort to a two-factor theory more parsimoniously in terms of schedules of reinforcement. Herzberg's (1966) finding that recognition is only a motivator if it is contingent on performance further documents the operant argument.

Another suggestion for job design from the operant tradition was suggested by Homans. He explored the relationship of the frequency of an activity and satisfaction to the amount of a reward. He concluded that satisfaction is generally positively related to the amount of reward whereas frequency of an activity is negatively related to the amount of reward the individual has received in the recent past. In order to have both high satisfaction and high activity, Homans (1961) suggested that tasks need to be designed in a manner such that repeated activities lead up to the accomplishment of some final result and get rewarded at a very low frequency until just before the final result is achieved. Then the reinforcement comes often. For example, consider the job of producing bottled soda. An optimal design would have the reward immediate on the completion of putting the caps on the bottles, but the task would be designed such that all the operations prior to capping were completed before any capping was done. Near the end of a work day, all the capping could be done. High output and satisfaction might then exist simultaneously. In general then, the operant approach suggests some interesting possibilities for designing jobs in ways which would maximize the power of reinforcers in the job itself.

A similar argument can be applied to some problems faced in administration and management. For example, it is commonly recognized that programmed tasks tend to be attended to before unprogrammed ones. It is quite obvious that programmed functions produce a product which is often tangible. The product itself is a reinforcer. An unprogrammed task often requires behavior which has not been reinforced in the past and will not produce a reward in the near future. It may be beneficial to provide rewards relatively early for behavior on unprogrammed tasks. This suggestion will be difficult to put into practice because of the very nature of unprogrammed tasks. Perhaps the best that can be done is to reward the working on such tasks.

Compensation and Alternative Rewards

Although whether money is a true "generalized reinforcer" as Skinner suggests, has not been demonstrated conclusively, for years operant principles have been applied in the form of monetary incentive systems. Opsahl and Dunnette (1966) concluded that such programs generally do increase output. However, the restriction of output and other unanticipated consequences are associated with these programs. Many writers have attributed these consequences to social forces, such as the desire for approval from one's peers. Gewitz and Baer (1958), for example, have shown that social approval has the same effects as other reinforcers in an operant situation. Dalton's (1948) famous study on rate-busters may be interpreted to show that people who are more "group-oriented" may place a higher value on social approval and hence are more apt to abide by group production norms than are less "group-oriented" people. Thus, it is not that money in piece-rate systems is not a potential reinforcer, but rather other reinforcers are more effective, at least after a certain level of monetary reward.

The successful use of the Scanlon Plan demonstrates the value of combining both economic and social rewards. This plan rewards improved work with several types of reinforcers, and often more immediately and directly than many incentive systems. The Scanlon Plan combines economic rewards, often given monthly, with social rewards. The latter are given soon after an employee's idea has been submitted or used.

Related arguments can be made for other group incentive programs. Often jobs are interdependent. The appropriate reinforcement for such tasks should be contingent upon interdependent responses, not individual ones. Even if the jobs are independent, the workers are social-psychologically interdependent. Social rewards are often obtainable by restricting output. It is hardly surprising that individual incentive programs have produced the unanticipated consequences so often noted. Further, since rewards and punishments from the informal group are apt to be administered immediately and frequently they are apt to be very powerful in controlling behavior.

In general then, money and other rewards must be made contingent on the desired responses. Further, the importance of alternative rewards to money must be recognized and incorporated into the design of the work environment. The widely known path-goal to productivity model expresses a similar point.

Another problem of compensation in organizations is also apparent in an operant contex. Often, means of compensation, especially fringe benefits, have the unanticipated consequence of reinforcing the wrong responses. Current programs of sick pay, recreation programs, employee lounges, work breaks, and numerous other personnel programs all have one point in common. They all reward the employee for not working or for staying away from the job. These programs are not "bad," since often they may act to reduce problems such as turnover. However, an employer who relies on them should realize what behavior he is developing by establishing these costly programs. Alternative expenditures must be considered. If some of the money that was allocated for these programs was used to redesign jobs so as to be more reinforcing in themselves, more productive effort could be obtained. This idea is certainly not new. A host of behavioral scientists have suggested that resources devoted to making performance of the job itself more attractive will pay social and/or economic dividends.

Another interesting application of conditioning principles has to do with the schedule on which pay is distributed. The conventional pay schedule is a fixed interval one. Further, pay often is not really contingent on one's performance. The response needed to be rewarded is often attending work on pay day. Not only is pay often not contingent upon performance, but the fixed interval schedule is not given to generating a high response rate. In a creative article, Aldis (1966) suggested an interesting compensation program employing a variable ratio schedule. Instead of an annual Christmas bonus or other types of such expected salary supplements, he suggested a lottery system. If an employee produced above an agreed upon standard, his name would be placed in a hat. A drawing would be held. The name(s) drawn would receive an amount of money proportionate to the number of units produced during that period of time. This system would approximate the desired variable ratio schedule.

In addition to the prosperity of the owners of gambling establishments, there is some direct evidence that variable ratio schedules will be of use to those charged with predicting and controlling human behavior. A leading St. Louis hardware company, although apparently unaware of the work of the operant conditioners, has applied an approximate variable ratio schedule of reinforcement to reduce absenteeism and tardiness. Although the complete data is not available, the personnel department has reported surprising success. A brief description of the system will be presented below. . . .

Under the lottery system, if a person is on time (that is, not so much as 1/2 minute late) for work at the start of his day and after his breaks, he is eligible for a drawing at the end of the month. Prizes worth approximately $20 to $25 are awarded to the winners. One prize is available for each 25 eligible employees. At the end of six months, people who have had perfect attendance for the entire period are eligible for a drawing for a color television set. The names of all the winners and of those eligible are also printed in the company paper, such that social reinforcement may also be a factor. The plan was introduced because tardiness and absenteeism had become a very serious problem. In the words of the personnel manager, absenteeism and tardiness ". . . were lousy before." Since the program was begun 16 months ago, conditions have improved greatly. Sick leave costs have been reduced about 62%. After the first month, 151 of approximately 530 employees were eligible for the drawing. This number has grown larger, although not at a steady rate to 219 for the most recent month. Although the comparable figures for the period before the program were unfortunately not available, management has noted great improvements. It would appear that desired behavior by organization participants in terms of tardiness and absenteeism can be readily and inexpensively developed by a variable ratio schedule of positive reinforcement. The possibilities for other areas are limited largely by the creativity of management.

The operant approach also has some additional implications for the use of money as a reward. First, many recent studies have shown money is not as important as other job factors in worker satisfaction. Herzberg, (1968) among others, has said explicitly that money will not promote worker satisfaction. Undoubtedly, in many situations, Herzberg is correct. However, crucial factors of reward contingencies and schedules have not been controlled in these studies. Again, it appears that the important distinction that can be made between Herzberg's motivators and hygiene factors is that the former set of rewards are contingent on an individual's responses and the latter are not. If a work situation were designed so that money was directly contingent on performance, the results might be different. A second point has to do with the perception of money as a reward. Opsahl and Dunnette (1966) have recently questioned pay secrecy policies. They maintained that pay secrecy leads to misperception of the amount of money that a promotion might mean. The value of the reinforcers are underestimated by the participants suggesting that they are less effective than they might otherwise be. Certainly, alternative rewards are likely to be "over chosen." By following policies of pay secrecy, organizations seem to be failing to utilize fully their available monetary rewards.

In addition to under utilization of money rewards, organizations seem to be almost totally unaware of alternative reinforcers, and in fact see punishment as the only viable method of control when existing reinforcers fail. What are some alternatives to a punishment centered bureaucracy? Some, such as job design, improved scheduling of reinforcement, and a search for new reinforcers have already been suggested. There are other possible reinforcers, a few of which are discussed below.

The important thing about reinforcers is that they be made immediately contingent on desired performance to the greatest degree possible. The potential reinforcers discussed here also require such a contingent relationship, although developing such relationships may be a severe test of an administrator's creativity. One of the more promising reinforcers is leisure. It would seem possible in many jobs to establish an agreed upon standard output for a day's work. This level could be higher than the current average. Once this amount is reached, the group or individual could be allowed the alternative of going home. The result of experiments in this direction would be interesting to all concerned. Quite possibly, this method might lead to a fuller utilization of our labor force. The individual may be able to hold two four-hour jobs, doubling his current contribution. Such a tremendous increase in output is quite possible as Stagner and Rosen (1966) have noted, when the situation possesses appropriate contingencies. Certainly, the problems of industrial discipline, absenteeism, and grievances which result in lower productivity might be ameliorated. Another possible reinforcer is information. Guetzkow (1965) noted that people have a strong desire to receive communication. Rewarding desired performance with communication or feedback may be a relatively inexpensive reinforcer. Graphs, charts, or even tokens which show immediate and cumulative results may serve this function. Some of the widely accepted benefits from participative management may be due to the reinforcing effect of communication. Certainly the "Hawthorne effect" can be described in these terms. In addition, social approval and status may be powerful reinforcers. Blau's classic study described by Homans (1961) on the exchange of approval and status for help is but one example. People will work for approval and status. If these are made contingent on a desired set of responses, the response rate can be increased. At present, often social approval is given by one's peers, but is contingent on behavior which is in conflict with organizational goals.

In addition to these reinforcers, there are certain social exchange concepts such as justice, equity, reciprocity, and indebtedness which deserve attention. Recent research has demonstrated that an unbalanced social exchange, such as one which is inequitable or leaves one person indebted to someone else, may be tension producing in such a way that individuals work to avoid them. In other words, unbalanced exchanges are a source of punishment. Relationships, such as those involving dependency, which result in such social imbalance can be expected to have the same latent consequences as punishment. Techniques which employ social imbalance to predict and control behavior can be expected to be less efficient in most respects than ones based on positive reinforcement.

The crucial variable in distributing any reward is contingency. Managers have been quick to point out that the problem with a "welfare-state" is that rewards do not depend on desired behavior. This point is well taken. It is surprising that the same point has not been recognized in current management practices.

Organizational Climate and Design

Important aspects of human behavior can be attributed to the immediate environment in which people function. The potential then exists to structure and restructure formal organizations in a manner to promote the desired behavior. Once this point is recognized and accepted by managers, progress can begin. The reaction of managers to this approach is often, "You mean my organization should reward people for what they ought to do anyway?" The answer is that people's behavior is largely determined by its outcomes. It is an empirical fact rather than a moral question. If you want a certain response and it does not occur, you had better change the reinforcement contingencies to increase its probable orrurence.

The first step in the direction of designing organizations on this basis involves defining explicitly the desired behaviors and the available reinforcers. The next step is to then make these rewards dependent on the emission of the desired responses. What are some of the implications of such reasoning for organizational design?

Already the importance of organizational climate has been discussed in connection with human development. Some additional implications merit brief consideration. A major one concerns conformity. Often today the degree to which people conform to a wide variety of norms is lamentably acknowledged and the question is asked, "Why do people do it?" The reasons in the operant view are quite clear: conformity is rewarded, deviance is punished. People conform in organizations because conformity is profitable in terms of the outcomes the individual achieves. In fact, Nord (in press) and Walker and Heyns (1962) presented considerable evidence that conformity has the same properties as other operant responses. If managers are really worried about the costs of conformity in terms of creativity and innovation, they must look for ways to reward deviance, to avoid punishing nonconformity, and to avoid rewarding conformity. Furthermore, the way in which rewards are administered is important. Generally, if rewards are given by a person or group of people, a dependency relationship is created, with hostility, fear, anxiety, and other emotional outcomes being probable. Dependence itself may be a discomforting condition. It is therefore desirable to make the rewards come from the environment. Rewards which have previously been established for reaching certain agreed upon goals are one such means. Meaningful jobs, in which achievement in itself is rewarding are another way. In general, to the degree that competition is with the environment or forces outside the organization, and rewards come from achievement itself, the more effective the reinforcers are apt to be in achieving desired responses.

A final point concerns the actual operation of organizations. Increasingly it is recognized that a formal organization, which aims at the coordination of the efforts of its participants, is dependent on informal relationships for its operation. As Gross (1968) noted,

In administration, also, "the play's the thing" and not the script. Many aspects of even the simplest operation can never be expressed in writing. They must be sensed and felt . . . Daily action is the key channel of operational definition. In supplying cues and suggestions, in voicing praise and blame, in issuing verbal instructions, administrators define or clarify operational goals in real life (p. 406).

More generally, what makes an organization "tick" is the exchange of reinforcers within it and between it and its environment. The nature of these exchanges involves both economic and social reinforcers. Many of these are given and received without explicit recognition or even awareness on the part of the participants. The operant approach, focuses attention on these exchange processes. As a result, it may prove to be an invaluable asset to both administrators and students of administration and organization.

A final advantage of the operant approach for current organizational theory and analysis may be the attention it focuses on planned and rational administration. Gouldner (1966) noted "Modern organizational analysis by sociologists is overpreoccupied with the spontaneous and unplanned responses which organizations make to stress, and too little concerned with patterns of planned and rational administration (p. 397)." The Skinnerian approach leads to rational planning in order to control outcomes previously viewed as spontaneous consequences. This approach could expand the area of planning and rational action in administration.

References

Aldis, O. Of pigeons and men. *In* R. Ulrich, T. Stachnik and J. Mabry (Eds.), *Control of Human Behavior*. Glenview, Ill.: Scott, Foresman, 1966. Pp. 218-221.

Ayllon, T. Intensive treatment of psychotic behavior by stimulus satiation and food reinforcement. *In* R. Ulrich, T. Stachnik and T. Mabry (Eds.), *Control of Human Behavior*. Glenview, Ill.: Scott, Foresman, 1966, 170-176.

Ayllon, T., and Azrin, N. H. The measurement and reinforcement of behavior of psychotics. *Journal of the Experimental Analysis of Behavior*, 1965, 8, 357-383.

Bijou, S. W., and Baer, D. M. *Child Development*. Vol. 1. New York: Appleton-Century-Crofts, 1961.

Dalton, M. The industrial 'rate-buster': a characterization. *Applied Anthropology*, 1948, 7, 5-18.

Fleishman, E. A. Leadership climate, human relations training, and supervisory behavior. *In* Fleishman, E. A. (Eds.), *Studies in Personnel and Industrial Psychology*. Homewood, Ill.: Dorsey, 1967, 250-263.

Free records given for E's, pupils report cards improve. *St. Louis Post Dispatch*, December 3, 1967.

Gewirtz, J. L., and Baer, D. M. Deprivation and satiation of social reinforcers as drive conditions. *Journal of Abnormal and Social Psychology*, 1958, 57, 165-172.

Gouldner, A. W. Organizational analysis. *In* Bennis, W. G., Benne, K. D., and Chin, R. (Eds.), *The Planning of Change*. New York: Holt, Rinehart, and Winston, 1966, 393-399.

Gross, B. M. *Organizations and their Managing*. New York: Free Press, 1968.

Guetzkow, H. Communications in Organizations. *In* March, J. G. (Ed.), *Handbook of Organizations*. Chicago: Rand McNally, 1965, 534-573.

Hamblin, R. L., Bushell, O. B., Buckholdt, D., Ellis, D., Ferritor, D., Merritt, G., Pfeiffer, C., Shea, D., and Stoddard, D. Learning, problem children and a social exchange system. Annual Report of the Social Exchange Laboratories, Washington University, and Student Behavior Laboratory, Webster College, St. Louis, Mo. August, 1967.

Herzberg, F. One more time: How do you motivate employees. *Harvard Business Review*, January-February, 1968, 53-62.

Herzberg, F. *Work and the Nature of Man*. Cleveland: World, 1966.

Homans, G. C. *Social Behavior: Its Elementary Forms*. New York: Harcourt, Brace and World, 1961.

Hulin, C. L., and Smith, P. A. An empirical investigation of two implications of the two-factor theory of job satisfaction. *Journal of Applied Psychology*, 1967, 51, 396-402.

Lindsay, C. A., Marks, E., and Gorlow, L. The Herzberg theory: a critique and reformulation. *Journal of Applied Psychology*, 1967, 51, 330-339.

Maltzman, I., Simon, S., Roskin, D., and Licht, L. Experimental studies in the training of originality. Psychological Monographs: General and Applied, 1960, 74 (6, Whole No. 493).

Maslow, A. *Eupsychian Management*. Homewood, Ill.: Dorsey, 1965.

McGregor, D. *The Human Side of Enterprise*. New York: McGraw-Hill, 1960.

McGregor, D. *Leadership and Motivation*. Cambridge, Mass.: M. I. T. Press, 1966.

Nord, W. R. Social exchange theory: an integrative approach to social conformity. *Psychological Bulletin*, (in press).

Northern Systems Company, A proposal to the department of labor for development of a prototype project for the new industries program. Part one.

Opsahl, R. L., and Dunnette, M. D. The role of financial compensation in industrial motivation. *Psychological Bulletin*, 1966, 66, 94-118.

Reese, E. P. *The Analysis of Human Operant Behavior*. Dubuque, Ia.: William C. Brown, 1966.

Roy, D. F. "Banana time"—job satisfaction and informal interaction. *In* Bennis, W. G., Schein, E. H., Berlew, D. E., and Steele, F. I. (Eds.) *Interpersonal Dynamics*. Homewood, Ill.: Dorsey, 1964, 583-600.

Schultz, D. P. Spontaneous alteration behavior in humans, implications for psychological research. *Psychological Bulletin*, 1964, 62, 394-400.

Skinner, B. F. *Science and Human Behavior*, New York: MacMillan, 1953.

Skinner, B. F. The science of learning and the art of teaching. *Harvard Educational Review*, 1954, 24, 86-97.

Skinner, B. F. *Walden Two*. New York: MacMillan, 1948.

Stagner, R., and Rosen, H. *Psychology of Union-Management Relations*. Belmont, Cal.: Wadsworth, 1966.

Sykes, A. J. M. The effect of a supervisory training course in changing supervisors' perceptions and expectations of the role of management. *Human Relations*, 1962, 15, 227-243.

Vinacke, E. W. Motivation as a complex problem. *Nebraska Symposium on Motivation*, 1962, 10, 1-45.

Walker, E. L., and Heyns, R. W. *An Anatomy of Conformity*. Englewood Cliffs, N. J.: Prentice-Hall, 1962.

Wolf, M. M. Paper read at Sociology Colluquium, Washington University, December 5, 1966.

Wolf, M. M., Risley, T., and Mees, H. Application of operant conditioning procedures to the behavior problems of an autistic child. *In* R. Ulrich, T. Stachnik and T. Mabry (Eds.), *Control of Human Behavior*. Glenview, Ill.: Scott, Foresman, 1966. Pp. 187-193.

SYSTEMS REWARDS
AND INDIVIDUAL REWARDS

DANIEL KATZ
ROBERT L. KAHN

Instrumental Satisfaction

. . . The first extension of machine theory beyond the rules is the addition of rewards to motivate performance. It is important to distinguish between rewards administered in relation to individual effort and performance and the system rewards which accrue to people by virtue of their membership in the system. In the former category are piece-rate incentives, promotion for outstanding performance, or any special recognition bestowed in acknowledgement of differential contributions to organizational functioning. The category of system rewards includes fringe benefits, recreational facilities, cost-of-living raises, across-the-board upgrading, job security, and pleasant working conditions.

Individual rewards properly administered help attract people to the system and hold them in it. A major factor in their effectiveness is the extent to which they are competitive with individual reward systems in other organizations. Individual rewards can also be effective in motivating people to meet and exceed the quantitative and qualitative standards of role performance. This effectiveness is limited, however, when large numbers of people are performing identical tasks, so that superior individual performance threatens the rewards and security of the majority. In other words, differential individual rewards are difficult to apply effectively to masses of people doing the same work and sharing a common fate in a mass production organization. It is no accident that large organizations have moved in the direction of converting individual rewards into system rewards.

Individual rewards are also difficult to apply to contributions that go beyond the formal requirements of role. Spectacular instances of innovative behavior can be singled out for recognition, of course, and heroism beyond the call of duty can be decorated. But the everyday cooperative activities which keep an organization from falling apart are more difficult to recognize and reward. Creative suggestions for organizational improvement are sometimes encouraged through financial rewards. In general, however, singling out of individuals for their extra contributions to the cause is not the most effective and reliable means of evoking high motivation for the accomplishment of organizational objectives.

Conditions Conducive to Effective Individual Instrumental Rewards

If rewards such as pay incentives are to work as they are intended, they must meet three primary conditions. (1) They must be clearly perceived as large enough in amount to justify the additional effort required to obtain them. (2) They must be perceived as directly related to the required performance and follow directly on

TABLE 1. Conditions Affecting the Use of Individual Monetary Rewards

Objective Conditions	Mediated by Psychological Variables	Outcome
1. Amount of reward for individual effort	1. Frame of reference in evaluating reward: what standards are used for comparison purposes	Possible reduction in turnover
2. Immediacy of reward	2. Temporal frame of reference of individual	Some reduction in absenteeism
3. Constancy of reward	3. Perception of dependability and no cutting back of rates;	Possible increases in productivity
	Other consequences of reward striving such as disapproval of peers	No necessary increase in cooperative or protective behavior
		Possible increases in creative suggestions

its accomplishment. (3) They must be perceived as equitable by the majority of system members, many of whom will not receive them. These conditions suggest some of the reasons why individual rewards can work so well in some situations and yet be so difficult of application in large organizations. The facts are that most enterprises have not been able to use incentive pay, or piece rates, as reliable methods for raising the quality and quantity of production (McGregor, 1960; Marriott, 1957).

In terms of the first criterion many companies have attempted incentive pay without making the differential between increased effort and increased reward proportional from the point of view of the worker. If he can double his pay by working at a considerably increased tempo, that is one thing. But if such increased expenditure means a possible 10 per cent increase, that is another. Moreover, there is the tradition among workers, and it is not without some factual basis, that management cannot be relied upon to maintain a high rate of pay for those making considerably more than the standard and that their increased efforts will only result in their "being sweated." There is, then, the temporal dimension of whether the piece rates which seem attractive today will be maintained tomorrow.

More significant, however, is the fact that a large-scale organization consists of many people engaging in similar and interdependent tasks. The work of any one man is highly dependent upon what his colleagues are doing. Hence individual piece rates are difficult to apply on any equitable basis. Group incentives are more logical, but as the size of the interdependent group grows, we move toward system rather than toward individual rewards. Moreover, in large-scale production enterprises the role performance is controlled by the tempo of the machines and their coordination. The speed of the worker on the assembly line is not determined by his decision but by the speed of the assembly line. An individual piece-rate just does not accord with the systemic nature of the coordinated collectivity. Motivational factors about the amount of effort to be expended on the job enter the picture not on the floor of the factory but during the negotiations of the union and management about the manning of a particular assembly line. Heads of corporations may believe in the philosophy of individual enterprise, but when they deal with reward systems in their own organizations they become realists and accept the pragmatic notion of collective rewards.

Since there is such a high degree of collective interdependence among rank-and-file workers the attempts to use individual rewards are often perceived as inequitable. Informal norms develop to protect the group against efforts which are seen as divisive or exploitive. Differential rates for subsystems within the organization will be accepted much more than invidious distinctions within the same subgrouping. Hence promotion or upgrading may be the most potent type of individual reward. The employee is rewarded by being moved to a different category of workers on a better pay schedule. Some of the same problems apply, of course, to this type of reward. Since differential performance is difficult to assess in assembly-type operations, promotion is often based upon such criteria as conformity to company requirements with respect to attendance and absenteeism, observance of rules, and seniority. None of these criteria is related to individual performance on the job. Moreover, promotion is greatly limited by the technical and professional education of the worker.

It is true, of course, that many organizations are not assembly-line operations, and even for those which are, the conditions described here do not apply to the upper echelons. Thus General Motors can follow a policy of high individual rewards to division managers based upon the profits achieved by a given division. A university can increase the amount of research productivity of its staff by making publication the essential criterion for promotion. In general, where assessment of individual performance is feasible and where the basis of the reward system is clear, instrumental individual rewards can play an important part in raising productivity.

System rewards differ from individual rewards in that they are not allocated on the basis of differential effort and performance but on the basis of membership in the system. The major basis for differential allocation of system rewards is seniority in the system. A higher pension for thirty years of service than for twenty years does not violate the principle of rewarding membership. Management often overlooks the distinction between individual and system rewards, and operates as if rewards administered across the board would produce the same effects as individual rewards.

System rewards are most effective for holding members within the organization. Since these rewards are often distributed on the basis of length of service, people will want to stay on to receive them. The limiting factor is competition with attractions in other systems. As the system increases its attractions, other things being equal, it should reduce its problems of turnover. In fact, it may sometimes have the problem of too little turnover, with many poorly motivated people staying on until retirement.

TABLE 2. Conditions Affecting the Use of System Rewards

Objective Conditions	Mediated by Psychological Variables	Outcome
1. Alternative system available to the individual	1. Perception of alternatives and law of least effort	Reduction in turnover
2. Relative advantages of system rewards in other available organizations	2. Perception and meaning to the individual of the differences	Some reduction in absenteeism Minimal quantity and quality of role performance
3. Uniformity of system rewards for all members or for major categories	3. Perception of equity	No creative contribution but some degree of cooperative and protective behavior and creation of favorable external environmental climate

System rewards will not lead to work of higher quality or greater quantity than is required to stay in the organization. Since rewards are given equally to all members or differentially in terms of seniority, people are not motivated to do more than meet the standards for remaining in the system. It is sometimes assumed that the liking for the organization created by system rewards will generalize to greater productive effort. Such generalization of motivation may occur to a very limited extent, but it is not a reliable basis for the expectation of higher productivity. Management may expect gratitude from workers because it has added some special fringe benefit or some new recreational facility. Employees will be motivated to remain in an enterprise with such advantages, but are unlikely to express gratitude by working harder for the company.

System rewards do little to motivate performance beyond the line of duty, with two possible exceptions. As people develop a liking for the attractions of the organization, they may be more likely to engage in cooperative relations with their fellows toward organizational goals. They may be more likely also to contribute to a favorable climate of opinion for the system in the external environment. It may be easier for a company to recruit personnel when employees have described it as a good place to work.

The effective use of system rewards requires their uniform application for all members of the system or for plausible major groupings within the system. If rewards are to be given by virtue of membership in the system, any allocation favoring some individuals over others is suspect. Management is frequently surprised by resentment over differential system rewards when there has been no resentment of differential individual rewards.

One public utility, for example, inaugurated an attractive retirement system for its employees before such fringe benefits were common. Its employees were objectively much better off because of the new benefits, and yet the most hated feature of the whole company was the retirement system. Employee complaints centered on two issues: years of employment in the company before the age of thirty did not count toward retirement pensions; and company officials, because of their higher salaries and correspondingly higher pensions, could retire on livable incomes. The employees felt intensely that, if they were being rewarded for service to the company, it was unfair to rule out years of service before age thirty. The service of a man who started to work for the company immediately after high school graduation was unrecognized for a dozen years. Moreover, workers felt that a lifetime of service to the company should enable them to retire on a livable income just as it enabled company officials to do so. The company house organ devoted considerable space over a few years to showing how much the workers actually benefited from the plan, as in fact was the case. On the occasion of a companywide survey, this campaign was found to have had little effect. The most common complaint was still the patent unfairness of the retirement system.

The critical point then is that system rewards have a logic of their own. Since they accrue to people by virtue of their membership or length of service in an organization, they will be perceived as inequitable if they are not uniformly administered. The perception of the organization member is that all members are equal in their access to organizational benefits. Office employees will not be upset by differences in individual rewards that recognize differences in responsibility. However, if their organization gives them free meals in a cafeteria and sets aside a special dining room for executives, many of them will be upset. In our culture we accept individual differences in income but we do not readily accept differences in classes of citizenship. To be a member of an organization is to be a citizen in that community, and all citizens are equal in their membership rights. Universities which do not extend to research workers the same tenure rights and fringe benefits accorded to the teaching staff have a morale problem on their hands.

The Citzenship Meaning of Membership in an Organization. There has been little systematic inquiry as to what it means for an individual to be a member of an organization or social system. By membership we do not necessarily mean that the individual pays or carries a card. We only mean that he is part of the system's operations, that he fulfills certain role obligations. Membership in this sense can be discussed in terms of the input a person regards as his due as a member of the system, and the output or behavior required of him to support the organization.

We have described the input side of this exchange in discussing system rewards. People in a democratic society feel that any system in which they are involved should accord them certain citizenship rights by virtue of their membership in the system. One such right is uniformity and equity in the distribution of system rewards. Another is equality of opportunity to earn the differential individual rewards available in the system. There should not be arbitrary discrimination against a worker because of race, religion, or social origin. Another right is that of due process of law, the right of the individual to be dealt with through established legal procedures and not through arbitrary, whimsical actions. Even though people are working for industrial organizations in which the power structure is oligarchical, they increasingly expect that their citizen rights in those organizations will be handled on the basis of democratic principles. Management in general also recognizes these citizen rights, and flagrant departures from them are not condoned. In fact, management goes even further in some instances and avoids the language of authority even though the citizen expectations of members do not demand a democratic authority structure.

There are many implications for organizations in the citizenship demands of members. The basic problem is the distribution of system rewards and privileges to different levels of workers, to different functional groups, and to the incumbents of different hierarchical positions.

The simple solution of uniform privileges and rewards for all organizational members regardless of position, type of work, or function would horrify the upper echelons. It would mean in a university, for example, that faculty members, research workers, clerks, and custodians would be entitled to the same provisions of tenure, retirement benefits, and vacations. When research workers and faculty members take ten days of vacation at Christmas, secretarial and administrative staffs would not be required to stay on the job. Though many would find this simple solution upsetting, the general trend is in this direction. Cost-of-living increases, which in many institutions are an important part of system rewards, are applied in a uniform fashion. Recreational facilities may be open to all members, and even parking permits, those coveted symbols of utility and prestige, are sometimes accorded to all.

A second solution is to translate inequitable system rewards into individual rewards. Instead of giving officials one plan of retirement and workers another, the retirement system can be the same for all, but the officials, by virtue of their individual positions and their unusual effort and achievement in those positions, can be given individual bonuses.

Another solution would be to find some acceptable rationale for distinguishing between functions and classes of citizens within an organization. In the university, the faculty perform a different function than clerical and custodial staff. Apart from meeting classes and conforming to other institutional requirements, faculty members can decide for themselves whether to work a thirty or a seventy hour week. Their Christmas vacation may in reality mean that they take less time from their professional duties than do their secretaries. In general, this distinction of functions is the major solution followed by most organizations in allocating system rewards. It has the merit of recognizing some of the realities of the situation, and encouraging a clear formulation of visible differences in functions, responsibilities, and obligations of different groups within the organization. On the other hand, this solution works against unification of all groups around the common goals of the organization, and it often encourages in-group loyalties and identifications at the expense of the total organization.

The problem of allocating system rewards is complicated by the functional sub-divisions of the organization and the division of the total structure into sectors of organizational space. If system rewards are distributed differentially according to the status, responsibility, and power of subgroups, the identity of these subgroups will be reinforced and their goals will tend to become more important than organiza-tional goals. If system rewards are distributed uniformly, the people whose positions carry more responsibility and require more effort and more investment in preliminary training will say that numerical equality is not genuine equality. Equal pay for equal work has the corollary that unequal pay should go with unequal work. The terms of the relations should not be lost.

The tendency of differential allocation of system rewards to intensify subgroup identification is greatest in an organization where the subgroup functions are in fun-damental opposition. A university needs scientists who can pursue the search for knowledge with maximum freedom. It also needs security police to protect its laboratories from theft and destruction. The conventional arrangement makes the se-curity police a subsystem of the university which ties directly to the top administra-tive structure and has no direct organizational tie to the functional units of the univer-sity whose premises the police are "protecting." As a result, none of the system rewards which accrue to the individual policeman—pay, promotion, timing and dura-tion of vacation, and the like—are determined by the university units in which he physically performs his job. He patrols the premises at times when members of these subunits are for the most part not present and he is in the odd position of having physical occupancy without membership. Thus, he has little knowledge of the mis-sion of the research group and little commitment to it. He may be just as suspicious of those he is protecting as he is of malicious intruders. An alternative arrangement would locate the security police in the subunit which they were protecting or at least woud allocate some of the system rewards on the basis of their performance as evaluated by the members of those subunits. This could lead to an embracing of the subsystem's mission by the security unit.

System rewards uniformly distributed will lead some people to identify with the larger organization, but more fundamental changes in organizational structure and roles make identification with the larger organization more likely. Specifically, this means broadening the role of members of the subgroup and giving them member-ship in some subsystem which is central to the mission of the organization. This could mean complete reorganization on the basis of teams concerned with problems rather than on the basis of functional specialization; it could mean assignment of a specialist to a team for limited periods, or it could mean maintaining the old group-ings of functional specialists with additional organization along task lines.

Hospital administrators have attempted reforms exemplifying the last of the above-mentioned alternatives. Attendants and nurses in mental hospitals tend to become more concerned with their custodial duties than with the major objective of improving the health of patients. The creation of teams involving doctors, adminis-trators, nurses, and attendants to discuss individual cases and alternative methods of dealing with them can help immeasurably in changing the conception of the job of the attendant and the nurse. One cannot make the security policeman a member of the scientific research team in the same sense, but he can be assigned to a particular laboratory and placed under the supervision of its director for the discharge of many of his duties. Thus he can learn that one of his functions is not to throw the scientist who has forgotten his identification card out of the laboratory, but to issue a new card for him. He can be given more responsibility rather than less in contributing to the mission of the organization.

The revision of organizational arrangements to involve peripheral and low-status groups in organizational goals has implications for system rewards. To the extent that the lowly member is now part of the team, it becomes more difficult to treat him as a third-class citizen in the distribution of organizational rewards. Professional baseball teams recognize this principle when they vote shares of the World Series bonus to players who have spent most of the season on the bench, to trainers, and to other nonplaying personnel. Football coaches follow the same principle by getting many of their first-squad members into a minute or more of playing in criterion games so that they can earn their varsity letters. Joint authorship, in which the names of all research workers are listed as responsible for a research report, is becoming a common practice. Where an obvious differentiation of individual contribution to the group product can be ascertained, it is feasible to set up individual rewards for differential effectiveness and effort. Where there are no palpable criteria for the determination of individual effort and where the emphasis is upon teamwork, system rewards are more feasible and lead to higher identification with the organization.

Though system rewards maintain the level of productivity not much above the minimum required to stay in the system, there still may be large differences *between* systems with respect to the quantity and quality of production as a function of system rewards. An organization with substantially better wage rates and fringe benefits than its competitors may be able to set a higher level of performance as a minimal requirement for its workers and still hold its employees. System rewards can be related to the differential productivity of organizations as a whole though they are not effective in maximizing the potential contributions of the majority of individuals within an organization. They may account for differences in motivation between systems rather than for differences in motivation between individuals in the same system. They operate through their effects upon the minimal standards for all people in the system. They act indirectly in that their effect is to make people want to stay in the organization; to do so people must be willing to accept the legitimately derived standards of role performance in that system. The direct mechanism for insuring performance is legal compliance, but the legal requirements of the organization will not hold members if demands are too great or rewards too meager in comparison to other organizations. The mediating variable in accounting for organizational differences based upon system rewards is the relative attractiveness of the system for the individual compared to other systems accessible to him.

The Rewards of Approval. Another instrumental satisfaction for group members derives, as we have mentioned earlier, from the approval and support of their leaders. This category has to do with the psychological rewards of leader approval and is distinct from the leader's use of more tangible rewards. The use of approval by organizational leaders is nevertheless subject to the same limitation as is use of other reward forms. He can avoid inequity and make his approval part of the system reward by speaking words of encouragement to every member meeting standards. Or he can single out for special approval the very few who perform above standard. In the former case, he may merely contribute to the feeling that this is a pleasant place to work. In the latter case, he may strengthen the motivation of a few "company" men and add to the resistance of the majority.

The actions of the superior in ministering to the dependency needs of his followers, moreover, may develop a satisfying interpersonal relationship which has, if anything, a negative effect upon organizational performance. The dependent employee may gravitate to the officer who can give him some psychological assurance in coping with personal problems. The support of the father figure, understandably enough, may not be given to the person who does the job well but to the dependent person on the basis of his needs. In turn, the superior may derive gratification from playing this supportive role. Though both individuals profit from the relationship, it may be so unrelated to the tasks to be performed that it merely subtracts from the productive time of both people. Kaye (1958) has provided data consistent with this interpretation.

Another type of reward is the approval of peers in the organization. Social support from peers can add to the attractiveness of the subsystem and can be a factor in the reduction of absenteeism and turnover. It will lead to increased productivity and quality of work, however, only if the norms of the peer group sanction such performance. In many industrial organizations, the norms of the peer group set informal standards for production which are not optimal from the company's point of view. In voluntary organizations, however, the norms of the group are often an important source of increased individual activity.

TABLE 3. Conditions Affecting the Use of Peer-Group Approval

Objective Conditions	Mediated by Psychological Variables	Outcome
1. Group cohesion	1. Individual's own attraction to group	Decreased turnover and absenteeism
	2. The relevance of group norms with respect to organizational objectives	Possible increases or decreases in productivity
		No necessary relations with behavior beyond the call of duty

Behavior beyond the formal requirements of role may be fostered or discouraged by the need for approval from peers. The norms of the local group generally sanction productive cooperation and support actions which protect the organization against disaster. The values of the work group seldom approve, however, of the eager member who wants to save the company money through some brilliant suggestion, or of the ambitious employees who seek to train themselves for better jobs. The work group tends to value seniority as the best principle for allocating privileges and benefits, and to be protective of the group rather than the organization.

References

Kaye, Carol. 1958. Some Effects of Organizational Change on the Personality of Key Role Occupants. Unpublished Doctoral Dissertation, University of Michigan.

McGregor, D. 1960. *The Human Side of Enterprise*. New York: McGraw-Hill.

Marriott, R. 1957. *Incentive Payment Plans*. London: Staple Press.

DYSFUNCTIONAL CONSEQUENCES OF PERFORMANCE MEASUREMENTS

V. F. RIDGWAY

There is today a strong tendency to state numerically as many as possible of the variables with which management must deal. The mounting interest in and application of tools such as operations research, linear programming, and statistical decision making, all of which require quantifiable variables, foster the idea that if progress toward goals can be measured, efforts and resources can be more rationally managed. This has led to the development of quantitative performance measurements for all levels within organizations, up to and including measurements of the performance of a division manager with profit responsibility in a decentralized company. Measurements at lower levels in the organization may be in terms of amount of work, quality of work, time required, and so on.

Quantitative measures of performance are tools, and are undoubtedly useful. But research indicates that indiscriminate use and undue confidence and reliance in them result from insufficient knowledge of the full effects and consequences. Judicious use of a tool requires awareness of possible side effects and reactions. Otherwise, indiscriminate use may result in side effects and reactions outweighing the benefits, as was the case when penicillin was first hailed as a wonder drug. The cure is sometimes worse than the disease.

It seems worth while to review the current scattered knowledge of the dysfunctional consequences resulting from the imposition of a system of performance measurements. For the purpose of analyzing the impact of performance measure-

Reprinted by permission of the author and the publisher from *Administrative Science Quarterly*, vol. 1, no 2 (Sept. 1956), pp. 240-47.

ments upon job performance, we can consider separately single, multiple, and composite criteria. Single criteria occur when only one quantity is measured and observed, such as total output or profit. Multiple criteria occur when several quantities are measured simultaneously, such as output, quality, cost, safety, waste, and so forth. Composite criteria occur when the separate quantities are weighted in some fashion and then added or averaged.

Single Criteria

A single criterion of performance was in use in a public employment agency studied by Peter M. Blau.[1] The agency's responsibility was "to serve workers seeking employment and employers seeking workers." Employment interviewers were appraised by the number of interviews they conducted. Thus the interviewer was motivated to complete as many interviews as he could, but not to spend adequate time in locating jobs for the clients. The organization's goal of placing clients in jobs was not given primary consideration because the measurement device applied to only one aspect of the activity.

Blau reports another case in a federal law enforcement agency which investigated business establishments. Here he found that work schedules were distorted by the imposition of a quota of eight cases per month for each investigator. Toward the end of the month an investigator who found himself short of the eight cases would pick easy, fast cases to finish that month and save the lengthier cases till the following month. Priority of the cases for investigation was based on length of the case rather than urgency, as standards of impartiality would require. This is one of many instances in which the existence of an "accounting period" adversely affects the over-all goal accomplishment of the organization.

Chris Argyris also reports this tendency to use easy jobs as fillers toward the end of a period in order to meet a quota.[2] In this case, a factory supervisor reported that they "feed the machines all the easy orders" toward the end of the month, rather than finish them in the sequence in which they were received. Such a practice may lead to undue delay of the delivery of some customers' orders, perhaps the most profitable orders.

David Granick's study of Soviet management reveals how the attention and glory that accrues to a plant manager when he can set a new monthly production record in one month leads to the neglect of repairs and maintenance, so that in ensuing months there will be a distinct drop in production.[3] Similarly, the output of an entire plant may be allowed to fall off in order to create conditions under which one worker can make a production record, when the importance of such a record is considered greater than over-all plant production.

Joseph S. Berliner's report on Soviet business administration points out sharply how the accounting period has an adverse effect upon management decisions.[4] The use of monthly production quotas causes "storming" at the end of the month to reach the quota. Repairs and maintenance are postponed until the following month, so that production lags in the early part of the month, and storming must again be resorted to in the following month. This has impact upon the rate of production for suppliers and customers who are forced into a fluctuating rate of operations with its attendant losses and wastes.

Standard costs as a criterion of performance is a frequent source of dissatisfaction in manufacturing plants.[5] The "lumpiness" of indirect charges that are allocated to the plants or divisions (indirect charges being unequal from month to month), variations in quality and cost of raw materials, or other factors beyond the control of the operating manager, coupled with inaccuracies and errors in the apportionment of indirect charges, causes distrust of the standards. A typical reaction of operating executives in such cases seems to be to seek explanations and justifications. Consequently, considerable time and energy is expended in discussion and debate about the correctness of charges. Only "wooden money" savings accrue when charges are shifted to other accounts and there is no increase in company profits. It should be pointed out, however, that having charges applied to the proper departments may have the advantage of more correctly directing attention to problem areas.

Granick discusses two measures of the success of the Soviet firm which have been considered and rejected as over-all measures by Soviet industrial leaders and economists.[6] The first, cost-reduction per unit of product, is considered inadequate because it does not provide a basis for evaluating new products. Further, variations in amount of production affect the cost-reduction index because of the finer division of overhead costs, quality changes, and assortment. The second over-all measure of a firm's performance, profitability, has been rejected as the basic criterion on the grounds that it is affected in the short run by factors outside the control of management, such as shortages of supplies. Profitability as a measure of success led to a reduction in experimental work and de-emphasized the importance of production quantity, quality, and assortment. Neither cost-reduction nor profitability was acceptable alone; each was only a partial index. The Soviets had concluded by 1940 that no single measure of success of a firm is adequate in itself and that there is no substitute for genuine analysis of all the elements entering into a firm's work.

Difficulties with single criteria have been observed in operations research, where one of the principal sources of difficulty is considered to be the choice of proper criteria for performance measurement.[7] The difficulty of translating the several alternatives into their full effect upon the organization's goal forces the operations researcher to settle for a criterion more manageable than profit maximization, but less appropriate. The efficiency of a subgroup of the organization may be improved in terms of some plausible test, yet the organization's efficiency in terms of its major goal may be decreased.

In all the studies mentioned above, the inadequacy of a single measure of performance is evident. Whether this is a measure of an employee at the working level, or a measure of management, attention is directed away from the over-all goal. The existence of a measure of performance motivates individuals to effort, but the effort may be wasted, as in seeking "wooden money" savings, or may be detrimental to the organization's goal, as in rushing through interviews, delaying repairs, and rejecting profitable opportunities.

Multiple Measurements

Recognition of the inadequacies of a single measure of success or performance leads organizations to develop several criteria. It is felt then that all aspects of the job will receive adequate attention and emphasis so that efforts of individuals will not be distorted.

A realization in the employment office studied by Blau that job referrals and placements were also important led eventually to their inclusion in measuring the performance of the interviewers.[8] Merely counting the number of referrals and placements had led to wholesale indiscriminate referrals, which did not accomplish the employment agency's screening function. Therefore, to stress the qualitative aspects of the interviewer's job, several ratios (of referrals to interviews, placements to interviews, and placements to referrals) were devised. Altogether there were eight quantities that were counted or calculated for each interviewer. This increase in quantity and complexity of performance measurements was felt necessary to give emphasis to all aspects of the interviewer's job.

Granick relates that no single criterion was universally adopted in appraising Soviet management.[9] Some managers were acclaimed for satisfying production quotas while violating labor laws. Others were removed from office for violating quality and assortment plans while fulfilling production quotas. Apparently there is a ranking of importance of these multiple criteria. In a typical interfirm competition the judges were provided with a long list of indexes. These included production of finished goods in the planned assortment, an even flow of production as between ten-day periods and as between months, planned mastery of new types of products, improvement in product quality and reduction in waste, economy of materials through improved design and changing of technological processes, fulfillment of labor productivity tasks and lowering of unit cost, keeping within the established wage fund, and increase in the number of worker suggestions for improvements in work methods and conditions and their adoption into operation. But no indication of how these indexes should be weighted was given. The pre-eminence of such indexes as quantity, quality, assortment of production, and remaining within the firm's allotment of materials and fuels brought some order into the otherwise chaotic picture. The presence of "campaigns" and "priorities" stressing one or more factors also has aided Soviet management in deciding which elements of its work are at the moment most important.

Without a single over-all composite measure of success, however, there is no way of determining whether the temporarily increased effort on the "cmapaign" criteria of the month represents new effort or merely effort shifted from other criteria. And the intangibility of some of these indexes makes it impossible to judge whether there has been decreased effort on other aspects. Hence even in a campaign period the relative emphases may become so unbalanced as to mitigate or defeat the purpose of the campaign.

The Soviet manager is working then under several measurements, and the relative influence or emphasis attached to any one measurement varies from firm to firm and from month to month. Profits and production are used, among other measurements, and these two may lead to contradictory managerial decisions.

Granick hypothesizes that some managers have refused complicated orders that were difficult to produce because it would mean failure to produce the planned quantities. Acceptance of these orders would have been very profitable, but of the two criteria, production quantity took precedence.

Numerous American writers in the field of management have stressed the importance of multiple criteria in evaluating performance of management. Peter Drucker, for example, lists market standing, innovation, productivity, physical and financial resources, profitability, manager performance and development, worker performance and attitude, and public responsibility.[10] This list includes many of the same items as the list used by Soviet management.

The consensus at a round-table discussion of business and professional men[11] was that although return on investment is important, additional criteria are essential for an adequate appraisal of operating departments. These other criteria are fairly well summed up in Drucker's list above.

Thus we see that the need for multiple criteria is recognized and that they are employed at different levels of the organization—lower levels as in the employment agency, higher levels as considered by Granick and Drucker. At all levels these multiple measurements or criteria are intended to focus attention on the many facets of a particular job.

The use of multiple criteria assumes that the individual will commit his or the organization's efforts, attention, and resources in greater measure to those activities which promise to contribute the greatest improvement to over-all performance. There must then exist a theoretical condition under which an additional unit of effort or resources would yield equally desirable results in over-all performance, whether applied to production, quality, research, safety, public relations, or any of the other suggested areas. This would be the condition of "balanced stress on objectives" to which Drucker refers.

Without a single over-all composite measure of performance, the individual is forced to rely upon his judgment as to whether increased effort on one criterion improves over-all performance, or whether there may be a reduction in performance on some other criterion which will outweigh the increase in the first. This is quite possible, for in any immediate situation many of these objectives may be contradictory to each other.

Composites

To adequately balance the stress on the contradictory objectives or criteria by which performance of a particular individual or organization is appraised, there must be an implied or explicit weighting of these criteria. When such a weighting system is available, it is an easy task to combine the measures of the various subgoals into a composite score for over-all performance.

Such a composite is used by the American Institute of Management in evaluating and ranking the managements of corporations, hospitals, and other organizations.[12] These ratings are accomplished by attaching a numerical grade to each of several criteria such as economic function, corporate structure, production efficiency, and the like. Each criterion has an optimum rating and the score on each for any particular organization is added to obtain a total score. Although there may be disagreement on the validity of the weighting system employed, the rating given on any particular category, the categories themselves, or the methods of estimating scores in the A.I.M. management audit, this system is an example of the type of over-all performance measurement which might be developed. Were such a system of ratings employed by an organization and found acceptable by management, it presumably would serve as a guide to obtaining a balanced stress on objectives.

A composite measure of performance was employed in Air Force wings as reported by K. C. Wagner.[13] A complex rating scheme covering a wide range of activities was used. When the organizations were put under pressure to raise their composite score without proportionate increases in the organization's means of achieving them, there were observable unanticipated consequences in the squadrons. Under a system of multiple criteria, pressure to increase performance on one criterion might be relieved by a slackening of effort toward other criteria. But with a composite criterion this does not seem as likely to occur. In Wagner's report individuals were subjected to tension, role and value conflicts, and reduced morale; air crews suffered from intercrew antagonism, apathy, and reduced morale; organization and power structures underwent changes; communications distortions and blockages occurred; integration decreased; culture patterns changed; and norms were violated. Some of these consequences may be desirable, some undesirable. The net result, however, might easily be less effective over-all performance.

These consequences were observable in a situation where goals were increased without a corresponding increase in means, which seems to be a common situation. Berliner refers to the "ratchet principle" wherein an increase in performance becomes the new standard, and the standard is thus continually raised. Recognition of the operation of the "ratchet principle" by workers was documented by F. J. Roethlisberger and William J. Dickson.[14] There was a tacit agreement among the workers not to exceed the quota, for fear that the job would then be rerated. Deliberate restriction of output is not an uncommon occurrence.

Although the experiences reported with the use of composite measures of performance are rather skimpy, there is still a clear indication that their use may have adverse consequences for the over-all performance of the organization.

Conclusion

Quantitative performance measurements—whether single, multiple, or composite—are seen to have undesirable consequences for over-all organizational performance. The complexity of large organizations requires better knowledge of organizational behavior for managers to make best use of the personnel available to them. Even where performance measures are instituted purely for purposes of information, they are probably interpreted as definitions of the important aspects of job or activity and hence have important implications for the motivation of behavior. The motivational and behavioral consequences of performance measurements are inadequately understood. Further research in this area is necessary for a better understanding of how behavior may be oriented toward optimum accomplishment of the organization's goals.

Notes

1. Peter M. Blau, *The Dynamics of Bureaucracy* (Chicago, Ill., 1955).
2. Chris Argyris, *The Impact of Budgets on People* (New York, 1952).
3. David Granic, *Management of the Industrial Firm in the U.S.S.R.* (New York, 1954).
4. Joseph S. Berliner, "A Problem in Soviet Business Management," *Administrative Science Quarterly,* Vol. 1, 1956, pp. 86-101.
5. H. A. Simon, H. Guetzkow, G. Kozmetsky, and G. Tyndall, *Centralization vs. Decentralization in Organizing the Controller's Department* (New York, 1954).
6. Granick, *op. cit.*
7. Charles Hitch and Roland McKean, "Suboptimization in Operations Problems," in J. F. McCloskey and Flora F. Trefethen (Eds.), *Operations Research for Management* (Baltimore, Md., 1954).
8. Blau, *op. cit.*
9. Granick, *op. cit.*
10. Peter M. Drucker, *The Practice of Management* (New York, 1954).
11. William H. Newman and James P. Logan, *Management of Expanding Enterprises* (New York, 1955).
12. *Manual of Excellent Managements* (New York, 1955).
13. Kenneth C. Wagner, "Latent Functions of an Executive Control: A Sociological Analysis of a Social System under Stress," *Research Previews,* Vol. II (Chapel Hill, N.C.: Institute for Research in Social Science, March, 1954), mimeo.
14. F. J. Roethlisberger and William J. Dickson, *Management and the Worker* (Cambridge, Mass., 1939).

TECHNOLOGY AND JOB SATISFACTION

LEONARD R. SAYLES
GEORGE STRAUSS

Automation and Continuous-process Technology

Perhaps a definition of automation is in order since the term has come into such widespread use. Although there is no single definition, most authors stress the following components: (1) use of high-speed computers for data processing or control, (2) use of "closed-loop feedback" techniques to facilitate self-control by machines themselves, (3) mechanization of transfer operations, (4) increased use of

Leonard R. Sayles and George Strauss, *Human Behavior in Organizations,* © 1966, pp. 59-67. Reprinted by permission of Prentice-Hall, Inc., Englewood Cliffs, New Jersey.

multiple-purpose equipment, and (5) the combination of jobs and work units in larger self-contained processes.[1]

Detroit Automation

Much "automation" leaves the intrinsic characteristics of jobs unchanged. Workers merely operate more productive machinery that positions the work, checks its accuracy, and transports materials from stage to stage automatically. But the operator continues to be a machine-tender, and a sharp status line continues to separate him from the engineers who install and maintain the equipment and the managers who supervise it. For the most part, this is what is called "Detroit Automation." Jobs may be somewhat less physically demanding, but there is also more pressure associated with the complicated, expensive and potentially very vulnerable processing techniques.[2] Should something go wrong, a great deal of production is lost. As a consequence, supervision may be even closer than before the changes.

Continuous-Process Technology

Something close to true automation does, however, exist today in some plants in the chemical and petroleum industries and in electrical power generation and steel manufacturing. Automation of this sort is most easily adapted to industries in which the product can flow continuously (particularly as a liquid or gas) from entering raw material to finished product through a number of interlinked stages. Continuous steel strip mills and electrical generating plants, where fuel or water power is used to make steam or is applied directly to power turbines, approximate the continuous flows of a chemical plant. In all such factories an employee spends much of his time monitoring gauges and control instruments, and his major work activities come only during breakdowns, and start-up and change-over periods.

Such work contrasts sharply with that of craftsmen and machine operators. As we have seen, a craftsman utilizes manual, motor, perceptual and conceptual skills. He manipulates materials, his own body, and ideas. Engineers have eliminated the conceptual and perceptual element from the job of the semiskilled machine-tender and the assembly-line worker, though they must still develop some manual dexterity and motor skill, but far less than the craftsmen. Automated employees, however, need few physical skills, but they are expected to use their "heads."[3]

Type of Worker	Skills Required			
Craftsman	Manual	Motor	Conceptual	Perceptual
Machine-tender and assembly-line worker	Manual	Motor		
Automation worker			Conceptual	Perceptual

Interest, Variety, and Movement

Most jobs in continuous-process plants require an irregular combination of surface attention and depth attention. The *job cycle* is a relatively long one. Dials have to be checked and adjustments made when readings are "off standard." In one case in a chemical plant, 50 different instruments are monitored every two hours.[4]

The pace of work is uneven, but in part it can be adjusted to the comfort, convenience, and natural "rhythms" of the employees. Although the checking operations must be periodic, they need not be done precisely on time:

> Sometimes when it's close to the time for 2 o'clock readings, we might have soup on the stove. You can eat the soup first and do the work later or take the readings at 1:45 and then eat your soup.[5]

In utility generating stations and in some parts of a refinery, the operators may be confined to a control room. In a chemical plant, however, they must take lengthy walks through widely dispersed equipment.

Aside from monitoring operations, the other part of automated jobs consists of handling unexpected breakdowns (and sometimes assisting in regular starting-up and shutting-down activities). In this phase depth attention is called for, and time is of utmost importance. Because of the enormous costs involved in idle equipment, management expects everyone to pitch in energetically when there is trouble. But if there are going to be sufficient personnel available for such emergencies, when things are going smooth, there is of necessity going to be a good deal of idle time.

Unlike a typical mass-production plant where a breakdown is a welcome relief, here a stoppage is a sign of failure. It is also a period of excitement, even drama. The unexpected breaks up the monotony. Locating, diagnosing, and fixing troubles can be absorbing, even though breakdowns also call for very hard work.

Accomplishment, Autonomy, and Identification

"Continuous-processing technology may serve to reverse the historic trend toward the greater division of labor and specialization."[6] It is this involvement in a tangible, complete activity (refining oil, producing electric power) that produces job interest and the satisfaction which grows out of meaningful activity. Employees feel *responsible* for keeping highly expensive technology going. Rather than concentrate on a small, essentially meaningless task, the employee develops a sense of commitment to the total process. Thus, he gains the satisfaction of knowing that in some measure he contributes to an observable, finished product:

> The worker's role changes from providing skills to accepting responsibility . . . the very definition of responsibility as a job requirement involves a meaningful connection between the worker's own function and the goals of entire enterprise.[7]

In contrast to the mass-production factory, there are not endless, impersonal rows of people repeating small tasks. Instead, relatively few men patrol and control a vast array of massive equipment, or they oversee a control room which is like a command post. Here employees accept some of the functions that supervisors exercise in other technologies.

Their sense of growth and development and importance is further enhanced by the career ladders that develop naturally. A refinery still or a production unit in a chemical plant is handled by a small crew which is differentiated in skill and experience; the lowest-ranking employee is usually called a helper and the top-skilled person can be a head operator stillman or crew chief. Because of the close inter-dependence of their jobs and the need to be familiar with a variety of complex tasks, new employees are brought in as part of general labor gangs and progress through a series of jobs as their experience increases and they evidence willingness to accept responsibility. Each successive job enables them to get a broader view of operations.

And here management, far more than in craft or mass-production industries, is willing to invest in continuing training. Hence, most employees experience a sense of steady progress in status and earnings. Highly important by-products are, for the employee, substantial job security and, for management, a workforce showing unusu-ally high identification with the company. Evidence of this opportunity to enjoy a real career and to progress is provided by wage differentials. In continuous-processing plants, unlike mass-production with its inherent limitations, jobs are arrayed in ascending ladders and there are considerable opportunities for promotions and steps upward in earnings.

The top skilled crew-chief positions involve enormous responsibility and chal-lenge in these industries. As an example, let us look at the chief melter in a newly computerized oxygen-furnace steel plant. Premixed, preweighted ingredients are transported to a huge pressure cooker (the furnace's converter), which heats them for about an hour and is then tapped. Here is a description of the work of the employee who handles the operation, Mr. Peral:

> Mr. Peral directs operations with the computer from a control room several feet from the vessel. He is in touch with his eight men through a loudspeaker system. . . . To make a batch of steel, called a heat, Mr. Peral first has his computer figure out the ingredients, based on orders for specific grades of steel. Then the vessel is tilted to the "charging" side. The press of a button sets off 75 to 80 tons of scrap—. . . . How does Mr. Peral know when it's time to tap? "You've got to know your end points," he says. "You notice how the carbon flame above the vessel is dying? It's about ready." . . . Mr. Peral orders the vessel tilted again toward the charging side. Protected by a metal shield, two of his assistants insert a long pole called a thermocouple into the vessel. . . . If the mixture is not hot enough, the vessel is turned upright again and heated some more. If it is too hot, Mr. Peral will have to have a look at it. . . . There is no device yet that will tell the melter about the heat that Mr. Peral can discover merely by peering into it through purple-tinted cobalt glasses. To Mr. Peral the process is "fascinating." . . . "On this process," he says, "I learn something new about steelmaking every day."[8]

Here, as elsewhere, machines do not completely displace employees; a number of critical jobs can still be performed more effectively by human beings.

The psychological satisfactions associated with these jobs has been highlighted by a recent study of an automated electricity-generating plant:

> It would appear that company managements through their design engineers are now in a position to restore to our working population some of the pride and

satisfaction that stems from performing interesting and challenging jobs. Rather than making men adjuncts to machines, automation seems to be capable of utilizing workers as human beings with a capacity for intellectual understanding.[9]

Job Pressures and Relations to Management

Under automation the speed-up that occurs during breakdowns or changeover periods is not resented as efforts by management to get more work done. Here the employees can see for themselves when hard work is required and the supervisor doesn't have to push them. Also, as we have seen, the technical leadership in these situations often is provided by the top-ranking member of the crew, the chief operator. Since he works right alongside the other members of the gang and shares their values and difficulties, his demands are likely to be interpreted as reasonable.[10]

Mistakes can be terribly expensive, so employees cannot be rushed or excessively pressured by management. Although a craft worker can redo poor-quality work and an assembler's mistakes can be remedied by a repairman farther down the line, an error by a continuous-process employee may cost thousands of dollars before it can be rectified. Checking and repairing involve mental processes which cannot be coordinated by stop watch.

In many circumstances, management is pleased when employees are not working hard—this indicates that things are going well. If the employees work wisely and effectively, there are few or no breakdowns. Under these conditions both employee relaxation and company product are maximized! One company considered developing an incentive payment plan under which employees would receive bonuses in proportion to how *little* time they had to work. Their work time was almost directly proportional to the amount of breakdown and loss of production, much of which reflected lack of employee foresight.

There are other reasons why management seldom appears oppressive to employees under this type of technology. Since at least the top-ranking workers are highly experienced and well informed, their opinions are often sought out by supervisors and by engineers. Particularly when pilot-plant operations are conducted, employees are likely to have contact with levels of management above their immediate supervisor and with staff engineers. Thus, in a modern continuous-process steel mill, there is less status distinction between skilled hourly workers and management and more personal relationships than are found in an automobile assembly plant, where relationships are highly formal and primarily limited to order-giving by the immediate manager.

Continuous-process industry is characterized by better human relations between management and employees over-all than those that prevail in other technologies. Since workers only indirectly control output, pressure on people is at a minimum. "The process foreman's job was to arrange things within limits, set by the plant, which both he and the operators understood and accepted."[11] And the small number of subordinates per manager helps improve human relations.

Since labor costs make up a much smaller percentage of total costs in automated plants than in nonautomated plants, management can provide more generous wages and fringe benefits. More important, since these plants are designed to operate with a minimum of employees, nearly all of whom are required no matter what the scale of operations, employees are less expendable during periods of recession. Furthermore, management as we have noted has a major investment in the career training of its workforce. The employees sense that they are not dealt with as a "variable cost," something that can be let go if business activity declines. Instead, they see themselves as having careers that will last their working life.[12]

Hours of Work

Many automated jobs require shift work and this is a source of dissatisfaction. To get maximum use of expensive equipment, it must be used round-the-clock. And, chemical plants and utilities operate day and night because their processes can't be turned "on" and "off" except at great cost.

Though a few employees like shift work, because it enables them to make alternative use of the daytime, most find that late hours interfere with normal family and social life. Many firms rotate shifts. This procedure avoids charges of discrimination and prevents jockeying for favorable schedules, but it requires employees to get used to constantly changing sleeping and waking hours, not an easy thing to do as anyone knows who has flown across a number of time zones.[13]

Social Relations

Most employees in automated industries work in teams. On some chemical operations there may be only two or three employees per shift; on others ten or so. The employees work closely together and must develop the ability to coordinate their efforts and help each other. In turn, close social relations develop on the team which may carry over into the community.

Whereas social-group boundaries are often ambiguous and vague in traditional industrial plants, they are more clear-cut here. Where hundreds of employees do similar operations under one roof or where an assembly line snakes for a mile or two past thousands working side by side, it is difficult for employees to identify with a specific group of fellow workers. The limited number of employees under automation and their specific relationship to a given process serves to unite a social group which has the same boundaries as the work unit.[14]

We should not exaggerate the beneficial effects of automation on social relations, however. Some automated plants have only a small number of employees, widely dispersed, who rarely see each other. Isolated locations plus noise may make difficult all but limited conversation.

Summary: Automation and Job Satisfaction

It would be a mistake to assume that all job-satisfaction problems are solved by the introduction of continuous-process automation. For there is substantial monotony associated with watching and waiting. Future research will likely emphasize the psychological reactions to this *surface-attention problem* since many military (for instance, missile bases and space ships) as well as civilian activities require "dial-watching" tasks to be performed over long periods of time.

Automation often requires a very high-level person for one hour a week and somebody who is capable of doing nothing for the other 39 hours. . . . You are going to have trouble keeping people from getting a kind of "turnpike fatigue" running one of these machines.[15]

In addition employees are likely to feel substantial anxiety about making costly errors.

More than balancing these dissatisfactions, however, are the through-the-job satisfactions derived from the relatively long work cycles, flexible work rhythms, and the opportunities to work as a team in emergencies. In fact, the entire relationship between management and workers is improved over what obtained in traditional manufacturing: There is more two-way communication and mutual understanding. People handle problems as they arise and there is little need for management to impose quotas and work standards. Employees can see themselves progressing over time on a career through a series of graded job steps. Relatively small numbers and management's investment in training give a sense of individualism which contrasts sharply with the impersonality of the traditional sprawling factory.

True automation is really the opposite of Taylorism and scientific management's mass-production methods. The former involves looking at work processes as a whole and giving employees a broader view and wider responsibilities. Mechanization and mass production foster a piecemeal approach: speeding up a machine here, eliminating an arm motion there, saving an operation some place else. It is hardly any wonder that employee reactions to these widely different technologies vary so dramatically.

A Note: Unskilled Work and Floating Labor

Automation is having one of its most profound effects in helping to eliminate some of those jobs that used to be filled by completely unskilled, often temporary, employees. Jobs such as those of yard gangs, sweepers, and loaders used to be reserved for "floating labor" who move endlessly from job to job and sometime from region to region. Lacking education, or handicapped by membership in a minority group, they are disqualified from the better jobs. Experience has "taught" them that they have little chance to get ahead, that there is no point even in trying. Just to hold on to what they have is hard enough. When they find a job they work until they get enough to meet their minimum needs, and when they are unemployed their friends support them. Immediate pleasures are their only goal. They show little "drive" or "ambition."

[Indeed,] only when one knows where his next week's or next month's shelter will come from, can he and his children afford to go in for long-term education and training, the endless search for opportunities, and the tedious apple polishing that the attainment of higher skills and occupational status requires.[16]

Since security and economic advancement mean little to these workers, they look for jobs that provide independence and a feeling of being one's own boss. They may not amount to much by middle-class standards, but they retain the freedom of telling off the boss and quitting their job whenever they want to.[17] Thus, in terms of commitment they represent the antithesis of the employee attitudes that can be fostered by continuous-process automation and its career lines. . . .

Notes and References

1. James Bright, *Automation and Management* (Boston: Harvard Business School, Division of Research, 1958); Floyd Mann and L. Richard Hoffman, *Automation and the Worker* (New York: Holt, Rinehart and Winston, 1960), p. 3; Charles R. Walker, *Toward the Automatic Factory* (New Haven, Conn.: Yale University Press, 1957).
2. *Cf.* William Faunce, "Automation in the Automobile Industry," *American Sociological Review,* Vol. 23, No. 4 (August 1958), pp. 401-407.
3. The table is adapted from Joan Woodward, *Industrial Organization: Theory and Practice* (London: Oxford University Press, 1965), pp. 63-64.
4. Robert Blauner, *Alienation and Freedom* (Chicago: University of Chicago Press, 1964), p. 134.
5. *Ibid.,* p. 138.
6. *Ibid.,* p. 143.
7. *Ibid.*
8. *The New York Times,* March 18, 1965, p. 43 and p. 50.
9. Mann and Hoffman, *op. cit.,* pp. 205-206.
10. One article suggests that leadership exercised by working, "inside" leaders was characteristic of man's earliest work groups: F. L. W. Richardson, "Managing Man's Animal Nature," *Pittsburgh Business Review,* Vol. 34, No. 11 (December 1964), p. 4.
11. Joan Woodward, *Management and Technology* (London: HMSO, 1960), p. 30.
12. Of course, this assumes that the employee exhibits reasonable energy and learning ability. In recent years some oil refineries have had to cope with what they termed "obsolete" employees, often through early retirement.
13. For a more complete treatment of the total subject of working hours see Clyde Dankert, Floyd Mann, and Herbert Northrop, eds., *Hours of Work* (New York: Harper and Row, 1965).
14. In Chapter 16 we shall see that many work frictions are caused by work environments in which the social group contains other members than the work group which must coordinate itself.
15. P. L. Cook, Jr., "Social and Economic Effects of Automation," *Twenty First Annual Midwest Conference on Industrial Relations* (Chicago: Graduate School of Business, University of Chicago, 1955), p. 10.
16. Allison Davis, "The Motivation of Underprivileged Workers," in William F. Whyte, ed., *Industry and Society* (New York: McGraw-Hill, 1946), p. 89.
17. See Richard Centers, "Motivation Aspects of Occupational Stratification," *Journal of Social Psychology,* Vol. 28 (November 1948), pp. 187-217.

PART SIX

Effective Leadership in the Organization

Leadership is the process by which an individual influences the behavior of another person or group. Compliance with this influence is important. If it can be assured, direction and guidance are likely to be followed, and administration is minimized. But compliance is not a unitary concept. Schein, in discussing the "psychological contract," pointed out that a large number of individual responses in organizations can be accounted for simply by the fact of membership. A person is there to do a job, and within reason, he will not disregard directives, suggestions, or policies. Behavior which falls within the boundaries of the psychological contract should not be considered a response to leadership.

Leadership occurs when an individual is able to influence another person or group to go *beyond* the boundaries of the psychological contract. Compliance with directives falling within the psychological contract is *administration*. To move an individual beyond those boundaries is leadership.

A basic assumption is that leadership is based on interpersonal relationships rather than on formal authority or position power. Position power gives an incumbent discretion over such matters as budgets or expenditures, and grants him the right of decision-making. Using this discretion, or administrative prerogative, any incumbent can extract the necessary compliance required for an acceptable level of performance. The effective use of organization structure—budgeting, job descriptions, policies, and so forth—can be taught. Leadership as an interpersonal skill may be more difficult, if not impossible, to teach.

When performance problems occur, there is a tendency to feel that they are a result of leadership deficiencies. Yet failure is often due to the fact that a manager may not *administer* as well as he could. Managers are unwilling, in most circumstances, to make use of the formal sanctions at their disposal. They are unwilling to criticize. They are shy about discussing performance deficiences. They cannot bring themselves to demote poor performers. They expect instead response to their "charismatic" appeals for better performance and commitment.

Given the concept of leadership as an interpersonal relationship, it is necessary to examine what factors are related to the ability to influence another interpersonally. If leadership is influence, and influence is the ability to extract compliance, then power is the force upon which influence is based. Power results from some type of dependence relationship, and may arise for a number of reasons.

An individual may comply with influence attempts simply because another person has the perceived capacity to reward or sanction. Power can be based upon the degree of individual control over the reward structure. Thus, a member may comply because he does not wish to incur negative effects, or because he hopes to be positively rewarded. Some rewards may be organizationally based; for example, promotion opportunities, pay increases, increased status, or any other factor which a manager has discretion to distribute among those who work for him. Rewards may also be socially or interpersonally based. For instance, there may be a high degree of personal attraction to another, so that one complies in order to be socially desirable to him.

When power is viewed as legitimate, the holder is viewed by others as having a right to expect compliance. Legitimate power may be organizationally based when certain rights and prerogatives are associated with certain positions. Under these circumstances, the holder has internalized the right to demand and expect compliance of others. To the extent that organizational definitions of jobs and positions are generally accepted, requests from individuals in those positions may be regarded as legitimate, increasing the likelihood of compliance.

A more complex problem in the consideration of leadership and administration is that it is easy to confuse these concepts. A leader is someone who is able to influence others. A manager is an individual in a particular organization position. While it certainly is true that most managers have discretion to make decisions about resource allocation and distribution which affect and influence subordinates, it is also possible that managers may not exert leadership influence, at least in the sense it has been defined here.

The relationships of leadership, managerial behavior, and performance have always been of interest to those concerned with improving results. However, extensive research has produced inconsistent conclusions about the relationship between leadership style and performance. Some research has found, for instance, that considerate leader behavior, an activity characterized by close relationships and concern for subordinates, is related to high performance by work groups. Other research has found a negative relationship between considerate leader behavior and performance. The selections by Fiedler and House attempt to shed some light on this apparent inconsistency.

It is widely acknowledged that effective leadership style is a function of the leader, the characteristics of the work group, and the situation. Fiedler's article describes situational characteristics which seem to be related to leadership effectiveness. While there is some criticism of his approach, it does force thinking about the leadership process in the direction of specification of what situational variables are important, and how they may be changed in order to improve effectiveness. Essentially, Fiedler's argument is that it is likely to be more productive to change situational characteristics to improve interpersonal interaction than to try to change the leadership style of an individual. Fiedler argues that the situation in which the leader operates determines his effectiveness as much as his own interpersonal skills and abilities do. When the situation and his behavioral style are incongruent, he is likely to be ineffective.

House takes a slightly different approach to integrating inconsistent findings in the leadership literature. He uses the path-goal motivation theory as a foundation for understanding why different leadership styles are likely to be more effective in different circumstances. The individual must know what is expected of him in a work situation. When the job is highly structured, directive leader behavior may have negative effects on employees. When the job is less clear, more ambiguous, or involves a good deal of managerial discretion, a directive style may clarify the relationship between individual activity and the objectives of the job. Thus, directive leader behavior may be positively related to individual performance and satisfaction.

By no means has the last word on leadership been spoken nor the last study conducted. New approaches and theories will be advanced as better measures and new theoretical constructs develop. We have provided in this part a set of concepts which have some practical value. There are, indeed, ways to restructure the work situation and to make assignments more clear. It is a simple matter, if a manager wishes, to change the power assigned to an individual. This can be done by simply delegating more responsibility or discretion to make decisions. A manager can also change the characteristics of the situation to improve leadership effectiveness. Rather than worry about inducing highly charismatic individuals to join an organization, or changing the leadership style of an individual, it may be more effective to restructure the environment to improve interpersonal interaction. Fiedler has suggested some of the ways that the job can be "engineered to fit the manager."

THE BASES OF SOCIAL POWER

JOHN R. P. FRENCH, JR.
BERTRAM RAVEN

The processes of power are pervasive, complex, and often disguised in our society. Accordingly one finds in political science, in sociology, and in social psychology a variety of distinctions among different types of social power or among qualitatively different processes of social influence (1, 6, 14, 20, 23, 29, 30, 38, 41). Our main purpose is to identify the major types of power and to define them systematically so that we may compare them according to the changes which they produce and the other effects which accompany the use of power. The phenomena of power and influence involve a dyadic relation between two agents which may be viewed from two points of view: (a) What determines the behavior of the agent who exerts power? (b) What determines the reactions of the recipient of this behavior? We take this second point of view and formulate our theory in terms of the life space of P, the person upon whom the power is exerted. In this way we hope to define basic con-

Reprinted by permission of the authors and the publisher, Institute for Social Research, from *Studies in Social Power* (1959).

cepts of power which will be adequate to explain many of the phenomena of social influence, including some which have been described in other less genotypic terms.

Recent empirical work, especially on small groups, has demonstrated the necessity of distinguishing different types of power in order to account for the different effects found in studies of social influence. Yet there is no doubt that more empirical knowledge will be needed to make final decisions concerning the necessary differentiations, but this knowledge will be obtained only by research based on some preliminary theoretical distinctions. We present such preliminary concepts and some of the hypotheses they suggest.

Power, Influence, and Change

Psychological Change

Since we shall define power in terms of influence, and influence in terms of psychological change, we begin with a discussion of change. We want to define change at a level of generality which includes changes in behavior, opinions, attitudes, goals, needs, values and all other aspects of the person's psychological field. We shall use the word "system" to refer to any such part of the life space.[1] Following Lewin (26, p. 305) the state of a system at time 1 will be denoted s_1 (a).

Psychological change is defined as any alteration of the state of some system *a* over time. The amount of change is measured by the size of the difference between the states of the system *a* at time 1 and at time 2: $ch(a) = s_2(a) - s_1(a)$.

Change in any psychological system may be conceptualized in terms of psychological forces. But it is important to note that the change must be coordinated to the resultant force of all the forces operating at the moment. Change in an opinion, for example, may be determined jointly by a driving force induced by another person, a restraining force corresponding to anchorage in a group opinion, and an own force stemming from the person's needs.

Social Influence

Our theory of social influence and power is limited to influence on the person, P, produced by a social agent, O, where O can be either another person, a role, a norm, a group or a part of a group. We do not consider social influence exerted on a group.

The influence of O on a system *a* in the life space of P is defined as the resultant force on system *a* which has its source in an act of O. This resultant force induced by O consists of two components: a force to change the system in the direction induced by O and an opposing resistance set up by the same act of O.

By this definition the influence of O does not include P's own forces nor the forces induced by other social agents. Accordingly the "influence" of O must be clearly distinguished from O's "control" of P. O may be able to induce strong forces on P to carry out an activity (i.e., O exerts strong influence on P); but if the opposing forces induced by another person or by P's own needs are stronger, then P will locomote in an opposite direction (i.e., O does not have control over

P). Thus psychological change in P can be taken as an operational definition of the social influence of O on P only when the effects of other forces have been eliminated.

It is assumed that any system is interdependent with other parts of the life space so that a change in one may produce changes in others. However, this theory focuses on the primary changes in a system which are produced directly by social influence; it is less concerned with secondary changes which are indirectly effected in the other systems or with primary changes produced by nonsocial influences.

Commonly social influence takes place through an intentional act on the part of O. However, we do not want to limit our definition of "act" to such conscious behavior. Indeed, influence might result from the passive presence of O, with no evidence of speech or overt movement. A policeman's standing on a corner may be considered an act of an agent for the speeding motorist. Such acts of the inducing agent will vary in strength, for O may not always utilize all of his power. The policeman, for example, may merely stand and watch or act more strongly by blowing his whistle at the motorist.

The influence exerted by an act need not be in the direction intended by O. The direction of the resultant force on P will depend on the relative magnitude of the induced force set up by the act of O and the resisting force in the opposite direction which is generated by that same act. In cases where O intends to influence P in a given direction, a resultant force in the same direction may be termed positive influence whereas a resultant force in the opposite direction may be termed negative influence.

If O produces the intended change, he has exerted positive control; but if he produces a change in the opposite direction, as for example in the negativism of young children or in the phenomena of negative reference groups, he has exerted negative control.

Social Power

The *strength of power* of O/P in some system *a* is defined as the maximum potential ability of O to influence P in *a*.

By this definition influence is kinetic power, just as power is potential influence. It is assumed that O is capable of various acts which, because of some more or less enduring relation to P, are able to exert influence on P.[2] O's power is measured by his maximum possible influence, though he may often choose to exert less than his full power.

An equivalent definition of power may be stated in terms of the resultant of two forces set up by the act of O: one in the direction of O's influence attempt and another resisting force in the opposite direction. Power is the maximum resultant of these two forces:

$$\text{Power of O/P(a)} = (f_{a,x} - f_{\overline{a,x}})\,\text{max}$$

where the source of both forces is an act of O.

Thus the power of O with respect to system *a* of P is equal to the maximum resultant force of two forces set up by any possible act of O: (a) the force which O can set up on the system *a* to change in the direction x, (b) the resisting force[3] in the opposite direction. Whenever the first component force is greater than the second, positive power exists; but if the second component force is greater than the first, then O has negative power over P.

It is necessary to define power with respect to a specified system because the power of O/P may vary greatly from one system to another. O may have great power to control the behavior of P but little power to control his opinions. Of course a high power of O/P does not imply a low power of P/O; the two variables are conceptually independent.

For certain purposes it is convenient to define the range of power as the set of all systems within which O has power of strength greater than zero. A husband may have a broad range of power over his wife, but a narrow range of power over his employer. We shall use the term "magnitude of power" to denote the summation of O's power over P in all systems of his range.

The Dependence of s (a) on O.

Several investigators have been concerned with differences between superficial conformity and "deeper" changes produced by social influence (1, 5, 6, 11, 12, 20, 21, 22, 23, 26, 36, 37). The kinds of systems which are changed and the stability of these changes have been handled by distinctions such as "public vs. private attitudes," "overt vs. covert behavior," "compliance vs. internalization," and "own vs. induced forces." Though stated as dichotomies, all of these distinctions suggest an underlying dimension of the degree of dependence of the state of a system on O.

We assume that any change in the state of a system is produced by a change in some factor upon which it is functionally dependent. The state of an opinion, for example, may change because of a change either in some internal factor such as a need or in some external factor such as the arguments of O. Likewise the maintenance of the same state of a system is produced by the stability or lack of change in the internal and external factors. In general, then, psychological change and stability can be conceptualized in terms of dynamic dependence. Our interest is focused on the special case of dependence on an external agent, O (31).

In many cases the initial state of the system has the character of a quasi-stationary equilibrium with a central force field around $s_1(a)$ (26, p. 106). In such cases we may derive a tendency toward retrogression to the original state as soon as the force induced by O is removed.[4] Let us suppose that O exerts influence producing a new state of the system, $s_2(a)$. Is $s_2(a)$ now dependent on the continued presence of O? In principle we could answer this question by removing any traces of O from the life space of P and by observing the consequent state of the system at time 3. If $s_3(a)$ retrogresses completely back to $s_1(a)$, then we may conclude that maintenance of $s_2(a)$ was completely dependent on O; but if $s_3(a)$ equals $s_2(a)$, this lack of change shows that $s_2(a)$ has become completely independent of O. In general the degree of dependence of $s_2(a)$ on O, following O's influence, may be defined as equal to the amount of retrogression following the removal of O from the life space of P:

$$\text{Degree of dependence of } s_2(a) \text{ on } 0 = s_2(a) - s_3(a)$$

A given degree of dependence at time 2 may later change, for example, through the gradual weakening of O's influence. At this later time, the degree of dependence of $s_4(a)$ on O, would still be equal to the amount of retrogression toward the initial state of equilibrium $s_1(a)$. Operational measures of the degree of dependence on O will, of course, have to be taken under conditions where all other factors are held constant.

Consider the example of three separated employees who have been working at the same steady level of production despite normal, small fluctuations in the work environment. The supervisor orders each to increase his production, and the level of each goes up from 100 to 115 pieces per day. After a week of producing at the new rate of 115 pieces per day, the supervisor is removed for a week. The production of employee A immediately returns to 100 but B and C return to only 110 pieces per day. Other things being equal, we can infer that A's new rate was completely dependent on his supervisor whereas the new rate of B and C was dependent on the supervisor only to the extent of 5 pieces. Let us further assume that when the supervisor returned, the production of B and C returned to 115 without further orders from the supervisor. Now another month goes by during which B and C maintain a steady 115 pieces per day. However, there is a difference between them: B's level of production still depends on O to the extent of 5 pieces whereas C has come to rely on his own sense of obligation to obey the order of his legitimate supervisors rather than on the supervisor's external pressure for the maintenance of his 115 pieces per day. Accordingly the next time the supervisor departs, B's production again drops to 110 but C's remains at 115 pieces per day. In cases like employee B, the degree of dependence is contingent on the perceived probability that O will observe the state of the system and note P's conformity (5, 6, 11, 12, 23). The level of observability will in turn depend on both the nature of the system (e.g., the difference between a covert opinion and overt behavior) and on the environmental barriers to observation (e.g., O is too far away from P). In other cases, for example that of employee C, the new behavior pattern is highly dependent on his supervisor, but the degree of dependence of the new state will be related not to the level of observability but rather to factors inside P, in this case a sense of duty to perform an act legitimately prescribed by O. The internalization of social norms is a related process of decreasing degree of dependence of behavior on an external O and increasing dependence on an internal value; it is usually assumed that internalization is accompanied by a decrease in the effects of level of observability (37).

The concepts "dependence of a system on O" and "observability as a basis for dependence" will be useful in understanding the stability of conformity. In the next section we shall discuss various types of power and the types of conformity which they are likely to produce.

The Bases of Power

By the basis of power we mean the relationship between O and P which is the source of that power. It is rare that we can say with certainty that a given empirical case of power is limited to one source. Normally, the relation between O and P will be characterized by several qualitatively different variables which are bases of power (30). Although there are undoubtedly many possible bases of power which may be distinguished, we shall here define five which seem especially common and important. These five bases of O's power are:

1. reward power, based on P's perception that O has the ability to mediate rewards for him;
2. coercive power, based on P's perception that O has the ability to mediate punishments for him;
3. legitimate power, based on the perception by P that O has a legitimate right to prescribe behavior for him;
4. referent power, based on P's identification with O;
5. expert power, based on the perception that O has some special knowledge or expertness.

Our first concern is to define the bases which give rise to a given type of power. Next, we describe each type of power according to its strength, range, and the degree of dependence of the new state of the system which is most likely to occur with each type of power. We shall also examine the other effects which the exercise of a given type of power may have upon P and his relationship to O. Finally, we shall point out the interrelationships between different types of power, and the effects of use of one type of power by O upon other bases of power which he might have over P. Thus we shall both define a set of concepts and propose a series of hypotheses. Most of these hypotheses have not been systematically tested, although there is a good deal of evidence in favor of several. No attempt will be made to summarize that evidence here.

Reward Power

Reward power is defined as power whose basis is the ability to reward. The strength of the reward power of O/P increases with the magnitude of the rewards which P perceives that O can mediate for him. Reward power depends on O's ability to administer positive valences and to remove or decrease negative valences. The strength of reward power also depends upon the probability that O can mediate the reward, as perceived by P. A common example of reward power is the addition of a piece-work rate in the factory as an incentive to increase production.

The new state of the system induced by a promise of reward (for example the factory worker's increased level of production) will be highly dependent on O. Since O mediates the reward, he controls the probability that P will receive it. Thus P's new rate of production will be dependent on his subjective probability that O will reward him for conformity minus his subjective probability that O will reward him even if he returns to his old level. Both probabilities will be greatly affected by the level of observability of P's behavior. Incidentally, a piece rate often seems to have more effect on production than a merit rating system because it yields a higher probability of reward for conformity and a much lower probability of reward for nonconformity.

The utilization of actual rewards (instead of promises) by O will tend over time to increase the attraction of P toward O and therefore the referent power of O over P. As we shall note later, such referent power will permit O to induce changes which are relatively independent. Neither rewards nor promises will arouse resistance in P, provided P considers it legitimate for O to offer rewards.

The range of reward power is specific to those regions within which O can reward P for conforming. The use of rewards to change systems within the range of reward power tends to increase reward power by increasing the probability attached to future promises. However, unsuccessful attempts to exert reward power outside the range of power would tend to decrease the power; for example if O offers to reward P for performing an impossible act, this will reduce for P the probability of receiving future rewards promised by O.

Coercive Power

Coercive power is similar to reward power in that it also involves O's ability to manipulate the attainment of valences. Coercive power of O/P stems from the expectation on the part of P that he will be punished by O if he fails to conform to the influence attempt. Thus negative valences will exist in given regions of P's life space, corresponding to the threatened punishment by O. The strength of coercive power depends on the magnitude of the negative valence of the threatened punishment multiplied by the perceived probability that P can avoid the punishment by conformity, i.e., the probability of punishment for nonconformity minus the probability of punishment for conformity (11). Just as an offer of a piece-rate bonus in a factory can serve as a basis for reward power, so the ability to fire a worker if he falls below a given level of production will result in coercive power.

Coercive power leads to dependent change also; and the degree of dependence varies with the level of observability of P's conformity. An excellent illustration of coercive power leading to dependent change is provided by a clothes presser in a factory observed by Coch and French (3). As her efficiency rating climbed above average for the group the other workers began to "scapegoat" her. That the resulting plateau in her production was not independent of the group was evident once she was removed from the presence of the other workers. Her production immediately climbed to new heights.[5]

At times, there is some difficulty in distinguishing between reward power and coercive power. Is the withholding of a reward really equivalent to a punishment? Is the withdrawal of punishment equivalent to a reward? The answer must be a psychological one—it depends upon the situation as it exists for P. But ordinarily we would answer these questions in the affirmative; for P, receiving a reward is a positive valence as is the relief of suffering. There is some evidence that conformity to group norms in order to gain acceptance (reward power) should be distinguished from conformity as a means of forestalling rejection (coercive power) (5).

The distinction between these two types of power is important because the dynamics are different. The concept of "sanctions" sometimes lumps the two together despite their opposite effects. While reward power may eventually result in an independent system, the effects of coercive power will continue to be dependent. Reward power will tend to increase the attraction of P toward O; coercive power will decrease this attraction (11, 12). The valence of the region of behavior will become more negative, acquiring some negative valence from the threatened punishment. The negative valence of punishment would also spread to other regions of the life space. Lewin (25) has pointed out this distinction between the effects of rewards and punishment. In the case of threatened punishment, there will be a resultant force on P to leave the field entirely. Thus, to achieve conformity, O must not only place a strong negative valence in certain regions through threat of punishment, but O must also introduce restraining forces, or other strong valences, so as to prevent P from withdrawing completely from O's range of coercive power. Otherwise the probability of receiving the punishment, if P does not conform, will be too low to be effective.

Legitimate Power

Legitimate power is probably the most complex of those treated here, embodying notions from the structural sociologist, the group-norm and role oriented social psychologist, and the clinical psychologist.

There has been considerable investigation and speculation about socially prescribed behavior, particularly that which is specific to a given role or position. Linton (29) distinguishes group norms according to whether they are universals for everyone in the culture, alternatives (the individual having a choice as to whether or not to accept them), or specialties (specific to given positions). Whether we speak of internalized norms, role prescriptions and expectations (34), or internalized pressures (15), the fact remains that each individual sees certain regions toward which he should locomote, some regions toward which he should not locomote, and some regions toward which he may locomote if they are generally attractive for him. This applies to specific behaviors in which he may, should, or should not engage; it applies to certain attitudes or beliefs which he may, should, or should not hold. The feeling of "oughtness" may be an internalization from his parents, from his teachers, from his religion, or may have been logically developed from some idiosyncratic system of ethics. He will speak of such behaviors with expressions like "should," "ought to," or "has a right to." In many cases, the original source of the requirement is not recalled.

Though we have oversimplified such evaluations of behavior with a positive-neutral-negative trichotomy, the evaluation of behaviors by the person is really more one of degree. This dimension of evaluation, we shall call "legitimacy." Conceptually, we may think of legitimacy as a valence in a region which is induced by some internalized norm or value. This value has the same conceptual property as power, namely an ability to induce force fields (26, p. 40-41). It may or may not be correct that values (or the superego) are internalized parents, but at least they can set up force fields which have a phenomenal "oughtness" similar to a parent's prescription. Like a value, a need can also induce valences (i.e., force fields) in P's psychological environment, but these valences have more the phenomenal character of noxious or attractive properties of the object or activity. When a need induces a valence in P, for example, when a need makes an object attractive to P, this attraction applies to P but not to other persons. When a value induces a valence, on the other hand, it not only sets up forces on P to engage in the activity, but P may feel that all others ought to behave in the same way. Among other things, this evaluation applies to the legitimate right of some other individual or group to prescribe behavior or beliefs for a person even though the other cannot apply sanctions.

Legitimate power of O/P is here defined as that power which stems from internalized values in P which dictate that O has a legitimate right to influence P and that P has an obligation to accept this influence. We note that legitimate power is very similar to the notion of legitimacy of authority which has long been explored by sociologists, particularly by Weber (42), and more recently by Goldhammer and Shils (14). However, legitimate power is not always a role relation: P may accept an induction from O simply because he had previously promised to help O and he values his word too much to break the promise. In all cases, the notion of legitimacy involves some sort of code or standard, accepted by the individual, by virtue of which the external agent can assert his power. We shall attempt to describe a few of these values here.

Bases for legitimate power. Cultural values constitute one common basis for the legitimate power of one individual over another. O has characteristics which are specified by the culture as giving him the right to prescribe behavior for P, who may not have these characteristics. These bases, which Weber (42) has called the authority of the "eternal yesterday," include such things as age, intelligence, caste, and physical characteristics. In some cultures, the aged are granted the right to prescribe behavior for others in practically all behavior areas. In most cultures, there are certain areas of behavior in which a person of one sex is granted the right to prescribe behavior for the other sex.

Acceptance of the social structure is another basis for legitimate power. If P accepts as right the social structure of his group, organization, or society, especially the social structure involving a hierarchy of authority, P will accept the legitimate authority of O who occupies a superior office in the hierarchy. Thus legitimate power in a formal organization is largely a relationship between offices rather than between persons. And the acceptance of an office as *right* is a basis for legitimate power—a judge has a right to levy fines, a foreman should assign work, a priest is justified in prescribing religious beliefs, and it is the management's prerogative to make certain decisions (10). However, legitimate power also involves the perceived right of the person to hold the office.

Designation by a legitimizing agent is a third basis for legitimate power. An influencer O may be seen as legitimate in prescribing behavior for P because he has been granted such power by a legitimizing agent whom P accepts. Thus a department head may accept the authority of his vice-president in a certain area because that authority has been specifically delegated by the president. An election is perhaps the most common example of a group's serving to legitimize the authority of one individual or office for other individuals in the group. The success of such legitimizing depends upon the acceptance of the legitimizing agent and procedure. In this case it depends ultimately on certain democratic values concerning election procedures. The election process is one of legitimizing a person's right to an office which already has legitimate range of power associated with it.

Range of legitimate power of O/P. The areas in which legitimate power may be exercised are generally specified along with the designation of that power. A job description, for example, usually specifies supervisory activities and also designates the person to whom the job-holder is responsible for the duties described. Some bases for legitimate authority carry with them a very broad range. Culturally derived bases for legitimate power are often especially broad. It is not uncommon to find cultures in which a member of a given caste can legitimately prescribe behavior for all members of lower castes in practically all regions. More common, however, are instances of legitimate power where the range is specifically and narrowly prescribed. A sergeant in the army is given a specific set of regions within which he can legitimately prescribe behavior for his men.

The attempted use of legitimate power which is outside of the range of legitimate power will decrease the legitimate power of the authority figure. Such use of power which is not legitimate will also decrease the attractiveness of O (11, 12, 36).

Legitimate power and influence. The new state of the system which results from legitimate power usually has high dependence on O though it may become independent. Here, however, the degree of dependence is not related to the level of observability. Since legitimate power is based on P's values, the source of the forces induced by O include both these internal values and O. O's induction serves to activate the values and to relate them to the system which is influenced, but thereafter the new state of the system may become directly dependent on the values with no mediation by O. Accordingly this new state will be relatively stable and consistent across varying environmental situations since P's values are more stable than his psychological environment.

We have used the term legitimate not only as a basis for the power of an agent, but also to describe the general behaviors of a person. Thus, the individual P may also consider the legitimacy of the attempts to use other types of power by O. In certain cases, P will consider that O has a legitimate right to threaten punishment for nonconformity; in other cases, such use of coercion would not be seen as legitimate. P might change in response to coercive power of O, but it will make a considerable difference in his attitude and conformity if O is not seen as having a legitimate right to use such coercion. In such cases, the attraction of P for O will be particularly diminished, and the influence attempt will arouse more resistance (11). Similarly the utilization of reward power may vary in legitimacy; the word "bribe" for example, denotes an illegitimate reward.

Referent Power

The referent power of O/P has its basis in the identification of P with O. By identification, we mean a feeling of oneness of P with O, or a desire for such an identity. If O is a person toward whom P is highly attracted, P will have a desire to become closely associated with O. If O is an attractive group, P will have a feeling of membership or a desire to join. If P is already closely associated with O he will want to maintain this relationship (39, 41). P's identification with O can be established or maintained if P behaves, believes, and perceives as O does. Accordingly O has the ability to influence P, even though P may be unaware of this referent power. A verbalization of such power by P might be, "I am like O, and therefore I shall behave or believe as O does," or "I want to be like O, and I will be more like O if I behave or believe as O does." The stronger the identification of P with O the greater the referent power of O/P.

Similar types of power have already been investigated under a number of different formulations. Festinger (7) points out that in an ambiguous situation, the individual seeks some sort of "social reality" and may adopt the cognitive structure of the individual or group with which he identifies. In such a case, the lack of clear structure may be threatening to the individual and the agreement of his beliefs with those of a reference group will both satisfy his need for structure and give him added security through increased identification with his group (16, 19).

We must try to distinguish between referent power and other types of power which might be operative at the same time. If a member is attracted to a group and he conforms to its norms only because he fears ridicule or expulsion from the group for nonconformity, we would call this coercive power. On the other hand if he conforms in order to obtain praise for conformity, it is a case of reward power. The basic criterion for distinguishing referent power from both coercive and reward power is the mediation of the punishment and the reward by O: to the extent that O mediates the sanctions (i.e., has means control over P) we are dealing with coercive and reward power; but to the extent that P avoids discomfort or gains satisfaction by conformity based on identification, regardless of O's responses, we are dealing with referent power. Conformity with majority opinion is sometimes based on a respect for the collective wisdom of the group, in which case it is expert power. It is important to distinguish these phenomena, all grouped together elsewhere as "pressures toward uniformity," since the type of change which occurs will be different for different bases of power.

The concepts of "reference group" (40) and "prestige suggestion" may be treated as instances of referent power. In this case, O, the prestigeful person or group, is valued by P; because P desires to be associated or identified with O, he will assume attitudes or beliefs held by O. Similarly a negative reference group which O dislikes and evaluates negatively may exert negative influence on P as a result of negative referent power.

It has been demonstrated that the power which we designate as referent power is especially great when P is attracted to O (2, 7, 8, 9, 13, 23, 30). In our terms, this would mean that the greater the attraction, the greater the identification, and consequently the greater the referent power. In some cases, attraction or prestige may have a specific basis, and the range of referent power will be limited accordingly: a group of campers may have great referent power over a member regarding campcraft, but considerably less effect on other regions (30). However, we hypothesize that the greater the attraction of P toward O, the broader the range of referent power of O/P.

The new state of a system produced by referent power may be dependent on or independent of O; but the degree of dependence is not affected by the level of observability to O (6, 23). In fact, P is often not consciously aware of the referent power which O exerts over him. There is probably a tendency for some of these dependent changes to become independent of O quite rapidly.

Expert Power

The strength of the expert power of O/P varies with the extent of the knowledge or perception which P attributes to O within a given area. Probably P evaluates O's expertness in relation to his own knowledge as well as against an absolute standard. In any case expert power results in primary social influence on P's cognitive structure and probably not on other types of systems. Of course changes in the cognitive structure can change the direction of forces and hence of locomotion, but such a change of behavior is secondary social influence. Expert power has been demonstrated experimentally (8, 33). Accepting an attorney's advice in legal matters is a common example of expert influence; but there are many instances based on much less knowledge, such as the acceptance by a stranger of directions given by a native villager.

Expert power, where O need not be a member of P's group, is called "informational power" by Deutsch and Gerard (4). This type of expert power must be distinguished from influence based on the content of communication as described by Hovland et al. (17, 18, 23, 24). The influence of the content of a communication upon an opinion is presumably a secondary influence produced after the *primary* influence (i.e., the acceptance of the information). Since power is here defined in terms of the primary changes, the influence of the content on a related opinion is not a case of expert power as we have defined it, but the initial acceptance of the validity of the content does seem to be based on expert power or referent power. In other cases, however, so-called facts may be accepted as self-evident because they fit into P's cognitive structure; if this impersonal acceptance of the truth of the fact is independent of the more or less enduring relationship between O and P, then P's acceptance of the fact is not an actualization of expert power. Thus we distinguish between expert power based on the credibility of O and informational influence which is based on characteristics of the stimulus such as the logic of the argument or the "self-evident facts."

Wherever expert influence occurs it seems to be necessary both for P to think that O knows and for P to trust that O is telling the truth (rather than trying to deceive him).

Expert power will produce a new cognitive structure which is initially relatively dependent on O, but informational influence will produce a more independent structure. The former is likely to become more independent with the passage of time. In both cases the degree of dependence on O is not affected by the level of observability.

The "sleeper effect" (18, 24) is an interesting case of a change in the degree of dependence of an opinion on O. An unreliable O (who probably had negative referent power but some positive expert power) presented "facts" which were accepted by the subjects and which would normally produce secondary influence on their opinions and beliefs. However, the negative referent power aroused resistance and resulted in negative social influence on their beliefs (i.e., set up a force in the direction opposite to the influence attempt), so that there was little change in the subjects' opinions. With the passage of time, however, the subjects tended to forget the identity of the negative communicator faster than they forgot the contents of his communication, so there was a weakening of the negative referent influence and a consequent delayed positive change in the subjects' beliefs in the direction of the influence attempt ("sleeper effect"). Later, when the identity of the negative communicator was experimentally reinstated, these resisting forces were reinstated, and there was another negative change in belief in a direction opposite to the influence attempt (24).

The range of expert power, we assume, is more delimited than that of referent power. Not only is it restricted to cognitive systems but the expert is seen as having superior knowledge or ability in very specific areas, and his power will be limited to these areas, though some "halo effect" might occur. Recently, some of our renowned physical scientists have found quite painfully that their expert power in physical sciences does not extend to regions involving international politics. Indeed, there is some evidence that the attempted exertion of expert power outside of the range of expert power will reduce that expert power. An undermining of confidence seems to take place.

Summary

We have distinguished five types of power: referent power, expert power, reward power, coercive power, and legitimate power. These distinctions led to the following hypotheses.
1. For all five types, the stronger the basis of power the greater the power.
2. For any type of power the size of the range may vary greatly, but in general referent power will have the broadest range.
3. Any attempt to utilize power outside the range of power will tend to reduce the power.
4. A new state of a system produced by reward power or coercive power will be highly dependent on O, and the more observable P's conformity the more dependent the state. For the other three types of power, the new state is usually dependent, at least in the beginning, but in any case the level of observability has no effect on the degree of dependence.
5. Coercion results in decreased attraction of P toward O and high resistance; reward power results in increased attraction and low resistance.
6. The more legitimate the coercion the less it will produce resistance and decreased attraction.

Notes

1. The word "system" is here used to refer to a whole or to a part of the whole.
2. The concept of power has the conceptual property of *potentiality;* but it seems useful to restrict this potential influence to more or less enduring power relations between O and P by excluding from the definition of power those cases where the potential influence is so momentary or so changing that it cannot be predicted from the existing relationship. Power is a useful concept for describing social structure only if it has a certain stability over time: it is useless if every momentary social stimulus is viewed as actualizing social power.
3. We define resistance to an attempted induction as a force in the opposite direction which is set up by the same act of O. It must be distinguished from opposition, which is defined as existing opposing forces which do not have their source in the same act of O. For example, a boy might resist his mother's order to eat spinach because of the manner of the induction attempt, and at the same time he might oppose it because he didn't like spinach.
4. Miller (33) assumes that all living systems have this character. However, it may be that some systems in the life space do not have this elasticity.
5. Though the primary influence of coercive power is dependent, it often produces secon-

dary changes which are independent. Brainwashing for example, utilizes coercive power to produce many primary changes in the life space of the prisoner, but these dependent changes can lead to identification with the aggressor and hence to secondary changes in ideology which are independent.

References

1. Asch, S. E. *Social psychology*, New York: Prentice-Hall, Inc., 1952.
2. Back, K. W. Influence through social communication. *J. abnorm. soc. Psychol.* 46 (1951): 9-23.
3. Coch, L., and French, J. R. P., Jr. Overcoming resistance to change. *Hum. Relat.* 1 (1948): 512-32.
4. Deutsch, M., and Gerard, H. B. A study of normative and informational influences upon individual judgment. *J. abnorm. soc. Psychol.* 51 (1955) 629-36.
5. Dittes, J. E., and Kelley, H. H. Effects of different conditions of acceptance upon conformity to group norms. *J. abnorm. soc. Psychol.* 53 (1956): 100-107.
6. Festinger, L. An analysis of compliant behavior. In Sherif, M, and Wilson, M. O., (Eds.). *Group relations at the crossroads*. New York: Harper & Row, Publishers, 1953, 232-56.
7. Festinger, L. Informal social communication. *Psychol. Rev.* 57 (1950): 271-82.
8. Festinger, L.; Gerard, H. B.; Hymovitch, B.; Kelley, H. H.; and Raven, B. H. The influence process in the presence of extreme deviates. *Hum. Relat.* 5 (1952): 327-46.
9. Festinger, L.; Schachter, S.; and Back, K. The operation of group standards. In Cartwright, D., & Zander, A. *Group dynamics: research and theory*. Evanston: Row, Peterson, 1953, 204-23.
10. French, J. R. P., Jr.; Israel; Joachim: and As, Dagfinn "Arbeidernes medvirkning i industribedriften. En eksperimentell undersokelse." Institute for Social Research, Oslo, Norway, 1957.
11. French, J. R. P., Jr.; Levinger, G.; and Morrison, H. W. The legitimacy of coercive power. In preparation.
12. French, J. R. P., Jr., and Raven, B. H. An experiment in legitimate and coercive power. In preparation.
13. Gerard, H. B. The anchorage of opinions in face-to-face groups. *Hum. Relat.* 7 (1954): 313-25.
14. Goldhammer, H., and Shils, E. A. Types of power and status. *Amer. J. Sociol* 45 (1939) 171-78.
15. Herbst, P. G. Analysis and measurement of a situation. *Hum. Relat.* 2 (1953): 113-40.
16. Hochbaum, G. M. Self-confidence and reactions to group pressures. *Amer. soc. Rev.*, 19 (1954) 678-87.
17. Hovland, C. I., Lumsdaine, A. A., and Sheffield, F. D. *Experiments on mass communication*. Princeton: Princeton Univer. Press, 1949.
18. Hovland, C. I., and Weiss, W. The influence of source credibility on communication effectiveness. *Publ. Opin. Quart.* 15 (1951): 635-50.
19. Jackson, J. M., and Saltzstein, H. D. The effect of person-group relationships on conformity processes. *J. abnorm. soc. Psychol.* 57 (1958): 17-24.
20. Jahoda, M. Psychological issues in civil liberties. *Amer. Psychologist* 11 (1956): 234-40.

21. Katz, D., and Schank, R. L. *Social psychology*. New York: John Wiley & Sons, 1938.
22. Kelley, H. H., and Volkart, E. H. The resistance to change of group-anchored attitudes. *Amer. soc. Rev.*, 17 (1952): 453-65.
23. Kelman, H. Three processes of acceptance of social influence: compliance, identification and internalization. Paper read at the meetings of the American Psychological Association, August 1956.
24. Kelman, H., and Hovland, C. I. "Reinstatement" of the communicator in delayed measurement of opinion change. *J. abnorm. soc. Psychol.* 48 (1953): 327-35.
25. Lewin, K. *Dynamic theory of personality*. New York: McGraw-Hill Book Company, 1935, 114-70.
26. Lewin, K. *Field theory in social science*. New York: Harper & Row, Publishers, 1951.
27. Lewin, K., Lippitt, R., and White, R. K. Patterns of aggressive behavior in experimentally created social climates. *J. soc. Psychol.* 10 (1939): 271-301.
28. Lasswell, H. D., and Kaplan, A. *Power and society: A framework for political inquiry*. New Haven: Yale Univer. Press, 1950.
29. Linton, R. *The cultural background of personality*. New York: Appleton-Century-Crofts, 1945.
30. Lippitt, R.; Polansky, N.; Redl, F.; and Rosen, S. The dynamics of power. *Hum. Relat.* 5 (1952): 37-64.
31. March, J. G. An introduction to the theory and measurement of influence. *Amer. polit. Sci. Rev.* 49 (1955): 431-51.
32. Miller, J. G. Toward a general theory for the behavioral sciences. *Amer. Psychologist* 10 (1955): 513-31.
33. Moore, H. T. The comparative influence of majority and expert opinion. *Amer. J. Psychol.* 32 (1921): 16-20.
34. Newcomb, T. M. *Social psychology*. New York: Dryden, 1950.
35. Raven, B. H. The effect of group pressures on opinion, perception, and communication. Unpublished doctoral dissertation, University of Michigan, 1953.
36. Raven, B. H., and French, J. R. P., Jr. Group support, legitimate power, and social influence. *J. Person.*, 26, 1958, 400-09.
37. Rommetveit, R. *Social norms and roles*. Minneapolis: Univer. Minnesota Press, 1953.
38. Russell, B. *Power: A new social analysis*. New York: Norton, 1938.
39. Stotland, E., Zander, A., Burnstein, E., Wolfe, D., and Natsoulas, T. Studies on the effects of identification. University of Michigan, Institute for Social Research. Forthcoming.
40. Swanson, G. E., Newcomb, T. M., and Hartley, E. L. *Readings in social psychology*. New York: Holt, Rinehart and Winston, 1952.
41. Torrance, E. P., and Mason, R. Instructor effort to influence: an experimental evaluation of six approaches. Paper presented at USAF-NRC Symposium on Personnel, Training, and Human Engineering. Washington, D.C., 1956.
42. Weber, M. *The theory of social and economic organization*. Oxford: Oxford Univer. Press, 1947.

SUPERVISORY STYLE AND PRODUCTIVITY: REVIEW AND THEORY

STEPHEN M. SALES

It is widely assumed that employees will work harder for supervisors who employ given styles of supervision than they will for supervisors who use other styles. This supposition clearly underlies much of supervisory training; it is a basic tenet of the writings of Morse (1953), Likert (1961), and many others. However, the theoretical underpinnings of this assumption are often unclearly stated (when they are stated at all); furthermore, the wide variety of studies investigating the validity of this position are rarely fully described. The present article will sketch a theory which accounts for the predicted differential in productivity and will review and evaluate the literature relevant to this theory.

Authoritarianism and Democracy

The styles to be discussed are the authoritarian and democratic dimensions. The distinction between these orientations has often been made in the literature; it will not be extensively elaborated here. Rather, we shall discuss only the major differences between these styles.

Authoritarian supervision, in general, is characterized by the relatively high degree of power wielded by the supervisor over the work group. As contrasted with democratic supervision, both power and all decision-making functions are absolutely concentrated in the person of the authoritarian. Democratic supervision, on the other hand, is characterized by a sharing of power and by participative decision-making. Under democratic supervision, the work group becomes in some ways co-equal with the supervisor; responsibility is spread rather than concentrated.

Differential Effectiveness

It is commonly assumed that, with other conditions held constant, employees will produce more under democratic supervision than they would have produced under autocratic supervision. (Such an assumption, of course, lies behind the entire human relations movement.) There is at least one good reason for this prediction. Specifically, the reinforcing value of work performed under democratic supervision should be higher than that of work performed under autocratic supervision.

It is a basic tenet of experimental psychology that high levels of performance will obtain in situations in which the reinforcement is large, whereas low performance levels will occur in those in which the reinforcement is small. In terms of industrial situations, the more reinforcement an employee receives for production,

Reprinted by permission of the author and the publisher from *Personnel Psychology*, vol. 19, no. 3 (1966)

the higher his production should be. (This is, of course, the assumption which underlies incentive systems, although reinforcement is rather narrowly defined in such programs.) Vroom (1962, pp. 26-43) in particular has explored the ramifications of this argument.

The importance of this point for the present consideration is that production is attended by two different levels of need-satisfaction under the two styles of supervision sketched above.Democratic supervision, by allowing subordinates freedom in determining the specific form and content of their work, implicates the personalities of the employees in the tasks they perform. This means that production, under democratic supervision, becomes a means for satisfying the employees' ego-esteem and self-actualization needs (see Maslow, 1954; Argyris, 1957). That is, the "greater opportunity for regulating and controlling their own activities [provided by democratic supervision] . . . should increase the degree to which individuals could express their various and diverse needs and could move in the direction of fully exploiting their potential while on the job" (Morse & Reimer, 1956). Authoritarian supervision, inasmuch as it makes work merely the carrying out of the supervisor's will, reduces the degree to which such need-satisfaction can be derived from production. Therefore, since productivity is less satisfying under autocratic than under democratic supervision, one would expect that workers would be less productive in the former condition than in the latter. (This effect, of course, should be accentuated for those individuals for whom the needs in question are most important.)

It should be noted that the above considerations do not involve between-style differences which rest upon uncontrolled factors (even when such factors might themselves follow from the style variation). For instance, if turnover were higher under one supervisory style than under the other, one would expect that the method resulting in higher turnover would be accompanied by the lower productivity rate (because of lowered effectiveness during learning periods). Factors of this sort would lead to productivity differences between the supervisory styles; however, such differences would not truly bear upon the question of effectiveness as usually posed. That is, statements about supervisory style center in general about the proposition that employees will work harder for some supervisors than for others. This statement cannot be supported by dependent variable differences which may be shown to result from between-condition variations other than that of supervisory style. The present discussion is concerned solely with productivity differences which follow *directly* from the style of supervision.

Relevant Investigations

Any review of the literature on supervision must be in some way limited if both the reviewer and the readers are to escape total exhaustion. For this reason, investigations employing non-production criteria will be excluded from this review as will studies in which methodological looseness clouds interpretation of the findings reported. Thus, investigations which operationalize the effectiveness of the supervisory styles used in terms of "increased acceptance of decisions" (e.g., Coch & French, 1948), morale, or similar criteria will not be reviewed, nor will unstandardized case studies of "participative management" or the Scanlon Plan.

Experimental Investigations

The original and best known study in this area is the experiment of Lewin, Lippitt, and White (e.g., Lippitt & White, 1958, pp. 496-510; White & Lippitt, 1962). These investigators employed as subjects thirty ten-year-old boys who met in six groups which ostensibly were recreational clubs. These groups were supervised by adults who had been trained to act in either a democratic, autocratic, or laisses-faire manner. (The last condition is not considered in the present discussion.) Each club was exposed to each of the three styles for six weeks.

The results of this experiment, in terms of productivity, are extremely difficult to establish. When exposed to autocratic supervision[1] the boys spent more time at work than they did under democratic supervision (74% of the total time as opposed to 50% under democratic supervision). However, the "work-mindedness" of the democratically-supervised boys appeared to be somewhat higher since under demo-cratic supervision the groups engaged in a slightly larger amount of "work-minded conversation." (There were 63 work-minded remarks per child under the democratic condition, whereas in the autocratic condition this figure fell to 52.) However, *no objective measure of pruductivity is reported by the authors, and therefore it is impossible to determine accurately which of the two styles evoked the higher produc-tion* (a fact often overlooked by reviewers of this study).

McCurdy and Eber (1953) examined supervisory style in an investigation on group problem-solving. In this experiment, three-man groups participated in a task in which the group determined the proper setting of three switches. In the authoritarian condition one subject was given the power to order the others at will, making him an "absolute" supervisor. The other subjects were instructed merely to obey orders. In the democratic condition the instructions emphasized equalitarian-ism, specifying that each subject could offer suggestions and that no individual could order the others in any way. No differences whatever appeared between the two conditions on a productivity criterion.

Shaw (1955), working with communication networks, also used problem-solving as a dependent variable in an investigation of supervisory style effects. Employing three different "nets," he instructed the subjects assigned to the position with the highest independence score within each structure[2] to behave either in an autocratic manner (e. g., by giving orders) or in a democratic manner (e.g., by making sugges-tions). Shaw found that the autocratically-supervised subjects (a) required less time to solve the problems, regardless of the communication net in which they were placed, and (b) made fewer errors.

Day and Hamblin (1964) trained a female student to employ "close" and "general" supervisory styles in leading groups of female subjects in an assembly-line task. These researchers found that subjects exposed to close supervision produced less than did subjects exposed to general supervision.

Sales (1964), like Day and Hamblin, replicated an industrial assembly-line set-ting in the laboratory. In Sales's experiment two male supervisors played democratic and autocratic roles over male and female groups. (Both role and sex of the sub-ordinates were fully counterbalanced in this experiment.) Sales reports no differential effectiveness whatever between the two styles; the productivity means for the two conditions were virtually identical.

Spector and Suttell (1957) report a relevant laboratory study with naval trainees as subjects. These authors trained supervisors to use either "single leadership" or "leadership sharing" styles, patterns which seem to parallel the democratic-autocratic distinction. The task consisted of problems in which team members cooperated in receiving, processing, and recording information. No differences were detected in the productivity of the groups under the two styles.

In the most extensive of the investigations reported in this area, Morse and Reimer (1956) created groups exposed either to democratic or to autocratic supervision by altering the style of supervision used in an on-going industrial setting. In two divisions ("participative treatment") an attempt was made to push down the level of decision-making. Supervisors were trained to employ more democratic supervisory methods, and they were given greater freedom of action than previously had been allowed. In two other divisions an "hierarchically-controlled treatment" was established by an increase in the closeness of supervision and a movement upward in the level at which decisions were made. The treatments were administered for a year's time to approximately five hundred employees.

Morse and Reimer found that both programs resulted in a significant increase in productivity. This increase was slightly higher for the hierarchically-controlled divisions; however, the actual difference between the treatments was quite small.

On balance, then, the experimental studies reviewed above show no consistent superiority of one style over the other in terms of a productivity criterion. Of the six studies for which objective production data are available, one (Day & Hamblin, 1964) reports democratic supervision to be more effective and one (Shaw, 1955) reports authoritarian supervision to be more effective. The other four investigations note no differences of consequence between the two styles.

Survey Investigations

Survey researches applied to the problem discussed herein follow a standard methodology. The supervisory style which exists in each of the work groups in the situation is determined (usually by means of questionnaires administered to the employees), and this variable is then related to productivity. Researchers using this methodology generally have found a clear relationship between style of supervision and work group productivity.

The extensive investigations performed by the Survey Research Center at the University of Michigan during the early 1950's (Katz, Maccoby & Morse, 1950; Katz, Maccoby, Gurin & Floor, 1951; Katz & Kahn, 1951, pp. 146-171) are representative of this approach. In a wide variety of industrial situations (including railway maintenance crews, insurance office staffs, and heavy industry production lines), these authors found (1) that general supervision was associated with high productivity whereas close supervision was associated with low productivity, and (2) that "employee-oriented" attitudes in the supervisor were associated with high productivity whereas "job-oriented" attitudes were associated with low productivity. It is unclear exactly what relationship these independent variables have to the democratic-autocratic dimension; however, it can certainly be assumed that employee-oriented attitudes and general supervision will tend to be associated with democracy (as here used) whereas job-oriented attitudes and close supervision will tend to be associated with authoritarianism. The data of Morse (1953) and Argyle, Gardner, and Cioffi (1957) support these assumptions.

Argyle *et al.* (1958) performed a successful replication of these earlier investigations in a British industrial situation. The authors report that foremen of high-producing work groups tended to use general rather than close supervision and were relatively more democratic in their behavior than were foremen of less productive work groups. Further, the attitudes of the more effective foremen tended to be more "employee-oriented" than those of the less effective foremen. In contrast to experimental findings, therefore, these survey data clearly seem to support the hypothesis that democratic supervision leads to higher production than does authoritarian supervision.

Discussion

The usual explanations offered for the failure of the experimental method to replicate survey findings rest upon either (a) the brevity of the experimental sessions or (b) the peripheral nature of the experimental tasks. It seems to the present author, however, that these explanations are respectively (a) too facile and (b) inadequately elaborated for proper handling of the problem.

Of the two, the "brevity" argument is the more open to attack. Experimental sessions are, of course, of relatively short duration. However, the entire science of experimental social psychology rests upon the assumption that experimental periods are sufficiently lengthy for treatments to "take," an assumption which is supported in every significant finding obtained in an experimental laboratory. To argue that the experiments reviewed here failed to demonstrate predicted productivity differences because of inadequate time periods (especially when these same time periods are sufficient to evoke morale differences—favoring the democratic supervisor—between the groups exposed to the two styles) seems somehow an unscientific and unsatisfactory way of explaining the findings. Furthermore, such an explanation fails to account for the quite small productivity differential which existed between the conditions created by Morse and Reimer in an experiment which continued over the course of an entire year.

It appears to the author that, rather than looking to brevity, one may best explain the equal experimental effectiveness of the two supervisory styles by concentrating upon the nature of the tasks involved. (This is, of course, the approach incompletely hinted at in the "peripheral nature" argument.) Specifically, it seems that no differences in effectiveness have been found between the two styles *because the tasks employed wholly fail to meet the conditions under which differential productivity was predicted.*

Democratic supervision, it will be remembered, was expected to be the more effective style because of the greater extent to which it makes productivity a means to need-satisfaction. This prediction rests upon the assumption that democratic supervision allows productivity to be a path to the satisfaction of self-actualization and ego-esteem needs, whereas autocratic supervision does not serve such a purpose.

These conditions do not seem to have been generated by the experimental investigations reported above. Democratic supervision, in these experiments, can hardly be seen as allowing the subjects to see production on the task involved as a path to self-actualization. *The thought is virtually absurd.* Regardless of the intent of the investigators, the decisions allowed by the democratic supervisors (e.g., suggesting possible solutions to simple problems) do not seem to implicate the unique personalities of the subjects in their tasks. This seems to have been true even in the Morse and Reimer investigation, for the authors report that "both groups of clerks indicated that their jobs throughout the course of the experiment did not give them a very high degree of self-actualization." To the extent that experimental studies fail to make productivity under democratic supervision a path to significantly greater need-satisfaction than it would be under autocratic supervision, there is no reason to suspect that they should demonstrate democratic supervision to be more effective. Such investigations simply fail to provide the conditions necessary for a test of the hypothesis in question.

It should not be inferred, however, that survey investigations provide a more adequate test of the hypothesis that workers will work harder for democratic supervisors, in spite of the satisfying direction of the findings. There are at least two reasons for approaching the results of these studies with caution, both of which rest upon the fact that spurious variables which clearly affect work group productivity accompany both these styles. To the extent that the effects of such variables cannot be discounted, survey methodology is incapable of offering convincing evidence concerning the relative effort expended by workers exposed to the styles in question.

In the first place, the supervisory styles discussed herein are accompanied by differential turnover and absenteeism (e.g., Mann & Baumgartel, 1953; Morse & Reimer, 1956; Argyle *et al.*, 1958). These effects do contribute to productivity differences between groups exposed to these styles, since the higher absenteeism and turnover evoked by autocratic supervision would lead to a productivity difference favoring democratic supervision. However, such a difference would be irrelevant to the hypothesis that democratic supervision leads directly to more concerted effort on the part of the employees involved. The effects of absenteeism and/or turnover could be removed from the analysis by means of simple statistical techniques, although no survey research known to the author has as yet attempted to do so.

A second consideration lies in the fact that supervisors who naturally affect a democratic style of supervision cannot be assumed to be otherwise similar to those who affect an authoritarian style. In particular, the author feels that democratically-oriented supervisors can be expected to be more intelligent than are autocratically-oriented supervisors. There are no direct data drawn from industry which bear on this statement. However, the fact that intelligence has clearly been shown to be negatively correlated with measured (*F*-scale) authoritarianism (e.g., Titus & Hollander, 1957), which in turn has been shown to be highly correlated with authoritarian behavior (McGee, 1955), seems sufficient to make the point.

It may be assumed that the intelligence of the supervisor should be of some importance in determining the productivity of the employees under him. The more intelligent supervisor might be expected to diagnose production difficulties more quickly than the less intelligent supervisor, and he might also be expected to take more effective remedial action. Therefore, inasmuch as authoritarian and democratic supervisors are differentiated on intelligence, one might expect them to be differentiated on their skill in dealing with day-to-day production problems. The advantage, of course, would go to the democratic supervisors.

The effect of this predicted difference between the two supervisory populations would be to make the work groups under democratic supervision more productive than those under autocratic supervision. However, as in the case of the different levels of turnover evoked by the two styles, such a finding would *not* necessarily imply that employees worked harder for supervisors affecting the democratic style. Like the effect of absenteeism, the effect of supervisory intelligence could be removed from the analysis by means of proper statistical techniques, but again there has been no survey research which has done so.

Therefore, in neither experimental studies nor survey investigations has an adequate test of the theory sketched above been made. Experimental studies have not created the conditions necessary for such a test; survey research has introduced at least two contaminating variables which render proper interpretation of the observed relationship extremely difficult. Such studies have not *disproved* the theory in question. They simply have not offered the unambiguous evidence administrative science must have in order to evaluate plans of action (e.g., supervisory training) tacitly based on this theory.

This should not be interpreted to mean that such a test cannot be made. Experimental investigations of the sort attempted by Morse and Reimer (1956), *using a technology in which self-actualization could occur under democratic supervision*, would provide an adequate test, as would survey investigations in which the intelligence of the supervisors and the turnover (and/or absenteeism) levels existing in the various work groups were assessed and partialled out of the correlation between the style of the supervisor and the productivity of the subordinates. (Research now in progress is directed toward this latter objective.) Without such conditions, however, the hypothesis that democratic supervision will evoke greater effort from employees than will autocratic supervision cannot truly be either supported or rejected.

Notes

1. Only the "submissive reaction" to autocracy will be here considered; the "aggressive reaction" is felt to be a function of the subjects and the situation employed by the investigators.
2. The research of Leavitt (1951) clearly suggests that these positions are the ones from which leadership is exercised.

References

Argyle, Michael, Gardner, Godfrey, and Cioffi, Frank. "The Measurement of Supervisory Methods." *Human Relations,* X (1957), 295-313.

Argyle, Michael, Gardner, Godfrey, and Cioffi, Frank. "Supervisory Methods Related to Productivity, Absenteeism, and Labour Turnover." *Human Relations,* XI (1958), 23-40.

Argyris, Chris. *Personality and Organization.* New York: Harper & Brothers, 1957.

Coch, L. and French, J. R. P., Jr. "Overcoming Resistance to Change." *Human Relations,* I (1948), 512-532.

Day, R. C. and Hamblin, R. L. "Some Effects of Close and Punitive Styles of Supervision." *American Journal of Sociology,* LXIX (1964), 499-510.

Katz, D. and Kahn, R. L. "Human Organization and Worker Motivation." In Tripp, L. Reed (Editor), *Industrial Productivity.* Madison, Wisconsin: Industrial Relations Research Association, 1951.

Katz, D., Maccoby, N., Gurin, G., and Floor, Lucretia. *Productivity, Supervision, and Morale Among Railroad Workers.* Ann Arbor, Michigan: Institute for Social Research, 1951.

Katz, D., Maccoby, N., and Morse, Nancy C. *Productivity, Supervision and Morale in an Office Situation.* Part 1. Ann Arbor, Michigan: Institute for Social Research, 1950.

Leavitt, Harold. "Some Effects of Certain Communication Patterns on Group Performance." *Journal of Abnormal and Social Psychology,* XLVI (1951), 16-30.

Likert, Rensis. *New Patterns of Management.* New York: McGraw-Hill, 1961.

Lippett, R. and White, R. K. "An Experimental Study of Leadership and Group Life." In Maccoby, E. E., Newcomb, T. N., and Hartley, E. L. (Editors), *Readings in Social Psychology,* Third Edition. New York: Holt, Rinehart, & Winston, 1958.

Maslow, A. H. *Motivation and Personality.* New York: Harper & Brothers 1954.

Mann, F. C. and Baumgartel, H. D. "Absences and Employee Attitudes in an Electric Power Company." Ann Arbor, Michigan: Institute for Social Research, 1953.

McCurdy, H. G. and Eber, H. W. "Democratic Versus Authoritarian: A Further Investigation of Group Problem-Solving." *Journal of Personality,* XXII (1953), 258-269.

McGee, H. M. "Measurement of Authoritarianism and its Relation to Teacher Classroom Behavior." *Genetic Psychological Monographs,* LII (1955), 89-146.

Morse, Nancy C. *Satisfactions in the White-Collar Job.* Ann Arbor, Michigan: Institute for Social Research, 1953.

Morse, Nancy C. and Reimer, E. "The Experimental Change of a Major Organizational Variable." *Journal of Abnormal and Social Psychology,* LI (1956), 120-129.

Sales, Stephen M. "A Laboratory Investigation of the Effectiveness of Two Industrial Supervisory Dimensions." Unpublished MS THesis, Cornell University, 1964.

Shaw, M. E. "A Comparison of Two Types of Leadership in Various Communication Nets." *Journal of Abnormal and Social Psychology,* L (1955), 127-134.

Spector, Paul, and Suttell, Barbara. *An Experimental Comparison of the Effectiveness of Three Patterns of Leadership Behavior.* Washington, D. C.: American Institute for Research, 1957.

Titus, H. E. and Hollander, E. P. "The California *F*-Scale in Psychological Research: 1950-1955." *Psychological Bulletin,* LIV (1957), 47-65.

Vroom, V. H. "Human Relations Research in Industry: Some Things Learned." In Baristow, Frances (Editor), *Research Frontiers in Industrial Relations Today.* Montreal: Industrial Relations Centre, 1962.

White, Ralph, and Lippitt, R. "Leader Behavior and Member Reaction in Three 'Social Climates.' " In Cartwright, Dorin, and Zander, Alvin (Editors), *Group Dynamics, Research and Theory,* Second Edition. Evanston, Illinois: Row, Peterson, 1962.

ENGINEER THE JOB TO FIT THE MANAGER

FRED E. FIEDLER

What kind of leadership style does business need? Should company executives be decisive, directive, willing to give orders, and eager to assume responsibility? Should they be human relations-oriented, nondirective, willing to share leadership with the men in their group? Or should we perhaps start paying attention to the more important problem of defining under what conditions each of these leadership styles works best and what to do about it?

The success or failure of an organization depends on the quality of its management. How to get the best possible management is a question of vital importance; but it is perhaps even more important to ask how we can make better use of the management talent which *we already have.*

To get good business executives we have relied primarily on recruitment, selection, and training. It is time for businessmen to ask whether this is the only way or the best way for getting the best possible management. Fitting the man to the leadership job by selection and training has not been spectacularly successful. It is surely easier to change almost anything in the job situation than a man's personality and his leadership style. Why not try, then, to fit the leadership job to the man?

Executive jobs are surprisingly pliable, and the executive manpower pool is becoming increasingly small. The luxury of picking a "natural leader" from among a number of equally promising or equally qualified specialists is rapidly fading into the past. Business must learn how to utilize the available executive talent as effectively as it now utilizes physical plant and machine tools. Your financial expert, your top research scientist, or your production genius may be practically irreplaceable. Their jobs call for positions of leadership and responsibility. Replacements for these men can be neither recruited nor trained overnight, and they may not be willing to play second fiddle in their departments. If their leadership style does not fit the job, *we must learn how to engineer the job to fit their leadership style.*

In this article I shall describe some studies that illuminate this task of job engineering and adaptation. It will be seen that there are situations where the authoritarian, highly directive leader works best, and other situations where the egalitarian, more permissive, human relations-oriented leader works best; but almost always there are possibilities for changing the situation around somewhat to match the needs of the particular managers who happen to be available. The executive who appreciates these differences and possibilities has knowledge that can be valuable to him in running his organization.

To understand the problems that a new approach would involve, let us look first at some of the basic issues in organizational and group leadership.

From "Engineer the Job to Fit the Manager," by Fred E. Fiedler, *Harvard Business Review*, vol. 43, no. 5 (1965), © 1965 by the President and Fellows of Harvard College; all rights reserved.

Styles of Leadership

Leadership is a personal relationship in which one person directs, coordinates, and supervises others in the performance of a common task. This is especially so in "interacting groups," where men must work together cooperatively in achieving organizational goals.

In oversimplified terms, it can be said that the leader manages the group in either of two ways. He can:

- Tell people what to do and how to do it.
- Or share his leadership responsibilities with his group members and involve them in the planning and execution of the task.

There are, of course, all shades of leadership styles in between these two polar positions, but the basic issue is this: the work of motivating and coordinating group members has to be done either by brandishing the proverbial stick or by dangling the equally proverbial carrot. The former is the more orthodox job-centered, autocratic style. The latter is the more nondirective, group-centered procedure.

Research evidence exists to support both approaches to leadership. Which, then, should be judged more appropriate? On the face of it, the first style of leadership is best under some conditions, while the second works better under others. Accepting this proposition immediately opens two avenues of approach. Management can:

- Determine the specific situation in which the directive or the nondirective leadership style works best, and then select or train men so that their leadership style fits the particular job.
- Or determine the type of leadership style which is most natural for the man in the executive position, and then change the job to fit the man.

The first alternative has been discussed many times before; the second has not. We have never seriously considered whether it would be easier to fit the executive's job to the man.

Needed Style?

How might this be done? Some answers have been suggested by a research program on leadership effectiveness that I have directed under Office of Naval Research auspices since 1951. This program has dealt with a wide variety of different groups, including basketball teams, surveying parties, various military combat crews, and men in open-hearth steel shops, as well as members of management and boards of directors. When possible, performance was measured in terms of objective criteria—for instance, percentage of games won by high school basketball teams; tap-to-tap time of open-hearth shops (roughly equivalent to the tonnage of steel output per unit of time); and company net income over a three-year period. Our measure of leadership style was based on a simple scale indicating the degree to which a man described, favorably or unfavorably, his least-preferred co-worker (LPC). This co-worker did not need to be someone he actually worked with at the time, but could be someone the respondent had known in the past. Whenever possible, the score was obtained before the leader was assigned to his group.

The study indicates that a person who describes his least-preferred co-worker in a relatively favorable manner tends to be permissive, human relations-oriented, and considerate of the feelings of his men. But a person who describes his least-preferred co-worker in an unfavorable manner—who has what we have come to call a low LPC rating—tends to be managing, task-controlling, and less concerned with the human relations aspects of the job. It also appears that the directive, managing, and controlling leaders tend to perform best in basketball and surveying teams, in open-hearth shops, and (provided the leader is accepted by his group) in military combat crews and company managements. On the other hand, the nondirective, permissive, and human relations-oriented leaders tend to perform best in decision- and policy-making teams and in groups that have a creative task—provided that the group likes the leader or the leader feels that the group is pleasant and free of tension.

Critical Dimensions

But in order to tell which style fits which situation, we need to categorize groups. Our research has shown that "it all depends" on the situation. After reviewing the results of all our work and the findings of other investigators, we have been able to isolate three major dimensions that seem to determine, to a large part, the kind of leadership style called for by different situations.

It is obviously a mistake to think that groups and teams are all alike and that each requires the same kind of leadership. We need some way of categorizing the group-task situation, or the job environment within which the leader has to operate. If leadership is indeed a process of influencing other people to work together effectively in a common task, then it surely matters how easy or difficult it is for the leader to exert his influence in a particular situation.

Leader-Member Relations. The factor that would seem most important in determining a man's leadership influence is the degree to which his group members trust and like him, and are willing to follow his guidance. The trusted and well-liked leader obviously does not require special rank or power in order to get things done. We can measure the leader-member relationship by the so-called sociometric nomination techniques that ask group members to name in their group the most influential person, or the man they would most like to have as a leader. It can also be measured by a group-atmosphere scale indicating the degree to which the leader feels accepted and comfortable in the group.

The Task Structure. The second important factor is the "task structure." By this term I mean the degree to which the task (a) is spelled out step by step for the group and, if so, the extent to which it can be done "by the numbers" or according to a detailed set of standard operating instructions, or (b) must be left nebulous and undefined. Vague and ambiguous or unstructured tasks make it difficult to exert leadership influence, because neither the leader nor his members know exactly what has to be done or how it is to be accomplished.

Why single out this aspect of the task rather than the innumerable other possible ways of describing it? Task groups are almost invariably components of a larger organization that assigns the task and has, therefore, a big stake in seeing it performed properly. However, the organization can control the quality of a group's performance only if the task is clearly spelled out and programmed or structured.

When the task can be programmed or performed "by the numbers," the organization is able to back up the authority of the leader to the fullest; the man who fails to perform each step can be disciplined or fired. But in the case of ill-defined, vague, or unstructured tasks, the organization and the leader have very little control and direct power. By close supervision one can ensure, let us say, that a man will correctly operate a machine, but one cannot ensure that he will be creative.

It is therefore easier to be a leader in a structured task situation in which the work is spelled out than in an unstructured one which presents the leader and his group with a nebulous, poorly defined problem.

Position Power. Thirdly, there is the power of the leadership position, as distinct from any personal power the leader might have. Can he hire or fire and promote or demote? Is his appointment for life, or will it terminate at the pleasure of his group? It is obviously easier to be a leader when the position power is strong than when it is weak.

Model for Analysis

When we now classify groups on the basis of these three dimensions, we get a classification system that can be represented as a cube; see Exhibit 1. As each group is high or low in each of the three dimensions, it will fall into one of the eight cells.

Exhibit 1. A model for classifying group-task situations.

From examination of the cube, it seems clear that exerting leadership influence will be easier in a group in which the members like a powerful leader with a clearly defined job and where the job to be done is clearly laid out (Cell 1); it will be difficult in a group where a leader is disliked, has little power, and has a highly ambiguous job (Cell 8).

In other words, it is easier to be the well-esteemed foreman of a construction crew working from a blueprint than it is to be the disliked chairman of a volunteer committee preparing a new policy.

I consider the leader-member relations the most important dimension, and the position-power dimension the least important, of the three. It is, for instance, quite possible for a man of low rank to lead a group of higher-ranking men in a structured task—as is done when enlisted men or junior officers conduct some standardized parts of the training programs for medical officers who enter the Army. But it is not so easy for a disrespected manager to lead a creative, policy-formulating session well, even if he is the senior executive present.

Varying Requirements

By first sorting the eight cells according to leader-member relations, then task structure, and finally leader position power, we can now arrange them in order according to the favorableness of the environment for the leader. This sorting leads to an eight-step scale, as in Exhibit 2. This exhibit portrays the results of a series of studies of groups performing well but (a) in different situations and conditions, and (b) with leaders using different leadership styles. In explanation:

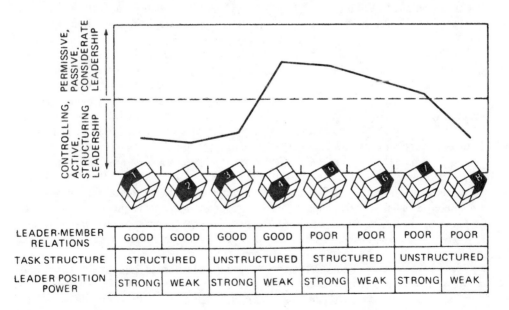

LEADER-MEMBER RELATIONS	GOOD	GOOD	GOOD	GOOD	POOR	POOR	POOR	POOR
TASK STRUCTURE	STRUCTURED		UNSTRUCTURED		STRUCTURED		UNSTRUCTURED	
LEADER POSITION POWER	STRONG	WEAK	STRONG	WEAK	STRONG	WEAK	STRONG	WEAK

Exhibit 2. How the style of effective leadership varies with the situation.

The *horizontal* axis shows the range of situations that the groups worked in, as described by the classification scheme used in Exhibit 1.

The *vertical* axis indicates the leadership style which was best in a certain situation, as shown by the correlation coefficient between the leader's LPC and his group's performance.

A positive correlation (falling above the midline) shows that the permissive, nondirective, and human relations-oriented leaders performed best; a negative correlation (below the midline) shows that the task-controlling, managing leader performed best. For instance, leaders of effective groups in situation categories 1 and 2 had LPC-group performance correlations of —.40 to —.80, with the average between —.50 and —.60; whereas leaders of effective groups in situation categories 4 and 5 had LPC-group performance correlations of .20 to .80, with the average between .40 and .50.

Exhibit 2 shows that both the directive, managing, task-oriented leaders and the nondirective, human relations-oriented leaders are successful under some conditions. Which leadership style is the best depends on the favorableness of the particular situation for the leader. In very favorable or in very unfavorable situations for getting a task accomplished by group effort, the autocratic, task-controlling, managing leadership works best. In situations intermediate in difficulty, the nondirective, permissive leader is more successful.

This corresponds well with our everyday experience. For instance:

● Where the situation is very favorable, the group expects and wants the leader to give directions. We neither expect nor want the trusted airline pilot to turn to his crew and ask, "What do you think we ought to check before takeoff?"

● If the disliked chairman of a volunteer committee asks his group what to do, he may be told that everybody ought to go home.

● The well-liked chairman of a planning group or research team must be nondirective and permissive in order to get full participation from his members. The directive, managing leader will tend to be more critical and to cut discussion short; hence he will not get the full benefit of the potential contributions by his group members.

The varying requirements of leadership styles are readily apparent in organizations experiencing dramatic changes in operating procedures. For example:

● The manager or supervisor of a routinely operating organization is expected to provide direction and supervision that the subordinates should follow. However, in a crisis the routine is no longer adequate, and the task becomes ambiguous and unstructured. The typical manager tends to respond in such instances by calling his principal assistants together for a conference. In other words, the effective leader changes his behavior from a directive to a permissive, nondirective style until the operation again reverts to routine conditions.

● In the case of a research planning group, the human relations-oriented and permissive leader provides a climate in which everybody is free to speak up, to suggest, and to criticize. Osborn's brainstorming method in fact institutionalizes these procedures. However, after the research plan has been completed, the situation becomes highly structured. The director now prescribes the task in detail, and he specifies the means of accomplishing it. Woe betide the assistant who decides to be creative by changing the research instructions!

Practical Tests

Remember that the ideas I have been describing emanate from studies of real-life situations; accordingly, as might be expected, they can be validated by organizational experience. Take, for instance, the dimension of leader-member relations described earlier. We have made three studies of situations in which the leader's position power was strong and the task relatively structured with clear-cut goals and standard operating procedures. In such groups as these the situation will be very favorable for the leader if he is accepted; it will be progressively unfavorable in proportion to how much a leader is disliked. What leadership styles succeed in these varying conditions? The studies confirm what our theory would lead us to expect:

● The first set of data come from a study of B-29 bomber crews in which the criterion was the accuracy of radar bombing. Six degrees of leader-member relations were identified, ranging from those in which the aircraft commander was the first choice of crew members and highly endorsed his radar observer and navigator (the key men in radar bombing), to those in which he was chosen by his crew but did not endorse his key men, and finally to crews in which the commander was rejected by his crew and rejected his key crew members. What leadership styles were effective? The results are plotted in Exhibit 3.

KEY: ———— AIR BOMBER CREWS
         —·—·— ANTI–AIRCRAFT CREWS
         — — — FARM SUPPLY COMPANIES

Exhibit 3. How effective leadership styles vary depending on group acceptance.

● A study of anti-aircraft crews compares the 10 most chosen crew commanders, the 10 most rejected ones, and 10 of intermediate popularity. The criterion is the identification and "acquisition" of unidentified aircraft by the crew. The results shown in Exhibit 3 are similar to those for bomber crew commanders.

● Exhibit 3 also summarized data for 32 small-farm supply companies. These were member companies of the same distribution system, each with its own board of directors and its own management. The performance of these highly comparable companies was measured in terms of percentage of company net income over a three-year period. The first quarter of the line (going from left to right) depicts endorsement of the general manager by his board of directors and his staff of assistant managers; the second quarter, endorsement by his board but not his staff; the third quarter, endorsement by his staff but not his board; the fourth quarter, endorsement by neither.

As can be seen from the results of all three studies, the highly accepted and strongly rejected leaders perform best if they are controlling and managing, while the leaders in the intermediate acceptance range, who are neither rejected nor accepted, perform best if they are permissive and nondirective.

Now let us look at some research on organizations in another country:

Recently in Belgium a study was made of groups of mixed language and cultural composition. Such teams, which are becoming increasingly frequent as international business and governmental activities multiply, obviously present a difficult situation for the leader. He must not only deal with men who do not fully comprehend one another's language and meanings, but also cope with the typical antipathies, suspicions, and antagonisms dividing individuals of different cultures and nationalities.

At a Belgian naval training center we tested 96 three-man groups, half of which were homogeneous in composition (all Flemish or all Walloon) and half heterogeneous (the leader differing from his men). Half of each of these had powerful leader positions (petty officers), and half had recruit leaders. Each group performed three tasks: one unstructured task (writing a recruiting letter); and two parallel structured tasks (finding the shortest route for ships through 10 ports, and doing the same for

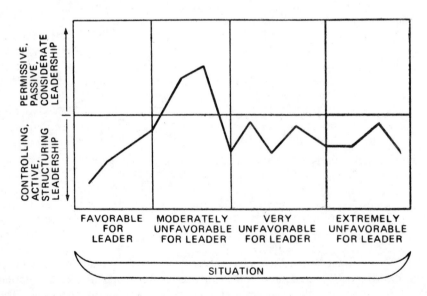

Exhibit 4. Effective leadership styles at the Belgian Naval Training Center.

12 ports). After each task, leaders and group members described their reactions—including group-atmosphere ratings and the indication of leader-member relations.

The various task situations were then arranged in order, according to their favorableness for the leader. The most favorable situation was a homogeneous group, led by a well-liked and accepted petty officer, which worked on the structured task of routing a ship. The situation would be especially favorable toward the end of the experiment, after the leader had had time to get to know his members. The least favorable situation was that of an unpopular recruit leader of a heterogeneous group where the relatively unstructured task of writing a letter came up as soon as the group was formed.

There were six groups that fell into each of these situations or cells. A correlation was then computed for each set of six groups to determine which type of leadership style led to best team performance. The results, indicated in Exhibit 4, support the conclusions earlier described.

Of particular interest is the fact that the difficult heterogeneous groups generally required controlling, task-oriented leadership for good performance. This fits the descriptions of successful leader behavior obtained from executives who have worked in international business organizations.

Conclusion

Provided our findings continue to be supported in the future, what do these results and the theory mean for executive selection and training? What implications do they have for the management of large organizations?

Selection and Training

Business and industry are now trying to attract an increasingly large share of exceptionally intelligent and technically well-trained men. Many of these are specialists whose talents are in critically short supply. Can industry really afford to select only those men who have a certain style of leadership in addition to their technical qualifications? The answer is likely to be negative, at least in the near future.

This being the case, can we then train the men selected in one leadership style or the other? This approach is always offered as a solution, and it does have merit. But we must recognize that training people is at best difficult, costly, and time-consuming. It is certainly easier to place people in a situation compatible with their natural leadership style than to force them to adapt to the demands of the job.

As another alternative, should executives learn to recognize or diagnose group-task situations so that they can place their subordinates, managers, and department heads in the jobs best suited to their leadership styles? Even this procedure has serious disadvantages. The organization may not always happen to have the place that fits the bright young man. The experienced executive may not want to be moved, or it may not be possible to transfer him.

Should the organization try to "engineer" the job to fit the man? This alternative is potentially the most feasible for management. As has been shown already, the type of leadership called for depends on the favorableness of the situation. The favorableness, in turn, is a product of several factors. These include leader-member relations, the homogeneity of the group, and the position power and degree to which the task is structured, as well as other, more obvious factors such as the leader's knowledge of his group, his familiarity with the task, and so forth.

It is clear that management can change the characteristic favorableness of the leadership situation; it can do so in most cases more easily than it can transfer the subordinate leader from one job to another or train him in a different style of interacting with his members.

Possibilities of Change

Although this type of organizational engineering has not been done systematically up to now, we can choose from several good possibilities for getting the job done:

1. *We can change the leader's position power.* We can either give him subordinates of equal or nearly equal rank or we can give him men who are two or three ranks below him. We can either give him sole authority for the job or require that he consult with this group, or even obtain unanimous consent for all decisions. We can either punctiliously observe the channels of the organization to increase the leader's prestige or communicate directly with the men of his group as well as with him in person.

2. *We can change the task structure.* The tasks given to one leader may have to be clarified in detail, and he may have to be given precise operating instructions; another leader may have to be given more general problems that are only vaguely elucidated.

3. *We can change the leader-member relations.* The Belgian study, referred to earlier, demonstrates that changing the group composition changes the leader's relations with his men. We can increase or decrease the group's heterogeneity by introducing men with similar attitudes, beliefs, and backgrounds, or by bringing in men different in training, culture, and language.

The foregoing are, of course, only examples of what could be done. The important point is that we now have a model and a set of principles that permit predictions of leadership effectiveness in interacting groups and allow us to take a look at the factors affecting team performance. This approach goes beyond the traditional notions of selection and training. It focuses on the more fruitful possibility of organizational engineering as a means of using leadership potentials in the management ranks.

A PATH GOAL THEORY
OF LEADER EFFECTIVENESS

ROBERT J. HOUSE

Introduction

Two major behavioral dimensions that have emerged from leadership research are those which sociologists have termed instrumental and social-emotional, or expressive, leadership behavior. Psychologists who have studied leadership have independently discovered these dimensions (Korman, 1966). The terms most frequently used to describe these behaviors are initiating structure and consideration. Leader initiating structure is used to describe the degree to which the leader initiates psychological structure for subordinates by doing such things as assigning particular tasks, specifying procedures to be followed, clarifying his expectations of subordinates, and scheduling work to be done. This dimension of leader behavior describes leaders who are similar to those prescribed by classical management theorists, that is, leaders who plan, organize, direct, and control. Leader consideration is used to describe the degree to which the leader creates a supportive environment of psychological support, warmth, friendliness, and helpfulness by doing such things as being friendly and approachable, looking out for the personal welfare of the group, doing little things for subordinates, and giving advance notice of change.

Research has indicated that leaders who initiate structure for subordinates are generally rated highly by superiors and have higher producing work groups than leaders who are low on initiating structure; and that leaders who are considerate of subordinates have more satisfied employees (Filley and House, 1969); however the evidence with respect to the relationship between initiating structure and satisfaction of subordinates is very mixed. Several studies have shown that initiating structure is frequently resented by unskilled and semiskilled employees and is a source of dissatisfaction (Filley and House, 1969), grievances, and turnover (Fleishman and Harris, 1962). However, employees in large groups have been found either to prefer initiating structure more or to dislike it less than employees in smaller groups (Hemphill, 1950; Mass, 1950; Vroom and Mann, 1960). And, Oaklander and Fleishman (1964) found initiating structure to be negatively correlated with intergroup conflict. Recent studies have shown that among high-level employees, initiating structure is positively related to satisfaction (House *et al.*, 1971a, 1971b), performance (House *et al.*, 1971b), and perceptions of organizational effectiveness, but negatively related to role conflict and ambiguity (Rizzo *et al.*, 1970).

This paper presents a theory of leader behavior that attempts to reconcile and integrate the conflicting results of previous studies under a set of general propositions from which they could have been deduced, and reports three studies designed to test eight hypotheses derived from the theory.

Reprinted by permission of the author and the publisher from *Administrative Science Quarterly*, vol. 16, no. 3 (Sept. 1971).

Theoretical Background

The theory advanced here is derived from the path-goal hypothesis advanced by Georgopoulos *et al.* (1957), and from previous research supporting the broad class of expectancy theory of motivation (Atkinson, 1958; Vroom, 1964; Porter and Lawler, 1967; Galbraith and Cummings, 1967; Graen, 1969; Lawler, 1968). The central concept of expectancy theories is that the force on an individual to engage in a specific behavior is a function of (*1*) his expectations that the behavior will result in a specific outcome; and (*2*) the sum of the valences, that is, personal utilities or satisfactions, that he derives from the outcome. The research findings indicate that the function is a nonlinear, monotonically increasing product of expectations and valences. Thus, according to this theory of motivation, an individual chooses the behaviors he engages in on the basis of (*1*) the valences he perceives to be associated with the outcomes of the behavior under consideration; and (*2*) his subjective estimate of the probability that his behavior will indeed result in the outcomes. Vroom (1964) formalized one perspective of expectancy motivation theory mathematically, and Galbraith and Cummings (1967) extended his formulation by pointing out that some of the valences associated with a specific behavior are intrinsic to the behavior itself and some are the extrinsic consequences of that behavior. To the extent that behavior is intrinsically valent it is also intrinsically motivational because the behavior is highly instrumental to the outcome of satisfaction. A person will be motivated to engage in such behavior because his expectancy that satisfaction will follow is nearly unity. That is, if the outcomes were contingent on an external rewarder—any significant other—the expectancy would be less than unity because the behavior might not be observed or recognized by the rewarder. However, when the reward is essentially self-administering, expectancy approaches unity.

The theory may be further extended and broken down into parts that have specific relevance for leadership using the concept of path instrumentality advanced by Evans (1968: 14): "This is the cognition of the degree to which following a particular path (behavior) will lead to a particular outcome, it is akin to (but not identical to) the concept of 'expectancy' introduced by Vroom." Evans (1968) has also advanced an extension of Vroom's (1964) theory and a path-goal theory of leadership. His theory is different from the one presented here in that its predictions are not contingent on situational variables, and it is not an attempt to account for the conflicting findings just revieweed.

According to the formulation advanced here, the individual makes probability estimates with respect to two linking points connecting behavior with its outcomes, and subjectively places values on the outcomes. The magnitude of these probability estimates indicates the degree of path instrumentality of his behavior for work-goal accomplishment and valence. This formulation can be expressed as the following formula:

$$M = IV_b + P_1 \left[IV_a + \sum_{i=1}^{n} (P_{2i}EV_i) \right]$$
$$i = 1, \ldots, n,$$

where:

  M = motivation to work;

  IV = intrinsic valence associated with goal-directed behavior;

  IV = intrinsic valence associated with work-goal accomplishment;

  EV = extrinsic valences associated with work-goal accomplishment;

  P_1 = path instrumentality of behavior for work-goal attainment;

  P_2 = path instrumentalities of work goal for extrinsic valences.

In work situations the individual estimates the path instrumentality, P_1, of his behavior for the accomplishment of some work goal. Here he considers such factors as his ability to behave in an appropriate and effective manner as well as the barriers to work-goal accomplishment in the environment, and the support he will receive from others to accomplish the work goal. In addition, he estimates the path instrumentality, P_2, of the work goal for attaining personal outcomes that have valence for him. For example, he estimates the probability that his superiors will recognize his goal accomplishment and reward him accordingly. He also considers, and places subjective values on the intrinsic valence associated with the behavior required to achieve the work goal, IV , the intrinsic valence associated with the achievement of the work goal, IV , and the extrinsic valences associated with the personal outcomes that he accrues as a result of achieving the work goal, EV .

The behavior of the leader is clearly relevant to all of the independent variables in this formulation. The leader, at least in part, determines what extrinsic rewards should be associated with work-goal accomplishment, EV . For example, he has some influence over the extent to which work-goal accomplishment will be recognized as a contribution and whether it will be rewarded with financial increases, promotion, assignment of more interesting tasks or opportunities for personal growth and development. Consequently, he influences the magnitude of the sum of the personal outcomes available. Second, the leader, through his interaction with the subordinate, can increase the subordinate's path instrumentality concerning the rewards forthcoming as a result of work-goal accomplishment, P_2. If he is consistent in his decision making with respect to recognizing and rewarding work-goal achievement, he will clarify the linkage between work-goal achievement and rewards. Thus, if he consistently rewards achievement, this will most probably increase the subordinate's path instrumentality, P_2, for valent personal outcomes. Third, through his own behavior he can provide support for the subordinate's efforts and thereby influence the probability that this effort will result in work-goal achievement, that is P_1. Fourth, the leader influences the intrinsic valences associated with goal accomplishment, IV , by the way he delegates and assigns tasks to subordinates, which determines the amount of influence the subordinate has in goal setting and the amount of control he is allowed in the task-directed effort. The greater the subordinate's opportunity to influence the goal and exercise control, the more intrinsically valent the work-goal accomplishment. Finally, the leader can increase the net intrinsic valence associated with goal-directed behavior, IV , by reducing frustrating barriers, being supportive in times of stress, permitting involvement in a wide variety of tasks, and being considerate of subordinate's needs.

Propositions

The above interpretation of motivation theory as applied to leadership suggests the following general propositions:

1. The motivation functions of a leader are to increase the net positive valences associated with work-goal attainment, increase the net positive valences associated with the path—behavior—to work-goal attainment, and increase the subordinate's path instrumentality with respect to work-goal attainment for personal outcomes and the behavior required for work-goal attainment. This statement assumes that when the subordinate is working under ambiguous path-goal relationships, his subjective probability estimates that his behavior will affect the valences he receives are less than the objective probabilities that his behavior will affect the valences he receives. When this assumption does not hold, that is, when under conditions of role ambiguity, his subjective probability estimates exceed the objective probabilities, then clarification of path-goal relationships will result in reduced motivation.

Stated less formally, the motivational functions of the leader consist of increas-ing personal pay-offs to subordinates for work-goal attainment, and making the path to these pay-offs easier to travel by clarifying it, reducing road blocks and pitfalls, and increasing the opportunities for personal satisfaction en route. The function of making the path easier and more satisfying to follow has been dealt with only implicitly in the leadership literature and, as will be shown, has significant implications for leader's behavior.

2. In increasing path instrumentality by clarifying path-goal relationships, the leader's behavior will have positive motivational effects to the extent that it reduces role ambiguity or makes possible the exercise of externally imposed controls. Reduction of role ambiguity results in increased motivation because role ambiguity is both negatively valent to subordinates (Rizzo *et al.*, 1970), and because it is usually associated with low path instrumentality. Externally imposed controls are motivational because they make possible the allocation of valences contingent on desirable behavior. Externally imposed control results in improved performance only to the extent that the rewards that are under the control of the leader are positively valent to the subordinates; punishments that are under the control of the leader are negatively valent to the subordinates; rewards and punishments are contingent on performance; and the contingency is clearly perceived by the subordinates. Whether performance motivated by external controls is satisfying to the subordinate, depends on his unconscious needs, conscious values, and perceptions of equity in the exchange of effort for rewards.

3. Where leader attempts to clarify path-goal relationships are redundant with existing conditions, that is, where path-goal relationships are apparent because of the routine of the tasks or objective system-fixed controls, attempts by the leader to clarify path-goal relationships will result in increased externally imposed control and will be seen by subordinates as redundant. Although such control may increase performance, it will also result in decreased satisfaction.

4. Leader behavior directed at need satisfaction of subordinates will result in increased performance to the extent that such satisfaction increases the net positive valence associated with goal-directed effort.

Hypotheses

From the above general propositions, several specific hypotheses concerning leader consideration, initiating structure, closeness of supervision, hierarchical influence, and authoritarianism can be derived. These hypotheses are consistent with empirical findings and thus illustrate how these prior findings could have been deduced from the general propositions of the theory. These hypotheses do not constitute an exhaustive list of relationships between the variables, but rather, serve to illustrate how the general propositions can be operationalized.

1. Leader initiating structure increases the path instrumentality for subordinates whose roles have nonroutine task demands by decreasing role ambiguity (Rizzo et al., 1970).

2. Informal leaders high in structure influence positively the subjective probabilities other group members assign to positively valent outcomes (Rim, 1965).

3. Leader initiating structure and consideration will have differential effects, depending on whether the task is satisfying or unsatisfying to the subordinate, and whether the task-role demands are clear or ambiguous.

The more satisfying the task, the less positive the relationship between consideration and subordinate satisfaction and performance (Fleishman, 1971: 13-14). These correlations will vary from insignificant to positive, depending on task satisfaction. For unsatisfying tasks, consideration will tend to offset dissatisfaction associated with the task; for satisfying tasks, consideration will be less important.

The less satisfying the task the more negative will be the relationship between structure and performance (Fleishman, 1971: 19-20). For unsatisfying tasks, structure will be viewed as an imposition of external control and, therefore dissatisfying, but will also be required to motivate subordinate effort toward goal achievement (Fleishman, 1971: 19-20).

The more ambiguous the task the more positive the relationship between leader initiating structure and subordinate satisfaction and performance. Structure serves to reduce role ambiguity and clarify path-goal relationships for ambiguous tasks but is viewed as unnecessary and redundant for nonambiguous tasks.

When task demands are self-evident due to a high degree of routinization, or where roles are clearly defined by such factors as mechanization, legal constraints, contracts, professional ethics, or group norms, initiating structure will not result in role clarification and will be unsatisfying to subordinates.

4. Where the follower's tasks are varied and interdependent and where teamwork norms are not developed within the group, initiating structure and close supervision will regulate and clarify path-goal relationships. Therefore, structure and close supervision will result in increased coordination, satisfaction, and performance (Patchen, 1962; Mass, 1950; Hemphill, 1950; Fleishman, 1971: 26).

5. Where tasks are interdependent, varied, and ambiguous, consideration will result in social support, friendliness among group members, increased cohesiveness, and team effort. These social outcomes will be positively valent to the members and thus increase the net sum of the positive valences associated with interdependent jobs requiring cooperation and team spirit (Oaklander and Fleishman, 1964; Fleishman, 1971: 13-14).

6. Where tasks and/or environment are frustrating and stress inducing, consideration will result in increased social support for followers and thus reduce negative valence associated with task-oriented behavior (Fiedler, 1967; Rim, 1965; Fleishman, 1971; 12-13.

7. Where stress is from sources external to the work unit and tasks are ambiguous, structure will result in increased ego protection, security, and satisfaction (Oaklander and Fleishman, 1964). In this instance, structure serves as an umbrella which protects followers from externally imposed stress.

8. Among hierarchically dependent employees under leaders with high upward influence, consideration will be positively related to satisfaction and performance of subordinates (Pelz, 1952). Among independent employees, or under leaders with low upward influence, consideration will have a lower positive relationship to subordinate satisfaction and performance (Wager, 1965; House *et al.*, 1971a; 1971b). Leader influence permits the leader to have more control over rewards for subordinates and thereby permits the leader to make subordinate valences contingent on performance and to make the outcomes of work-goal attainment more valent or less valent.

9. Under conditions of authoritarian or punitive leadership, both leader initiating structure and leader hierarchical influence will be negatively related to subordinate satisfaction. Under such conditions, both structure and influence will be seen as bases of authoritarian power by subordinates.

Reconciliation of Prior Findings

The usefulness of the theory can be illustrated by showing how it can be applied to reconcile what appear to be conflicting results of prior research cited earlier.

Fleishman and Harris (1962) found that when the leader's consideration toward subordinates' needs was used as a moderating variable—that is, when separate correlations are computed for high-considerate, medium-considerate, and low-considerate leaders—the relationship between leader structure and grievances and turnover varied. Specifically they found that there was no relationship between structure and grievances or turnover for highly considerate leaders; but for leaders with low consideration, the relationship was positive and significant.

House *et al.* (1971b) attempted to conduct a replication of the findings of Fleishman and Harris (1962), using the same scales for the predictor and moderator variables and eight measures of satisfaction with subordinate role expectations as criterion variables. The populations studied were salaried engineers, scientists, and technicians in three large research, design and development organizations. Unexpectedly, the data not only failed to replicate Fleishman and Harris' (1962) findings but suggested their opposite. Specifically it was found that leader initiating structure had a significant linear—unmoderated—positive relationship to half the satisfaction measures in two of the three companies, and significant positive correlations, .36, $p < 05$, with satisfaction with the company management in all three companies studied. Furthermore, in one company under conditions of high leader consideration, leader initiating structure had significant positive curvilinear relationships to measures of satisfaction with job freedom, advancement, security, and family attitudes toward the respondent's job, with the eta correlation ranging from .36 to .50.

In a subsequent study of 192 nontechnical corporate office employees of a chemical manufacturing company, House *et al.* (1970) failed to replicate the findings of Fleishman and Harris (1962) and showed significant positive relationships between leader initiating structure and six measures of satisfaction.

The following three hypotheses derived from the theory serve to reconcile these findings.

Leader initiating structure can be hypothesized to clarify path-goal relationships for higher occupational level jobs which are frequently ambiguously defined. Such clarification reduces role ambiguity and increases the employee's perceived instrumentality of effort toward goal attainment. That is, it increases his subjective probability estimates that his efforts will result in goal attainment. Thus, the path-goal theory advanced here offers an explanation for the positive correlations between leader initiating structure and satisfaction among the high occupational level groups studied by House *et al.* (1970, 1971a, 1971b). The theory also explains the negative relationships found at lower occupational levels by Fleishman and Harris (1962). If it can be assumed that lower level jobs are generally more routine, that their path-goal relationships are usually self-evident, and that the job itself is frequently not intrinsically satisfying, then it can be hypothesized that leader initiating structure would be viewed by subordinates as an imposition of external control that does little to clarify path-goal relationships and is viewed by subordinates as being directed at keeping them working at unsatisfying activities. Although such control is likely to increase productivity by preventing soldiering, work restriction, or slowdowns, it is also a source of dissatisfaction to employees.

Another hypothesis derived from path-goal theory explains the findings concerning the moderating effect of consideration in some studies and not in others. Where the path is not viewed as satisfying, that is, for lower level jobs, it can be hypothesized that consideration serves as a source of extrinsic social satisfaction and support to the employee, thus making the path easier to travel. Consequently, for Fleishman and Harris' (1962) blue-collar workers, leader consideration moderated the unsatisfying effects of leader structure; whereas, for higher level jobs, where the path was intrinsically satisfying, the need for such support was lower and consequently consideration would be expected to have little or no moderating effect on the relationship between initiating structure and satisfaction.

Similarly in the International Harvester study reviewed by Fleishman (1971: 19-20), high leader initiating structure was found to be related to foremen ratings of proficiency, but also higher grievances; high leader consideration was found to be related to lower proficiency ratings, a tendency more pronounced in production than in other departments. The specific variable that was subsequently discovered to account for the differential relations across departments was pressure for output. If it can be assumed that the tasks in the production departments were less satisfying, then it follows that under conditions of high pressure for output, leader initiating structure would be viewed as an externally imposed form of control. Such control would be more acceptable to higher managers, but resented by the subordinates on whom it was imposed. Leader consideration is more likely to serve as a stress reducer as tasks become more unsatisfying and pressure for output increases. Thus the differential relationship found across types of departments can be explained in terms of differences in task satisfaction, that is, path valence and pressure for production differences. This explanation is directly deducible from the path-goal theory presented here and again illustrates the ability of the theory to accommodate and explain otherwise confusing empiric findings.

Three studies were conducted in which eight hypotheses specifically derived from the theory were tested, and three of these hypotheses were retested. . . .*

Conclusion

The theory advanced here has been shown to reconcile apparently conflicting findings from previous research. It has also been shown to provide an integrated explanation of the results of findings about authoritarianism in leader hierarchical influence, closeness of supervision, initiating structure, and consideration.

The theory was tested by correlational tests of 8 hypotheses derived from general propositions. The tests are somewhat weak in that the theoretical constructs, such as intrinsic task satisfaction and ambiguity of task-role demands, were inferred from situational measures of task autonomy and job scope and from occupational characteristics of the populations studied. These inferences make the tests susceptible to the error of rejecting a valid hypothesis, so that the tests are conservative ones. A further limitation is inherent in cross-sectional survey research, which can rule out invalid hypotheses, but cannot establish causal relationships among the variables.

The findings, when viewed collectively, generally support the theory. Among high-occupational groups, leader initiating structure was generally positively related to subordinate satisfaction and performance. This relationship was accounted for in terms of variance in subordinate role ambiguity, which was shown to have a negative correlation with initiating structure. The relationships between leader structure and subordinate role ambiguity, and satisfaction, although significant and in the theoretically predicted direction, were quite low, probably because it was not possible to control for contaminating variables that would be expected to suppress these relationships. The relationships between initiating structure and consideration, and subordinate satisfaction and performance varied significantly and widely in the directions predicted when moderated by job scope. When moderated by task autonomy the theoretical predictions were supported by one sample and not supported by another which raised a question about the appropriateness of task autonomy as an indicator of ambiguity of task-role demands and satisfaction among blue-collar workers as well as a question about the validity of the general proposition from which the hypothesis was derived.

On balance, the ability of the theory to reconcile and integrate earlier findings, together with moderate-to-strong support, for seven of the eight hypotheses tested, two of which were replicated in a second study, suggests that the theory shows promise and warrants further testing with more direct measurement of the theoretical constructs using experimental as well as correlational methods.

---

*Editor's Note: The results of the research studies, which generally support the hypotheses presented by House, are not included here. They are likely to be of great interest to students of leadership or to those who would like to see how theoretical formulations may be supported by empirical research evidence.

References

Atkinson, J. W. "Towards experimental analysis of human motivation in terms of motives, expectancies, and incentives." In J. W. Atkinson (ed.), Motives in Fantasy, Action and Society. New York: Van Nostrand. 1958.

Bescoe, Robert O., and C. H. Lawshe. "Foreman leadership as perceived by superiors and subordinates." Personnel Psychology, 12: 573-582. 1959.

Campbell, Donald T., and Donald W. Fiske. "Convergent and discriminant validation by the multitrait, multimethod matrix." Psychological Bulletin, 56: 81-105. 1959.

Evans, Martin G. The Effects of Supervisory Behavior upon Worker Perception of Their Path-Goal Relationships. Doctoral dissertation, Yale University. 1968.

——. "Convergent and discriminant validites of the Cornell job descriptive index and a measure of goal attainment." Journal of Applied Psychology, 55: 102-106. 1969.

Fiedler, Fred E. A Theory of Leadership Effectiveness. New York: McGraw-Hill. 1967.

Filley, Alan C., and Robert J. House. Managerial Process and Organizational Behavior. Glenview, Ill.: Scott Foresman. 1969.

Fleishman, Edwin A. "Twenty years of consideration and structure." In Symposium on Contemporary Development in the Study of Leadership. Carbondale: Southern Illinois University, in press. 1971.

Fleishman, Edwin A., and Edwin F. Harris. "Patterns of leadership behavior related to employee grievances and turnover." Personnel Psychology, 15: 43-56. 1962.

Galbraith, Jay, and Larry L. Cummings. "An empirical investigation of the motivational determinants of past performance: interactive effects between instrumentality, valence, motivation and ability." Organizational Behavior and Human Performance 2: 237-257. 1967.

Georgopoulous, Basil S., Gerald M. Mahoney, and Nyle W. Jones, Jr. "A path-goal approach to productivity." Journal of Applied Psychology, 41: 345-353. 1957.

Graen, George. "Instrumental theory of work motivation: some empirical results and suggested modifications." Journal of Applied Psychology, 53: 1-25. 1969.

Halpin, Andrew W. "The leader behavior and effectiveness of aircraft commanders." In Ralph H. Stogdill and A. E. Coons (eds.), Leader Behavior Its Description and Measurement. Ohio State University, Bureau of Business Research. 1957.

Hemphill, John K. "Relations between the size of the group and the behavior of superior leaders." Journal of Abnormal and Social Psychology, 32: 11-12. 1950.

House, Robert J., Alan C. Filley, and Domo N. Gujarati. "Leadership style, hierarchical influence and the satisfaction of subordinate role expectations: a test of Likert's influence proposition." Journal of Applied Psychology, in press. 1971.

House, Robert J., Alan C. Filley, and Steven Kerr. "Relation of leader consideration and initiating structure to R and D subordinate satisfaction." Administrative Science Quarterly, 16: 19-30. 1971b.

House, Robert J., Lawrence A. Wigdor, and Kenneth Shulz. "Leader behavior, psychological participation, employee satisfaction and performance: an extension of prior investigations and a motivation theory interpretation." In W. M. Frey (ed.), Proceedings Seventh Annual Conference of Eastern Academy of Management: 179-195. Amherst: University of Massachusetts. 1970.

Korman, Abraham K. "Consideration, initiating structure and organizational criteria—a review." Personnel Psychology, 19: 349-361. 1966.

Lawler, Edward E. III. "Ability as a moderator of the relationship between job attitudes and job performance." Personnel Psychology, 19: 153-164. 1966.

———. "A correlation-causal analysis of the relationship between expectancy attitudes and job performance." Journal of Applied Psychology, 52: 462-468. 1966.

Mass, H. S. "Personal and group factors in leader's social perception." Journal of Abnormal and Social Psychology, 45: 54-63. 1950.

Oaklander, Harold, and Edwin A. Fleishman. "Patterns of leadership related to organizational stress in hospital settings." Administrative Science Quarterly, 8: 520-532. 1964.

Patchen, Marvin. "Supervisory methods and group performance norms." Administrative Science Quarterly, 7: 275-294. 1962.

Pelz, Donald C. "Influence: a key to effective leadership in the first-line supervisor." Personnel 29: 209-221. 1952.

Porter, Lyman, and Edward E. Lawler, III. Managerial Attitudes and Performance. Homewood, Ill.: Irwin Dorsey. 1967.

Rim, Y. "Leadership attitudes and decisions involving risk." Personnel Psychology, 18: 423-430. 1965.

Rizzo, John R., Robert J. House, and Sidney E. Lirtzman. "Role conflict and ambiguity in complex organizations." Administrative Science Quarterly, 15: 150-153. 1970.

Siegel, Sidney. Nonparametric Statistics. New York: McGraw-Hill. 1956.

Stogdill, Ralph M. Manual for the Leader Behavior Description Questionnaire. Columbus: Ohio State University of Business Research. 1965.

Vroom, Victor H. Work and Motivation. New York: Wiley. 1964.

Vroom, Victor, and Floyd Mann. "Leader authoritarianism and employee attitudes." Personnel Psychology, 13: 125-139. 1960.

Wager, Wesley L. "Leadership style, influence and supervisory role obligations." Administrative Science Quarterly, 9: 391-420. 1965.

Wigdor, Larry. "Effectiveness of Various Management and Organization Characteristics on Employee Satisfaction and Performance as a Function of Employees Need for Independence. Doctoral dissertation, Bernard M. Baruch College, City University of New York. 1969.

PART SEVEN

Organizational Change and Development

Organization change can be treated at both the organizational and the individual level. At the organizational level, change is involved with how organizations adjust or adapt their structure to be consistent with the organization's environment. In the first part of this book, Terreberry concludes that organization change is externally induced: when the environment changes from turbulent to stable, organic organizations will become more mechanistic—and vice versa. Structural change of this type is an evolutionary process. The manager can do little but react to it. Awareness of alternative structural forms should facilitate adaptation rather than resistance. Under changing conditions, resisting a change in organization structure to a more appropriate form is certainly likely to restrict the effectiveness of the system.

Individual change is generally of greater concern to the managers. Change at the individual level means changing people, singly or in groups, to improve the effectiveness of the organization. The focus is on changing knowledge, attitudes, skills, and/or the capability to perform a job.

A different strategy of change can be applied, at both the individual and organizational level, for each of the following sets of conditions:

1. The organization structure may be appropriate to the environment, and the individuals within the system may have effectively adapted. This, of course, means that the system is functioning relatively well and surviving. Under these conditions, there is little need to attempt any change of a major nature. Introducing such efforts would be self-defeating, disturbing the equilibrium of the organization-environment-individual relationship.

2. The structure may not be appropriate for the environmental conditions, and the individuals may not possess required skills and attitudes. For instance, a mechanistic structure in a dynamic environment, staffed largely by people who function reasonably well in a fairly structured setting, is a situation which needs major change. Under such conditions major structural change, along with personnel changes, may be required.

It is unlikely that this problem will exist for a total organization, since a whole organization so incongruent with the environment is not likely to survive long. Rather, this may be a problem for a particular subunit; for instance, a shift in the technological environment may alter the kind of work done by a research and development group. If the nature of the shift is dynamic to stable, more routine policies and procedures may be required in the lab. Personnel changes might be required, such as replacing research chemists with chemical engineers.

3. It is possible that the organization structure is inappropriate for effective environmental adaptation, but the members have the capacity to perform effectively if it were changed. There is no people problem here—the system itself is inappropriate. This might occur when an organization structure is imposed without regard to external conditions. For example, a director of manufacturing might be assigned control of the R and D lab and impose relatively rigid rules and policies which could seriously hamper its effectiveness. The solution seems to be the revision of the structural system. Of course, structural alteration may be possible only by putting someone else in charge, but within the unit the prescription for change is structural.

4. The structure may be appropriate, but the attitudes, values, and/or skills of the members are inconsistent or incongruent. In this case, it is clear that some sort of *organizational development* is necessary. The need for major structural alterations is less likely. Although some minor policy adjustments may be necessary, the major thrust must be on changing individuals or groups.

One strategy for change is the selection approach. An attempt can be made to replace current employees with new ones who possess attributes compatible with the system. A second, more likely, alternative, would be training and development.

The fourth condition, involving organizational development, is the one treated in the readings in this part of the book.

In a set of three articles, Hersey and Blanchard provide an overview of organizational change problems. In the first selection they define four levels or types of change: knowledge change, attitude change, individual-behavior change, and group behavior change. Each type along the line involves a substantial increase over the previous one in both time and difficulty. This is so because more factors must be dealt with at each level in order to induce and maintain new performance patterns. It may be necessary, for instance, to alter leadership relationships *and* a complex set of structural factors to induce *major* individual and group change.

Hersey and Blanchard describe how positive and negative reinforcement may affect the behavior and attitudes of individuals, and go on to consider some of the general problems of implementing organizational change. They note that there are forces which drive an organization toward an equilibrium state, and that to induce change, these forces must be altered.

The methods described by Hersey and Blanchard attempt to change the behavior or attitudes of individuals. Too often, however, change programs have not taken into account the environment within which an individual works or the initial values and beliefs of those who are subjects of the environment. Organizational Development (OD) aims not only at individuals, but at the organization as a whole. The objective is a coordinated, planned change of all factors which may cause interpersonal problems in the organization. OD solutions may range from intervention methods, such as T-groups, to changing the nature of the structural characteristics, such as the compensation system, accounting system, or production system. A review of part 5 will suggest once more how these structural factors can affect performance and attitudes.

A broad overview of organizational development is given by French. He details the necessary conditions for OD to be successful. He clearly stresses the underlying humanistic orientation of OD as one of its fundamental premises. Basically, OD is a general approach to dealing with the problem of changing the effectiveness of organizations. It may be any one or a combination of a number of techniques and methods designed to induce more effective interaction among individuals. The techniques range from lectures, to sensitivity-training, to the redesign or organization structure.

The most important aspect of OD may well be the *diagnostic effort* to determine problem areas. Organization diagnosis may uncover problems otherwise left untouched. Effective diagnosis will focus problem-solving where it can have the most impact.

OD efforts are likely to work best when there is top-management commitment to change. But commitment means more than a statement of support. It must be exhibited in practice, which means that top managers must operate in ways consistent with what they expect subordinates to do. "Do as I say, not as I do," does not work with OD, or any other change effort.

We have argued earlier that systemic factors, one of which is the characteristics of the work itself, affect behavior patterns. In discussing "job enrichment," Paul et al, provide useful insights into the manner in which jobs may be restructured and redesigned and show data which indicate that improved performance can obtain. Their point is that when a work setting is a performance deterrent, trying to change people may have little impact; therefore, the job itself must be changed. Yet not all jobs can be altered. When such is the case, the manager must be prepared to live with the problem created by the job environment, or eliminate the job through automation.

The development of stable, predictable performance patterns is a major part of a manager's job. This can be regarded as a form of behavioral manipulation. Motivation strategies, the design of organization structure, and the implementation of change programs, especially those which use positive reinforcement methods, represent forms of behavior modification. These methods can be powerful, and yet they may be applied without the awareness of those they affect. In the closing article of the book, Kanfer analyzes the ethical questions involved in this issue and discusses safeguards against misapplication of change efforts.

ORGANIZATION DEVELOPMENT:
OBJECTIVES, ASSUMPTIONS, AND STRATEGIES

WENDELL FRENCH

Organization development refers to a long-range effort to improve an organization's problem solving capabilities and its ability to cope with changes in its external environment with the help of external or internal behavioral-scientist consultants, or change agents, as they are sometimes called. Such efforts are relatively new but are becoming increasingly visible within the United States, England, Japan, Holland, Norway, Sweden, and perhaps in other countries. A few of the growing number of organizations which have embarked on organization development (OD) efforts to some degree are Union Carbide, Esso, TRW Systems, Humble Oil, Weyerhaeuser, and Imperial Chemical Industries Limited. Other kinds of institutions, including public school systems, churches, and hospitals, have also become involved.

Organization development activities appear to have originated about 1957 as an attempt to apply some of the values and insights of laboratory training to total organizations. The late Douglas McGregor, working with Union Carbide, is considered to have been one of the first behavioral scientists to talk systematically about and to implement an organization development program[1] Other names associated with such early efforts are Herbert Shepard and Robert Blake who, in collaboration with the Employee Relations Department of the Esso Company, launched a program of laboratory training (sensitivity training) in the company's various refineries. This program emerged in 1957 after a headquarters human relations research division began to view itself as an internal consulting group offering services to field managers rather than as a research group developing reports for top management.[2]

Objectives of Typical OD Programs

Although the specific interpersonal and task objectives of organization development programs will vary according to each diagnosis of organization problems, a number of objectives typically emerge. These objectives reflect problems which are very common in organizations:

1. To increase the level of trust and support among organization members.

2. To increase the incidence of confrontation of organization problems, both within groups and among groups, in contrast to "sweeping problems under the rug."

3. To create an environment in which authority of assigned role is augmented by authority based on knowledge and skill.

4. To increase the openness of communications laterally, vertically, and diagonally.

5. To increase the level of personal enthusiasm and satisfaction in the organization.

6. To find synergistic solutions[3] to problems with greater frequency. (Synergistic

Reprinted from *California Management Review*, vol. 12, no. 2, pp. 23-46, by permission of The Regents; © 1969, by The Regents of the University of California.

solutions are creative solutions in which 2+2 equals more than 4, and through which all parties gain more through cooperation than through conflict.)

7. To increase the level of self and group responsibility in planning and implementation.[4]

Difficulties in Categorizing

Before describing some of the basic assumptions and strategies of organization development, it would be well to point out that one of the difficulties in writing about such a "movement" is that a wide variety of activities can be and are subsumed under this label. These activities have varied all the way from inappropriate application of some "canned" management development program to highly responsible and skillful joint efforts between behavioral scientists and client systems.

Thus, while labels are useful, they may gloss over a wide range of phenomena. The "human relations movement," for example, has been widely written about as though it were all bad or all good. To illustrate, some of the critics of the movement have accused it of being "soft" and a "hand-maiden of the Establishment," of ignoring the technical and power systems of organizations, and of being too naively participative. Such criticisms were no doubt warranted in some circumstances, but in other situations may not have been at all appropriate. Paradoxically, some of the major insights of the human relations movement, e.g., that the organization can be viewed as a social system and that subordinates have substantial control over productivity have been assimilated by its critics.

In short, the problem is to distinguish between appropriate and inappropriate programs, between effectiveness and ineffectiveness, and between relevancy and irrelevancy. The discussion which follows will attempt to describe the "ideal" circumstances for organization development programs, as well as to point out some pitfalls and common mistakes in organization change efforts.

Relevancy to Different Technologies and Organization Subunits

Research by Joan Woodward[5] suggests that organization development efforts *might be more relevant to certain kinds of technologies and organizational levels, and perhaps to certain workforce characteristics, than to others.* For example, OD efforts may be more appropriate for an organization devoted to prototype manufacturing than for an automobile assembly plant. However, experiments in an organization like Texas Instruments suggest that some manufacturing efforts which appear to be inherently mechanistic may lend themselves to a more participative, open management style than is often assumed possible.[6]

However, assuming the constraints of a fairly narrow job structure at the rank-and-file level, organization development efforts may inherently be more productive and relevant at the managerial levels of the organization. Certainly OD efforts are most effective when they start at the top. Research and development units—particularly those involving a high degree of interdependency and joint creativity among group members—also appear to be appropriate for organization development activities, if group members are currently experiencing problems in communicating or interpersonal relationships.

Basic Assumptions

Some of the basic assumptions about people which underlie organization development programs are similar to "Theory Y" assumptions[7] and will be repeated only briefly here. However some of the assumptions about groups and total systems will be treated more extensively. The following assumptions appear to underlie organization development efforts.[8]

About People

● Most individuals have drives toward personal growth and development, and these are most likely to be actualized in an environment which is both supportive and challenging.

● Most people desire to make, and are capable of making, a much higher level of contribution to the attainment of organization goals than most organizational environments will permit.

About People in Groups

● Most people wish to be accepted and to interact cooperatively with at least one small reference group, and usually with more than one group, e.g., the work group, the family group.

● One of the most psychologically relevant reference groups for most people is the work group, including peers and the superior.

● Most people are capable of greatly increasing their effectiveness in helping their reference groups solve problems and in working effectively together.

● For a group to optimize its effectiveness, the formal leader cannot perform all of the leadership functions in all circumstances at all times, and all group members must assist each other with effective leadership and member behavior.

About People in Organizational Systems

● Organizations tend to be characterized by overlapping, interdependent work groups, and the "linking pin" function of supervisors and others needs to be understood and facilitated.[9]

● What happens in the broader organization affects the small work group and vice versa.

● What happens to one subsystem (social, technological, or administrative) will affect and be influenced by other parts of the system.

● The culture in most organizations tends to suppress the expression of feelings which people have about each other and about where they and their organizations are heading.

● Suppressed feelings adversely affect problem solving, personal growth, and job satisfaction.

● The level of interpersonal trust, support, and cooperation is much lower in most organizations than is either necessary or desirable.

● "Win-lose" strategies between people and groups, while realistic and appropriate in some situations, are not optimal in the long run to the solution of most organizational problems.

• Synergistic solutions can be achieved with a much higher frequency than is acutally the case in most organizations.

• Viewing feelings as data important to the organization tends to open up many avenues for improved goal setting, leadership, communications, problem solving, intergroup collaboration, and morale.

• Improved performance stemming from organizational development efforts needs to be sustained by appropriate changes in the appraisal, compensation, training, staffing, and task-specialization subsystem—in short, in the total personnel system.

Value and Belief Systems of Behavioral Scientist-change Agents

While scientific inquiry, ideally, is value-free, the applications of science are not value-free. Applied behavioral scientist-organization development consultants tend to subscribe to a comparable set of values, although we should avoid the trap of assuming that they constitute a completely homogenous group. They do not.

One value, to which many behavioral scientist-change agents tend to give high priority, is that the needs and aspirations of human beings are the reasons for organized effort in society. They tend, therefore, to be developmental in their outlook and concerned with the long-range opportunities for the personal growth of people in organizations.

A second value is that work and life can become richer and more meaningful, and organized effort more effective and enjoyable, if feelings and sentiments are permitted to be a more legitimate part of the culture. A third value is a commitment to an action role, along with a commitment to research, in an effort to improve the effectiveness of organizations.[10] A fourth value—or perhaps a belief—is that improved competency in interpersonal and intergroup relationship will result in more effective organizations.[11] A fifth value is that behavioral science research and an examination of behavioral science assumptions and values are relevant and important in considering organizational effectiveness. While many change agents are perhaps overly action-oriented in terms of the utilization of their time, nevertheless, as a group they are paying more and more attention to research and to the examination of ideas.[12]

The value placed on research and inquiry raises the question as to whether the assumptions stated earlier are values, theory, or "facts." In my judgment, a substantial body of knowledge, including research on leadership, suggests that there is considerable evidence for these assumptions. However, to conclude that these assumptions are facts, laws, or principles would be to contradict the value placed by behavioral scientists on continuous research and inquiry. Thus, I feel that they should be considered theoretical statements which are based on provisional data.

This also raises the paradox that the belief that people are important tends to result in their being important. The belief that people can grow and develop in terms of personal and organizational competency tends to produce this result. Thus, values and beliefs tend to be self-fulfilling, and the question becomes "What do you choose to want to believe?" While this position can become Pollyannaish in the sense of not seeing the real world, nevertheless, behavioral scientist-change agents, at least this one, tend to place a value on optimism. It is a kind of optimism that says people can do a better job of goal setting and facing up to and solving problems, not an optimism that says the number of problems is diminishing.

It should be added that it is important that the values and beliefs of each behavioral science-change agent be made visible both to himself and to the client. In the first place, neither can learn to adequately trust the other without exposure—a hidden agenda handicaps both trust building and mutual learning. Second, and perhaps more pragmatically, organizational change efforts tend to fail if a prescription is applied unilaterally and without proper diagnosis.

Stragegy in Organization Development: an Action Research Model

A frequent strategy in organization development programs is based on what

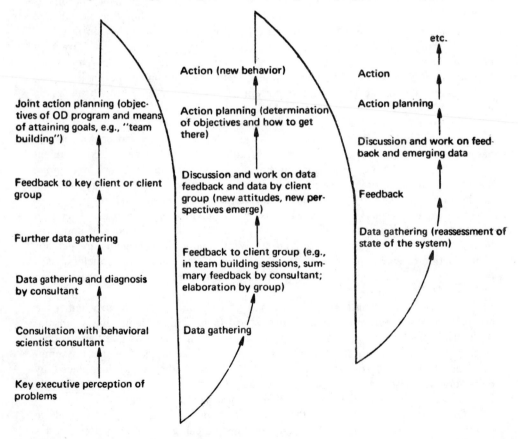

Figure 1. An action research model for organization development.

behavioral scientists refer to as an "action research model." This model involves extensive collaboration between the consultant (whether an external or an internal change agent) and the client group, data gathering, data discussion, and planning. While descriptions of this model vary in detail and terminology from author to author, the dynamics are essentially the same.[13]

Figure 1 summarizes some of the essential phases of the action research model, using an emerging organization development program as an example. The key aspects of the model are *diagnosis, data gathering, feedback to the client group, data discussion and work by the client group, action planning,* and *action.* The sequence tends to be cyclical, with the focus on new or advanced problems as the client group learns to work more effectively together. Action research should also be considered a process, since, as William Foote Whyte says, it involves ". . . a continuous gathering and analysis of human relations research data and the feeding of the findings into the organization in such a manner as to change behavior."[14] (Feedback we will define as nonjudgmental observations of behavior.)

Ideally, initial objectives and strategies of organization development efforts stem from a careful diagnosis of such matters as interpersonal and intergroup problems, decision-making processes, and communication flow which are currently being experienced by the client organization. As a preliminary step, the behavioral scientist and the key client (the president of a company, the vice president in charge of a division, the works manager or superintendent of a plant, a superintendent of schools, etc.), will make a joint initial assessment of the critical problems which need working on. Subordinates may also be interviewed in order to provide supplemental data. The diagnosis may very well indicate that the central problem is technological or that the key client is not at all willing or ready to examine the organization's problem-solving ability or his own managerial behavior.[15] Either could be a reason for postponing or moving slowly in the direction of organization development activities, although the technological problem may easily be related to deficiencies in interpersonal relationships or decision making. The diagnosis might also indicate the desirability of one or more additional specialists (in engineering, finance, or electronic data processing, for example) to simultaneously work with the organization.

This initial diagnosis, which focuses on the expressed needs of the client, is extremely critical. As discussed earlier, in the absence of a skilled diagnosis, the behavioral scientist-change agent would be imposing a set of assumptions and a set of objectives which may be hopelessly out of joint with either the current problems of the people in the organization or their willingness to learn new modes of behavior. In this regard, it is extremely important that the consultant *hear and understand* what the client is trying to tell him. This requires a high order of skill.[16]

Interviews are frequently used for *data gathering* in OD work for both initial diagnosis and subsequent planning sessions, since personal contact is important for building a cooperative relationship between the consultant and the client group. The interview is also important since the behavioral scientist-consultant is interested in spontaneity and in feelings that are expressed as well as cognitive matters. However, questionnaires are sometimes successfully used in the context of what is sometimes referred to as survey feedback, to supplement interview data.[17]

Data gathering typically goes through several phases. The first phase is related to diagnosing the state of the system and to making plans for organizational change.

This phase may utilize a series of interviews between the consultant and the key client, or between a few key executives and the consultant. Subsequent phases focus on problems specific to the top executive team and to subordinate teams. (See Figure 2.)

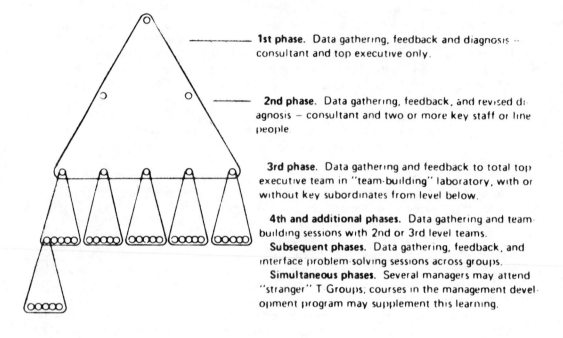

1st phase. Data gathering, feedback and diagnosis -- consultant and top executive only.

2nd phase. Data gathering, feedback, and revised diagnosis – consultant and two or more key staff or line people.

3rd phase. Data gathering and feedback to total top executive team in "team-building" laboratory, with or without key subordinates from level below.

4th and additional phases. Data gathering and team-building sessions with 2nd or 3rd level teams.
Subsequent phases. Data gathering, feedback, and interface problem-solving sessions across groups.
Simultaneous phases. Several managers may attend "stranger" T Groups; courses in the management development program may supplement this learning.

Figure 2. Organization development phases in a hypothetical organization.

Typical questions in data gathering or "problem sensing" would include: What problems do you see in your group, including problems between people, that are interfering with getting the job done the way you would like to see it done?; and what problems do you see in the broader organization? Such open-ended questions provide wide latitude on the part of the respondents and encourage a reporting of problems *as the individual sees them*. Such interviewing is usually conducted privately, with a commitment on the part of the consultant that the information will be used in such a way as to avoid unduly embarrassing anyone. The intent is to find out what common problems or themes emerge, with the data to be used constructively for both diagnostic and feedback purposes.

Two- or three-day offsite *team-building or group problem-solving sessions* typically become a major focal point in organization development programs. During these meetings the behavioral scientist frequently provides *feedback* to the group in terms of themes which emerged in the problem-sensing interviews.[18] He may also encourage the group to determine which items or themes should have priority in terms of maximum utilization of time. These themes usually provide substantial and meaningful data for the group to begin work on. One-to-one interpersonal matters, both positive and negative, tend to emerge spontaneously as the participants gain confidence from the level of support sensed in the group.

Different consultants will vary in their mode of behavior in such sessions, but will typically serve as *"process" observers and as interpreters of the dynamics of the group interaction* to the degree that the group expresses a readiness for such intervention. They also typically encourage people to take risks, a step at a time, and to experiment with new behavior in the context of the level of support in the group. Thus, the trainer-consultant(s) serves as a stimulant to new behavior but also as a protector. The climate which I try to build, for example is "Let's not tear down any more than we can build back together."[19] Further, the trainer-consultant typically works with the group to assist team members in improving their skills in diagnosing and facilitating group progress.[20]

It should be noted, however, that different groups will have different needs along a task-process continuum. For example, some groups have a need for intensive work on clarifying objectives; others may have the greatest need in the area of personal relationships. Further, the consultant or the chief consultant in a team of consultants involved in an organization development program will play a much broader role than serving as a T-group or team-building trainer. He will also play an important role in periodic data gathering and diagnosis and in joint long-range planning of the change efforts.[21]

Laboratory Training and Organization Development

Since organization development programs have largely emerged from T-group experience, theory, and research, and since laboratory training in one form or another tends to be an integral part of most such programs, it is important to focus on laboratory training per se. As stated earlier, OD programs grew out of a perceived need to relate laboratory training to the problems of on-going organizations and a recognition that optimum results could only occur if major parts of the total social system of an organization were involved.

Laboratory training essentially emerged around 1946, largely through a growing recognition by Leland Bradford, Ronald Lippitt, Kenneth Benne, and others, that human relations training which focused on the feelings and concerns of the participants was frequently a much more powerful and viable form of education than the lecture method. Some of the theoretical constructs and insights from which these laboratory training pioneers drew stemmed from earlier research by Lippitt, Kurt Lewin, and Ralph White. The term "T-Group" emerged by 1949 as a shortened label for "Basic Skill Training Group", these terms were used to identify the programs which began to emerge in the newly formed National Training Laboratory in Group Development (now NTL Institute for Applied Behavioral Science).[22] "Sensitivity Training" is also a term frequently applied to such training.

Ordinarily, laboratory training sessions have certain objectives in common. The following list, by two internationally known behavioral scientists,[23] is probably highly consistent with the objectives of most programs:

Self-objectives
- Increased *awareness* of own feelings and reactions, and own impact on others.
- Increased *awareness* of feelings and reactions of others, and their impact on self.
- Increased *awareness* of dynamics of group action.
- *Changed attitudes* toward self, others, and groups, i.e., more respect for, tolerance for, and faith in self, others, and groups.
- Increased *interpersonal competence*, i.e., skill in handling interpersonal and group relationships toward more productive and satisfying relationships.

Role Objectives
- Increased *awareness* of own organizational role, organizational dynamics, dynamics of larger social systems, and dynamics of the change process in self, small groups, and organizations.
- *Changed attitudes* toward own role, role of others, and organizational relationships, i.e., more respect for and willingness to deal with others with whom one is interdependent, greater willingness to achieve collaborative relationships with others based on mutual trust.
- Increased *interpersonal competence* in handling organizational role relationships with superiors, peers, and subordinates.

Organizational Objectives
- Increased *awareness* of, *changed attitudes* toward, and increased *interpersonal competence* about specific organizational problems existing in groups or units which are interdependent.
- *Organizational improvement* through the training of relationships of groups rather than isolated individuals.

Over the years, experimentation with different laboratory designs has led to diverse criteria for the selection of laboratory participants. Probably a majority of NTL-IABS human relations laboratories are "stranger groups," i.e., involving participants who come from different organizations and who are not likely to have met earlier. However, as indicated by the organizational objectives above, the incidence of special labs designed to increase the effectiveness of persons already working together appears to be growing. Thus terms like "cousin labs," i.e., labs involving people from the same organization but not the same subunit, and "family labs" or "team-building" sessions, i.e., involving a manager and all of his subordinates, are becoming familiar. Participants in labs designed for organizational members not of the same unit may be selected so as to constitute a heterogeneous grouping by rank ("diagonal slice"). Further, NTL-IABS is now encouraging at least two members from the same organization to attend NTL Management Work Conferences and Key Executive Conferences in order to maximize the impact of the learning in the backhome situation.[24]

In general, experienced trainers recommend that persons with severe emotional illness should not participate in laboratory training, with the exception of programs designed specifically for group therapy. Designers of programs make the assumptions, as Argyris states them,[25] that T-Group participants should have:

1. A relatively strong ego that is not overwhelmed by internal conflicts.

2. Defenses which are sufficiently low to allow the individual to hear what others say to him.

3. The ability to communicate thought and feelings with minimal distortion.

As a result of such screening, the incidence of breakdown during laboratory training is substantially less than that reported for organizations in general,[26] However, since the borderline between "normalcy" and illness is very indistinct, most professionally trained staff members are equipped to diagnose severe problems and to make referrals to psychiatrists and clinical psychologists when appropriate. Further, most are equipped to give adequate support and protection to participants whose ability to assimilate and learn from feedback is low. In addition, group members in T-Group situations tend to be sensitive to the emotional needs of the members and to be supportive when they sense a person experiencing pain. Such support is explicitly fostered in laboratory training.

The duration of laboratory training programs varies widely. "Micro-Labs," designed to give people a brief experience with sensitivity training, may last only one hour. Some labs are designed for a long weekend. Typically, however, basic human relations labs are of two weeks duration, with participants expected to meet mornings, afternoons, and evenings, with some time off for recreation. While NTL Management Work Conferences for middle managers and Key Executive Conferences run for one week, team-building labs, from my experience, typically are about three days in length. However, the latter are usually only a part of a broader organization development program involving problem sensing and diagnosis, and the planning of action steps and subsequent sessions. In addition, attendance at stranger labs for key managers is frequently a part of the total organization development effort.

Sensitivity training sessions typically start with the trainer making a few comments about his role—that he is there to be of help, that the group will have control of the agenda, that he will deliberately avoid a leadership role, but that he might become involved as both a leader and a member from time to time, etc. The following is an example of what the trainer might say:

> This group will meet for many hours and will serve as a kind of laboratory where each individual can increase his understanding of the forces which influence individual behavior and the performance of groups and organizations. The data for learning will be our own behavior, feelings, and reactions. We begin with no definite structure or organization, no agreed-upon procedures, and no specific agenda. It will be up to us to fill the vacuum created by the lack of these familiar elements and to study our group as we evolve. My role will be to help the group to learn from its own experience, but not to act as a traditional chairman nor to suggest how we should organize, what our procedure should be, or exactly what our agenda will include. With these few comments, I think we are ready to begin in whatever way you feel will be most helpful.[27]

The trainer then lapses into silence. Group discomfort then precipitates a dialogue which, with skilled trainer assistance, is typically an intense but generally highly rewarding experience for group members. What goes on in the group becomes the data for the learning experience.

Interventions by the trainer will vary greatly depending upon the purpose of the lab and the state of learning on the part of the participants. A common intervention, however, is to encourage people to focus on and own up to their own feelings about what is going on in the group, rather than to make judgments about others. In this way, the participants begin to have more insight into their own feelings and to understand how their behavior affects the feelings of others.

While T-Group work tends to be the focal point in human relations laboratories, laboratory training typically includes theory sessions and frequently includes exercises such as role playing or management games.[28] Further, family labs of subunits of organizations will ordinarily devote more time to planning action steps for back on the job than will stranger labs.

Robert J. House has carefully reviewed the research literature on the impact of T-Group training and has concluded that the research shows mixed results. In particular, research on changes as reflected in personality inventories is seen as inconclusive. However, studies which examine the behavior of participants upon returning to the job are generally more positive.[29] House cites six studies, all of which utilized control groups, and concludes:

> All six studies revealed what appear to be important positive effects of T-Group training. Two of the studies report negative effects as well . . . all of the evidence is based on observations of the behavior of the participants in the actual job situations. No reliance is placed on participant response; rather, evidence is collected in his normal work activities.[30]

John P. Campbell and Marvin D. Dunnette,[31] on the other hand, while conceding that the research shows that T-Group training produces *changes in behavior*, point out that the usefulness of such training in terms of *job performance* has yet to be demonstrated. They urge research toward "forging the link between training-induced behavior changes and changes in job-performance effectiveness."[32] As a summary comment they state:

> . . . the assumption that T-Group training has positive utility for organizations must necessarily rest on shaky ground. It has been neither confirmed nor disconfirmed. The authors wish to emphasize . . . that utility for the organization is not necessarily the same as utility for the individual.[33]

At least two major reasons may account for the inconclusiveness of research on the impact of T-Group training on job performance. One reason is simply that little research has been done. The other reason may center around a factor of cultural isolation. To oversimplify, a major part of what one learns in laboratory training, in my opinion, is how to work more effectively with others in group situations, *particularly with others who have developed comparable skills*. Unfortunately, most participants return from T-Group experiences to environments including colleagues and superiors who have not had the same affective (emotional, feeling) experiences, who are not familiar with the terminology and underlying theory, and who may have anxieties (usually unwarranted) about what might happen to them in a T-Group situation.

This cultural distance which laboratory training can produce is one of the reasons why many behavioral scientists are currently encouraging more than one person from the same organization to undergo T-Group training and, ideally, all of the members of a team and their superior to participate in some kind of laboratory training together. The latter assumes that a diagnosis of the organization indicates that the group is ready for such training and assumes such training is reasonably compatible with the broader culture of the total system.

Conditions and Techniques for Successful Organization Development Programs

Theory, research, and experience to date suggest to me that *successful* OD programs tend to evolve in the following way and that they have some of these characteristics (these statements should be considered highly tentative, however):

● There is a strong pressure for improvement from both outside the organization and from within.[34]

● An outside behavioral scientist-consultant is brought in for consultation with the top executives and to diagnose organizational problems.

● A preliminary diagnosis suggests that organization development efforts, designed in response to the expressed needs of the key executives, are warranted.

● A collaborative decision is made between the key client group and the consultant to try to change the culture of the organization, at least at the top initially. The specific goals may be to improve communications, to secure more effective participation from subordinates in problem solving, and to move in the direction of more openness, more feedback, and more support. In short, a decision is made to change the culture to help the company meet its organizational goals and to provide better avenues for initiative, creativity, and self-actualization on the part of organization members.

● Two or more top executives, including the chief executive, to to laboratory training sessions. (Frequently, attendance at labs is one of the facts which precipitates interest in bringing in the outside consultant.)

● Attendance in T-Group program is voluntary. While it is difficult to draw a line between persuasion and coercion, OD consultants and top management should be aware of the dysfunctional consequences of coercion (see the comments on authentic behavior below). While a major emphasis is on team-building laboratories, stranger labs are utilized both to supplement the training going on in the organization and to train managers new to the organization or those who are newly promoted.

● Team-building sessions are held with the top executive group (or at the highest point where the program is started). Ideally, the program is started at the top of the organization, but it can start at levels below the president as long as there is significant support from the chief executive, and preferably from other members of the top power structure as well.

● In a firm large enough to have a personnel executive, the personnel-industrial relations vice president becomes heavily involved at the outset.

● One of two organizational forms emerges to coordinate organization development efforts, either (a) a coordinator reporting to the personnel executive (the personnel executive himself may fill this role), or (b) a coordinator reporting to the chief executive. The management development director is frequently in an ideal position to coordinate OD activities with other management development activities.

• Ultimately, it is essential that the personnel-industrial relations group, including people in salary administration, be an integral part of the organization development program. Since OD groups have such potential for acting as catalysts in rapid organizational change, the temptation is great to see themselves as "good guys" and the other personnel people as "bad guys" or simply ineffective. Any conflicts between a separate organization development group and the personnel and industrial relations groups should be faced and resolved. Such tensions can be the "Achilles heel" for either program. In particular, however, the change agents in the organization development program need the support of the other people who are heavily involved in human resources administration and vice versa; what is done in the OD program needs to be compatible with what is done in selection, promotion, salary administration, appraisal, and vice versa. In terms of systems theory, it would seem imperative that one aspect of the human resources function such as any organization development program must be highly interdependent with the other human resources activities including selection, salary administration, etc. (TRW Systems is an example of an organization which involves top executives plus making the total personnel and industrial relations group an integral part of the OD program.[35])

• Team-building labs, at the request of the various respective executives, with laboratory designs based on careful data gathering and problem diagnosis, are conducted at successively lower levels of the organization with the help of outside consultants, plus the help of internal consultants whose expertise is gradually developed.

• Ideally, as the program matures, both members of the personnel staff and a few line executives are trained to do some organization development work in conjunction with the external and internal professionally trained behavioral scientists. In a sense, then, the external change agent tries to work himself out of a job by developing internal resources.

• The outside consultant(s) and the internal coordinator work very carefully together and periodically check on fears, threats, and anxieties which may be developing as the effort progresses. Issues need to be confronted as they emerge. Not only is the outside change agent needed for his skills, but the organization will need someone to act as a "governor"—to keep the program focused on real problems and to urge authenticity in contrast to gamesmanship. The danger always exists that the organization will begin to punish or reward involvement in T-Group kinds of activities per se, rather than focus on performance.

• The OD consultants constantly work on their own effectiveness in interpersonal relationships and their diagnostic skills so they are not in a position of "do as I say, but not as I do." Further, both consultant and client work together to optimize the consultant's knowledge of the organization's unique and evolving culture structure, and web of interpersonal relationships.

• There needs to be continuous audit of the results, both in terms of checking on the evolution of attitudes about what is going on and in terms of the extent to which problems which were identified at the outset by the key clients are being solved through the program.

• As implied above, the reward system and other personnel systems need to be readjusted to accommodate emerging changes in performance in the organization. Substantially improved performance on the part of individuals and groups is not likely to be sustained if financial and promotional rewards are not forthcoming. In short, management needs to have a "systems" point of view and to think through the interrelationships of the OD effort with the reward and staffing systems and the other aspects of the total human resources subsystem.

In the last analysis, the president and the "line" executives of the organization will evaluate the success of the OD effort in terms of the extent to which it assists the organization in meeting its human and economic objectives. For example, marked improvements on various indices from one plant, one division, one department, etc., will be important indicators of program success. While human resources administration indices are not yet perfected, some of the measuring devices being developed by Likert, Mann, and others show some promise.[36]

Summary Comments

Organization development efforts have emerged through attempts to apply laboratory training values and assumptions to total systems. Such efforts are organic in the sense that they emerge from and are guided by the problems being experienced by the people in the organization. The key to their viability (in contrast to becoming a passing fad) lies in an authentic focus on problems and concerns of the members of the organization and in their confrontation of issues and problems.

Organization development is based on assumptions and values similar to "Theory Y" assumptions and values but includes additional assumptions about total systems and the nature of the client-consultant relationship. Intervention strategies of the behavioral scientist-change agent tend to be based on an action-research model and tend to be focused more on helping the people in an organization learn to solve problems rather than on prescriptions of how things should be done differently.

Laboratory training (or "sensitivity training") or modifications of T-Group seminars typically are a part of the organizational change efforts, but the extent and format of such training will depend upon the evolving needs of the organization. Team-building seminars involving a superior and subordinates are being utilized more and more as a way of changing social systems rapidly and avoiding the cultural-distance problems which frequently emerge when individuals return from stranger labs. However, stranger labs can play a key role in change efforts when they are used as part of a broader organization development effort.

Research has indicated that sensitivity training generally produces positive results in terms of changed behavior on the job, but has not demonstrated the link between behavior changes and improved performance. Maximum benefits are probably derived from laboratory training when the organizational culture supports and reinforces the use of new skills in ongoing team situations.

Successful organization development efforts require skillful behavioral scientist interventions, a systems view, and top management support and involvement. In addition, changes stemming from organization development must be linked to changes in the total personnel subsystem. The viability of organization development efforts lies in the degree to which they accurately reflect the aspirations and concerns of the participating members.

In conclusion, *successful organization development tends to be a total system effort; a process of planned change—not a program with a temporary quality; and aimed at developing the organization's internal resources for effective change in the future.*

Notes and References

This article is largely based on the . . . second edition of my *The Personnel Management Process: Human Resources Administration* (Boston: Houghton Mifflin Company, 1970), chap. 28.

1. Richard Beckhard, W. Warner Burke, and Fred I. Steele, "the Program for Specialists in Organization Training and Development," mimeographed, NTL Institute for Applied Behavioral Science, Dec. 1967, p. ii; and John Paul Jones, "What's Wrong With Work?" in *What's Wrong With Work?* (New York: National Association of Manufacturers, 1967), p. 8. For a history of NTL Institute for Applied Behavioral Science, with which Douglas McGregor was long associated in addition to his professorial appointment at M.I.T. and which has been a major factor in the history of organization development, see Leland P. Bradford, "Biography of an Institution," *Journal of Applied Behavioral Science*, III:2 (1967), 127-143. While we will use the word "program" from time to time, ideally organization development is a "process," not just another new program of temporary quality.

2. Harry D. Kolb, Introduction to *An Action Research Program for Organization Improvement* (Ann Arbor: Foundation for Research in Human Behavior, 1960), p. i.

3. Cattell defines synergy as "the sum total of the energy which a group can command." Daniel Katz and Robert L. Kahn, *The Social Psychology of Organizations* (New York: John Wiley and Sons, 1966), p. 33.

4. For a similar statement of objectives, see "What is OD?" *NTL Institute: News and Reports from NTL Institute for Applied Behavioral Science*, II (June 1968), 1-2. Whether OD programs increase the overall level of authority in contrast to redistributing authority is a debatable point. My hypothesis is that both a redistribution and an overall increase occur.

5. Joan Woodward, *Industrial Organization: Theory and Practice* (London: Oxford University Press, 1965).

6. See M. Scott Myers, "Every Employee a Manager," *California Mangement Review*, X (Spring 1968), 9-20.

7. See Douglas McGregor, *The Human Side of Enterprise* (New York: McGraw-Hill Book Company, 1960), pp. 47-48.

8. In addition to influence from the writings of McGregor, Likert, Argyris, and others, this discussion has been influenced by "Some Assumptions About Change in Organizations," in notebook "Program for Specialists in Organization Training and Development," NTL Institute for Applied Behavioral Science, 1967; and by staff members who participated in that program.

9. For a discussion of the "linking pin" concept, see Rensis Likert, *New Patterns of Management* (New York: McGraw-Hill Book Company, 1961).

10. Warren G. Bennis sees three major approaches to planned organizational change, with the behavioral scientists associated with each all having "a deep concern with applying social

science knowledge to create more viable social systems; a commitment to action, as well as to research . . . and a belief that improved interpersonal and group relationships will ultimately lead to better organizational performance." Bennis, "A New Role for the Behavioral Sciences: Effecting Organizational Change," *Administrative Science Quarterly* VIII (Step. 1963), 157-158; and Herbert A. Shepard, "An Action Research Model," in *An Action Research Program for Organization Improvement*, pp. 31-35.

11. Bennis, "A New Role for the Behavioral Sciences," 158.

12. For a discussion of some of the problems and dilemmas in behavioral science research, see Chris Argyris, "Creating Effective Relationships in Organizations," in Richard N. Adams and Jack J. Preiss, eds., *Human Organization Research* (Homewood, Ill.: The Dorsey Press, 1960), pp. 109-123; and Barbara A. Benedict. et al., "The Clinical Experimental Approach to Assessing Organizational Change Efforts," *Journal of Applied Behavioral Science*, (Nov. 1967), 347-380.

13. For further discussion of action research, see Edgar H. Schein and Warren G. Bennis, *Personal and Organizational Change Through Group Methods* (New York: John Wiley and Sons, 1966), pp. 272-274.

14. William Foote Whyte and Edith Lentz Hamilton, *Action Research for Mangement* (Homewood, Ill.: Richard D. Irwin, 1964), p. 2.

15. Jeremiah J. O'Connell appropriately challenges the notion that there is "one best way" of organizational change and stresses that the consultant should choose his role and intervention strategies on the basis of "the conditions existing when he enters the client system" (*Managing Organization Innovation* [Homewood, Ill.: Richard D. Irwin, 1968], pp. 10-11).

16. For further discussion of organization diagnosis, see Richard Beckhard, "An Organization Improvement Program in a Decentralised Organization," *Journal of Applied Behavioral Science*, 1 (Jan.—March 1966), 3-4, "OD as a Process," in *What's Wrong with Work?*, pp. 12-13.

17. For example, see Floyd C. Mann, "Studying and Creating Change," in Timothy W. Costello and Sheldon S. Zalkind, eds., *Psychology in Administration—A Research Orientation* (Englewood Cliffs: Prentice-Hall, 1963), pp. 321-324, See also Delbert C. Miller, "Using Behavioral Science to Solve Organization Problems," *Personnel Administration*, XXXI (Jan.—Feb. 1968), 21-29.

18. For a description of feedback procedures used by the Survey Research Center, Univ. of Michigan, see Mann and Likert, "The Need for Research on the Communication of Research Results," in *Human Organization Research*, pp. 57-66.

19. This phrase probably came from a management workshop sponsored by NTL Institute for Applied Behavioral Science.

20. For a description of what goes on in team-building sessions, see Beckhard, "An Organizational Improvement Program," 9-13; and Newton Margulies and Anthony P. Raia, "People in Organizations—A Case for Team Training," *Training and Development Journal*, XXII (August 1968), 2-11. For a description of problem-solving sessions involving the total management group (about 70) of a company, see Beckhard, "The Confrontation Meeting," *Harvard Business Review*, XLV (March—April 1967), 149-155.

21. For a description of actual organization development programs, see Paul C. Buchanan, "Innovative Organizations—A Study in Organization Development," in *Applying Behavioral Science Research in Industry* (New York: Industrial Relations Counselors, (1964), pp. 87-107; Sheldon A. Davis, "An Organic Problem-Solving Method of Organizational Change," *Journal of Applied Behavioral Science*, III:1 (1967), 3-21; Cyril Sofer, *The Organization from Within* (Chicago: Quadrangle Books, 1961); Alfred J. Marrow, David G. Bowers, and Stanley E. Seashore, *Management by Participation* (New York: Harper and Row, 1967); Robert R. Blake, Jane S. Mouton, Louis B. Barnes, and Larry E. Greiner, "Breakthrough in Organiza-

tion Development," *Harvard Business Review*, XLII (Nov.—Dec. 1964), 133-155; Alton C. Bartlett, "Changing Behavior as a Means to Increased Efficiency," *Journal of Applied Behavioral Science*, III:3 (1967), 381-403; Larry E. Greiner, "Antecedents of Planned Organization Change," *ibid.*, III:1 (1967), 51-85; and Robert R. Blake and Jane Mouton, *Corporate Excellence Through Grid Organization Development* (Houston, Texas: Gulf Publishing Company, 1968).

22. From Bradford, "Biography of an Institution." See also Kenneth D. Benne, "History of the T-Group in the Laboratory Setting," in Bradford, Jack R. Gibb, and Benne, eds., *T/Group Theory and Laboratory Method* (New York: John Wiley and Sons, 1964), pp. 80-135.

23. Schein and Bennis, p. 37.

24. For further discussion of group composition in laboratory training, see Schein and Bennis, pp. 63-69. NTL-LABS now include the Center for Organization Studies, the Center for the Development of Educational Leadership, the Center for Community Affairs, and the Center for International Training to serve a wide range of client populations and groups.

25. Chris Argyris, "T-Groups for Organizational Effectiveness," *Harvard Business Review*, XLII (March—April 1964), 60-74.

26. Based on discussions with NTL staff members. One estimate is that the incidence of "serious stress and mental disturbance" during laboratory training is less than one percent of participants and in almost all cases occurs in persons with a history of prior disturbance (Charles Seashore, "What is Sensitivity Training," *NTL Institute News and Reports*, II [April 1968], 2).

27. *Ibid.*, 1.

28. For a description of what goes on in T-groups, see Schein and Bennis, pp. 10-27; Bradford, Gibb, and Benne, pp. 55-67; Dorothy S. Whitaker, "A Case Study of a T-Group," in Galvin Witaker, ed., *T-Group Training: Group Dynamics in Mangement Education*, A.T.M. Occasional Papers, (Oxford: Basil Blackwell, 1965), pp. 14-22; Irving R. Weschler and Jerome Reisel, *Inside a Sensitivity Training Group* (Berkeley: University of California, Institute of Industrial Relations, 1959); and William F. Glueck, "Reflections on a T-Group Experience," *Personnel Journal*, XLVII (July 1968), 501-504. For use of cases or exercises based on research results ("instrumented training") see Robert R. Blake and Jane S. Mouton, "The Instrumented Training Laboratory," in Irving R. Weschler and Edgar H. Schein, eds., *Five Issues in Training* (Washington: National Training Laboratories, 1962), pp. 61-76; and W. Warner Burke and Harvey A. Hornstein, "Conceptual vs. Experimental Mangement Training," *Training and Development Journal*, XXI (Dec. 1967), 12-17.

29. Robert J. House, "T-Group Education and Leadership Effectiveness: A Review of the Empiric Literature and a Critical Evaluation." *Personnel Psychology*, XX (Spring 1967), 1-32. See also Dorothy Stock, "A Survey of Research on T-Groups," in Bradford, Gibb, and Benne, pp. 395-441.

30. House, *ibid.*, pp. 18-19.

31. John P. Campbell and Marvin D. Dunnette, "Effectiveness of T-Group Experiences in Managerial Training and Development," *Psychological Bulletin*, LXX (August 1968), 73-104.

32. *Ibid.*, 100.

33. *Ibid.*, 101. See also the essays by Dunnette and Campbell and Chris Argyris in *Industrial Relations*, VIII (Oct. 1968), 1-45.

34. On this point, see Larry E. Greiner, "Patterns of Organization Change," *Harvard Business Review*, XLV (May—June 1967), 119-130.

35. See Sheldon A. Davis, "An Organic Problem-Solving Method."

36. See Rensis Likert, *The Human Organization: Its Mangement and Value* (New York: McGraw-Hill Book Company, 1967).

THE MANAGEMENT OF CHANGE

PAUL HERSEY
KENNETH H. BLANCHARD

In the dynamic society in which today's organizations exist, the question of whether change will occur is no longer relevant. Instead, the issue now is how do managers cope with the inevitable barrage of changes which confront them daily in attempting to keep their organizations viable and current. While change is a fact of life, effective managers (if they are to be effective), can no longer be content to let change occur as it will, they must be able to develop strategies to plan, direct and control change. The purpose of [this three-part] article on "The Management of Change" is to provide practitioners with a general framework of change theory, hopefully with some strategies that can be used in planning and implementing change in their own environments.

In the first [part], "Change and the Use of Power," we will discuss two kinds of power, position power and personal power, then examine the use of both in varying situations. We will examine various levels of change from knowledge and attitude to individual behavior and organizational performance. These levels of change will then be analyzed in terms of two change cycles—participative and coerced.

In the second [part], "Change Through Behavior Modification," we will look at how managers can create an environment to move people from one level of maturity and responsibility to a higher level. Behavior modification will be examined as a tool for making changes at the operational level for both individuals and groups and we will discuss what implications reinforcement theory can have for the practitioner or change agent.

In the final [part], "Planning and Implementing Change," we will attempt to integrate much that we discussed in the first two articles into some theoretical frameworks that can be used to develop specific change strategies in various situations. In particular, we will examine force field analysis and the process of change and then look at the impact of change on the total system.

Part One: Change and the Use of Power

In developing a change strategy, the practitioner must be conscious of whatever power he has and be able to determine how this power might be appropriately used.

Sources of Power

Amitai Etzioni discusses the difference between *position power* and *personal power*.[1] His distinction springs from his concept of power as the ability to induce or influence behavior. He claims that power is derived from an organizational office, personal influence or both. An individual who is able to induce another individual to do a certain job because of his position in the organization is considered to have position power, while an individual who derives his power from his followers is considered to have personal power. Some individuals can have both position and personal power.

Etzioni postulates that the best situation for a leader is when he has both personal and position power. But in some cases it is not possible to build a relationship on both. Then the question becomes whether it is more important to have personal power or position power. Happiness and human relations have been culturally reinforced over the past several decades. With this emphasis, most people would pick personal power as being the most important, but there may be another side of the coin.

Machiavelli in the fifteenth century in his treatise *The Prince* presents an interesting viewpoint when he raises the question—whether it is better to have a relationship based upon love (personal power) or fear (position power).[2] Machiavelli, as Etzioni, contends it is best to be both loved and feared. If, however, you cannot have both, he suggest a relationship based on love alone tends to be volatile, short run and easily terminated when there is no fear of retaliation. On the other hand, Machiavelli contends a relationship based upon fear tends to be longer lasting since the individual must be willing to incur the sanction (pay the price) before terminating the relationship. This is a difficult concept for many people to accept; and yet one of the most difficult roles for a leader, whether he be a boss, teacher or parent, to engage in is disciplining someone about whom he cares. Yet to be effective we sometimes have to sacrifice short-term friendship for long-term respect if we are interested in the growth and development of the people with whom we are working. Machiavelli warns, however, that one should be careful that fear does not lead to hatred. For hatred often evokes overt behavior in terms of retaliation, undermining and attempts to overthrow.

Successful Leadership versus Effective Leadership

If an individual attempts to have some effect on the behavior of another, we call this stimulus attempted leadership. The response to this leadership attempt can be successful or unsuccessful. Since a manager's basic responsibility in any type of organization is to get work done with and through people, his success is measured by the output or productivity of the group he leads. With this thought in mind, Bernard M. Bass suggests a clear distinction between *successful* and *effective* leadership or management.[3]

Suppose manager A attempts to influence individual B to do a certain job. It is not really an either/or situation. A's success could be depicted on a continuum (Figure 1) ranging from very successful to very unsuccessful with gray areas in between which would be difficult to ascertain as either.

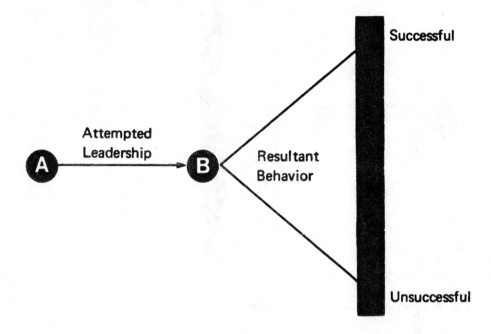

Figure 1. Successful-unsuccessful leadership continuum.

Let us assume that A's leadership is successful. In other words, B's response to A's leadership stimulus falls on the successful side of the continuum. This still does not tell the whole story of effectiveness.

If A's leadership style is not compatible with the expectations of B and, if B is antagonized and does the job only because of A's position power, then we can say that A has been successful but not effective. B has responded as A intended because A has control of rewards and punishment, and not because B sees his own needs being accomplished by satisfying the goals of the manager or organization.

On the other hand, if A's attempted leadership leads to a successful response, and B does the job because he wants to do it and finds it rewarding, then we consider A as having not only position power but also personal power. B respects A and is willing to cooperate with him realizing that A's request is consistent with his own personal goals. In fact, B sees his own goals as being accomplished by this activity. This is the meaning of effective leadership, keeping in mind that effectiveness also appears as a continuum which can range from very effective to very ineffective as illustrated in Figure 2.

Success has to do with how the individual or group behaves. On the other hand,

Figure 2. Successful and effective leadership continuums.

effectiveness describes the internal state or predisposition of an individual or group and thus is attitudinal in nature. If an individual is interested only in success, he tends to emphasize his position power and uses close supervision.

However, if he is effective he will depend also on personal power and be characterized by more general supervision. Position power tends to be delegated down from the organization, while personal power is generated from below through follower acceptance.

In the management of organizations, the difference between successful and effective often explains why many supervisors can get a satisfactory level of output only when they are right there, looking over the worker's shoulder. But as soon as they leave output declines and often such things as horseplay and scrap loss increase.

The phenomenon described applies not only to business organizations but also to less formal organizations like the family. If parents are successful and effective, have both position and personal power, their children accept family goals as their own. Consequently, if the husband and wife leave for the weekend, the children behave no differently than if their parents were there. If, on the other hand, the parents continually use close supervision and the children view their own goals as being stifled by their parents' goals, the parents have only position power. They maintain order because of the rewards and punishments they control. If these parents went away on a trip leaving the children behind, upon returning they might be greeted by havoc and chaos.

In summary, a manager could be successful, but ineffective, having only short-run influence over the behavior of others. On the other hand if a manager is both successful and effective, his influence tends to lead to long-run productivity and organizational development.

Levels of Change

We have to look at changes from more than just a behavioral viewpoint because often changes in behavior are a result of changes in knowledge and attitude. In fact, there are four levels of change in people: (1) knowledge changes, (2) attitudinal changes, (3) behavior changes and (4) group or organizational performance changes.[4] The time relationship and relative difficulty involved in making each of these levels of change are illustrated in Figure 3.

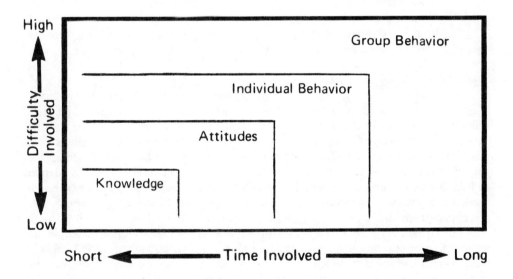

Figure 3. Time and difficulty involved in making various changes.

Changes in knowledge tend to be easiest to make; all one has to do is give a person a book or article to read, or have someone whom he respects tell him something new. Attitude structures differ from knowledge structures in that they are emotionally charged in a positive or negative way. The addition of emotion often makes attitudes more difficult to change than knowledge.

Changes in individual behavior seem to be significantly more difficult and time consuming than either of the two previous levels. For example, a person may have knowledge about the potential dangers of smoking, even actually feel that smoking is a bad habit he would like to change and still be unable to stop smoking because a habit pattern has been reinforced over a long period of time. It is important to point out that we are talking about change in patterned behavior and not a single event. In our example, anyone can quit smoking for a short period of time; the real test comes months later to see if a new long term pattern has evolved.

While individual behavior is difficult enough to change, when we get to the implementation of group or organizational performance, it is compounded because at this level we are concerned with changing customs, mores and traditions. Being a group, it tends to be a self-reinforcing unit and therefore a person's behavior as a member of a group is more difficult to modify without first changing the group norms.[5]

The Change Cycles

The levels of change become very significant when we examine two different change cycles—the participative change cycle and the coerced change cycle.

Participative Change

A participative change cycle is implemented when new knowledge is made available to the individual or group. It is hoped that the group will accept the data and will develop a positive attitude and commitment in the direction of the desired change. At this level the strategy may be direct participation by the individual or group in helping to select or formalize the goals or new methods for obtaining the goals. This is group participation in problem-solving. The next step is to attempt to translate this commitment into actual behavior. This tends to be the real tough barrier to overcome. For example, it is one thing to be concerned (attitude) about a social problem but another thing to be willing to actually get involved in doing something (behavior) about the problem. One strategy that is often useful is to attempt to identify informal as well as formal leaders within the group and concentrate on gaining their acceptance and behavior. Once this is accomplished you have moved a long way in getting others in the group to begin to pattern their behavior after those persons whom they respect and perceive in leadership roles. This participative change cycle is illustrated in Figure 4.

Coerced Change

We've all probably been faced with a situation similar to one in which there is an announcement on Monday morning that "as of today all members of this organization shall begin to operate in accordance with Form 10125." This is an example of a coerced change cycle. This cycle begins by imposing change on the total organization. This will tend to affect the interaction—influence system at the individual level. The new contacts and modes of behavior create new knowledge

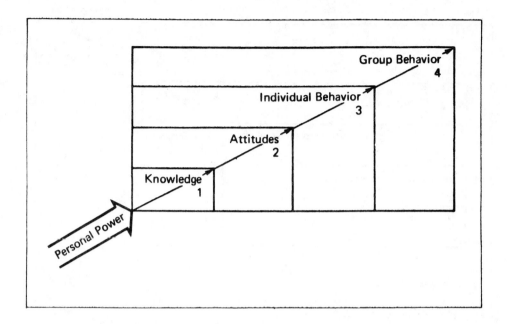

Figure 4. Participative change cycle.

which tend to develop predispositions toward or against the change. The coerced change cycle is illustrated in Figure 5.

The intention of this coerced change cycle is that the new behavior creates the kind of knowledge which creates commitment to the change and therefore approximates a participative change cycle as it reinforces the individual and group behavior.

Differences Between Change Cycles

The participative change cycle tends to be more appropriate for working with mature groups since they tend to be achievement-motivated and have a degree of knowledge and experience that may be useful in developing new strategies for accomplishing goals.[6] Once the change starts, mature people are much more capable of assuming responsibilities for implementation. On the other hand, with immature people the coerced change cycle might be more productive because they are often dependent and not willing to take new responsibilities unless forced to do so. In fact, by their very nature, these people might prefer direction and structure to being faced with decisions that might be frightening to them.

There are some other significant differences between these two change cycles. The participative change cycle tends to be effective when induced by leaders with personal power, while the coerced cycle necessitates significant position power—rewards, punishments and sanctions.

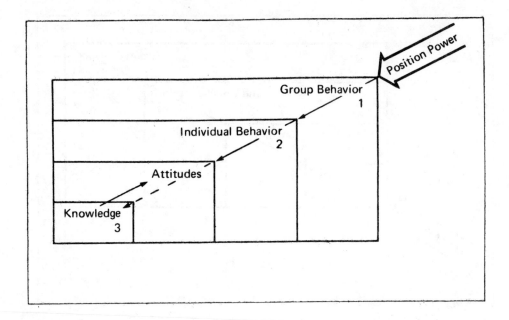

Figure 5. Coerced change cycle.

With the participative cycle, the main advantage is that once accepted it tends to be long-lasting, since the people are nighly committed to the change. Its disadvantage is that it tends to be slow and evolutionary. On the other hand, the advantage of the coerced cycle is speed. Using his position power, the leader can often impose change immediately. The disadvantage of this cycle is that it tends to be volatile. It can only be maintained as long as the leader has position power to make it stick. It often results in animosity, hostility and in some cases overt and covert behavior to undermine and overthrow.

These cycles have been described as if they were either/or positions. In reality, it is more a question of the proper blend of each, depending upon the situation.

Part Two: Change Through Behavior Modification

Rensis Likert found that employee-centered supervisors who use general supervision tend to have higher producing sections than job-centered supervisors who use close supervision.[7] We underline the word "tend" because this seems to be high probability in our society, yet we also must realize there are exceptions to this tendency which are even evident in Likert's data. What Likert found was that a subordinate generally responds well to a superior's high expectations and genuine confidence in him and tries to justify his boss's expectations of him. His resulting high performance will reinforce his superior's high trust for him, for it is easy to trust and respect the man who meets or exceeds your expectations. This occurrence could be called the effective cycle.

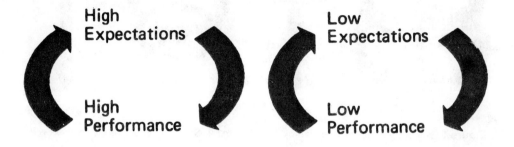

Figure 1. Effective cycle.   **Figure 2.** Ineffective cycle.

Yet, since top management often promotes on the basis of short run output alone, managers tend to overemphasize task accomplishment, placing extreme pressure on everyone to achieve high levels of productivity. This task-oriented leader behavior style, in some cases, does not allow much room for a trusting relationship with employees. Instead, subordinates are told what to do and how to do it. With little consideration, subordinates respond with minimal effort and resentment; low performance results in these instances. Reinforced by low expectations, it becomes a vicious cycle. Many other examples could be given which result in this all too common problem in organizations as shown in Figure 2.

These cycles are depicted as static but in reality they are very dynamic. The situation tends to get better or worse. For example, high expectations result in high performance, which reinforces the high expectations and produces even higher productivity. It almost becomes a spiral effect as illustrated in Figure 3.

In many cases, this spiraling effect is caused by an increase in leverage created through the use of what Frederick Herzberg calls "motivators."[8] In analyzing the data from his research, Herzberg concluded that man has two different categories of needs which are essentially independent of each other and affect behavior in different ways. He found that when people felt dissatisfied about their jobs, they were concerned about the environment in which they were working. On the other hand, when people felt good about their jobs, this had to do with the work itself. Herzberg called the first category of needs *hygiene factors* because they describe man's environment and serve the primary function of preventing job dissatisfaction. He called the second category of needs *motivators* since they seemed to be effective in motivating people to superior performance.

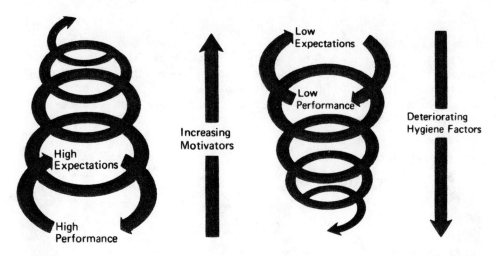

Figure 3. Spiraling effect of effective cycle.   **Figure 4.** Spiraling effect of ineffective cycle.

Company policies and administration, supervision, working conditions, interpersonal relations, money, status and security may be thought of as hygiene factors. There are not an intrinsic part of a job, but are related to the conditions under which a job is performed. Herzberg relates his use of the word "hygiene" to its medical meaning (preventative and environmental). Hygiene factors produce no growth in worker output capacity; they only prevent losses in worker performance due to work restriction.

Satisfying factors that involve feelings of achievement, professional growth and recognition that one can experience in a job which offers challenge and scope are referred to as motivators. Herzberg used this term because these factors seem capable of having a positive effect on job satisfaction often resulting in an increase in one's total output capacity. In terms of the upward spiraling effect, as people perform they are given more responsibility and opportunities for achievement and growth and development, which results in higher productivity and continued high expectations.

Ineffective Cycle

This spiraling effect can also occur in a downward direction as shown in Figure 4. Low expectations result in low performance, which reinforces the low expectations and produces even lower productivity. It becomes a spiral effect like a whirlpool as shown in Figure 4.

If this downward spiraling continues long enough, the cycle may reach a point where it cannot be turned around in a short period of time because of the large reservoir of negative past experience which has built up in the organization. Much of the focus and energy is directed toward the perceived problems with hygiene factors rather than the work itself. This takes such form as hostility, undermining and slow-down in work performance. When this happens, even if a manager actually changes his behavior, the credibility gap based on long-term experience is such that the response is still distrust and skepticism rather than change.

Style Change

One alternative that is sometimes necessary at this juncture is to bring in a new manager from the outside. The reason this has a higher probability of success is that the sum of the past experience of the people involved with the new manager is likened to a "clean slate," and thus different behaviors are on a much more believable basis. This was vividly illustrated by Robert H. Guest in a case analysis of organizational change.[9] He examined a large assembly plant of an automobile company, Plant Y, and contrasts the situation under two different leaders.

Under Mr. Stewart, plant manager, working relationships at Plant Y were dominated by hostility and mistrust. His high task style was characterized by a continual attempt to increase the driving forces pushing for productivity. As a result, the prevailing atmosphere was that of one emergency following on the heels of another, and the governing motivation for employee activity was fear—fear of being "chewed out" right on the assembly line, fear of being held responsible for happenings in which one had no clear authority, fear of losing one's job. Consequently, of the six plants in this division of the corporation, Plant Y had the poorest performance record, and it was getting worse.

Mr. Stewart was replaced by Mr. Cooley, who seemed like a truly effective leader. Three years later, dramatic changes had occurred. In various cost and performance measures used to rate the six plants, Plant Y was now truly the leader; and the atmosphere of interpersonal cooperation and personal satisfaction had improved impressively over the situation under Stewart. These changes, moreover, were effected through an insignificant number of dismissals and reassignments. Using a much higher relationships style, Cooley succeeded in "turning Plant Y around."

Expectations Change

On the surface, the big difference was style of leadership. Cooley was a good leader. Stewart wasn't. But Guest points out clearly in his analysis that leadership style was only one of two important factors. "The other was that while Stewart received daily orders from division headquarters to correct specific situations, Cooley was left alone. Cooley was allowed to lead; Stewart was told how to lead."[10] In other words, when productivity in Plant Y began to decline during changeover from wartime to peacetime operations. Stewart's superiors expected him to get productivity back on the upswing by taking control of the reins and they put tremendous pressure on him to do just that. Guest suggests that these expectations forced Stewart to operate in a very crisis-oriented, autocratic way. However, when Cooley was given charge as plant manager, a "hands off" policy was initiated by his superiors. The fact that the expectations of top management had changed enough to put a moratorium on random, troublesome outside stimuli from headquarters gave Cooley an opportunity to operate in a completely different style. One could raise the question, what might have happened if instead of hiring Cooley, top management had given Stewart this same kind of support and "free hand"? Could he have turned the plant around like Cooley did? Probably not. The ineffective cycle seemed to have been in a downward spiral far past the point where Stewart would have had a good opportunity to make significant change. But with the introduction of a new manager with whom the employees had no past experience, now-significant changes were possible.

While a new manager may be in a better position to initiate change in a situation which has been spiraling downward, he still does not have an easy task. Essentially, he has to break the ineffective cycle. There are at least two alternatives available to him. He can either fire the low performing personnel and hire people who he expects to perform well or respond to low performance with high expectations and trust.

The latter choice for the manager is difficult. In effect, the attempt is to change the expectations or behavior of his subordinates. It is especially difficult for a manager to have high expectations about people who have shown no indication that they deserve to be trusted. The key, then, is to change appropriately. This is where the concepts of behavior modification might be helpful.

Behavior Modification

In the normal work environment, managers feel that either close supervision and pressure (task-oriented behavior) or consideration and trust (relationship-oriented behavior) are the only ways to focus a subordinate on his task or change patterns of behavior. They use these methods even when they prove unsuccessful, because they are often unaware of better techniques. At one time, managers were too structured, rigid and punishing. Now there seems to be a swing to the overly trusting, unstructured manager. Both these strategies when inappropriate have created problems. Another alternative is behavior modification,[11] which can provide a strategy for shifting leadership style appropriately to stimulate changes in maturity. In order to illustrate the differences between these three strategies—task behavior, relationships behavior and behavior modifications—we can compare how a manager using each might handle a potential problem-worker.

Tony, a new employee right out of high school, is a very aggressive, competitive individual. During his first day on the job, he argues over tools with another young employee. Table I attempts to illustrate the possible reactions of a high task manager, a high relationships manager and a manager using behavior modification techniques.

Behavior modification (often referred to as operant conditioning or reinforcement theory) is based upon *deserved* behavior and not internal psychological feelings or attitudes.[12] Its basic premise is that *behavior is controlled by its immediate consequences*. Any behavior will be made stronger or weaker by what happens immediately after it occurs. If what happens is positive, it tends to increase the frequency of that behavior occurring again. Positive reinforcement is anything that is rewarding to the individual being reinforced. Reinforcement, therefore, depends on the individual. What is reinforcing to one person may not be reinforcing to another. Money might motivate some people to work harder, but to others money is not a high strength need; the challenge of the job might be the most rewarding incentive. Managers must look for unique differences in their people and recognize the dangers of generalizing.

Positive Reinforcement

In order for a desirable behavior to be obtained, the slightest positive behavior exhibited by the individual in that direction must be rewarded as soon as possible. This is called reinforcing positively successive approximations toward a goal. For example, when an individual's performance is low, one cannot expect drastic changes over night, regardless of changes in expectations or other incentives. Similar to the child learning some new behavior, we do not expect high levels of performance at the outset. So, as a parent or teacher, we would use *positive reinforcement* as the child's behavior approaches the desired level of performance. Therefore, the manager must be aware of any progress of his subordinate, so he is in a position to reinforce appropriately this change.

This is compatible with the concept of setting interim rather than final goals and then reinforcing appropriate progress toward the final goal as interim goals are accomplished. In this process, the role of a manager is not always setting goals for his followers. Instead, effectiveness may be increased by providing an environment where subordinates can play a role in setting their own goals. Research indicates that commitment increases when a person is involved in his own goal setting. If an individual is involved, he will tend to engage in much more goal-directed activity before he becomes frustrated and gives up. On the other hand, if the boss sets the goal for him, he is apt to give up more easily because he perceives these as his boss's goals and not as his own. Goals should be set high enough so a person has to stretch to reach them but low enough so that they can be attained.

So often final goals are set and the person is judged only in terms of success in relation to this terminal goal. Suppose, in our example, the manager had expected Tony to become a "perfect" employee overnight. Suppose after the first week Tony is better but still causes some problems. The result is usually the manager reprimanding him (punishment) even though he has shown improvement. If this reprimanding continues to occur, there is a high probability that Tony may stop trying. His behavior, rather than improving, may become worse. An alternative for the manager is setting interim realistic goals which move in the direction of the final goals as they are attained. Then with a change in the desired direction, even though only moderate, positive reinforcement may be used rather than some form of punishment.

Negative Reinforcement

While positive reinforcement tends to be more effective in working with people, experiencing some unpleasant consequences or *negative reinforcement* can sometimes

TABLE 1
DIFFERENT APPROACHES USED IN DEALING WITH A DISRUPTIVE WORKER

	HIGH TASK MANAGER	HIGH RELATIONSHIPS MANAGER	BEHAVIOR MODIFICATION MANAGER
Manager Reaction	"This worker is going to be a trouble-maker. This behavior must be stopped!"	"Oh dear, I hope I can get them interacting and happy."	"Feels Tony needs to learn to cope in positive ways to replace aggressive behavior!" Separates conflicting workers without hostility or comment.
Supervisor Subordinate Interaction	"Hey, you. Knock it off! We don't allow fighting around here," said with coldness or anger.	"How would you both like to give me a hand on a job over here."	Manager watches for any positive behavior he can immediately reinforce. Supervisor sets limits on some behavior and carefully ignores others.
Worker Reaction	Tony builds resentment and hostility. Next few days, behavior becomes more aggressive.	Tony finds he can get attention of supervisor by being disruptive because the supervisor wants to be "understanding." He causes trouble and watches supervisor's reaction. Supervisor pays more and more attention as his behavior gets worse. Disruptive behavior reinforced.	Tony finds the supervisor appreciates good things about him. Wants to gain his respect. Supervisor Strategy: 1. Watches for any occurrences of positive behavior to reinforce. 2. Decides which new behaviors Tony needs to learn first. 3. Plans strategy to get desired behavior. 4. Attempts to better understand Tony in an effort to use incentives appropriate for his need structure. 5. Uses the incentives to reinforce behavior Tony needs to learn. 6. Continues to evaluate to make sure incentives are still appropriate since these tend to change with time.
Outcome	Tony feels disliked by supervisor. Self-image deteriorates as he attempts to defend ego from assaults. Becomes more hostile and aggressive or withdrawn. Avoids supervisor and learning tasks.	Aggressiveness remains. Becomes more obnoxious as other workers withdraw. Creates incidents to get attention and assigned to those jobs he wants. Does not learn. No friends. Low self-image covered by bravado.	Outcome in two or three weeks. Tony's work and acceptance by other members of his work group continue to improve. Builds new self-image on basis of new behavior he has learned. Hostile and aggressive behavior toward other employees stops. Begins to have a sense of accomplishment. Inner needs and feelings start to change. Aggressiveness used in constructive ways. Has friends and becomes a positive rather than a disruptive influence on his work group.

strengthen a particular behavior. For example, suppose a manager reprimands Al, one of his subordinates, for sloppy work, rather than giving him his usual "praise." If Al becomes just anxious enough, finds out what he did wrong, then does it right and gets his boss's praise, the unpleasantness of the reprimand becomes a negative "reinforcer." In this case, the manager was not just trying to punish Al because he wanted to make him feel badly but was giving him negative feedback because he wanted him to do better. Al responded as he had hoped he would, giving the manager a chance to use positive reinforcement with him again.

A leader or manager has to be careful in using negative reinforcement or punishment because he does not always know what he is reinforcing in a person when he uses these methods. He might be reinforcing lying, manipulation or all kinds of undesirable behavior because the individuals involved may use these behaviors, rather than improved performance, to eliminate punishment or further negative reinforcement. Another possible reaction to punishment is that the individual may begin to use avoidance behaviors such as attempting to eliminate communications and interactions between himself and the person who makes him feel threatened.

Extinction

Another way to respond to behavior besides positive or negative reinforcement is to not reinforce it at all. This is called *extinction* because it tends to get rid of a behavior. For example, suppose a worker is disruptive to get the attention of his supervisor. What would happen if his supervisor paid no attention to him? After engaging in this behavior on several occasions without accomplishing anything, he soon would be trying other behaviors.

People do not tend to continue doing things that do not provide positive reinforcement. This is even true sometimes when they are behaving well. Parents often get into this situation when they tend to pay attention to their children only when they are behaving poorly. When children are behaving appropriately adults may pay little or no attention to them, which in a sense could put that behavior on extinction. If a child wants attention from his parents (it is rewarding to him), he may be willing to endure what the parent thinks is punishment for that attention. In the long run the parents might be reinforcing the very behavior they don't want and extinguishing more appropriate behavior.

Psychotherapy Not Appropriate

Behavior modification seems like a useful tool for practitioners since it can be applied, to some extent, in most environments. Therefore, it has relevance for most people interested in accomplishing goals through others. This was not the case with psychotherapy. This process was based upon the assumption that to change behavior one had to first start with the feelings and attitudes within an individual.

The problem with psychotherapy from a practitioner's viewpoint is that it is too expensive and is appropriate for use only by trained professionals. This is true because the emphasis in psychotherapy is on analyzing the reasons underlying behavior which often requires extensive probing into the early experiences in the life of an individual. Behavior modification, on the other hand, is not as complex since it concentrates on observed behavior using goals or rewards outside the individual to modify behavior.

Part Three: Planning and Implementing Change

In evaluating effectiveness, perhaps more than 90 per cent of managers in organizations look at measures of output alone. Thus, the effectiveness of a business manager is often determined by net profits, the effectiveness of a college professor may be determined by the number of articles and books he has published, and the effectiveness of an athletic coach may be determined by his won-lost record.

Others feel that it is unrealistic to think only in terms of productivity or output in evaluating effectiveness. According to Rensis Likert,[13] another set of variables should be taken into consideration in determining effectiveness. These are *intervening variables* which reflect the current condition of the human resources in an organization and are represented in its skills, loyalty, commitment to objectives, motivations, communications, decision-making and capacity for effective interaction. These intervening variables are concerned with building and developing the organization and tend to be long-term considerations. Managers are often promoted, however, on the basis of short-run output variables such as increased production and earnings, without concern for the long-run and organizational development. This creates a dilemma.

Organizational Dilemma

One of the major problems in industry today is that there is a shortage of successful managers. Therefore, it is not uncommon for a manager to be promoted in six months or a year if he is a "producer." Let's look at the example of Mr. X, a manager who realizes that the basis on which top management promotes is often short-run output, and therefore attempts to achieve high levels of productivity by over-emphasizing task accomplishment and placing extreme pressure on everyone, even when it is inappropriate.

The immediate or short-run effect of Mr. X's behavior will probably be increased productivity. Yet if his task-oriented style is inappropriate for those involved, and if it continues over a long period, the morale and climate of the organization will deteriorate. Some indications of deterioration resulting from these intervening variables may be turnover, absenteeism, increased accidents, scrap loss and numerous grievances. Not only the number of grievances, but the nature of grievances is important. Are grievances really significant problems or do they reflect pent-up emotions due to anxieties and frustration? Are they settled at the complaint stage between the employee and supervisor or are they pushed up the hierarchy to be settled at higher levels or by arbitration? The organizational dilemma is that in many instances a manager like Mr. X, who places pressure on everyone and produces in the short run, is promoted out of this situation before the disruptive aspects of the intervening variables catch up.

Time Lag

There tends to be a time lag between declining intervening variables and significant restriction of output by employees under such management climate. Employees tend to feel "things will get better." Thus, when Mr. X is promoted rapidly, he often stays "one step ahead of the wolf."

The real problem is faced by the next manager, Mr. Y. Although productivity records are high, he has inherited many problems. Merely the introduction of a new manager may be enough to collapse the slowly deteriorating intervening variables. A tremendous drop in morale and motivation leading almost immediately to significant decrease in output can occur. Change by its very nature is frightening; to a group whose intervening variables are declining, it can be devastating.

Regardless of Mr. Y's style, the present expectations of the followers may be so distorted, that much time and patience will be needed to close the now apparent "credibility gap" between the goals of the organization and the personal goals of the group. No matter how effective Mr. Y might be in the long run, his superiors, in reviewing a productivity drop, may give him only a few months to improve performance. But as Likert's studies indicate, rebuilding a group's intervening variables in a small organization may take one to three years, and in a large organization, may extend to seven years.

Short and Long Term

It should be made clear that the choice for a manager is not whether to concentrate on output or intervening variables but often a matter of how much emphasis to place on each. The decision is between short- and long-range goals. If the accepted goal is building and developing an organization for the future, then the manager should be evaluated on these terms and not entirely on his present productivity.

While intervening variables do not appear on balance sheets, sales reports or accounting ledgers, we feel that these long-term considerations can be just as important to an organization as short-term output variables. Therefore, although difficult to measure, intervening variables should not be overlooked in determining organizational effectiveness.

In summary, we feel that effectiveness is actually determined by whatever the manager and the organization decide are their goals and objectives, but should consider these factors: output variables, intervening variables, short-range goals and long-range goals.

Force Field Analysis

Force field analysis, a technique for diagnosing situations developed by Kurt Lewin, may be useful in looking at the variables involved in determining effectiveness and in developing strategies for changing in particular the condition of the output or intervening variables.[14]

Lewin assumes that in any situation there are both driving and restraining forces which influence any change which may occur. *Driving forces* are those forces affecting a situation which are "pushing" in a particular direction; they tend to initiate a change and keep it going. In terms of improving productivity in a work group, pressure from a supervisor, incentive earnings and competition may be examples of driving forces. *Restraining forces* are forces acting to restrain or decrease the driving forces. Apathy, hostility and poor maintenance of equipment may be examples of restraining forces against increased production. Equilibrium is reached when the sum of the driving forces equals the sum of the restraining forces. In our example, equilibrium represents the present level of productivity as shown in Figure 1.

This equilibrium or present level of productivity can be raised or lowered by changes in the relationship between the driving and restraining forces. For illustrations, let us look again at the dilemma of Mr. Y, the new manager who takes over a work group where productivity is high but Mr. X, his predecessor, drained the human resources (intervening variables). Mr. X had upset the equilibrium by increasing the driving forces (i.e., being autocratic and keeping continual pressure on his men) and thus achieving increases in output in the short run. By doing this though, new restraining forces developed, such as increased hostility and antagonism, and at the time of his departure the restraining forces were beginning to increase and the results manifested themselves in turnover, absenteeism and other restraining forces which lowered productivity shortly after Mr. Y arrived. Now a new equilibrium at a significantly lowered productivity is faced by the new manager.

Now just assume that Mr. Y decides not to increase the driving forces, but to reduce the restraining forces. He may do this by taking time away from the usual production operation and engaging in problem-solving and training and development. In the short run, output will tend to be lowered still further. However, if commitment to objectives and technical know-how of his group are increased in the long run, they may become new driving forces, and that, along with the elimination of the hostility and apathy which were restraining forces, will now tend to move the balance to a higher level of output.

A manager, in attempting to implement change, is often in a position where he must consider not only output but also intervening variables, not only short-term but also long-term goals, and a framework which is useful in diagnosing these interrelationships is available through force field analysis.

Process of Change

In developing a change strategy, another important aspect that must be taken into consideration is the process of change. Kurt Lewin, in his pioneer work in

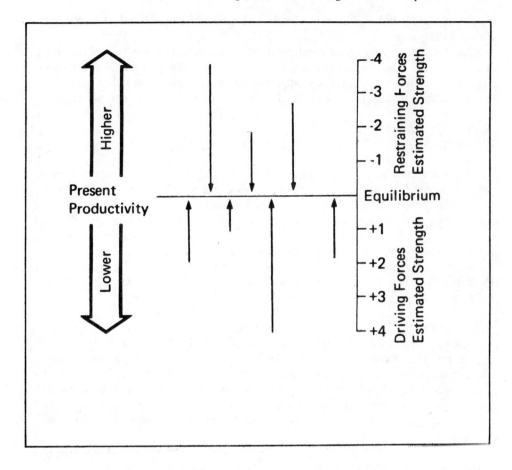

Figure 1. Driving and restraining forces in equilibrium.

change, identified three phases of the change process.[15] These are unfreezing, changing and refreezing.

Unfreezing

The aim of unfreezing is to motivate and make the individual or group ready to change. It is a "thawing out" process where the forces acting on an individual are rearranged so now he sees the need for change. According to Edgar H. Schein, some elements that unfreezing situations seem to have in common are: (1) the physical removal of the individual being changed from his accustomed routines, sources of information and social relationships; (2) the undermining and destruction of all social supports; (3) demeaning and humiliating experience to help the individual being changed to see his old self as unworthy and thus to be motivated to change;

(4) the consistent linking of reward with willingness to change and of punishment with unwillingness to change.[16]

In brief, unfreezing is the breaking down of the mores, customs, and traditions of an individual—the old ways of doing things—so he is ready to accept new alternatives. In terms of force field analysis, unfreezing may occur when either the driving forces are increased or the restraining forces that are resisting change are reduced.

Changing

Once the individual has become motivated to change, he is now ready to be provided with new patterns of behavior. This process is most likely to occur by one of two mechanisms: identification and internalization.[17] *Identification* occurs when one or more models are provided in the environment from whom an individual can learn new behavior patterns by identifying with them and trying to become like them. *Internalization* occurs when an individual is placed in a situation where new behaviors are demanded of him if he is to operate successfully in that situation. He learns these new behavior patterns not only because they are necessary to survive but as a result of new high strength needs induced by coping behavior.

> Internalization is a more common outcome in those influence settings where the direction of change is left more to the individual. The influence which occurs in programs such as Alcoholics Anonymous, in psychotherapy or counseling for hospitalized or incarcerated populations, in religious retreats, in human relations training of the kind pursued by the National Training Laboratories (1953), and in certain kinds of progressive education programs is more likely to occur through internalization or, at least, to lead ultimately to more internalization.[18]

Identification and internalization are not either/or courses of action and effective change is often the result of combining the two into a strategy for change.

Force or compliance is sometimes discussed as another mechanism for inducing change.[19] It occurs when an individual is forced to change by the direct manipulation of rewards and punishment by someone in a power position. In this case, behavior appears to have changed when the change agent is present, but often is dropped when supervision is removed. Thus, rather than discussing force as a mechanism of changing, we would rather think of it as a tool for unfreezing.

Refreezing

The process by which the newly-acquire behavior comes to be integrated as patterned behavior into the individual's personality and/or ongoing significant emotional relationships is referred to as *refreezing*. As Schein contends, if the new behavior has been internalized while being learned, "this has automatically facilitated refreezing because it has been fitted naturally into the individual's personality. If it has been learned through identification, it will persist only so long as the target's relationship with the original influence model persists unless new surrogate models are found or social support and reinforcement is obtained for expressions of the new attitudes.''[20]

This highlights how important it is for an individual engaged in a change process to be in an environment which is continually reinforcing the desired change. The effect of many a training program has been short-lived when the person returns to an environment that does not reinforce the new patterns or, even worse, is hostile toward them.

What we are concerned about in refreezing is that the new behavior does not get extinguished over time. To insure this not happening, reinforcement (rewards and incentives) must be scheduled in an effective way. There seem to be two main reinforcement schedules: continuous and intermittent.[21] Continuous reinforcement means that the individual being changed is rewarded every time he engages in the desired new pattern. With intermittent reinforcement on the other hand, not every desired response is reinforced. Reinforcement can be either completely random or scheduled according to a prescribed number of responses occurring or a particular interval of time elapsing before reinforcement is given.

With continuous reinforcement, the individual learns the new behavior quickly, but if his environment changes to one of nonreinforcement, extinction (elimination of the behavior) can be expected to take place relatively soon. With intermittent reinforcement, extinction is much slower because the individual has been conditioned to go for periods of time without any reinforcement. Thus for fast learning, a continuous reinforcement schedule should be used. But once the individual has learned the new pattern, a switch to intermittent reinforcement should insure a long lasting change.

Change Process—Some Examples

To see the change process in operation, several examples could be cited.

A college basketball coach recruited for his team Bob Anderson, a 6' 4'' center from a small town in a rural area. In his district, 6' 4'' was good height for a center. This fact, combined with his deadly turn-around-jump shot, made Anderson the rage of his league and enabled him to average close to 30 points a game.

Recognizing that 6' 4'' is small for a college center, the coach hoped that he could make Anderson a forward, moving him inside only when they were playing a double pivot. One of the things the coach was concerned about, however, was when Anderson would be used in the pivot, how he could get his jump shot off when he came up against other players ranging in height from 6' 8'' to 7'. He felt that Anderson would have to learn to shoot a hook shot, which is much harder to block, if he was going to have scoring potential against this kind of competition.

The approach that many coaches use to solve this problem would probably be as follows: The first day of practice when Anderson arrived, the coach would welcome Anderson and then explain the problem to him as he had analyzed it. As a solution he would probably ask Anderson to start to work with the varsity center, Steve Cram, who was 6' 10'' and had an excellent hook. ''Steve can help you start working on that new shot, Bob,'' the coach would say. Anderson's reaction to this interchange might be one of resentment and he would go over and work with Cram only because of the coach's position power. After all, he might think to himself, "Who does he think he is? I've been averaging close to 30 points a game for three years now and the first day I show up here the coach wants me to learn a new shot." So he may start to work with Cram reluctantly, concentrating on the hook shot only when the coach is looking but taking his favorite jump shot when he wasn't being observed. Anderson is by no means unfrozen or ready to learn to shoot another way.

Another Approach

Let's look at another approach the coach could have used to solve this problem. Suppose on the first day of practice he sets up a scrimmage between the varsity and freshmen. Before he starts the scrimmage he gets big Steve Cram, the varsity center, aside and tells him, "Steve, we have this new freshman named Anderson who has real potential to be a fine ball player. What I'd like you to do today though, is not to worry about scoring or rebounding, just make sure every time Anderson goes up for a shot you make him eat it. I want him to see that he will have to learn to shoot some other shots if he is to survive against guys like you."

So when the scrimmage starts, the first time Anderson gets the ball and turns around to shoot Cram leaps up and "stuffs the ball right down his throat." Time after time this occurs. Soon Anderson starts to engage in some coping behavior, trying to fall away from the basket, shooting from the side of his head rather than the front, in an attempt to get his shot off.

After the scrimmage, Anderson comes off the court dejected. The coach says, "What's wrong Bob?" He replies, "I don't know, Coach, I just can't seem to get my shot off against a man as big as Cram. What do you think I should do, Coach?" he asks. "Well, Bob, why don't you go over and start working with Steve on a hook shot. I think you'll find it much harder to block. And with your shooting eye I don't think it will take long for you to learn." How do you think Anderson feels about working with Cram now? He's enthusiastic and ready to learn. Having been placed in a situation where he learns for himself that he has a problem, Anderson is already in the process of unfreezing his past patterns of behavior. Now he's ready for identification. He has had an opportunity to internalize his problem and is ready to work with Steve Cram.

So often the leader who has knowledge of an existing problem forgets that until the people involved recognize the problem as their own, it is going to be much more difficult to produce change in their behavior. Internalization and identification are not either/or alternatives but can be parts of developing specific change strategies appropriate to the situation.

The Military Example

Another example of the change processes in operation can be seen in the military, particularly in the induction phase. There are probably few organizations that have entering their ranks people who are less motivated and committed to the organization than the recruits the military gets. Yet in a few short months, they are able to mold these men into a relatively effective combat team. This is not an accident. Let's look at some of the processes that help accomplish this.

The most dramatic and harsh aspects of the training are the unfreezing phase. All four of the elements that Schein claims unfreezing situations have in common are present. A specific example follows.

(1) The recruits are *physically removed from their accustomed routines, sources of information and social relationships* in the isolation of a place such as Parris Island.

> During this first week of training at Parris Island, the recruit is . . . hermetically sealed in a hostile environment, required to rise at 4:55 a.m., do exhausting exercises, attend classes on strange subjects, drill for hours in the hot sun, eat meals in silence and stand at rigid attention the rest of the time; he has no television, no radio, no candy, no coke, no beer, no telephone—and can write letters only during one hour of free time a day.[22]

(2) *The undermining and destruction of social supports* is one of the DI's (Drill Instructor) tasks. "Using their voices and the threat of extra PT (physical training), the DI . . . must shock the recruit out of the emotional stability of home, pool hall, street corner, girl friend or school."[23]

(3) *Demeaning and humiliating experiences* are commonplace during the first two weeks of the training as the DI's help the recruits *see themselves as unworthy and thus motivated to change* into what they want a Marine to be. "It's a total shock . . . Carrying full seabags, 80 terrified privates are herded into their 'barn,' a barracks floor with 40 double-decker bunks. Sixteen hours a day, for two weeks, they will do nothing right."[24]

(4) Throughout the training there is *consistent linking of reward with willingness to change and punishment with unwillingness to change.*

> Rebels or laggards are sent to the Motivation Platoon to get "squared away." A day at Motivation combines constant harrassment and PT (physical training), ending the day with the infiltration course. This hot, 225-yard ordeal of crawling, jumping and screaming through ditches and obstacles is climaxed by the recruits dragging two 30-pound ammo boxes 60 yards in mud and water. If he falters he starts again. At the end, the privates are lined up and asked if they are ready to go back to their home platoons . . . almost all go back for good.[25]

While the recruits go through a severe unfreezing process, they quickly move to the changing phase, first identifying with the DI and then emulating informal leaders, as they develop. "Toward the end of the third week a break occurs. What one DI calls 'that five per cent—the slow fat, dumb or difficult' have been dropped. The remaining recruits have emerged from their first-week vacuum with one passionate desire—to stay with their platoon at all costs."[26]

Internalization takes place when the recruits through their forced interactions develop different high strength needs. "Fear of the DI gives way to respect, and survival evolves into achievement toward the end of training." "I learned I had more guts than I imagined" is a typical comment.[27]

Since the group tends to stay together throughout the entire program, it serves as a positive reinforcer which can help refreeze the new behavior.

Impact of Change on Total System

The focus in [this three-part] article has been on the management of human resources and as a result we have spent little time on how technical change can have an impact on the total system. And yet, the importance of combining the social and technical into a unified social systems concept is stressed by Robert Guest.

On his part the social scientist often makes the error of concentrating on human motivation and group behavior without fully accounting for the technical environment which circumscribes, even determines, the roles which the actors play. Motivation, group structure, interaction processes, authority—none of these abstractions of behavior take place in a technological vacuum.[28]

A dramatic example of the consequences of introducing technical change and ignoring its consequences on the social system is the case of the introduction of the steel axe to a group of Australian aborigines.[29]

This tribe remained considerably isolated, both geographically and socially, from the influence of Western cultures. In fact, their only contact was an Anglican mission established in the adjacent territory.

The polished stone axe was a traditionally basic part of the tribe's technology. Used by men, women and children, the stone axe was vital to the subsistence economy. But more than that, it was actually a key to the smooth running of the social system; it defined interpersonal relationships and was a symbol of masculinity and male superiority. "Only an adult male could make and own a stone axe; a woman or a child had to ask his permission to obtain one."[30]

The Anglican mission in an effort to help improve the situation of the aborigines introduced the steel axe, a product of European technology. It was given indiscriminately to men, women and children. Because the tool was more efficient than the stone axe, it was readily accepted but it produced severe repercussions unforeseen by the missionaries or the tribe. As Stephan R. Cain reports:

The adult male was unable to make the steel axe and no longer had to make the stone axe. Consequently, his exclusive axe-making ability was no longer a necessary or desirable skill, and his status as sole possessor and dispenser of a vital element of technology was lost. The most drastic overall result was that traditional values, beliefs, and attitudes were unintentionally undermined.[30]

This example illustrates that an organization is an "open social system," that is, all aspects of an organization may have an impact on other parts or the organization itself. Thus a proposed change in one part of an organization must be carefully assessed in terms of its likely impact on the rest of the organization.

Notes and References

1. Etzioni, Amitai, *A Comparative Analysis of Complex Organizations*, The Free Press of Glencoe, New York, 1961.
2. Machiavelli, Niccolo, *The Prince and the Discources*, Chapter XVII, "Of Cruelty and Clemency, Whether It Is Better to be Loved or Feared," Random House, New York, 1950.
3. Suggested by Bernard M. Bass in *Leadership, Psychology, and Organizational Behavior*, Harper & Bros., New York, 1960.
4. R. J. House discusses similar concepts in *Management Development: Design, Implementation and Evaluation*, Bureau of Industrial Relations, University of Michigan, Ann Arbor, Mich., 1967.
5. Brown, J.A.C., *The Social Psychology of Industry*, Penguin Books, Baltimore, Md., 1954, p. 249.
6. For a definition of maturity and a discussion of the relationship between leadership style and the maturity of one's followers see Paul Hersey and Kenneth H. Blanchard "Life Cycle Theory of Leadership," *Training and Development Journal*, May, 1969.
7. Likert, Rensis, *New Patterns of Management* McGraw-Hill, New York, 1961, p. 7.
8. Frederick, Herzberg, Bernard Mausner and Barbara Synderman, *The Motivation to Work*, John Wiley, New York, 1959 and Herzberg, *Work and the Nature of Man*, World Publishing Co., New York, 1966.
9. Guest, Robert H., *Organizational Change: The Effect of Successful Leadership*, Dorsey Press and Irwin Inc, Homewood, Ill., 1964.
10. Perrow, Charles, *Organizational Analysis: A Sociological View*, Wadsworth Publishing Co., Inc., Belmont, Calif., 1970, p. 12.
11. A discussion of behavior modification by Glema G. Holsinger in *Motivating the Reluctant Learner*, Motivity, Inc., Lexington, Mass., 1970, was very helpful in developing this section.
12. The most classic discussions of behavior modification or operant conditioning have been done by B. F. Skinner. See Skinner, *Science and Human Behavior*, Macmillan, New York, 1953, and *Analysis of Behavior*, McGraw-Hill, New York, 1961.
13. Likert, *op. cit.*, p. 2.
14. Lewin, Kurt, "Frontiers in Group Dynamics: Concept, Method and Reality in Social Science; Social Equilibria and Social Change," *Human Relations*, Vol. 1, No. 1, June, 1947, pp. 5-41.
15. *Ibid.*
16. Schein, Edgar H., "Management Development as a Process of Influence" in David R. Hampton, *Behavioral Concepts in Management*, Dickinson publishing Co., Belmont, Cal., 1968, p. 110. Reprinted from the *Industrial Management Review*, Vol. II, No. 2, May, 1961, pp. 59-77.
17. The mechanisms are taken from H. C. Kelman "Compliance, Identification and Internalization: Three Processes of Attitude Change," *Conflict Resolution*, 1958, II, pp. 51-60.
18. Schein, *op. cit.*, p. 112.
19. Kelman discussed compliance as a third mechanism for attitude change.
20. Schein, *op cit.*, p. 112.
21. See C. B. Ferster and B. F. Skinner, *Schedules of Reinforcement*, Appleton-Century Crofts, New York, 1957.
22. "Marine Machine," *Look Magazine*, Aug. 12, 1969.

23. *Ibid.*
24. *Ibid.*
25. *Ibid.*
26. *Ibid.*
27. *Ibid.*
28. Guest, *op. cit.* p. 4.
29. Sharp, Lauriston, "Steel Axes for Stone Age Australians," in *Human Problems in Technological Change*, ed. Edward H. Spicer, Russell Sage Foundation, New York, 1952, pp. 69-94.
30. Cain, Stephen R., "Anthropology and Change" taken from *Growth and Change*, Vol. 1, No. 3, July, 1970, University of Kentucky.
31. *Ibid.*

JOB ENRICHMENT PAYS OFF

WILLIAM J. PAUL, JR.
KEITH B. ROBERTSON
FREDERICK HERZBERG

In his pioneering article, "One More Time: How Do You Motivate Employees?" Frederick Herzberg put forward some principles of scientific job enrichment and reported a successful application of them involving the stockholder correspondents employed by a large corporation. According to him, job enrichment seeks to improve both task efficiency and human satisfaction by means of building into people's jobs, quite specifically, greater scope for personal achievement and its recognition, more challenging and responsible work, and more opportunity for individual advancement and growth. It is concerned only incidentally with matters such as pay and working conditions, organizational structure, communications, and training, important and necessary though these may be in their own right. But like a lot of pioneering work, Herzberg's study raised more questions than it answered. Some seemed to us to merit further consideration, particularly those in regard to the (1) generality of the findings, (2) feasibility of making changes, and (3) consequences to be expected. Consider:

1. *Generality*—Can similarly positive results be obtained elsewhere with other people doing different jobs? How widespread is the scope or need for equivalent change in other jobs? Can meaningful results be obtained only in jobs with large

numbers of people all doing the same work and where performance measures are easily available?

2. *Feasibility*—Are there not situations where the operational risk is so high that it would be foolhardy to attempt to pass responsibility and scope for achievement down the line? Because people's ability and sense of responsibility vary so much, is it not necessary to make changes selectively? Do all employees welcome having their jobs enriched, or are there not some who prefer things to be left as they are? Can one enrich jobs without inevitably facing demands for higher pay or better conditions to match the new responsibilities? And, in any case, is not the best route to motivational change through participation?

3. *Consequences*—In view of so many possible difficulties in the way, are the gains to be expected from job enrichment significant or only marginal? Do they relate primarily to job satisfaction or to performance? What are the consequences for supervision if jobs are loaded with new tasks taken from above—i.e., does one man's enrichment become another's impoverishment? Finally, what are the consequences for management if motivational change becomes a reality? Is the manager's role affected? If so, how? And what are the implications for management development?

There are undoubtedly more questions that could be raised and investigated. But these seem particularly important from a corporate point of view if job enrichment is to take place on a widespread basis, as part of management practice rather than as a research activity. Accordingly, the purpose of this article is to probe into the complexities of job enrichment in an attempt to shed light on these questions and to determine how the concept may be most effectively applied in furthering the attainment of corporate business objectives.

In order to do this, we shall report in Part I on five studies carried out in Imperial Chemical Industries Limited and other British companies. Two of the studies—covering laboratory technicians in an R&D department and sales representatives in three companies—will be examined in some detail. The other three—encompassing design engineers, production foremen on shift work, and engineering foremen on day work—will be summarized. In Part II, the main conclusions emerging from the studies will be presented in the form of answers to the questions raised at the beginning of this article.

Each study was initiated in response to a particular problem posed by management, and the conclusions drawn from any one can be only tentative. Among them, however, they cover not only widely different business areas and company functions, but also many types and levels of jobs. Collectively, they provide material which adds to our understanding of both theory and practice.

Part I: The Job Enrichment Studies

As in all studies on job satisfaction and performance, the need to measure results introduced certain constraints which do not exist in normal managerial situations. Consequently, three main features were common to the studies we are reporting in this discussion:

First, the "hygiene" was held constant. This means that no deliberate changes were made as part of the investigation, in matters such as pay, security, or working conditions. The studies were specifically trying to measure the extent of those gains which could be attributed solely to change in job content.

Second, recognition of the normal hygiene changes led to the need to have an "experimental group" for whom the specific changes in job content were made, and a "control group" whose job content remained the same.

Third, the studies had to be kept confidential to avoid the well-known tendency of people to behave in an artificial way when they know they are the subject of a controlled study. Naturally, there was no secret about the changes themselves, only about the fact that performance was being measured.

All studies set out to measure job satisfaction and performance for both the experimental and control groups over a trial period following the implementation of the changes. The trial period itself generally lasted a year and was never less than six months. The performance measures always were specific to the group concerned and were determined by local management of the subject company. To measure job satisfaction, we relied throughout on a job reaction survey which measures the degree of people's satisfaction with the motivators in their job as they themselves perceive them.

Laboratory Technicians

Managers in an industrial research department were concerned about the morale of laboratory technicians, or "experimental officers" (EOs). This group's job was to implement experimental programs devised by scientists. The EOs set up the appropriate apparatus, recorded data, and supervised laboratory assistants, who carried out the simpler operations. The EOs were professionally qualified people, but lacked the honors or doctorate degrees possessed by the scientists.

The average age of the experimental officers was increasing. A quarter of them had reached their salary maximums, and fewer now had the chance to move out of the department. Their normal promotion route into plant management had become blocked as manufacturing processes grew more complex and more highly qualified people filled the available jobs. Management's view of the situation was confirmed by the initial job reaction survey. Not only were the EOs' scores low, but many wrote of their frustration. They felt their technical ability and experience was being wasted by the scientists' refusal to delegate anything but routine work.

Against this background, the research manager's specific objective was to develop the EOs into "better scientists." If job enrichment was to be useful, it would have to contribute to the attainment of that goal.

Changes and Experimental Design. Here is the specific program of action devised and implemented for the experimental officers.

Technical: EOs were encouraged to write the final report, or "minute," on any research project for which they had been responsible. Such minutes carried the author's name and were issued along with those of the scientists. It was up to each EO to decide for himself whether he wanted the minute checked by his supervisor before issue, but in any case he was fully responsible for answering any query arising from it.

EOs were involved in planning projects and experiments, and were given more chance to assist in work planning and target setting.

They were given time, on request, to follow up their own ideas, even if these went beyond the planned framework of research. Written reports had to be submitted on all such work.

Financial: EOs were authorized to requisition materials and equipment, to request analysis, and to order services such as maintenance, all on their own signature.

Managerial: Senior EOs were made responsible for devising and implementing a training program for their junior staff. In doing so, they could call on facilities and advice available within the company.

Senior EOs were involved in interviewing candidates for laboratory assistant jobs, and they also acted as first assessor in any staff assessment of their own laboratory assistants.

These changes drew on all the motivators. Each one gave important chances for achievement; together, they were designed to make the work more challenging. Recognition of achievement came in the authorship of reports. Authority to order supplies and services was a responsibility applying to all the EOs involved. The new managerial responsibilities reserved to senior EOs opened up room for advancement within the job, while the technical changes, particularly the opportunity for self-initiated work, gave scope for professional growth.

Some 40 EOs in all were involved in the study. Two sections of the department acted as experimental groups (N=15) and two as control groups (N=29). One experimental and one control group worked closely together on the same type of research, and it was anticipated that there would be some interaction between them. The other two groups were separate geographically and engaged on quite different research.

The changes were implemented for the experimental groups during October and November 1966, and the trial period ran for the next twelve months. After six months, the same changes were introduced into one of the control groups, thus converting it into an experimental group (N=14). This was done to see whether a similar pattern of performance revealed itself, thereby safeguarding against any remote possibility of coincidence in the choice of the original groups.

Research work is notoriously difficult to measure, but as the aim was to encourage more scientific contribution from EOs, this was what had to be judged in as objective a way as possible. All EOs were asked to write monthly progress reports of work done. Those written by experimental and control group EOs were assessed by a panel of three managers, not members of the department, who were familiar with the research work concerned.

Reports were scored against eight specifically defined criteria thought to reflect the kind of growth being sought: *knowledge, comprehension, synthesis, evaluation, original thought, practical initiative, industry,* and *skill in report writing.* Whenever the assessor found particular evidence of one of these qualities in a report, he would award it one mark, the total score for a report being simply the sum of these marks.

In order to establish a baseline for clarifying standards and testing the assessors' consistency of marking, reports were collected for three months prior to the introduction of any job enrichment changes. The very high consistency found between the marking of the three assessors encouraged confidence in the system. The assessors, naturally, were never told which were the experimental and control groups, though it became easy for them to guess as the trial period went on.

The other main measure was to use the same system to assess research minutes written by the EOs. These were compared against an equivalent sample of minutes written by scientists over the same period, which were submitted to the panel for assessment, again without identification.

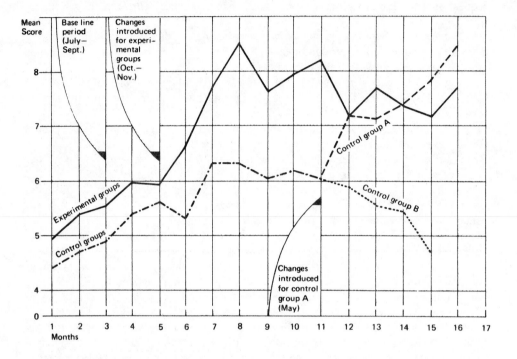

Exhibit 1. Assessment of EOs monthly reports.

Motivational Results. The assessment of monthly reports written by the experimental officers is given in Exhibit 1, which compares the mean score achieved by all experimental group EOs each month with that achieved by all control group EOs. On occasions when a monthly report had obviously suffered because of the attention devoted to writing a research minute covering much the same ground, a marginal weighting factor was added to the score depending on the quality of the minute concerned. Both experimental and control groups improved their monthly report scores at about the same rate during the first five months. There is no doubt that with practice all were getting better at report writing, and it may be that the mere fact of being asked to write monthly reports itself acted as a motivator for both groups.

Once the changes had been fully implemented in the experimental groups, however, performance began to diverge. Although the reports of the control groups continued to improve for a time, they were far outpaced by those of the experimental groups. With some fluctuations, this performance differential was maintained throughout the rest of the trial period. When, after six months, the motivators were fed into one of the two control groups, its performance improved dramatically, following the pattern achieved by the original experimental groups. Meanwhile, the performance of the other control group, unaffected by what was happening elsewhere, began to slip back toward its original starting point.

During the 12 months of the trial period, a total of 34 research minutes were written by EOs, all from the experimental groups, compared with 2 from the department as a whole during the previous 12-month period. There were also a number of minutes jointly authored by scientists and EOs, which are excluded from this analysis. Of the 34 being considered, 9 were written by EOs in the control group which was converted into an experimental group, but all came from the time after the changes had been introduced.

It is one thing for laboratory technicians to write research minutes, but whether the minutes they write are any good or not is a different matter. Exhibit 2 shows the quality of the EOs' minutes compared with that of the scientists'. The EOs' mean score was 8.7; the scientists' 9.8. All EO scores except three fell within the range of scores obtained by the scientists; the three exceptions were written by one man. Three of the EOs' minutes, one in fact written by a laboratory assistant with guidance from an EO, were judged to be as good as the best of the scientists' minutes.

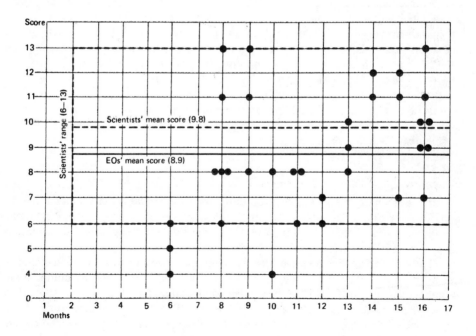

Exhibit 2. Assessment of EOs research minutes.

Encouraged by the success of a training scheme designed for laboratory assistants, the EOs initiated one for themselves. It aimed to give them the opportunity to come to terms with the ideas and terminology of chemical engineering. Managers judged it to have been of considerable value, and one EO summed it up by saying, "A couple of pages of chemical engineering calculations and formulas won't frighten us off now."

One original idea followed up, as the changes now permitted, by an EO from an experimental group resulted in an important discovery with possible applications in certain kinds of national emergency. The idea was investigated further by a government department, which described it as the most promising of some 200 ideas submitted on that topic.

Three staff assessments on EOs were carried out—at the beginning, middle, and end of the trial period. Each followed the normal company procedure. The only group which showed a consistent improvement was one of the experimental groups.

The job reaction survey was given both before and after the trial period. In the initial survey, experimental and control group EOs could not be specifically identified, and so an exact comparison of the before and after scores of each group cannot be made. The overall mean score attained by all EOs in the department was no higher at the end of the trial period than it had been at the beginning. Although managers believed there had been a positive change in job satisfaction, that is not a conclusion which can be supported with data.

An internal company report, written by the personnel officer who managed and coordinated the study throughout, concluded that there had been definite evidence of growth among the EOs, particularly in one group, and that much useful work had been accomplished during the exercise. One of the experimental groups had been able to keep abreast of its commitments even though it lost the services of two of its six scientists during the trial period and functioned without a manager for the last five months of the study. There can be little doubt that job enrichment in this case helped to further the research manager's objective of tackling a morale problem by getting at the root of the matter and developing experimental officers as scientists in their own right.

Sales Representatives

To investigate the potential of job enrichment in the sales field, work has been done in three British companies dealing with quite different products and markets, both wholesale and retail. In only one study, however, were experimental conditions strictly observed.

The company concerned had long enjoyed a healthy share of the domestic market in one particular product range, but its position was threatened by competition. A decline in market share had been stabilized before the study began, but 1967 sales still showed no improvement over those of 1966. So far as could be judged, the company's products were fully competitive in both price and quality. The critical factor in the situation appeared to be sales representatives' effort.

The representatives' salaries—they were not paid a commission—and conditions of employment were known to compare well with the average for the industry. Their mean score in the job reaction survey, like that of other groups of salesmen, was higher than most employees of equivalent seniority, which suggested that they enjoyed considerable job satisfaction.

The problem in this case, therefore, was that for the vital business objective of regaining the initiative in an important market, sustained extra effort was needed from a group of people already comparatively well treated and reasonably satisfied with their jobs. Here, job enrichment would stand or fall by the sales figures achieved.

Changes and Experimental Design. Here is the specific program of action devised and implemented for the sales representatives.

Technical: Sales representatives were no longer obliged to write reports on every customer call. They were asked simply to pass on information when they thought it appropriate or request action as they thought it was required.

Responsibility for determining calling frequencies was put wholly with the representatives themselves, who kept the only records for purposes such as staff reviews.

The technical service department agreed to provide service "on demand" from the representatives; nominated technicians regarded such calls as their first priority. Communication was by direct contact, paperwork being cleared after the event.

Financial: In cases of customer complaint about product performance, representatives were authorized to make immediate settlements of up to $250 if they were satisfied that consequential liability would not be prejudiced.

If faulty material had been delivered or if the customer was holding material for which he had no further use, the representative now had complete authority, with no upper limit in sales value, to decide how best to deal with the matter. He could buy back unwanted stock even if it was no longer on the company's selling range.

Representatives were given a discretionary range of about 10% on the prices of most products, especially those considered to be critical from the point of view of market potential. The lower limit given was often below any price previously quoted by the company. All quotations other than at list price had to be reported by the representative.

The theme of all the changes was to build the sales representative's job so that it became more complete in its own right. Instead of always having to refer back to headquarters, the representative now had the authority to make decisions on his own—he was someone the customer could really do business with. Every change implied a greater responsibility; together they gave the freedom and challenge necessary for self-development.

The company sold to many different industries, or "trades." In view of the initial effort needed to determine limit prices and to make the technical service arrangements, it was decided that the study should concentrate on three trades chosen to be typical of the business as a whole. These three trades gave a good geographical spread and covered many types of customers; each had an annual sales turnover of about $1 million.

The experimental group ($N=15$) was selected to be representative of the sales force as a whole in age range, experience, and ability. An important part of each member's selling responsibility lay within the nominated trades. The rest of the sales force ($N=23$) acted as the control group. The changes were introduced during

December 1967, and the trial period ran from January 1 to September 30, 1968.

The background of static sales and the objective of recapturing the market initiative dictated that sales turnover would be the critical measure, checked by gross margin. The difficulties of comparing unequal sales values and allowing for monthly fluctuations and seasonal trends were overcome by making all comparisons on a cumulative basis in terms of the percentage gain or loss for each group against the equivalent period of the previous year.

Since they were selling in the same trades in the same parts of the country, the performance of all the representatives was presumably influenced by the same broad economic and commercial factors. In two of the trades, the experimental group had the bigger share of the business and tended to sell to the larger customers. In these cases it may be surmised that prevailing market conditions affected the experimental group's performance, favorably or unfavorably, more than the control group's. As it happened, in one of these trades commercial trends were favorable, while in the other they were distinctly unfavorable. In the third trade, the experimental and control groups were evenly matched. Taken together, then, the three trades give as fair a comparison as can be obtained between the performances of sales representatives under those two sets of conditions.

Motivational Results. During the trial period the experimental group increased its sales by almost 19% over the same period of the previous year, a gain of over $300,000 in sales value. The control group's sales in the meantime declined by 5%. The equivalent change for both groups the previous year had been a decline of 3%. The difference in performance between the two groups is statistically significant at the 0.01 level of confidence.

Exhibit 3 shows the month-to-month performance of the two groups, plotted cumulatively. It can be seen that the control group in fact started the year extremely well, with January/February sales in the region of 30% above the equivalent 1967 figures. This improvement was not sustained, however, and by May cumulative sales had dropped below their 1967 level. By the last five months of the trial period, performance was running true to the previous year's form, showing a decline of about 3%.

The experimental group, on the other hand, started more modestly, not exceeding a 20% improvement during the first quarter. During the second quarter, outstanding results in May compensated for poorer figures in April and June. The third quarter showed a steady, if slight, rise in the rate of improvement over 1967. This sustained increase of just under 20% was in marked contrast to the previously declining performance of the trades as a whole.

Comparisons with other trades suffer from the disadvantage that different economic and commercial factors affect the various parts of the business. Nevertheless, the experimental group's performance was consistently between 6% and 7% better than that for the rest of the business. Exhibit 4 shows the month-to-month picture. It can be seen not only that the experimental group maintained a higher rate of improvement than the rest of the business throughout the trial period, but that the gap widened if anything as time went on. At the 1967 rates of turnover, this performance differential in all trades would be worth $1.5 million in sales value in a full year.

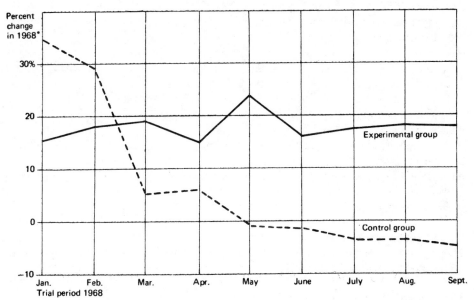

*Against corresponding 1967 period, plotted cumulatively.

Exhibit 3. Sales turnover within trades chosen as typical of the business as a whole.

In view of the greater negotiating authority granted to the experimental group representatives, it is important to check whether their substantial increase in turnover was achieved at the expense of profit. As all quotations other than at list price were reported by the representatives, it was possible to analyze the gross margin achieved by both groups. The analysis showed without doubt that the gross margin of the experimental group's sales was proportionally as high, if not higher, than that of the control group's sales.

Managers had the impression that representatives actually used their price discretion less often than they had previously asked for special prices to be quoted by the sales office. Also, in the sales manager's view, once the representatives were given real negotiating authority, they discovered that price was not the obstacle to sales which they had always imagined it to be. Under the new arrangements, they were able to assess more completely what the true obstacles to sales were in each individual case.

Over the trial period the control group's mean score in the job reaction survey remained static. In contrast, the experimental group's score rose by 11%.

Design Engineers
The engineering director of one of the divisions of ICI wanted to see whether the job of design engineer might lend itself to motivational change. His design department faced an increasing work load as more design work for the division's plants was being done internally. The situation was exacerbated by difficulties in

Exhibit 4. Sales turnover: experimental group and rest of business.

recruiting qualified design engineers. People at all levels in the department were being overloaded and development work was suffering.

Changes and Experimental Design. Here is the specific program of action devised and implemented for the design engineers.

Technical: Experienced engineers were given a completely independent role in running their projects; the less experienced technical men were given as much independence as possible. Occasions on which reference to supervision remained obligatory were reduced to an absolute minimum. The aim was that each engineer should judge for himself when and to what extent he should seek advice.

Group managers sponsored occasional investigatory jobs, and engineers were encouraged to become departmental experts in particular fields. They were expected to follow up completed projects as they thought appropriate.

When authority to allocate work to outside consultants was given, the engineers were to have the responsibility for making the choice of consultants.

Financial: Within a sanctioned project with a budget already agreed on, all arbitrary limits on engineers' authority to spend money were removed. They themselves had to ensure that each "physical intent" was adequately defined and that an appropriate sum was allocated for it in the project budget. That done, no financial ceiling limited their authority to place orders.

Managerial: Engineers were involved in the selection and placing of designers (drawing office staff). They manned selection panels, and a recruit would only be allocated to a particular engineer if the latter agreed to accept him.

Experienced engineers were asked to make the initial salary recommendations for all their junior staff members.

Engineers were allowed to authorize overtime, cash advances, and traveling expenses for staff.

Motivational results. In summary fashion, these are the deductions that can be drawn from this study:

● Senior managers saw a change in both the amount and the kind of consultation between experimental group design engineers and their immediate supervisors. The supervisors' routine involvement in projects was much reduced, and they were able to give more emphasis in their work to technical development. Some engineers still needed frequent guidance; others operated independently with confidence. The point is that not all were restricted for the benefit of some; those who could were allowed to find their own feet.

● The encouragement of specialist expertise among design engineers was a long-term proposition, but progress was made during the trial period.

● The removal of any financial ceiling on engineers' authority to place orders within an approved project with an agreed budget proved entirely effective. Whereas before the design engineers had to seek approval from as many as three higher levels of management for any expenditure over $5,000—a time-consuming process for all concerned—now they could, and did, place orders for as much as $500,000 worth of equipment on their own authority.

● There is no evidence of any poor decision having been taken as a result of the new arrangements. In fact, at the end of the trial period, none of the senior managers concerned wanted to revert to the old system.

● The changes involving the engineers in supervisory roles were thought by the senior managers to be at least as important as the other changes, possibly more so in the long term.

● There was no doubt about the design engineers' greater involvement in the selection process, which they fully accepted and appreciated. Significantly, they began to show a greater feel for the constraints involved in selection.

● The responsibility for overtime and travel claims was fully effective and taken in people's stride. There was no adverse effect from a budgetary control point of view.

● The involvement of design engineers in making salary recommendations for their staff was considered by the senior managers to have been a major improvement. If anything, engineers tended to be "tighter" in their salary recommendations than more senior management. There was general agreement that the effectiveness of this change would increase over time.

● Senior managers felt that none of the changes of its own accord had had an overriding effect, nor had all problems been solved. But there was no doubt that the cumulative effect of the changes had been significant and that the direction of solutions to some important problems had been indicated.

The changes may have been effective, but in this particular study the important question was whether they had a significant impact on job satisfaction. Some of the motivators introduced into the experimental groups had been in operation in the control group for some time; others—because of the specialist nature of the control group's work—were not as important to it as to the experimental groups. The control group had scored high in the initial job reaction survey, while the experimental groups had both achieved very low scores. If the experimental groups' scores did not improve, doubt would inevitably be cast on the relationship between job content and job satisfaction. As it turned out, comparison results of the before and after job reaction surveys revealed that the mean scores of the two experimental groups had increased by 21% and 16%, while those of the control group and all other design engineers in the department had remained static.

Factory Supervisors

The final two studies, one in ICI and one in another British company, concerned factory supervisors: production foremen on shift work fabricating nonferrous metals, and engineering foremen on day work providing maintenance services. As the two studies seem to be complementary, they are considered jointly.

In both cases management was concerned about the degree to which the traditional role of the foreman had been eroded in recent years. The increasing complexity of organizational structures, plant and equipment, and industrial relations had left the foreman isolated. Decisions in the areas of planning, technical control, and discipline—originally in his province—were now passed up the line or turned over to a specialist staff. Many managers believed that as a consequence small problems too often escalated unnecessarily, managers were being overloaded, and day-to-day relationships between the foreman and his men had been weakened.

Changes and Experimental Design. Here is the specific program of action devised and implemented for the production and engineering foremen.

Technical: Foremen were involved more in planning. Production foremen were authorized to modify schedules for loading and sequencing; engineering foremen were consulted more about organizational developments, given more responsibility for preventive maintenance, and encouraged to comment on design.

All were assigned projects on specific problems such as quality control, and could draw on the necessary resources for their implementation.

Other changes included giving foremen more "on the spot" responsibility, official deputizing for engineers, the writing of monthly reports, and more recognition of foremen's achievement of plans.

Financial: Engineering foremen were given complete control of certain "on cost" budgets. Production foremen were encouraged to make all decisions on non-standard payments.

Managerial: Production foremen were given the authority to hire labor against agreed manning targets. They interviewed candidates for jobs and made the decision on their selection.

All the foremen were given complete disciplinary authority, except for dismissal. They decided what disciplinary action to take, consulted the personnel department if they thought it necessary, conducted the interviews, and kept the records.

All were given formal responsibility for the assessment, training, and development of their subordinates, and in some cases for the appointment of their own deputies. On the production side, a newly appointed training officer acted as a resource person for the foremen. Engineering foremen were involved more in the application of a job appraisement scheme and in joint consultation and negotiation with union officials.

The objective of integrating the foreman more fully into the managerial team dictated that responsibility should be the motivator chiefly concerned in these changes. Control of his own labor force, backed up by more technical and financial responsibility, was designed to give the foreman more opportunities for achievement and personal growth in the job. The main issue in these studies was whether foremen would prove themselves capable of carrying the increased responsibility. Thus, in monitoring the effectiveness of the changes, the aim was primarily to detect any instability or shortcomings in performance.

Motivational Results. In summary fashion, these are the deductions that can be drawn from this study:

• In six months the production foremen recruited nearly 100 men, and were judged by the personnel officer to be "hiring a better caliber of man at an improved rate." Their immediate supervisors were categorical in their approval and noted that the foremen were taking special care to "design their own shifts." Recruitment interviews were said to have improved the foremen's ability to handle encounters with existing staff and shop stewards.

• Training was handled equally successfully by the production foremen. For each job it was specified that there should be a certain number of men trained to take over in an emergency. During the trial period, the margin by which the target number was missed was reduced from 94 to 55; the number of operators unable to do another's job fell by 12%, and the number of assistants unable to do the job of the man they assisted fell by 37%. No comparable improvement was achieved in the control group.

• It became clear from both studies that foremen were fully capable of carrying disciplinary responsibility. An analysis of all cases arising during the trial year showed that there had been a reduction in the number of "repeat offenses" among employees with poor disciplinary records and a substantial reduction in short-term work stoppages. The analysis concluded that foremen were not prone to take one kind of action rather than another, they had developed a purposeful approach to such problems, and there had been no adverse union reaction.

About 50% of the engineering foremen's monthly reports during the trial year referred to consultation and negotiation with union officials—this on a site not noted for its harmonious industrial relations. Topics included demarcation, special payments, and the easing of bans imposed on "call outs." The incidence of such reports was spread evenly throughout the experimental group; their frequency increased during the trial period as the foremen became more confident of their abilities. All such matters appear to have been handled capably.

• From both studies came evidence, confirming what has long been demonstrated in training courses, that special investigatory projects give foremen much needed opportunity to contribute their experience and expertise to the solution of long-standing technical and organizational problems. In only three cases where financial evaluation was possible, the estimated annual savings totaled more than $125,000.

• Regarding the engineering foremen's control of budgets, in some cases the aim was to meet the target exactly; in others it was to reduce costs as much as possible. Both aims were achieved by the foremen at least as well as they had been by the managers. There is no evidence that plant efficiency or work effectiveness suffered in any way as a result of cost savings achieved by the foremen.

• In the case of the engineering foremen, the experimental group's staff assessments at the end of the trial year were markedly better than those of the control groups. Despite the attempt made in the initial selection of experimental and control groups to achieve as good a balance as possible in ability and experience, there can be little doubt that the experimental group did in any case contain some more able men. But no one anticipated that such a large difference would show itself at the end of the trial period. As evidence of development, 45% of the experimental group's assessments referred to significant improvements in performance during the year, and 36% made particular mention of how effectively the foreman had dealt with increased responsibility received during the year. These assessments were written by managers who were not party to the study.

• In the production foremen's study, superintendents reported that the new conditions were "separating the wheat from the chaff"; some of those who had previously been thought to be among the best of the foremen had not lived up to their reputations in a situation which placed little value on compliance, while others had improved enormously.

• The production foremen's job reaction survey scores showed no particular improvement over the trial period. In the case of the engineering foremen, the experimental group's mean score showed a 12% increase, while the control group's had only risen by 3%

Part II: The Main Conclusions

What has been described in the first part of this article is the consistent application of theory in an area where custom and practice are normally only challenged by individual hunch or intuition. As we have seen, each study posed a separate problem concerning a different group of employees; the only common element among them was the conceptual framework brought to bear on the problem, enabling a specific program of action to be devised and implemented. Much was learned in the process, by ourselves and managers alike.

Now in Part II, the main conclusions which emerged from the job enrichment studies are presented in the form of answers to the questions raised at the beginning of this article.

Generality of findings
Can similarly positive results be obtained elsewhere with other people doing different jobs?

Yes. The studies reflect a diversity of type and level of job in several company functions in more than one industry. From the evidence now available, it is clear that results are not dependent on any particular set of circumstances at the place of study. Our investigation has highlighted one important aspect of the process of management and has shown that disciplined attention to it brings results. The findings are relevant wherever people are being managed.

How widespread is the scope or need for equivalent change in other jobs?

The scope seems enormous. In brainstorming sessions held to generate ideas for change in the jobs covered by the studies, it was not uncommon for over a hundred suggestions to be entertained. The process of change in these particular jobs has started, not finished. In many places it has not even started. Though there probably are jobs which do not lend themselves to enrichment, we have never encountered a level or a function where some change has not seemed possible. It is difficult to say in advance what jobs are going to offer the most scope; the most unlikely sometimes turn out to have important possibilities. We have certainly not been able to conclude that any area of work can safely be left out of consideration.

The need is as deep as the scope is wide. The responsiveness of so many people to changes with a common theme suggests that an important and widespread human need has indeed been identified in the motivators. Moreover, it would seem to be a need which manifests itself in a variety of ways. If, from a company point of view, a gain once demonstrated to be possible is accepted as a need, then the performance improvements registered in these studies would seem to betray an organizational need which is far from fully recognized as yet.

Can meaningful results be obtained only in jobs with large numbers of people all doing the same work, and where performance measures are easily available?

No. Meaningful results can be obtained in situations very far from the experimental ideal. Indeed, the very awkwardness of many "real-life" situations leads to perceptions which could not come from a laboratory experiment.

Organizational changes are made, work loads fluctuate, people fall sick, managers are moved, emergencies have to be dealt with. The amount of attention which can be given to managing changes designed to enrich people's jobs is often slight. When a man's immediate supervisor does not even know that study is taking place, there is no vested interest in its success. In circumstances such as these, whatever is done stands or falls by its own merits.

In few of the studies could members of the experimental groups be said to be doing exactly the same work. Changes sometimes had to be tailor-made to suit specific individual jobs. Yet from the diversity of application came an understanding of the commonality of the process. Although laboratory technicians were engaged in quite different kinds of research, they were all doing research work; although foremen were looking after radically different operations, they were all supervising.

The changes that seemed to have the most impact were precisely those which related to the common heart and substance of the role played by people whose jobs differed in many important details. More than this, it became clear that all of them—the laboratory technician following up an original idea, the design engineer buying equipment, the foreman taking disciplinary action, the sales representative negotiating in the customer's office—are essentially in the same situation, the crux of which is the private encounter between an individual and his task. Only a change which impacts on this central relationship, we believe, can be truly effective in a motivational sense.

Real-life conditions not only give an investigation authenticity; they highlight the problem of measurement. What is most meaningful to a manager, of course—a foreman's proprietary attitude toward his shift, for example—is not always quantifiable. An important discovery, however, was that the better the motivator, the more likely it was to provide its own measure. Employees' "sense of responsibility," judged in a vacuum, is a matter of speculation; but the exercise of a specific responsibility, once given, is usually capable of meaningful analysis. Laboratory technicians may or may not be thought to have innate potential; the number and quality of their research minutes can be measured. Several times managers commented that job enrichment had opened up measurement opportunities which not only allowed a more accurate assessment of individual performance, but often led to a better diagnosis of technical problems as well.

Feasibility of Change
Are there not situations where the operational risk is so high that it would be foolhardy to attempt to pass responsibility and scope for achievement down the line?

Probably there are, but we have not encountered one. The risks attached to some of the changes in the sales representatives' study seemed frightening at the time. Few managers who have not tried it can accept with equanimity the thought of their subordinates placing orders for $500,000 worth of equipment on their own authority, even within a sanctioned project. The research manager in the laboratory technicians' study concluded that a change was only likely to be motivational for his subordinates if it made him lose sleep at nights.

Yet in no case did disaster result. In reviewing the results of the studies with the managers concerned, it was difficult in fact for us as outsiders not to have a sense of anticlimax. By the end of the trial period, the nerve-racking gambles of a few months before were hardly worth a mention. The new conditions seemed perfectly ordinary. Managers had completely revised their probability judgments in the light of experience.

Theory provides an explanation for the remarkable absence of disaster experienced in practice. Bad hygiene, such as oppressive supervision and ineffectual control systems, constrains and limits performance, and may even lead to sabotage. Administrative procedures that guard against hypothetical errors and imaginary irresponsibility breed the very carelessness and apathy which result in inefficiency. With too many controls, responsibility becomes so divided that it gets lost. Hygiene improvements at best lift the constraints.

The motivators, on the other hand, make it possible for the individual to advance the base line of his performance. The road is open for improvement, while present standards remain available as a reference point and guide. When a man is given the chance to achieve more, he may not take that chance, but he has no reason to achieve less. The message of both theory and practice is that people respond cautiously to new responsibility; they feel their way and seek advice. When responsibility is put squarely with the person doing a job, he is the one who wants and needs feedback in order to do his job. His use of the motivators, not our use of hygiene, is what really controls performance standards.

As managers, we start having positive control of the job only when we stop concentrating on trying to control people. Mistakes are less likely, not more likely, than before; those which do occur are more likely to be turned to account, learned from, and prevented in the future, for they are seen to matter. Monitoring continues, but its purpose has changed. Now it provides the jobholder with necessary information and enables management to see how much more can be added to a job rather than how much should be subtracted from it. That way, continual improvement, while not being guaranteed, at least becomes possible as the scope for the motivators is extended. It is the nearest thing to a performance insurance policy that management can have.

Such is the theory, and from the evidence of the studies, practice bears it out. If the studies show anything, they show that it pays to experiment. No one is being asked to accept anything on faith; what is required is the courage to put old assumptions and old fears to the test. For the manager, the process is like learning to swim: it may not be necessary to jump in at the deep end, but it surely is necessary to leave the shallow end. Only those who have done so are able to conquer the fear which perverts our whole diagnosis of the problem of managing people.

Because people's ability and sense of responsibility vary so much, is it not necessary to make changes selectively?

No. To make changes selectively is never to leave the shallow end of the pool. We are in no position to decide, before the event, who deserves to have his job enriched and who does not. In almost every study managers were surprised by the response of individuals, which varied certainly, but not always in the way that would have been forecast. As the job changed, so did the criteria of successful performance change. Some people who had been thought to be sound and responsible under the old conditions turned out merely to have been yes-men once those conditions were changed; their performance was the same as it had always been, but now compliance was no longer valued so highly. At the other extreme was one classic example of an awkward employee, about to be sacked, who turned out to be unusually inventive and responsible when he has given the opportunity to be so.

In one study, not reported, a promising set of changes brought relatively disappointing results—the changes had been implemented selectively. When pressed to explain the grounds on which people had been chosen, the manager quoted as an example someone who had already carried similar responsibility in a previous job. It is exactly this kind of vicious circle that job enrichment seeks to break.

When changes are made unselectively, the genuinely good performers get better. Some poor performers remain poor, but nothing is lost. Because the changes are opportunities and not demands, all that happens is that the less able ignore them and go on as before. Some people, however, develop as they never could under the old conditions, and do better than others originally rated much higher. This is the bonus from job enrichment. Not only is overall performance improved, but a clearer picture emerges of individual differences and potential.

So long as a foundation of new job opportunities available to all is firmly established, there is no harm in restricting certain changes to the more senior of the jobholders. Such changes can be seen in both the laboratory technicians' and the design engineers' studies. This is a very different matter from introducing changes selectively in the first place. It is a way of providing scope for personal advancement within the job and recognizing the achievements of those who build well on the foundation of opportunity already provided.

Do all employees welcome having their jobs enriched, or are there not some who prefer things to be left as they are?

Individual reaction to job enrichment is as difficult to forecast in terms of attitudes as it is in terms of performance. Those already genuinely interested in their work develop real enthusiasm. Not all people welcome having their jobs enriched, certainly, but so long as the changes are opportunities rather than demands, there is no reason to fear an adverse reaction. If someone prefers things the way they are, he merely keeps them the way they are, by continuing to refer matters to his supervisor, for example. Again, there is nothing lost.

On the other hand, some of the very people whom one might expect to duck their chance seize it with both hands, developing a keenness one would never have anticipated. In attitudes as well as in performance, the existence of individual differences is no bar to investigating the possibilities of job enrichment.

Can you enrich jobs without inevitably facing demands for higher pay or better conditions to match the new responsibilities?

Yes. In no instance did management face a demand of this kind as a result of changes made in the studies. It would seem that changes in working practice can be made without always having a price tag attached.

Here, as in the matter of oprational risk, what is surprising in practice is easily explicable in terms of theory. The motivators and the hygiene factors may not be separate dimensions in a manager's analysis of a situation, but they are in people's experience. It is time that our diagnosis of problems took more account of people's experience. The studies demonstrate again that, when presented with an opportunity for achievement, people either achieve something or they do not; when allowed to develop, they either respond or stay as they are. Whatever the result, it is a self-contained experience, a private encounter between a person and his task.

It is something quite separate when the same person becomes annoyed by his poor working conditions, worries about his status or security, or sees his neighbors enjoying a higher standard of living. The cause-effect relationship between hygiene and motivation scarcely exists. Motivation is not the product of good hygiene, even if bad hygiene sometimes leads to sabotage. Higher pay may temporarily buy more work, but it does not buy commitment. Nor does commitment to a task, by itself, bring demand for better hygiene.

Managers often complain of their lack of room for maneuver. In doing so, they are generalizing from the rules of the hygiene game to the total management situation. There is little evidence that the workforce in fact prostitutes its commitment to a task, although incentive bonus schemes, productivity bargaining, and the like assiduously encourage such prostitution. Before the process goes too far, it seems worth exploring more fully the room for maneuver freely available on the motivator dimension.

This is not to say, however, that the motivators should be used as an alibi for the neglect of hygiene. If people genuinely are achieving more, taking more responsibility, and developing greater competence, that is no reason to take advantage of them for a short-term profit. Any tendency to exploitation on management's part could destroy the whole process.

Is not the best route to motivational change through participation?

Yes and no. We have to define our terms. So far as the process of job enrichment itself is concerned, experimental constraints in the studies dictated that there could be no participation by jobholders themselves in deciding what changes were to be made in their jobs. The changes nevertheless seemed to be effective. On the other hand, when people were invited to participate—not in any of the reported studies—results were disappointing. In one case, for example, a group of personnel specialists suggested fewer than 30 fairly minor changes in their jobs, whereas their managers had compiled a list of over 100 much more substantial possibilities.

It seems that employees themselves are not in a good position to test out the validity of the boundaries of their jobs. So long as the aim is not to measure experimentally the effects of job enrichment alone, there is undoubtedly benefit in the sharing of ideas. Our experience merely suggests that it would be unwise to pin too many hopes to it—or the wrong hopes.

Participation is sometimes held, consciously or unconsciously, to be an alternative to job enrichment. Instead of passing responsibility down the line and possibly losing control, the manager can consult his subordinates before making a decision, involve them, make them feel part of the team. It all seems to be a matter of degree, after all. Participation, in this sense of consultation, is seen as a safe halfway house to job enrichment, productive and satisfying to all concerned.

A multitude of techniques are available to help the manager be more effective in consultation: he can be trained to be more sensitive to interpersonal conflict, more sophisticated in his handling of groups, more ready to listen, more oriented toward valuing others' contributions. Better decisions result, especially in problem-solving meetings that bring together colleagues or opponents in different roles or functions.

But in the specific context of the management of subordinates, it is worth asking who is motivated in this kind of participation. The answer would seem to be the person who needs a second opinion to make sure he comes to the right decision—the manager in fact. The subordinate does not have the same professional or work-inspired need for the encounter, for he is not the one who has to live with responsibility for the decision. It is doubtful whether his "sense of involvement" even makes him feel good for long, for an appeal to personal vanity wears thin without more substance. However well-intentioned, this halfway-house kind of participative management smacks of conscience money; and receivers of charity are notoriously ungrateful. In the case of professional staff it is downright patronizing, for the subordinate is paid to offer his opinion anyway.

Theory clarifies the position. It is not a matter of degree at all. The difference between consultation and enrichment is a difference in kind. Consultation does not give a subordinate the chance for personal achievement which he can recognize; through involvement, it subtly denies him the exercise of responsibility which would lead to his development, however humbly, as an executive in his own right. Far from being the best route to motivational change, this kind of participation is a red herring. It is hygiene masquerading as a motivator, diverting attention from the real problem. It may help to prevent dissatisfaction, but it does not motivate.

The laboratory technicians, sales representatives, design engineers, and foremen did indeed participate, but not in a consultative exercise designed to keep them happy or to help their managers reach better decisions. Nor was it participation in ambiguity—an all too common occurrence in which, although no one quite knows where he stands or what may happen, the mere fact of participation is supposed to bring success. The participation of employees involved in the studies consisted of doing things which had always previously been done by more senior people. In all cases consultation continued, but now it was consultation upward. In consultation upward there is no ambiguity; tasks and roles are clear. Both parties are motivated, the subordinate by the need to make the best decision, to satisfy himself, to justify the trust placed in him, to enhance his professional reputation; the manager by the need to develop his staff.

When design engineers consulted tneir more senior colleagues, it was on questions of technical difficulty, commercial delicacy, or professional integrity—all more to the point than the more price of a piece of equipment. Foremen consulted their managers on unusual budgetary worries, or the personnel department on tricky disciplinary problems. Sales representatives consulted headquarters on matters such as the stock position on a certain product before negotiating special terms with a customer.

Participation is indeed the best route to motivational change, but only when it is participation in the act of management, no matter at what level it takes place. And the test of the genuineness of that participation is simple—it must be left to the subordinate to be the prime mover in consultation on those topics where he carries personal responsibility. For the manager, as for the subordinate, the right to be consulted must be earned by competence in giving help. Therein lies the only authority worth having.

Expected Consequences
In view of so many possible difficulties in the way, are the gains to be expected from job enrichment significant or only marginal?

We believe the gains are significant, but the evidence must speak for itself. In all, 100 people were in the experimental groups in the studies described. A conservative reckoning of the financial benefit achieved, arrived at by halving all estimated annual gains or savings, would still be over $200,000 per year. Cost was measurable in a few days of managers' time at each place.

Do the gains relate primarily to job satisfaction or to performance?

Contrary to expectation, the gains, initially at least, seem to relate primarily to performance. Wherever a direct measure of performance was possible, an immediate gain was registered. In one or two instances, performance seemed to peak and then drop back somewhat, though it stayed well above its starting point and well above the control group's performance. Elsewhere there seemed to be a more gradual improvement; if anything it gained momentum through the trial period. We have no evidence to suggest that performance gains, once firmly established, are not capable of being sustained.

In the short term, gains in job satisfaction would seem to be less spectacular. Attitudes do not change overnight. Satisfaction is the result of performance, not vice versa, and there is a long history of frustration to be overcome. When direct measurement of job satisfaction was possible, the most significant gains seemed to come when the trial period was longest. There is every reason to think that in the long term attitudes catch up with performance and that job enrichment initiates a steady and prolonged improvement in both.

What are the consequences for supervision if jobs are loaded with new tasks taken from above—i.e., does one man's enrichment become another's impoverishment?

The more subordinates' jobs are enriched, the more superfluous does supervision, in its old sense, become. Several of the studies showed that short-term absences of the experimental groups' supervisors could be coped with more easily as day-to-day concern for operational problems shifted downward. The need for the supervisor to be always "on the job" diminished; greater organizational flexibility was gained.

But though supervision may become redundant, supervisors do not. Fears of loss of authority or prestige were never realized. Far from their jobs being impoverished, supervisors now found that they had time available to do more important work. Design engineers' supervisors were able to devote more effort to technical development; production foremen's supervisors found themselves playing a fuller managerial role.

The enrichment of lower-level jobs seems to set up a chain reaction resulting in the enrichment of supervisors' jobs as well. Fears that the supervisor may somehow miss out are based on the premise that there is a finite pool of responsibility in the organization which is shared among its members. In practice new higher-order responsibilities are born.

Even when subordinates are given responsibilites not previously held by their own supervisors, as happened in the sales representatives' study and to a lesser extent in some of the others, there is no evidence that supervisors feel bypassed or deprived, except perhaps very temporarily. It soon becomes apparent to all concerned that to supervise people with authority of their own is a more demanding, rewarding, and enjoyable task than to rule over a bunch of automatons, checking their every move.

Finally, what are the consequences for management if motivational change becomes a reality? Is the manager's role affected? If so, how? And what are the implications for management development?

The main consequence is that management becomes a service, its purpose to enable, encourage, assist, and reinforce achievement by employees. Task organization and task support are the central features of the manager's new role. In task *organization* two complementary criteria emerge: (1) tasks have to be authentic—i.e., the more opportunity they give employees to contribute to business objectives, the more effective they are likely to be motivationally; (2) tasks have to be motivational—i.e., the more they draw upon the motivators, the more likely they are to produce an effective contribution to business objectives. In task *support*, factors such as company policy and administration, technical supervision, interpersonal relations, and working conditions all have to be pressed into the service of the motivators. Control of the job is achieved by providing people with the tools of their trade, with the information they require, with training as appropriate, and with advice when sought.

The job itself becomes the prime vehicle of all individual development, of which management development is only one kind. In aiding the process of development, our starting point, as always, is problem diagnosis—in this case, assessment of individual abilities, potentials, and needs. When people are underemployed, we have no way of distinguishing between those who are near the limit of their abilities and those who have a great deal more to contribute. All too often, potential has to be inferred from risky and subjective judgments about personality. Such judgments, once made, tend to be static; people become categorized. The studies show that when tasks are organized to be as authentic and motivational as possible, management receives a more accurate and a continuing feedback on individual strengths and weaknesses, ability, and potential. Task support becomes a flexible instrument of management, responsive to feedback.

If the job itself is the prime vehicle of individual development, task support is the means by which management can influence it. We still think of individual development, especially management development, far too much as something which can be imposed from outside. We pay lip service to on-the-job training but go on running courses as a refuge. We speak of self-development, but we are at a loss to know how to encourage it. Now, however, we can postulate a criterion: self-development is likely to be most effective when the task a person is engaged in is authentic and motivational and when in doing it he receives understanding, imaginative, and capable support. When these conditions are met, the job itself becomes a true learning situation, its ingredients the motivators.

Though only one study set out specifically to measure individual development, the most pervasive impression from all was one of development and personal growth achieved. The latent inspirational value of jobs appeared to have been released. People were able to demonstrate and utilize skills they already possessed, and go on to learn new ones. Each new facet of the task required a response in terms of individual development, and results suggest that that response was seldom lacking.

The best evidence of development came, however, not from the experimental groups in the studies, but from the managers who put the studies into effect. It is sometimes said that attitude change is the key to success. But in seeking to improve the performance of our business, perhaps we rely too much on efforts to change managers' attitudes. These studies went ahead without waiting for miracles of conversion first. Just as the experimental groups in the studies represented a cross section of employees engaged on those jobs, so the managers who put the studies into effect represented a cross section of managers. Enthusiasts and skeptics alike agreed to judge the studies by their results. They did, and the effect was clear for the observer to see. Success proved to be the key to attitude change. In retrospect, who would want it otherwise?

ISSUES AND ETHICS IN
BEHAVIOR MANIPULATION

FREDERICK H. KANFER

Whenever a science is ready to apply its principles or methods to the control of man's social and physical environment, public attention demands that the consequences of such application be carefully examined. This scrutiny often results in argumentative debates and emotional alignment of the public vis-a-vis the science, its contents and its practitioners. The merciless beam of the public spotlight has by no means been confined to psychology. In our own time chemistry, physics and biology have repeatedly provided discoveries which the public viewed and discussed with alarm. Public concern usually declined gradually as scientific contributions were absorbed into the social fabric. Nevertheless, the vigor of recent public reactions to progress in the study and control of human behavior has taken our academically-minded science by surprise. Perhaps the sudden widespread concern with test makers, public opinion swayers, and adjustment manipulators simply indicates that psychology finally may have something to offer which has applicability to everyday life. The hope for eventual development of the psychology of behavioral control also raises the problem of the ethics of manipulating the behavior of another person. The most surprising aspect of the psychologist's dilemma posed by this problem is its recency. After all, the maniuplation of behavior reportedly first took place when Eve whetted Adam's appetite in the Garden of Eden. For centuries, the issues of morality and the control of one human being over another either have been kept separated or, in fact, combined in such absurd fashion that the most cruel methods of control were perpetrated under the guise of morality. The slaughter during the crusades, the elimination of witchcraft, the conquest of the American Indian, the "liberation" of Europe by the Nazis represent a few choice historical examples of human misbehavior and the use of the ultimate in behavior control through physical force and extermination. By comparison, the minor infraction committed currently when a psychotherapist subtly alters a neurotic patient's value system or his social behavior pattern seems rather mild. Nevertheless, numerous recent popular articles and books reflect the increasing public concern with the use of psychological methods in education, in industry, in the treatment of the mentally ill, and in politics.

The purpose of this paper is to discuss several issues concerning use of psychological principles in the manipulation of human behavior. These issues may arise in the context of psychology practiced in the clinic, in industry, by the military, or by governments. This paper will focus on behavior control by psychotherapy. The issues concern: (1) the methods of control, (2) the domain of controlled behavior, and (3) the selection of ends for which control is exercised.

Reprinted with permission of author and publisher: Kanfer, F. H., "Issues and Ethics in Behavior Manipulation," from *Psychological Reports*, 1965, 16, 187-96.

Control by Reward versus Punishment

With regard to the "psychology of behavior control" (Krasner, 1962a) in a clinic, the current sensitivity to the ethical issues stems largely from an increased proficiency in the control of behavior, and especially from a fear of one special kind of manipulation.[1] In the past, efforts toward improving control over adult behavior have been mainly directed at finding better methods of aversive control, e.g., threat, coercion, or physical force. Currently, there is a tendency toward increasing use of control by positive reinforcement in all areas of life. This shift to promises, rewards, and seductions rather than coercion represents, in our opinion, the pith of public concern. In his discussion of methods used by controlling agencies, Skinner (1953) suggests that government, law, and religion mainly use practices of threat of punishment, withdrawal of positive reinforcers, or presentation of negative reinforcers to achieve obedience. Further, with use of these methods by social agencies the usual "effect of group control is in conflict with a strong primarily reinforced behavior of the individual" (Skinner, 1953, p. 327). In contrast, economic control, education, and psychotherapy rely more heavily on positive reinforcement. Recently, control by positive reinforcement has been used extensively in programs of "ideological totalism" (Lifton, 1961). In practice, such control is heightened when used only after achievement of complete control over the individual's environment and thought processes by force. As in laboratory animals, positive reinforcement is most effective following severe deprivation. If such deprivations can be created in human groups, success in behavior control should be markedly enhanced for the possessor of the positive reinforcers. The deliberate application of methods reserved earlier mostly for education, work achievement, child rearing and therapy, in politics and government represents a major innovation. Coupled with extension from control over individuals to control over groups, this advance in control techniques raises public concern. The shift in methods of control is illustrated in the history of psychotherapy by the progress from straitjackets, padded cells, and beatings to therapeutic communities, insight therapy, and counter-conditioning.

It is interesting to speculate why control by positive reinforcement might be more dangerous than control by coercion. Manipulation by aversive control creates its own hazards. The person under aversive control usually knows it. He suffers pain, experiences humiliation, anger, or other emotional discomfort. It is also likely that aversive control inevitably breeds attempts at counter-control. Even in the young child the first response to being slapped is to try to slap back. Aversive control thus motivates behavior aimed at reducing such control by annoying, teasing, or destroying the controller. Further, aversive control is difficult to maintain by a small group. To use force effectively you have to be bigger, stronger, or more numerous than your adversary. Thus aversive control by an individual over a large group, or by a small minority is doomed to failure in the long run. Finally, as Skinner (1953) has indicated, aversive control affects only public behavior. It is of limited use in "thought control" because a person can escape some aversive consequences by thinking silently or by nonconforming behavior in his private experiences.

In contrast, manipulation by positive control produces none of these disturbing by-products. By definition these methods use reinforcing stimuli which have the inherent potential for increasing or maintaining behaviors which procure these stimuli. People respond in blind faith to reward, to promises, and to reassurances. Large scale use of these methods, however, has not concerned people because the age-old deceptions of the Pied Piper have been assumed to be sufficiently transparent to allow most adults to recognize them as false promises and to resist temptation by persuasion. Recently, Browning's Pied Piper of Hamlin has become more sophisticated. He has put on the disguise of a gray flannel suit, of a human relationship expert, a psychotherapist, or a friendly interrogator in a prison camp. His pipe has turned into other instruments promising such sweet things as affection and happiness to a juvenile delinquent, money-back guaranteed satisfaction with soaps and cereals, or a political paradise for the masses, all without pain, coercion, or physical violence. This increased professionalism and sophistication in the application of psychological principles has caused uneasiness to the public because the methods have lost some of their transparency and amateurish quality. Although there is contradictory experimental evidence on the question of behavioral modification without awareness (Eriksen, 1962; Kanfer & Marston, 1961), these studies also clearly indicate that Ss cannot verbalize all aspects of the controlling stimuli which affect their behavior.

Certainly, the increase in psychological sophistication has also made it easier for the controller to disguise his own motives in order to mislead Ss of his controlling influence. In addition, he can manipulate conditions which would make his positive reinforcement more effective. Frank (1961) makes this point in discussing methods of thought reform: "the essence of the relationship is that the persuader invests great effort to bring about changes in the sufferer's bodily state or attitudes that he regards as beneficial . . . (and the setting) . . . occurs in the context of hope and potential support from the persuader and the group" (1961, p. 95). Since our democratic principles also uphold the right of consent of the governed, any use of control resulting in a change of behavior without S's awareness of the methods of influence and the intent of his controllers would be ethically objectionable to our society. Even though these emphases placed upon self-control, self-government, and self-determination are accepted by our culture and its scientist members, a deterministic behavioral psychology cannot disavow its implication that behavior is controlled by an organism's previous history and its environment, regardless of its ability to describe verbally these controlling variables. Regardless of ethic or social interest the fiction of the complete Rational Man as the captain of his own destiny, is as naive to behavioristic psychology as it was to Freudian psychoanalysis (although for different reasons).

In psychotherapy, social pressures or other devices attempting to maniupulate the patient's behavior by coercion are rarely used as a primary method of control. Therapeutic operations are more likely to stress positive goals, to reduce tensions, to reinforce and strengthen new behaviors. The therapist is, of course, at an additional disadvantage in the use of aversive controls. When the therapist acts as a noxious stimulus the patient can counter by "resistance," by failing to keep his appointments, or by leaving the field altogether. Patients under strong aversive control by parental pressure or court order are notoriously poor risks for psychotherapy.

Control of Private Experiences

The invitability of mutual influence in a clinical relationship is well domumented by recent research and some of its implications have been discussed by Krasner (1962a).

What are some of the features then which make the psychotherapeutic interaction or other similar relationships especially suited for the manipulation or control of behavior?

One factor is the distress and discomfort of the patient. The social role of the patient has been described by Parsons (Parsons & Fox, 1958). In our society the sick person can claim certain privileges. It is assumed that he is not responsible for his incapacity, and his state of sickness exempts him from his normal social obligations. In turn, it is understood that he will attempt to get well and that he has an obligation to seek help and cooperate with others who treat him. As Parsons states, the latter implies a dependency of the sick person on the healer. The act of coming for help signifies the patient's realization that he cannot cope with the problem and that he wishes another person to take responsibility for treating it. This dependency status should tend to increase the effectiveness of the therapist's reinforcing operations (cf. research on the role of dependency, prestige, and other therapist-patient variables in verbal conditioning; Greenspoon, 1962, Krasner, 1962b).

A second feature concerns the *content* of the interactions. Most psychologists agree that the specific content of the patient's verbalizations in psychotherapy is far less important than was believed by earlier theorists. One common element in all therapeutic interactions is the therapist's insistence that the patient talk about those private experiences, fears, attitudes, and beliefs which are usually not shared with other people. Recent reviews by William Sargant (1957), Jerome Frank (1961) and Robert Lifton (1961) of methods of persuasion, thought reform, and therapy all suggest that the most successful methods of behavior manipulation, including magic, religion, and political coercion, share the requirement that the person publicly expose at least some of his privately held beliefs and attitudes. This accessibility to personal and private behavior, in turn, makes the person more vulnerable to control. The more behavior is exposed to the controlling agent the easier it is to set up conditions which modify behavior. Lifton (1961) points out that the admissions of guilt over minimal crimes against the state in Chinese "brainwashing" camps and universities provide the opportunity for the controller to reinforce such self-accusing behavior, to promise relief from guilt by self-punishing procedures and generally to weaken existing behavior and introduce new responses.

Privacy, the inaccessibility of much personal behavior in a democratic society, probably represents the bulwark of democracy because it allows for variability, and for divergence of attitudes and beliefs. What is jealously guarded as a right to privacy in everyday life is, in fact, surrendered in the psychotherapeutic hour. The consequences of this making accessible of the patient's private experiences have been discussed elsewhere (Kanfer, 1961). The potentials for controlling important behavioral sequences, usually not subject to control by direct social reinforcement, increase very much the extent of the therapist's influence.

Metavalues and Personal Values

Clinicians are beginning to accept the thesis that the therapist's value system tends to affect the direction of the patient's change in treatment (Rosenthal, 1955; Schrier, 1953). Among the many problems raised by this recognition are the methods of handling value material (e.g., Ellis, 1962; Meehl, 1959; Segal, 1959), and the ethical implications of the intrusion of personal values into psychotherapy (Williamson, 1958; Weisskopf-Joelson, 1953). Existential analysis (Weisskopf-Joelson, 1958) assumes that the purpose of treatment is the realization of creative and attitudinal values and this school frankly admits its value-orientation.

Although the term "value" is difficult to define, two separate aspects relating to the problem in psychotherapy are worthy of mention.

There are clear cut rules for many behaviors which are common to practically all members of a given culture. These rules are usually also accepted by the therapist and his client. We will call these *metavalues* (cultural values). In addition, there is a variety of situations in which several alternate behaviors and goal hierarchies are equally tolerated by society but which differ in the degree to which they lead to satisfaction in the individual. These alternatives are determined primarily by the individual's past experience. We shall call these alternatives *personal values*. Complications arise both in the patient's value system and in the psychotherapy relationship because of the inconsistencies between metavalues and personal values. Interpretation of the cultural metavalues further varies as a function of membership in a subgroup such as a socio-economic, religious, or geographic affiliation. The outcome of therapy should provide a wider choice of alternative behaviors for the patient with only the restriction that the new behaviors must also be compatible with the metavalues of the patient's cultural environment. The problem lies mainly in producing those changes which lead to socially acceptable behavior even while they result in sweeping changes in the life pattern of the patient. For example, therapists generally do not disagree whether to manipulate behavior which may avert a suicide, but they *do* disagree whether a client's vocational or marital choice should be modified. In complete absence of standards for such personal and private modes of behavior the therapist's judgments are based mainly on his theoretical orientation, on his own experiences, and on his own personal values. These therapist experiences then become the standards for selecting the goals for a particular patient in psychotherapy.[2]

In most cases the neurotic patient can be of little help in deciding what personal values need changing and what range of alternatives would be tolerated both by him and by his environment. When a patient *is* able to do this, the therapist's job does not involve the problem of values. The patient might indicate that he wishes to improve his study habits or seek technical help in making a vocational choice. In these cases technical skills by the psychologist may be applied directly to a problem with an outcome defined clearly by the client himself. Unfortunately, therapists sometimes become suspicious even in these cases and the desirability of the patient's stated goal is often questioned by therapists from the viewpoint of their own personal value systems. Endowed with a tradition of depth-probing, many a therapist is tempted to substitute his own goal for that of the patient. Instead of rendering technical assistance in a circumscribed area, the therapist may then attempt to change the patient's total pattern of living.

Rules for Control

The most heated arguments are generated by the question, "Who establishes the legitimacy of means and ends in behavioral control?" The writer does not presume to have a solution to this question, but wishes to present a few thoughts designed to stimulate further debate.

The APA attempted to indicate the limitations of appropriate means and ends for psychological practice in its early code of ethics (1953). Principle 1.12-1 (p. 7) reads in part: "the psychologists's ultimate allegience is to society, and his professional behavior should demonstrate awareness of his social responsibilities. The welfare of the profession and of the individual psychologist are clearly subordinate to the welfare of the public." Further, Principle 1.13-1 (p. 10): "The psychologist should express in his professional behavior a firm commitment to those values which lie at the foundation of a democratic society, such as freedom of speech, freedom of research, and respect for the integrity of the individual." While these statements arouse the unqualified support of all good psychologists, they do not help to resolve the conflict inherent in the problem of treating neurotic patients. On the one hand, as citizens in a democratic society, psychologists believe that every person has the right to make his own free choice about his way of life. On the other hand, as professionals they also recognize that people who are in difficulties should be helped and choices must often be made for them. The clinical psychologist is an expert in assessing and modifying human behavior by virtue of his training. Regardless of the limitations of psychological theories and methods, psychologists constitute a profession (some say the only profession) which offers extensive training in behavior theory and in methods used to assist people with psychological problems. Therefore, the psychologist is better prepared to apply his knowledge than the layman.[3] However, as noted above, there is a difference between competence in bringing about behavioral changes and in judging the desirability of the behavior and the value system to be substituted. The clinician cannot accept sole responsibility for judging the adequacy of the individual's value system, nor can he become the ultimate interpreter of cultural metavalues to the patient by psychotherapy or education. In clinical practice, the patient, social milieu and other significant persons in his life must all be considered in selecting appropriate goals for therapy.

Nor can psychology be held responsible for the application of its principles and methods by social agencies or industry in the fields of government, economics, or education. Decisions concerning the legitimacy of means and ends in use of behavioral control methods are no more the responsibility of the psychologist than is the question whether to use atomic weapons in a war in the area of competence of the physicist, or the decision to adopt sterilization procedures with some humans in the domain of the biologist. In the absence of any specific mandate from the social community through its legal, political, religious, or social agencies psychologists will continue to use methods of control which are sometimes not acceptable to the public and use these for purposes about which there is some debate.

There has already been some indication that psychological knowledge is gradually becoming incorporated into the legal system, providing some standards of behavior which are more consistent with our knowledge of man than many current laws. There is, however, a considerable lag between mores and their incorporation into the legal structure of a society. During this lag professional groups will have to provide leadership in working out rules which describe the goals for which individual human behavior may be manipulated, and the restrictions upon methods under which this purpose is to be accomplished.

When the psychologist leaves his immediate work setting, his conduct falls under the rules by which other social groups operate. A social scientist who publicly gives opinions about the implications of behavioral control techniques for international politics, education, or consumer behavior must expect the same treatment as other public figures who champion controversial issues. It is probably this change in the accustomed reaction from student or patient audiences which has made psychologists so reluctant to participate in public debate and to provide information and guidance to social groups. An additional problem, of course, lies in the thin line of distinction between fact and opinion, between researcher and reformer.

From these considerations, it seems that several specific contributions can be made by psychologists to further public recognition of the social implications of recent advances in psychology.

(1) In their roles as scientists, continuing research on behavioral control methods and on factors limiting their effects to special circumstances should provide clearer understanding of the extent of the problem in practical situations. Research findings already exist which tend to suggest that total behavioral control requires a totally controlled environment; that verbal (and attitudinal) behavior can be influenced by a variety of variables toward maximal or minimal change; and that self-control training can modify the effect of incentives, thereby reducing greatly the utility of many conditioning procedures. Knowledge of these factors should permit a better estimate of the actual threat inherent in practical methods to which objections are currently raised. If recently described methods turn out to be no more effective than previous controlling devices, or if easy countermeasures are available, no further concern or action would be warranted.

(2) With no special prerogatives to dictate to society the rules by which its members should be educated, controlled, or changed, psychologists as educated citizens can make a contribution as resource persons to established social agencies. These activities demand of the consultant that he explicitly distinguish between facts, interpretation of facts, and his personal opinion.

(3) Our discussion suggests that continued public awareness of the growing effectiveness of psychological techniques may present the best safeguards against their misapplication. Ultimately, the products of any science become public property and only the informed public can wisely regulate their use.

(4) If psychologists have a service to perform in society's effort to evaluate itself, it is the scientific analysis of current psychological practices, embedded in our social matrix. Among those are many which appear to have relevance to the control of *individual* behavior, i.e., practices in education, in law-enforcement, in

treatment of emotional adjustment, in consumer persuasion, and industrial personnel procedures. Contributions to each of these fields lie not only in suggestions for changes but also in a thorough analysis of the present practices and their consequences.

Notes

1. While skeptics can point to evidence of current ignorance of even the most common determinants of individual behavior, few will doubt that rapid progress has been made in the last decade. We assume here that modification of individual behavior is feasible, though all the necessary controlling variables are not yet known.
2. If all mental health workers were to share a single set of values their influence would carry with it the same dangers as any system of total control. A requirement of strict conformity to the norms and values set up by the therapist's model of behavior is also tantamount to the complete subservience imposed by totalistic control systems.
3. We recognize that personality variables as yet unexplored may be important determinants of therapist effectiveness. But no scientifically grounded professional can fail to assume that additional didactic training is a necessary, if not sufficient, condition for practice.

References

Ellis, A., *Reason and emotion in psychotherapy.* New York: Lyle Stuart, 1962.

Eriksen, C. W., (Ed.) *Behavior and awareness.* Durham: Duke Univer. Press, 1962.

Frank, J. D., *Persuasion and healing: a comparative study of psychotherapy.* Baltimore: Johns Hopkins Press, 1961.

Greenspoon, J., Verbal conditioning and clinical psychology. In A. J. Bachrach (Ed.), *Experimental foundations of clinical psychology.* New York: Basic Books, 1962.

Kanfer, F. H., Comments on learning in psychotherapy. *Psychol. Rep.,* 1961, 9, 681-699.

Kanfer, F. H., & Marston, A. R., Verbal conditioning, ambiguity, and psychotherapy. *Psychol. Rep.,* 1961, 9, 461-475.

Krasner, L., Behavior control and social responsibility. *Amer. Psychologist,* 1962, 17, 199-204. (a)

Krasner, L., The therapist as a social reinforcement machine. In H. Strupp & L. Luborsky (Eds.), *Research in psychotherapy.* Washington: APA, 1962. Pp. 61-95.

Lifton, R. J., *Thought reform and the psychology of totalism.* New York: Norton, 1961.

Meehl, P. E. Some technical and axiological problems in the therapeutic handling of religious and valuational material. *J. counsel. Psychol.,* 1959, 6, 255-259.

Parsons, T. & Fox, R., Illness, therapy and the modern urban family. In E. G. Jaco (Ed.), *Patients, physicians, and illness.* Glencoe: Free Press, 1958. Pp. 234-245.

Rosenthal, D., Changes in some moral values following psychotherapy. *J. consulting Psychol.,* 1955, 19, 131-136.

Sargant, W., *Battle for the mind: a physiology of conversion and brainwashing.* New York: Doubleday 1957.

Schrier, H., The significance of identification in therapy. *Amer. J. Orthopsychiat.,* 1953, 23, 585-604.

Segal, S. J., The role of the counselor's religious values in counseling. *J. counsel. Psychol.,* 1959, 6, 270-274.

Skinner, B. F., *Science and human behavior.* New York: Macmillan, 1953.

Weisskopf-Joelson, E., Some suggestions concerning Weltanschauung and psychotherapy. *J. abnorm. soc. Psychol.,* 1953, 48, 601-604.

Weisskopf-Joelson, E., Logotherapy and existential analysis. *Acta Psycholther., psychosomat. Orthopaed.,* 1958, 6, 193-204.

Williamson, E. G., Value orientation in counseling. *Personnel Guid. J.,* 1958, 36, 520-528.